Identity, Sexuality, and Relationships among Emerging Adults in the Digital Age

Michelle F. Wright
Masaryk University, Czech Republic

A volume in the Advances in Human and Social Aspects of Technology (AHSAT) Book Series

IGI GLOBAL
DISSEMINATOR OF KNOWLEDGE

www.igi-global.com

Published in the United States of America by
IGI Global
Information Science Reference (an imprint of IGI Global)
701 E. Chocolate Avenue
Hershey PA, USA 17033
Tel: 717-533-8845
Fax: 717-533-8661
E-mail: cust@igi-global.com
Web site: http://www.igi-global.com

Library of Congress Cataloging-in-Publication Data

Names: Wright, Michelle F., editor.
Title: Identity, sexuality, and relationships among emerging adults in the digital age / Michelle F. Wright, editor.
Description: Hershey, PA : Information Science Reference, 2017. | Includes bibliographical references and index.
Identifiers: LCCN 2016048126| ISBN 9781522518563 (hardcover) | ISBN 9781522518570 (ebook)
Subjects: LCSH: Internet and youth. | Internet--Social aspects. | Identity (Psychology) | Interpersonal relations. | Youth--Sexual behavior.
Classification: LCC HQ799.9.I58 I34 2017 | DDC 004.67/80835--dc23 LC record available at https://lccn.loc.gov/2016048126

This book is published in the IGI Global book series Advances in Human and Social Aspects of Technology (AHSAT) (ISSN: 2328-1316; eISSN: 2328-1324)

British Cataloguing in Publication Data
A Cataloguing in Publication record for this book is available from the British Library.

For electronic access to this publication, please contact: eresources@igi-global.com.

Advances in Human and Social Aspects of Technology (AHSAT) Book Series

Ashish Dwivedi
The University of Hull, UK

ISSN:2328-1316
EISSN:2328-1324

Mission

In recent years, the societal impact of technology has been noted as we become increasingly more connected and are presented with more digital tools and devices. With the popularity of digital devices such as cell phones and tablets, it is crucial to consider the implications of our digital dependence and the presence of technology in our everyday lives.

The **Advances in Human and Social Aspects of Technology (AHSAT) Book Series** seeks to explore the ways in which society and human beings have been affected by technology and how the technological revolution has changed the way we conduct our lives as well as our behavior. The AHSAT book series aims to publish the most cutting-edge research on human behavior and interaction with technology and the ways in which the digital age is changing society.

Coverage

- Cyber Bullying
- Technology and Freedom of Speech
- Digital Identity
- Information ethics
- Cultural Influence of ICTs
- Technoself
- Human-Computer Interaction
- End-User Computing
- Human Rights and Digitization
- Technology Adoption

The Advances in Human and Social Aspects of Technology (AHSAT) Book Series (ISSN 2328-1316) is published by IGI Global, 701 E. Chocolate Avenue, Hershey, PA 17033-1240, USA, www.igi-global.com. This series is composed of titles available for purchase individually; each title is edited to be contextually exclusive from any other title within the series. For pricing and ordering information please visit http://www.igi-global.com/book-series/advances-human-social-aspects-technology/37145. Postmaster: Send all address changes to above address.

Titles in this Series

For a list of additional titles in this series, please visit: www.igi-global.com

Enriching Urban Spaces with Ambient Computing, the Internet of Things, and Smart City Design
Shin'ichi Konomi (University of Tokyo, Japan) and George Roussos (University of London, UK)
Engineering Science Reference • copyright 2017 • 323pp • H/C (ISBN: 9781522508274) • US $210.00 (our price)

Handbook of Research on Individualism and Identity in the Globalized Digital Age
F. Sigmund Topor (Keio University, Japan)
Information Science Reference • copyright 2017 • 645pp • H/C (ISBN: 9781522505228) • US $295.00 (our price)

Information Technology Integration for Socio-Economic Development
Titus Tossy (Mzumbe University, Tanzania)
Information Science Reference • copyright 2017 • 385pp • H/C (ISBN: 9781522505396) • US $200.00 (our price)

Handbook of Research on Human-Computer Interfaces, Developments, and Applications
João Rodrigues (University of Algarve, Portugal) Pedro Cardoso (University of Algarve, Portugal) Jânio Monteiro (University of Algarve, Portugal) and Mauro Figueiredo (University of Algarve, Portugal)
Information Science Reference • copyright 2016 • 663pp • H/C (ISBN: 9781522504351) • US $330.00 (our price)

Human Development and Interaction in the Age of Ubiquitous Technology
Hakikur Rahman (BRAC University, Bangladesh)
Information Science Reference • copyright 2016 • 384pp • H/C (ISBN: 9781522505563) • US $185.00 (our price)

Examining the Evolution of Gaming and Its Impact on Social, Cultural, and Political Perspectives
Keri Duncan Valentine (West Virginia University, USA) and Lucas John Jensen (Georgia Southern University, USA)
Information Science Reference • copyright 2016 • 456pp • H/C (ISBN: 9781522502616) • US $190.00 (our price)

Handbook of Research on Human Social Interaction in the Age of Mobile Devices
Xiaoge Xu (Botswana International University of Science and Technology, Botswana)
Information Science Reference • copyright 2016 • 548pp • H/C (ISBN: 9781522504696) • US $325.00 (our price)

Defining Identity and the Changing Scope of Culture in the Digital Age
Alison Novak (Rowan University, USA) and Imaani Jamillah El-Burki (Lehigh University, USA)
Information Science Reference • copyright 2016 • 316pp • H/C (ISBN: 9781522502128) • US $185.00 (our price)

IGI GLOBAL
DISSEMINATOR OF KNOWLEDGE

www.igi-global.com

701 E. Chocolate Ave., Hershey, PA 17033
Order online at www.igi-global.com or call 717-533-8845 x100
To place a standing order for titles released in this series, contact: cust@igi-global.com
Mon-Fri 8:00 am - 5:00 pm (est) or fax 24 hours a day 717-533-8661

Editorial Advisory Board

Table of Contents

Detailed Table of Contents

In this chapter, the authors explore the role that networked platforms play in identity development during emerging adulthood. They use the stories of two youth to highlight dominant themes from existing research and to examine the developmental implications of forming one's identity in a networked era. The inquiry is theoretically informed by the work of the psychologist Erik Erikson, who depicted identity development as a process of exploration that ultimately results in a sense of personal continuity and coherence. The authors consider what insights this theory—formulated in the mid-twentieth century—has to offer in a digital world. The chapter concludes with a discussion of the practical implications relating to education, policy, and the design of new technologies.

In this chapter, the author is interested in studying more about self-comparison through social media; especially in Jakarta, Indonesia. In Indonesia, social media are commonly used and widely used by various groups. As many as 93% of Internet users in Indonesia are accessing Facebook. Jakarta is even referred as the capital of a text-based social media. The use of social media can be influenced by the collective culture in Indonesia. In this case social media is not just a tool but also the social environment, in which social interaction occurs. This is also influences how individuals view themselves. The topic of the psychological effects of social media has been much discussed. A lot of research conducted on the effect of social on development of self-concept and including self-esteem. Social media becoming a place for comparing oneself to others and it turn out it has a great effect.

High mobility of Brazilian athletes has increased significantly due to the globalization of soccer. It is very common to observe young athletes moving from their hometowns to a different place as a demand of the profession/career. During this process, youth face the process of acculturation, known as the transition to a different culture as a job demand (to play soccer) and feeling confused about his/her cultural identity. In addition, these young athletes assume responsibilities of adults in a period of development - adolescence and the transition to adulthood - characterized by the identity consolidation. The process of identity of football players is emphasized since the early childhood. The aim of this chapter is to discuss the process of acculturation in young Brazilian soccer athletes elucidating related aspects and the development of identity, concerning its cultural dimension surrounded by information and communication technologies of a digital age.

Previous studies have found that the use of social networking sites (SNSs) is associated with the user's positive outcomes such as perceived social support and psychological well-being. To seek those positive influences, those with health issues such as physical illness or mental illness actively use SNSs. The first aim of this chapter is to describe previous studies on the use of SNSs by those with health issues such as mental illnesses, HIV/AIDS, cancer, intellectual disabilities, and diabetes. The second aim is to propose a new direction of research on the use of SNSs by those with health issues: the impact of stigma on communication on SNSs.

We use a developmental tasks framework to guide the exploration of digital media and the development of lesbian, gay, bisexual, transgender, and questioning (LGBTQ) youth. Since digital contexts are ubiquitous, it is clear that youth use them in the service of developmental tasks such as formation of identity, pursuit of intimacy, and development of sexuality. Research suggests that LGBTQ youth use digital media more often than their peers, likely due to the challenges they face. At the same time, electronic peer-victimization and sexual health are concerns since LGBTQ youth are more likely to be at risk. Drawing on extant research we will show that digital media use is associated with stigma-related stressors and risks while concurrently offering opportunities for healthy development. The chapter concludes with recommendations for future research that should help bolster our understanding of how digital contexts may predict the development and well-being of LGBTQ youth.

Cyberstalking is a rapidly growing phenomenon, which is becoming more common among youth nowadays. The study aimed at investigating: 1) the prevalence, behaviors, and tactics of both victims and perpetrators among a sample of Greek undergraduate students, 2) the correlates of victimization and perpetration with personality, attachment style, and relating to others, and 3) the impact of cyberstalking on victims' mental health. Results showed that 23.9% of the students were victims and 9% were perpetrators, with females, disproportionately both experiencing and inflicting cyberstalking. Negatively close relating (i.e., intrusive, restrictive and possessive relating) increased the risk of cyberstalking perpetration, whereas negatively distant relating (suspicious, avoidant, and self-reliant relating) decreased the risk of cyberstalking victimization. Agreeableness decreased the risk of perpetration. Mother's affectionless control increased the risk of both perpetration and victimization and mother's neglectful parenting increased the risk of perpetration only.

This chapter describes a study with the objective to examine cyber aggression involvement among emerging adults across technologies and relationships. Another purpose was to investigate the bidirectional associations between emerging adults' cyber aggression involvement and adjustment difficulties over four years. Participants were 1,483 emerging adults (Mage = 24.67; 60% female) from Southeastern universities in the United States. Emerging adults completed questionnaires on their cyber aggression involvement and adjustment difficulties. The most frequently utilized digital technologies and tool to harm others were text messages. Ex-friends were frequently involved in cyber aggression. Cyber aggression involvement predicted all adjustment difficulties across four years and all adjustment difficulties predicted cyber aggression involvement, suggesting bidirectional relationships among these variables. There were magnitude differences such that the bidirectional relationships were stronger when predicting all adjustment difficulties from cyber aggression and cyber victimization.

Preface

The purpose of this book is to provide a new framework for understanding emerging adults and how they navigate developmental tasks and issues utilizing digital technologies. Emerging adulthood is a developmental period in the human lifespan. It is a period between adolescence and adulthood. Some of these individuals do not live on their own and many do not have sufficient income to be fully independent in their early to late 20s. It is a period characteristic of identity exploration, instability, self-focus, and feeling in between. These individuals utilize a variety of means to explore their identity to find out about themselves. They grew up in a digital era, many of them not knowing a time in which digital media was not a huge part of their lives. Digital media is often used to help explore, develop, and maintain emerging adults' identity, sexuality, and interpersonal relationships.

The aim of this book is to synthesize the research on emerging adults' digital technology use and how these technologies hinder or help their identity development and formation, contribute to aggressive and prosocial behaviors, understand their sexuality, and describe how these technologies benefit or hinder their relationships with their parents, friends, and romantic partners. In places where the published research on a topic is missing, research from the face-to-face context was used to provide a starting point for understanding the same topics in relation to digital technologies. Gaps in the literature were identified and future research were proposed on these topics. Topics include relationship with parents, friendships, love, romantic relationships, sexting, aggression, prosocial behavior, technology addiction, identity development and formation, and the self.

THE ORGANIZATION OF THE BOOK

This book is organized according to various contexts of how emerging adults connect with digital technologies. These contexts involve their identity, sexuality, and interpersonal relationships. Some of the chapters include overlapping information, especially when describing the nature of emerging adulthood. It is often difficult to conceptualize of one context separate from the others or how such contexts might overlap. Authors of chapters employ different terminology to refer to the emerging adulthood period, including adults, youths, young people, college students, students, and young adults.

Chapters 1 through 4 focus on emerging adults' identity development, exploration, and formation as augmented by digital technologies. The purpose of Chapter 1 is to explore the role of networked platforms in the development of identity during emerging adulthood utilizing Erik Erikson's theory as a theoretical framework. The authors describe identity development within the context of two case studies.

They conclude their chapter by discussing practical implications of new digital technologies on identity development in emerging adulthood. Chapter 2 focuses on Indonesian emerging adults' self-comparisons through social media. The author also explains how social media influences how emerging adults view themselves. The authors of Chapter 3 examine identity consolidation of highly mobile Brazilian athletes. Digital technologies are explored as a context to help the acculturation process of these athletes. Chapter 4 discusses the potential of social networking websites to provide social support and help the psychologically well-being of individuals with health issues. The chapter concludes with a proposal about how social networking websites can be used to explore identity among individuals with health issues.

Chapters 5 through 7 focus on emerging adults' sexuality. Using the developmental task framework, the authors of Chapter 5 explore the development of lesbian, gay, bisexual, transgender, and questioning (LGBTQ) youths through the digital media. The authors conclude with recommendations for future research to broaden our understanding of how digital contexts predict the development and well-being of LGBTQ youths. The purpose of Chapter 6 is to analyze online participation on LGBTQ websites among youths in Spain. The authors explain how social networking websites can help with alternative sexual identity. Chapter 7 describes the changes in sex education among young adults in Uganda and Kenya. In contrast to sex education previously being taught by paternal aunts and grandparents, the authors describe how social media has shifted sex education to social media. The authors explain the positives and negatives associated with using social media for sexuality-related information.

Chapters 8 through 16 focus on interpersonal relationships. More chapters are included in the context of interpersonal relationships, highlighting how far research has come on this topic. The authors of Chapters 8 and 9 explore how digital technologies are being used in the context of parent-emerging adult relationships. Chapter 8 summarizes research related to the influence of digital technologies on parent-emerging adult relationships from a Family Systems perspective. The authors of Chapter 9 content analyzed the online messages of Chinese international students who were studying and living in the United States. Their findings revealed that the students often sought out and provided assistance to their peers regarding understanding and acculturating to family life in the United States via a popular online forum. The aim of Chapters 10 through 13 was to describe how emerging adults navigate romantic relationships in the digital age. Chapter 10 focuses on the online dating experiences of people with disabilities by describing how these people communicate with potential partners and escape disability stigma. The authors of Chapter 11 applied thematic analysis to understanding Nigerian emerging adults' use of social networking websites, particularly Facebook. They found that many of the dating couples spent hours on Facebook, although they did not feel comfortable with the hours their partner spent chatting with friends on Facebook. Chapter 12 reviews the existing literature on the nature of pornography use among emerging adults and how pornography impacts their romantic relationships. Chapter 13 reviews the existing literature on emerging adults' engagement in and evaluations of sexting. The authors also describe risk factors associated with sexting victimization, such as attachment style and rejection sensitivity. In Chapter 14, the authors introduce research on the association between the online and offline lives of emerging adults. They also explain the factors that predict problematic digital technology use among emerging adults. The authors of Chapter 15 and 16 explore two forms of cyber harassment: Cyberstalking and cyber aggression. Chapter 15 describes the author's research on the prevalence, behaviors, and tactics of cyberstalking perpetrators. She also explains the correlates of cyberstalking perpetration and victimization, including personality characteristics, attachment styles, and relating to others. The final chapter, Chapter 16, describes the author's research on the longitudinal relationships between adjustment difficulties and cyber aggression involvement among emerging adults. The author discusses future research directions for understanding the adjustment difficulties associated with emerging adults' cyber aggression perpetration and victimization, and explains possible intervention programs aimed at reducing these behaviors.

Chapter 1
Identity Development in the Digital Age:
An Eriksonian Perspective

Katie Davis
University of Washington, USA

Emily Weinstein
Harvard University, USA

ABSTRACT

In this chapter, the authors explore the role that networked platforms play in identity development during emerging adulthood. They use the stories of two youth to highlight dominant themes from existing research and to examine the developmental implications of forming one's identity in a networked era. The inquiry is theoretically informed by the work of the psychologist Erik Erikson, who depicted identity development as a process of exploration that ultimately results in a sense of personal continuity and coherence. The authors consider what insights this theory—formulated in the mid-twentieth century—has to offer in a digital world. The chapter concludes with a discussion of the practical implications relating to education, policy, and the design of new technologies.

INTRODUCTION

Questions of identity are central to adolescents and emerging adults. Questions like "Who am I?" and "What is my role in society?" represent focal objects of reflection, shaping youth's thoughts, actions, and commitments (Arnett, 2004; Erikson, 1968). For contemporary adolescents and emerging adults, the tasks of identity development take place in a world of ubiquitous social media use. It is increasingly challenging, if not entirely impossible, to disentangle 'digital life' from the contexts in which today's adolescents and emerging adults navigate key developmental tasks. Among 18 to 29-year-olds, 85% own smartphones and 82% of those who use the Internet are social media users (Duggan, Ellison, Lampe, Lenhart & Madden, 2015; Smith, 2015). Among a slightly younger group, 92% of 13 to 17-year-olds use the Internet on a daily basis, 88% have access to mobile phones, and 76% use social media (Lenhart,

DOI: 10.4018/978-1-5225-1856-3.ch001

2015). Moreover, more than 90% of these youth access the Internet on mobile devices, meaning that app use and digital communications accompany young people through the breadth of environments they inhabit during their daily activities.

Social media platforms like Instagram, Snapchat, and Facebook have introduced new ways for young people to engage in self-expression: Posting selfies on Instagram, updating statuses on Facebook, sharing mashups of daily activities on Snapchat. Although the motivation for these self-expressions may be recognizable, they nevertheless appear distinct from pre-networked identity expressions. Contributing to this distinctiveness are the particular qualities of networked technologies, such as asynchronous communication, 24/7 connectivity, feelings of anonymity and pseudonymity, and the public, persistent nature of online communication. These qualities introduce new dynamics to the act of self-expression. In pre-networked times, images captured by a camera were typically seen by one's immediate friends and family members. The photos that young people post of themselves online today, by contrast, may be seen—now and years from now—by much larger, more diverse audiences, some of them intended, others not.

In this chapter, we ask: How do youth's expressions on and through digital apps and devices intersect with, enable, or impede their identity development? We draw on the stories of two youth, Lilli and Trevor, to characterize the forms that identity expression takes in a networked world. We use these stories as case studies to examine how the attributes of networked technologies shape the identities that young people express online. In the process, we synthesize current research investigating the opportunities and challenges associated with forming one's identity in a networked world. Lilli and Trevor are adolescents; yet, their experiences highlight core themes from research on emerging adults. In addition, the decisions that Lilli and Trevor make as adolescents will directly influence their experiences as emerging adults; in particular, they will eventually have to reconcile their online adolescent and emerging adult selves. In this way, their stories highlight the kinds of challenges that emerging adults are increasingly managing as they move from adolescence to emerging adulthood in a digital context. We therefore use the stories of Lilli and Trevor as entry-points for exploring the experiences of emerging adults in a digital age. Our analysis is framed theoretically by the work of the psychologist Erik Erikson, whose foundational writing on identity largely shaped how psychologists viewed identity development during adolescence and emerging adulthood during the second half of the twentieth century. What insights, if any, does Erikson's theory have to offer in today's digital world? We also frame our investigation with an historical overview of scholarship addressing identity expression in a digital age, charting major themes from an early wave of internet research in the 1990s through to present day. We conclude the chapter with a discussion of the practical implications related to education, policy, and the design of new technologies.

BACKGROUND

An Eriksonian View of Identity Development

Erikson (1950, 1968, 1980) depicted the development of a satisfying identity as the central developmental task of adolescence. As more people living in Western societies postpone major life milestones, such as marriage and children in favor of pursuing further education and establishing a career path, it is now widely recognized that the work of developing one's identity extends into emerging adulthood (Arnett, 2004). Indeed, Erikson (1968) himself acknowledged that identity development is a lifelong process that individuals revisit periodically as they engage in subsequent developmental tasks such as intimacy, generativity, and wisdom. Nevertheless, adolescence and emerging adulthood represent the first and potentially most important period for identity development during the lifecycle.

Erikson (1968) portrayed the process of identity development as a conflict between identity synthesis and identity confusion. During a period of suspended consequences—what Erikson termed a psychosocial moratorium—individuals try on different identities, gain feedback and affirmation from others, and reflect on their beliefs, values, and goals. They successfully resolve the conflict between synthesis and confusion if they are able to achieve a sense of "self-sameness and inner continuity" (Erikson 1968, p.50). Those who are unsuccessful experience the fragmentation and instability associated with identity confusion.

Though both adolescents and emerging adults engage in identity exploration, the nature and expression of these explorations may differ. In adolescence, the focus of identity exploration lies largely in reflecting on who one is in relation to one's family, peers, and immediate community (Davis, 2010). As individuals enter emerging adulthood, their perspective shifts as they start to reflect on their place and purpose in the broader society (Damon, Menon, & Bronk, 2003). Thus, identity exploration during emerging adulthood involves reflection on how one's interests and abilities intersect with societal values and concerns. Emerging adults consider such things as their desired career path, long-term romantic partners, and general lifestyle choices (Arnett, 2004).

The following excerpt from Erikson's writing illustrates his conception of a successful outcome of identity development:

The wholeness to be achieved at this stage [of development] I have called a sense of inner identity. The young person, in order to experience wholeness, must feel a progressive continuity between that which he has come to be during the long years of childhood and that which he promises to become in the anticipated future; between that which he conceives himself to be and that which he perceives others to see him and to expect of him. (Erikson, 1968, p.87)

According to Erikson, coherence and consistency lie at the heart of a healthy, satisfying identity (Cote, 2009; Schwartz, 2007). He recognized that social context shapes identities in important ways, requiring people to show different aspects of themselves in different circumstances. Yet, he claimed that these different facets of the self could—and should—be united into a coherent, whole identity. In this way, Erikson's writings bear resemblance to an earlier theorist of the self, William James (1890), who emphasized the synthetic nature of personal identity.

Subsequent work by identity scholars has emphasized the integrative function of identity development. These scholars have depicted identity as an informal theory about the self (Berzonsky, 2003a, 2003b); a story that brings together different aspects of the self (McAdams, 1996, 1997); and a foundational structure for understanding who one is in the world (Adams & Marshall, 1996). According to Baumeister (1993), "[I]dentity furnishes a basis for making stable, coherent, consistent choices" (p.182). These characterizations are united by a belief that identity provides structure and meaning to an individual's disparate experiences.

Postmodern views of identity are defined more by multiplicity than consistency, raising the question of whether an Eriksonian conception of identity holds relevance in today's world. According to Gergen (2000), achieving a sense of personal coherence is not possible in such a rapidly changing, socially and technologically complex world. As we discuss in the subsequent section, early investigations into identity in a digital age emphasized the opportunities that the Internet provides for crafting and expressing multiple identities.

At the same time, one could argue that as our experiences become increasingly varied and distributed, the search for an overarching structure that organizes and imparts meaning to these disparate experiences becomes ever more important. Scholars, such as Giddens (1991) and Lifton (1993), asserted that the multiplicity that defines our postmodern experience does not preclude us from searching for and achieving a sense of personal coherence. Indeed, this sense of personal coherence may be essential for navigating successfully the challenges associated with living in a postmodern world.

A 'Dogged' Pursuit to Understand Identity Expression in a Digital Age

Be Who You Want to Be

A series of three cartoons - published in 1993, 2007, and 2015, respectively - offer witty popular culture portrayals of shifting trends highlighted by scholars who study identity in a networked context. The first cartoon, created by Peter Steiner and published in *The New Yorker* in 1993, features two dogs. One dog is sitting at a desk in front of a desktop computer, speaking to second dog who looks on with curiosity; the caption reads, "On the Internet, nobody knows you're a dog" (Steiner, 1993).

An early wave of research in the 1990s underscored opportunities for identity play online. In her 1995 book, *Life on the Screen: Identity in the Age of the Internet*, Sherry Turkle described how the potential for anonymity online translated to seemingly boundless opportunities for identity experimentation. Turkle referenced Steiner's cartoon as an entry point to her discussion of identity expression within Multi-User Dungeons (MUDs). MUDs, Turkle explained, enabled players "to express multiple and often unexplored aspects of the self, to play with their identity and try out new ones" (p. 12). Turkle even saw the potential for MUDs to function as therapeutic contexts in which players could do meaningful identity 'work' that translated to RL (i.e., real life) benefits.

In a similar vein, Stone (1991) and Waskul and Douglass (1997) wrote during the same period as Turkle (1995) about how the disembodied nature of online identity directly facilitated exploration. Stone highlighted the fluidity of gender, exemplified by "computer crossdressing" (p. 84), while Waskul and Douglass described how the identities of multiple "cyberselves" could "emerge" due to the disembodied, anonymous, and faceless nature of the communicative context (p. 395). Because cyberselves in the 1990s generally existed as distinct from offline life and relationships, it was left to each individual to decide whether – and when – to adopt a different identity or to express a more authentic, 'true' self. One of Waskul and Douglass' (1997) participants commented: "You can be anything. I may stretch the truth, and be with whoever I want - no inhibitions" (p. 389). Another participant similarly found the online context liberating, but for a different reason: "The anonymity allows me to be myself, allowing a certain freedom of expression in which I rarely indulge in person" (p. 389). Indeed, in spite of the potential for dramatic identity play, other research from this period (e.g., Baym, 1995; Kendall, 1999, Kennedy, 2006; Miller, 1995; Tetzlaff, 2000) similarly found that Internet users nevertheless often created online identities consistent with their offline selves.

Be Recognizable

A second cartoon, created by Rob Cottingham in 2007, bears close resemblance to Peter Steiner's 1993 illustration – though the dogs are seated in front of a slimmer, laptop computer. In this version, the caption reads: "On Facebook, 273 people know I'm a dog. The rest can only see my limited profile" (Cottingham, 2007).

In the beginning of the 2000s, social networking sites (SNSs) "hit the mainstream" (boyd & Ellison, 2007, p. 216). Early SNSs, including MySpace and Friendster, allowed users to create their own profiles and form explicit, ongoing connections to others' profiles. Aided by these affordances, SNSs started to "bridge the physical and digital" (boyd & Heer, 2006, p. 9). The connection between offline and online selves became even more pronounced with the rise of platforms like Facebook. Launched in 2004, Facebook explicitly facilitates the creation of online profiles grounded in an individual's offline identity and connections. Although privacy settings (e.g., the aforementioned 'limited profile') allow users to share selectively with different audiences, the platform forbids users from maintaining more than one profile (Facebook, 2015).

Facebook is but one of the digital contexts through which adolescents and emerging adults connect and communicate. Yet in the years following the platform's release, scholars began to document the consistent and considerable overlap between young people's online and offline social networks (Davis, 2010; Reich, Subrahmanyam, & Espinoza, 2012; Subrahmanyam, Reich, Weachter, & Espinoza, 2008). As offline friends became a defining part of individuals' online lives, cyberselves ceased to be faceless, disembodied, and anonymous. To the contrary, existing friends expect their friends' online identity representations to be recognizable, familiar, and consistent with offline behavior (Davis, 2012a; 2014). Notably, one benefit of using social networking sites to connect with friends from offline life is that digital disclosure and communication can enhance closeness and strengthen peer relationships offline (Davis, 2012a; Valkenburg & Peter, 2011).

Be Who You Are

A third cartoon, created in 2015 by Kaamran Hafeez, features two dogs again. In the 2015 version, the dogs both sit on the floor while their owner occupies the seat in front of the computer. The caption – seemingly a comment from the first dog to the second dog – reads, "Remember when, on the Internet, nobody knew who you were?" (Hafeez, 2015).

For Facebook's CEO Mark Zuckerberg, it is unlikely that Hafeez's cartoon would evoke feelings of nostalgia about fewer opportunities for identity play. To the contrary, Zuckerberg criticizes the mere practice of adjusting identity portrayals for different contexts. As he told author David Kirkpatrick:

You have one identity. The days of you having a different image for your work friends or co-workers and for the other people you know are probably coming to an end pretty quickly...Having two identities for yourself is an example of a lack of integrity. (Kirkpatrick, 2011, p.199)

To be sure, there exists a plethora of apps and platforms that still purport to offer anonymity (e.g., Whisper, Insider, mood; see Roose, 2014). Yet digital life increasingly intertwines with offline life, and users as young as 13 years old – just entering the throes of identity development – are welcomed to Facebook, Instagram, and other contemporary SNSs that tend to anchor digital selves in real names, images, affiliations, and connections to offline peers. What, then, are the implications of navigating the ongoing processes of identity development and expression in digital spaces that increasingly presume consistency, authenticity, and accountability across contexts as feasible and worthwhile objectives?

TWO CASE STUDIES

Meet Lilli

When [sixteen-year-old Lilli] Hymowitz first joined Instagram, in middle school, her account was private, but by the time she started high school she had opened it to the public. She has posted thousands of photos, but fewer than 500 are extant because she began to realize that many of the things she used to care about didn't fit with her current persona. "I deleted a bunch of the photos I didn't like anymore," she says. "Now I think I'm at a place where I don't really change that much." ...The oldest photo Hymowitz has not deleted, and thus the earliest moment she has deemed relevant to her current self-image, is of a marijuana-leaf bracelet, posted when she was 13. (Wiedeman, 2015)

For an identity scholar who lived and studied adolescents and emerging adults solely in a pre-digital era, certain aspects of the above excerpt would almost certainly be confusing. The word 'Instagram' would be unfamiliar, as would the concepts of 'opening one's account to the public' and 'deleting' old photographs. Yet other practices characteristic of identity development during adolescence and emerging adulthood would seem entirely familiar: Experimentation with various roles, exploration, and evidence of a shift toward greater continuity and self-coherence.

Crafting a Curated Online Identity

Lilli Hymowitz's narrative presumes a connection between her online, Instagram self and her offline self. She does not anonymously post in a digital world akin to the faceless context described by Sherry Turkle and others in the 1990s. Rather, Lilli uses her real name on her Instagram account. She is not faceless; her face is quite literally a focal point of many of her posts and identity expressions. Although she does not personally know all of her followers, her close friends are among them.

Lilli's digital representation offers a carefully crafted, 'glammed up' (Davis, 2014) portrayal of her life. Indeed, online identity expressions often constitute heavily curated, idealized constructions of self and life (Gardner & Davis, 2013; Zhao, Grasmuck, & Martin, 2008). In Lilli's words, "You can edit your life on Instagram" (Wiedeman, 2015). Lilli's friends note that her Instagram "definitely" does not fully capture her personality. "[Lilli's] Instagram is like, 'She does cool stuff.' It's a lifestyle that people want to live," one of her friends observed. Yet, although her identity expressions online offer a thin, edited version of her life, they are neither fictitious nor unrecognizable. Adolescents and emerging adults engage in a kind of identity editing through an intentional, effortful selection process, which they use to determine which moments and expressions to post online.

In their book, *The App Generation,* Gardner and Davis (2013) described the pervasive contemporary pressure to present a polished and packaged self online. They voiced a concern that pressure from an early age to present a well-curated, clearly articulated identity may prompt premature identity foreclosure among young people, who in turn avoid exploring alternative identities and roles. Such premature foreclosure bypasses the psychosocial moratorium described by Erikson (1968) as an important component of the identity development process.

Outgrowing Past Identity Expressions

Hymowitz also describes a second type of 'editing': Removing old expressions or posts that she no longer feels are representative of her current identity. In a similar vein, Davis (2010) documented self-described shifts in online expression as female bloggers moved from adolescence to emerging adulthood. Drawing on her interviews with these youth, Davis differentiated adolescent practices from those characteristic of emerging adulthood. As adolescents, the bloggers regularly restructured blog layout, wrote emotionally-charged posts, and were heavily influenced by friends in both deciding to create their blogs and in crafting their posts. As emerging adults, they described increased stability and greater self-assuredness in their expressions, a shift from focusing heavily on personal issues to a greater emphasis on issues of social concern, and a more pronounced and explicit orientation toward the future. Perhaps unsurprisingly, these practices and emphases are closely aligned with attributes that characterize and differentiate adolescence and emerging adulthood (e.g., Arnett, 2004; Markus & Nurius, 1986).

Weinstein and colleagues (2015) also documented a shift in young people's approaches to online expression in their longitudinal study of youth with strong civic and political identities. In Weinstein's (2014) original interviews, the researchers found that most youth – 50 of their 70 participants (72%) – tended to express their civic interests through personal social media accounts. Approximately two years later, Weinstein, Rundle, and James (2015) followed up with participants in an effort to understand whether their approaches to online expression remained stable. Forty-one of the 70 original participants participated in the follow-up study; these participants spanned late adolescence and emerging adulthood (ages 16-25) at the time of their initial interviews and were all emerging adults (ages 18-27) at the time of the follow-up study.

More than 40% of participants had changed their approaches to online expression, with most participants moving in the direction of greater restraint for what they posted (Weinstein et al., 2015). These participants cited a range of considerations related to their quieting expression, including more salient concerns about the future, unintended consequences, and their careers. Those who modified their expression patterns also contributed to a group level shift. Whereas most young people shared the civic aspects of their identities online at Time 1, a majority quieted or entirely withheld their civic expression on social media two years later.

Gavin, for example, was 16 at the time of her initial interview, and she reported that she clearly portrayed her civic identity and political interests on her Facebook page (Weinstein et al., 2015). Two years later, as an 18-year-old, Gavin described herself as "much more cautious about the information [she] shared with others online." She explained that she still openly discusses her views offline, but "would rather not risk ever being penalized for what I posted on Facebook as a teenager."

Taken together, these studies and Lilli Hymowitz's more recent personal narrative underscore several points related to online identity expression. First, young people do indeed alter their online identity expressions, including both the content and nature of their posts, over time and as they develop (Davis, 2010; Weinstein, Rundle, & James, 2015). Hymowitz's more recent practices also include retroactively reviewing and removing previous posts (Wiedeman, 2015). Second, the motivation for altering identity expressions may stem from simply feeling like previous expressions from earlier adolescent years no longer 'fit' one's current identity. Or they may instead be symptomatic of shifting concerns characteristic of development into and through emerging adulthood, such as less anxiety about fitting into one's immediate peer group and conveying 'who I am' right now, alongside greater concern about society and setting oneself up for 'who I will become.'

Revisionist History?

Herein lies a central question for today's emerging adults, who are tasked with navigating digital identity expressions as their identities develop and change: How should they manage past identity expressions from earlier childhood and adolescent years, which increasingly remain persistent, searchable, and linked to their online identities long after they are personally relevant? In her 2010 TED talk, cyborg anthropologist Amber Case explains that managing digital profiles and identities from a younger age means that:

a lot of people now, especially adolescents, have to go through two adolescences. They have to go through their primary one, that's already awkward, and then they go through their second self's adolescence, and that's even more awkward because there's an actual history of what they've gone through online.

Hymowitz describes her deliberate practice of deleting old posts, likely in an effort to revise the history to which Case (2010) refers. Yet posts can easily live on in digital copies that are downloaded, saved, or stored elsewhere. Therefore, retroactively removing old posts is an imperfect strategy for cleansing one's digital footprint from adolescent activities, expressions, and experimentation.

Essena O'Neill, an Australian youth, model, and Instagram celebrity, serves as a case-in-point. In November 2015, O'Neill decided that her Instagram account was an inauthentic representation of her life and determined that she wanted to remove her old posts (Hunt, 2015). However, she preceded the mass-removal of her posts with a phase of editing their captions to reveal additional context, including how she felt at the time when they were taken (e.g., lonely, insecure) and how much effort she put into capturing the 'perfect' shot. While crafting a curated version of her life for Instagram is seemingly an entertaining pastime for Lilli Hymowitz, Essena O'Neill reveals the considerable discomfort and stress generated by her Instagram portrayal. O'Neill explained, "I made myself into a machine that gave others what they wanted from me, never knowing or valuing my true self. I was lost to expectations, pressures and a fearful desire to be accepted" (Safronova, 2015). As of late November, 2015, O'Neill deleted all of her Instagram posts from her account – yet because posts were downloaded or 'screenshotted' before they were taken down, many of her old posts are still easily retrieved with a quick Google Image search.

Meet Trevor

Not too long ago, the first author of this chapter received an unexpected phone call from a public defender's office in a small city on the West Coast of the United States. The investigator was seeking an expert witness in the case of a 17-year-old boy accused of murdering his grandmother. The boy had recently moved to a new state to live with his grandmother after experiencing several years living in a turbulent household. The detective described Trevor as a shy, insecure boy desperately seeking acceptance from his peers. As it happened, the peers from whom he most wanted acceptance were involved in gang activity.

To appeal to these peers, Trevor (pseudonym) created a persona on Instagram in which he depicted himself as a hard-hitting, seasoned 'gangsta.' The first author of this chapter spent an afternoon scrolling through three years' worth of Instagram posts that included pictures of Trevor with wads of cash stuffed in his mouth, flipping gang signs, and holding guns, as well as a steady stream of violent, misogynistic quotes from hip-hop songs. Since moving out of state, the only way for him to stay in contact with his friends back home was through social media and texting, and so his Instagram posts became more important than ever.

The prosecution wanted to use Trevor's social media postings as evidence in the case against him. Specifically, they wanted to make the argument that his Instagram persona proved that he was involved in gang activity and capable of committing such a horrible crime against his grandmother. Trevor's legal team wanted the first author of this chapter to help them make the counter-argument that the identities that young people display online are sometimes quite different from those that they express offline.

On the face of it, Trevor's story seems worlds apart from Lilli's. Indeed, the facts of their life circumstances stand in stark contrast, geographically, socioeconomically, racially, and culturally. It is no surprise, then, that their Instagram feeds bear little resemblance to one another: Bikini shots by pools versus guns, gang signs, and mouthfuls of cash. And yet, both Instagram feeds reflect a desire—typical and strong among adolescents and emerging adults—to portray an identity that they believe is attractive to the particular peer group with whom they identify and from whom they seek acceptance.

Online Identity, Then and Now

From an Eriksonian perspective, Trevor's actions can be understood as an attempt to search for and establish an identity that is both personally satisfying and recognized by others (Erikson, 1950, 1968, 1980). If Erikson were alive today and had access to Trevor's Instagram account, he would likely view his posts as an attempt to carve out a 'psychosocial moratorium' where he could try on a new identity and assess the reaction it elicited from his peers. The key to such exploration is that it is done in a context in which there are no grave consequences for one's identity expressions. Erikson believed young people needed a safe space to explore different identities and see which of them fit.

Sherry Turkle, writing in 1995, described how the nature of MUDs supported the Eriksonian concept of a psychosocial moratorium. Turkle explained:

The adolescent moratorium is a time of intense interaction with people and ideas. It is a time of passionate friendships and experimentation. The moratorium is not on significant experiences but on their consequences…The moratorium facilitates the development of a core self, a personal sense of what gives life meaning. This is what Erikson called identity. (Turkle, 1995, p. 204)

In other words, actions and identity moves in MUDs could remain safely disconnected from offline life and repercussions, and thereby facilitate the kind of exploration and experimentation paradigmatic of the Eriksonian moratorium.

In stark contrast to the world of early online environments, Underwood and Faris' (2015) contemporary study of thirteen-year-olds reveals today's apparent dissipation of boundaries between online and offline life. The authors observe:

Examining the social media communication of... 13-year-olds made clear that there is no firm line between their real and online worlds. Social media is an extension of their social lives, a context in which real and meaningful relationships develop and at times take some seriously wrong turns, and is very much integrated with their ongoing daily lives and their offline interactions. (Underwood & Faris, 2015, p.1)

As this excerpt suggests, friends play a central role in the desire for consistency across online and offline contexts. Davis described the "anchoring role" of peers in her explanation of how friends' expectations influence youth's online identities (Davis, 2014, p. 18). The adolescents interviewed for her study noted that friends would disapprove of online expressions that seemed inconsistent with offline behavior. Friends tolerate digital portrayals that are, to some extent, "glammed up" (p. 20). Yet a firm and recognizable anchoring in offline identity is paramount in order to avoid seeming "two-faced" (p. 19).

Who Is Most Likely to Experiment Online?

Though consistency in self-representation represents the stated ideal for most young people (Davis, 2014; Gardner & Davis, 2013), there do exist contexts and situations in which some youth feel comfortable with and motivated to explore identities online that differ substantially from the day-to-day identities they convey offline. This motivation is fairly common among youth whose interests lie outside the mainstream activities of their peer group, for instance, youth who write fan fiction or play certain types of video games (Gardner & Davis, 2013). The identities that youth express in these online interest-driven communities may appear quite different from the identities they express when they are hanging out with their peers offline. One college freshman interviewed by Gardner and Davis (2013) reflected on her use of LiveJournal to express her identification with fan culture:

I can definitely be more of a deranged fan girl in my LiveJournal than I can in real life...I don't have to like kind of censor myself. It's not even really censoring myself in real life; it's kind of recognizing that people aren't that interested and kind of dropping off before I freak them out. (p.90)

Some youth try out new identities in anonymous or pseudonymous online environments before they feel comfortable enough to claim those identities officially offline. In her ethnographic study of teens' networked lives, for instance, boyd (2014) described one girl who was exploring her sexuality at the time she was interviewed. Living in a conservative state in the Midwestern United States, the girl did not feel comfortable conducting this exploration in her everyday offline environment, and particularly not with her parents' knowledge. She found an online chatroom in which other queer girls shared their personal experiences as well as helpful LGBT-related resources. Although it took concerted effort on her part (effort that likely would not have been needed twenty years earlier), the girl was able to achieve some measure of anonymity online, enabling her to explore her sexuality in a non-threatening environment.

Youth who are insecure, shy, or lonely offline are also more likely to explore different identities online (Barker, 2009; Davis, 2012a, 2013). In her study of college freshmen, Barker (2009) found that participants low in self-esteem were less likely to use SNSs to communicate with their offline peer group. Similarly, participants low in *collective* self-esteem—perceiving their social group to be unpopular—were more likely to use SNSs for social compensation, or to distance themselves from their offline peer group and align themselves with a more desirable peer group. These results are consistent with Davis' (2013) finding that greater online identity experimentation and lower levels of online peer communication were connected to lower self-concept clarity among high school students.

This body of research sheds light on the apparent disjunction between Trevor's online and offline personas. Trevor was described to the first author as an insecure boy who desperately wanted to be accepted by a group of peers whom he admired. He used his Instagram account to craft an identity that he believed fit with this group but which bore little resemblance to the way he actually presented himself offline, which was more reserved and shy.

Colliding Contexts

The challenge with such identity exploration today is that it is increasingly difficult to control the audiences that see it (boyd, 2014). Trevor's Instagram posts were intended for one particular audience, but they were ultimately seen by an audience that he never anticipated. This convergence of diverse audiences in one online setting is a distinguishing characteristic of networked environments and one that makes it difficult for youth to use the Internet as a site for low-stakes self-exploration. The girl discussed in the previous section, who went online to explore her sexuality, took deliberate measures to keep her various online and offline contexts separate. boyd (2014) described how she used different browsers for Facebook and LGBT-related chatrooms and websites, and she was careful to erase her browser history after each use.

In her book *It's Complicated*, boyd (2014) recounted the story of an African American boy who was not so successful at keeping his contexts separate. This boy had written a strong college essay about his desire to escape the gangs in his community by attending college and getting a high-quality education. The admissions officer at the Ivy League University to which he had applied conducted a Google search that brought up the boy's MySpace page. She was concerned to see references to gang activities and images of gang symbols. Which version of the boy's identity was true? According to boyd, both versions were true and appropriate to the different contexts in which they were expressed. The boy expressed an identity on MySpace that allowed him to gain acceptance from his peer group and community at home. At the same time, he aspired to an education and recognized that he would have to express a different side of himself in order to secure that opportunity. Though these identities were appropriate to the audiences for which they were intended, their expression was complicated by the convergence of multiple disparate audiences online.

Far from providing a low-stakes context for expression, then, many of today's social media platforms instead create a digital history that may be searched years later by college admissions officers and future employers (e.g., Singer, 2013; Smith, 2013). In Trevor's case, his social media postings were discovered by law enforcement and used to portray his personality and actions offline. In such a networked world, can today's adolescents and emerging adults still find spaces for valuable identity experimentation and exploration with a moratorium on consequences?

Finding a Space to Play Online

Recent trends in youth's online activities suggest they are actively looking for ways to carve out spaces for low-stakes identity exploration. In November 2015, Valeriya Safronova wrote an article for *The New York Times* in which she described the increasingly common practice among teens and young adults of creating fake Instagram ('finstagram') accounts. Safronova (2015) explained:

Some young adults, weary of trying to live up to their annoyingly perfect online avatars, have created 'finstagrams,' or fake Instagram accounts, that present truer versions of themselves than their main profiles. These locked, pseudonymous accounts capture something rarely seen by people who follow these same users on their main accounts: reality.

The rise of practices like maintaining finstagrams and of apps like Snapchat, which are characterized by an intentionally ephemeral nature, may be symptomatic of a search for digital spaces that allow for less carefully curated, performative, and lasting identity expressions. Some policymakers, too, are advancing legislative efforts such as California's 'eraser button' law, which requires sites to provide minors with the option to remove or anonymize previously posted content (Ingis, Signorelli, & Wolf, 2014). Evolving practices and policies are illustrative of ongoing efforts to address the puzzles that attend coming of age in a digital world.

FUTURE DIRECTIONS

As new technologies are introduced at an increasingly fast pace, new opportunities and challenges associated with identity expression will undoubtedly follow suit. Emerging trends like finstagrams and Snapchat are important for scholars to track, as they shed light on how youth navigate identity development in an ever-changing digital age. These recent trends suggest that youth feel the pressure to be perfect online, which has grown with the rise of widely used SNSs like Facebook, Instagram, and Twitter, and they are pushing back by carving out spaces to be less polished. What do these practices tell us about young people's needs and desires around self-expression? What insight can we gain about the challenges youth face when their needs and desires bump up against the distinct properties of networked technologies? What strategies do youth use to cope with such challenges, and with what effects on their self-expressions? Future research should explore such questions in order to provide continued and evolving insight into the impact of digital technologies on emerging adults' processes of identity development.

If the opportunity for an Eriksonian moratorium is deemed valuable for individuals and society, the onus is on researchers, policymakers, educators, and designers of new technologies to attend to the ways in which digital life can support or interfere. Educators can use insights gained from research to develop curricula aimed at helping youth to become self-reflective about their online identity expression and to help them navigate the particular identity-related challenges they face in different networked environments. Policymakers can use these insights to promote policies that recognize the challenges associated with growing up in a networked world and seek to shield youth as they inevitably make mistakes while navigating these challenges. Technology developers can take research insights into account as they design devices and applications that satisfy young people's need to explore their identities in a safe, low-stakes environment. What might it mean to deliberately 'design for identity development' in recognition of the possibility that users will grow up on and through their sites?

CONCLUSION

This chapter has documented the considerable changes to online life over the last twenty years. These changes have precipitated a movement away from the anonymity of the 1990s Internet toward an increasing interweaving of online and offline life. As a result, offline connections exert a profound influence on emerging adults' online identity expressions. Digital connections to offline friends, family members, and colleagues often facilitate closeness and enhance relationships. At the same time, the increasing overlap between online and offline life fuels pressure for consistency and accountability across contexts.

To cope with the challenge of managing developing identities in the face of persistent digital footprints, emerging adults often respond by carefully packaging, editing, and curating their online identity portrayals. They still find places and adopt practices that enable them to explore and experiment online. Yet contexts from offline life often collapse online, sometimes to the knowledge of the individual, other times in ways beyond what that individual ever anticipated.

Decades after Erikson developed his influential work on identity, his theory continues to provide a valuable framework for understanding youth's motivations and behaviors. Adolescents and emerging adults are in the midst of exploring different identities, expressing their identities to others, and seeking and interpreting social feedback. The online world offers a ripe context for both expression and feedback. Erikson would likely be unsurprised to learn that youth indeed explore their identities online, seeking spaces that function as psychosocial moratoria. Eriksonian theory highlights the value of preserving online spaces for youth to try on and try out different identities without lasting consequences.

At the same time, Erikson's concept of identity coherence also has its place in a digital age. While recognizing the multiplicity of online life, Erikson would likely assert that the search for a coherent sense of self is not merely possible in a digital age, it is essential for gaining a sense of mastery over this multiplicity. This is not to say that individuals should strive to be singular beings both online and offline; indeed, Erikson would no doubt express concern about the pressure young people experience to portray fully realized, polished selves before they have adequately explored alternatives. Rather, his focus on coherence underscores the value of seeking to coordinate one's self-expressions in such a way that imparts a meaningful, purposeful sense of self.

There are few endeavors more salient during adolescence and emerging adulthood than the construction of a synthesized identity. At the same time, there are few daily practices more universal among contemporary youth living in developed countries than checking, connecting, and communicating through digital devices and platforms. This chapter has focused on the intersection between identity development and the digital age, synthesizing the current state of research in this area. Through this synthesis, we have sought to characterize the distinct opportunities and challenges that emerging adults face growing up in a networked world and pave the way forward for continued research and public discourse.

REFERENCES

Adams, G. R., & Marshall, S. K. (1996). A developmental social psychology of identity: Understanding the person-in-context. *Journal of Adolescence*, *19*(5), 429–442. doi:10.1006/jado.1996.0041 PMID:9245296

Arnett, J. (2004). *Emerging adulthood: The winding road from the late teens through the twenties*. New York, NY: Oxford University Press.

Barker, V. (2009). Older adolescents motivations for social network site use: The influence of gender, group identity, and collective self-esteem. *Cyberpsychology & Behavior*, *12*(2), 209–213. doi:10.1089/cpb.2008.0228 PMID:19250021

Baumeister, R. F. (1993). Conceptions of self and identity: A modern retrospective on Allport's view. In K. H. Craik, R. Hogan, R. N. Wolfe, K. H. Craik, R. Hogan, & R. N. Wolfe (Eds.), *Fifty years of personality psychology* (pp. 177–186). New York, NY: Plenum Press. doi:10.1007/978-1-4899-2311-0_12

Baym, N. K. (1995). The emergence of community in computer-mediated interaction. In S. G. Jones (Ed.), *Cybersociety: Computer-mediated communication and community* (pp. 138–163). Thousand Oaks, CA: Sage.

Berzonsky, M. D. (2003a). Identity style and well-being: Does commitment matter? *Identity*, *3*(2), 131–142. doi:10.1207/S1532706XID030203

Berzonsky, M. D. (2003b). The structure of identity: Commentary on Jane Krogers view of identity status transition. *Identity*, *3*(3), 231–245. doi:10.1207/S1532706XID0303_04

boyd, d. & Ellison, N. (2007): Social network sites: Definition, history, and scholarship. *Journal of Computer-Mediated Communication, 13*(1).

boyd, d., & Heer, J. (2006, January). Profiles as conversation: Networked identity performance on Friendster. In *System Sciences, 2006. HICSS'06. Proceedings of the 39th Annual Hawaii International Conference on* (Vol. 3, pp. 59c-59c). IEEE.

boyd, d. (2014). *It's complicated: The social lives of networked teens.* New Haven, CT: Yale University Press.

Case, A. (2010, December). *Amber Case: We are all cyborgs now* [video file]. Retrieved from https://www.ted.com/talks/amber_case_we_are_all_cyborgs_now/transcript?language=en

Cote, J. E. (2009). *Identity formation and self-development in adolescence.* In R. M. Lerner & L. D. Steinberg (Eds.), Handbook of adolescent psychology (3rd ed.; pp. 266–304). Hoboken, NJ: John Wiley & Sons, Inc.

Cottingham, R. (2007, June 23). *"On Facebook, nobody knows..."* [web log post; cartoon]. Retrieved from http://www.socialsignal.com/blog/rob-cottingham/on-facebook-nobody-knows

Damon, W., Menon, J., & Cotton, B. K. (2003). The development of purpose during adolescence. *Applied Developmental Science*, *7*(3), 119–128. doi:10.1207/S1532480XADS0703_2

Davis, K. (2010). Coming of age online: The developmental underpinnings of girls blogs. *Journal of Adolescent Research, 25*(1), 145–171. doi:10.1177/0743558409350503

Davis, K. (2012a). Friendship 2.0: Adolescents experiences of belonging and self-disclosure online. *Journal of Adolescence*, *35*(6), 1527–1536. doi:10.1016/j.adolescence.2012.02.013 PMID:22475444

Davis, K. (2012b). Tensions of identity in a networked era: Young peoples perspectives on the risks and rewards of online self-expression. *New Media & Society*, *14*(4), 634–651. doi:10.1177/1461444811422430

Davis, K. (2013). Young peoples digital lives: The impact of interpersonal relationships and digital media use on adolescents sense of identity. *Computers in Human Behavior*, *29*(6), 2281–2293. doi:10.1016/j.chb.2013.05.022

Davis, K. (2014). Youth identities in a digital age: The anchoring role of friends in youth's approaches to online identity expression. In A. Bennett & B. Robards (Eds.), *Mediated youth cultures: The internet, belonging, and new cultural configurations* (pp. 11–25). New York, NY: Palgrave Macmillan. doi:10.1057/9781137287021_2

Duggan, M., Ellison, N. B., Lampe, C., Lenhart, A., & Madden, M. (2015). Social media update 2014. Washington, DC: Pew Research Center. Retrieved from http://www.pewinternet.org/2015/01/09/social-media-update-2014/

Erikson, E. H. (1950). *Childhood and society* (1st ed.). New York, NY: Norton.

Erikson, E. H. (1968). *Identity, youth, and crisis* (1st ed.). New York, NY: Norton.

Erikson, E. H. (1980). *Identity and the life cycle*. New York, NY: Norton.

Facebook. (2015). *Terms of service*. Retrieved from https://www.facebook.com/legal/terms

Gardner, H., & Davis, K. (2013). *The App Generation: How today's youth navigate identity, intimacy, and imagination in a digital world*. New Haven, CT: Yale University Press.

Gergen, K. J. (2000). *The saturated self: Dilemmas of identity in contemporary life*. New York, NY: Basic Books.

Giddens, A. (1991). *Modernity and self-identity: Self and society in the late modern age*. Stanford, CA: Stanford University Press.

Hafeez, K. (2015, February 23). Remember when, on the Internet, nobody knew who you were. [Cartoon]. *The New Yorker*. Retrieved from http://www.condenaststore.com/-sp/Remember-when-on-the-Internet-nobody-knew-who-you-were-New-Yorker-Cartoon-Prints_i13126074_.htm

Hunt, E. (2015, November 3). Essena O'Neill quits Instagram claiming social media 'is not real life'. *The Guardian*. Retrieved from http://www.theguardian.com/media/2015/nov/03/instagram-star-essena-oneill-quits-2d-life-to-reveal-true-story-behind-images

Ingis, S., Signorelli, M., & Wolf, A. (2014). California eraser button law. *The Download*. Retrieved from http://www.lexology.com/library/detail.aspx?g=5112686b-104a-46fc-8091-09aca02b2b1b

James, W. (1890). *The principles of psychology*. New York, NY: H. Holt. doi:10.1037/11059-000

Kendall, L. (1999). Recontextualizing "cyberspace": Methodological considerations for on-line research. In S. G. Jones (Ed.), *Doing Internet research: Critical issues and methods for examining the Net* (pp. 57–74). Thousand Oaks, CA: Sage. doi:10.4135/9781452231471.n3

Kennedy, H. (2006). Beyond anonymity, or future directions for internet identity research. *New Media & Society*, *8*(6), 859–876. doi:10.1177/1461444806069641

Kirkpatrick, D. (2012). *The Facebook effect: The real inside story of Mark Zuckerberg and the world's fastest growing company*. New York, NY: Simon Schuster.

Lenhart, A. (2015). Teens, social media & technology. Washington, DC: Pew Research Center. Retrieved from http://www.pewinternet.org/2015/04/09/teens-social-media-technology- 2015/

Lifton, R. J. (1993). *The protean self: Human resilience in an age of fragmentation*. New York, NY: BasicBooks.

Markus, H., & Nurius, P. (1986). Possible selves. *The American Psychologist*, *41*(9), 954–969. doi:10.1037/0003-066X.41.9.954

McAdams, D. P. (1996). Personality, modernity, and the storied self: A contemporary framework for studying persons. *Psychological Inquiry*, *7*(4), 295–321. doi:10.1207/s15327965pli0704_1

McAdams, D. P. (1997). The case for unity in the (post)modern self: A modest proposal. In R. D. Ashmore, L. J. Jussim, R. D. Ashmore, & L. J. Jussim (Eds.), *Self and identity: Fundamental issues* (pp. 46–78). New York, NY: Oxford University Press.

Miller, H. (1995, June). The presentation of self in electronic life: Goffman on the Internet. In Embodied knowledge and virtual space conference (Vol. 9). Academic Press.

Roose, K. (2014, June 13). The complete guide to anonymous apps. *New York Magazine*. Retrieved from http://nymag.com/daily/intelligencer/2014/06/complete-guide-to-anonymous-apps.html

Safranova, V. (2015, November 18). On fake Instagram, a chance to be real. *The New York Times*. Retrieved from http://www.nytimes.com/2015/11/19/fashion/instagram-finstagram-fake-account.html?_r=0

Schwartz, S. J. (2007). The structure of identity consolidation: Multiple correlated constructs or one superordinate construct? *Identity*, *7*(1), 27–49. doi:10.1080/15283480701319583

Singer, N. (2013, November 9). They loved your GPA then they saw your tweets. *The New York Times*. Retrieved from http://www.nytimes.com/2013/11/10/business/they-loved-your-gpa-then-they-saw-your-tweets.html

Smith, A. (2015). U.S. smartphone use in 2015. Washington, DC: Pew Research Center. Retrieved from http://www.pewinternet.org/2015/04/01/us-smartphone-use-in-2015/

Smith, J. (2013, April 16). How your social media can help (or hurt) you in your job search. *Forbes*. Retrieved from http://www.forbes.com/sites/jacquelynsmith/2013/04/16/how-social-media-can-help-or-hurt-your-job-search/

Steiner, P. (1993). On the Internet, nobody knows you're a dog. *The New Yorker, 69*(20), 61.

Stone, A. R. (1991). Will the real body please stand up?. *Cyberspace: First Steps*, 81-118.

Subrahmanyam, K., Reich, S. M., Waechter, N., & Espinoza, G. (2008). Online and offline social networks: Use of social networking sites by emerging adults. *Journal of Applied Developmental Psychology*, *29*(6), 420–433. doi:10.1016/j.appdev.2008.07.003

Tetzlaff, D. (2000). Yo-ho-ho and a server of warez. In *The World Wide Web and contemporary cultural theory*, (pp. 99-126). Academic Press.

Turkle, S. (1995). *Life on the screen: Identity in the age of the Internet*. New York, NY: Simon & Schuster.

Underwood, M., & Faris, R. (2015). *#Being thirteen: Social media and the hidden world of young adolescents' peer culture*. Retrieved from https://assets.documentcloud.org/documents/.../being-13-report.pdf

Valkenburg, P. M., & Peter, J. (2011). Online communication among adolescents: An integrated model of its attraction, opportunities, and risks. *The Journal of Adolescent Health*, *48*(2), 121–127. doi:10.1016/j.jadohealth.2010.08.020 PMID:21257109

Waskul, D., & Douglass, M. (1997). Cyberself: The emergence of self in on-line chat. *The Information Society*, *13*(4), 375–397. doi:10.1080/019722497129070

Weinstein, E. (2014). The personal is political on social media: Online civic expression patterns and pathways among civically engaged youth. *International Journal of Communication*, *8*(24), 210–233.

Weinstein, E., Rundle, M., & James, C. (2015). A hush Falls over the crowd: Diminished online civic expression among young civic actors. *International Journal of Communication*, *9*(23), 84–105.

Wiedeman, R. (2015, September 23). The prom queen of Instagram. *New York Magazine.* Retrieved from http://nymag.com/thecut/2015/09/lilli-hymowitz-prom-queen-of-instagram.html#

Zhao, S., Grasmuck, S., & Martin, J. (2008). Identity construction on Facebook: Digital empowerment in anchored relationships. *Computers in Human Behavior*, *24*(5), 1816–1836. doi:10.1016/j.chb.2008.02.012

KEY TERMS AND DEFINITIONS

Asynchronous Communication: The ability to communicate with others at different points in time and in different geographic locations.

Finstagram: 'Fake' Instagram accounts in which people limit the audiences that can see their Instagram posts in order to express themselves in a style that is often different from their 'real' Instagram accounts.

Fragmentation: An inability to coordinate the multiple facets of one's self into a coherent whole.

Identity Confusion: A failure to craft a coherent and consistent picture of one's self.

Identity Synthesis: The achievement of a coherent and personally meaningful sense of self.

Pseudonymity: A state of partial anonymity in which one is recognized by an invented alias rather than one's real name.

Psychosocial Moratorium: Described by Erikson as a period of suspended consequences during which one is free to explore a variety of values and goals before making commitments to any of them.

Social Media: Networked platforms that support content sharing and interpersonal communication to various audiences.

Social Networking Sites: A type of social media platform that allows users to create individual profiles and link them to the profiles of other users.

Chapter 2
Self-Comparison:
The Self in Digital World

Clara Moningka
Gunadarma University, Indonesia

ABSTRACT

In this chapter, the author is interested in studying more about self-comparison through social media; especially in Jakarta, Indonesia. In Indonesia, social media are commonly used and widely used by various groups. As many as 93% of Internet users in Indonesia are accessing Facebook. Jakarta is even referred as the capital of a text-based social media. The use of social media can be influenced by the collective culture in Indonesia. In this case social media is not just a tool but also the social environment, in which social interaction occurs. This is also influences how individuals view themselves. The topic of the psychological effects of social media has been much discussed. A lot of research conducted on the effect of social on development of self-concept and including self-esteem. Social media becoming a place for comparing oneself to others and it turn out it has a great effect.

INTRODUCTION

Mashall McLuhan, communication theorist, coined the phrase, "the medium is the message" (Steers, Wickham, & Acitelli, 2014). Steers and colleagues stated that McLuhan did not mean to imply that individuals should ignore messages communicated through a certain medium, but that people should not only be aware of a medium's obvious properties but also be aware of how it subtly influences culture. He argued that important technological advances have the potential to become extensions of the people using them and, in turn, may redefine human interactions.

The use of social media is growing rapidly worldwide. Brenner and Smith (2014) found that Facebook and Twitters were the most popular social media websites among Indonesian emerging adults. Facebook is the most popular social media all over the world (Steers et al., 2014). Social media is used by various age groups. Kimbrough, Guadagno, Muscannel, and Dill (2013) argue that social media users usually are young people, especially women. Statistics showed that the biggest users groups of Facebook are teens and emerging adults; young emerging adults over the age of 18 years occupy 42% of total users,

DOI: 10.4018/978-1-5225-1856-3.ch002

followed by the older emerging adults aged 25-34 years at 21% (Sandra 2012). Kemp (2011) suggested that Indonesian internet users are some of the most social people on earth and Indonesian youth see social media as an everyday *necessity*. These youths will readily sacrifice other 'luxuries' to ensure their phones have sufficient credit to access mobile data. Indonesian youths between the ages of 13 and 24 years old have the highest level of interactions through the internet when compared to other cohorts. Comparing these youths, Indonesian emerging adults are the highest users of social media. Arnett (2006) defines emerging adulthood as a specific phase around the ages of 18 to 25. Emerging adulthood is characterized by instability and the search for stability and transition. The transition from adolescence to emerging adulthood is a crucial period in the formation of self-concept.

Self is an important part of human. The self relates to how we see ourselves and it also helps us to adapt to the environment. It is formed from the interaction between the potential that exists within us and within the environment. The environment might include parenting style, schools, neighborhoods, and the peer group. The digital world is becoming part of our environment. This aim of this chapter is to examine how the effects of social media on the self. The use of social media is massively increasing. This phenomenon can affect the formation of self. Social media allows people to easily view, access, and know information about other people's lives. It can also lead to upward or downward self-comparison. This comparison can affect how we see ourselves. This is the concern of this chapter, particularly in relation to social media use.

BACKGROUND

Mazzoni and Zanazzi (2014) described changes in global market that have affected social structure, specifically the transition from communication medium to another might have changed the personal need for social integration, which allowed people to find new channels of communication and to maintain their social networks. One well known social networking website in Indonesia is Facebook. Arakali (2015) reported that approximately 63 million people in Indonesia access Facebook at least once a month in 2015. This year also marked the culmination of mobile phone use. Indonesia has the 3rd largest country population accessing Facebook, after United State and India; the percentage of Facebook users from Indonesia who access the platform via mobile phones is higher than in any other country. By the end of 2015, it is estimated that users of social media will reach 100 million, and will continue to increase in 2016. Furthermore, Indonesia will reach the top five of internet users in 2017, overtaking Japan. Social media is like a two-sided coin. On one hand, social media can help us build social networks, expanding social interaction, but on the other hand, social media also have some risks that could affect aspects of human life, whether cognitive, affective, or behavioral. Sandra (2012) suggests that good self-concept is a result of good interaction in the cyberspace and also in the real environment.

The need to control the use of social media. In 2013, Japan's Ministry of education estimates that about 518,000 children in Japan were addicted to internet and should be rehabilitated (Samakow, 2013). The Government was concerned that this addiction would disrupt children's development. One way to deal with addiction is to send children to Internet fasting camps, where there is no internet connection. This camp tries to encourage children to communicate directly with others. This is an important rehabilitation because children and adolescents who use the internet intensely are more likely to experience depression, obesity, and developmental disorders.

The use of social media allows us for a more intense interaction. We often do not realize the impact of social media. Andriani (2016) explained that social media can make it easier for us to communicate in real time, but it can also be used for negative behaviors, such as taunting and arguing. Mocking behavior can disrupt children's development. Sometimes these behaviors are referred to as cyberbullying. Furthermore, Vogel et al. (2014) explained that social media, such as Facebook, provides abundant social comparison opportunities. Uhlir (2016) also explained the Facebook depression phenomenon, which is caused by social comparison of oneself to others who post on social media. This phenomenon occurs because the individual can easily open social media and see other people's lives. Social comparison is sometimes done to boost self-esteem, but it does not always work. It can make people envious of others.

Self in the Digital World

Formation of the Self

At birth, we were given a name that became part of our identity. Along with our physical and mental development, we also develop other types of identity, such as gender identity and a concept of who we are. The knowledge about ourselves is known as self-concept. Self-concept is defined as a person's sense of self, shaped through interaction with the environment and other people. Sandra (2014) and Sanderson (2010) elaborate further that self-concept is a picture of how people describe themselves, which covers their point of view and how they think and judge themselves. A positive self-concept is very important for improving mental health and various behaviors, such as academic achievement and the resiliency to cope with negative interactions (Chapman, Tunmer, & Prochnov, 2000)

The formation of self-concept is not limited to the interaction with the family, school, and the peer group, which can occur offline or through cyberspace. Technological developments and improvements make it possible for us to be closer to each other, even when we are far from each other. Social networking websites allow us to easily see the activities of other individuals. These activities shown might include fun activities or something that makes someone proud (Moningka, 2015). Uhlir (2016) also argued that social media users may post photos and statuses that reflect the most exciting parts of their lives, such as parties with friends and glamorous vacation, to create a flattering depiction of themselves. Kim and Lee (2011) argued that this activity is a way to present themselves to others, which is known as self-presentation. They also explained that self-presentation involves users presenting themselves in a selective manner, emphasizing favorable and appropriate images. This behavior can lead to self-comparison. It is human nature for people to see others who are luckier and better than their selves. Such comparison may relate to the formation of the self and may influence psychological wellbeing. People can choose to present their ideal self or false self on social media. They might do so for deception, exploration or impressing others. Discrepancies between the ideal self and real self can lead to devaluation of the self and presentation of the false self. It is also linked to low self-esteem and depression.

Interaction between Self and Self-Comparison

Around the world, children are growing up in high-technology environments. Children are masters of technology, including the Internet and how to interact in social media. Foo (2003) suggests that the interaction with the Internet leads to the development of unlimited self-identity. Development of information technology can encourage the growth of creativity and knowledge, but also increases interactions on social networking websites, where people expect positive feedback from such interaction. Research conducted by Jackson, Zhao, Witt, Fitzgerald, Von Eye, and Harold (2009) revealed that interactions in the virtual world can build positive self-concepts. Good interaction through social networking websites also lead to life satisfaction and better relationships in the real world. Sandra (2012) conducted research in four large cities in Indonesia, Jakarta (Capital City), Yogyakarta (Central Java), and Denpasar (Bali). Findings from this research revealed that Internet use also has negative impacts. For instance, people tend to pretend and present an unreal self-identity. Social media allows people to be anyone they want to be. The Indonesian Commission for Child Protection also stated that there were 784 cases of child abuse in Indonesia in year 2014, and from that number, 20% occurred in cyberspace (Setyawan, 2014).

Self-comparison theory was purposed by Leon Festinger. This theory explains that individuals tend to compare themselves to others, when they need guidance or a standard to compare their ability to. Individuals process information from their social environment by comparing themselves to established similarities and differences. This information might be sought for a reason or purpose (Krayer, Ingledew, & Iphofen, 2008). Sanderson (2010) stated that self-comparison explains what we think about ourselves and can be different for each person, depending on the nature of comparison we are making. People make social comparisons to reduce uncertainty about their performance or abilities. Therefore, they need an external standard to compare with. White, Langer, Yariv, and Welch, 2006 explained that social-comparison can be used as a coping mechanism. For instance, when we compare ourselves with others who are less fortunate than us, we sometimes feel relieve.

Self-comparison plays an important role in evaluating our abilities. Sanderson, 2010 explained that first year college students suddenly feel not so smart, even though they used to be a star in their previous school. The new environment of college means that they are surrounded by smart students, which can lower self-esteem. A contemporary psychoanalyst, Bolt (2010), explained that some people were raised in a society that taught them to compare themselves with others. Children might learn this early on as some parents compare their children with other children in order to control their children's undesirable behavior. Such comparisons might reduce or boost egos. Bolt (2010) explained that the effects of social comparison has two distinct outcomes, depending on the meaning we assigned to the comparison. A person who does not measure up to the comparison might feel exhausted and depressed, withdrawing from others. On the other hand, when an individual feels that he or she is superior to other individuals, feelings of superiority increase. White, Langer, Yariv, and Welch (2006) explained that frequent social comparison are associated with destructive emotions and behaviors, such as envy and depression.

Dark Side of Social Comparison

Lyubomirsky and Ross (1997) found that unhappy people tend to compare themselves to others. The comparison occurs spontaneously and frequently. These findings are also similar with research from Giordano, Wood, and Michela (2000) and Swallow and Kuiper (1992). This research found that unhappy people make frequent comparisons. Swallow and Kuiper also found that people with depression made frequent social comparison. Furthermore, Stapel and Blanton (2004) explained that social comparison occurs automatically, meaning that we do are oftentimes not aware that we are doing it. With social media, people can easily compare themselves with others, either automatically or purposefully.

White, Langer, Yarif, and Welch (2006) suggests that individuals who often make social comparisons with others are dissatisfied with themselves. Frequent social comparison positively correlated with destructive emotions and behaviors, such as envy, guilt, regret, and lying. Many studies have revealed that envy affects behaviors. Smith and Kim (2007) explained that Facebook is an easier place to engage in comparisons. Furthermore, Krasnova, Wenninger, Widjaja, and Buxmann (2013) also stated that the more people use Facebook, the more envious these individuals feel and the more dissatisfied they are with their lives.

Moningka (2015) conducted research in Jakarta, Indonesia regarding social. The research was conducted in Jakarta, because it is the metropolis city and also the capital city of the country in which the population of social media users is quite high. This study's aim was to understand the purpose of using social media and what participants felt when they used it. From the 90 respondents (ages ranged from 17 to 45), more than 80% used social media as a tool to entertain themselves. They also accessed social media daily and used it on average more than 1 hours a day. More than 40% respondent felt anxious or irritated if they were not able to access social media other respondents indicated that not being able to access social media would be boring. Other respondents indicated that they would feel relief if they could not access social media. Some of the respondents who answered that they would feel relief indicated that they would feel a sense of freedom from social media. Social media is important to their lives and can affect their emotions. These findings were similar to the results from a study conducted in Semarang, Central Java. In her research on 100 undergraduate students, Soliha (2015) found a positive correlation between social anxiety and dependence on social media.

Moningka (2015) also explained that activities on social media consisted of updating statuses or seeing other people's statuses and photos. Participants felt excited to read other status or knowing their friend's activities. This preliminary research also found that most of the respondents felt envious about what was happening on social media and sometimes they lied to boost their self-esteem. These activities are unhealthy and can lead to stress, even depression. After interviewing eight people, Moningka (2015) that these individuals were quite happy with their self; however, when they accessed social media frequently, they felt that others were happier and luckier. They pretended like things were going well in their lives to boost their self-esteem. They mentioned that they felt happy for their friends and colleagues for accomplishments but because they did not experience the success themselves, they sometimes felt negative emotions. These findings are consistent with a study carried out by Lyuborsky and Ross (1997). In their study, they found that unhappy people felt worse when paired with better performers. These unhappy people compared themselves with worse performers. In contrast, happy people were unaffected by other's performance. Social media gives us a lot of chances to compare ourselves to others. We might do so unconsciously at first.

Vogel et al. (2014) also found that the social media users with more exposure to Facebook tended to evaluate themselves more poorly while average users reported more upward comparisons than downward social comparison. Comparisons on Facebook allow individuals to compare themselves on a variety of topics, including their looks or physical performance. Women tend to compare their activities and their performance to their Facebook friends' more than men (Moningka, 2015). Furthermore, women were generally more curious about what their Facebook friends did and where their friends went in comparison to men. Sagioglou and Greitemeyer (2014) also found similar patterns. Even though both genders experiences negative moods resulting from their social comparisons. Fardouly, Diedrichs, Vartanian, and Halliwell (2015) found that women reported more negative mood safter brief exposure in Facebook than after exposure to an appearance-neutral website. Social comparison through media images and messages are used to form identity development (Krayer, Ingledew, & Iphofen, 2008). This research also revealed that body dissatisfaction increases when individuals viewed or read appearance-focused material or were exposed to peer messages about thinness.

Sandra (2012) also explained that people try to get noticed or gain attention in cyberspace. Furthermore, people desire to be accepted via cyberspace as well by altering change their names or profile updates to fit in with others. In another study, Vaswani (2012) explained that young people in Indonesia, especially in the big city or urban areas, use social media because it is one way for young Indonesians to feel connected to some of the more famous and powerful people. To be connected with someone famous might boost their self-esteem. These individuals identify themselves with the social figure they followed and sometimes they compare themselves with the social figure and adopt his or her way of thinking.

Self-esteem can predict positive emotion, leading to happiness; however, when we frequently compare ourselves to others, we might feel dissatisfied with ourselves, leading to negative emotions and behaviors. In support of this conclusion, Vogel and colleagues (2014) found that frequent Facebook users believed that other users were happier and more successful than themselves. It appears that the people compared their realistic self with their idealized online selves of others. Kim and Lee (2011) explained that self-presentation on Facebook is reinforced by improvements in mood and self-esteem; social media in some ways can increase happiness, although social comparison is a mediator in the association between Facebook and depressive symptoms.

SOLUTIONS AND RECOMMENDATIONS

Social media is intended to facilitate communication and expression. However, there is a darker side to social media. It can become a place to boast. People often compare themselves with others on social media, which can make them feel stress and depressed. These comparisons can lower self-esteem and affect psychological well-being. Social media is not to blame, but rather how individuals can control themselves and use social media more wisely.

REFERENCES

Andriani, I. (2016). *Model of cyberbullying behavior influenced by external and internal factors* (Unpublished Doctoral Dissertation). University of Gunadarma, Jakarta.

Arakali, H. (2015). *Emerging Markets Like Indonesia, India Top US In Facebook Mobile Access.* Retrieved January 30, 2016 from http://www.ibtimes.com/emerging-markets-indonesia-india-top-us-facebook-mobile-access-1792686Bolt

Bolt, J. (2010, August 9). How to Wreck Your Self Esteem: Compare Yourself with Others. *Psychology Today*. Retrieved from http://www.psychologytoday.com/blog/your-zesty- self/201008/how-wreck-your-self-esteem-compare-youself-others

Chapman, J., Turner, W., & Prochnow, J. (2000). Early reading related to performance, reading self-concept and the development of academic self-concept. *Journal of Educational Psychology*, *92*(4), 703–708. doi:10.1037/0022-0663.92.4.703

Fardouly, J., Diedrichs, P. C., Vartanian, L. R., & Halliwell, E. (2015). Social comparison on social media: The impact of Facebook on young womans body image concern and mood. *Body Image*, *13*, 38–45. doi:10.1016/j.bodyim.2014.12.002

Foo, C. T. (2003). Child of the internet. *Cyberpsychology & Behavior*, *6*(2), 195–199. doi:10.1089/109493103321640392

Giordano, C., Wood, J. V., & Michela, J. L. (2000). Depressive personality style, dysphoria, and social comparison in everyday life. *Journal of Personality and Social Psychology*, *79*(3), 438–451. doi:10.1037/0022-3514.79.3.438

Jackson, L. A., Zhao, Y., Witt, E. A., Fitzgerald, H. E., Von Eye, A., & Harold, R. (2009). Self-concept, self-esteem, gender, race, and information technology use. *Cyberpsychology & Behavior*, *12*(4), 437–440. doi:10.1089/cpb.2008.0286

Kemp, S. (2011). *Social, digital, and mobile in Indonesia*. Retrieved January 5, 2016 from http://weare-social.sg/blog/2011/12/social-digital-mobile-indonesia/

Kim, J., & Lee, J. R. (2011). The Facebook paths to happiness: Effects of the number Facebook friends and self-presentation on subjective well-being. *Cyberpsychology, Behavior, and Social Networking*, *14*(6), 359–364. doi:10.1089/cyber.2010.0374

Kimbrough, A. M., Guadagno, R. E., Muscanell, N. L., & Dill, J. (2013). Gender differences in mediated communication:Women connect more than do men. *Computers in Human Behavior*, *29*(3), 896–900. doi:10.1016/j.chb.2012.12.005

Krasnova, H., Wenninger, H., Widjaja, T., & Buxmann, P. (2013). "Envy on Facebook: A Hidden Threat to Users' Life Satisfaction?" (2013). *Wirtschaftsinformatik Proceedings 2013*. Retrieved from http://www.ara.cat/tecnologia/facebook_ARAFIL20130128_0001.pdf

Krayer, A., Ingledew, D. K., & Iphofen, R. (2008). Social comparison and body image in adolescence: A grounded theory approach. *Health Education Research*, *23*(5), 892–903. doi:10.1093/her/cym076

Lyubormirsky, S., & Ross, L. (1997). Hedonic consequnces of social comparison: A contrast of happy and unhappy people. *Journal of Personality and Social Psychology*, *73*(6), 1141–1157. doi:10.1037/0022-3514.73.6.1141

Mazzoni, E., & Zanazzi, L. (2014). Comparing the use of SNSs among adults and emerging adults. *Journal of e-Learning and knowledge. Society*, *10*(3), 25–36.

Moningka, C. (2015). *The use of social media in Jakarta. Unpublished research*. Jakarta: Gunadarma University.

Sagioglou, C., & Greitemeyer, T. (2014). Facebooks emotional consequences: Why Facebook causes a decrease in mood and why people still use it. *Computers in Human Behavior, 35*, 359–363. doi:10.1016/j.chb.2014.03.003

Samakow, J. (2013). *Japan Internet 'Fasting Camps' Aim To Treat Screen-Addicted Kids.* Retrieved January, 8, 2016 from http://www.huffingtonpost.com/2013/08/28/japan-internet-fasting-camp_n_3824697.html

Sanderson, C. A. (2010). *Social psychology*. New York: John Wiley & Sons, Inc.

Sandra, L. (2012). *The dynamics interaction of psychological self-concept and on-line identity* (Unpublished Doctoral Dissertation). University of Gajah Mada, Yogyakarta.

Setyawan, D. (2014). *KPAI ingatkan orang tua: waspadai kejahatan seksual pada anak melalui media sosial.* Retrieved, January, 8, 2016 from http://www.kpai.go.id/berita/kpai-ingatkan-orang-tua-waspadai-kejahatan-seksual-pada-anak-melalui-media-sosial/

Smith, R. H., & Kim, S. H. (2007). Comprehending envy. *Psychological Bulletin, 133*(1), 46–64. doi:10.1037/0033-2909.133.1.46

Soliha, S. F. (2015). Tingkat ketergantungan pengguna media sosial dan kecemasan sosial. *Jurnal Interaksi, 4*(1), 1–10.

Srivastava, R., & Joshi, S. (2014). Relationship between self-concept and self-esteem in adolescent. *Journal of Advanced Research, 2*(2), 36–43.

Stapel, D. A., & Blanton, H. (2004). From seeing to being: Subliminal social comparison affect implicit and explicit self-evaluation. *Journal of Personality and Social Psychology, 87*(4), 468–481. doi:10.1037/0022-3514.87.4.468

Steers, M. N., Wickham, R. E., & Acitelli, L. K. (2014). Seeing everyone elses highlight reels: How Facebook usage is linked to depressive symptoms. *Journal of Social and Clinical Psychology, 33*(8), 701–731. doi:10.1521/jscp.2014.33.8.701

Swallow, S. R., & Kuiper, N. A. (1992). Mild depression and frequency of social comparison behavior. *Journal of Social and Clinical Psychology, 11*(2), 167–180. doi:10.1521/jscp.1992.11.2.167

Uhlir, J. L. (2016). *Social comparison and self-presentation on social media of depressive symptoms.* Scripps Senior Theses Paper 756. Retrieved, August 18, 2016 from http://scolarship.claremont.edu/scripps_theses/756

Vaswani, K. (2012). *Indonesia's love affair with social media.* Retrieved, January 8, 2016 from http://www.bbc.com/news/world-asia-17054056

Vogel, E. A., Rose, J. P., Roberts, L. R., & Eckles, K. (2014). Social comparison, social media, and self-esteem. *Psychology of Popular Media Culture, 3*(4), 206–222. doi:10.1037/ppm0000047

White, J. B., Langer, E. J., Yariv, L., & Welch, J. C. IV. (2006). Frequent social comparison and destructive emotions and behaviors: The dark side of social comparison. *Journal of Adult Development, 13*(1), 36–44. doi:10.1007/s10804-006-9005-0

KEY TERMS AND DEFINITIONS

Collective Culture: Culture which is oriented in togetherness or doing something together. It usually occurs in Asian Culture.

On-Line Identity: Social identity that internet user uses in on-line community; it can be real identity or fake identity.

Self-Comparison: The act of comparing oneself to others in order to gain personal worth. It consist of upward social comparison and downward social comparison.

Self-Concept: The sense of self.

Self-Esteem: Person's evaluation of his/her own worth.

Social Media: Computer-mediated communication that allow people or organization to create, share, or exchange information.

Chapter 3
The Process of Acculturation and Transition for Adulthood in Young Brazilian Soccer Players in a Digital Age

Fernanda Faggiani
Pontifícia Universidade Católica do Rio Grande do Sul, Brazil

Carolina Saraiva de Macedo Lisboa
Pontifícia Universidade Católica do Rio Grande do Sul, Brazil

ABSTRACT

High mobility of Brazilian athletes has increased significantly due to the globalization of soccer. It is very common to observe young athletes moving from their hometowns to a different place as a demand of the profession/career. During this process, youth face the process of acculturation, known as the transition to a different culture as a job demand (to play soccer) and feeling confused about his/her cultural identity. In addition, these young athletes assume responsibilities of adults in a period of development - adolescence and the transition to adulthood - characterized by the identity consolidation. The process of identity of football players is emphasized since the early childhood. The aim of this chapter is to discuss the process of acculturation in young Brazilian soccer athletes elucidating related aspects and the development of identity, concerning its cultural dimension surrounded by information and communication technologies of a digital age.

INTRODUCTION

The objective of this chapter is to discuss the acculturation process and identity construction of Brazilian teenage athletes and their transition to adulthood, while considering the cultural dimensions that influence universal aspects of this process. The world's globalization, in part, is influenced by information and communication technologies. This globalization has provoked changes in adolescence and adulthood. The process which the individual goes through - moving to a new place culturally different from his own

DOI: 10.4018/978-1-5225-1856-3.ch003

- impacts performance, identity, and mental health. The contextual aspects that influence the process of acculturation and identity as well as the discussion of this subject in the area of sports psychology are theoretical and practical challenges for psychologists and other professionals who work with Brazilian soccer athletes. This process can be facilitated by communication and information technologies. The possibility of being in frequent contact with people from the individual's country of birth may make it more difficult to adapt to the transition to living in a new country.

BACKGROUND

The Soccer Player Formation in Brazil

Soccer, besides being a sport, is one of the great cultural institutions. It can influence and consolidate national identities. Becoming a soccer athlete in Brazil consists of increasingly refining techniques, due to the strained competition in this sport. Among the components of the athletes' training are physical contexts or formation centers, living accommodations, training environment, and changing rooms.

The organizational principles of a soccer player are hinged from the economic investment, clubs' and companies' political interests, and the preparation for games and professional exercises. These are adjusted according to the availability and the requirements of the club. This process is managed by experts, former players, physical education teachers, and agency networks that represent athletes.

Becoming a soccer player is a highly competitive processes and physically and emotionally stressful. There are approximately 5000 hours of investments on physical training, distributed over the course of about ten years, directed to the body, in tightly disciplined routines that are both exhausting and commonly monotonous. Training athletes are teens, ages from 10 to 20 years, and many came from vulnerable environments and from different Brazilian regions and countries. Coaches, family, media, clubs, and fans have high expectations of these youths, which makes them vulnerable to stress (Afif, 1997). These athletes face, from a very early age, the pressure to become players and having their professional identity shaped from the perspectives/expectations of adults (e.g., relatives, entrepreneurs, leaders, technicians), before they even have their own sense of self.

The career of these athletes starts and sometimes ends in the formation center. In the formation center, athletes can remain until they are 20 years old. The next step, if they are selected, is to be a professional soccer player. If the athlete does not reach the requirements/criteria needed to advance, the athlete will have to search for another alternative. Many of these athletes that cannot advance in their career leave behind their chances at a soccer career. Formation centers are specialized in learning the fundamentals of soccer. These centers are focused on improving the physical, technical, tactical, and psychological skills of athletes during their career development. Athletes' access to these locations is not mandatory, which is why the strict compliance with the training and the residence rules is necessary. To have a soccer career, athletes' motivation is important. Once integrated in the sport's club, the youth needs to devote himself or herself to the intensive workouts and routines. The youth will eventually abdicate from other forms of social interaction, friendship, entertainment, and family (Damo, 2007, 2014). Some Brazilian soccer athletes devalue school and academic development.

Young athletes from different Brazilian regions and countries bring their customs, values, and habits to the soccer clubs. The adaptation to a different culture can generate culture shock. The athletes face new customs in training and in daily life. Accepting and understanding the new culture is important because athletes can encounter cultural differences in issues related to family, region, social relationships, and professional activities, as well as experience an abrupt transition from childhood to adulthood. Guidelines, accompaniments, and clarifications are important so these athletes can adapt in a healthy way to local customs. While athletes are subjected to medical and dental examinations, they must be accompanied by psychologists and social workers, and receive school and cultural education to guarantee a healthy adaptation to the new environment (Afif, 1997).

Playing professional soccer is a dream desired by many athletes, particularly among Brazilian youths. This dream represents the potential to change one's financial status. Some poor or vulnerable families urge their children to play soccer more than studying or going to university in order to achieve better socioeconomic conditions for themselves and their families. Playing professional soccer can become a reality for some youths (Ciampa, Helm, & Souza, 2010). However, many youths are unaware of the pressures and stress of everyday life and sports practice. The dream for many professional players starts in childhood and the process of soccer player identity formation overlaps with their own process of individuation, throughout their development. These youths seek professional soccer careers for social recognition, believing in an omnipotent perspective that they "can do anything" while disregarding their physical and emotional limitations (Ciampa, Helm, & Souza, 2010). Sports provides these youths with visibility, financial security, expansion of personal ties, improved social status, the acquisition of material goods (e.g., home ownership and luxury items), and the ability to contribute to their family's well-being. The expectation to reach professionalism influences not only the identity of the athlete, but also represents the dreams of his or her family. These youths face risks inherent in the sport, in addition to being expected to perform well by coaches, family, and the public. Facing professional challenges and being away from their families, athletes often connect to families and friends digitally through social networks (Abreu, 2013; Gross, 2004; Matos, 2015; Salgado, Boubeta, Tobío, Mallou & Couto, 2004; Wendt & Lisboa, 2014; Young, 1999).

Identity and Transition to Adulthood

According to the World Health Organization (WHO), adolescence involves the period between 10 and 19 years in which significant changes occur biologically, psychologically, and socially. During this period, individuals experience different forms of relationship, have new social roles and abilities, and assume new attitudes in everyday situations (Rodrígues & Damásio, 2014; Santos, Neto & Koller, 2014). In adolescence, concerns related to being inserted in the social group (peer group), involvement in risk groups, and search for social identity parallel the process of forming one's own identity and being autonomous from one's parents. The period also marks biopsychosocial changes, including sexual maturity, interest in the opposite sex, and sex (Smith, 2011; Santos, Neto, & Koller, 2014). It is the period in which the transition from child dependency to adult autonomy occurs (Muuss, 1969). In the digital age, the "likes" of friends and others seem to gain special importance that even concern psychologists and health professionals (Abreu, 2013; Salgado, Boubeta, Tobío, Mallou, & Couto, 2014; Wendt & Lisboa, 2014; Young, 1999).

In adolescence, individuals develop new cognitive skills, such as the acquisition of abstract forms of thought (Piaget, 1960; Rodrígues, & Damásio, 2014). With these new skills, teenagers have a greater ability to reflect about himself or herself and about others, and how he or she fits into the world. Therefore, the massive information available on social networking websites dictate social patterns that affect individuals' subjectivity and personal opinions.

It is in this phase that teenagers establish their relationships with others. They might intensify their friendships and intimacy, experimenting with new social roles and becoming closer to their peers. Many teenagers face social challenges like meeting new people with different beliefs and values (Marcelli & Branconnier, 2007; Rodrígues & Damásio, 2014). These internal contradictions can cause confusion and distress in adolescents, raising anxiety levels (Rodríguez & Damásio, 2014).

A later stage after adolescence, which is still very similar in characteristics, is the transition to emerging adulthood (Arnett, 2004; Dutra-Thomas & Koller, 2014). This stage of life refers to a chronological period between 18 and 25 years old. This is a period in which individuals are becoming adults. In adolescence, many individuals are attending school and are systematically monitored by their parents. In adulthood, individuals tend to express their desire to or get married or have children, maintain a steady job, and realize themselves as adults (Dutra-Thomé, 2013).

The transition to adulthood is a stage of the life cycle in which young people from developed countries devote more time to their studies and postpone the experience of marriage and having children. Postponing these tasks gives them the opportunity to explore different employment opportunities (Arnett, 2004, 2007). In developing countries, such as Brazil, the insertion of the young people into the work market seems to happen increasingly earlier than in developed countries. This fact can be explained by the important social inequality existing in the country and mainly due to the need of individuals, from a very early age, to financially support their families. However, even having financial independence, Brazilian youths are staying longer in their families' home (Delhi-Thomé, 2013).

In Brazil, the transition to adulthood is characterized by a stage of identity exploration and changes in work, education, and relationships. Moreover, it is at this stage that individuals continue to focus on themselves and their desires, because they tend to have a vision of freedom and/or high hopes about the future as well as ambivalence and oscillations between teenagers' and adults' attitudes and behaviors. It is noted that the transition to adulthood is not a universal phenomenon, but shows specific characteristics in different countries. It is also a topic of incipient study in developing countries. The characteristics of this process occur due to cultural differences (Arnett, 2007; Delhi-Thomas & Koller, 2014).

The transition to adulthood is an individual process, which is characterized by emotional ambivalence; the individual no longer feels like an adolescent and does not understood himself or herself as an adult (Arnett, 2000). Many young people experiencing the transition to adulthood feel ambivalent about their roles as teenagers and adults because there is an accumulating set of activities that need to be undertaken, such as paying bills, taking care of the house and household chores, and sending money to their parents. For young soccer players, the transition to adulthood may occur earlier than for other individuals. These players assume adult responsibilities and have less leisure time. Also, these young adults may move quickly to adulthood by earning more money and establishing family bonds (marriage) that they may not be ready to do.

The social and relational aspects through which these young people pass in the period of adolescence and subsequent transition to adult life influence their conception of themselves and the constitution of their identity (Rodrígues & Damásio, 2014). Identity can be described as a set of beliefs and significant goals that allow, in a coherent and consistent way, the person to understand who he or she is and who he or she hopes to become in the future (Bronk, 2011). Furthermore, identity is based on self-concept, self-esteem, and self-efficacy. The individual perceives elements of himself or herself that make up who he or she is individually (self-concept), his or her values concerning those elements (self-esteem), and trust in himself or herself regarding receiving desired result from his or her goals (self-efficacy). The individual is confronted with the characteristics of the surrounding environment and the characteristics of the different people he or she meets during his or her life to establish an identity. The identity process demands having a clear sense of who someone is. The clarity of this information promotes the organization of personal actions, gives meaning to existence, and allows the individual to establish a link with the world (Rodrígues & Damásio, 2014).

Identity is a social process. More specifically, identity includes beliefs about oneself that are often contrasted with the views of others, particularly significant others in our lives, to establish a real and ideal sense about oneself (Harter, 2003; Rodrígues & Damásio, 2014). Social and cultural contexts are important to understanding the construction of identity. The digital age influences the construction of identity (Gardner & Steinberg, 2005; Gross, 2004; Lapidot-Lefler & Barak, 2012; Luna, 2013; Moss, 2015; Salgado, Boubeta, Tobío, Mallou & Couto, 2004; Wendt & Lisboa, 2014)

Each society is characterized by cultural elements, which provide identification and perpetuation of values, customs, and beliefs. Cultural norms and expectations help to determine the nature of emerging adulthood and thus assume an important role in identity construction (Santos, Neto, & Koller, 2014). Transitions throughout the process of identity can result in cultural conflicts and, consequently, doubts or questions about identity.

Research demonstrates the culturally significance of identity, and failure to establish a strong identity might be a risk factor for anxiety, depression, stress, and poor social skills (Cuadrado & Tabernero, 2014, Schwartz, Unger, Zamboanga & Szapocznik, 2010). Cultural identity is the part of the self-concept that integrates the significant values and emotions of belonging and identify within a specific cultural group. The more identified and attached to the standards and cultural elements belonging to one's place of origin (city, state, country) the greater the risk of experiencing stress and difficulties adapting to a new cultural group (Cuadrado & Tabernero, 2014). A study with adolescents from twenty different countries revealed that higher degree of identification with traditional family values was related to greater difficulties with acculturation (Cuadrado & Tabernero, 2014). Cultural identity was stronger among immigrants compared to natives, indicating that cultural identity shows marked importance to those groups that are far from their original culture.

The process of adaptation to different environments can be easier for children and adolescents than for adults, because children and adolescents have higher cognitive and emotional flexibility (Cheung, Heine, & Chudek, 2011; Schwartz, Unger, Zamboanga & Szapocznik, 2010; Cuadrado & Tabernero, 2014). They have greater physical energy to learn new behaviors. When it comes to youths, efforts occur during identity construction and a new cultural context could contribute to a fluid and easy acquisition of new cultural practices, values, and identifications.

Gonzales and Oliveira (2011) observed changes in the personality of young adults who moved from one region to another culturally different region. Individuals reported an identity change linked to the challenges associated with moving to a new area. They described spiritual, emotional, self-concept, and personality changes to adapt to the new culture. The acculturation process directly influenced their construction and maintenance of identity.

Migration and Acculturation in Brazilian Soccer Players

Soccer players transition through different sport clubs and cultures to progress in their career. Besides having a steady job as a soccer player, athletes take on adult responsibilities while in the middle of transitioning between developmental periods. Due to the transition, the athlete's identity might be reconstructed. Many athletes identify as a soccer player early on in their lives. The passion for the sport sometimes continues as a lifelong pursuit. Soccer promotes a rapprochement between people, encourages dialogue and exchange of information, is conducive to human development. and promotes social identity formation (Ciampa, Helm, & Souza, 2010).

The desire to develop an identity may facilitate the generation of goals and objectives that are meaningful to adolescents and emerging adults (Rodríguez & Damásio, 2014). As soccer players, they might feel the need to achieve a status, to earn money, and be socially recognized. Consequently, their identity might be characterized by constant changes and pressures (Ciampa, Helm, & Souza, 2010; Tibbert, Andersen, & Morris, 2015). A recent study conducted with young soccer players who migrated from other European countries to play in England found that these players believed their development was enhanced due to their experiences (Richardson, Litterwood, Neti, & Benstead, 2012).

Transitioning between cultures leads to cultural value changes. These values include those that are widespread across ethnic groups. Values, such as individualism, collectivism, familiarity, sexism, feminism, respect, kindness, conformity, family recognition, emotional self-control, and humility, are important for healthy adaptation. Individualistic attitudes and values increase the risk for negative psychological consequences, while collectivist attitudes and values seem protective and assist with proper adaptation to a new culture (Schwartz, Unger, Zamboanga, & Szapocznik, 2010). On the other hand, Weedon (2011) and Schinke, McGannon, Battochio, Wells (2013) explained that individual cultural perspectives should be activated as resources to negotiate the experiences, values, and behaviors of athletes, while integrating and reinforcing their self-concept and identity.

Richardson and colleagues (2012) suggest that integrated support, focusing on the identity of the player, rather than on the practice of various techniques (e.g. relaxation) and psychological skills (e.g. concentration), results in better adaptation to the new environment. Therefore, support for athletes requires basic skills counseling with an emphasis on developing self-knowledge, self-confidence (Ravizza, 2002), and identity (Erickson, 1997).

In 2010, the Brazilian Confederation of soccer (CBF) announced that approximately 1,029 professional soccer athletes moved from a Brazilian team to play in a foreign one (Brandão, Magnani, Tega, & Medina, 2013). According to the CBF, 683 (66%) of this athletes returned to Brazil before the end of the first year. Furthermore, professional soccer athletes residing in another country reported that they were in the country in passing (Rial, 2008). For these athletes, the culture reference is not the national-local, but the culture of the soccer club is. The 40 Brazilian athletes in this study also indicated that they lived in "bubbles" that protect and control them, mediating their relationships with the outside world.

The transition process and the individual's adjustment to a new culture is defined as acculturation (Andreason, 2003). This is the approach of two distinct or similar cultures, in which the individual absorbs aspects from both of them, internalizing a new culture. This process involves a wide range of emotional and psychological reactions of the individual and his or her ability to deal with cultural differences and move on to face new forms of socializing. Acculturation is the interpretation of culture, through the direct and continuous contact with groups of individuals who are representatives of different cultures (Pereira, Pimentel, & Kato, 2005; Ferreira, 1997). The terms that have been used in international investigations to explain the transition from one country to another are acculturation (Schinke, McGannon, Battochio, & Wells, 2013), migration (Evans & Stead, 2014), and migratory transition (Richardson, Litterwood, Neti, & Benstead, 2012). The term that is used in Brazil is expatriate (Brandão, Magnani, Tega, & Medina, 2013; Pereira, Pimentel, & Kato, 2005). The different terminology may not impact the phenomenon itself, but it certainly impacts the research and academic exchanges on advancing our understanding of acculturation and intervening strategies to help with this transition.

Acculturation is an emergent phenomenon in surveys with professional sports athletes (Ryska, 2001; Agergaard, 2008; Rial, 2008; Weedon, 2011; Evans & Stead, 2014; Richardson, Litterwood, Nesti & Benstead, 2012; Brandão, Magnani, Tega & Medina, 2013; Agergaard & Ryba, 2014; Blodgett et al., 2014; Tibbert, Andersen & Morris, 2015), because the process impacts athletes' performance (Mendenhall & Oddou, 2014; Lee & Kartika, 2014). Performance levels and quality have an important effect on the adaptation of the expatriate athlete, decreasing levels of depression and work conflicts (Lee & Kartika, 2014). However, the process of acculturation may be a challenge and depends on numerous factors.

Desirable adaptation to the new environment involves healthy adjustment to work, as well as to the social and cultural contexts. Also important for success in this process are individual factors, such as self-awareness, self-efficacy, emotional stability, empathy, flexibility, and tolerance (Brandão, Magnani, Tega & Medina, 2013; Mor, Morris & Joh, 2013). Communication skills and fluency in the language of the location in which the individual resides are relevant to a proper adaptation to a new culture (Andreason, 2003; Richardson, Litterwood, Neti & Benstead, 2012; Mendenhall & Oddou, 2014).

Family support is an important factor for athletes' healthy adaptation to the new environment (Lee & Kartika, 2014). Factors, such as cultural values and beliefs, communication, family relationships, and social relationships are highlighted as important elements for the adaptation of the whole family to a new culture (Pereira, Pimentel & Kato, 2005). A survey conducted by Pereira, Pimentel, and Kato (2005) revealed that companies need to support the adaptation of their employees abroad. They emphasized the importance of a support network (e.g. employees of the new institution), which can contribute to language learning and culture training to reduce the risk of repatriation.

Successful adjustment to a new culture may be related to cultural flexibility. Cultural flexibility involves the ability of individuals to trade activities in their original country for new activities typical of the host country. Consequently, cultural flexibility allows individuals to manage stress and adapt more easily to a new culture (Downes, Varner & Hemmasi, 2010). The ability to develop new and long-lasting friendships with new hosts fosters resilience and healthy adaptation (Mendenhall & Oddou, 2014). In the digital age, the use of digital tools, such as Facebook, Whatsapp, facetime, and skype, are important and protective to athletes. These tools help them to maintain contact with their families and friends. The easy access to anyone through digital technologies can facilitate athletes' feelings of closeness to significant people and this can help them deal with the difficulties found in the new environment (Prensky, 2001).

Acculturated individuals with high emotional intelligence tend to better understand their emotions. Emotional intelligence is the ability to perceive, evaluate, and express emotions accurately. In addition, another important element for the adjustment to a new environment is cultural intelligence, understanding the ability to collect information, interpret, and operate effectively in cross-cultural environments and in multi-cultural situations (Lee & Kartika, 2014).

A major risk in the process of acculturation is the inability to adjust to the new environment. The individual tends to deal initially with a cultural shock, a reaction to the new, unpredictable environment (Andreason, 2003). In addition, personality and emotional immaturity also result in difficult adapting to the new cultural context. The lack or insufficiency of technical skills, little motivation to work, and high levels of anxiety, stress, and depression are considered risks that may led to maladjustment (Pereira, Pimentel, & Kato, 2005).

The main barrier to an effective adaptation between cultures involves the lack of communication skills and language difficulties (Andreason, 2003; Agergaard, & Ryba, 2014; Weedon, 2011, Richardson, Litterwood, Nesti, & Benstead, 2012; Baines, 2013; Schinke, McGannon, Battochio, & Wells, 2013; Evans & Stead, 2014). When activities carried out at the place of origin are not found in the place of residence, feelings of loneliness, isolation, and frustration can arise, which contributes to cultural shock (Downes, Varner & Hemmasi, 2010). The differences between the place of origin and the new residence in terms of beliefs, values, knowledge, and language increase the difficult with adapting to the new culture (Brandão, Magnani, Tega & Medina, 2013). Daily language can be a challenge to acculturate young adult athletes. Digital, "universal" language might be perceived as more attractive of an option for communication. Pictures and symbols are largely used as expressions in digital contexts and represent a language shared by everyone.

Some aspects of the acculturation process have been investigated in research by Richardson, Litterwood, Neti, and Benstead (2012). They investigated the transition of young soccer players from Europe to English clubs. Richardson and colleagues found that there were many social and psychological demands of the athletes in the process of moving to the new country. First, athletes dealt with the increased attention that they received for migrating to a new club. Second, athletes left their families and their homes to move to a new city or country. Athletes often lived in a sports residence or with a new family. Communication skills in a foreign language, making new friends, and establishing a relationship with the coach and collaborators are required. However, athletes from this study reported that it was not possible to establish friendships, because there are frequent changes of athletes between different teams. Consequently, athletes reported that their family and childhood friends remained their primary source of social support. Furthermore, athletes preferred to seek help from their family than from the club professionals (Richardson, Litterwood, Neti & Benstead, 2012). The increased use of digital technologies makes athletes feel close and receive support from friends and families. This might be particularly important in Brazil because it is a huge country, which makes it difficult for athletes to travel during weekends to visit to their families and friends. Having digital tools to easily contact distant family members and friends can help athletes adapt to the new environment and maintain good sport performance. Isolation and pressure, which is especially pertinent among emerging adulthood, increases the risk for negative digital technology use, including cyberbullying, sexual harassment, and technology addiction (Abreu, 2013; Gross, 2004; Lapidot-Lefler & Barak, 2012; Luna, 2013; Prensky, 2001; Salgado, Boubeta, Tobío, Mallou & Couto, 2004; Wendt & Lisboa, 2014; Young, 1999).

SOLUTIONS AND RECOMMENDATIONS

Brazilian athletes might experience feelings of fear and insecurity, but also amazement when changing cities. They might experience financial pressure but have no opportunities for emotional reflection. They must have affective and psychosocial balance to progress and improve their sports performance. In addition, they begin to take on adult responsibilities, such as paying bills and taking on household chores. This might potentially lead to ambivalence between being a teenager and adult.

Interventions to help these athletes adjust to the changes in their life are needed. Teaching adaptive skills can help athletes adjust to a new culture and prevent psychological difficulties. Dealing with work adversities and the environment change is not easy. It might be more difficult for these athletes to establish their identity and deal with emotional oscillation.

Intervention programs should consider the effects of the acculturation process of these athletes and its influences on identity, health, and job performance. It is necessary to consider the mental health of athletes by striving to improve their well-being. These interventions should consider the cultural values associated with young athletes' new residence. There should be open dialogue between the soccer training department and psychology professionals to help promote and maintain the mental health of young athletes.

CONCLUSION

The aim of this chapter was to discuss aspects related to the process of acculturation, identity construction, and transition to emerging adulthood among Brazilian soccer players. The process of acculturation is important to study among this population because of their high levels of mobility. High levels of mobility can impact these athletes' identity process. It can lead these individuals to take on adult responsibilities, accelerating their transition from adolescence to adulthood, when they are not ready.

To achieve the desired career as a soccer player, young athletes face isolation, competitiveness, family distance, media and fans harassment, and loss of privacy. Teenage athletes residing in soccer clubs come from different regions of their countries and abroad. These adolescents arrive in new cultural contexts, without knowing any information about the place that they will reside; they know much less about the typical foods, political issues, and beliefs of the region. These individuals may live in intense conflict in relation to their personal and cultural identity.

Even if the athletes are motivated for a sports career, the challenges resulting from this trajectory include adaptation to a new style of training and other difficulties. These difficulties can lead to isolation and difficulties in interpersonal relationships. These consequences affect athletes' performance and can generate stress and other emotional vulnerabilities. Sport globalization in a digital age and the increasing mobility of athletes require that athletes' workplaces urgently develop strategies to intervene and promote the mental health of these acculturated individuals, particularly during their transition to emerging adulthood.

REFERENCES

Abreu, C. (2013). Dependência de internet. In *Vivendo esse mundo digital* (pp. 95–103). Porto Alegre: Artmed.

Afif, J. C. B. A. (1997). *Futebol 100% profissional.* São Paulo: Editora Gente.

Agergaard, S., & Ryba, T. V. (2014). Migration and Carrer Transition in professional sport: Transitional athletic careers in a psychological and sociological perspective. *Sociology of Sport Journal*, *31*(2), 228–247. doi:10.1123/ssj.2013-0031

Andreason, A. W. (2003). Expatriate adjustment to foreign assignments. *International Journal of Commerce & Management*, *1*(1), 42–60. doi:10.1108/eb047459

Arnett, J. J. (2004). *Emerging adulthood: The winding road from the late tens through the twenties.* New York, NY: Oxford University Press.

Arnett, J. J. (2007). Emerging adulthood: What is it, and what is it good for? Child Devlopment. *Perspectives*, *1*, 68–73. doi:10.1111/j.1750-8606.2007.00016.x

Baines, R. (2013). Translation, Globalization and the Elite Migrant Athlete. *The Translator*, *19*, 207-228.

Blodgett, A. T., Schinke, R. J., McGannon, K. R., Caholic, D. A., Enosse, L., Peltier, D., & Pheasant, C. (2014). Navigating the inseder-outsider hyphen: A qualitative exploration of the acculturation challenges on aboriginal athletes pursuing sport in Euro-Canadian context. *Psychology of Sport and Exercise*, *15*(4), 345–355. doi:10.1016/j.psychsport.2014.02.009

Brandão, M. R. F., Magnani, A., Tega, E., & Medina, J. P. (2013). Além da cultura nacional: O expatriado no futebol. *Revista Brasileira Ciência e Movimento*, *21*(2), 177–182. doi:10.18511/0103-1716/rbcm.v21n2p177-182

Bronk, K. C. (2011). The role of purpose in life in healthy identity formation: A grounded model. *New Directions for Youth Development*, *132*(132), 31–44. doi:10.1002/yd.426 PMID:22275277

Cheung, B. Y., Chudek, M., & Heine, S. J. (2011). Evidence for a sensitive period for acculturation: Younger immigrants report acculturating at faster rate. *Psychological Science*, *22*(2), 146–152. doi:10.1177/0956797610394661 PMID:21189354

Ciampa, A. C., Leme, C. G., & Souza, R. F. (2010). Considerações sobre a formação e transformação da identidade profissional de atleta de futebol no Brasil. *Diversidade. Perspectiva em Psicologia*, *6*, 27–36.

Confederação Brasileira de Futebol. (2015, Março 15). Retrieved from http://www.cbf.com.br/stjd/publicacoes-pautas#.VYA3V-eXHeQ

Cuadrado, E., Tabernero, C., & Briones, E. (2014). Dispositional and psychosocial variables as longitudinal predictors of acculturative stress. *Applied Psychology*, *63*(3), 441–479. doi:10.1111/j.1464-0597.2012.00531.x

Damo, A. S. (2007). *Do dom à profissão: a formação de futebolistas no Brasil e na França*. São Paulo: Anpocs.

Damo, A. S. (2014). Training soccer players in Brazil. *Soccer and Society*, *15*(1), 93–107. doi:10.1080/14660970.2013.854570

DeSousa, D. A., Salum, G. A., Isolan, R. L., & Manfro, G. G. (2013). Sensitivity and Specificity of the Screen for Child Anxiety Related Emotional Disorders (SCARED): A Community-Based Study. *Child Psychiatry and Human Development*, *44*(3), 391–399. doi:10.1007/s10578-012-0333-y PMID:22961135

Downes, M., Varner, I. I., & Masoud, H. (2010). Indvidual profile as predictors of expatriate effectiveness. *International Business Journal*, *20*, 235–247.

Dutra-Thomé, L. (2013). *Emerging adulthoodin Southern Brazilians from differing socioeconomic status: social e subjective markers* (Unpublished doctoral dissertation). Universidade Federal do Rio Grande do Sul, Porto Alegre, Brazil.

Dutra-Thomé, L., & Koller, S. H. (2014). Emerging adulthood in brazilians of differing socioeconomic status: Transition to adulthood. *Paidéia*, *24*, 313–322.

Dutra-Thomé, L., Koller, S. H., McWhirter, E., & McWhirter, B. (2015). Application of the Future Expectation Scale for Adolescents (FESA) in Brazil. *Psicologia: Reflexão e Crítica, 28*(2), 331–339. doi:10.1590/1678-7153.201528213

Erikson, E. H. (1997). *The life cycle completed.* New York: W. W. Norton.

Evans, A. B., & Stead, D. E. (2014). Its long way to the super leaguw: The experiences of Australisian professional rugby league migrants in the United Kingdon. *International Review for the Sociology of Sport, 49*(6), 707–727. doi:10.1177/1012690212464700

Ferreira, A. B. H. (1997). *Minidicionário Aurélio de língua portuguesa.* Rio de janeiro: Nova Fronteira.

Gardner, M., & Steinberg, L. (2005). Peer influence on risk taking, risk preference, and risky decision making in adolescence and adulthood: An experimental study. *Developmental Psychology, 41*(4), 625–635. doi:10.1037/0012-1649.41.4.625 PMID:16060809

Giulianotti, R. (2010). *Sociologia do Futebol: Dimensões históricas e sociocülurais do esporte das multidões.* São Paulo: Nova Alexandria.

González, J. M. R., & Oliveira, J. A. (2011). Os efeitos da expatriação sobre a identidade: Estudo de caso. *Caderno EBAPE, 9*(4), 1122–1135. doi:10.1590/S1679-39512011000400011

Gross, E. F. (2004). Adolescent Internet use: What we expect, what teens report. *Journal of Applied Developmental Psychology, 25*(6), 633–649. doi:10.1016/j.appdev.2004.09.005

Guterman, M. (2009). *O futebol explica o Brasil – Uma história da maior expressão popular do país.* São Paulo: Contexto.

Harter, S. (2003). The development of self-representations during childhood and adolescence. In M. R. Leary & J. P. Tangney (Eds.), *Hand-book of self and Identity* (pp. 610–642). New York: Guilford.

Lapidot-Lefler, N., & Barak, A. (2012). Effects of anonymity, invisibility, and lack of eye-contact on toxic online disinhibition. *Computers in Human Behavior, 28*(2), 434–443. doi:10.1016/j.chb.2011.10.014

Lee, L., & Kartika, N. (2014). The influence of individual, family, and social capital factors on expatriate adjustment and performance: The moderating effect of psychology contract and organizational support. *Expert Systems with Applications, 41*(11), 5483–5494. doi:10.1016/j.eswa.2014.02.030

Luna, C. (2013). Uma *web* perturbada pela violência. In *Vivendo esse mundo digital* (pp. 60–71). Porto Alegre: Artmed.

Marcelli, D., & Branconnier, A. (2007). *Adolescência e Psicopatologia.* Porto Alegre: Artmed.

Matos, M. (2015). *Adolescentes em navegação segura, por águas desconhecidas.* Lisboa: Coisas de ler.

McWhirter, E. H., & McWhirter, B. T. (2008). Adolescente future expectations of work, education, Family and community: Development of a nem measure. *Youth & Society, 40*(2), 182–202. doi:10.1177/0044118X08314257

Mendenhall, M., & Oddou, G. (2014). The dimensions of expatriate acculturation: A review. *Academy of Management Review, 10*, 39–47.

Mor, S., Morris, M., & Joh, J. (2013). Identifying and training adaptive cross-cultural management skills: The crucial role of cultural metacognition. *Academy of Management Learning & Education, 12*(3), 453–475. doi:10.5465/amle.2012.0202

Muuss, R. E. (1969). *Teorias da Adolescência.* Belo Horizonte: Editora do Professor.

Pereira, N. A. F., Pimentel, R., & Kato, H. T. (2005). Expatriação e estratégia internacional: O papel da família como fator de equilíbrio na adaptação do expatriado. *Revista de administração. Contemporanea (Bologna, Italy), 9*, 53–71.

Piaget, J. (1960). *The psychology of intelligence.* Patterson: Littlefield-Adams.

Prensky, M. (2001). Digital Natives, Digital Immigrants. *On the Horizon, 9*(5), 1–6. doi:10.1108/10748120110424816

Ravizza, K. (2002). A philosophical costruct: A framework for performance enhancement. *International Journal of Sport Psychology, 33*, 4–18.

Reifman, A., Arnett, J. J., & Colwell, M. J. (2007). *Emerging Adulthood*: Theory, assessment and application. *Journal of Youth Development, 2*(1).

Rial, C. (2008). *Rodar*: A circulação dos jogadores de futebol brasileiros no exterior. *Horizontes Antropológicos, 14*(30), 21–75. doi:10.1590/S0104-71832008000200002

Richardson, D., Litterwood, M., Nesti, M., & Benstead, L. (2012). An examination of the migratory transition of elite young European soccer players to the english premier league. *Journal of Sports Sciences, 30*(15), 1605–1618. doi:10.1080/02640414.2012.733017 PMID:23098129

Rodrigues, N. (2013). *A pátria das chuteiras.* Rio de Janeiro: Nova Fronteira.

Rodríguez, S. N., & Damásio, B. F. (2014). Desenvolvimento da identidade e sentindo de vida na adolescência. In L. F. Habigzang, E. Diniz, & S. H. Koller (Eds.), *Trabalhando com adolescentes: teoria e intervenção psicológica* (pp. 30–41). Porto Alegre: Artmed.

Salgado, P. G., Boubeta, A. R., Tobío, T. B., Mallou, J. V., & Couto, C. B. (2014). Evaluation and early detection of problematic Internet use in adolescents. *Psicothema, 26*(1), 21–26. PMID:24444725

Santos, E. C., Neto, O. C. M., & Koller, S. H. (2014). Adolescentes e Adolescências. In Trabalhando com adolescentes: teoria e intervenção psicológica. Porto Alegre: Artmed.

Schinke, R. J., McGannon, K. R., Battochio, R. C., & Wells, G. D. (2013). Acculturation in elite sport: A thematic analysis of immigrant athletes and coaches. *Journal of Sports Sciences, 31*(15), 1676–1686. doi:10.1080/02640414.2013.794949 PMID:23688005

Schwartz, S. J., Unger, J. B., Zamboanga, B. L., & Szapocznik, J. (2010). Rethinking the concept of acculturation: Implications for theory and research. *The American Psychologist, 65*(4), 237–251. doi:10.1037/a0019330 PMID:20455618

Smith, P. K. (2011). *Understanding children's development* (5th ed.). Chichester, UK: John Wiley & Sons Ltd.

Spitz, C. (2012). PIB do esporte cresce mais do que o do país. *O Globo*. Retrieved from http://oglobo.globo.com/economia/pib-do-esporte-cresce-mais-do-que-do-pais-5028799#ixzz3AHwi5EIJ

Tibbert, S. J., Andersen, M. B., & Morris, T. (2015). What a difference a Mentally Toughening year makes: The acculturation of a rookie. *Psychology of Sport and Exercise*, *17*, 68–78. doi:10.1016/j.psychsport.2014.10.007

Wendt, G., & Lisboa, C. (2014). Adolescência no contexto das novas tecnologias de informação e comunicação. In *Trabalhando com adolescentes: teoria e intervenção psicológica* (pp. 180–190). Porto Alegre: Artmed.

Young, K. S. (1999). Internet addiction: symptoms, evaluation and treatment. *Innovations in clinical practice: A source book, 17*, 19-31.

Chapter 4
Use of Social Networking Sites by People with Health Issues

Tatsuya Imai
Nanzan University, Japan

ABSTRACT

Previous studies have found that the use of social networking sites (SNSs) is associated with the user's positive outcomes such as perceived social support and psychological well-being (Ellison, Steinfield, & Lampe, 2007; Nabi, Prestin, & So, 2012). To seek those positive influences, those with health issues such as physical illness or mental illness actively use SNSs (e.g., Shpigelman & Gill, 2014a; Gowen, Deschaine, Gruttadara, & Markey, 2012). The first aim of this chapter is to describe previous studies on the use of SNSs by those with health issues such as mental illnesses, HIV/AIDS, cancer, intellectual disabilities, and diabetes. The second aim is to propose a new direction of research on the use of SNSs by those with health issues: the impact of stigma on communication on SNSs.

INTRODUCTION

Today, it is difficult to find people who do not use any social networking sites (SNSs). In 2015, 90% of American young adults (18 to 29 years) used at least one SNS, compared with 12% in 2005 (Perrin, 2015). The time spent on SNSs among emerging adults is high, around 52 minutes every day (Coyne, Padilla-Walker, & Howard, 2013; Jacobsen & Forste, 2011). Emerging adults use SNSs for various purposes, such as maintaining friendships (Barker, 2009) and developing romantic relationships (Fox, Warber, & Makstaller, 2013). Thus, the use of SNSs is associated with various positive outcomes for the users. In particular, the number of Facebook friends is related to perceived social support, reduced stress, and less physical illness (Nabi, Prestin, & So, 2013). The use of Facebook is also related to psychological well-being, especially for those with low self-esteem and low life satisfaction (Ellison, Steinfield, & Lampe, 2007).

Consequently, it is not surprising that people with health issues use SNSs with the intent to improve their quality of life (e.g., Gowen, Deschaine, Gruttadaro, & Markey, 2012; Horvath et al., 2012; Shpigelman & Gill, 2014a). Shpigelman and Gill (2014a) surveyed individuals suffering from disabilities, such

DOI: 10.4018/978-1-5225-1856-3.ch004

as physical disability, Autism, hearing disability, and mental illness, to examine these individuals' use of Facebook. Results showed that 69% of the participants visited Facebook at least once a day and 48% of them reported having up to 200 Facebook friends. In addition, 10.1% of them reported that they did not have Facebook friends with disabilities, while 89.9% of them indicated that they had Facebook friends with disabilities. Furthermore, findings from this study also revealed that the participants mainly used Facebook to connect with nondisabled friends rather than to connect with disabled friends. Qualitative analyses of responses to the open-ended questions suggested that people with disabilities use Facebook to seek support and advice from other users. These findings revealed that SNSs play an important role for those with health issues in maintaining and developing interpersonal relationships.

However, when using SNSs, those with health issues might experience stigma associated with their health issues, similar to the stigma they might experience offline (e.g., Goffman, 1963; Imai & Dailey, 2015; Schneider, 2005). The stigma those with health issues experience may threaten their identity (Newman, Lauterbach, Munson, Resnick, & Morris, 2011; Schabert, Browne, Mosely, & Speight, 2013). For example, some individuals struggling with diabetes may want to share their health condition on SNSs to seek emotional support (Newman et al., 2011). However, they are concerned about the possibility that disclosing their health issue threatens their socially desired identity. This might be particularly concerning for emerging adults, whose main task is to establish a sense of identity (Schwartz, Donnellan, Ravert, Luyckx, & Zamboanga, 2013).

Despite the significant effect of stigma associated with health issues on SNSs, little research has been conducted on this topic. Thus, this chapter describes the current state of the literature on SNSs use by those with health issues and the stigma associated with various health issues. This chapter first introduces past studies investigating how those individuals with various health issues use SNSs for different purposes. Next, the effects of stigma on SNS users with health issues are considered. Finally, this chapter describes future research directions on stigmatizing effects of SNSs on emerging adults with health issues.

USE OF SOCIAL NETWORKING SITES BY THOSE WITH HEALTH ISSUES

Past studies have investigated the use of SNSs by people with health issues utilizing both quantitative and qualitative approaches. These studies have focused on the use of SNSs by those with a mental illness, HIV/AIDS, cancer, an intellectual disability, and diabetes.

Mental Illness

Five features of mental illnesses are described by Stein et al. (2010). First, a mentally ill individual demonstrates a clinically significant behavioral or psychological syndrome or pattern. Second, the syndrome or pattern is related to present distress or disability or to a considerably increased risk of suffering death, pain, disability, or an important loss of freedom. Third, the syndrome or pattern is not an expectable and culturally sanctioned response to a specific event (e.g., the death of a loved one). Fourth, the individual shows a behavioral, psychological, or biological dysfunction. Finally, neither deviant behaviors nor conflicts between the individual and society can be classified as mental illness, unless the deviance or conflict is a symptom of dysfunction in the individual. Fitting these criteria, there are a variety of types of mental illnesses, such as schizophrenia, substance-related disorders, mood disorders, anxiety disorders, and eating disorders as described in the *Diagnostic and Statistical Manual of Mental Disorders* (DSM-V; American Psychiatric Association, 2013). Based on the results of a meta-analysis of mental health surveys conducted worldwide from 1980 through 2013, one in five adults (17.6%) has suffered from mental disorders within the past 12 months and 29.2% across their lifetime (Steel et al., 2014).

Past studies delineate how and why those with mental illness use SNSs, such as Facebook and MySpace. Gowen et al. (2012) surveyed 207 emerging adults (18 to 24 years) comprised of 128 individuals with a mental illness and 79 individuals without a mental illness. Results showed that 94% of those with mental illness used SNSs for a variety of purposes. Compared with those without a mental illness, mentally ill people tended to use SNSs more often to make new friends, share interests, and blog. The main communication methods they use on SNSs were sending private messages, posting public messages, sharing information and links, and commenting on blogs. Through SNSs, those with mental illness desire to find information on independent living skills, strategies to overcome social isolation, and ways to develop interpersonal relationships. This research illustrates mentally ill emerging adults' active use of SNSs to gain various support that would not be available in face-to-face (FtF) interactions.

Specifically, MySpace has played a significant role in providing such support through health-related online communities. For instance, the most popular health-related communities on MySpace were ones focusing on depression and the second most popular communities were ones focusing on bipolar disorders (Seeman, 2008). Another study showed that a quarter of Facebook users who are juniors and seniors in a college posted comments that meet the criteria as symptoms of depression received social support from Facebook friends (Moreno et al., 2011). Taken together, many mentally ill emerging adults actively use SNSs for various purposes.

HIV/AIDS

There were approximately 34 million people living with HIV/AIDS in 2014 (WHO, 2015). The WHO (2015) reports that in 2014 about 1.2 million people died from HIV-related causes and approximately 2 million people became newly infected with HIV globally. There is no cure for the HIV infection, but effective treatments with antiretroviral drugs are available to control the virus, leading to healthy and productive lives of those with HIV.

Specifically, about 57,200 emerging adults (18 to 24 years) were living with HIV in the United States at the end of 2012 (Centers for Disease Control & Prevention, 2016). Among them, 25,300 were living with undiagnosed HIV, that was the highest rate of undiagnosed HIV in any age group. Also, 21% of them were prescribed HIV medicines and 16% had a suppressed viral load, that is the lowest rates of any age group.

Some research illustrates the use of SNSs by those individuals living with HIV/AIDS. Horvath et al. (2012) surveyed individuals living with HIV regarding their use of SNSs and found that 76% of these individuals used SNSs at least once a week. The most widely used SNS was Facebook, which was used by 62% of individuals living with HIV in this study. In addition, 22% of the participants reported that they participated in at least one of two online groups focusing on HIV. Several themes emerged from the open-ended questions assessing their ideal SNS. Forty-five percent of the participants reported that their ideal SNS would be one in which they could connect with other people, whether the people live with HIV or not. On the other hand, another 14% of them reported that they would not like to participate in a SNS focusing on HIV. An additional 26% of them were concerned about the privacy issues related to their participating in HIV-focused SNSs. For example, some users living with HIV were worried that others would find out they were HIV positive by participating in online groups focusing on HIV. Overall, people living with HIV use SNSs to develop interpersonal relationships and participate in online communities focusing on HIV, although privacy is a barrier to using SNSs.

In order to closely investigate online interaction of individuals living with HIV/AIDS, Mo and Coulson (2008) analyzed the contents of 1,138 messages exchanged in an online HIV/AIDS support group. Of these messages, there were 171 unique message sender names identified in the selected threads and the HIV status of 145 members could be identified as HIV-positive on their profiles. Among all the messages, 986 messages contained at least one type of social support and the supportive messages were categorized into five social support message types: information support (44.5%), emotional support (35.2%), esteem support (12.4%), network support (6.9%), and tangible assistance (1.0%). Information support is advice messages providing suggestions or guidance for coping with HIV/AIDS symptoms. Emotional support is offered by messages to express care and concern to other members. Esteem support is provided through compliment messages, which convey positive assessments of the recipient and his or her abilities. Network support involves messages that broaden the recipients' social network by developing access to new members. Tangible support involves messages in which senders are offering to perform a direct task related to a request.

In short, SNSs and online support communities for those living with HIV/AIDS could help them seek various types of information and support. Even though these studies did not focus on emerging adults, the information of HIV/AIDS provided in online communities are helpful for emerging adults living with HIV who tend to lack enough accurate information of the disease (Centers for Disease Control & Prevention, 2016).

Cancer

Cancer represents around 12% of all-cause mortality worldwide (International Agency for Research on Cancer, 2008). In 2012, there were 14.1 million new cancer cases, 8.2 million cancer deaths, and 32.6 million people living with cancer (WHO, 2012). In the world, the most common causes of cancer death are cancers of the lungs (1.59 million deaths), liver (745,000 deaths), stomach (723,000 deaths), colorectal (694,000 deaths), breast (521,000 deaths), and oesophageal cancer (400,000 deaths).

SNSs play an important role in providing a variety of support for people having cancer. The third most popular types of health-related communities on MySpace are ones focusing on cancer (Seeman, 2008). Furthermore, Bender, Jimenez-Marroquin, and Jadad (2011) examined 620 breast cancer groups on Facebook to identify the purposes, use, and creators of the groups. They analyzed the contents of the groups and found four main types of breast cancer groups: fundraising groups, awareness-raising groups, support groups, and "promote-a-site" groups. The fundraising groups are created to attract financial resources for breast cancer through events, products, or services. The awareness-raising groups aim to bring attention to the significance of breast cancer in general. Support groups attempt to meet the information and emotional needs or breast cancer survivors or affected family members or friends. The "promote-a-site" groups are formed to increase the prominence of external websites raising funds. Participating in support groups regarding cancer was associated with increased social support, leading to reduced stress and depression (Beaudoin & Tao, 2007).

The population of these studies was not emerging adults. However, one study interviewing emerging adults (20 to 25 years) with cancer revealed that their needs such as necessary information and interpersonal support were not met (Patterson, Millar, Desille, & McDonald, 2012). Thus, if emerging adults with cancer participate in the support groups on SNSs, their needs could be met through interaction with other SNS users.

Intellectual Disability

According to the American Association of Intellectual and Developmental Disabilities (AAIDD; 2013), an intellectual disability (ID) is defined as significant limitations on both intellectual functions and in adaptive behavior, which includes everyday conceptual, social, and practical skills, and this disability originates before the age of 18. The adaptive behavior specifically includes language, literacy, interpersonal skills, self-esteem, occupational skills, and transportation. Approximately 200 million people in the world have an intellectual disability (Special Olympics, 2015).

There has been little research on the use of SNSs by those with an intellectual disability. Shpigelman and Gill (2014b) examined the use of Facebook by 58 people with a learning disability and/or ADD/ADHD. The participants visited Facebook at least once a week (67.2%) and they used it mainly for connecting with people they meet in face-to-face settings, such as friends, family members, and caregivers. The results also revealed that 68% of the participants reported that making new friends is easier on Facebook than in person. Also, 82% of them said that they felt more comfortable talking with people on Facebook than face to face. Some responses to open-ended questions referred to the emotional effect of communication on Facebook. For instance, Facebook helped the participants feel connected with others when they felt lonely.

Research found that young adults with ID reported that their interpersonal networks were composed of only a few people who tended to be support professionals, leading to feelings of being isolated from others (Starke, 2013). To help emerging adults with ID develop relationships with other youth, SNS may be useful as shown in the results of the study by Shpigelman and Gill (2014b).

Diabetes

Diabetes is the eighth leading cause of death in the world (WHO, 2014a). In 2014, the global prevalence of diabetes was estimated to be 9% among adults (WHO, 2014b). Common symptoms of diabetes are urinating often, feeling very thirsty, extreme fatigue, and blurry vision (American Diabetes Association, 2015).

Previous studies have examined individuals with diabetes' use of SNSs. Greene, Choudhry, Kilabuk, and Shrank (2010) qualitatively examined the 15 most recent wall posts and the 15 most recent discussion topics from the 10 largest Facebook groups focusing on diabetes management. The study sample included 690 individual posts on wall pages and discussion board posts written by 480 users. The main themes identified included posts about information-sharing, patient-centered management, and community-building. As for the main function of the Facebook groups, 62% of the posts involved sharing of personal experiences with diabetes management. Furthermore, 24% of posts contained sensitive aspects of patient-centered diabetes management. For instance, posts described how to count carbohydrates to enable extended alcoholic drinking sessions among individuals with Type I Diabetes. Some posts also functioned to form a supportive community to seek interpersonal support from group members. These findings imply that Facebook groups specifically focusing on diabetes allow diabetes patients to share and seek information related to their illness.

To understand further why and how people with diabetes share their health information on SNSs and online support communities, Newman et al. (2011) interviewed 14 individuals struggling with diabetes and weight loss management. By analyzing the contents of transcripts of the interviews, Newman and colleagues found that the main goal of the individuals using SNSs and online support communities was to receive emotional support. Through online support communities, it was easier to find people who have similar struggles, so the participants could obtain positive and encouraging messages from other users. The researchers also revealed that SNS users with diabetes had concerns regarding their identity management on SNSs. Although they would emphasized their identity as healthy people, they wanted to obtain support by being open about their struggles.

One study focusing on young adults with diabetes found that they believed that talking about their diabetes-related distress with others and joining peer support groups moderate their distress caused by diabetes (Balfe, Doyle, Smith, Sreenan, Brugha, Hevey, & Conroy, 2013). Considering findings of past studies (Green et al., 2010; Newman et al., 2011), SNSs might help emerging adults with diabetes join online support groups where they can talk about their distress with other users to moderate the distress.

In summary, the studies introduced in this section suggest that SNSs could help users with health issues improve their quality of life by sharing and seeking important information on their conditions through SNS and developing online interpersonal relationships. However, if the users with health issues feel stigmatized while using SNSs as they do in a real life (e.g., Goffman, 1963; Schneider, 2005), they might be discouraged from using SNSs. Such a stigmatizing effect on SNSs has not been fully examined. The next section introduces the definition and characteristics of stigma followed by previous studies focusing on various influences of illness or disability stigma on communication.

STIGMA

Stigma is defined as an attribute or characteristic that conveys a social identity that is discredited and devalued in a particular context (Goffman, 1963; Schneider, 2005). Link and Phelan (2001) argue that a set of events need to take place in order for stigma to manifest. First, people distinguish and label targets based on the differences they have from others. Second, the differences are associated with negative stereotypes. Third, the labels are given for specific categories that separate "us" from "them." Fourth, people who receive stigmatizing labels experience status loss and discrimination, leading to unequal outcomes. Finally, the stigmatization the targets experience is related to social, economic, and political power that may identify their differences, construct stereotypes, and separate them into distinct categories.

Additionally, stigma has six dimensions (Jones et al., 1984). The essential dimension is concealability. For example, facial disfigurement and physical disabilities are harder to conceal than a history of mental illness, a prison record, or homosexuality. The second dimension is called time course. Some conditions, such as AIDS, may worsen over time whereas other conditions, such as diabetes, may improve. On the other hand, some types of physical disabilities, such as blindness and paralysis, may not change. The third dimension is aesthetic value. For instance, obesity, facial scars, and body disfigurement are related to physical attractiveness whereas AIDS may not be associated with attractiveness. How stigmatized conditions are generated is another crucial dimension called stigma origins. This dimension is related to whether a stigmatized individual is seen as responsible for the stigma. For example, some conditions, including obesity, a criminal record, and homosexuality, may be seen as matters of choice. However, other conditions, such as cancer and physical disability, are perceived to be outside of the control of the stigmatized individuals. People often blame or devalue individuals with conditions that are seen to be caused by their choice or to be in their control. The fifth dimension is whether the stigmatizing condition is perceived to put other people in danger. For example, people might see those with criminal records to be dangerous. People with HIV may make others more afraid of contamination than those diagnosed with cancer. The final dimension is disruptiveness—the degree to which the stigma interrupts social interactions. For example, interactions with schizophrenic individuals might be disruptive because they often have symptoms of speech dysfunctions.

STIGMA ASSOCIATED WITH SPECIFIC HEALTH ISSUES

Previous studies suggest that different illnesses and disabilities carry different stigmas.

Mental Illness

Stigma associated with a general label of "mental illness" (i.e., not a specific mental illness) impacts interpersonal communication in various ways. First, Modified Labeling Theory explains how a mental illness label influences those labeled in various situations, such as interpersonal interactions, job opportunities, and quality of life (Link, 1982). According to this theory, if people believe a mentally ill individual is devalued and rejected, they worry that they would also be rejected if they have a mental illness. When they realize that they have a mental illness, the belief (e.g., people with mental illness are rejected) will bring them negative consequences, such as demoralization, income loss, and unemployment. Furthermore, Link, Cullen, Struening, Shrout, and Dohrenwend (1989) found several possible consequences associated with the fear of being labeled with a mental illness, including secrecy, withdrawal, and education. Secrecy involves concealing a history of treatment, such as being hospitalized and being prescribed medications. Labeled individuals may also withdraw from potentially threatening situations, such as a party with people who stigmatize mentally ill individuals. Education includes the active attempt at educating others in hopes of enlightening them to ward off negative attitudes. Among these strategies, the withdrawing behaviors may lead to poorer social support from others.

Second, mental illness stigma also affects others' interpersonal behaviors toward those with mental illness. Sibicky and Dovidio (1986) found that people who believed that an individual is mentally ill leads to negative perceptions and behaviors toward that individual. In their study, participants were told that their interactant was a regular undergraduate student or a student seeking psychotherapy. After they interacted, the audio of the interaction was coded. Results revealed that the participants in the experimental condition had a more negative impression of their interactant and the coded speech of the participants toward their interactant was less open and secure compared with the control condition. In short, when individuals believe that someone is mentally ill, their perceptions and behaviors toward the person tend to be negative. Mental illness stigma may impact mentally ill individuals as well as others around them.

Depression

Depressed individuals are perceived as more violent than those without any mental illness (Link, Phelan, Bresnahan, Stueve, & Pescosolido, 1999). People also believe that depressed individuals tend to be angry, afraid, alone, tired, sad, unhappy (Horowitz, French, Lapid, & Wecker, 1982), and dependent (Rippere, 1977). These negative ideas of depression make people reject those with depression (Link et al., 1999).

Several theoretical accounts explain how the stigma of depression impacts others' perceptions toward depressed individuals. Cane and Gotlib (1985) argued that stereotypes of depression function as a cognitive framework influencing people's interpretations of depressed individuals' characteristics and behaviors. Thus, people are likely to perceive behaviors engaged in by depressed individuals consistent with depression stereotypes, such as being alone and sad. In addition, Sacco and Vaughan (2006) developed the Social-Cognitive Interpersonal Process Model with an emphasis on interpersonal factors influencing depression. Similar to the ideas of Cane and Gotlib (1985), this model argues that people explain behaviors of depressed individuals in negative ways because of a negative schema associated with depressed individuals.

These theoretical frameworks are consistent with findings of empirical studies on the stigma of depression. Individuals who interacted with a confederate who they believed to be depressed evaluated the confederate more negatively on both depression-related traits and depression-unrelated traits as compared to a control condition (Nicholson & Sacco, 1999). In another study conducted by Yarkin, Harvey, and Bloxom (1981), participants were told before interacting with a confederate that the confederate was distressed or not distressed (the distressing behaviors were similar to symptoms of depression), but the confederate behaved neutrally in both conditions. The confederate in the distressed condition was evaluated more negatively than that in the control condition.

These negative evaluations of depressed individuals might lead people to reject those with depression. In the study by Yarkin et al. (1981), participants who believed that a confederate was distressed maintained a larger distance from the confederate, displayed shorter durations of eye contact, engaged in a more negatively-valenced conversation, and spoke for shorter periods of time than those who were not told that the confederate was distressed. In addition, Nicholson and Sacco (1999) revealed that participants who interacted with a confederate who they believed to be depressed showed that they were less willing to interact with the confederate again than a nondepressed confederate. Furthermore, participants who only imagined interactions with depressed individuals indicated more rejecting attitudes than did participants in a control group (Gotlib & Beatty, 1985). Taken together, depression stereotypes negatively affect others' perceptions of depressed individuals' behaviors, leading to rejection of these individuals.

Schizophrenia

Individuals suffering from schizophrenia are more seriously stigmatized than those with depression. Compared with depressed individuals, schizophrenic individuals tend to be seen as more dangerous and unpredictable and consequently, they are more often rejected (Angermeyer & Matschinger, 1997, 2003; Link et al., 1999). A depressed individual could elicit more positive emotions in others, such as a desire to help and empathy, whereas a schizophrenic individual elicits more fear, uneasiness, and insecurity in others (Angermeyer & Matschinger, 2003). People may have such negative feelings toward a schizophrenic individual because they believe schizophrenia is difficult to cure. For example, people believe schizophrenia is caused by biological factors, such as a chemical imbalance in the brain, more than depression and alcohol dependence (Link et al., 1999). Angermeyer and Matschinger (2003) also found that depression is believed to be caused by social factors, such as stress at work, and life events, whereas schizophrenia is perceived to be caused by more biological and genetic factors, such as brain disease and heredity; consequently, schizophrenia is believed to be more likely to deteriorate and be harder to cure than depression.

Previous studies further reveal a strong negative effect of the stigma attached to schizophrenia on interpersonal communication. Jenkins and Carpenter-Song (2009) interviewed those diagnosed with schizophrenia and 96% of them reported experiencing stigmatization across a variety of social settings, including interactions with strangers, in work places, and within close relationships. Schizophrenic individuals reported that verbal and nonverbal communication by strangers was expressed in a way to signal that a schizophrenic individual is strange, frightening, and has less intellectual/social capacity (Jenkins & Carpenter-Song, 2009). The experience of being stigmatized was associated with low quality interpersonal relationships and with low frequency of contact with friends and acquaintances (Lysaker, Roe, & Yanos, 2007). Norman et al. (2010) assessed others' perception of schizophrenic individuals in an experiment and found people possessing stigmatizing attitudes toward schizophrenic individuals did not desire to be physically close to them. In sum, research has revealed that schizophrenic individuals are more seriously stigmatized than those with depression, and consequently these individuals often treated more negatively.

HIV/AIDS

Although the perception of HIV/AIDS has improved over the past 20 years (Herek, 2014), among those without correct knowledge about HIV transmission, 34% of them reported that they would be uncomfortable working with people with HIV and 65% of them reported that they would be uncomfortable about having food prepared by people with HIV (Washington Post & Kaiser Family Foundation, 2012). Because individuals with HIV are aware of the stigma associated with HIV, they may hesitate to disclose their diagnosis even to people they feel close to (Greene, 2009). In fact, after disclosing their HIV-positive status, they receive negative emotional reactions and perceive being treated differently (Greene & Faulkner, 2002). Consequently, those with HIV perceive that they receive social rejection and social isolation (File & Wright, 2000). Furthermore, people often associate HIV/AIDS with homosexuality and IV drug use, and they believe that the patient is responsible for having HIV/AIDS because they engaged in such deviant behaviors.

Cancer

The stigma attached to cancer is caused primarily by fear of the illness itself (File & Wright, 2000). For instance, people tend to associate cancer with death (Chapple, Ziebland, & McPherson, 2004). Results of a survey conducted in India, Italy, Japan, Mexico, and South Africa to examine people's perceptions of cancer showed that 30% of these individuals believed that people with cancer cannot survive (Neal et al., 2010). Sixteen percent of them believed that cancer is contagious and 25% of them believed that people with cancer bring it on themselves. These negative images associated with cancer make people reject those with cancer (File & Wright, 2000). People with cancer have difficulties obtaining social resources and their social activities are restricted (Bloom & Kessler, 1994).

Intellectual Disability

Past research suggests that there are negative stereotypes attached to people with ID. Some people believe that those with ID are aggressive (Slevin & Sines, 1996) and threatening (van Alphen, Dijker, Bos, van Den Borne, & Curfs, 2012), so people are sometimes fearful of those with ID (Jahoda, Wilson, Stalker, & Cairney, 2010). These stereotypes make those with ID experience stigmatization in various social contexts. In school, some individuals with ID are ridiculed and called names by other students and teachers sometimes refuse to help them (Cooney, Jahoda, Gumley, & Knott, 2006). Parents are willing to include children with mild and moderate ID in school, but they oppose the inclusion of children with severe ID (Rafferty, Boettcher, & Griffin, 2001). The teacher-student relationship of children with ID are of poorer quality than that of typically developing students (McIntyre, Blacher, & Baker, 2006). Stigma associated with ID also plays a role in employment. Only 21% of working-age people with ID are employed, according to U.S. Bureau of Labor Statistics (2010). Even when they get a job, they tend to be bullied and ignored in the workplace (Johoda et al., 2010). In fact, some individuals would like to avoid working with those with ID (Bickley, 1990).

Diabetes

Studies have shown that people who do not have diabetes are likely to perceive diabetes as a non-stigmatized condition (e.g., Schabert, Brown, Mosely, & Speight, 2013), but those with diabetes experience being stigmatized (e.g., Brod, Kongso, Lessard, & Christensen, 2009). To treat diabetes, patients may have to use syringes, but using them in public may make them feel embarrassed and afraid of being rejected (Brod et al., 2009). Those with diabetes might have to be careful about what they eat, so they sometimes need to refuse unhealthy food at social events, leading to embarrassment (Wellard, Rennie, & King, 2008). Patients also feel that few people around them understand diabetes correctly, so they are afraid of disclosing their health status even to their fiancés and parents (Sato et al., 2003). Some patients reported that they were afraid to lose their job if they disclosed their health status to people they work with (Shiu, Kwan, & Wong, 2003). Patients who worry about stigmatization described above are likely to suffer from depression and psychological distress (Schabert, Brown, Mosely, & Speight, 2013).

Taken together, past studies indicate that different illnesses and disabilities are associated with various stigmas. As mentioned in the previous section, the stigma associated with health issues on SNSs has not been fully researched. However, some research implies that people with health issues experience stigma while using SNSs. For example, some Facebook users with diabetes avoid showing their concerns and distress about their health issue because of the stigma associated with diabetes even though they desire support from others on SNSs by disclosing their inner state (Newman et al., 2011). Bender et al. (2011) also suggest that features of SNSs such as the visibility of user profiles and personal networks reduce the anonymity, so users who are concerned about stigma associated with their health issue might hesitate sharing their experience on SNSs. Thus, stigma of health issues may prevent SNS users with health issues from seeking information and support on SNSs. Especially for emerging adults, most of whom are struggling to manage their identity (Schwartz et al., 2013), the negative effect of stigma on SNSs might be significant. In fact, on Facebook, emerging adults try to engage in identity management by presenting multiple facets of the self such as the real self, the ideal self, and the false self (Michikyan, Dennis, & Subrahmanyam, 2015).

FUTURE DIRECTIONS: STIGMA OF HEALTH ISSUES ON SNS

The previous sections introduce research on the use of SNSs by individuals with health issues and the stigma associated with specific health issues. Considering the frequency of SNSs use by individual with health issues and their negative experiences related to the stigma, it is necessary to investigate how stigma impacts SNSs use. People evaluate others based on the social categories that they belong to (e.g., a group of mentally ill patients, Asians, females), according to Social Identification Model of Deindividuation Effects (Postmes, Spears, & Lea, 2000). This effect is no different through computer-mediated communication. Therefore, on SNSs, people might have negative perceptions of an individual with health issues due to the effects of the stigma associated with the health issues.

On SNSs, health issues can be revealed in various ways. For example, SNS users with a health issue may disclose their health issues on a wall that other users can see. People could also disclose their health issue by sending a message only to someone they want to disclose their illness to. People may realize others' illness by seeing interactions on SNSs that are open to other users or by seeing that others belong to an organization to which only people with a specific health issue are allowed to belong.

There are various situations in which people with a health issue communicate with others on SNSs, but little research has examined stigma effects of a specific health issue on online communication. Thus, the following sections discuss how stigma of a specific health issue influences communication on SNSs with Facebook as a particular focus, since this SNS has the highest number of users (Pew Research Center, 2014) and 82% of emerging adults who use the Internet use Facebook; the percentage is the highest of any age group (Pew Research Center, 2015). Also, Facebook has been used as the main SNS by many people with a health issue (e.g., Bender et al., 2011; Shpigelman & Gill, 2014a). Possible research questions are also proposed to drive research in these areas.

Sending and Receiving Messages

On most SNSs, users can send and receive private online messages to each other. If people realize that their interactant has a health issue, they may change their message to the interactant. For instance, people may see someone's wall in which the person's friends discuss a health issue the person has. After realizing the person has the issue, messages sent to the person may be negatively altered. To address the possibility that mental illness stigma influences online messages to a mentally ill individual, Imai and Dailey (2015) examined mental illness stigma effects on a request for a favor from a mentally ill individual on Facebook. Participants (97% of them were emerging adults: 18 to 29 years) interacted with a hypothetical target on Facebook, who was believed to have schizophrenia, depression, or a cavity (i.e., the control group). Participants were asked to rate the favor request in terms of face threat in addition to writing a response which was then coded by researchers. Results indicated that a request by a schizophrenic target threatened participants' positive face more significantly than that of a target with depression or without any mental illness. Also, participants' responses to the schizophrenic target were more likely to be polite, but less warm, whereas responses to the depressed target were more likely to be accepting messages. The results indicate that emerging adults who realize that their interactant on SNSs has a health issue, their message to the interactant may be negatively altered.

Stigma may also influence messages those with health issues send to others. Disclosing health issues to someone may be effective in obtaining social support from others (e.g., Chesney & Smith, 1999). Thus, it is possible for those with health issues to disclose their illness or disability by using online messages because these exchanged messages are not seen by others except for the specific recipient. However, people may decide not to disclose their illness because of the stigma associated with the illness (Greene, 2009). Research shows that people living with HIV hesitate to disclose their HIV positive status because of expected negative reactions caused by the stigma of HIV (Miller & Rubin, 2007).

Especially for emerging adults, it is difficult to talk about their health issues through online messages. Research interviewing youth living with HIV (17 to 21 years) revealed that most participants had great difficulty disclosing their diagnosis (Hosek, Harper, & Domanico, 2000). One participant told that he or she could not disclose the diagnosis even to his or her parents because of the stigma attached to HIV. Another study specifically examining diagnosis disclosure of adolescents living with HIV found that one third of the participants disclosed their diagnosis only to immediate family members and a few close friends (Wiener & Battles, 2006). Taken together, as the previous studies show possible stigma effects of messages exchanged on SNSs, future research should examine the effects by exploring the following research questions:

RQ1: If people know their Facebook friend has a health issue, will their online message to the friend be negatively influenced?
RQ2: If people with a health issue expect to be stigmatized after disclosing their issue, will they be unwilling to disclose their issue through the use of online messages?

Communication on Walls

Facebook users can write comments on their own and their friend's walls. For example, they can post an update status on their wall that allows them to show other Facebook friends what they are doing and how they are feeling. In turn, their Facebook friends can write comments on the updated status. Also, Facebook users can use a Like button to let other users know they like other's postings such as a status updates, pictures, and shared websites. These functions play important roles in communication on Facebook.

If people know their Facebook friend has health issues, their communication on walls involving the friend might negatively affected. For example, some individuals struggling with weight loss management reported that when they mentioned they worried about their weight on a Facebook wall, they received sarcastic and negative comments from others (Newman et al., 2011). To avoid the negative feedback from others, people with health issues often hesitate to reveal their health condition on their SNS wall. Thus, stigma of health issues could influence interaction on walls by those with and without the health issues.

To research the stigma effect on interaction on SNSs, Modified Labeling Theory (Link, 1982) is useful. This theory specifically focuses on mental illness stigma, but some concepts in this theory are applicable to other health issues. One of the ideas of the theory is that mentally ill individuals would try to educate other Facebook friends to obviate the negative effects of mental illness stigma. They may share websites that show the facts of mental illnesses to combat the myths of mental illnesses. They may also write comments on friends' walls if the friends write incorrect information about mental illnesses. Modified Labeling Theory also suggests stigmatized individuals may avoid interaction on walls where they would be rejected by Facebook friends. For instance, if those with health issues are afraid of being rejected or ignored by other Facebook friends, they may not participate in conversations taking place on walls.

The stigma impact on interaction using the wall may be significant particularly for emerging adults. Schwartz et al. (2013) suggest that emerging adults undertake experimentation to explore who they are through interpersonal interaction. For example, to establish their identity, emerging adults may show their different facets of the self to others to see if they get feedback that is consistent with who they think they are. In fact, emerging adults present the real self, the ideal self, and even the false self on Facebook to explore their identity (Michikyan et al., 2015). Thus, if they are aware that their health issues are stigmatized, they would not reveal the information about the issues on walls of SNSs. Based on these theoretical ideas, future research should examine the following research questions:

RQ3: If people know their Facebook friend has a health issue, will their comments on the friend's wall be negatively influenced?
RQ4: If an individual with a health issue believes their health status is known by Facebook friends, will the individual try to educate the friends by providing information related to the health issue?
RQ5: If an individual with a health issue believes their health status is known by Facebook friends, will the individual decline to participate in conversations taking place on walls?

Mixed-Mode Relationships

Past research argues that some online relationships migrate to FtF settings (Anthenunis, Valkenburg, & Peter, 2012). Such relationships are called mixed-mode relationships (MMRs), in which people meet online and migrate offline (Walther & Parks, 2002). Those with health issues actively seek new relationships on SNSs (e.g., Gowen et al., 2012), so it is possible for them to try to meet people they met on SNSs in a FtF setting.

However, stigma associated with health issues might influence the decision for SNS users with or without health issues to meet in FtF settings. For instance, people tried to avoid physically meeting a schizophrenic individual they know only on Facebook because of the stigma associated with the illness (Imai, in press). Stigma may also impact people with health issues' decision to meet others offline. Modified Labeling Theory (Link 1982) suggests that people with health issues try to avoid potentially threatening situations, such as social gatherings where they may be rejected and isolated. Thus, people may avoid physically meeting someone they know only on SNSs because they are afraid to lose the social ties they developed online.

Research showed that the main motive to use SNSs for emerging adults is to stay in touch with friends they know offline, but one third of them use SNSs to meet and make friends with new people (Subrahmanyam, Reich, Waechter, & Espinoza 2008). The stigma associated with their health issues may prevent emerging adults with health issues from developing new relationships online. According to these accounts, the following research questions are posed:

RQ6: If people know their Facebook friend has a health issue, will they avoid meeting the friend in FtF settings?
RQ7: If individuals with health issues believe their health status is known by their Facebook friends, will the friend decline to meet in FtF settings?

CONCLUSION

Previous research revealed that some emerging adults with health issues have a hard time developing close relationships with others and obtaining interpersonal support (Patterson et al., 2012; Starke, 2013). SNSs could provide valuable opportunities for them to achieve such relationships and support (e.g., Barker, 2009; Nabi, Prestin, & So, 2013). However, those with health issues are at risk of experiencing stigma while using SNSs (Imai & Dailey, 2015; Newman et al., 2011) and this experience may have a negative impact on emerging adults' identity management (Schwartz et al., 2013). Despite the predicted risk, there has been little research investigating the stigma effect on SNS users with health issues. To facilitate research on this issue, this chapter described the current literature on the use of SNSs by individuals with health issues. Previous research has revealed that people with health issues actively use SNSs to obtain various types of support. However, these studies are also concerned with how individuals with health issues manage their identity by sharing or withholding their health information on SNSs. To help researchers examine this topic, this chapter poses research questions that future studies should explore. Addressing these questions will make SNSs better places for emerging adults with health issues to develop interpersonal relationships and improve their quality of life.

REFERENCES

American Association of Intellectual and Developmental Disabilities. (2013). *Definition of intellectual disability*. Retrieved from http://aaidd.org/intellectual-disability/definition#.Vd0xTKaZ5EI

American Diabetes Association. (2015). *Diabetes symptoms*. Retrieved from http://www.diabetes.org/diabetes-basics/symptoms/

American Psychiatric Association. (2013). *Diagnostic and statistical manual of mental disorders* (5th ed.). Arlington, VA: American Psychiatric Publishing.

Angermeyer, M. C., & Matschinger, H. (1997). Social distance towards the mentally ill: Results of representative surveys in the Federal Republic of Germany. *Psychological Medicine*, *27*(1), 131–141. doi:10.1017/S0033291796004205

Angermeyer, M. C., & Matschinger, H. (2003). Public beliefs about schizophrenia and depression: Similarities and differences. *Social Psychiatry and Psychiatric Epidemiology*, *38*(9), 526–534. doi:10.1007/s00127-003-0676-6

Anthenunis, M. L., Valkenburg, P. M., & Peter, J. (2012). The quality of online, offline, and mixed-mode friendships among users of a social net- working site. *Cyberpsychology: Journal of Psychosocial Research on Cyberspace, 6,* Article 6. Retrieved from http://www.cyberpsychology.eu/view.php? cislo clanku=2012120304&article=6

Balfe, M., Doyle, F., Smith, D., Sreenan, S., Brugha, R., Hevey, D., & Conroy, R. (2013). Whats distressing about having type 1 diabetes? A qualitative study of young adults perspectives. *BMC Endocrine Disorders*, *13*(1), 1–14. doi:10.1186/1472-6823-13-25

Barker, V. (2009). Older adolescents motivations for social network site use: The influence of gender, group identity, and collective self-esteem. *Cyberpsychology & Behavior, 12*(2), 209–213. doi:10.1089/cpb.2008.0228

Beaudoin, C. E., & Tao, C. C. (2007). Benefiting from social capital in online support groups: An empirical study of cancer patients. *Cyberpsychology & Behavior, 10*(4), 587–590. doi:10.1089/cpb.2007.9986

Bender, J. L., Jimenez-Marroquin, M. C., & Jadad, A. R. (2011). Seeking support on facebook: A content analysis of breast cancer groups. *Journal of Medical Internet Research, 13*(1), e16. doi:10.2196/jmir.1560

Bickley, S. R. (1990). Dental hygienists' attitudes towards dental care for people with a mental handicap and the perceptions of adequacy of their training. *Dental Education, 168*, 361–364.

Bloom, J. R., & Kessler, L. (1994). Emotional support following cancer: A test of the stigma and social activity hypotheses. *Journal of Health and Social Behavior, 35*(2), 118–133. doi:10.2307/2137360

Brod, M., Kongso, J. H., Lessard, S., & Christensen, T. L. (2009). Psychological insulin resistance: Patient beliefs and implications for diabetes management. *Quality of Life Research: An International Journal of Quality of Life Aspects of Treatment, Care and Rehabilitation, 18*(1), 23–32. doi:10.1007/s11136-008-9419-1

Cane, D. B., & Gotlib, I. H. (1985). Implicit conceptualizations of depression: Implications for an interpersonal perspective. *Social Cognition, 3*(4), 341–368. doi:10.1521/soco.1985.3.4.341

Centers for Disease Control & Prevention. (2016). *HIV Among Youth.* Retrieved from http://www.cdc.gov/hiv/group/age/youth/

Chapple, A., Ziebland, S., & McPherson, A. (2004). Stigma, shame, and blame experienced by patients with lung cancer: Qualitative study. *British Medical Journal, 328*(7454), 1470–1473. doi:10.1136/bmj.38111.639734.7C

Chesney, M. A., & Smith, A. W. (1999). Critical delays in HIV testing and care: The potential role of stigma. *The American Behavioral Scientist, 42*(7), 1162–1174. doi:10.1177/00027649921954822

Cooney, G., Jahoda, A., Gumley, A., & Knott, F. (2006). Young people with learning disabilities attending mainstream and segregated schooling: Perceived stigma, social comparisons and future aspirations. *Journal of Intellectual Disability Research, 50*(6), 432–445. doi:10.1111/j.1365-2788.2006.00789.x

Coyne, S. M., Padilla-Walker, L. M., & Howard, E. (2013). Emerging in a digital world: A decade review of media use, effects, and gratifications in emerging adulthood. *Emerging Adulthood, 1*(2), 125–137. doi:10.1177/2167696813479782

Ellison, N. B., Steinfield, C., & Lampe, C. (2007). The benefits of Facebook friends: Social capital and college students use of online social network sites. *Journal of Computer-Mediated Communication, 12*(4), 1143–1168. doi:10.1111/j.1083-6101.2007.00367.x

File, B. L., & Wright, E. R. (2000). The dimensionality of stigma: A comparison of its impact on the self of persons with HIV/AIDS and cancer. *Journal of Health and Social Behavior, 41*(1), 50–67. doi:10.2307/2676360

Fox, J., Warber, K. M., & Makstaller, D. (2013). The role of Facebook in romantic relationship development: An exploration of Knapps relational stage model. *Journal of Social and Personal Relationships*, *30*(6), 771–794. doi:10.1177/0265407512468370

Goffman, E. (1963). *Stigma: Notes on the management of spoiled identity*. Englewood Cliffs, NJ: Prentice Hall.

Gotlib, I. H., & Beatty, M. E. (1985). Negative responses to depression: The role of attribution style. *Cognitive Therapy and Research*, *9*(1), 91–103. doi:10.1007/BF01178753

Gowen, L. K., Deschaine, M., Gruttadaro, D., & Markey, D. C. (2012). Young adults with mental health conditions and social networking websites: Decreasing social isolation. *Psychiatric Rehabilitation Journal*, *35*, 245–250. doi:10.2975/35.3.2012.245.250

Greene, J. A., Choudhry, N. K., Kilabuk, E., & Shrank, W. H. (2010). Online social networking by patients with diabetes: A qualitative evaluation of communication with facebook. *Journal of General Internal Medicine*, *26*(3), 287–292. doi:10.1007/s11606-010-1526-3

Greene, K. (2009). An integrated model of health disclosure decision-making. In T. D. Afifi & W. A. Afifi (Eds.), *Uncertainty, information management, and disclosure decisions: Theories and applications* (pp. 226–253). New York: Routledge.

Greene, K., & Faulkner, S. L. (2002). Self-disclosure in relationships of HIV-positive African American adolescent females. *Communication Studies*, *53*, 297–317. doi:10.1080/10510970209388595

Herek, G. M. (2014). HIV-related stigma. In P. W. Corrigan (Ed.), *The stigma of disease and disability: Empirical models and implications for change* (pp. 121–138). Washington, DC: American Psychological Association.

Horowitz, L. M., French, R. de S., Lapid, J. S., & Weckler, D. A. (1982). Symptoms and interpersonal problems: The prototypes as an integrating concept. In J. C. Anchin & D. J. Kiesler (Eds.), Handbook of interpersonal psychotherapy (pp. 168-189). New York: Pergamon.

Horvath, K. J., Danilenko, G. P., Williams, M. L., Simoni, J., Amico, K. R., Oakes, J. M., & Rosser, B. R. S. (2012). Technology use and reasons to participate in social networking health websites among people living with HIV in the US. *AIDS and Behavior*, *16*(4), 900–910. doi:10.1007/s10461-012-0164-7

Hosek, S. G., Harper, G. W., & Domanico, R. (2000). Psychological and social difficulties of adolescents living with HIV: A qualitative analysis. *Journal of Sex Education and Therapy*, *25*, 269–276.

Imai, T. (in press). Influences of mental illness stigma in a computer-mediated communication context: Investigating mediating roles of predicted outcome value and negative affect. *Japanese Journal of Communication Studies, 45*.

Imai, T., & Dailey, R. M. (2015). Influences of mental illness stigma on perceptions of and responses to requests for favors. *Health Communication*.

International Agency for Research on Cancer. (2008). *World Cancer Report 2008* (P. Boyle & B. Levin, Eds.). Lyon, France: Author.

Jacobsen, W. C., & Forste, R. (2011). The wired generation: Academic and social outcomes of electronic media use among university students. *Cyberpsychology, Behavior, and Social Networking*, *14*(5), 275–280. doi:10.1089/cyber.2010.0135

Jahoda, A., Wilson, A., Stalker, K., & Cairney, A. (2010). Living with stigma and the self perceptions of people with mild learning disabilities. *The Journal of Social Issues*, *66*(3), 521–534. doi:10.1111/j.1540-4560.2010.01660.x

Jenkins, J. H., & Carpenter-Song, E. A. (2009). Awareness of stigma among persons with schizophrenia: Marking the contexts of lived experience. *The Journal of Nervous and Mental Disease*, *197*(7), 520–529. doi:10.1097/NMD.0b013e3181aad5e9

Jones, E. E., Farina, A., Hastorf, A. H., Markus, H., Miller, D. T., & Scott, R. A. (1984). *Social stigma: The psychology of marked relationships*. New York: Freeman.

Link, B. G. (1982). Mental patient status, work, and income: An examination of the effects of a psychiatric label. *American Sociological Review*, *47*(2), 202–215. doi:10.2307/2094963

Link, B. G. (1987). Understanding labeling effects in the area of mental disorders: An assessment of the effects of expectations of rejection. *American Sociological Review*, *52*(1), 96–112. doi:10.2307/2095395

Link, B. G., Cullen, F. T., Struening, E., Shrout, P. E., & Dohrenwend, B. P. (1989). A modified labeling theory approach to mental disorders: An empirical assessment. *American Sociological Review*, *54*(3), 400–423. doi:10.2307/2095613

Link, B. G., & Phelan, J. C. (2001). Conceptualizing stigma. *Annual Review of Sociology*, *27*(1), 363–385. doi:10.1146/annurev.soc.27.1.363

Link, B. G., Phelan, J. C., Bresnahan, M., Stueve, A., & Pescosolido, B. A. (1999). Public conceptions of mental illness: Labels, causes, dangerousness and social distance. *American Journal of Public Health*, *89*(9), 1328–1333. doi:10.2105/AJPH.89.9.1328

Lysaker, P. H., Roe, D., & Yanos, P. T. (2007). Toward understanding the insight paradox: Internalized stigma moderates the association between insight and social functioning, hope, and self-esteem among people with schizophrenia spectrum disorders. *Schizophrenia Bulletin*, *33*(1), 192–199. doi:10.1093/schbul/sbl016

McIntyre, L. L., Blacher, J., & Baker, B. L. (2006). Transition to school: Adaptation in young children with and without developmental delays. *Journal of Intellectual Disability Research*, *50*, 349–361. doi:10.1111/j.1365-2788.2006.00783.x

Michikyan, M., Dennis, J., & Subrahmanyam, K. (2015). Can you guess who I am? Real, ideal, and false self-presentation on Facebook among emerging adults. *Emerging Adulthood*, *3*(1), 55–64. doi:10.1177/2167696814532442

Miller, A. N., & Rubin, D. L. (2007). Factors leading to self-disclosure of a positive HIV diagnosis in Nairobi, Kenya. *Qualitative Health Research*, *17*(5), 586–598. doi:10.1177/1049732307301498

Mo, P. K. H., & Coulson, N. S. (2008). Exploring the communication of social support within virtual communities: A content analysis of messages posted to an online HIV/AIDS support group. *Cyberpsychology & Behavior, 11*(3), 371–374. doi:10.1089/cpb.2007.0118

Moreno, M. A., Jelenchick, L. A., Egan, K. G., Cox, E., Young, H., Gannon, K. E., & Becker, T. (2011). Feeling bad on Facebook: Depression disclosures by college students on a social networking site. *Depression and Anxiety, 28*(6), 447–455. doi:10.1002/da.20805

Nabi, R. L., Prestin, A., & So, J. (2013). Facebook Friends with (Health) Benefits?: Exploring the Palliative Effects of Social Network Sites Compared to Interpersonal Networks. *Cyberpsychology, Behavior, and Social Networking, 16*, 721–727. doi:10.1089/cyber.2012.0521

Neal, C., Beckjord, E., Rechis, R., Schaeffer, J., Berno, D., & Duchover, Y. (2010). *Cancer stigma and silence around the world: A LIVESTRONG report.* Retrieved from http://images.livestrong.org/downloads/flatfiles/what-we-do/our-approach/reports/cancer-stigma/LSGlobalResearchReport.pdf

Newman, M. W., Lauterbach, D., Munson, S. A., Resnick, P., & Morris, M. E. (2011). It's not that I don't have problems, I'm just not putting them on Facebook: Challenges and opportunities in using online social networks for health. In *Proceedings of the ACM 2011 Conference on Computer Supported Cooperative Work* (pp. 341- 350). Hangzhou, China: ACM. doi:10.1145/1958824.1958876

Nicholson, K. J., & Sacco, W. P. (1999, August). *Interpersonal responses to depression: Negative social-cognition, affect, and non-genuine support.* Poster session presented at the annual meeting of the American Psychological Association, Boston, MA.

Norman, R. M. G., Gawronski, G., Hampson, E., Sorrentno, R. M., Szeto, A., & Ye, Y. (2010). Physical proximity in anticipation of meeting someone with schizophrenia: The role of explicit evaluations, implicit evaluations and cortisol levels. *Schizophrenia Research, 124*(1-3), 74–80. doi:10.1016/j.schres.2010.07.021

Patterson, P., Millar, B., Desille, N., & McDonald, F. (2012). The unmet needs of emerging adults with a cancer diagnosis: A qualitative study. *Cancer Nursing, 35*(3), 32–40. doi:10.1097/NCC.0b013e31822d9105

Perrin, A. (2015). *Social media usage 2005-2015.* Retrieved from http://www.pewinternet.org/2015/10/08/social-networking-usage-2005-2015/

Pew Research Center. (2014). *Social networking fact sheet.* Retrieved from http://www.pewinternet.org/fact-sheets/social-networking-fact-sheet/

Pew Research Center. (2015). *The demographics of social media users.* Retrieved from http://www.pewinternet.org/2015/08/19/the-demographics-of-social-media-users/

Postmes, T., Spears, R., & Lea, M. (2000). The formation of group norms in computermediated communication. *Human Communication Research, 26*(3), 341–371. doi:10.1111/j.1468-2958.2000.tb00761.x

Rafferty, J., Boettcher, C., & Griffin, K. W. (2001). Benefits and risks of reverse inclusion for preschoolers with and without disabilities: Parents perspectives. *Journal of Early Intervention, 24*(4), 266–286. doi:10.1177/105381510102400403

Rippere, V. (1977). Commonsense beliefs about depression and antidepressive behaviour: A study of social consensus. *Behaviour Research and Therapy, 15*(6), 465–473. doi:10.1016/0005-7967(77)90002-X

Sacco, W. P., & Vaughan, C. A. (2006). Depression and the response of others: A social-cognitive interpersonal process model. In T. E. Joiner, J. S. Brown, & J. Kistner (Eds.), *The interpersonal, social and cognitive nature of depression*. Mahwah, NJ: Lawrence Erlbaum Associates.

Sato, E., Ohsawa, I., Kataoka, J., Miwa, M., Tsukagoshi, F., Sato, J., & Sato, Y. et al. (2003). Socio-psychological problems of patients with late adolescent onset type 1 diabetes – analysis by qualitative research. *Nagoya Journal of Medical Science*, *66*, 21–29.

Schabert, J., Browne, J. L., Mosely, K., & Speight, J. (2005). Social stigma in diabetes: A framework to understand a growing problem for an increasing epidemic. *Patient*, *6*(1), 1–10. doi:10.1007/s40271-012-0001-0

Schneider, D. J. (2005). *The psychology of stereotyping*. New York: Guilford Press.

Schwartz, S. J., Donnellan, M. B., Ravert, R. D., Luyckx, K., & Zamboanga, B. L. (2013). Identity development, personality, and well-being in adolescence and emerging adulthood: Theory, research, and recent advances. In Handbook of psychology: Developmental psychology (vol. 6, pp. 339-364). New York: John Wiley and Sons.

Seeman, N. (2008). Web 2.0 and chronic illness: New horizons, new opportunities. *ElectronicHealthcare*, *6*, 104–110.

Shiu, A. T., Kwan, J. J. Y., & Wong, R. Y. (2003). Social stigma as a battier to diabetes self-management: Implications for multi-level interventions. *Journal of Clinical Nursing*, *12*(1), 149–150. doi:10.1046/j.1365-2702.2003.00735.x

Shpigelman, C.-N., & Gill, C. J. (2014a). Facebook use by persons with disabilities. *Journal of Computer-Mediated Communication*, *19*(3), 610–624. doi:10.1111/jcc4.12059

Shpigelman, C.-N., & Gill, C. J. (2014b). How do adults with intellectual disabilities use Facebook? *Disability & Society*, *29*(10), 1601–1616. doi:10.1080/09687599.2014.966186

Sibicky, M., & Dividio, J. F. (1986). Stigma of psychological therapy: Stereotypes, interpersonal reactions, and the self-fulfilling prophecy. *Journal of Counseling Psychology*, *33*(2), 148–154. doi:10.1037/0022-0167.33.2.148

Slevin, E., & Sines, D. (1996). Attitudes of nurses in general hospital towards people with learning disabilities: Influences of contact, and graduate – non-graduate status, a comparative study. *Journal of Advanced Nursing*, *24*(6), 1116–1126. doi:10.1111/j.1365-2648.1996.tb01016.x

Special Olympics. (2015). *What is intellectual disability?* Retrieved from http://www.specialolympics.org/Sections/Who_We_Are/What_Is_Intellectual_Disability.aspx

Starke, M. (2013). Everyday life of young adults with intellectual disabilities: Inclusionary and exclusionary processes among young adults of parents with intellectual disability. *Intellectual and Developmental Disabilities*, *51*(3), 164–175. doi:10.1352/1934-9556-51.3.164

Steel, Z., Marnane, C., Iranpour, C., Chey, T., Jackson, J. W., Patel, V., & Silove, D. (2014). The global prevalence of common mental disorders: A systematic review and meta-analysis 19802013. *International Journal of Epidemiology*, *43*(2), 476–493. doi:10.1093/ije/dyu038

Stein, D. J., Phillips, K. A., Bolton, D., Fulford, K. W. M., Sadler, J. Z., & Kendler, K. S. (2010). What is a mental/psychiatric disorder? From DSM-IV to DSM-V. *Psychological Medicine*, *40*(11), 1759–1765. doi:10.1017/S0033291709992261

Subrahmanyam, K., Reich, S. M., Waechter, N., & Espinoza, G. (2008). Online and offline social networks: Use of social networking sites by emerging adults. *Journal of Applied Developmental Psychology*, *29*(6), 420–433. doi:10.1016/j.appdev.2008.07.003

U.S. Bureau of Labor Statistics. (2010). *Employment status of the civilian population by sex, age, and disability status, not seasonally adjusted* [Data file]. Retrieved from http://www.bls.gov

Van Alphen, L. M., Dijker, A. J. M., Bos, A. E. R., Van den Borne, B., & Curfs, L. M. G. (2012). The influence of group size and stigma severity on social acceptance: The case of people with intellectual disability moving into neighborhoods. *Journal of Community & Applied Social Psychology*, *22*(1), 38–50. doi:10.1002/casp.1094

Walther, J. B., & Parks, M. R. (2002). Cues filtered out, cues filtered in: Computer-mediated communication and relationships. In M. L. Knapp & J. A. Daly (Eds.), *Handbook of interpersonal communication* (3rd ed.; pp. 529–563). Thousand Oaks, CA: Sage.

Washington Post-Kaiser Family Foundation. (2012). *2012 survey of Americans of HIV/AIDS*. Retrieved from https://kaiserfamilyfoundation.files.wordpress.com/2013/01/8334-f.pdf

Wellard, S. J., Rennie, S., & King, R. (2008). Perceptions of people with type 2 diabetes about self-management and the efficiency of community based services. *Contemporary Nurse*, *29*(2), 218–226. doi:10.5172/conu.673.29.2.218

Wiener, L. S., & Battles, H. B. (2006). Untangling the web: A close look at diagnosis disclosure among HIV-infected adolescents. *The Journal of Adolescent Health*, *38*(3), 307–309. doi:10.1016/j.jadohealth.2005.03.024

World Health Organization. (2012). *Cancer fact sheet*. Retrieved from http://globocan.iarc.fr/Pages/fact_sheets_cancer.aspx

World Health Organization. (2014a). *The top 10 causes of death*. Retrieved from http://www.who.int/mediacentre/factsheets/fs310/en/

World Health Organization. (2014b). *Diabetes*. Retrieved from http://www.who.int/mediacentre/factsheets/fs312/en/

World Health Organization. (2015). *HIV/AIDS*. Retrieved from http://www.who.int/mediacentre/factsheets/fs360/en/

Yarkin, K. L., Harvey, J. H., & Bloxom, B. M. (1981). Cognitive sets, attribution, and social interaction. *Journal of Personality and Social Psychology*, *41*(2), 243–252. doi:10.1037/0022-3514.41.2.243

KEY TERMS AND DEFINITIONS

AIDS: The final stage of HIV infection in which the body is vulnerable to diseases and those with AIDS may develop various serious health conditions.

Cancer: A group of different and distinctive diseases caused by an uncontrolled abnormal cell growth.

Diabetes: A group of metabolic diseases in which the body cannot control the amount of sugar in blood.

HIV: HIV interferes with the function of the immune system that fights off diseases.

Intellectual Disability: A disability characterized by impaired intellectual abilities and a lack of skills necessary for day-to-day life.

Mental Illness: A mental health condition that interferes with an individual's cognitive, emotional, or behavioral functioning.

Social Networking Sites: A web-based services that enable users to create a public profile and develop relationships with other users online.

Stigma: A negative stereotype associated with a specific group of people, leading to the unequal treatment for them.

Chapter 5
The Digital Development of LGBTQ Youth:
Identity, Sexuality, and Intimacy

Tyler J. Hatchel
California State University – Los Angeles, USA

Kaveri Subrahmanyam
California State University – Los Angeles, USA

Michelle Birkett
Northwestern University, USA

ABSTRACT

We use a developmental tasks framework to guide the exploration of digital media and the development of lesbian, gay, bisexual, transgender, and questioning (LGBTQ) youth. Since digital contexts are ubiquitous, it is clear that youth use them in the service of developmental tasks such as formation of identity, pursuit of intimacy, and development of sexuality. Research suggests that LGBTQ youth use digital media more often than their peers, likely due to the challenges they face. At the same time, electronic peer-victimization and sexual health are concerns since LGBTQ youth are more likely to be at risk. Drawing on extant research we will show that digital media use is associated with stigma-related stressors and risks while concurrently offering opportunities for healthy development. The chapter concludes with recommendations for future research that should help bolster our understanding of how digital contexts may predict the development and well-being of LGBTQ youth.

INTRODUCTION

Emerging adulthood is believed to be a distinct developmental period, although that uniqueness may vary as a function of culture (Arnett, 2006). Nevertheless, there is a high degree of affinity for digital media among most emerging adults regardless of where they live (Brown, 2006; Arnett, 2014). This may be because digital media can help in dealing with developmental tasks such as identity formation,

DOI: 10.4018/978-1-5225-1856-3.ch005

expressing autonomy, as well as exploring relationships (Coyne, Padilla-Walker, & Howard, 2013). According to a Ipsos/Google survey, emerging adults are essentially always connected and that 92% of them often use more than one device at a time (Google, 2012). One cross-sectional survey showed that nearly 100% of emerging adults in the U.S. reported that they used the Internet with some regularity (Jones, 2002). More specifically, another study found that emerging adults reported spending about 3.5 hours a day on the Internet, often via social media (Padilla-Walker, Nelson, Carroll, & Jensen, 2010). Additionally, they report spending at least 45 minutes a day using digital devices such as smart phones (Jacobsen & Forste, 2011). There has been considerable research done on emerging adults and digital media in general, but few studies have examined specific groups.

Much of the research concerning lesbian, gay, bisexual, transgender, and questioning (LGBTQ) youth is specific to older adolescents as well as emerging adults (e.g., 16-24), and therefore we use the term youth to encompass this broader age range. Survey data suggest that LGBTQ youth are even more likely to use digital media than non-LGBTQ peers (GLSEN, CiPHR, & CCRC, 2013). However, it is not especially clear why LGBTQ youth use digital media more often and whether this use is related to their development and well-being. The research on LGBTQ youths' digital media use has also yielded mixed and inconsistent results. Some findings suggest that digital media use may leave LGBQ youth at heightened risk for peer victimization or poor sexual health (Cooper & Blumenfield, 2012; Bolding, Davis, Hart, Sherr, & Elford, 2007), whereas others indicate that digital media may enable them to develop in a healthy and educated manner (Magee, Bigelow, DeHaan, & Mustanski, 2012; Mustanski, Greene, Ryan, & Whitton, 2014). Moreover, despite the increased risk of exposure to threats such as electronic peer victimization (i.e., cyberbullying), LGBTQ youth are more likely than their peers to report using digital media for peer support, health information, and civic engagement (GLSEN, CiPHR, & CCRC, 2013).

Given these polarized findings, it is important to explore how digital media may predict the development and well-being of LGBTQ youth, topics that have not been thoroughly addressed in the literature. These limitations are magnified by the notion that adolescence and emerging adulthood are critical transitional phases when well-being may be tenuous (Steinberg, 2008; Arnett, 2000). To address these shortcomings, this chapter describes the role of digital media in the lives of LGBTQ youth. Specifically, we start by exploring the unique challenges faced by LGBTQ youth as that offers insights into how digital media may be unique for this population. Next we present the developmental framework guiding the chapter, followed by a discussion of the role of digital media as youth deal with the key developmental tasks of exploring identity, coming to terms with their sexuality, and pursuing intimacy. This developmental framework offers a useful way to conceptualize and synthesize the extant literature on LGBTQ youth and digital media. Our synthesis suggests a modest, albeit beneficial, theoretical foundation for future work to be built upon. Finally, the conclusion identifies gaps in the literature, as well as future directions for research and program design.

BACKGROUND

Unique Challenges Faced by LGBTQ Youth

To understand the relation between LGBTQ youths' digital media use and well-being, we begin by examining the stigma, health disparities, and unique developmental challenges that they face (Mustanski, Birkett, Greene, Hatzenbuehler, & Newcomb, 2014). In particular, LGBTQ youth are exposed to stressors related to their minority status such as victimization and uncertainties regarding their identity. The combination of typical daily stressors and stigma-related stressors leaves them at an increased risk for psychopathology and poor psychosocial adjustment (Meyer, 2003; Bos, Sandfort, de Bruyn, & Hakvoort, 2008). Other difficulties specific to LGBTQ youth development include accessibility of supportive friend and romantic partners, acceptance of one's own identity, as well as challenges surrounding sexuality and support (Mustanski, Birkett, Greene, Hatzenbuehler, & Newcomb, 2014). Moving forward, we will frame these difficulties within a traditional developmental framework.

Developmental Framework

To further understand the implications of LGBTQ youths' digital media usage, we draw from extant research on developmental psychology and digital media to offer a guiding framework for this chapter. Adolescence and emerging adulthood are transitional periods when youth are faced with the developmental tasks of solidifying their identity, forming intimate relationships with peers and romantic partners, as well as accepting their sexuality (Arnett, 2000; Sternberg, 2008). In addition, the transitions of emerging adulthood due to moving from home for college or work may further emphasize youths' reliance on peers and romantic partners for much needed support (Collins & van Dulmen, 2006). The unique features of emerging adulthood – not quite independent financially or otherwise – means that youth have additional time to deal with the aforementioned developmental tasks (Arnett, 2000). Importantly, social contexts including the family and peer group play a vital role during these transitional stages (Arnett, 2000; Hill, 1983). Similarly, research has shown that aspects of the social context such as school climate, peer relations, as well as parental dynamics predict the development and well-being of LGBTQ youth (D'Augelli, 2012). Scholars have argued that digital worlds present youth with opportunities to interact and communicate with peers and thus have become an important social context where sexuality, identity, and intimacy are played out (Subrahmanyam, Greenfield, Tynes, 2004; Subrahmanyam, Smahel, & Greenfield, 2006). On this view, digital media may be another important social context for LGBTQ youth, and similar to other contexts, play a role as youth deal with the developmental tasks facing them. In the next sections, we adopt this approach to examine the role of digital media in key areas of LGBTQ youth development.

DIGITAL MEDIA AND LGBTQ YOUTHS' IDENTITY DEVELOPMENT

One of the most distinctive features of emerging adulthood is the exploration and development of identity (Arnett, 2000). Although identity exploration begins in adolescence (Erikson, 1968), it continues into emerging adulthood. Aspects of identity such as one's vocation and worldview require more experience, thought, and time to truly form. Research also suggests that during the same phase, there is continued cognitive growth as complex forms of contemplation, self-reflection, and a sense of self develop (Arnett, 2006). However, the exact timing and processes surrounding identity development may vary. Although the above statements apply to all youth, nonetheless it is very likely that LGBTQ youth may go through the identify formation process differently than their non-LGBTQ peers due to the unique challenges facing them.

Research on identity development among LGBTQ youth reveal that digital media are being used to find information to facilitate the exploration of self, for development of a sense of self, and understanding the implications of emergent identities (Bond, Hefner, & Drogos, 2009; DeHaan, Kuper, Magee, Bigelow, & Mustanski, 2013; Hamer, 2003; Hillier & Harrison, 2007). These findings are consistent with previous research, which has shown that social media, online videos, and other digital contexts provide a safe atmosphere for all youth to express themselves and explore their identity (Subrahmanyam & Šmahel, 2012). Digital media and the Internet appear to offer new resources and contexts that enable LGBTQ youth to achieve tasks associated with identity development that historically occurred offline. Nevertheless, one qualitative study on LGBTQ emerging adults showed that factors such as context, culture, and relationships seemed to predict exactly how digital media were used (Kuper & Mustanski, 2014). For example, those who were seemingly isolated or rejected by parents were more likely to utilize digital media as supplementary resources in ways that promoted healthy identity development by encouraging self-acceptance. Another qualitative study of 63 gay or bisexual male youth found that the participants utilized a wide range of digital tools (e.g., social media, mobile apps, informational resources) to explore and ultimately come to accept their identities; they also reported using digital media to increase self-awareness of sexual identity and to learn more about the LGBTQ community (Harper, Serrano, Bruce, & Bauermeister, 2015). Other studies have also shown that digital tools are more likely to be used by LGBTQ youth in the pursuit of developing identities, intimacies, and sexualities when offline resources are insufficient (DeHaan et al., 2013; Hillier & Harrison, 2007).

LGBTQ youth's preconceived notions about the nature of digital media as well as previous experiences specific to the Internet may predict their perceptions about how helpful digital media could be for their identity development (Kuper & Mustanski, 2014). Specifically, if LGBTQ youth had negative perceptions of the online LGBTQ community, then they were less likely to utilize them as helpful resources. It is possible that internalized homophobia, potentially as an artifact of stigma-related stressors, contributed to negative perceptions of the online LGBTQ community. Making sense of emerging sexual and romantic identities are critical tasks for which digital media may be utilized (Kuper & Mustanski, 2014). Again, LGBTQ youth seem to utilize digital tools when offline resources that supplement development are either unavailable or lacking.

Nevertheless, sometimes limitations in support can cascade or be reproduced online. In other words, an LGBTQ youth's susceptibility may be triggered by offline experiences which, then, may leave her/him more vulnerable to negative online experiences. The combination of negative experiences across online and offline contexts appears to diminish healthy identity development by interfering with the formation of self-acceptance (Kuper & Mustanski, 2014). The additional stress of difficulties online may also have deleterious consequences for LGBTQ youth when pursuing the development of intimacy.

DIGITAL MEDIA AND LGBTQ YOUTH'S INTIMACY DEVELOPMENT

Studies have found that during adolescence and emerging adulthood, youth are more concerned with peer relations than familial relations (Collins & Laursen, 2004). Since youth largely use digital tools to communicate with peers, these digital platforms become increasingly important at this point in their lives (Subrahmanyam & Šmahel, 2012). Friends and romantic partners are critical sources of support and intimacy for older adolescents and emerging adults (Coyne, Padilla-Walker, & Howard, 2013). Yet, the vital nature of peer relations may leave some at risk for peer victimization or poor sexual health.

These topics warrant exploration with regard to LGBTQ public health, since they are often related to poor outcomes such as suicidality (Ybarra, Mitchell, Kosciw, & Korchmaros, 2015; Birkett, Espelage, & Koenig, 2009) or contraction of infectious diseases (Mustanski et al., 2014). In the next section, we will explore how digital media might augment or weaken the healthy development of intimacy among LGBTQ youth.

Peer Victimization

Digital media can be sources of stigma-related stressors such as peer victimization (i.e., being victimized by an act of aggression from a similarly-aged peer). For instance, compared to their heterosexual and cisgender peers, LGBTQ youth were more likely to report being victimized via digital media, feeling just as unsafe online as offline, and being victimized online and offline simultaneously (Cooper & Blumenfield, 2012). For LGBTQ youth, electronic peer victimization has been found to have similar outcomes as offline peer victimization including poor mental health, feelings of loneliness, and reduced academic achievement (GLSEN, CiPHR, & CCRC, 2013). Additionally, like offline victimization, electronic peer victimization is often related to a victim's actual or perceived gender expression (i.e., gender nonconformity), gender identity, and/or sexuality (GLSEN, CiPHR, & CCRC, 2013) which is in line with minority stress theory since these appearances and expressions tend to elicit stigmatization from peers. However, electronic peer victimization may be more insidious because it can occur at any time, leave little to no escape, is relatively permanent, and may have a larger audience. Additionally, because of the potential for anonymity and disembodiment within digital contexts, electronic peer victimization can be more extreme than offline victimization (Kowalski, Giumetti, Schroeder, & Lattanner, 2012; Kowalski, Limber, & Agatston, 2012; Suler, 2004). Although digital contexts can be a source of victimization, they also offer opportunities for healthy relationships and social support, the topic of the next section.

Social Support

In addition to being a safe platform to explore identity, digital media enable youth to access peer-based social support in meaningful ways (Subrahmanyam & Šmahel, 2012). Social support is the perception that one is part of a social network and/or the actuality of being cared for by others. In other words, digital media provide a platform for self-disclosure, closeness, and developing relationships, all key to the pursuit of intimacy. Connecting to and exploring online communities associated with one's identity can encourage the evolution of LGBTQ youths' self-acceptance offline (Hillier & Harrison, 2007). Coming to terms with one's sexual orientation or gender identity is vital for self-acceptance and is positively correlated with self-esteem and mental health (Savin-Williams, 1994). Thus it is possible that due to increased acceptance or social support, LGBTQ youth are more likely to self-disclose and develop intimate relationships online. These notions are supported by data showing that LGBTQ youth often reveal their identities online before doing so offline (GLSEN, CiPHR, & CCRC, 2013). Furthermore, Savin-Williams (2005) speculates that the trend towards revealing one's sexuality or gender identity earlier in life is partially attributable to the growth and availability of virtual communities and digital social support.

The nature of social support and affinity for type of support (i.e., peer-based, parental, and romantic) is believed to be dynamic and generally carries positive implications for development and well-being. For example, one cross-sectional study on 97 LGBQ youth found that all social support has a protective role in their psychosocial adjustment, even in the face of peer victimization (Williams, Connolly, Pepler, & Craig, 2005). Research has also shown that youth who had clear support from a peer were less likely to be victimized offline and displayed lower levels of internalizing symptoms such as depression (Hodges, Boivin, Vitaro, & Bukowski, 1999). Often victimization and its consequences are defined by social contexts such as a youth's environment and social support, which serve as buffering agents (Espelage & Swearer, 2008). Therefore, social support likely moderates the relation between victimization and poor outcomes for all youth, but may be especially critical for stigmatized youth like those who identify as LGBTQ. The protective role of digital support for LGBTQ youth is not as well established, but one cross-sectional study of 5,542 U.S. youth did find that LGBT youth were more likely to report that online friends were important due to the emotional support they provided (Ybarra, Mitchell, Palmer, & Reisner, 2015). More research needs to be done in this area to validate the findings.

Eliason and Schope (2007) suggest that peer support is integral to the beginning stages of sexual minority development and resolving feelings of being different. Although somewhat of a dilemma, it demonstrates the unique situation of LGBTQ youth, wherein disclosure of identity simultaneously puts them at risk for alienation, but also in a position to acquire much needed support. Furthermore, the fear of ostracism may hinder youth's self-disclosure about their identity, making it difficult to utilize social support, and therefore further delaying healthy development. Digital media can potentially help to reconcile these challenges.

Research is limited regarding the value of online intimacy for LGBTQ youth, yet some recent findings are pertinent to this issue. Using a resiliency-based framework to examine whether openness about one's LGBTQ identity shaped well-being, one cross-sectional study on 7,816 LGBTQ youth found that openness did relate to higher rates of victimization; however, openness was also indicative of higher self-esteem and lower levels of depression, suggesting that online presentation of identity may have the potential to facilitate healthy development, including intimacy (Kosciw, Palmer, & Kull, 2014). As expected, youth who revealed their LGBTQ identities in rural environments were more likely to be subjected to victimization, indicating that digital media may be essential for youth in more isolated environments. Digital media can offer a more controlled and safe environment for LGBTQ youth to develop their relationships, while diminishing risks associated with disclosure (i.e., peer victimization). Digital media can also offer a sense of belonging and acceptance. However, another cross-sectional study of 425 LGB youth aged 16-24 reported that although perceived offline social support did offer a certain compensatory effect, it did not fully reduce the negative effects associated with offline peer victimization (Mustanski, Newcomb, & Garofalo, 2011). This suggests that although social support is important, it is not sufficient when it comes to mending the consequences associated with peer victimization.

Another consideration for intimacy is whether relationships formed (e.g., friends and/or romantic partners) online are as meaningful as offline relationships. Early studies specific to heterosexual youth suggest that online relationships were perceived as not being as 'real' (Šmahel, 2003). These youth mostly connect online with peers who they already know offline (Subrahmanyam & Šmahel, 2012), and thus digital media can serve as a tool to develop and enrich those relationships. More recent studies have found that digital media do contribute to developing relationships, connectedness, and social support (Davis, 2012; Grieve, Indian, Witteveen, Tolan, & Marrington, 2013). This was especially true when offline affairs were inherently challenging or lacking (Indian & Grieve, 2014). Therefore we speculate that digital media may be helpful for LGBTQ youth who often feel isolated and are subject to unique developmental challenges. One cross-sectional study on LGBQ Dutch youth aged 16-24 years found that they often utilized digital media to find social support (Baams, Jonas, Utz, Bos, & van der Vuurst, 2011). Others have found that the LGBTQ youths' perception of online relationships and support was predicted by background and experience with the online community (Kuper & Mustanski, 2014). In sum, online social support is likely more valuable for youth who are stigmatized or lacking offline support (Hillier, Mitchell, & Ybarra, 2012), yet some LGBTQ youth may find digital resources more useful than others.

LGBTQ YOUTH SEXUALITY AND DIGITAL MEDIA

Although emerging adults do not necessarily have to cope with the physical and sexual changes brought on by puberty like adolescents do, they are still faced with coming to terms with their sexual self (Erikson, 1968). Similar to other discussed developmental tasks, digital media may serve as both a resource and liability within the domain of developing sexualities. For example, digital media have enabled youth to access sexually explicit content with considerable ease. For all youth, there are concerns that exposure to sexually explicit content may distort the youth's understanding of sexual norms or healthy behavior (Greenfield, 2004; Lo & Wei, 2005). Yet, others suggest that exposure to sexually explicit content may be an important component of sex education (Watson & Smith, 2012), especially when other sources of information are lacking, which is often the case for LGBTQ youth.

Sexual Health

Despite the concerns about sexual risk stemming from LGBTQ youths' use of digital media, it is important to consider some ways in which digital tools can foster healthy development. The Internet is a treasure trove of sex-related health information which is used by health care providers and youth alike (Fox & Jones, 2009). Magee and colleagues (2012) completed a mixed-methods study on 32 LGBT youth aged 16-24 years and found that healthy sexual development, including feeling comfortable with one's maturing body and accepting the new or stronger feelings of sexual arousal (Steinberg, 2008; Brooks-Gunn & Paikoff, 1993), largely occur within the context of websites, video content, social media, and smart phone applications. Similarly, one mixed method study of 329 sexual minority men aged 18-24 years found that sexually explicit content found online played a significant role by reinforcing and facilitating a better understanding of sexual attraction and arousal (Mustanski et al., 2011a). The content may validate LGBTQ youth's sexual feelings as being normative despite previous exposure to stigma, and thus, promotes personal acceptance.

Most youth are particularly concerned with sexual health information as they search for it more than any other health-related topic (Buhi, Daley, Fuhrmann, & Smith, 2009). Searching for sexual health information may be crucial for LGBTQ youth since schools and their sex education programs typically fall short when providing information specific to this population. Moreover, digital media may act as a bridge to offline sexual health resources like community centers and therefore facilitate the healthy development of sexuality. However, online health resources are not equally credible, and youth may need training in searching for information and source credibility (Mustanski et al., 2014). Researchers should continue to examine the integrity of online information as well as the processes by which LGBTQ youth determine the quality of these online resources.

Sexual Risk

LGBTQ youth often use the Internet and digital tools to meet sexual partners. Bolding, Davis, Hart, Sherr, and Elford (2007) conducted a longitudinal study on 810 young men who have sex with men, and found that over a few years, there was a significant increase in participants reporting that they found their first sexual partner online (i.e., 2.6-61.0%). Finding partners online presents an important opportunity for them, as they may be isolated and not be able to explore romantic intimacy otherwise (DeHaan et al., 2013). At the same time, research indicates that LGBTQ youth are at an increased risk to engage in high risk sexual behaviors (Mustanski, Garofalo, Herrick, & Donenberg, 2007). Additionally, a meta-analysis of 15 studies found that online sex-seeking behavior among sexual minority youth was linked to a history of unprotected sex (Liau, Millet, & Marks, 2006). These findings should be interpreted with some caution as several of the studies included in the meta-analysis had limitations, such as the use of a retrospective design that did not allow researchers to determine if the online sex-seeking and engagement in high risk sexual behavior were clearly related (Mustanski, Lyons, & Garcia, 2011). Studies without these limitations did not support the findings that online sex-seeking behavior was associated with increased sexual risk (Mustanski et al., 2007). The propensity to make poor sexual health decisions is likely a separate factor from how partners are met (Mustanski et al., 2011a). It is also important to consider that the desire to develop romantic intimacy and come to terms with one's sexuality, without access to typical offline outlets or peers, could, theoretically, leave LGBTQ youth at an increased risk for online solicitation or exploitation by older adults.

Sexting describes the sending or receiving of sexually suggestive pictures or messages via digital media. Specific to all youth, the prevalence of sexting ranges from 10% to 35% with older youth being more likely to engage in this behavior (Klettke, Hallford, & Mellor, 2014). Concerns about youth sexting focus on the associated risks, including the distribution of content without consent, being charged with producing/owning/transmitting child pornography, and the potential for distress or mental health issues (Judge, 2012). The Youth Risk Behavior Survey (n = 1839) suggests that LGBTQ youth are more likely to engage in sexting, possibly because of their isolation and reliance on digital media to explore intimacy and sexuality (Rice, et al., 2012). Longitudinal research with LGBTQ youth is needed to further investigate the relationship between sexting and possible poor outcomes like engaging in sexually risky behaviors.

Digital media may present risks for LGBTQ youths' understanding of healthy sexual relationships as sexually explicit content and online forums are two of the few means of accessing sexual health-related information and the available content is not always accurate or helpful (Magee et al., 2012; Mustanski, Greene, Ryan, & Whitton, 2014). Nevertheless, a study examining the development of sexuality and sexual health as a function of exposure to digital content would illuminate this uncertainty and is another topic that demands further investigation.

CONCLUSION AND FUTURE RESEARCH

Development is a process which may attenuate well-being and this may be especially true for LGBTQ youth given their unique developmental challenges. Throughout this chapter, the extant literature has been reviewed to illustrate how digital media may enhance the healthy development and well-being of LGBTQ youth. It is intuitive that a population who are subjected to challenges, like coming to terms with sexuality or gender identity, would utilize tools available to them. We suspect that LGBTQ youth are more likely to use digital media in the pursuit of developmental tasks, but this strategy is not necessarily risk free. Digital media are important social contexts, wherein stigma-related stressors and protective factors can be realized, and are also a forum where the development of identity, intimacy, and sexuality unfold. Our synthesis offers support for the notion that using a developmental framework for understanding the role of digital media in the lives of LGBTQ youth is warranted. Furthermore, our conceptualization could serve as a foundation for rigorous research or sophisticated model development.

There is a clear demand for additional studies on LGBTQ youth that utilize creative research designs and examine contextual factors such as digital media. Ignoring social contexts, such as digital media, when investigating the development and well-being of LGBTQ youth, would profoundly distort our understanding of this population (D'Augelli, 2012). Similarly, it is important to incorporate the role of digital media when studying the developmental tasks faced by LGBTQ youth to further augment our understanding of their well-being. The development of tuned measures and refined conceptualization of constructs concerning LGBTQ youth and digital media would further enhance our understanding. For example, it is still unclear how exactly online social support should be examined for LGBTQ youth. It may be the medium through which the support is received or perhaps the origination of the relationship which tends to predict the potential buffering roles. Alternatively, a sense of belonging or community could be the features which prove the most meaningful. Also, measures specific to electronic peer victimization do not necessarily account for the motive like offline measures designed for LGBTQ youth do. In other words, offline measures seek to illustrate that the victimization is particular to LGBTQ youth's identity or gender expression and this dovetails nicely with minority stress theory. Furthermore, the nature of online peer victimization may vary as a function of platform or source.

Although it is tempting to suggest that digital tools are simply risky or supportive, these dynamics are more likely predicted by the unique developmental challenges facing LGBTQ youth (i.e., exposure to victimization, having access to safe social support, and accurate health-related information (see Table 1). That said, our review was not able to find sufficient scholarship concerned with how to magnify the opportunities afforded by digital media. Additional translational research needs to be done to assess the effectiveness of programs that target victimization, offer a safe online environment, as well as foster accessibility and accuracy of health-related information. Moreover, there is a clear dearth of research examining how digital media relate to transgender or gender nonconforming youth. Finally, studies that could help illustrate exactly what predisposes LGBTQ youth to utilize digital resources while avoiding risks would further enhance our understanding of their well-being.

Table 1. Relations among LGBTQ youth development, risk, and opportunity within the context of digital media use

Youth Developmental Tasks	Digital Media Use	
	Opportunity	**Risks**
Sexuality	• Information • Social Support	• Misinformation • Exploitation
Identity	• Identity Exploration • Development of sense of self	• Isolation • Exposure to negative identity-related experiences
Intimacy	• Social Support • Access to Relationships	• Solicitation • Victimization

LGBTQ youth appear to be utilizing digital media to access opportunities since findings have shown they can be tools to promote healthy development (Magee, Bigelow, DeHaan, & Mustanski, 2012; Mustanski, Greene, Ryan, & Whitton, 2014; GLSEN, CiPHR, & CCRC, 2013; Bond, Hefner, & Drogos, 2009; Hamer, 2003; Hillier & Harrison, 2007). Digital media may be instrumental for LGBTQ youth since their offline worlds often restrict the development of key milestones due to stigma-related stressors and other difficulties (Mustanski, Birkett, Greene, Hatzenbuehler, & Newcomb, 2014; Meyer, 2003). LGBTQ youth face unique developmental challenges and digital media may help lessen these restrictions. Although digital media are not without risks, with proper use, they may largely contribute to the well-being and healthy development of LGBTQ youth. These new media are clearly a significant contextual factor and may predict the development of LGBTQ youth, but we still do not understand what predisposes a youth to utilize them as a resource, while avoiding or coping with the risks. It may be a trait the youth has (i.e., resilience), other contextual factors (i.e., school climate or social support), or specific resources offered by digital platforms.

REFERENCES

Arnett, J. J. (2000). Emerging adulthood: A theory of development from the late teens through the twenties. *The American Psychologist*, *55*(5), 469–480. doi:10.1037/0003-066X.55.5.469 PMID:10842426

Arnett, J. J. (2006). Emerging adulthood: Understanding the new way of coming of age. In J. J. Arnett & J. L. Tanner (Eds.), *Emerging adults in America: Coming of age in the 21st century* (pp. 1–19). Washington, DC: American Psychological Association. doi:10.1037/11381-001

Arnett, J. J. (2014). *Emerging adulthood: The winding road from the late teens through the twenties.* OUP Us. doi:10.1093/acprof:oso/9780199929382.001.0001

Baams, L., Jonas, K. J., Utz, S., Bos, H. M. W., & van der Vuurst, L. (2013). Internet use and online social support among same sex attracted individuals of different ages. *Computers in Human Behavior*, *27*(5), 1820–1827. doi:10.1016/j.chb.2011.04.002

Birkett, M., Espelage, D., & Koenig, B. (2009). LGB and questioning students in schools: The moderating effects of homophobic bullying and school climate on negative outcomes. *Journal of Youth and Adolescence*, *38*(7), 989–1000. doi:10.1007/s10964-008-9389-1 PMID:19636741

Bolding, G., Davis, M., Hart, G., Sherr, L., & Elford, J. (2007). Where young MSM meet their first sexual partner: The role of the Internet. *AIDS and Behavior*, *11*(4), 522–526. doi:10.1007/s10461-007-9224-9 PMID:17347876

Bond, B. J., Hefner, V., & Drogos, K. L. (2009). Information-seeking practices during the sexual development of lesbian, gay, and bisexual individuals: The influence and effects of coming out in a mediated environment. *Sexuality & Culture*, *13*(1), 32–50. doi:10.1007/s12119-008-9041-y

Bos, H. M., Sandfort, T. G., de Bruyn, E. H., & Hakvoort, E. M. (2008). Same-sex attraction, social relationships, psychosocial functioning, and school performance in early adolescence. *Developmental Psychology*, *44*(1), 59–68. doi:10.1037/0012-1649.44.1.59 PMID:18194005

Brooks-Gunn, J., & Paikoff, R. (1993). *Sex is a gamble, kissing is a game: Adolescent sexuality and health promotion. In Promoting the health of adolescents: New directions for the twenty-first century* (pp. 180–208). New York, NY: Oxford University Press.

Buhi, E. R., Daley, E., Oberne, A., Smith, S., Schneider, T., & Fuhrmann, H. (2010). Quality and accuracy of sexual health information web sites visited by young people. *The Journal of Adolescent Health, 47*(2), 206–208. doi:10.1016/j.jadohealth.2010.01.002 PMID:20638014

Collins, W., & Laursen, B. (2004). Changing relationships, changing youth. *The Journal of Early Adolescence, 24*(1), 55–62. doi:10.1177/0272431603260882

Cooper, R. M., & Blumenfeld, W. J. (2012). Responses to cyberbullying: A descriptive analysis of the frequency of and impact on LGBT and allied youth. *Journal of LGBT Youth, 9*(2), 153–177. doi:10.1080/19361653.2011.649616

Coyne, S. M., Padilla-Walker, L. M., & Howard, E. (2013). Emerging in a digital world a decade review of media use, effects, and gratifications in emerging adulthood. *Emerging Adulthood, 1*(2), 125–137. doi:10.1177/2167696813479782

DAugelli, A. R. (2012). Restoring Lives: Developmental Research on Sexual Orientation. *Human Development, 55*(1), 1–3. doi:10.1159/000336251

Davis, K. (2012). Friendship 2.0: Adolescents experiences of belonging and self-disclosure online. *Journal of Adolescence, 35*(6), 1527–1536. doi:10.1016/j.adolescence.2012.02.013 PMID:22475444

DeHann, S., Kuper, L. E., Magee, J. C., Bigelow, L., & Mustanski, B. S. (2013). The interplay between online and offline explorations of identity, relationships, and sex: A mixed-method study with LGBT youth. *Journal of Sex Research, 50*(5), 421–434. doi:10.1080/00224499.2012.661489 PMID:22489658

Eliason, M. J., & Schope, R. (2007). Shifting sands or solid foundation? Lesbian, gay, bisexual, and transgender identity formation. In The health of sexual minorities (pp. 3-26). Springer US.

Erikson, E. H. (1968). *Identity: Youth and crisis*. New York, NY: Norton; doi:10.1007/978-0-387-31334-4_1

Espelage, D. L., & Swearer, S. M. (2008). Addressing research gaps in the intersection between homophobia and bullying. *School Psychology Review, 37*(2), 155–159.

Fergus, S., & Zimmerman, M. A. (2005). Adolescent resilience: A framework for understanding healthy development in the face of risk. *Annual Review of Public Health, 26*(1), 399–419. doi:10.1146/annurev.publhealth.26.021304.144357 PMID:15760295

Fox, S., & Jones, S. (2009). The social life of health information. Washington, DC: Pew Internet and American Life Project. Retrieved from http://www.pewinternet.org/2009/06/11/the-social-life-of-health-information/

GLSEN, CiPHR, & CCRC. (2013). *Out online: The experiences of lesbian, gay, bisexual and transgender youth on the Internet*. New York: GLSEN. Retrieved from http://www.glsen.org/sites/default/files/Out%20Online%20FINAL.pdf

Google. (2012). *Hyper-connected teens and twenty-somethings*. Retrieved from https://www.thinkwithgoogle.com/infographics/the-media-habits-of-teens-and-young-adults.html

Grieve, R., Indian, M., Witteveen, K., Tolan, G. A., & Marrington, J. (2013). Face-to-face or Facebook: Can social connectedness be derived online? *Computers in Human Behavior*, *29*(3), 604–609. doi:10.1016/j.chb.2012.11.017

Hamer, J. S. (2003). Coming-out: Gay males' information seeking. *School Libraries Worldwide*, *9*(2), 73–89.

Harper, G. W., Serrano, P. A., Bruce, D., & Bauermeister, J. A. (2015). The Internet's multiple roles in facilitating the sexual orientation identity development of gay and bisexual male adolescents. *American Journal of Men's Health*. PMID:25585861

Hill, J. P. (1983). Early Adolescence: Research agenda. *The Journal of Early Adolescence*, *3*(1-2), 1–21. doi:10.1177/027243168331002

Hillier, L., & Harrison, L. (2007). Building realities less limited than their own: Young people practicing same-sex attraction on the Internet. *Sexualities*, *10*(1), 82–100. doi:10.1177/1363460707072956

Hillier, L., Mitchell, K. J., & Ybarra, M. L. (2012). The Internet as a safety net: Findings from a series of online focus groups with LGB and non-LGB young people in the U.S. *Journal of LGBT Youth*, *9*(3), 225–246. doi:10.1080/19361653.2012.684642

Hodges, E. V. E., Boivin, M., Vitaro, F., & Bukowski, W. M. (1999). The power of friendship: Protection against an escalating cycle of peer victimization. *Developmental Psychology*, *35*(1), 94–101. doi:10.1037/0012-1649.35.1.94 PMID:9923467

Indian, M., & Grieve, R. (2014). When Facebook is easier than face-to-face: Social support derived from Facebook in socially anxious individuals. *Personality and Individual Differences*, *59*, 102–106. doi:10.1016/j.paid.2013.11.016

Jacobsen, W. C., & Forste, R. (2011). The wired generation: Academic and social outcomes of electronic media use among university students. *Cyberpsychology, Behavior, and Social Networking*, *14*(5), 275–280. doi:10.1089/cyber.2010.0135 PMID:20961220

Jones, S. (2002). The Internet goes to college: How students are living in the future with today's technology. Washington, DC: Pew Internet & American Life Project. Retrieved from http://files.eric.ed.gov/fulltext/ED472669.pdf

Judge, A. M. (2012). Sexting among U.S. adolescents: Psychological and legal implications. *Harvard Review of Psychiatry*, *20*(2), 86–96. doi:10.3109/10673229.2012.677360 PMID:22512742

Klettke, B., Hallford, D. J., & Mellor, D. J. (2014). Sexting prevalence and correlates: A systematic literature review. *Clinical Psychology Review*, *34*(1), 44–53. doi:10.1016/j.cpr.2013.10.007 PMID:24370714

Kosciw, J. G., Palmer, N. A., & Kull, R. M. (2014). Reflecting resiliency: Openness about sexual orientation and/or gender identity and its relationship to well-being and educational outcomes for LGBT students. *American Journal of Community Psychology*, *55*(1-2). doi:10.1007/s10464-014-9642-6 PMID:24691967

Kowalski, R. M., Giumetti, G. W., Schroeder, A. N., & Lattanner, M. R. (2012). Bullying in the digital age: A critical review and meta-analysis of cyberbullying research among youth. *Psychological Bulletin*, *140*(4), 1073–1137. doi:10.1037/a0035618 PMID:24512111

Liau, A., Millett, G., & Marks, G. (2006). Meta-analytic examination of online sex-seeking and sexual risk behavior among men who have sex with men. *Sexually Transmitted Diseases*, *33*(9), 576–584. doi:10.1097/01.olq.0000204710.35332.c5 PMID:16540884

Madden, M., Lenhart, A., Duggan, M., Cortesi, S., & Gasser, U. (2013). Teens and technology. Washington, DC: Pew Research Center. Retrieved from http://www.pewinternet.org/files/old-media/Files/Reports/2013/PIP_TeensandTechnology2013.pdf

Magee, J. C., Bigelow, L., DeHann, S., & Mustanski, B. S. (2012). Sexual health information seeking online: A mixed-method study among lesbian, gay, bisexual, and transgender young people. *Health Education & Behavior*, *39*(3), 276–289. doi:10.1177/1090198111401384 PMID:21490310

Meyer, I. H. (2003). Prejudice, social stress, and mental health in lesbian, gay, and bisexual populations: Conceptual issues and research evidence. *Psychological Bulletin*, *129*(5), 674–697. doi:10.1037/0033-2909.129.5.674 PMID:12956539

Mustanski, B., Birkett, M., Greene, G. J., Hatzenbuehler, M. L., & Newcomb, M. E. (2014). Envisioning an American without sexual orientation inequities in adolescent health. *American Journal of Public Health*, *104*(2), 218–225. doi:10.2105/AJPH.2013.301625 PMID:24328618

Mustanski, B., Garofalo, R., Herrick, A., & Donenberg, G. (2007). Psychosocial health problems increase risk for HIV among urban young men who have sex with men: Preliminary evidence of a syndemic in need of attention. *Annals of Behavioral Medicine*, *34*(1), 37–45. doi:10.1007/BF02879919 PMID:17688395

Mustanski, B., Greene, G. J., Ryan, D., & Whitton, S. W. (2015). Feasibility, acceptability, and initial efficacy of an online sexual health promotion program for LGBT youth: The Queer Sex Ed intervention. *Journal of Sex Research*, *52*(2), 220–230. doi:10.1080/00224499.2013.867924 PMID:24588408

Mustanski, B., Lyons, T., & Garcia, S. C. (2011a). Internet use and sexual health of young men who have sex with men: A mixed- methods study. *Archives of Sexual Behavior*, *40*(2), 289–300. doi:10.1007/s10508-009-9596-1 PMID:20182787

Mustanski, B., Newcomb, M., & Garofalo, R. (2011). Mental health of lesbian, gay, and bisexual youth: A developmental resiliency perspective. *Journal of Gay and Lesbian Social Services, 23*, 204– 225. doi: 10.1080=10538720.2011.561474

Padilla-Walker, L. M., Nelson, L. J., Carroll, J. S., & Jensen, A. C. (2010). More than a just a game: Video game and Internet use during emerging adulthood. *Journal of Youth and Adolescence*, *39*(2), 103–113. doi:10.1007/s10964-008-9390-8 PMID:20084557

Rice, E., Rhoades, H., Winetrobe, H., Sanchez, M., Montoya, J., Plant, A., & Kordic, T. (2012). Sexually explicit cell phone messaging associated with sexual risk among adolescents. *Pediatrics*, *130*(4), 667–673. doi:10.1542/peds.2012-0021 PMID:22987882

Roberts, D., Foehr, U., & Rideout, V. (2005). *Generation M: Media in the lives of 8-18 year olds*. Menlo Park, CA: Kaiser Family Foundation. Retrieved from http://kff.org/other/event/generation-m-media-in-the-lives-of/

Savin-Williams, R. C. (1994). Verbal and physical abuse as stressors in the lives of lesbian, gay male, and bisexual youths: Associations with school problems, running away, substance abuse, prostitution, and suicide. *Journal of Consulting & Clinical Psychology, 62*, 261–269. doi: .26110.1037/0022-006X.62.2

Savin-Williams, R. C. (2005). *The new gay teenager*. Cambridge, MA: Harvard University Press. doi:10.4159/9780674043138

Šmahel, D. (2003). *Psychology and Internet: Children being adults, adults being children*. Prague: Triton.

Steinberg, L. (2008). *Adolescence*. New York, NY: McGraw-Hill.

Subrahmanyam, K., & Greenfield, P. M., & Tynes, B. M. (2004). Constructing sexuality and identity in an online teen chat room. *Journal of Applied Developmental Psychology, an International Lifespan Journal, 25*, 651-666. doi:10.1016/j.appdev.2004.09.007

Subrahmanyam, K., Šmahel, D., & Greenfield, P. M. (2006). Connecting developmental constructions to the internet: Identity presentation and sexual exploration in online teen chat rooms. *Developmental Psychology*, *42*(3), 395–406. doi:10.1037/0012-1649.42.3.395 PMID:16756432

Subrahmanyam, K. S., & Šmahel, D. (2012). *Digital youth: The role of media in development*. New York, NY: Springer.

Suler, J. (2004). The online disinhibition effect. *Cyberpsychology & Behavior*, *7*(3), 2004. doi:10.1089/1094931041291295 PMID:15257832

Williams, T., Connolly, J., Pepler, D., & Craig, W. (2005). Peer victimization, social support, and psychosocial adjustment of sexual minority adolescents. *Journal of Youth and Adolescence*, *34*(5), 471–482. doi:10.1007/s10964-005-7264-x

Ybarra, M. L., Mitchell, K. J., Kosciw, J. G., & Korchmaros, J. D. (2015). Understanding linkages between bullying and suicidal ideation in a national sample of LGB and heterosexual youth in the United States. *Prevention Science*, *16*(3), 451–462. doi:10.1007/s11121-014-0510-2 PMID:25322949

Ybarra, M. L., Mitchell, K. J., Palmer, N. A., & Reisner, S. L. (2015). Online social support as a buffer against online and offline peer and sexual victimization among US LGBT and non-LGBT youth. *Child Abuse & Neglect*, *39*, 123–136. doi:10.1016/j.chiabu.2014.08.006 PMID:25192961

Chapter 6
Alternative Sexualities and Virtual Communities:
Aspects of LGBT Participation on Social Networking Sites in Spain

Leonor Acosta
University of Cadiz, Spain

Esperanza Moreno
University of Cadiz, Spain

Sebastian Molinillo
University of Malaga, Spain

Beatriz Gomez-Ortiz
University of Malaga, Spain

ABSTRACT

The purpose of this chapter is to analyze online participation on LGBT websites in Spain in order to contribute to the field of social networking site usage and the users' mode of participation with the aim of identifying their expectations and reasons to do it. The main concern is to focus on specific social network sites which are meant to ideologically and politically construct alternative sexual identities, such as lesbians, gays, transsexuals and bisexuals, which could have a difficult access to social recognition and which could be silenced on some heteronormative social networks. Uses and Gratifications Theory has been used as the basic model for the display of constructs, variables and hypotheses, to confirm the identity politics inherent in these practices, which are rather connected with social recognition than with some other needs as companionship or finding sexual partners.

INTRODUCTION

The codification of identity is related to the categories of sex, gender, sexuality, sexual orientation, social class, nationality, race, and ethnic group. These topics have been the object of analysis for most theories about culture in contemporary times. From the deconstructive project, originating in the second half of the past century, this issue has provoked a huge amount of literature belonging to disciplines, such as philosophy, sociology, anthropology, and literary studies. In order to understand how this chapter approaches the concept of alternative sexualities, which are increasingly present in connection with social

DOI: 10.4018/978-1-5225-1856-3.ch006

activities, media productions, and legal documents, it is necessary to go back to the history of LGBT construction through a historic–cultural explanation. This academic approach highlights basic tenets, which acknowledges that identity categories are mostly constructed in the process of adapting oneself to the world.

The investigation of emerging adults' access to alternative sexualities needs to be addressed, within an explanatory frame of how LGBT identity was formed and developed over time. Two hypotheses are considered: a) that social activities of LGBT emerging adults can be safer in online communities than in offline life, and b) that LGBT virtual communities may be structuring experiences without age limits, establishing an online space for sharing, asking, consuming, dating, and constructing alternative sexuality. The analysis of online experience in this chapter makes the claim that virtual communities which gather LGBT people are a source of increasing debate concerning these people's needs and anxieties in the contemporary world. To approach this phenomenon properly, the concept of alternative sexualities in the last years of the past century and as developed within the academic framework provided by cultural studies is necessary to consider.

Once stated, the point of departure lies in situating the chapter in this precise manner of understanding LGBT as an alternative sexuality, constructed in a specific time of Western history. The chapter locates this specific identity in its connection with online activities and its use of virtual communities on the Internet with the idea of showing the benefits of social networking sites created with this sense of belonging. The Uses and Gratifications Theory is the analytical tool selected for the evaluation of an online questionnaire, distributed within some LGBT communities in Spain, with 75 respondents with a specific deadline and a focus on contemporaneity as regards the responses. This makes the study a cross-sectional analytical survey of what is happening in LGBT virtual communities in Spain just at the moment of the questionnaire distribution. The fact of limiting this distribution to a Spanish context is justified by the opportunity for appreciating the relevance of LGBT political claims and achievements in recent years, which have seen the approval of certain modifications of the Spanish Civil code which promulgated same-sex marriage as official and legal in 2005.

From the beginning of this century, but more specifically since 2005, Spanish networking sites have been taken over by groups of LGBT users, creating a voice and a political agenda for the development of this alternative identity. The social networks devoted to this agenda are, in a sense, creating a new idea about the particular characteristics and the specific problems LGBT people have in contemporary Spain. This is the reason for the selection of some of these groups for the questionnaire distribution, which was finally sent to the following websites of five well-known LGBT associations in Spain: a) An online magazine dealing with LGBT cultural production and social journalism, b) two feminist associations situated in the South of Spain, and c) two transgender activist groups, whose use of the virtual community is mostly focused on political action.

The application of the Use and Gratification Theory upon the questionnaire results provides the chapter with some important insights about why and how LGBT people in Spain are accessing the Internet for reasons of identity construction and development, and also proves that emergent adults participating in these virtual communities are benefiting from the particular achievements of this online experience when in virtual contact with elders. The Spanish scenario produces another critical point since, in this national context, the main areas of identity formation, focusing on relevant decisions in life (Arnett, 2000), are put at stake because of the particular circumstances conditioning emergent adults' life in Spain. With around a 40% unemployment rate amongst Spanish emerging adults, the main tenets of the concept of age distinction is questioned in a very powerful manner, provoking new ways of accessing adulthood which are far from the experience in other Western countries. The facts of being economically dependent and of having to live at home with their family produce a different perception of this transient age, which tends to be perceived as a prolonged adolescence or an unadjusted adulthood. A positive consequence of this situation is that a greater proportion of these emergent adults' engage in academic formation and intellectual preparation, which, in the case of LGBT people, covers relevant formation in feminist and transgender theories. The reason for this specific characteristic is that Gender Studies are implemented at different levels of the education system in Spain, covering from monitoring Primary and Secondary Education for a transversal inclusion of gender discussion in schools, to the overall implantation of Gender Studies at Spanish universities: nearly 50% of them currently offer Master's Degrees on Gender Studies, Feminist Criticism and Equality Policies, and there is an increasing number of PhD theses dealing with gender from different academic approaches.

HISTORICAL BACKGROUND: ELEMENTS ALLOWING ALTERNATIVE SEXUALITIES TO ENTER THE CULTURAL SCENARIO

Western societies have experienced a radicalized demand for social, cultural and political changes, and numerous social movements desired civil rights and for a voice in political discourse. The 1960s was a global period of revolutions—social, sexual, cultural and political. The following years saw a global radicalization of critical theory, coming from poststructuralism, which originated in France. The principle objective of the poststructuralist movement is the dismantling of all the conceptualizations taken for granted in the past. The deconstructionist method focused on exploring the multiplicity of contemporary social phenomena, by interrogating the workings of language, the codification of identity, the relativity of history, and the impossible impartiality of knowledge (Sarup, 1993).

Though this intellectual project embraced all areas of human knowledge and covered all issues around the movement called Postmodernism, the most important issue for this research is the questioning around human identity. The concept of identity is certainly the center of different academic disciplines, including philosophy, anthropology, sociology, and psychology. Nevertheless, out of the multiple approaches proposing new conceptualizations of identity, feminist theory was the one which proposed a global shift in the understanding of the individual, mainly in its focus on women's lives, women's conditions, and the conventional way of dealing with 'womanhood' (De Beauvoir, 1949).

The deconstruction of sexuality, nevertheless, was not only a feminist concern at the time. It was also highlighted from another philosophical perspective, covered by Michel Foucault, who paved the way for its development in the 1980s.[1] Explorations about sexuality and its practice turned to an analysis of how power relations govern social exchange. Since the moment in which Michel Foucault destabilized the conventional 'knowledge' about sexuality, detaching it from any essentialism, his ideas were constantly brought to the front by all scholars dealing with the overall interest in sexuality and the codification of gender.

Thus, while the first feminist theories attacked the biological identification between sex and gender, laying bare the 'conventionalities' organizing the idea of 'womanhood' in Western societies, Foucault's ideas acknowledged the fallacy of understanding human sexuality as something essential to the individual. Sexuality is anything but 'natural'. Rather, it is a pre-given script, more connected with social control over individuals than with an inherent personal tendency. Sexuality, considered from this perspective, is intimately linked to the materiality of the discourses which creates the idea of personality, subjectivity and individuality.

A significant step forward was taken by Judith Butler in the 1990s, by introducing the idea about gender as an accumulation of performative acts. In her seminal book, *Gender Trouble: Feminism and the Subversion of Identity* (1990), Butler argued that conventional feminist thought failed when inscribing sexuality within the binarism of 'female' and 'male' sex and the idea of patriarchy as dominating social relations. Her project reinforces the impossibility of separating biological sex from sexual identity. The application of the idea of performativity to the issue of gender brought to the forefront a deconstruction of this human category as a stable component of identity, since gender becomes a question of performing conventional acts modelled by culture and society. From this perspective, there is always the possibility of questioning heteronormativity by modifying the performances of gender. By interrogating the norm of masculine vs. feminine, Butler's proposal converged in a common line with Foucault's idea of resistance to the hegemonic thinking about sexuality and its connection with his assumption about the workings of power.[2] Resistance must be interpreted, under this line of thought, as the instrument for transformation and political change, and this change is, nowadays, the object of transgender people trying to construct their identity by means of technological devices, which place them within a cybernetic world full of possibilities.

The study presented in this chapter focuses on this cybernetic interaction among people who are resisting heteronormativity, from a specific nation (Spain) and at a specific time in history (nowadays), through the creation and participation in websites, social networking sites, and Internet online groups, with the objective of exploring their experiences as 'queer' identities. Following the thesis proposed by Judith Halberstam (2005), the chapter proposes an analytical approach to the way in which social networking sites are providing a new cybernetic space to develop a perspective (ideological, cultural, social and political) which transforms the idea of gender into the concept of transgender, a perspective which transcends the binary perception of experience by focusing on alternative options for understanding the individual as agent of alternative subcultural practices in our contemporary globalized world. With this argument in mind, the principle hypothesis, which this chapter explores and demonstrates, is that LGBT Spanish users of social networking sites enter the cybernetic realm in search of a safe place for the development of gender, identity, and sexuality.

The virtual community users' participation and presence in the online world have been approached by several theoretical frameworks, such as Social Identity Theory, Plan Behavior Theory, Sense of Virtual Community Theory, and Usage and Gratification Theory. To understand the motivations and influential aspects which guide the individuals to participate in social networking sites, the study uses different theories. Social Identity Theory (Tajfel & Turner, 1986; Kim, Zheng, & Gupta, 2011) states that people participate in virtual communities to create their own identity through their connection with other people. Dholakia, Bagozzi, and Pearo (2004) use the social psychological model of goal-directed behavior and social identity theory to explain the individual's participation in virtual communities from two types of key determinants (i.e. group norms and social identity), together with a series of motivating and mediating components. Moreover, Network Theory takes as a starting point the idea that established relations in social networks, such as virtual communities, create emotional links among members, as well as help the construction of a common identity (Lee, Lee, Taylor, & Lee, 2011). Sense of Community

Theory (McMillan, 1996; Blanchard, 2007) explains the way in which the communities' users construct a specific sense of community, which is key to understanding the influence on the users' behavior. Self-determination Theory (Deci & Ryan, 2002) introduces different ways of explaining participation in communities, from the perspective of the individuals' needs and motivation. The Theory of Planned Behavior (Ajzen, 1991) asserts that the individual's intentions and behaviors are the result of his or her attitude toward the manner in which he or she perceives behavior and subjective norms.

Though these theories contributed to the study in explaining the different aspects of people's participation in virtual communities, Uses and Gratifications Theory (Lasswell, 1948) seems to holistically explain many of the diverse reasons why individuals use social networking sites. The basic assumption is that people search for social media which may satisfy their needs and lead them to find gratification (Lariscy, Tinkham, & Sweetser, 2011). The theory intends to explain the social and psychological needs which make people participate in social networking websites and other social media (Katz, Blumber, & Gurevitch, 2003). Instead of questioning what media and social networking provoke in the individual, this theory asks 'What does an active audience do with social media? Why? With what effect?' (Lasswell, 1948). Uses and Gratification Theory has been studied and developed over 60 years. The recent rise of social networking sites produced a revival of the interest in uses and gratifications as relevant elements in the phenomenon; this theory provides a fresh theoretical approach for the preliminary phases of all mass media (Ruggiero, 2000).

The study described in this chapter begins with the assumption that Uses and Gratification Theory offers a theoretical framework to explain how people make use of media for social capital purposes. It is also a suitable theory to explain the users' gratification when participating in social media. In recent years, several authors have applied this theory to social media in connection with the users' participation (De Valck, Van Bruggen &Wierenga, 2009; Lariscy, Tinkham, & Sweetser, 2011; Lawlor & Rowley, 2010; Whiting & Williams, 2013). Nevertheless, this theory has not been applied to the study of online communities formed around LGBT identities. The great amount of interest in exploring this technological phenomenon has produced some hypotheses about how the virtual community might gain the users' attention and favors the users' engagement. To increase successful outcomes, any virtual community should promote its members' participation and presence, since these communities can provide the fulfillment of the users' expectations and widen its scope (Oestreicher-Singer & Zalmanson, 2013; Sung et al., 2010; Tickle, Adebanjo & Michaelides, 2011; Zhao et al., 2012).

The analysis begins with a description of the relationship among several variables, which might justify the great success of virtual communities connected with alternative sexualities. It continues with the creation of an integrating approach, since it is possible to assemble relevant concepts based on the level of identification with the community, the sense of belonging, and personal engagement. This made it necessary to design a list of hypotheses from which to build a theoretical model to explain the phenomenon of participation in online communities for the development of queer/transgender sexual identities.

This theoretical model was empirically examined using questionnaire-based data, structured by questions about the informers' demographics, their Internet usage, and other issues related to their motivation and participation and engagement in a particular virtual community. Though the questionnaire was, in its first step, tested on a small group of people, use of online questionnaires was the procedure selected because of the advantages they offer. Online questionnaires are more time-efficient, flexible, convenient, low cost, and geographically unrestricted, and data entry and analysis are easier.

QUEER THEORY AND ALTERNATIVE SEXUALITIES: THE POSSIBILITIES OFFERED BY VIRTUAL COMMUNITIES

The origin of queer associations began in New York in 1990, when activists founded the group Queer Nation, connected with the artistic environment of the city. This group carried out performances in public spaces, with the objective to make queer affective acts outside heteronormativity. These performances gave visibility to the alternative ways of understanding human relations, without the restrains of hegemonic discourses about how to represent sexuality and human relations in general. The relation of this activism with the so called 'Queer theory' was established by Teresa de Lauretis in the lecture given in 1990 entitled "Queer Theory: Gay and Lesbian Sexualities" (De Lauretis, 1991). Nevertheless, the term 'queer' went through some problematic phases in its appropriation by the academic world, just because of the connotation of the reality it wanted to refer to. At the very time in which Judith Butler was becoming a sort of 'mother-figure' for alternative comprehensions of gender, her intervention was fundamental for the future of 'queerness' and Queer Theory. In her book, *Body that Matters* (1993), Butlers proposes a flexible application of the term to avoid essentialism and other constraints, since the entrance of the term into the semiotics of academia could possibly shift its revolutionary project.

If the term 'queer' is to be a site of collective contestation, the point of departure for a set of historical reflections and future imaginings, it will have to remain that which is, in the present, never fully owned, but always and only redeployed, twisted, queered from a prior usage towards the direction of expanding political purposes (Butler, 1993). This has been the case in Queer Studies, queer practices, and queer activism around the turn of the 21st century, something that is explored by Judith Halberstam in her book, *In a queer time and place. Transgender bodies, subcultural lives* (2005).

Queer uses of time and space develop, at least in part, in opposition to the institutions of family, heterosexuality, and reproduction. They also develop according to other logics of location, movement, and identification. If we try to think about queerness as an outcome of strange temporalities, imaginative life schedules, and eccentric economic practices, we detach queerness from sexual identity. The queer 'way of life' will encompass subcultural practices, alternative methods of alliance, forms of transgender embodiment, and those forms of representation dedicated to capturing these willfully eccentric modes of being (Halberstam, 2005).

In her account on queer lives as lived practices, which breaks the normative logics of time and space, Halberstam (2005) allows the possibility of a new experience of social life, separate from the traditional temporality and spatiality as conditioning the heteronormative identity. In part due to globalization, which affects human life worldwide, and, fundamentally, due to the overall inclusion of technology and the Internet in social practices, the construction of subcultural identities has been transformed, modified, and shifted from a physical scenario to the out-of-the-limits online experience. With the systematic use of social networks, queer identities have found a rich virtual space in which to present and express themselves. In the 21st century, social networking has become a meaningful platform for empowering queer people and for the development of a whole discourse about subcultural lives, alternative sexualities, revisited theories, and personal archives about 'queerness'. Thus, from a passive status of being the 'Other' to heteronormativity, now queer people are able to build up an increasingly growing community, expanding their interests, their political movements, their artistic manifestations, and their anxieties in coping with society.

In 1997, Celia Romm, Nava Pliskin, and Rodney Clarke analyzed the workings of virtual communities in the article "Virtual Communities and Society: Toward an Integrative Three Phase Model". In a period in which virtual communities were capturing society's attention and congregating an increasingly large group of people, their objective was to create a model to investigate the connection between online practices and the social functions and experiences of the individual. Keeping in mind that online platforms had previously been used for shopping and business exchanges, the challenge, in the late 1990s, was to focus on other consequences which Internet networking was bringing to the forefront. In consonance with Barry Wellman and Milena Gulia (1997), Romm and her colleagues explained that this new mode of social interaction was changing the way in which people participated and felt a sense of belonging different from traditional face-to-face community relations.

Along the turn of the century, research on virtual communities was engaged in several thematic lines, such as the possible identification between virtual and face-to-face communities, the functions of virtual communities (informative, supportive, entrepreneurial), the dehumanizing effect of a virtual society, and the magnificent possibilities of this virtual exchange for the construction of groups with the same interests but with the particular circumstance of not meeting in 'real' time and space. A recollection of all the theoretical frameworks devoted to the analysis and study of the users' intervention in online communities was published in 2012, with the title "Virtual community participation and motivation: Cross-disciplinary theories" (Li, 2012), with the intention to present the topic under the light of different perspectives which highlight the great interest the topic has gained for a great number of scholars.

Topics on virtual communities include virtual community participation, virtual involvement, or virtual community behavior, describing members' various activities including posting messages, browsing messages, posting diaries, and blogging. Virtual community participation is also the prerequisite for knowledge accumulation. For this reason, virtual community participation has gained large attention from researchers from diversified disciplines, such as psychology, communication, sociology, education, information systems, business, marketing, and engineering (Li, 2012).

One of the fields, which can be of great relevance for virtual community studies, and which is not included in the previous compilation, is Gender Studies. One advance can be found in Modzelewski's "Virtual togetherness: Sense of identity and community in cyberspace" (2013), an article which takes Cultural Studies and its definition of identity as the theoretical basis for its approach.[3] The positive factor that gives online communities their particular relevance is the consideration of Internet networks as a non-aggressive environment, which is able to promote humanistic values for education, and keep associations of people informed throughout the world, regardless of race, gender, nationality, and other social and cultural categories. In this line of thought, virtual communities become a site for the intervention of identities in conflict with the standards of society, and, as such, they provide a site of struggle for the construction of debate and information about alternative positions in the individual's life.

When addressing lesbian, gay, bisexual, and transsexual (LGBT) identities, these Internet networks have formed a political arena for the visibility of the LGBT civil rights movement and the 'queer' embodiment of this social group. The alliance of these disaggregated people is made increasingly stronger and more affectionate than in real life, and might be producing a worldwide phenomenon which would perhaps not be possible within the strict limits of local associations. In the moment in which these queer virtual communities were more and more visible, they served diverse purposes in the creation of queer identity, forming an archive of personal experiences, of artistic manifestations, of meaningful documents, and of relevant news around the LGBT movement, as well as producing a certain feeling of being together. The mobilization of people living in faraway countries and within such different social and cultural environments is also made possible, and channels the diverse experience of allies throughout the activities and events organized by local groups. Moreover, social networking sites become more and more aware of the presence, participation, and sense of belonging of these LGBT communities, which might be producing a clear effect on future generations, thereby having some specific impact on the future.

USES AND GRATIFICATIONS OF LGBT SOCIAL NETWORKING SITES

Uses and gratifications theory assumes that individuals actively use media to fulfil their particular needs. This theory, which originated in the 1940s, has been applied to a lot of studies about expanding technologies, such as Internet and social networking websites, among others. Park, Kee, and Valenzuela (2009) reveal four primary needs for participating in groups within Facebook: socializing, entertainment, self-status seeking, and information seeking. Pai and Arnott (2013) identify four main values derived from social networking site use: belonging, hedonism, self-esteem, and reciprocity. Dholakia and colleagues (2004) categorize the fulfilment of different needs into five values: purposive value, self-discovery, social enhancement value, maintaining interpersonal connectivity, and entertainment value. Couch and Liamputtong (2008), Lawson and Leck (2006), and Wang and Chang (2010) developed qualitative studies in various cultural contexts, and revealed that online dating site use is driven by such motives as companionship, seeking sexual partners, romance, freedom from commitment, and ease meeting new people.

According to Meyrowitz (1985), members of the active audience are not passive recipients of social media stimuli; rather, they are purposive and conscious about selecting messages that fulfil personal needs (such as 'keeping in touch with important events' or 'escape from boredom'). Uses and gratification theory has been widely employed in investigating a wide range of traditional media, such as newspapers, radios, and telephones. The Internet and other web based applications enhanced uses and gratification theory's predictive power because, in computer-mediated communication (CMC) settings, users become empowered, as it is relatively easy for them to switch from one medium to another providing similar services or content. Xu and colleagues (2012) affirm that these studies identified a list of gratifications, such as affection, convenience, coordination, entertainment, relaxation, escape, fashion, interpersonal utility, information seeking, sociability, and self-expression, that influence different media use.

Specially regarding the application of uses and gratification theory to LGBT studies, Clemens and colleagues (2015) explained that "historically, those who are attracted to the same sex have been isolated from peer contact and support;" and that, "however, the Internet has proved to be a safe haven, offering anonymity, an unparalleled sense of security, and a breadth of choices across geographical boundaries; this make it possible for users to find others with sexual and relational interests similar to their own." LGBT people, who can be considered marginalized individuals in society, could capitalize on the Internet's ability to transcend geographical boundaries and provide pseudonymous or anonymous communication (McKenna & Bargh, 1998). Fox and Warber (2015) consider that these affordances give LGBT individuals new opportunities to develop relationships by identifying similar others and self-disclosing in ways they may not have been able to accomplish offline. Other online affordances, such as asynchronicity and the ability to selectively edit one's self-presentation, also promote relationship development, as users feel more secure and self-disclosure is less inhibited (Fox, Warber, & Makstaller, 2013; Walther, 1996).

Among LGBT users, Erosheva et al. (2016) affirms that women have larger social networks than men, that older adults with higher levels of education tend to have larger social networks (Ajrouch, Blandon, & Antonucci, 2005), and those with higher incomes have larger and more diverse networks. Gudelunas

(2012) examined the uses and gratifications of online social networks for gay men and found that they often juggled multiple identities across platforms. For example, they may be completely out and visible on a dating site, but choose to keep their sexual identity off of Facebook. In a content analysis of Facebook pages, Drushel (2010) found that gay users had fewer total friends than heterosexual or bisexual users, but posts indicated their friends interacted frequently and, thus, gay users were maintaining social capital on the site. Fox and Warber (2015) affirm that little is known about how queer individuals experience social networking sites, particularly as co-cultural group members.

It seems that those who identify themselves as gay or lesbian spend more time on the Internet and on social networking websites than heterosexual individuals. Social networks, in a broad sense, are relationships with family, friends, coworkers, neighbors, members of a community, acquaintances, and even members in online networking sites (Erosheva et al., 2016). In a study on the role of affective identity, Dholokia and colleagues (2004) maintained that being affiliated with a virtual community has emotional and evaluative meaning. According to this study, affective identification with one's community membership creates emotional commitment to a community. Some of the affective manifestations may include, among others, affective identification with community, commitment, and emotional attachment. Thus, it is plausible that emotional identity provides members of a community with emotional exchange, empathy, and collective intelligence, which serve as motives for social networking site use (Yoon, 2014).

In making use of all these theoretical approaches for the purpose of this chapter, the conceptual framework that guides this research was taken from them the most relevant constructs to build a theoretical model to test the effect of gratification on LGTB community usage (See Figure 1).

Figure 1. Research model: testing gratification on LGBT

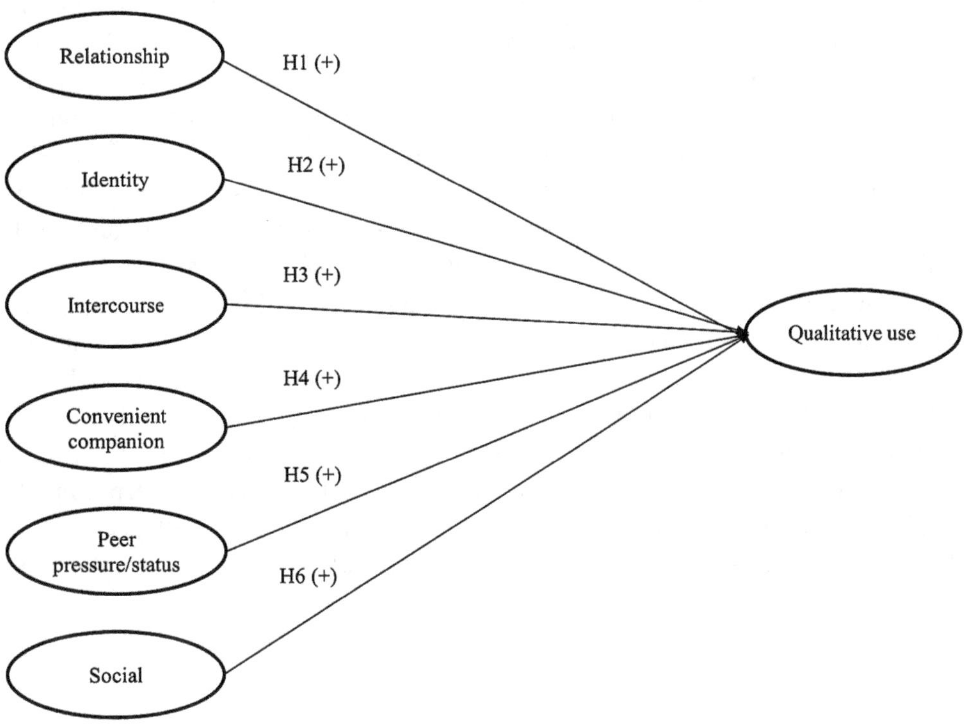

The Study: Methodology

All the ideas developed above form the basic context for understanding the main objective of the present study. By using an empirical approach, the intention is to describe the way in which social networking sites are providing a new cybernetic space to construct transgender identity for reasons of personal self-assertion, social cohesion, and political activism. The empirical data are recollected through the analysis of an online questionnaire, designed with some basic parameters such as:

1. A previous selection of websites for the questionnaire distribution,
2. A planning of questions to address the specific phenomenon of LGBT movement in Spain and
3. A cross-sectional perspective in the design of the study.

These basic parameters are justified by the preliminary idea about the LGBT movement in Spain as something growing in visibility and embracing all issues about the alternative positions in social, cultural, and political life in contemporary Spain.

Research Design and Sample

The empirical data for this project were collected through an online survey from January to February 2016. The target for this research was Spanish-speaking users. The questionnaire was embedded into transgender virtual communities on Spanish websites. The preliminary process for selection of these websites followed one basic criterion, that of being committed to transgender exploration and queer association. With this criterion in mind, apart from some personal blogs, the questionnaire was sent to the following websites: *Revista Pikara Magazine*, the activist group *Ideadestroyingmuros*, the transgender group *Colectivo Lambda,* and the feminist associations *Equiláteras* and *Arcoiris Cádiz*. The questionnaire was also posted in some widespread social networking websites, such as Facebook, Twitter, and Tumblr, to consider an ample range of responses which might depend on the particular website characteristics. In addition to this, snowball sampling was used in this study because it gives access to populations, people are less reluctant to take part in the research, and results can be produced quickly (Atkinson & Flint, 2001).

A total of 50 answered questionnaires were retained for study after questionnaires with incomplete data or invalid responses were removed. As an interpretative context for understanding the variables contained in the questionnaire regarding personal profiles (see Table 1), it seems that it does not only take into consideration people with a conscious sexual orientation within the limits of LGBT identities but also heterosexual informers with a certain level of participation in these gendered-aimed communities. It is also necessary to indicate that the categories related to family situation include marriage as a relevant item, since homosexual couples have legal access to this social institution in Spain. Table 1 shows the range of categories displayed in the questionnaire in regards to the specific social and demographic profiles of the participants. Remarkable conclusions can be drawn by interpreting this data, in a broader sense, in relation to the great number of women's participation, as well as regarding the family situation selected in this part of the questionnaire, which is clearly supported by single women and men with a high level of education.

Table 1. Characteristics of the respondents

Demography	Category	Percentage (%)
Biological Sex	Male	29.4
	Female	66.7
	Transsexual	3.9
Transgender	Yes	27.4
	No	72.6
Sexual Orientation	Gay	9.8
	Lesbian	23.5
	Bisexual	15.7
	Heterosexual	13.7
	Other	37.3
Age	18-24	19.6
	25-34	41.2
	35-44	25.5
	45-54	9.8
	55-64	3.9
	65 or more	0
Family Situation	Single	43.1
	Divorced	7.8
	Widow(er)	0
	Married/with partner without children	31.4
	Married/with partner with children	5.9
	Other	11.8
Educational Level	Uneducated	0
	Primary Education	0
	Secondary Education	2.0
	High School	3.9
	Job Training	5.9
	Undergraduate	43.1
	Postgraduate	45.1
	Other	0
Employment Status	Part-time employment	7.8
	Full time employment	25.5
	Self-employed	29.4
	Unemployed	21.6
	Student	15.7
	Housework	0
	Retired	0
Family Income	No Income	19.6
	Less than 650 €	11.8
	651 €-900 €	27.4
	901 €-1200 €	2.0
	1201 € -1500 €	19.6
	1501 €- 1800 €	7.8
	1801 €- 2400 €	5.9
	2401 € - 3000 €	2.0
	More than 3000 €	3.9

Instrument Development

The questionnaire used in this research consists of 41 items, divided into three sections:

1. Items concerned with the qualitative use of the social networking site,
2. Items related to the usage and gratifications of social networking sites, and
3. Questions about social and demographic factors.

The measurement items were developed on the basis of previous studies and checked for reliability and validity. Likert-type scale questions, ranging from one (*strongly disagree*) to five (*strongly agree*) were used; for instance, rate your level of agreement with the following statement, "The community is part of everyday life", on a scale of 1 (*disagree strongly*) to 5 (*agree strongly*). In particular, the measurement scale for gratifications and motivations in the use of LGBT virtual communities was adapted from Clemens et al. (2015) by differentiating six constructs: relationship, identity, intercourse, convenient companion, peer pressure/status, and social. Networking use was measured by means of a qualitative approach, as developed by Yoon (2014).

Data Analysis

The theoretical model was contrasted by means of a specific variant of Structural Equation Modelling (SEM) analysis called Partial Least Squares (PLS). As stated by Wold, who is considered the father of PLS: "this technique enables the researcher to specify the relation between the conceptual factors of interest and the measures for each construct" (1985, p.234). Traditionally SEM analysis is based on co-variances (CB-SEM), while PLS-SEM is based on variances. Unlike CB-SEM, PLS-SEM analysis does not require the application of confirmatory factor analysis, and is suitable when there is no guarantee about data normality, allowing the study of small samples (Hair, Hult, Ringle, & Sarstedt, 2014). PLS is considered instead of CBS because, according to Kolmogorov-Smirnov test results, data are distributed in a non-normalized way (asymmetrical), and because the analysis was conducted with a smaller sample, which is very near to the minimum of ten times the largest number of inner model paths directed at a particular construct in the inner model (Barclay, Higgins, & Thompson, 1995).

The first evaluation consists of implementing the content validity test (Pavlou & El Sawy, 2006), the Cronbach alpha test of reliability and convergent validity, the composite reliability test, the loadings of the indicators and AVE (Chin, 1998) and a test for discriminant validity (Fornell & Larcker, 1981), all of which are conducted on the reflective items. As for the formative items, the tests chosen were the following: content validity (Pavlou & El Sawy, 2006), multicollinearity level (Petter, Straub, & Rai, 2007), and evaluation of the weights and evaluation of the factorial loadings (Chin, 1998). Lastly, regarding the evaluation of the structural model, the measurement analysis focused on the magnitude, the level of significance of the coefficients and the predictive quality (Chin, 1998), as well as the percentage of the variance explained for each of the latent variables (Falk & Miller, 1992).

In regards to a cultural approach for data analysis in light of emerging adults' participation in the study, it seems remarkable that the scope of categories related to the respondents shows some of the previously mentioned characteristics of Spanish society in the contemporary globalized world, which differentiate it from some other Western countries. It is quite significant to cross lines of argumentation for the categories of employment status, educational level, and family income. When observing the results of this demographic schema, the questionnaire gives a particular panorama about current Spanish social circumstances, proving that the unemployment rate is high among emerging adults, which could explain the possible inconsistency of this concept for Spanish people. It also shows that in spite of their low income, the respondents possess a high degree of academic formation, due perhaps to the failure in finding a job, and also due to the specific situation of public universities in Spain (low cost fees, number of universities per province).

MAIN RESULTS OF THE STUDY

Measure Assessment

The data analysis is distributed into two models committed with measurement and structure. Along the first evaluation, it was convenient to determine which of the items were formative or reflective, by using the most complete reference framework which has been proved up to this date. This reference framework is explored and planned in the works by Jarvis, MacKenzie and Podsakoff (2003) and MacKenzie, Podsakoff and Jarvis (2005). In both articles, the authors propose four criteria to be taken into account as an essential part of the quantitative analysis.

The first criterion is connected with the causality implication between the construct and its indicators. For the models with formative indicators, the construct is determined by its measures, for the matter of which changes in the indicators should cause changes in the aggregated construct. In this case, the measurements represent defining features which collectively convey the construct meaning. However, in the models with reflective indicators, such as the one used, the casualty implication goes between the construct and the items. This entails that changes in the construct produce changes in the indicators. As a result, the indicators become manifestations in the latent variable.

The second criterion questions whether measurements can be exchanged in terms of conceptualization. In this case, they are regarding the formative indicators, they are exogenous determinants of the construct, and they do not need to share a common concept, and this makes them able to capture unique aspects from the conceptual domain which belong to the latent variable. There is no expectation about the possible interchangeability of such measures, since the deletion of any indicator could vary the conceptual domain of the construct. However, the reflective indicators share a common topic, since they became equivalent manifestations of the same construct, and, as such, they might be interchangeable.

The third criterion is intimately related to the covariance shown by the measurements. The features presented in the aggregated latent models make it is possible to state that their formative indicators do not demand covariance among each other. Nevertheless, a high degree of covariance might be required in the indicators working within models of reflective constructs, since they share a common topic. In the model presented here, all correlations between the different reflective items in each of the seven constructs are meaningful and positive, according to Pearson's correlation coefficient.

Finally, the fourth criterion addresses the similarity within the indicators' nomological networks. In this sense, it is convenient to consider the issue of measurements having the same antecedents and consequences. The reflective indicators, being projections or manifestations of the same underlying construct, should show the same antecedents and consequences, as occurs in the model here, because they are meant to be interchangeable. In contrast, the formative averages do not need to present the same antecedents and consequences.

Within the analysis of the measurement model, having verified that the items are reflective, the model has been examined by applying the following tests to its components: the content validity test (Pavlou & El Sawy, 2006), Cronbach's reliability and convergent validity-alpha test, indicator loading and AVE (Barclay, Higgins, & Thompson, 1995; Chin, 1998), and the discriminant validity test (Fornell & Larcker, 1981).

Finally, in regards to the structural model evaluation, the magnitude, the significance levels of coefficients, and predictive quality (Chin, 1998), as well as the variance percentage as explained by each latent variable (Falk & Miller, 1992) were calculated.

The reflective measurement model is evaluated by its reliability and validity. Cronbach's alpha offers an assessment of reliability (Chin, 1998; Henseler, Ringle & Sinkovics, 2009), and it can be observed that punctuation is greater than the recommended 0.50 (Barclay et al., 1995; Chin, 1998) for all reflective constructs. The same thing happens with composite reliability, which surpasses 0.50 (Chin, 1998) in all cases. Concerning indicator loadings, used also to evaluate reliability, they are high and significant (higher than 0.50). The study of validity was made through the analysis of convergent and discriminant validity, which is confirmed for all the latent constructs, given that, in the first case, AVE>0.50 for all constructs, and, in the second, the square root of AVE is greater than the bivariate correlation among all the constructs in the model (Chin 1998) (see Tables 2 and 3).

Hypothesis Testing Results

The structural model evaluates the weight and the magnitude of the relations between the different variables. To carry out an appropriate interpretation of the internal or structural model in PLS modeling, the following questions—amongst others—had to be answered (Falk & Miller, 1992): What quantity of variance of the endogenous variables is explained by the constructs which predict them, and to what extent do the predictive variables contribute to the variance explained by the endogenous variables. To answer both questions, we used two indexes: R2 and the standardized ß paths.

As shown in Figure 2, statistical results indicate that not all relationships have the appropriate sign, contributing just some of the "partial empirical validation of the theoretical relationships between the latent variables assumed" (Henseler et al., 2009, p. 304). First, the magnitude and level of significance of the coefficients were measured. These have to be over 0.20 to be considered significant (Chin, 1998). It should be noted that not all the coefficients of the relations between the different variables of the structural model meet this requirement. The effects of some of the estimated weights are not, therefore, according to their importance. This leads to the conclusion that not all the proposed hypotheses are confirmed:

1. Relationships do not influence qualitative use, and this produces the rejection of H1;
2. Identity influences qualitative use, which leads to the confirmation of H2;
3. Intercourse does not influence social networking site qualitative use, which rejects H3;
4. Convenient companion does not influence qualitative use, and this rejects H4;
5. Peer pressure/status does not influence qualitative use of the networking sites, which rejects H5;
6. Finally, social issues influence networking site qualitative use, and this confirms H6.

In summary, it is possible to say that the study confirms that only identity and social issues influence and affect the qualitative usage of the networking sites, and social aspects stand out as having the most significant influence.

Table 2. The measurement model loadings

Measurements	Loadings
Relationship. a: .9141 rc: .9177	
Find someone for a serious relationship	0.834
Fall in love	0.847
Establish an intimate connection with someone	0.882
Build an emotional connection with someone	0.847
Seek out someone to date	0.649
Meet a future husband or wife	0.595
Find companionship	0.780
Find people like me	0.621
Meet new people	0.585
Identity. a: .8672 rc: .8965	
Live out a fantasy	0.783
Escape who I am	0.689
Experience things I cannot in the real world	0.828
Try out new identities	0.705
Be accepted for my ideas	0.791
Feel important	0.809
Intercourse. a: .8857 rc: .9099	
Find a friend to have sex with	0.814
Live out a sexual fantasy	0.876
Find a one-night stand	0.766
Increase my sexual experience	0.910
Seek out someone with similar sexual interests	0.715
Convenient Companion. a: .7908 rc: .8593	
When there is no one else to talk to or be with	0.847
When I'm feeling lonely	0.827
Because it makes me feel less alone	0.781
Peer Pressure/Status. a: .7851 rc: .8959	
Because everyone else does	0.844
Gain status	0.954
Social. a: .7731 rc: .8692	
Stay in touch with people I don't see very often	0.860
Get advice and support	0.759
Get information to pass on to other people.	0.869
Qualitative Use. a: .8281 rc: .8815	
The community is part of everyday life	0.760
I take pride in using this community	0.768
I feel the lack of realism when I don't use this community	0.591
I feel this community is part of my community	0.931
I would feel sorry when this community is not around me.	0.794

Table 3. Convergent and discriminant validity

Construct	AVE	Relationship	Identity	Intercourse	Convenient Companion	Peer Pressure / Status	Social	Qualitative Use
Relationship	0.5594	**0.7479**						
Identity	0.5919	0.6377	**0.7694**					
Intercourse	0.6708	0.5202	0.4686	**0.819**				
Convenient Companion	0.6708	0.5672	0.4378	0.1359	**0.819**			
Peer Pressure / Status	0.8121	0.1633	0.2923	0.319	0.0084	**0.9011**		
Social	0.6898	0.4703	0.4689	0.2924	0.5466	0.2704	**0.8306**	
Qualitative Use	0.6027	0.3722	0.5378	0.2659	0.3678	0.2944	0.7149	**0.7763**

Figure 2. Results of LGBT social networking sites use model

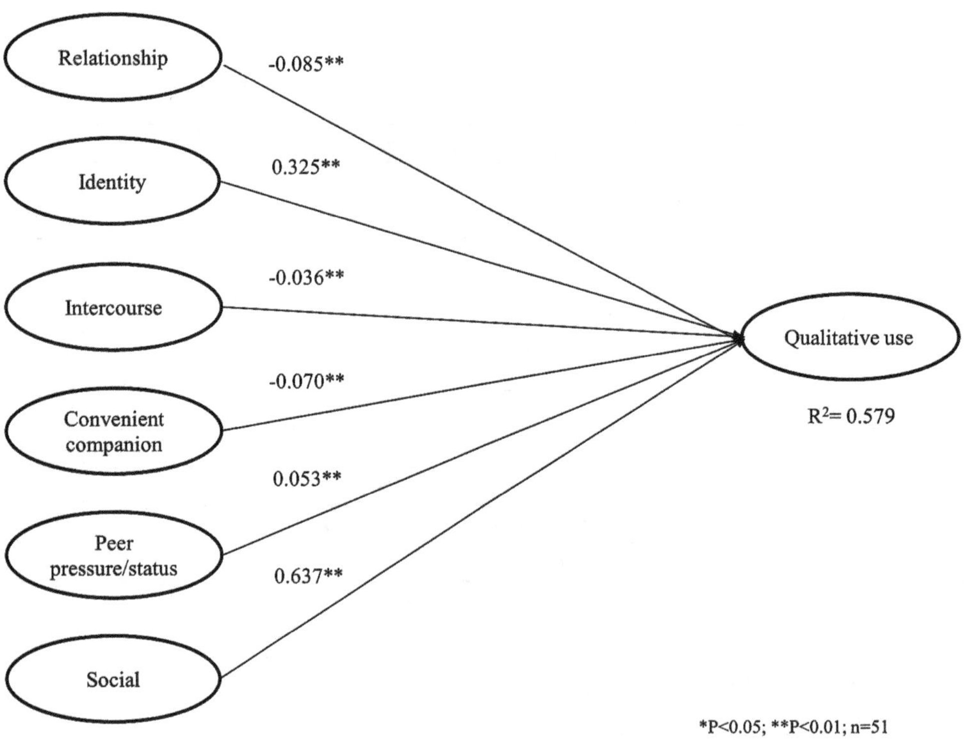

On the other hand, the explanatory power (R2) of the predictive constructs is 57.9%. This measure indicates the quantity of the construct's variance which is explained by the model and whose values, around 0.19, 0.33 and 0.67, are considered weak, moderate and substantial, respectively (Chin, 1998). Specifically, for qualitative use R2= 0.579, as a result of which its predictive quality would be between moderate and substantial. Therefore, it fulfils the criterion of Falk and Miller (1992), who state that values over 0.10 are always considered to have a good predictive quality.

Next, to know the extent to which the predictive variables contribute to the variance explained of the endogenous variables, we turn to Falk and Miller (1992). These authors point out that a reasonable index of variance explained in an endogenous construct by another latent variable is given by the absolute value of the result of multiplying the coefficient path (ß) by the corresponding coefficient correlation between both variables. From this we obtain that 17.478% of the qualitative use variance is explained by the value of the latent variable of identity and that 1.560% of the qualitative use variance is explained by peer pressure/status and that 45.539% of the qualitative use variance is explained by Social. All the cases fulfill the rule of Falk and Miller (1992), according to which a predictive variable should explain at least 1.5% of a predicted variable's variance.

Therefore, the conclusions indicate that the model proposed, along with its measurement structure, does not support all the preliminary hypotheses.

CONCLUSION

The investigation of technology as a source of new online experiences of life and the possibilities it provides for the construction and exploration of alternative sexualities is the principal objective accomplished throughout this study. The multiple expressions of cultural and social resistance found on Internet networks leads to the understanding that this cybernetic space has now become a site of struggle for people positioning outside the standards of mainstream society. The study presented here takes this phenomenon as the corpus for analysis and produces a systematic methodology for empirical examination. With the aid of structural equation modeling it is possible to find adequate procedures for the better understanding how people participate, create and feel safe in the use of these online spaces. The implementation of this methodology provides the study with a specific ability to impute relationships between unobserved constructs (latent variables) from observable variables. In the study which has been carried out here, the model works as a relevant tool to understand these relations, which seem, at first sight, to be unattainable. The feelings and emotional responses of people navigating the Internet and participating in virtual communities would be difficult to assess without the use of this methodological approach, and, when applied, it helps in drawing conclusions about levels of participation and the motivation individuals have for accessing the networking sites and intervening in them. The basic assumptions given by Uses and Gratifications Theory are of great value for attaining some relevant outcomes in this research, because they established a background for the comprehension of the degree of satisfaction in using and participating in the specific websites that are included as the corpus of the study.

The constructs used within the research model, however, are strongly attached to LGBT activism, which is clearly centered on the political movement of a minority of people feeling themselves to be outsiders of the heteronormative social system. The basic parameters used in designing the online questionnaire and in pre-selecting the specific websites for reasons of LGBT identification and social participation in Spanish society organize the results within the particular framework of a national differentiation. Choosing a cross-sectional study serves to survey Spanish LGBT associations in a panoramic fixed situation, given that the popular feeling is that LGBT identity is covering a great part of media production, and a huge amount of social participation in offline life and online activities. These actions result in a search for self-assertion and community reinforcement, apart from being inherently connected with sentimental or sexual quest for partners in the same terms as the already studied online dating sites (ODS). The main purpose of the research model was to analyse the qualitative use of the websites for the needs of relationships, identity confirmation, intercourse, companionship, status and social recognition, and, in the development of the study, it was possible to confirm that participation and usage of these websites pointed more to issues connected with recognition of LGTB identity and its social integration than to the other constructs used within the model. This outcome produces another relevant conclusion, which links this online activity with the concept of a specific 'queer space' for the construction of alternative sexualities out of the norm of standardized society, and with the consequence of providing LGBT people and communities with a sense of safety and inspiration for their individual development.

This is part of the study's originality, since there is an insistence on the existence of LGBT practices taking place on the web for political and social interests, in the same sense that there are, for instance, brand communities which are establishing an online phenomenon in commercial contexts. However, it is convenient to highlight some other relevant outcomes in this research, which point to the great opportunity of approaching the functioning of virtual communities from a multidisciplinary perspective, by using the large amount of literature derived from the study of identity and sexuality done by Gender Studies and Cultural Studies together with an implementation of structural equation modeling to make theoretical frameworks merge with empirical analysis. By implementing the cultural conceptualization of the model, the questionnaire is organized with a strong theoretical bias regarding different academic approaches to the issue of gender and sexuality in LGBT identities. This original point of departure has provided the questions with an intimate connection with these identities and their social construction in contemporary Spain. An important part of the results analyzed in the chapter shows that LGBT communities in Spain are possibly inconsistent with the idea of emergent adulthood as limited by age in a society with few people having a job, with a very low level of mobility in the Spanish geography due to the effects of unemployment. It is also remarkable that the results point to the idea that these communities in Spain are largely prepared, academically speaking, for their understanding as alternative transgender people, and this produces a relevant conclusion about the role of social networking activities in terms of sexual politics and in terms of affective online relations within the virtual community.

The questionnaire design, and the theoretical model presented are, in this sense, enriched by specific theories about LGTB communities, queer theory, and concepts about transgender identities and expressions, requiring the intervention of a critical background, which, in a sense, becomes a refreshing method for scholars doing Cultural Theory and Research.

For further investigation on the topic, it is possible to think about ameliorating the questionnaire scope in terms of geographical target and size. Keeping Spanish as the vehicle for the questionnaire would be useful for a cross-survey with South American countries which seem to be actively concerned with LGBT experience and social visibility. Colombia, Mexico, Chile and Argentina are countries with LGBT political movements that are fighting for civil rights, and they could become a target for spreading the study.

REFERENCES

Ajrou, K. J., Blandon, A. Y., & Antonucci, T. C. (2005). Social networks among men and women: The effects of age and socioeconomic status. *The Journals of Gerontology. Series B, Psychological Sciences and Social Sciences*, *60*(6), S311–S317. doi:10.1093/geronb/60.6.S311 PMID:16260713

Ajzen, I. (1991). The theory of planned behavior. *Organizational Behavior and Human Decision Processes*, *50*(2), 179–211. doi:10.1016/0749-5978(91)90020-T

Arnett, J. J. (2000). Emerging adulthood. A theory of development from the late teens through the twenties. *The American Psychologist*, *55*(5), 469–480. doi:10.1037/0003-066X.55.5.469 PMID:10842426

Atkinson, R., & Flint, J. (2001). Accessing hidden and hard-to-reach populations: Snowball research strategies. *Social Research Update*, *33*(1), 1–4.

Barclay, D. C., Higgins, C., & Thompson, R. (1995). The partial least squares approach to causal modelling: Personal computer adoption and use as an illustration. *Technology Studies*, *2*, 285–308.

Blanchard, A. L. (2007). Developing a sense of virtual community measure. *CyberPsychology & Behaviour*, *10*(6), 827–830. doi:10.1089/cpb.2007.9946 PMID:18085972

Blumler, J. G., & Katz, E. (Eds.). (1974). *The Uses of Mass Communications: Current Perspectives on Gratifications Research* (Vol. 3). Beverly Hills, CA: Sage Annual Reviews of Communication Research.

Butler, J. (1993). *Bodies that matter: On the discursive limits of sex*. London: Routledge.

Butler, J. (1999). *Gender trouble. Feminism and the subversion of identity*. New York: Routledge.

Chin, W. W. (1998). The partial least squares approach for structural equation modelling. In G. A. Marcoulides (Ed.), Modern Methods for Business Research (pp. 295-336). London: Lawrence Erlbaum Associates.

Clemens, C., Atkin, D., & Krishnan, A. (2015). The influence of biological and personality traits on gratification obtained through online dating websites. *Computers in Human Behavior*, *49*, 120–129. doi:10.1016/j.chb.2014.12.058

Couch, D., & Liamputtong, P. (2008). Online dating and mating: The use of the Internet to meet sexual partners. *Qualitative Health Research*, *18*(2), 268–279. doi:10.1177/1049732307312832 PMID:18216345

De Beauvoir, S. (1989). *The second sex*. New York: Vintage Books.

De Lauretis, T. (1991). Queer theory. Lesbian and gay sexualities. *Differences: A Journal of Feminist Cultural Studies*, *3*(2), 3–18.

De Valck, K., Van Bruggen, G. H., & Wierenga, B. (2009). Virtual communities: A marketing perspective. *Decision Support Systems*, *47*(3), 185–203. doi:10.1016/j.dss.2009.02.008

Deci, E. L., & Ryan, R. M. (2002). *Handbook of self-determination research*. Rochester, NY: University of Rochester Press.

Dholakia, U. M., Bagozzi, R., & Pearo, L. (2004). A social influence model of consumer participation in network and small group based virtual communities. *International Journal of Research in Marketing*, *21*(3), 241–263. doi:10.1016/j.ijresmar.2003.12.004

Drushel, B. E. (2010). Virtually supportive: Self-disclosure of minority sexualities through online social networking sites. In C. Pullen & M. Cooper (Eds.), *LGBT Identity and Online New Media* (pp. 62–72). New York: Routledge.

Erosheva, E. A., Kim, H.-J., Emlet, C., & Fredriksen-Goldsen, K. I. (2016). Social networks of lesbian, gay, bisexual, and transgender older adults. *Research on Aging*, *38*(1), 98–123. doi:10.1177/0164027515581859 PMID:25882129

Falk, R. F., & Miller, N. B. (1992). *A primer for soft modeling*. Akron, OH: University of Akron Press.

Fornell, C., & Larcker, D. F. (1981). Evaluating structural equation models with unobservable variables and measurement error. *JMR, Journal of Marketing Research*, *18*(1), 39–50. doi:10.2307/3151312

Foucault, M. (1978). The history of sexuality:Vol. 1. *An introduction*. New York: Pantheon Books.

Fox, J., & Warber, K. M. (2015). Queer identity management and political self-expression on social networking sites: A co-cultural approach to the spiral of silence. *Journal of Communication*, *65*(1), 79–100. doi:10.1111/jcom.12137

Fox, J., Warber, K. M., & Makstaller, D. (2013). The role of Facebook in romantic relationship development: An exploration of Knapps relational stage model. *Journal of Social and Personal Relationships*, *30*(6), 771–794. doi:10.1177/0265407512468370

Gudelunas, D. (2012). Theres an app for that: The uses and gratifications of online social networks for gay men. *Sexuality & Culture*, *16*(4), 347–365. doi:10.1007/s12119-012-9127-4

Hair, J. F., Hult, G. T. M., Ringle, C. M., & Sarstedt, M. (2014). *A primer on partial least squares structural equation modeling (PLS-SEM)*. Thousand Oaks, CA: Sage.

Halberstam, J. (2005). *In a queer time and place. Transgender bodies, subcultural lives*. New York: New York University Press.

Henseler, J., Ringle, C. M., & Sinkovics, R. R. (2009). The use of partial least squares modeling in international marketing. *Advances in International Marketing*, *20*, 277–319.

Jarvis, C. B., MacKenzie, S. B., & Podsakoff, P. M. (2003). A critical review of construct indicators and measurement model misspecification in marketing and consumer research. *The Journal of Consumer Research*, *30*(2), 199–218. doi:10.1086/376806

Katz, E., Blumler, J. G., & Gurevitch, M. (2003). Utilization of mass communication by the individual. In V. Nigthingale & K. Ross (Eds.), *Critical Readings: Media and Audiences* (pp. 35–51). Maidenhead, UK: Open University Press.

Kim, H. W., Zheng, J. R., & Gupta, S. (2011). Examining knowledge contribution from the perspective of an online identity in blogging communities. *Computers in Human Behavior*, *27*(5), 1760–1770. doi:10.1016/j.chb.2011.03.003

Lariscy, R. W., Tinkham, S. F., & Sweetser, K. D. (2011). Kids these days: Examining differences in political uses and gratifications, internet political participation, political information efficacy, and cynicism on the basis of age. *The American Behavioral Scientist*, *55*(6), 749–764. doi:10.1177/0002764211398091

Lasswell, H. D. (1948). The structure and function of communication in society. *The Communication of Ideas*, *37*, 215–228.

Lawlor, D. A., & Rowley, M. (2010). Young Peoples Use of Online Social Networking Sites - a Uses and Gratifications Perspective. *Journal of Research in Interactive Marketing*, *4*(1), 46–58. doi:10.1108/17505931011033551

Lawson, H., & Leck, K. (2006). Dynamics of internet dating. *Social Science Computer Review*, *24*(2), 189–208. doi:10.1177/0894439305283402

Lee, H. J., Lee, D. H., Taylor, C. R., & Lee, J. H. (2011). Do online brand communities help build and maintain relationships with consumers? A network theory approach. *Journal of Brand Management*, *19*(3), 213–227. doi:10.1057/bm.2011.33

Li, H. (Ed.). (2012). *Virtual community motivation and participation: Cross-disciplinary theories.* Hershey, PA: Information Science Reference. doi:10.4018/978-1-4666-0312-7

MacKenzie, S. B., Podsakoff, P. M., & Jarvis, C. B. (2005). The problem of measurement model misspecification in behavioural and organizational research and some recommended solutions. *The Journal of Applied Psychology*, *90*(4), 710–730. doi:10.1037/0021-9010.90.4.710 PMID:16060788

McKenna, K.-Y. A., & Bargh, J. A. (1998). Coming out in the age of the Internet: Identity demarginalization through virtual group participation. *Journal of Personality and Social Psychology*, *7*(3), 681–694. doi:10.1037/0022-3514.75.3.681

McMillan, D. W. (1996). Sense of community. *Journal of Community Psychology*, *24*(4), 315–325. doi:10.1002/(SICI)1520-6629(199610)24:4<315::AID-JCOP2>3.0.CO;2-T

Meyrowitz, J. (1985). *No sense of place. The impact of social electronic in social behavior*. Oxford, UK: Oxford University Press.

Modzelewski, R. (2013). Virtual togetherness: Sense of identity and community in cyberspace. *Crossroads: A Journal of English Studies, 1,* 37–53.

Oestreicher-Singer, G., & Zalmanson, L. (2013). Content or community? A digital business strategy for content providers in the social age. *Management Information Systems Quarterly*, *37*(2), 591–616.

Pai, P., & Arnott, D. C. (2012). User adoption of social networking sites: Eliciting uses and gratifications through a means–end approach. *Computers in Human Behavior*, *29*(3), 1039–1053. doi:10.1016/j.chb.2012.06.025

Park, N., Kee, K. F., & Valenzuela, S. (2009). Being immersed in social networking environment: Facebook groups, uses and gratifications, and social outcomes. *Cyberpsychology & Behavior*, *12*(6), 729–733. doi:10.1089/cpb.2009.0003 PMID:19619037

Pavlou, P. A., & El Sawy, O. A. (2006). From IT competence to competitive advantage in turbulent environments: The case of new product development. *Information Systems Research*, *17*(3), 198–227. doi:10.1287/isre.1060.0094

Petter, S., Straub, D. W., & Rai, A. (2007). Specifying formative constructs in information systems research. *Management Information Systems Quarterly*, *31*, 623–656.

Romm, C., Pliskin, N., & Clarke, R. (1997). Virtual communities and society: Toward an integrative three phase model. *International Journal of Information Management*, *11*(4), 261–270. doi:10.1016/S0268-4012(97)00004-2

Ruggiero, T. E. (2000). Uses and gratifications theory in the 21st century. *Mass Communication & Society*, *3*(1), 3–37. doi:10.1207/S15327825MCS0301_02

Sarup, M. A. (1993). *Introductory guide to Poststructuralism and Postmodernism*. Athens, GA: University of Georgia Press.

Tajfel, H., & Turner, J. C. (1986). The social identity theory of intergroup behaviour. In S. Worchel & W. G. Austin (Eds.), *Psychology of Intergroup Relations* (2nd ed.; pp. 7–24). Chicago, IL: Nelson-Hall.

Tickle, M., Adebanjo, D., & Michaelides, Z. (2011). Developmental approaches to B2B virtual communities. *Technovation*, *31*(7), 296–308. doi:10.1016/j.technovation.2011.04.002

Wakeford, N. (2002). New technologies and 'cyber-queer' research. In D. Richardson & S. Seidman (Eds.), *The Handbook of Lesbian and Gay Studies* (pp. 115–144). Thousand Oaks, CA: Sage Publications. doi:10.4135/9781848608269.n9

Walther, J. B. (1996). Computer-mediated communication: Impersonal, interpersonal, and hyperpersonal interaction. *Communication Research*, *23*(1), 3–43. doi:10.1177/009365096023001001

Wang, C., & Chang, Y. (2010). Cyber relationship motives: Scale development and validation. *Social Behavior and Personality: An International Journal*, *38*(3), 289–300. doi:10.2224/sbp.2010.38.3.289

Ward, P., Clark, T., Zabriskie, R., & Morris, T. (2014). Paper/pencil versus online data collection: An exploratory study. *Journal of Leisure Research*, *46*(1), 84–105.

Wellman, B., & Guilia, M. (1999). Net surfers don't ride alone: Virtual communities as communities. In P. Kollock & M. Smith (Eds.), *Communities and cyberspace* (pp. 167–194). New York: Routledge.

Whiting, A., & Williams, D. (2013). Why people use social media: A uses and gratifications approach. *Qualitative Market Research: An International Journal*, *16*(4), 362–369. doi:10.1108/QMR-06-2013-0041

Wold, H. (1985). Introduction to the second generation of multivariate analysis. In H. Wold (Ed.), *Theoretical Empiricism: A general rationale for scientific model-building* (pp. 9–11). New York: Paragon House.

Xu, C., Ryan, S., Prybutok, V., & Wen, C. (2012). It is not for fun: An examination of social network site usage. *Information & Management*, *49*(5), 210–217. doi:10.1016/j.im.2012.05.001

ENDNOTES

1 Michel Foucault published his *History of sexuality* in three volumes (1976-1984), but the most relevant out of the three for his methodological shift is the first one, *The will to knowledge (La volonté de savoir),* published in 1976 by Êditions Gallimard in Paris. This volume served as an introduction to Foucault's assumptions and future theorization of identity, discourse, and power,

and it was translated into English as early as 1978, which favored its use in a broader academic domain.

2 Taking as a point of departure that Foucault sees power as omnipresent in all human relations and not only, as argued by Marxist theory, in the political domain within the State, the mere possibility of resistance and transformation makes power a flexible and changeable force, an outcome in this dialogic negotiation and not a static entity.

3 The author mentions Stuart Hall's definition of identity as his point of departure: a non- fixed, unstable and constantly constructed entity. Stuart Hall is one of the founders of Cultural Studies, a discipline emerging from the cultural breakouts of the 1960s. It is in this sense a point of view which coincides with the feminist perspective taken as primary assumptions in this chapter.

Chapter 7
Likes and Comments:
The Untamed Facebook Sex Education in Uganda and Kenya for Emerging Adults

David Mugambe Mpiima
Makerere University, Uganda

Ruth Kendagor
Karatina University, Kenya

Sarah Wairimu Ndung'u Njau
Moi University, Kenya

ABSTRACT

This chapter focuses on the changes in sex education among young adults in Uganda and Kenya. Sex education was previously done through paternal aunties and grandparents. However, in the recent past, the proliferation of social media especially Facebook has seen sex education shift to this social media. Using mostly qualitative methods and limited quantitative information, the chapter explores the ease with which sex information; some laced with sexually explicit photographs, has become so easy to access. Some of the shared information is empowering say about fashion, information about safe sex, relationship advice, connecting with people of the opposite sex as well developing identity formation and the freedom about one's body through the likes and positive comments made on Photos posted on Facebook walls. However, some of this information has led to cases of risk behavior like freelance sex, exposure to nudity, sharing of nude photos with boyfriends and girlfriends as well as pathological revenge porn by jilted lovers.

INTRODUCTION AND BACKGROUND

In most African societies, sex education and sexuality are treated as taboo matters that can only be whispered about or left unaddressed (Odek, 2007; Kabaabetswe & Norr, 2002). Sex education encompasses behavior, sexual knowledge, beliefs, and attitudes (Magoon, 2010). In Uganda and Kenyan communities, there are essentially two layers of cultural influences on individuals: the household or family and com-

DOI: 10.4018/978-1-5225-1856-3.ch007

munity. The two layers inform one's sexual values, traditions, and behaviors, varying among individuals and communities. In Uganda, especially among the Baganda and Basoga cultures, the *Sengas* (paternal aunt) play a key role in preparing emerging adults (girls) for marriage. The *Senga* wound take action as the betrothal event drew near to prepare her niece for a successful marriage. She would do this by teaching her general good conduct as a growing female and wife but mostly about sex. This long standing tradition is similar to the Swahili culture among the Kenyan coastal community. In this culture, the bride is subjected to a one week or more of teaching by her aunts on how to take care of the husband on various issues, especially on sex and other bedroom matters. It should be noted that there is no such arrangements for emerging adult males.

In other communities, sex educators could be grandparents; for instance, among the Kisi, sex education is not the parents' role but it is carried out by the grandparents. These are the confidants of the grandchildren. While among the Luo and the Maragoli, sexual education targets older children who are kept in separate huts or homes of elderly community members. Sex knowledge is passed on during the initiation ceremonies (Odek, 2007). All this sex education takes place in the homesteads of these various elders as the girls became adults.

The 2011 Uganda Demographic and Health Survey (UDHS) shows that by 15 years, 12 percent of girls and 18 percent of the boys have engaged in sexual activity and by the time they reach the age of 18, 6 out of 10 adolescents (58%) and 47% of the boys have engaged in sex (Uganda Bureau of Statistics (UBOS) & ICF International Inc., 2012). The 2012 Kenya Demographic and Health Survey (KHDS) reveals that 7% of young adolescents between the ages of 12 and 14 years have reported ever having sex, with the median age at first sex encounter as 10 years old. Among young adults aged 15 to 24 years, 66% of women and 59% of men have ever had sex. Of those, 21% had reported sexual activity before 15 years of age, compared to 25% in Kenya Aids Indicator Survey (KAIS) of 2007 (Kenya National Bureau of Statistics, 2015). In addition, 4% of women and 30% of men who were sexually active between the ages of 15 and 24 years reported multiple sexual partners (2 or more partners) in the past 12 months. Furthermore, 57% of women and 38% of men reported that they were aware of their sex partners' HIV status. Regarding condom use, 11% of women and 43% of men reported consistent condom use with partners of unknown or discordant HIV status. According to the report, half of all new HIV infections occur among young people between the ages of 15 and 24 years. Adolescent girls are twice as likely to be infected as boys of the same age. Thus by the time Kenyans and Ugandans get into the bracket of emerging adulthood, many are sexually active.

The heightened sexual activity is triggered by the rapid urbanization, increased levels of education, preference for boarding schools, especially for the urban dwellers, reduced contact with the traditional sex education providers, the culture that eliminates parents from sex education, and the proliferation of both the internet and availability of mobile phones. It is considered embarrassing for parents to discuss sexual information with their own child in African culture, hence emerging adults hardly get open sex education from their parents. With increased detachment from the more secure traditional system that filters sex education messages for emerging adults, the contemporary system leaves them to fend for themselves, often relying on their peers and social media, including Facebook. Thus, they transfer identity explorations for sex to social media platforms, leading to diverse sex education results.

With the lessening of the cultural arrangements for sex education, other groups have sprung up to fill the void. In Kenya, for instance, the emergence of emerging adults meetings known as *Chamas* (self-groups), has been noted. Bridal shower groups in Uganda have also emerged, where sexuality and sex issues are discussed. The bride to be is taught how to sexually satisfy a husband, how to dress appealingly when at home, and how to speak to a man.

Schools are also among the emerging structures that have tried to fill the void by incorporating sex education in their curriculum, especially given the widespread occurrence of HIV/AIDS that is partly driven by a lack of the necessary behavioral information. Thus, schools have sex education programs focused on reducing risky sexual behavior, reducing the spread of STDs and HIV/AIDs, and reducing pregnancies among school girls (Ridini, 1998). In Kenya, there is a yet to be discussed Reproductive Health Bill 2014 which is being pushed by nominated Senator Judith Sijeny because of resistance from other senators. The bill proposes that adolescents and emerging adults should be given access to comprehensive sex education and confidential services, meaning that parental consent, will not be necessary for these services. One of the key functions of the bill is that it urges the national and county governments to make family planning services available. The argument advanced is that sex education should include contraceptive options, counseling, and information and education. These services should be offered to children beginning at the age of 13 because sexual activity begins around this age.

The need for early sex education has become one of the unintended consequences of social networking sites. The popularity of social networking sites has been fanned by the proliferation of smart mobile phones and increased accessibility to the internet in East African region. There are several social media websites, like MySpace, Cyworld, Bebo, Mychurch, Xanga, Twitter, WhatsApp Friendster and Facebook (Nsibirano & Consolata, 2014). WhatsApp has become especially famous for its easy photo sharing ability and its ability to limit chatting to only those people who are included in the user's phone contacts. Facebook, to which this chapter is limited, is a broader social network platform as it allows information sharing with strangers, friends, family, and the wider public. This wider reach and appeal has led to Facebook's popularity. Facebook is noted by various researchers as the leading social media platform (Kreutz, 2009).

Globally, there were 1.79 billion active Facebook users at the beginning of April 2016 according to Stastica an online statistics portal (Stastica, 2016). Facebook as a communication platform has dramatically shifted from being a platform for students to stay connected with one another, to a global platform that facilitates communication and interaction across a wide range and array of social dimensions (Ellison, Steinfield, & Cliff, 2007; Schoon & Cain, 2011; Quan-Haase & Young, 2010; Wachira, 2010). It is this heightened communication that has become rich with sex information. In the first half of 2016, Uganda had over 7.6 million internet users, a 19% penetration rate (Internet Live Stats, 2016). By 2014, Uganda had over 19.5 million mobile phone users (Uganda Communications Commission, 2014) and 1.8 million Facebook users (World Internet Stats, 2015). Kenya has over 4.5 million active Facebook users (Rick, 2015) In addition; Kenya also has had a high internet penetration percentage of 21,273,738 million internet users, which is 47.3% of the total population in 2013. This internet penetration provides fertile ground for social media based communication. Facebook is largely used to learn about social events, to keep in touch with friends, and as a diversion from school work (Wachira, 2010; Quan-Haase & Young, 2010). Facebook has created a cultural shift in how we share information and with whom we choose to share our information.

Facebook derived its popularity from allowing users to interact, flirt, and network. Furthermore, it also allows users to add friends, send messages, and update personal profiles. In addition, Facebook users can also form and join virtual groups, develop applications, host content, and learn about each other's' interests, hobbies, and relationship status through users' online profiles (McMahon, 2010). Facebook plays an important role in mediating the boundaries between individuals and groups, and in setting the boundaries between personal and public life (Schoon & Cain, 2011). This need for connection has accounted for the long hours that emerging adults spend on their phones (Coyne, Padilla-Walker, & Howard, 2013).

The most common internal motivation is the desire to keep in touch with friends and social capital which are the benefits received from relationships with other people (Ellison, Heino, & Gibbs, 2006; Joinson, 2008). Social capital is created through interactions with others, thus bringing a sense belonging to a group not individuals (Coleman, 1988). Therefore, according to Ellison et al. (2006), emerging adults who use Facebook tend to have a higher bridging social capital as well as higher bonding capital. East Africans still enjoy a high degree of social capital either through the extended family system or a high sense of community. This is amplified through the use of Facebook. Facebook as a social media tool helps in the maintenance of relationships with both acquaintances and close friends. Therefore, Facebook users can communicate directly with a small group of friends by posting comments or messages indicating strong ties; they can also follow their friends through passive means, such as viewing friends' news feed and browsing (Burke, Marlow, & Thomas, 2010). In addition, Facebook use helps fulfill social grooming needs, such as gossip and small talk (Dunbar, 1998; Gosling, 2009). Facebook can be used to minimize loneliness, to relieve boredom, and to pass time (Wilson, Graham, & Graham, 2012). Another reason to use Facebook is to access sex information being shared. However, Facebook can also increase jealousy, envy, and surveillance behaviors among emerging adults, leading to exacerbation of existing difficulties with trust (Nitzburg & Farber, 2013).

This study focuses on two themes: firstly, the ways in which young adults use Facebook as a source of sex education is examined, and secondly, the costs and benefits associated with using Facebook for sexual education is investigated.

THEORETICAL FRAMEWORK

This paper utilises the theory of emerging adulthood espoused by Arnett (2015). Emerging adulthood is a rapidly growing theoretical explanation that is mostly focused on the ages of 18-25. Arnett argues that the age bracket of 18-25 is the period in-between adolescence and the stable commitments of adulthood (Arnett, 2000). This is a period when one accepts responsibility for their actions, makes independent decisions, and becomes financially independent. The theory has five key features: identity exploration, instability, self-focus, feeling in-between, and possibilities or optimism. Identity exploration involves self-awareness by trying out different options especially in love and work, thus making unending decisions and life choices (Arnett, 2000). Young adults seek more emotional and physical intimacy, with strong focus on identity and exploration of a wide range of romantic and sexual relationships. It is a stage wrought with risky behavior including unprotected sex in a sensation seeking trait that includes pornography (Arnett, 2005; Arnett, 2000; Coyne, Padilla-Walker, & Howard, 2013). Some emerging adults are not close to their parents as well, limiting their ability to freely interact with their parents on sexual matters. Instability is most pronounced during this stage (Arnett, 2005) and there are frequent changes in terms of love, work, and place of residence.

Feeling in-between is a transition period; the emerging adult is neither an adolescent nor an adult. The fifth feature is of possibilities, meaning that hopes are at their highest with boundless opportunities to transform their lives. Many emerging adults are living away from their parents and stay with either their friends or alone. Self-focus doesn't simply mean being selfish but rather being freer to make more independent decisions compared to other age groups (Arnett, 2005). Their friends are the strongest social network. Despite greater freedoms, emerging adults have parents to answer to and in most African societies, they also answer to the community in which they stay and are thus closely monitored. Social media thus provides greater freedom from parents, and the community offers more connections with friends, and more choice to the emerging adult on content accessed and a chance to build new relationships including intimate ones (Coyne, Padilla-Walker, & Howard, 2013). Thus at this stage, the emerging adults have the shackles of an adolescent and the responsibilities of an adult. Some of the shackles are the cultural restrictions on pre-marital sex with African societies encouraging sexual piety through proper dressing, proper sitting postures that do not expose sexual zones, maintaining of virginity among girls, and proper relations with the opposite sex.

By the end of the late twenties, most emerging adults have made choices with lifelong repercussions (Arnett, 2000). This stage changes the identities of the emerging adults as they try to navigate life's changes at emotional, sexual, and work levels (Sharp, Coatsworth, Darling, Cumsille, & Ranieri, 2007). However, change, exploration, and instability wane as the emerging adult enters the late 20s.

The personality traits of social media users are very important for their online engagement (Correa, Hinsley, & Gil de Zuniga, 2010). Some use social media to influence their body image perceptions and also raise their self-esteem, especially among women, even when social media does not provide an accurate account of body size and weight for emerging adults (Coyne, Padilla-Walker, & Howard, 2013). Thus, more exploration and instability, which are the most dangerous, fluid features of emerging adulthood. These characteristics manifest even on social media as the emerging adults seek sex education, identity construction and achievement, and social acceptance through their Facebook activity. These concerns mostly affect male and female emerging adults with negative affectivity and neuroticism. Some emerging adults use social media for pathological reasons and hurt others through abusive language or sharing inappropriate sexual materials (Coyne, Padilla-Walker, & Howard, 2013). Because of these vile attacks, many emerging adults restrict their profiles so that they are only accessible to their Facebook friends (Patchin & Hinduja, 2010).

Emerging adulthood is a theory proposed in developed countries with a clear trajectory for these individuals, such as moving away for college, seeking work, and postponing marriage to the mid and late twenties. The theory might also apply to other societies, like East Africa, where there is a high illiteracy rate and a high rate of teenage mothers who do not go through the same trajectory as emerging adults in the developed world. Cultural beliefs, norms, and differences in socialization have been noted to impact the trajectory of emerging adults in East African settings (Arnett, 2005; Nelson & Chen, 2007).

METHODOLOGICAL NOTE

Data was collected through documents and online interviews through Facebook's in-box chat platform. This study is largely qualitative with a limited use of quantitative information where figures and statistics were needed. Observations were also employed on Facebook pages where the researchers could access Facebook walls. A total of 16 Ugandans and 20 Kenyans participated in this study with women constituting half of the participants in both countries. All respondents had to have active Facebook accounts. The respondents ranged from the ages of 16-25 to capture the demographic of young mothers with statistics showing that girls start giving birth at the age of thirteen among the urban poor and the rural areas. Arnett (2005) is cognisant of these differences in the category of emerging adults especially in rural areas and most developing countries which impacted the methodological choices of this study.

WHEN EVERYONE IS A SEX EDUCATOR

The advent of Facebook has provided opportunities to emerging adults to explore and learn about intimacy and sex. Most Facebook commentaries are on varied issues including: relationships, religion, personal issues, politics, and other social debates. This confirms that Facebook is one of the leading social media sites that are used by various individuals as a tool of visual representation, especially among those seeking fame and self-presentation. Furthermore, Facebook users with motivations to explore and impress others or even for mate-seeking behaviors, design their online profiles with photographs on their walls and on their profiles, depicting romantic images that they wish to expose. This relates to earlier findings that concluded that the emerging adults stage is the peak for identity exploration as well as risky behaviors (Arnett, 2015; Arnett, 1992). This is evident with the photos that are uploaded on profiles as well as the high numbers of comments and likes from friends.

Comments on one's profile are used to nurture and maintain social capital as well as intensify the friendships and identity exploration. Observations revealed that sexual matters are dominantly used for romantic attraction and they have led to fame as people who post elaborate and revealing photos of breasts, bums, and other eroticized body parts get a large following and become instant Facebook celebrities (Alpizar, Islas-Alvarado, Warren, & Fiebert, 2012). In line with this argument, a male Kenyan respondent had this to say:

It is evident that sexual matters have dominated Facebook users because if a user posts a very witty post and another posts a sexual post, the sexual post gets more likes and comments compared to the witty post.

Having heavily invested in good looks and sexual appeal by skin bleaching, and breast, bums, and hips enhancement, emerging adult female posts on Facebook draw massive following. Some of these Facebook users have even gone to the extent of creating applications in their names where their followers can view them and play with their bodies. Nsibirano and Kabonesa (2014) term this a continuation of the stereotypical masculine and feminine identities and sexualities. Whereas this is a personal choice of the individual to feel comfortable in her own body, it can elicit both positive and negative reviews from friends and family basing on personal definitions of sexuality.

However, it has been noted that emerging adult male and female Facebook users are leading in engaging in mate seeking behaviors than those in a relationship. Through sexual information sharing, changing of pictures and exchange of comments, categorized as a *social butterfly,* such users hope to achieve the potential of a future relationship (Alpizar, Islas-Alvarado, Warren, & Fiebert, 2012). This is a confirmation of identity exploration among emerging adults. Facebook is in a way a self teaching tool that will tell you about the relationship status of the account user, the likes of the user, and dislikes. It is a pseudo anonymous dating tool even when one has never met the other party. Thus, facebook becomes a space for both men and women to interact and enjoy themselves in ways they have not before (Nsibirano & Kabonesa, 2014). It has a liberating force around it.

Recent studies have identified significant gender differences in how emerging adults use Facebook especially for intimacy. It has been noted that females are more likely than males to institute intimacy through discussion and self disclosure and their relationships on Facebook. Emerging adults (girls) tend to receive more comments and likes, especially when they post pictures depicting their sexuality. To achieve good relationships, women use language full of relationship building words to draw both sympathy and advice from their readers about their looks, relationships, or family matters. On the other hand, men focus on shared activities and experiences and they are more likely to establish intimacy through shared activities (Rau, Gao, & Ding, 2008). Because of this liberty, it is not uncommon for young girls to tell it all through Facebook as revealed by a Ugandan female respondent:

We discuss sex issues and share experiences with each other. These can range from the sex styles they know and practice, how many boys one has had sex with and who was the best, to how their genitals look like and those of their boyfriends. They also discuss how it feels having sex, whether it is painful or whatever they imagined the experience would be.

Facebook without photos would be incomplete as it is one of the biggest activities on Facebook. It is reported that by the turn of 2013, over 250 billion photos had been uploaded on the Facebook platform and that over 350 million photos were finding their way onto Facebook on a daily basis and the number was expected to have doubled after 12 months (Smith, 2013). If as they say a photo is worth a thousand words, these are already infinite words spoken by these billions of photos! Research by Kissmetrics (2013), an online statistics agency, revealed that photos get 53% more likes, 104% more comments, and 84% more clicks compared to text based posts guaranteeing 39% more interaction in the process. Photos placed on people's walls and Facebook albums are intended in some way to enhance their sexuality and attract admirers in an effort to feel handsome or beautiful. Photos are also a mark of social status. They communicate social economic status of the user. A female Ugandan respondent had this to say:

In some cases, negative comments are deleted and if one insists on posting negative comments, they can be blocked or 'unfriended'. The 'brave ones' even come to your inbox and abuse you and start a verbal fight.' However, some people just love taking photos and sharing them so a positive or negative comment will not be taken badly because some actually post funny photos for fun. Negative comments are loathed because they lower self esteem of the girls especially if it is the guys commenting negatively. No one wants to be told that you are ugly, especially the girls. Boys normally like eroticized photos showing a lot of cleavage, thighs, and other seductive body parts.

She added that:

Non-sexualized photos of fashion will only elicit comments from fellow girls since they appreciate fashion and sexuality more than men do. Fashion enhances our sexuality and self esteem especially if you do it well. So if you have one photo that can communicate that new sexuality freedom to the public, you share it.

Thus, most women post and in many cases tag Facebook friends to their personal photographs taken when they are smiling and dressed nicely so as to capture people's views on how they look. This affirms self-focus and could enhance their level of connection as it was noticed that the individual could get more than three friend requests from strangers after posting an appealing photo and most of them were gladly accepted. Self-focus enhances the female identity as communicators with their interest in social interaction (Nsibirano & Kabonesa, 2014).

Facebook actually has a lot of free sex information on people's walls. These status attracts a lot of comments and likes from individuals who are friends with the person who shared the information and even those who are not as long as the post was public. This information was previously a preserve of paternal aunties and grandparents but it is now available freely to emerging adults who have Facebook accounts. This has been enhanced by the rate at which individuals spend observing the activities of other Facebook users and their personal interests on sexual information (Alpizar, Islas-Alvarado, Warren, & Fiebert, 2012). It is from such posts and comments that a lot of sexual information is shared amongst facebook friends. A male respondent had this to say about comments and posts:

The freedom to use Facebook defines the comments raised by the individual Facebook users which can either be positive or negative depending on the individual perception of the post. Sometimes these comments are made to make the post's author feel good or to educate others and also negatively to rebuke the post's author if they belief the information is vulgar.

Despite the negative information posted, sexual related information has always attracted many likes and comments either in support or opposition. Such comments drive sexuality related information as people comment about girl's shapes and sizes, sex styles, appearances, and so forth (Coyne, Padilla-Walker, & Howard, 2013)

It is in the Facebook groups, especially the women only groups or men only groups, that more sexual information is shared. These groups are normally closed and thus other Facebook users cannot access the content therein. It shields emerging adults and dating partners from being labeled by their partners as abnormal. This increases both self-focus and the freedom of emerging adults (Arnett, 2005; Coyne, Padilla-Walker, & Howard, 2013). A female Ugandan respondent who is in several such groups had this to share:

We discuss many things, i.e., how to seduce a guy who is bragging on Facebook and take him to bed and actually you can later tell other girls whether he is worth the bravado or not! You just inform them that he is up to no good and I wonder why he brags that much! However, if he is any good, then you tell the girls that he was such a tiger but the problem is that they too will want to have a share of him and get to know his prowess first hand. The girls in these closed groups do not care so much who they sleep with because they do not take sex seriously but as long as a guy gets approval from some in the groups, they will hunt for him.

In Kenya this has led to the popularity of the term 'Team *Mafisi' and* 'Team *Mafiset'* (both are loosely derived from a hyena's greed of wanting more of everything) among emerging adults. This means that an emerging adult male's or female's sexual appeal is high if she/he is in either category. As a sign of self-focus, members of these emerging adults groups dream of having sex because of the kind of sexual information they are exposed to. They want to go and try out things and see how these things work. The discussions are at times sexually exciting to the group members which are used to drive decisions to engage in sexual activity to new highs which inadvertently leads to risky behavior. This is an anti-thesis to what is propagated at home and in the schools where sex education is aimed more at self-preservation, avoiding and preventing diseases, especially HIV, and meeting the right partner for marriage. Facebook seems to encourage sexual liaisons whether on or off Facebook because of the uncontrolled nature in which sex education takes place.

If men designed their online profiles well, they would be able to date gorgeous women (Miedema, 2009). Well-put together online profiles include pictures, personal descriptions, comments, and interests. These areas he argues should be well designed to be captivating. Miedema further cites a lot of sexual information that could be useful in winning women online, such as saying 'you are hot,' 'gorgeous,' etc. It can be concluded, therefore, that effective online dating is enhanced through the availability and use of sexual information by the key interested parties to capture the attention of their targets. A male Ugandan respondent seemed to concur by stating:

It is believed that online dating is effective and in fact some girls have jokingly got husbands and men have got wives, settled down, and married.

Apart from online websites being used for dating, Facebook is also used as a platform where individuals can receive relationship advice from peers that help them solve their relationship problems and grow their relationships (Miedema, 2009). They do this by posting information on their Facebook walls, making comments on posts, and joining groups where they can freely share their ideas. Some online groups are good at building relationships as members objectively solve relationship problems for fellow members which helps mend and grow such relationships. It has been argued that the social networks of the emerging adults are built within their friendships and Facebook offers an outlet for constant contact among friends. A female Ugandan respondent had this to say about social support via social networking sites:

Girls talk about pregnancies - whether they conceived, plan to conceive, and if there are other girlfriends who are pregnant and they seek advice from those who have been there before them. Girls generally discuss relationships and advise one another.

EMPOWERING OR DISEMPOWERING? ONLINE FREEDOM AND SEXUALITY EDUCATION

Although many Facebook users, especially women, feel that their sexuality is liberated with the pictures that they post on their profiles. Posting pictures is a type of exploration (Arnett, 2015). At times, emerging adults post pure pornographic material which is well known for leading to other forms of abuse, including cyber bullying and cyber harassment, intimate partner violence, online stalking, sexting, child exploitation, and sex trafficking (Fairbairn, Bivens, & Dawson, 2013). Emerging adults (females) seem to be the biggest culprits of taking and sharing nude photos with their boyfriends which has haunted some when relationships go sour as the photos end up in the press or on Facebook walls in form of revenge porn.

There are many cases of men and women making advances to the opposite sex. Some emerging adults might deem the opposite sex as being knowledgeable in sexual matters based on the kind of information one posts on his or her wall or through other people's comments. sexual freedom, mixed with the freedom of Facebook, might make some emerging adults vulnerable to abuse. This age group is not typically controlled by their parents and thus they have more lee-way to engage in illicit sexual behavior. This leads to instability, social upheaval, and bitter relationship fights. Indeed, some emerging adults use Facebook for pathological reasons (Coyne, Padilla-Walker, & Howard, 2013). A female Ugandan respondent cautioned:

When things go bad, say a spouse or partner finds out, ugly fights ensue on people's walls as revenge. They write about them on their walls in long elaborate stories, attacking them, leaking nude photos that were shared earlier on in the glory days either in the press or on facebook to shame them or blackmail them.

Female sexuality is highly regulated in the African context and having freedom to explore one's sexuality breaks social norms of female sexuality (Nsibirano and Kabonesa, 2014). Given that emerging adulthood is a period of exploration, there is a lot of sexual and intimacy exploration using the information posted by other social media users.

There is also a tendency of over trivialization of some posts where clearly the author needs some sort of assistance. Instead of receiving serious comments, the post is ignored or simply receives funny comments. Consequently, the problem might not receive a solution. This could lead to depression. In one sample, 79% of these people who post personal information were depressed (Fearnow, 2014). Given that friends are the strongest social network as argued by Arnett (2005), emerging adults who post personal information are unconsciously reaching out to their friends for approval. This might help to ward of negative feelings, such as depression.

The threat of HIV from sex liaisons is real; too much information sharing might drive girls to try out the same men due to the men's documented sexual prowess. In such scenarios, simple sex rules, like taking HIV tests before engaging in sexual liaisons with strangers, will be broken. This affirms the assertion by Arnett (2005) that emerging adults engage in high risky behavior that includes unprotected sex as a form of sensation seeking.

Some emerging adult (female) Facebook users who also belong to groups that become sexually explicit admitted that Facebook has 'advertised' prostitution. Vulgar language is frowned upon in African culture, yet Facebook seems to have made it usable depending on the forum one is using. Consequently, emerging adults are breaking away from societal norms. For emerging adults (females) to engage in prostitution, they are slowly introduced to the trade by those with whom they share sexy information with, even though the act is deemed illegal in East Africa. This affirms the fact that emerging adulthood is a period of exploration and thus emerging adult females are exploring the options available to them with lifelong repercussions (Arnett, 2000). A female Ugandan Facebook user had this to say:

It starts slowly and people start taking their facebook friends out with other guys and once they see that it is simple, they join the prostitution trade since they do not have to stand at Speke Road[1]! They sleep with men for petty things like drinks!

The promotion of charms and witch craft, especially in female only groups, as aphrodisiacs is common place. The use of aphrodisiacs was reported from both Kenyan and Ugandan respondents. This leads young adult females into shrines, where they might fall prey to sexual abuse, engage in sex for a fee to be able to get enough finances to pay for the charms, and visit the shrines to get the men of their dreams. This behavior affirms emerging adulthood as both a phase of exploration and risky behavior since there is limited guidance from elders who would have otherwise cautioned against some of the risky adventures that have become so attractive.

Some groups add very young adolescents who ideally aren't supposed to be part of such adult leaning groups. It is not uncommon to find 15-year-old girls added to Facebook groups that are teaching explicit sexual matters to emerging adults. Not verifying the age of young adolescents before adding them to these groups might increase risky sexual behavior, which might increase in emerging adulthood, contributing to teenage pregnancies in both Kenya and Uganda.

CONCLUSION: PRESSING FORTH BUT LOOKING BACKWARDS

Sex information has been typically shared by elders in most African communities. In particular, sex information was passed on through the paternal aunt and the grandparents in East Africa but this role has been overtaken by recent technological developments. Facebook has helped to contribute knowledge about sex to emerging adults, regardless of whether the knowledge is right or wrong. Some of the information is empowering, like knowing about fashion that enhances ones' sexuality, relationship advice, connecting with people of the opposite sex, and making someone feel good about himself or herself through the posts and comments they make or the Photos that he or she post on Facebook walls.

Emerging adults have heightened sexual exploration, experience increases in the engagement of risky behaviors, and a spike in self-focus that is driven by increased freedom through the use of Facebook. However, some of the posted information may not necessarily be useful but it might be acknowledged since there are no prying eyes and ears of parents, elders, or teachers. Consumption of this information translates into the now well documented cases of freelance sex, exposure to nudity, and the sharing of nude photos with boyfriends, girlfriends, and total strangers. These negative consequences associated with receiving sex information via social networking sites suggests that parents, teachers, and other well meaning elders need to impart much needed and well guided sexuality education to emerging adults.

REFERENCES

Alpizar, K., Islas-Alvarado, R., Warren, C., & Fiebert, M. (2012). 'Gender, Sexuality and Impression Management on Facebook'. *International Review of Social Sciences and Humanities*, *4*(1), 121–125.

Arnett, J. J. (1992). Reckless Behaviour in Adolescence: A developmental Perspective. *Developmental Review*, *12*(4), 339–373. doi:10.1016/0273-2297(92)90013-R

Arnett, J. J. (2000). Emerging Adulthood: A Theory of Development from the Late Teens Through the Twenties. *The American Psychologist*, *55*(5), 469–480. doi:10.1037/0003-066X.55.5.469 PMID:10842426

Arnett, J. J. (2005). The Developmental Context of Substance Use in Emerging Adulthood. *Journal of Drug Issues*, *35*(2), 235–254. doi:10.1177/002204260503500202

Arnett, J. J. (2015). *Emerging Adulthood: The Winding Road from the Late Teens Through the Twenties*. Oxford, UK: Oxford University Press. doi:10.1093/oxfordhb/9780199795574.013.9

Burke, M., Marlow, C., & Thomas, L. (2010). Social Networking Activity and Social Wellbeing. *CHI 2010 April 10-15*. Atlanta, GA: CHI.

Coleman, J. S. (1988). Social Capital in the Creation of Human Capital. *American Journal of Sociology*, *94*, S95–S120. doi:10.1086/228943

Correa, T., Hinsley, A. W., & Gil de Zuniga, H. (2010). Who Interacts on the Web? The Intersection of Users Personality and Social Media Use. *Computers in Human Behavior*, *26*(2), 247–253. doi:10.1016/j.chb.2009.09.003

Coyne, S. M., Padilla-Walker, L. M., & Howard, E. (2013). Emerging in a Digital World of Media Use, Effects, and Gratifications in Emerging Adulthood. *Emerging Adulthood*, *1*(2), 125–137. doi:10.1177/2167696813479782

Dunbar, R. (1998). *Grooming, Gossiping and the Evolution of Language*. Cambridge, MA: Harvard University Press.

Ellison, N. B., Heino, R., & Gibbs, J. (2006). Managing Impression Online: Self-Presentation Process in the Online Dating Environment. *Journal of Computer-Mediated Communication*, *11*(2), 415–441. doi:10.1111/j.1083-6101.2006.00020.x

Ellison, N. B., Steinfield, C., & Cliff, L. (2007). The Benefits of Facebook Friends: Social Capital and College Students Use of Online Social Netework Sites. *Journal of Computer-Mediated Communication*, *12*(4), 1143–1168. doi:10.1111/j.1083-6101.2007.00367.x

Fairbairn, J., Bivens, R., & Dawson, M. (2013). *Sexual Violence and Social Media: Building a Framework for Prevention*. Ottawa: Crime Prevention Ottawa.

Fearnow, B. (2014, May 25). *Study: Facebook Users Who Share Too Much Information More Lonely, Depressed*. Retrieved August 9, 2016, from CBS Atlanta: http://atlanta.cbslocal.com/2014/05/25/study-facebook-users-who-share-too-much-information-more-lonely-depressed/

Gosling, S. (2009, March 20). *The Ancient Psychological Roots of Facebook Behaviour*. Retrieved August 9, 2016, from Harvard Business Review: https://hbr.org/2009/03/the-ancient-psychological-root.html

Internet Live Stats. (2016, August 9). *Internet Live Stats*. Retrieved August 9, 2016, from Uganda Internet Users: http://www.internetlivestats.com/internet-users/uganda/

Joinson, A. N. (2008). 'Looking at', 'Looking up', or 'Keeping Up' with People? Motives and Uses of Facebook. CHI 2008 Proceedings: Online Social Newtworks (pp. 1027-1036). Florence, Italy: ACM.

Kabaabetswe, P., & Norr, K. F. (2002). Behavioural Change, Goals and Means. In *Aids in Africa* (2nd ed.). New York: Kluwer Academic Publishers. doi:10.1007/0-306-47817-X_33

Kenya National Bureau of Statistics (KNBS). (2015). *Kenya National Bureau of Statistics*. Retrieved August 9, 2016, from 2014 Kenya Demographic and Health Survey (2014 KDHS): http://www.knbs.or.ke/index.php?option=com_content&view=article&id=308:2014-kenya-demographic-and-health-survey-2014-kdhs&catid=82:news&Itemid=593

KISSmetrics. (2013). *Infographics: How to Get More Likes on Facebook*. Retrieved August 9, 2016, from KISSmetrics: https://blog.kissmetrics.com/more-likes-on-facebook/

Kreutz, C. (2009, June). *The Next Billion-The Rise of Social Networking sites in Developing Countries*. Retrieved November 17, 2015, from Web2forDev.com: http://www.web2fordev.net/en/component/content/article/1-latest-news/69-social-networks

Magoon, K. (2010). *Sex Education in Schools*. Abdo Consulting Inc.

McMahon, F. (2010). Use Social Media. *Sound and Video Contractor*, *28*(3), 50–53.

Miedema, J. (2009). *Slow Reading*. Duluth, MN: Litwin.

Nelson, L. J., & Chen, X. (2007). Emerging Adulthood in China: The Role of Social and Cultural Factors. *Society for Research in Child Development, 1*(2), 86–91.

Nitzburg, G., & Farber, B. A. (2013). Putting Up Emotional (Facebook) Walls? Attachment Status and Emerging Adults Experiences of Social Networking Sites. *Journal of Clinical Psychology, 69*(11), 1183–1190. doi:10.1002/jclp.22045 PMID:23996299

Nsibirano, R., & Consolata, K. (2014). Internet Use and Reconstruction of Gender Identity Among University Students in Uganda. In G. B. Kyomuhendo, F. K. Muhanguzi, S. Gerrard, & J. Ahikire (Eds.), *Gender, Poverty and Social Transformation: Reflections on Fractures and Continuities in Contemporary Uganda* (pp. 139–168). Kampala: Fountain Publishers.

Odek, T. (2007). *Cultural Challenges and Sex Education in Mageta Island, Kenya: Post Sexuality Leadership Development Report Series 3*. Nairobi: Africa Sexuality Centre.

Patchin, J. W., & Hinduja, S. (2010). Changes in Adolescent Online Social Networking Behaviours from 2006 to 2009. *Computers in Human Behavior, 26*(6), 1818–11821. doi:10.1016/j.chb.2010.07.009

Quan-Haase, A., & Young, A. L. (2010). Uses and Gratifications of Social Media: A Comparison of Facebook and Instant Messaging. *Bulletin of Science and Technology, 30*(5), 350–361. doi:10.1177/0270467610380009

Rau, P., Gao, Q., & Ding, Y. (2008). Relationship Between the Level of Intimacy and Lurking in Online Social Network Services. *Computers in Human Behavior, 24*(6), 2757–2770. doi:10.1016/j.chb.2008.04.001

Rick, W. (2015, September 10). *Reuters*. Retrieved August 9, 2016, from Facebook Rakes in Users in Nigeria and Kenya, Eyes Rest of Africa: http://www.reuters.com/article/us-facebook-africa-idUSKCN0RA17L20150910

Ridini, S. P. (1998). *Health and Sexuality Education in Schools*. West Port: Green Wood Publishing Group, Inc.

Schoon, E. W., & Cain, C. (2011). Facebooks Boundaries. *Contexts, 10*(2), 70–71. doi:10.1177/1536504211408925

Sharp, E. H., Coatsworth, J. D., Darling, N., Cumsille, P., & Ranieri, S. (2007). Gender Differences in the Self-Defining Activities and Identity Experiences of Adolescents and Emerging Adults. *Journal of Adolescence, 30*(2), 251–269. doi:10.1016/j.adolescence.2006.02.006 PMID:16600358

Smith, C. (2013, September 18). *Facebook Users Are Uploading 350 Million New Photos Each Day*. Retrieved August 9, 2016, from Business Insider: Tech: http://mybilliondollarapp.com/how-many-photos-on-facebook-how-about-240-billion/

Stastica. (2016, August 9). *Stastica*. Retrieved August 9, 2016, from Statistical Online Portal: http://www.statista.com/statistics/264810/number-of-monthly-active-facebook-users-worldwide/

Stats, I. W. (2015, November 15). *Internet World Stats*. Retrieved August 9, 2016, from Usage and Population Statistics: http://www.internetworldstats.com/stats1.htm

Uganda Bureau of Statistics (UBOS), & ICF International Inc. (2012). *Uganda Demographic and Health Survey 2011.* UBOS and Calverton.

Uganda Communications Commission. (2014). *Uganda Communications Commission.* Retrieved August 9, 2016, from Uganda Communications Commission: http://www.ucc.co.ug/data/qmenu/3/Facts-and-Figures.html

Wachira, K. (2010). Kenya Digital Life 2010. *MSRA Conference.* Nairobi: TNS Research International.

Wilson, R. E., Graham, S. D., & Graham, L. T. (2012). A Review of Facebook Research in Social Sciences. *Perspectives of Pyschology Science, 7*(3), 203–220. doi:10.1177/1745691612442904 PMID:26168459

ENDNOTE

1 Speke Road is famed for having prostitutes in Kampala, Uganda.

Chapter 8
Parent–Emerging Adult Relationships in the Digital Age:
A Family Systems Theoretical Perspective

Justin Peer
University of Michigan – Dearborn, USA

ABSTRACT

Emerging adulthood is a period of life characterized by increased individuation and independence. For emerging adults to successfully navigate this process, many aspects of the parent-child relationship must be renegotiated, including rules and expectations related to communication. The emergence of digital communication technology has provided an added layer to this process. This chapter summarizes research related to the influence of digital technology on parent-emerging adult relations. Early findings suggest that digital influence on this stage of development is complex. This chapter employs a Family Systems perspective to offer insight into how current and historical family functioning influences choices related to the use of digital communication technology and how these choices affect the development of emerging adults. Implications for practice as well as avenues for future research are offered.

INTRODUCTION AND BACKGROUND

Emerging adulthood, the time of life between the ages of 18 and 29, is characterized by exploration and instability. The goal of this period is the development of autonomy and self-sufficiency (Arnett, 2015). Though many emerging adults navigate the journey toward adulthood successfully (Arnett, 2007), the instability that coincides with self-exploration triggers increased stress (Arnett, 2015; Asberg, Bowers, Renk, & McKinney, 2008; Peer, Hillman, & Van Hoet, 2015) and self-doubt (Peer & McAuslan, 2016) for some. Social support is critical for buffering the negative impacts during this time (Masten, Obradović, & Burt, 2006). Parents serve as primary sources of such support, particularly during the early stages of emerging adulthood when individuals are beginning the process of establishing an identity independent of their family. As emerging adults work toward individuation, they maintain emotional connections

DOI: 10.4018/978-1-5225-1856-3.ch008

with their parents (Lee, Mazaros, & Colvin, 2009). Moreover, healthy development during this stage of life is intimately related to family relationships, yet change and instability in these relationships are also part of emerging adult experiences (Aquilino, 2006).

Digital technology has revolutionized the manner in which emerging adults and their parents communicate with each other (Clark, 2011). As "digital natives," emerging adults consume approximately 12 hours of digital media per day (Arnett, 2015). Cell phone usage, text messaging, and social media websites have become the preferred methods of communication among emerging adults. Digital technology has also become a main platform for communication for families and has greatly expanded the opportunities and frequency for emerging adults and their parents to communicate. Digital technology allows emerging adults and their parents to be in contact constantly and nearly instantly, wherever they may be and at any time.

Digital communication technology acts as an "electronic tether" between emerging adults and their parents (Hofer, 2008), which may impact emerging adult development and adjustment (Ramsey, Gentzler, Morey, Oberhauser, & Westerman, 2013). On the one hand, digital communication can enhance autonomy through the provision of a tool that individuals can use to efficiently gain needed support from parents, sometimes making it easier and less stressful to make important decisions. Emerging adults, for example, have reported that they rely on the support that they receive from their family through digital technology modalities (Arnett, 2015). On the other hand, this "instant access" can also serve to stifle developmental progress through overreliance on parents and in some cases through a continuation of dysfunctional family patterns via a new means. It is therefore critical to understand how evolving digital technologies influence the changing nature of parent-child relationships and how they can support and/or hinder healthy development of the emerging adult. In turn, it is also important to assess various factors related to the quality of the parent-child relationship (i.e., level and types of support provided, emotional closeness, level of conflict, and attachment patterns) and how they influence the use of digital technology to communicate (Ramsey et al., 2013).

In this chapter, I explain the potential effects of digital communication on parent-child relations during this stage of development. I use a theoretical framework, especially the Family Systems Theory (Bertalanffy, 1968; Goldenberg & Goldenberg, 1996), for understanding the impact of various aspects of family functioning on the successful integration of digital technologies into communication between parents and emerging adults. Specifically, I point to the importance of parents and children renegotiating their relationship during this period by discussing and creating new rules, expectations, and boundaries. Finally, the chapter concludes with a discussion about applications for family life education and clinical practice as well as implications and opportunities for future research based on the current research findings.

THE POTENTIAL IMPACT OF DIGITAL TECHNOLOGY ON PARENT-CHILD RELATIONS DURING EMERGING ADULTHOOD

In Western society, adulthood is highlighted by independence and self-sufficiency. Emerging adults experience a sense of feeling "in-between," as they have achieved some level of independence that differentiates them from adolescents, yet they still require emotional, material, and financial support from parents (Arnett, 2015). To successfully navigate this time of life, emerging adults must move toward self-responsibility and away from dependency upon their parents. The very nature of their relationship with their parents must evolve for this to be fully realized.

The parent-child relationship during this period moves toward a relationship based on mutual respect between two adults, rather than a relationship based on authority and control between a parent and their dependent child (Aquilino, 2006). Emerging adults and parents see each other more as humans rather than simply as a "parent" or as a "child." As the parent-emerging adult relationship changes, a renegotiation of many aspects of the relationship is required, including expectations and patterns of communication. This is a bi-directional process. Parents should respect their child's growing maturity and privacy, while the emerging adult should be respectful of their parents' responsibilities and availability for communication. While the underlying foundation of emotional support remains, the parent-child relationship should evolve into one highlighted by parental support of their child's self-sufficiency and autonomy (Aquilino, 2006). Developmentally, the critical concern for emerging adults is their ability to balance personal autonomy and connection with their parents. For parents specifically, it is vital to acknowledge and support their child's growing sense of independence while also maintaining a strong connection and open line of communication.

As the emerging adult develops more independent decision-making ability, new and a wider range of topics of conversation between parents and emerging adults arise (Arnett, 2015). For example, more open and freer conversations involve financial, career, and child-rearing matters. Parents are also able to offer "coaching" on a variety of topics. Furthermore, the technological revolution has allowed contact between emerging adults and their parents to increase dramatically and these advances have made communication accessible and affordable for most (Arnett, 2015).

Digital technology has offered not only a new avenue for communication between emerging adults and their parents but also another area up for renegotiation as independence is established. The 24-hour, instant access that digital technology allows could provide a sense of parental support for emerging adults or could be an area of conflict if boundaries are not established or enforced. Digital social media (Facebook, for example) provides potentially both positive and negative impacts for parent-child relations (Child & Westermann, 2013). The upside to digital mediums like Facebook is that they provide a convenient and easy way for family members to maintain an open line of communication. However, there is also the potential for serious conflict stemming from parental privacy intrusions and/or poor respect for personal boundaries, which could be initiated by both parent and emerging adult. Furthermore, though digital technology may benefit the relationship through the almost instant accessibility offered, some theorists believe that technology could possibly hinder the emerging adult's maturational process through the emerging adult's dependence on this instant access to their parents for decision-making purposes versus actively problem solving and making decisions on their own (Miller-Ott, Kelly, & Duran, 2014).

In their book, *The iConnected Parent,*Hofer and Moore (2010) explore in detail the process of parents remaining connected with their college-aged children while also learning to appreciate their child's emerging independence. They define "iConnected parenting" as "a culture of parents deeply involved in their children's lives, even as they approach adulthood, that uses technology of instant communication to enhance their connection" (p. 2), and they argue that this represents a new age in parenting. They state that the instant access afforded by digital communication explains why the frequency with which emerging adults and their parents communicate has risen rather dramatically in recent times. Parents, for example, believe that contact with their emerging adult is significantly greater than the contact they had had with their parents during emerging adulthood (Arnett, 2015). It is important to note that this process is bi-directional. Parents are contacting their kids more frequently and emerging adults are also contacting their parents more often. Some emerging adults contact their parents using cell phones multiple times per day and, in some circumstances, desire even more frequent contact with their family (Chen & Katz, 2009).

Hofer and Moore (2010) contend that the instant access that cell phones and computers allow creates a closeness conflict for parents. Although emotional closeness and communication are key to emerging adult development, parents must "stay in touch while letting them (their emerging adult children) grow" (Hofer & Moore, 2010, p. 12). They believe that this has become more difficult given the instant access parents have to their children through digital technology, as this instant access provides an "electronic tether" between parent and child that could hinder emerging adult autonomy. This could also lead to potential conflict and relationship dissatisfaction for the child and/or the parent. To avert this conflict, the renegotiation of digital communication rules and expectations for both emerging adults and their parents is of critical importance. The ability to effectively negotiate digital communication likely buffers relationship issues and positively impacts an emerging adult's ability to develop a sense of independence.

DIGITAL COMMUNICATION AND PARENT-EMERGING ADULT RELATIONS USING A FAMILY SYSTEMS PERSPECTIVE

Being able to successfully communicate through digital media is a process not solely determined by the current state of the parent-child relationship. This adaptation is occurring within a dynamic family system. Relationships are evolving and adjusting given the developmental needs of individual family members involved (both the emerging adult and parents). The quality of ties and the ability/willingness to discuss and integrate digital technology into their relationship is rooted within the complexity of developmental needs, as well as the functioning of the family historically. What occurs relationally between emerging adults and their parents currently, including the use of digital means of communication, mirrors explicit/implicit rules and roles utilized within the family unit over time. Understanding communication between emerging adults and their parents within this type of framework offers significant insight into the dynamics that contribute to successful integration of digital technology into family communication patterns. It complements the interplay between the family system and society, and acknowledges the bi-directional influences among family members within the overall family system as well as sub-components within this system.

Family Systems Theory, born from General Systems Theory (Bertalanffy, 1968; Goldenberg & Goldenberg, 1996), provides a framework for understanding how families are organized and the interdependence among members of the family system. Within this framework, the focus is on relationships between family members rather than on individuals in isolation. Structurally, family systems are usually composed of a generally stable set of relationships among members who tend to function in typical ways within that specific system. Interactions among family members serve to strengthen or weaken the stability (wholeness) of the family system. Family interaction "typically follows organized, established patterns, based on the family structure; these patterns enable each person to learn what is permitted or expected of him or her as well as others in the family transactions" (Goldenberg & Goldenberg, 1996, p. 44). In other words, individuals within the system are best understood through interactions with other family members. These interactions are governed by rules, boundaries between family members, and openness to change that all serve to maintain a sense of stability within the system.

The family strives for a sense of balance, or homeostasis, per this framework. Emerging adulthood and the developmental changes associated with it can create a sense of instability within the family system. This is due to the changing needs of the individual during this stage. Family Systems Theory is an applicable and suitable framework for exploring the multiple paths through which digital media may affect family functioning (Lanigan, 2009). Though this theory is not sufficient for exploring the characteristics of a particular technology and its influence on family relations, through the emphasis on the family unit, Family Systems Theory does provide a useful framework for exploring the process through which families discuss, and potentially integrate, digital technology into their structure and routines. Further, it explains the effects that the integration of digital media may have on the family system and the ability of the system to adapt to these changes.

Only one known study (Lanigan, Bold, & Chenoweth, 2009) has directly applied a systems perspective to the impact of technology on family life. Within their study, Lanigan et al. (2009) found that families believed that communication through a personal computer (e-mail, instant messaging, etc.) increased the sense of family connection. The authors support that using a systems perspective provides a framework for understanding how computer use influences family dynamics. However, their study does not focus solely on the emerging adult-parent relationship nor does it consider other forms of digital communication. Applying this framework to a broader range of communication technologies provides a more detailed view of family processes during emerging adulthood.

STABILITY AND CHANGE IN THE FAMILY SYSTEM

Renegotiation and other necessary steps associated with emerging adulthood impact the sense of normalcy within the family, thus disrupting the system's sense of homeostasis. According to Family Systems Theory, the family takes part in multiple processes to assure a sense of balance. Through these processes, the family rules that define relationships within the system may become activated. Adaptability becomes a crucial aspect of functioning for families. The system's ability to adapt to the developmental needs, including those related to communication, of the emerging adult will predict how satisfactory and productive relations will become. A cardinal characteristic of the family system is that it is constantly evolving while attempting to establish a new sense of balance.

In family systems terminology, the parental struggle between supporting their emerging adult and "letting go" is described as a dilemma of "morphogenesis" and "morphostasis." In other words, it is the parent-child relationship's ability to adapt and grow (morphogenesis) while simultaneously maintaining a sense of emotional support (morphostasis) that potentially creates conflict (Goldenberg & Goldenberg, 1996). The family system must be flexible and open to changes within the emerging adult and responsive to their communication needs. Families that are able to achieve and maintain stability in the midst of change are thought to be stronger (Goldenberg & Goldenberg, 1996).

Parental monitoring of digital media should be considered within this context. As emerging adults mature, parents adapt by respecting the developing autonomy of their child. Part of this adaptation is relinquishing a sense of control related to how their children use digital media and what content they consume. Although not an active part of communicating through social/digital media, expectations around parental mediation can certainly impact quality of relationships within families with emerging adults. Mediation (including viewing media with emerging adults, discussing digital media, and actively monitoring bills and content that is viewed) could aid emerging adults as they transition toward adulthood. However, it could also negatively affect the parent-child relationship if parental mediation is not negotiated and is seen as a means of control (Coyne, Padilla-Walker, & Howard, 2013; Vaterlaus, Beckert, & Bird, 2015). Minimal research has been conducted to thoroughly explore this area, but intuitively, it makes sense that for emerging adults to attain developmental and relational success, rules and expectations related to parental mediation of digital media must be discussed. Filtered through the family systems perspective, there are various reasons why a parent would or would not mediate their child's digital media usage. According to the principle of morphogenesis (Goldenberg & Goldenberg, 1996), a family that is flexible and open to change is responsive to the growth and development of their emerging adult. However, striving for familial balance must continue. Remaining sensitive to the stability of previously established, warm relationships with their child (morphostasis), the family adapts by accepting their child's budding autonomy and having a collaborative discussion regarding digital media (morphogenesis). Parents display adaptability through their willingness to discuss the use of media, content of media, and ways in which they could assist their child, seeking feedback from their emerging adult as part of this discussion. The emerging adult gains new insight regarding the use of digital media and new rules are implemented regarding how parents may monitor and be supportive of the child's digital technology use. Thus, the family has "grown" by establishing a new way of functioning that integrates continued parental support and monitoring (morphostasis) with education, rules, and expectations that support the emerging adult's autonomy (morphogenesis). This stabilizes the family and promotes healthy parent-child relationships. A dynamic balance in the midst of change allows for this to occur.

The sheer number of digital technologies available also must be considered within the context of stability and change. As the family unit evolves, the types and number of digital technologies utilized to communicate contribute to the complexity of the parent-child relationship, potentially impacting both quality and satisfaction. Schon (2014) found that the more technologies that parents and emerging adults used to communicate the more positive the impact was on communication satisfaction and relationship satisfaction. Though the total number of technologies used by participants in the study was low (mean number of 3.49 technologies for emerging adult/mother communications and 3.11 for emerging adult/father communications), there still was modest positive impact on relationship satisfaction. Findings relating satisfaction with the number of technologies utilized suggest that part of a healthy morphogenetic process should include negotiating rules and expectations around what is discussed via digital media, when it should be discussed, and through what means it is discussed. The Media Multiplexity Theory (Haythornthwaite, 2005) is based on the idea that people with stronger emotional/social ties to others will use media more to communicate than those with weaker ties. Based on this theory, those with "stronger ties" are going to use more forms of communication (Schon, 2014). Schon's study supports healthy morphostatic functioning as it was found that "communication competence" explained a greater amount of variance for relationship satisfaction than the number of technologies utilized. Communication competence is a collective term for multiple quality factors including supportiveness, empathy, and self-disclosure (Rubin & Martin, 1994).

Families who are unable to adapt, who remain rigidly tied to old rules, and who resist change within relationship dynamics are likely to experience an inability to grow and develop effectively. An over-reliance on morphostatic functioning can be attributed to various factors. Dysfunctional roles and rules within the system, trauma, substance abuse, and mental illness are examples of variables that can contribute to the system's resistance to change. Even a parent's own anxiety, real or perceived, about their child's wellness may promote an unhealthy morphostasis through the parent's unwillingness to relinquish their monitoring role (Hofer & Moore, 2010). Overly rigid or porous boundaries between parent and emerging adult may also contribute to the family's inability to negotiate rules and related expectations regarding the use of digital communication. Relationship satisfaction in the digital world may also parallel parent-child relationship quality in the "real world." Gentzler, Oberhauser, Westerman, and Nadorff (2011) found that emerging adults who experienced supportive and satisfying relationships with their parents spoke to their parents more often on the phone. But satisfaction with communication through digital technology differed based on the channel of communication utilized. Emerging adults who communicated with their parents through texting, e-mail, and social networking sites actually reported higher levels of loneliness, anxious parent-child attachment patterns, and conflict with their parents. Gentzler et al. (2011) explain this finding using the Theory of Electronic Propinquity (Korzenny, 1978), which is built on the idea that individuals use electronic devices as a means to maintain closeness to others. Using this theory, the authors state that the use of the cell phone as a method of communication with parents provides the optimal balance of independence and closeness that is developmentally appropriate during emerging adulthood.

Emerging adults and their parents must also consider the method of communication when negotiating rules and expectations. Families should not force emotionally laden cell phone conversations, for example, if this is not the preferred communication method among members within the family system. As the family adapts, attention and care should be given to preferences among all members. The system must "cut the wireless cord" (Lee et al., 2009) if a particular method is not preferred. Neglecting to do so may increase conflict and impede growth of both the system and the individual members within the system.

Additionally, the connection among non-cell phone digital methods of communication, anxious attachment, and parental conflict is efficiently explained through Family Systems Theory. Given that attachment relationships are determined through early parent-child interactions, relational issues and attachment problems at the emerging adult stage represent a remnant of historical role, rule, and boundary disturbances among members of the family system. The balance within the system was likely conflicted, which provided an atmosphere in which anxious attachment patterns could develop and persist within parent-child dyads. This pattern likely remained part of the equilibrium within the system and continues to be demonstrated in a novel way as emerging adults have reported higher levels of conflict with their parents (Gentzler et al., 2011). Further, utilizing these written methods of digital communication (e-mail, texting) may offer a way for emerging adults to avoid speaking to parents with whom they have an established anxious emotional connection.

Other researchers have also evaluated the influence of digital technology on parent-emerging adult attachment relationships. Lee et al. (2009) assessed the function of cell phones for emerging adult college students and its effects on their perceived attachment relationships with their parents. Individuals who were considered to be "connected" cell phone users reported greater attachment to their parents, particularly to their mother. Factors that identified a "connected" user were those who prefer the cell phone for social interactions, use the various functions that cell phones provide regularly, view the cell phone as a necessary component of living in modern society, and feel safer having access to a cell phone. Lee et al. (2009) suggest that "connected" users may feel more attached to their mothers based on their preference for using cell phones. "Connected" users may reach out to their parents for more reasons than those who use cell phones less frequently and are less reliant on this mode of communication. Talking to parents on cell phones, in turn, increases a sense of emotional attachment to their parents, especially their mother. Similarly, Ramsey et al. (2013) found that those parent-emerging adult dyads that used cell phones for regular communication reported the highest quality of parent-child relationships. Specifically, emerging adults who had regular contact with their parents via cell phone reported greater parental support, intimacy/closeness, and relationship satisfaction. The authors suggest that this may be due to the intimacy that is created through hearing a loved one's voice versus reading a text message, e-mail, or other similar technology. Collectively, these studies address how historical systemic functioning relates strongly to current parent-emerging adult attachment, relationship quality, and satisfaction, among other important indicators.

Digital technology also serves to maintain and strengthen current relationships between emerging adults and their parents. In a study of the relationship between the use of electronic communication technologies and parent-child attachment relationships during the transition to college, Sarigiani, Trumbell, and Camarena (2013) found that students viewed electronic communication as a way to stay in touch with their parents, ease the negative feelings associated with missing their family, and "maintain a deep parent-child bond" (p. 53). The authors believe that electronic communication is a protective factor that helps students buffer the stress associated with the college transition and promotes healthy adjustment. From a systemic perspective, electronic communication technology serves as a method for maintaining healthy morphostatic functioning. However, digital communication technology could also play a role in increasing relational conflict between emerging adults and their parents if rules and expectations are not discussed. Digital technology may serve to maintain both positive and negative relationships among members of the family system.

RULES WITHIN THE FAMILY SYSTEM

Rules are established patterns of interaction that denote expectations of family members. Miller-Ott et al. (2014) argue that communication rules allow parents and emerging adults to standardize and organize their interactional patterns while also establishing healthy boundaries. Most family rules are unstated, are learned through experience within the family unit, and govern the effectiveness of family functioning. Family rules may exist where "children do not challenge their parents" or "children do not have a voice." These rules may follow a "redundancy principle" (Jackson, 1965) whereby they are repeated over and over during the family life cycle. The emerging adult's ability to renegotiate frequency and expectations associated with digital communication may be influenced by these types of rules. If the implicit rule within the home is "the child does not have a voice," then the emerging adult may feel distressed in relation to the potential of being perceived as "challenging" their parent regarding rules of communication. In a system where family rules are based on equality and openness, this is likely not an issue.

Privacy management within families is a prime example of an embedded family rule that could potentially affect parent-emerging adult digital communication satisfaction. In a study on privacy rules and emerging adult responses to parental Facebook friend requests, Child and Westermann (2013) state that "the interior family privacy orientation is cultivated through both direct communication within the family and the occurrence of such practices among sub-groups within the family as concealing secrets from one another" (p. 49). This orientation is reported to be positively related with family functioning and satisfaction. To support this assertion, the authors reference previous work (Hawk, Keijsers, Hale, & Meeus, 2009) that reveals that the level of privacy invasion relates reciprocally with conflict among parents and young adults. Consistent with Family Systems Theory, Child and Westermann (2013) found that emerging adults who accepted Facebook friend requests, primarily from their mothers, were from families in which rules allowing for the sharing of private information between family members were already established. These individuals accepted the requests without changing any privacy rule settings within Facebook before doing so. Interpreted through a systems perspective, family rules related to the open sharing of personal/private information were ingrained in the system and allowed to occur via digital technology means. Within family systems with a closed line of communication and/or rules that discouraged open disclosure, the invitations would likely be ignored or turned down, potentially leading to conflict among members of the system. This suggests that embedded within family rules are values related to open versus closed communication practices. This is important as it helps to explain family dynamics in relation to the decision by emerging adults to allow/establish a line of communication with their parents via social media (Child & Westermann, 2013).

BOUNDARIES WITHIN THE FAMILY SYSTEM

Family systems are composed of various subsystems that carry out numerous tasks. The parental subsystem, one of the most enduring subsystems, serves the function of raising and nurturing children and moving them toward a sense of autonomy and self-determination. An integral component of the parental subsystem is boundaries, which are "invisible lines of demarcation" (Goldenberg & Goldenberg, 1996, p. 55) that differentiate family members and establish autonomy among the separate individuals within the subsystem. As within the larger family system, boundaries within subsystems must be flexible without becoming overly porous or rigid. Thus, rules should be established that govern the boundaries within the subsystem. Boundaries are directly related to negotiations of digital communication between emerging adults and their parents. If healthy boundaries are established and maintained, emerging adults and their parents engage in patterns of communication that are supportive yet respectful. In families where boundaries are porous and/or rigid, parents may be overly involved in the emerging adult's life, stifling their journey toward independence and creating an atmosphere that is conflictual and potentially highly dysfunctional.

Digital communication technologies, most notably cell phones, produce opportunities for boundary violations among emerging adults and their parents (Miller-Ott et al., 2014). Without establishing rules for how cell phones will be utilized for communication, the temptation of instant contact may weaken boundaries or exacerbate historical boundary disturbances between emerging adults and parents. In a study of relationship satisfaction related to having cell phone rules, Miller-Ott et al. (2014) explored the symbiotic relationship between rules and boundaries within the parent-emerging adult subsystem. They found that cell phone usage is frequent between emerging adults and their parents, particularly their mothers. The authors analyzed multiple rules (examples include availability, repeated contact, and arguments over the cell phone) related to cell phone communication and found that rules between emerging adults and their mothers were associated with relationship satisfaction and feelings of closeness. Miller-Ott et al. (2014) note that rules may counterbalance relational tension associated with autonomy and closeness within the mother-emerging adult dyad. They further described that, without rules, emerging adults may avoid parent phone calls or otherwise limit their access as a part of establishing a sense of independence. From a systemic perspective, this would disrupt homeostasis within the family system. Parents may respond to this disruption by actions designed to re-establish stability within the system. Parents may engage in intrusive behaviors—including monitoring their child's cell phone usage, making calls to their child that are not welcomed, and eavesdropping on calls to exert control—all conducted, from within the system's framework, in an effort to return the system to homeostasis. However, this behavior can lead to conflict and can compromise the emerging adult's drive for independence, further emphasizing the importance of role/rule negotiation and boundary establishment/maintenance.

HISTORICAL FAMILY FUNCTIONING

Current patterns of digital communication between emerging adults and their parents likely reflect both the quality of "offline" communication patterns and historical patterns of communication. Ramsey et al. (2013) suggest that parent-emerging adult satisfaction with the utilization of communication technology for correspondence reflects the quality of other relationship factors (support, intimacy, conflict) that occur outside of the digital realm. Members of the system rely on historical/redundant rules and patterns of communication with one another instead of opening the system to the full menu of behavioral patterns available to them. This explains the mirroring effect that the literature suggests, pertaining to satisfaction with digital communication between emerging adults and their parents. To understand how they will relate in the "digital world," the rules and expectations for communication in the "real world" must be clear. Analyzing rules, roles, and positive/negative feedback loops (information about past systemic functioning being "looped" back into the system as a way of controlling the system) in face-to-face interactions is likely predictive of systemic functioning when utilizing digital technology.

It is critical to consider historical systemic functioning when gauging the quality and satisfaction of digital relationships. Multiple studies (Gentzler et al., 2011; Lee et al., 2009; Sarigiani et al., 2013) describe the relationship between aspects of digital communication and the quality of attachment relationships between emerging adults and their parents. Given that attachment patterns are representative of early parent-child interactions and considered enduring (Bowlby, 1969), understanding the quality of current systemic functioning related to digital technology within the context of historical relational quality is important. From a systems perspective, this could again reflect redundancy within the system. Even more, the structure and organization of the system must be considered. Anxious or ambivalent patterns of attachment that persist from infancy into emerging adulthood may reflect a "closed system." A closed system is one that resists change, lacks constructive feedback to its members, and struggles to adapt (Goldenberg & Goldenberg, 1996). Opposing, "open systems" are flexible and adapt to change effectively, and are marked by open, constructive communications among members of the system. Current research reveals that present digital communication satisfaction is likely influenced by systemic functioning historically (Gentzler et al., 2011; Lee et al., 2009; Sarigiani et al., 2013). Attachment relationships represent, in this context, an indicator of how the system has functioned over time. The integration of digital technology serves to exacerbate and perpetuate the nature and quality of these attachments. Thus, to fully understand satisfaction among emerging adults and their parents, it is crucial to consider the historical context within which this relationship occurs.

SOLUTIONS AND RECOMMENDATIONS

Understanding parent-emerging adult relationships in the digital age is critical. Having knowledge of how digital communication and media impacts parent-child relations deepens our awareness of how completely technology has permeated our relationships. Not only does digital communication affect the quality of parent-emerging adult relations, but it may also directly and/or indirectly influence healthy psychological adjustment, independence/autonomy, and identity formation during this time of life. Although there remains a paucity of research devoted to this area of inquiry, the research that has been conducted speaks to the multifaceted ways that digital communication technology can influence parent-child relationship quality and satisfaction during emerging adulthood. This is not a linear relationship.

Satisfaction with digital communication relates to means of communication, current and historical family system functioning, parent-child roles within the family system, and expectations/rules for when contact can be made and what can be discussed, among other influential factors. The complexity of this relationship provides multiple implications for family life educators as well as clinical mental health professionals who work with emerging adults and/or their parents.

Preventatively, family life educators should provide information for emerging adults and/or their parents regarding the multiple ways that digital technology should be discussed and negotiated. Included in this information should be rules and expectations regarding when digital technology can be used, what can be discussed through digital technology, what is the preferred type of digital technology to be used to communicate, and how to competently utilize digital technology (primarily for parents) when communicating. Providing parents with information about the developmental goals of emerging adulthood and the importance of allowing for change while maintaining the stability of close emotional ties with their child, and considering how digital communication technology may facilitate and/or hinder this process, is important.

Mental health professionals (such as individual therapists working with emerging adults and family therapists) should assess the ways that relevant digital technology may be creating and/or perpetuating parent-emerging adult conflict. Further, aiding emerging adults and/or their parents to establish functional rules and expectations around the use of technology for communication purposes may help in reducing conflict and increasing a sense of cohesiveness and support within the family system. Professionals should also consider historical patterns of attachment when conceptualizing current family conflict regarding the use of digital communication technology.

For family life educators and mental health professionals, utilizing a systems perspective to conceptualize how rules, roles, boundaries, and historical functioning influence electronic communication on parent-emerging adult relations is useful. This perspective provides a framework for both understanding and explaining the nuanced ways that technology impacts the health and quality of relationships during this time. Further, it is critical for professionals to consider the implications stemming from the failure of the family system to renegotiate rules and roles, observe appropriate boundaries, and adapt to the use of digital technology effectively. The inability to adapt places the family at risk for entropy (Goldenberg & Goldenberg, 1996), which is marked by systemic decay, disorganization, and disordered functioning. It increases the likelihood of conflict within the family during a critical phase of human development. This conflict, in turn, may negatively influence the developmental trajectory of the emerging adult. From a broader perspective, the inability to adapt and grow effectively may hinder the family's ability to respond to demands in times of prolonged stress and/or crisis. During this time there may be a regression toward old, ineffective rules for communication. The professional plays a vital role in preventing this regression from occurring through the use of systemic assessment/intervention and the provision of information that aids the ability for families to clarify rules, roles, and boundaries related to technological integration successfully.

FUTURE RESEARCH DIRECTIONS

Though the current base of literature on the influence of digital technology on parent-emerging adult relationships provides foundational knowledge on the topic, there are still many unanswered questions that warrant exploration. This area of scientific inquiry is still in its infancy, and further quantitative and qualitative research is necessary to enhance our knowledge of how technology influences parent-child relations during emerging adulthood. In a review of digital media and emerging adult development, Coyne et al. (2013) note that "we know almost nothing about how emerging adults and parents use media and this represents a particularly useful area for future research" (p. 133). Emphasized here is the importance of forging new lines of inquiry exploring various aspects of the relationship between digital media and family functioning during emerging adulthood. Doing so will potentially explain differences within different family systems and subsystems, as well as address the heterogeneity that exists within our emerging adult population.

One area of future research is analyzing the role of fathers in parent-emerging adult digital communications. Having supportive relationships from both parents likely increases the emerging adult's sense of comfort and confidence as they move toward independence. The literature base suggests differential relationships among emerging adults, mothers, and fathers in relation to digital communication (Child & Westermann, 2013; Hofer & Moore, 2010; Lee et al., 2009; Miller-Ott et al., 2014; Sarigiani et al., 2013). Research suggests a more active role being played by mothers, while fathers are more passive and distant in their digital relationships with emerging adult children. Hofer and Moore (2010) strongly encourage fathers to initiate and sustain contact with their children. Further research is warranted to tease out the factors that differentiate mothers and fathers and should especially investigate the roles, rules, and history functioning within the family system that contributes to the father's place within the periphery of digital communication with their emerging adult child. From a family systems perspective, understanding family organization is pivotal for understanding interactional patterns and overall functioning. Finding the underlying historical, cultural, and systemic reasons for this difference could provide answers that bring fathers into a more active role within their child's life and, in turn, increase both relationship satisfaction and successful developmental outcomes for emerging adults.

Future research should also expand the subject base. The literature base currently relies heavily, if not exclusively, on digital communication between parents and emerging adults who are making the transition from high school to college. Given that emerging adulthood ranges from ages 18 to 29, it is logical to assert that digital relationships may evolve as the emerging adult moves closer and closer to the independence, self-sufficiency, and personal responsibility associated with adulthood. Little is known about how digital relationships change during the course of emerging adulthood. Longitudinal and cross-sectional studies that compare the influence of digital technology on parent-emerging adult relationships across this entire period are needed. This could shed light on the stability of digital communications during this stage and could potentially highlight shifts in their use over time. Research in this area may emphasize the changing needs and expectations/rules related to digital communication for emerging adults as they mature.

The current research base relies heavily on the use of undergraduate college students, thus neglecting potential differences in digital communication quality, style, and patterns among parents and other subsections of the emerging adult population. Little, for example, is known about how emerging adults who do not attend college and their parents relate within this "digital age." Arnett (2015) describes the developmental period of emerging adulthood as one that contains significant heterogeneity among its members. There are multiple paths toward adulthood and differences within this group should be acknowledged and appreciated. Providing research attention to how digital technology influences relationship quality/satisfaction for non-college attending emerging adults and their parents is significant. Coyne et al. (2013) echoes the need for investigating digital media use among non-college samples. They suggest, in line with Aquilino (2006), that researchers focus more on samples that contain emerging adults who do not attend college or who attend community colleges or vocational/technical schools. To offer even more depth and texture to the current base of literature, studies that sample emerging adults who live at home versus independently should also be conducted.

Finally, examining other forms of digital technology may lead to a greater understanding of emerging adulthood and parent-child communication. As forms of digital technology are ever evolving, future research should focus on how more recent social media platforms (Snapchat, Instagram, Twitter) serve to facilitate or inhibit parent-emerging adult communication.

CONCLUSION

Digital technology has revolutionized how individuals communicate with one another. We now enjoy instant access to others, regardless of their location. A primary developmental task of emerging adulthood is the renegotiation of rules between emerging adults and their parents. Rules for use of digital communication between emerging adults and their parents is a critical component of this renegotiation. The available limited literature suggests that digital technology undoubtedly affects the relationship quality and satisfaction between emerging adults and their parents. Research reveals that satisfaction with digital communication among emerging adults and their parents is related to various factors associated with the type of technology utilized, rules/expectations for media use, competence related to media use, and present and historical family functioning. Family Systems Theory provides a useful framework for understanding this impact. As the emerging adult strives for autonomy, the family system must adapt to accommodate this pivotal developmental goal. This framework aids in understanding how the family balances relational change and stability within the digital world. Further, it provides a solid theoretical foundation for future research, family life education, and clinical practice involving family communication during emerging adulthood as new technologies become available.

REFERENCES

Aquilino, W. S. (2006). Family relationships and support systems in emerging adulthood. In J. J. Arnett, J. L. Tanner, J. J. Arnett, & J. L. Tanner (Eds.), *Emerging adults in America: Coming of age in the 21st century* (pp. 193–217). Washington, DC: American Psychological Association. doi:10.1037/11381-008

Arnett, J. J. (2007). Emerging adulthood: What is it, and what is it good for? *Child Development Perspectives*, *1*(2), 68–73. doi:10.1111/j.1750-8606.2007.00016.x

Arnett, J. J. (2015). *Emerging adulthood: The winding road from the late teens through the twenties* (2nd ed.). New York: Oxford University Press. doi:10.1093/oxfordhb/9780199795574.013.9

Asberg, K. K., Bowers, C., Renk, K., & McKinney, C. (2008). A structural equation modeling approach to the study of stress and psychological adjustment in emerging adults. *Child Psychiatry and Human Development*, *39*(4), 481–501. doi:10.1007/s10578-008-0102-0

Bowlby, J. (1969). Attachment and loss:Vol. I.*Attachment*. New York, NY: Basic Books.

Chen, Y., & Katz, J. E. (2009). Extending family to school life: College students use of the mobile phone. *International Journal of Human-Computer Studies*, *67*(2), 179–191. doi:10.1016/j.ijhcs.2008.09.002

Child, J. T., & Westermann, D. A. (2013). Lets be Facebook friends: Exploring parental Facebook friend requests from a Communication Privacy Management (CPM) perspective. *Journal of Family Communication*, *13*(1), 46–59. doi:10.1080/15267431.2012.742089

Clark, L. S. (2011). Parental mediation theory for the digital age. *Communication Theory*, *21*(4), 323–343. doi:10.1111/j.1468-2885.2011.01391.x

Coyne, S. M., Padilla-Walker, L. M., & Howard, E. (2013). Emerging in a digital world a decade review of media use, effects, and gratifications in emerging adulthood. *Emerging Adulthood*, *1*(2), 125–137. doi:10.1177/2167696813479782

Gentzler, A. L., Oberhauser, A. M., Westerman, D., & Nadorff, D. K. (2011). College students use of electronic communication with parents: Links to loneliness, attachment, and relationship quality. *Cyberpsychology, Behavior, and Social Networking*, *14*(1-2), 71–74. doi:10.1089/cyber.2009.0409

Goldenberg, I., & Goldenberg, H. (1996). *Family therapy: An overview* (4th ed.). Pacific Grove, CA: Brooks/Cole Publishing.

Hawk, S. T., Keijsers, L., Hale, W. I., & Meeus, W. (2009). Mind your own business! Longitudinal relations between perceived privacy invasion and adolescent-parent conflict. *Journal of Family Psychology*, *23*(4), 511–520. doi:10.1037/a0015426

Haythornthwaite, C. (2005). Social networks and internet connectivity effects. *Information Communication and Society*, *8*(2), 125–147. doi:10.1080/13691180500146185

Hofer, B. K. (2008). The electronic tether: Parental regulation, self-regulation, and the role of technology in college transitions. *Journal of the First-Year Experience & Students in Transition*, *20*(2), 9–24.

Hofer, B. K., & Moore, A. S. (2010). *The iConnected parent: Staying close to your kids in college (and beyond) while letting them grow up*. New York: The Free Press.

Jackson, D. D. (1965). The study of the family. *Family Process*, *4*(1), 1–20. doi:10.1111/j.1545-5300.1965.00001.x

Korzenny, F. (1978). A theory of electronic propinquity: Mediated communications in organizations. *Communication Research*, *5*(1), 3–24. doi:10.1177/009365027800500101

Lanigan, J. D. (2009). A sociotechnological model for family research and intervention: How information and communication technologies affect family life. *Marriage & Family Review*, *45*(6-8), 587–609. doi:10.1080/01494920903224194

Lanigan, J. D., Bold, M., & Chenoweth, L. (2009). Computers in the family context: Perceived impact on family time and relationships. *Family Science Review*, *14*, 16–32.

Lee, S., Meszaros, P. S., & Colvin, J. (2009). Cutting the wireless cord: College student cell phone use and attachment to parents. *Marriage & Family Review*, *45*(6-8), 717–739. doi:10.1080/01494920903224277

Masten, A. S., Obradović, J., & Burt, K. B. (2006). Resilience in emerging adulthood: Developmental perspectives on continuity and transformation. In J. J. Arnett, J. L. Tanner, J. J. Arnett, & J. L. Tanner (Eds.), *Emerging adults in America: Coming of age in the 21st century* (pp. 173–190). Washington, DC: American Psychological Association; doi:10.1037/11381-007

Miller-Ott, A. E., Kelly, L., & Duran, R. L. (2014). Cell phone usage expectations, closeness, and relationship satisfaction between parents and their emerging adults in college. *Emerging Adulthood*, *2*(4), 313–323. doi:10.1177/2167696814550195

Peer, J. W., Hillman, S. B., & Van Hoet, E. (2015). The effects of stress on the lives of emerging adult college students: An exploratory analysis. *Adultspan Journal*, *14*(2), 90–99. doi:10.1002/adsp.12007

Peer, J. W., & McAuslan, P. (2016). Self-doubt during emerging adulthood: The conditional mediating influence of mindfulness. *Emerging Adulthood*, *4*(3), 176–185. doi:10.1177/2167696815579828

Ramsey, M. A., Gentzler, A. L., Morey, J. N., Oberhauser, A. M., & Westerman, D. (2013). College students use of communication technology with parents: Comparisons between two cohorts in 2009 and 2011. *Cyberpsychology, Behavior, and Social Networking*, *16*(10), 747–752. doi:10.1089/cyber.2012.0534

Rubin, R. B., & Martin, M. M. (1994). Development of a measure of interpersonal communication competence. *Communication Research Reports*, *11*(1), 33–44. doi:10.1080/08824099409359938

Sarigiani, P. A., Trumbell, J. M., & Camarena, P. M. (2013). Electronic communications technologies and transition to college: Links to parent-child attachment and adjustment. *Journal of the First-Year Experience & Students in Transition*, *25*(1), 35–60.

Schon, J. (2014). Dad doesnt text: Examining how parents use of information communication technologies influences satisfaction among emerging adult children. *Emerging Adulthood*, *2*(4), 304–312. doi:10.1177/2167696814551786

Vaterlaus, J. M., Beckert, T. E., & Bird, C. V. (2015). At a certain age its not appropriate to monitor ones child: Perceptions of parental mediation of emerging adult interactive technology use. *Emerging Adulthood*, *3*(5), 353–358. doi:10.1177/2167696815581277

von Bertalanffy, L. (1968). *General systems theory: Foundation, development, applications*. New York: Braziller.

KEY TERMS AND DEFINITIONS

Boundaries: Established limits that distinguish a family system and differentiate the members within the family system.

Closed System: A system that struggles to adapt, resists change, and lacks constructive communication between family members.

Digital Communication Technology: An electronic method of interaction among individuals, such as text messaging, cell phone calls, or social media websites.

Emerging Adulthood: A theory describing human development between the ages of 18 and 29. This period is marked by several distinctive features.

Entropy: Disorder or chaos resulting from lack of information or input from outside of the family system as a means of resolving a crisis or problem.

Family Systems Theory: A theoretical framework that suggests that the family is composed of a variety of relational subsystems that influence each other and the family unit as a whole. The system organizes to adapt to the changing needs of its members while simultaneously working to maintain a sense of balance.

Homeostasis: The ability of the family system to use outside information and feedback processes to maintain internal stability.

iConnected Parenting: A cultural trend in parenting in which technology is utilized to communicate and enhance parental connection with their child.

Morphogenesis: The ability for the family system to adapt and grow.

Morphostasis: The ability for the family system to maintain a sense of balance and stability.

Open System: A family that is flexible, adapts to change, and has open, constructive communication between members.

Redundancy Principle: The tendency for family members to interact using rules/roles in a repetitive sequence.

Chapter 9
Chinese International Students' Messages on the Family Forum:
Topics, Objectives, and Types of Assistance

Chenwei Wu
University of Arkansas, USA

Lynne M. Webb
Florida International University, USA

ABSTRACT

We content analyzed the online messages of Chinese international students who are currently studying and living in the United States. We examined messages within the students' ethnic group as they sought and provided assistance to each other in understanding and acculturating to family life in the United States via a popular online forum. We randomly sampled 50 recent, original posts and their accompanying threads (147 pages of text containing 108,723 words). Thematic analysis indicated that students use the forum to achieve three objectives (seeking informational/emotional support, offering information/emotional support, offering topics for discussion) across a wide variety of family issues (e.g., conflict, child rearing/education, appropriate behaviors for husbands and wives). Users provided multiple types of assistance (e.g., informational/emotional support, topics of discussion, questions based on the original posts, self-disclosure, positive feedback, and negative feedback) to the posters.

INTRODUCTION

Emerging Adult Theory argues that a distinct life stage exists between adolescence and adulthood, a time when individuals "have not yet settled into the long-term choices and life-paths that make up adulthood" (Bigham, 2012, p. 533). As originally conceived by Arnett (2000, 2015), this life stage extended from late teens through the 20s when individuals address the challenging tasks that typically accompany the transition into adulthood. Munsey (2006) identified five features of emerging adulthood:

DOI: 10.4018/978-1-5225-1856-3.ch009

- Identity exploration concerning life styles and believe systems (religion, politics).
- **Instability:** Individuals may change residents frequently, moving frequently for education, work, and/or family reasons. They may change intimate partners and friends frequently as well. The challenge for emerging adults is to find stability including negotiating on-going, positive interpersonal relationships and moving along a chosen career path that allows life in primarily one location. Particularly relevant to this research report, emerging adults must redefine family relationships to work functionally as adult-adult relationships including relationships with siblings (Brockhage & Phillips, 2016; Halliwell, 2016) and parents (Hays & Metts, 2015; Milevsky, 2005; Padilla-Walker, Nelson, & Knapp, 2014; Willoughby, Olson, Carroll, Nelson, & Miller, 2012).
- **Self-Focus:** Given the above described instability and focus on identity exploration, emerging adults remain self-focused until they begin making commitments to a specific career path and to significant others—commitments that lead to adulthood.
- **Feeling in Between:** Individuals know they are not children or teenagers any more, but often do not see themselves as adults yet.
- **Endless Possibilities:** This time of exploration and confusion leaves emerging adults with a sense of incompleteness but also with a sense of wonder and endless possibilities. That experience of endless possibilities can lead to a sense of empowerment or feeling overwhelming by too many options.

The Theory of Emerging Adulthood is not without its critics (Hendry & Kloep, 2007). Some adherents have argued that tying the definition of emerging adulthood to its challenges rather than specific ages is more sensible, given that individuals complete development tasks at differing paces (Bigham, 2012). Additionally, researchers argue that ethnicity (Munsey, 2006) and culture (Arseth, Kroger, Martinussen, & Bakken, 2009; Badger, Nelson, & Barry, 2006; Nelson, Badger, & Wu, 2004) may influence how individuals experience this life stage. Finally, a new line of research attempts to examine how emerging adulthood plays out in online behaviors (Davis, 2012; Stephenson-Abetz & Holman, 2012; Sumter, Vandenbosch, & Ligtenberg, 2017).

This chapter reports the findings of an original research study that continues an exploration of emerging adulthood among these newer concerns (i.e., extended age-frame, cultural differences, and online behaviors). Our study examined posts from one discussion board designed for Chinese nationals living in the United States. Specifically, we examined posts on a family forum to see what kinds of problems emerging-adult users discussed (and thus identified) as well as the social support strategies they employ in their responses to posts by other users to provide assistance in coping with challenges related to family life during their extended emerging adulthood in a foreign land. The majority of the discussion board users were:

1. Students completing higher education degrees,
2. Their spouses who emigrated with the students, or
3. Recent graduates looking for employment.

Because education figured so prominently in the users lives, for the balance of the chapter, we refer to our posters as students.

BACKGROUND

The United States, a desired destination for higher education and immigration, has served as a major recipient of international students since the 1960s (Hazen & Alberts, 2006). China, considered as a "major sending country" (IIE, 2010), sent 895,392 students to the United States for further education in 2009 alone; these students brought with them 40,956 spouses and children (U. S. Department of Homeland Security, 2010). Compared to native U. S. students, international students can suffer from more physical, mental, and academic-related problems (Lewthwaite, 1996). Thus, Chinese international students can face a variety of challenges and difficulties adapting to new cultural and academic environments (Sullivan, 2010), while bringing economic benefits to the United States (NAFSA, 2010) and contributing to cultural diversity in the higher education classroom (U. S. Department of State, 2009).

Researchers have identified multiple problems experienced by Chinese international students including acculturative stress (Li, Liu, Wei, & Lan, 2013; Sullivan, 2010; Ye, 2006a, 2006b; Wei et al., 2012), identity clashes (Brown, 2009), feeling like an outsider (Zhang, 2009), and loneliness (Wang & Sun, 2008). Other researchers have explored how Chinese international students' computer mediated communication with their ethnic group can assist with acculturative problems (Kim, Izumi, & McKay-Semmler, 2009; Zhang, 2009; Wang & Sun, 2008; Ye, 2006) via blogs (Zhang, 2009), social support networks (Cao & Bathhurst, 2012), and web browsing (Zhou & Cai, 2002; Yang, Wu, Zhu, & Southwell, 2004; Wang & Sun, 2008). However, we could locate no previously published research on Chinese international students' use of online forums—the subject of our study. Researchers have previously examined Chinese users' discussions in Web-based forums, specifically fan-based forums (Lin & Tong, 2009), forums for older adults (Xie, 2008), and protest forums (Yang, 2010)—but not forums for students studying abroad and not for forums focused on family issues.

Chinese international students' communication within their ethnic group about family problems, especially young adult Chinese nationals living in the U.S with their families, remains unexplored. Given the recent finding that family issues contribute to Chinese international students' socio-cultural stress (Yan & Berliner, 2013) and given the Chinese cultural value of family recognition through academic achievement (Liao & Wei, 2014), Chinese students who are studying and living in the United States are likely to perceive more pressure from family "back home" than international students from other countries. In the study here reported, we explored how Chinese international students communicate about family issues in one popular online forum, MITBBS.

Cross Cultural Adaption Theory

In addition to any stress associated with emerging adulthood issues, Chinese nationals studying abroad must also face acculturation issues. Cross-cultural adaptation theory, developed by Korean scholar Young Yun Kim (2001), posits that, when entering a new culture, individuals can face problems becoming involved in the host culture and adapting to life in the host culture. The major challenge is to learn "to live with unfamiliarity and uncertainty" (Yang, Wu, Zhu & Southwell, 2004, p. 82) caused by cultural differences. Non-natives live under pressure to survive stressful events and transform themselves to meet the demands of a new cultural environment (Kim, 2001). Language acquisition (Wang, Wei, & Chen, 2015) and communication with members of the host culture (Gallagher, 2013) can reduce the stress of intercultural adaption. However, communication (interpersonal, group, and mass communication) with their other ethnically Chinese students living abroad can facilitate intercultural adjustment and intercultural competency (Lin, 2006) as well as provide "material, informational, emotional, and other forms of social support" (De Cocq, 1976, as cited in Kim, 1988, p.64).

Using Kim's (2001) cross-cultural adaptation theory as a second theoretical framework, this study explores Chinese international students' communication within their ethnic group (including requests and offers of assistance with family issues) on one popular online forum, MITBBS. Because family is of paramount importance to Chinese people, family issues may require more attention than other acculturation issues.

Chinese Family

Given its collective nature, Chinese culture emphasizes family relationships and support. Chinese families have experienced significant changes in recent decades fueled by socioeconomic development that ultimately resulted in structural changes in family life. The typical Chinese family has changed from a three-generational household to a nuclear family. Furthermore, many Chinese families have experienced changes in family dynamics associated with the one-child policy. Nonetheless, family remains a primary source of social support to Chinese people and is still valued by most individuals who are culturally Chinese (Xu, Xie, Liu, Xia & Liu, 2007). Indeed, Montgomery and Borg (2010) report that many Chinese students studying in the United States communicate daily with at least one parent, typically through email or text. Furthermore, Chinese students living in the United States continue to rely on family for health-related information (Xu, 2010). Thus, information on strength of Chinese family, on Chinese marriage, Chinese family structure, and potential problems experience in Chinese families were relevant to our study and are reviewed below.

- **Strength of Chinese Family:** In 1996, Xie, DeFrain, Meredith, and Combs identified four important strengths of Chinese families: loyalty, family support, enjoying time together, and harmony. Following a study of Chinese immigrants to the United States, Xie, Xia and Zhou (2004) identified an alternative set of four strengths of Chinese families: social support from friends and community, communication among family members, balancing host and heritage cultures, and spiritual wellbeing. Both of these studies identified the importance of family support, and their findings are consistent with the popular metaphor in China that family is always everyone's safe harbor. Indeed, among the Chinese, almost all personal problems, including mental health problems, are addressed within the family (Lim et al., 2010). Regardless of structural and dynamic changes, families remain a crucial part of any Chinese person's support network (Logan, Bian, and Bian, 1998). In difficult situations, Chinese nationals turn to family members for mutual support socially, economically, and emotionally. But what happens when there are conflicts with family members, especially family members back home? Perhaps Chinese nationals abroad are more likely to turn to peers on a discussion board for social support and helpful suggestions.
- **Chinese Marriage:** Arranged marriages were a common practice in China until the Marriage Law of 1950 (Xu & Martin, 1990) and based on the Chinese belief in "Men Dang Hu Dui" (i.e., the social and economic status of the wife's family should be similar to the husband's family or conflicts will result). Into the early 20th century, Chinese parents and matchmakers often make decisions on the engagement of young couples based upon "Men Dang Hu Dui," regardless of young couples' feelings or preferences. Today, arranged marriages are decreasing and Chinese

young adults experience more freedom to choose their mates and marriages (Xu et al., 2007). Contemporary Chinese young adults care more about the personality, affection, and health of potential partners than the family backgrounds (Li, 1989; Liu, 1996; Fei & Xie, 1995; as cited in Xu et al., 2007). Many Chinese international students bring a spouse and/or children with them when they enter the United States to study (U. S. Department of Homeland Security, 2010) or hope to acquire a spouse during their time abroad (Montgomery & Borg, 2010).

- **Structure of Chinese Family and Family Communication:** Until recently, Chinese citizens typically lived in three-generational households. After the Chinese government instituted the one-child policy to control high birthrates, married couples began to live with their only children as "nuclear families." Today, the structure of the typical Chinese family is four grandparents, two parents, and one child, called the 4-2-1 family (Jiang & Sa´nchez-Barricarte, 2011).

In the past, husbands served as the primary income earners in Chinese families and wives managed the households. Then, in the 1950s, the Chinese government enacted policies that encouraged women to seek employment outside the home (Xu et al., 2007). Today, most Chinese women work outside the home. As a result, women's decision-making power has increased in the home (Xu et al., 2007). However, Chinese working women can experience substantial stress as they typically retain primary responsibilities for the care for the households and children.

Given its collective orientation, Chinese culture values social stability and harmony within the family. Furthermore, Chinese people value "face." If conflicts take place within the family, Chinese nationals typically are unwilling to let others outside the family know. A common saying in China is that what happens within the family stays in the family.

Potential problems within Chinese families include the following:

- In the 4-2-1 family mode, six adults focus their attention on the only child; it is challenging for six adults to reach agreement about child-rearing, including decisions related to a child's education. Disagreements can be particularly contentious with mothers-in-law (Lim & Lim, 2012).
- The Chinese social security system is not well developed and family remains the major elder-care agency (Zhang, 2001). There are typically four senior citizens in a Chinese family but only one husband and wife couple. Can two working adults provide adequate care for four seniors and a child? If not, how should they prioritize their care?
- Chinese wives face the challenge of taking care of the family, while simultaneously working or studying. Additionally, wives of male Chinese student studying in the United States often experience the challenge of attempting to care for the family while locating employment among limited opportunities for foreign nationals (Chen, 2009).

Studying abroad may lead to additional family problems including the following:

- Changes in gender roles and relationships occurring during acculturation may lead to marital conflicts (Zhang, Smith, Swisher, Fu, & Fogarty, 2010).
- Following graduation, the return of culturally altered adult-children to their native country may lead to real or imagined conflict with elderly parents (Chang, 2010).

Online Support Networks and Overseas Chinese Nationals' Internet Use

Online networks, also known as virtual communities, are "gathering points for people with common interests, beliefs, and ideas" (Bakardjieva, 2003, p. 297). Users can find social support in online communities (Bakardjieva, 2003; Cao & Bathhurst, 2012; Qian & Mao, 2010; Xie, 2008) via interpersonally supportive interactions (Baym, 2001). Members of online groups can engage in a variety of activities such as expressing emotion (Quan & Ren, 2010), sharing personal stories, information, and providing social support to others (Turner, Grube & Meyers, 2001).

Compared to personal blogs and instant message services, forums provide open venues for discussions and flexible conversations. After a thread-starter posts a topic, all registered users in and visitors to the community can view the post and comment freely. Because the post remains on the bulletin board unless the thread-starter deletes it, readers may reply at any time, reply repeatedly as the conversation evolves, or elect simply read and not comment.

The more eager the user is to receive assistance from the online group, the more active she/he will be participating in online conversation (Ye, 2006). Because users share common characteristics and interests that form the basis for their online community, the users are comfortable turning to the forum for assistance; ironically, forum users can obtain various types of assistance from online groups given that the users come from a variety of backgrounds and experiences *within* their commonalities (Turner et al., 2001).

Chinese international students use specific types of mass media for differing purposes (Wang & Sun, 2008). When they suffer from loneliness and stressful events they are more likely to use the Internet than other media to contact and interact with their ethnic groups (Wang & Sun, 2008). The study here reported examined internet messages between Chinese international students on a popular online forum, specifically on the Family Forum of MITBBS.

MITBBS http://www.mitbbs.com/, literally meaning "Unnamed Space," is one of the most influential Chinese bulletin board system sites in the oversea Chinese community (Lei, Liu, Zhou, & Zhang, 2008). Founded in 1996, MITBBS is considered the most popular oversea Chinese web portal with over a hundred thousand registered users (Unknown Space, 2003). Most of its users are young and well-educated Chinese/Chinese Americans with an average age of 28; 98% of the users have received at least an undergraduate college degree (Unknown Space, 2003). The primary languages of MITBBS are Mandarin Chinese and English.

Several characteristics distinguish MITBBS from other Chinese online forums: It is not under the censorship of the Chinese government (Lei et al., 2008) and thus allows for free speech and the free flow of information among its users. About 85% of the forum's traffic is generated from the United States. The forum is bilingual with posts and responses appearing in English and Mandarin. The MITBBS has more than 300 forums on various topics including "Arts and Sciences," "Jobs and Financials," "Leisure and Entertainment," and "Life" (see the Appendix for a list of the major forums). The forums provide users with a venue for contacting other Chinese people who share similar experiences living in the United States to discuss specific issues/problems and to seek assistance. The MITBBS' Family Forum provides Chinese nationals who are living in the eastern United States a platform to communicate with other Chinese nationals about family issues related to living abroad.

The purpose of this study was to closely examine the messages about family matters posted on a popular online forum (i.e., MITBBS Family Forum) to learn how emerging adults living as Chinese nationals in the United States employed the medium to addresses the challenges of the transition to adulthood related to family matters. To that end, we posed three research questions:

RQ1: When discussing family matters, what objectives (e.g., seeking informational support; seeking emotional support; offering information; offering topic of discussion) do users seek to achieve via the forum?
RQ2: What kinds of family issues are discussed on the forum?
RQ3: Does the forum appear to provide its users assistance on family matters?

METHOD

Sample

Social scientific studies of online communication examine primarily two objects of study: the users who create online messages or the messages per se. Each option offers unique insights. In this study, we directly examined messages to objectively assess their content. The Family Forum of the MITBBS was selected for sampling as it was more likely to contain family-related posts than other forums on the popular MITBBS. The posts on the forum covered various types of family issues, working problems, and university experiences, indicating that users of Family Forum were currently studying or working in the United States

A total of 6,450 posts were posted to the Family Forum during the three years prior to data collection (the period of May 2008 to May 2011). We randomly sampled 50 original posts and their subsequent responses from among the most recent 500 posts listed on the forum. Because the study analyzed the flow of conversations among the forum users, we analyzed the 50 sampled "threads" (i.e., all the comments from the 50 sampled thread-starters and other users who responded to the thread-starter). These 50 threads were cut and pasted into a document file, yielding 147 pages of text containing 108,723 words.

The 50 sampled posts selected for analysis represented less than one per cent (specifically, 0.80%) of all the posts in Family Forum on the date of data collection. Users viewed the sampled posts, on average, 5941 times (Range = 173-32,110 times); each sampled post received, on average, 28 replies/ comments (Range = 1-104 responses). On average, 19 users participated in the conversation about each post (Range = 1-67 users). Among the 50 posts, 33 were related to family issues; 35 sought social support (22/35 were family orientated) while 14 other posts aimed to offer information or start discussion (11/14 related to family issues).

Given the anonymity of online discussion boards, we cannot ascertain demographic information about the users who created the messages. Furthermore, we could not ask the users directly as we were not in contact with the message creators to request their information. However, two indirect sources of demographic information were available to us and we report findings from those sources below:

1. The discussion board creators' report of data about their users as a whole offers demographic information about the user population who created the messages on the discussion board. According to the discussion board website, all the registered users in the Family Forum were Chinese or Chinese Americas living in the eastern part of the United States. Almost all users came to the United States to pursue higher education. However, some users live in the United States as spouses or as other family members of students holding F2/F2/J2 visas.
2. Additionally, we approximated limited user characteristics by inferring data from users' avatars, names, and statements made in their posts (e.g., "When I gave birth to my first child…" was probably said by a female). Among the 50 thread-starters, 39 provided information from which we deduced their biological sex and 28 provided information related to marital status. Among the ten males who reported their sex, six reported being married and the marital statuses of the other four remains unknown. Among the 29 females who reported their gender, 25 reported being married.

Procedures

Sampling Procedure

The sample frame consisted of the most recent 500 posts on the Family Forum at the time of data collection. We employed random sampling to select threads for the four pretests and the research sample. We drew original samples of 5, 7, and 7 threads for pretests 1 through 3 respectively. For pretest 4, we randomly selected 16 posts from among the 50 posts that comprised the research sample.

Pretest 1

Like many researchers before us who examined online text (e.g., Lee, 2013), we conducted textual analysis, a common form for analyzing textual data scraped from the Internet (Webb & Wang, 2013). Using a grounded theory approach (Corbin and Strauss, 2008), the first coder built a coding sheet based on data from the first pretest. Any common idea that emerged in three or more posts was considered as a category for the coding sheet. Additionally, observable demographic characters of the thread-starters (biological sex, marital status) became categories.

To code the pre-test data, the first coder read the sampled posts three times, highlighting and taking notes on potential themes and interesting statements. After the third reading, the coder reviewed the highlighted and noted statements, sorted them into categories and then devised a coding sheet. Categories like "issues," "family member involved," "responses from the thread-starter," "types of comments" were selected and added in the coding sheet. The thread-starters' enacted biological sex (either by directly stating their biological sex or by the sex of their posted avatar), marital status, number of reads, number of posted responses, the date of the posts, and the UAL link of the poster were added to the coding sheets.

Pretests 2 and 3

The first coder applied the newly developed coding sheet to the data drawn for the second pretest. Coding difficulties led to modifications and refinements to the coding sheet. In the third pretest, the viability of the modified coding sheet was further tested and proved workable.

Pretest 4

After the coder completed the first three pretests, a second coder was recruited. The second coder, like the original coder, was a Chinese student who spoke fluent English and who shared a similar cultural and educational background with the first coder. Following a one-hour training session, both coders examined the same fifteen posts, randomly selected from among the 50 sampled threads that comprised the research data. They independently coded the 15 posts (30% of the sample) using the same coding sheets. Their inter-coder agreement was 77.30%. All disagreements were settled amicably through discussions via online video chat. Following the above described session, a category was added to list the objective of the post (e.g., seeking support or offering information/discussion). The final coding sheet is displayed in the Appendix.

Coding and Analysis

The original coder coded each post in the sample. The coding process was completed within a week. Categories such as "Sex of the Thread-starter," "Marital Status of the Thread-starter," "Issues," "Response form the Thread-starter (Yes/No)," "Number of Browsing," "Number of Response," "Date of the Post," and "UAL Link of the Post" were gathered directly from the messages. Other categories including "Type of Comment" and "Objective of the Post" required a judgement and the coder consistently followed a set of rules developed across the four pretests in making such judgments.

The coder identified eight types of comments:

1. **Informational Support:** Advice, suggestions, information, ideas, or opinions, etc.
2. **Emotional Support:** Comments like "I feel you," "I am on your side," or "I feel sorry for you," etc.
3. **Self-Disclosure:** Self storytelling and personal experiences.
4. **Positive Feedback:** Messages expressing agreement or thankfulness.
5. **Negative Feedback:** Disagreement, blame, doubt, or debate, etc.
6. **Question Based on the Original Topic:** Question related to the post.
7. **Off Topic:** Comment unrelated to the post.
8. **N/A:** No response.

The posts typically exemplified two types of objectives–offering or seeking. They included the following:

1. **Offering Informational Support:** Provide information, suggestion, or advice.
2. **Offering Both Informational and Emotional Support:** Provide information, suggestion, or advice while providing encouragement.
3. **Offering Topic of Discussion:** Provide a topic and lead discussion.
4. **Seeking Emotional Support:** Self-disclosing to receive understanding, spiritual support, or encouragement without asking for suggestions.
5. **Seeking Informational Support:** Consult for opinions, suggestions, or advice.
6. **Seeking Both Emotional and Informational Support:** Ask for suggestions, understanding, and/or spiritual support.

7. **Seeking Emotional and Offering Informational Support:** Ask for understanding or spiritual support and then provide suggestions or advice.

RESULTS

Results Relevant to RQ1: Users' Objectives When Posting on the Family Forum

Most ($N = 33$; 66%) of the 50 sampled posts were related to family matters. Within the 33 family-related posts, forum users sought to achieve various objectives as displayed in Figure 1, including seeking informational support, seeking emotional support, offering information, and introducing a topic for discussion. Note that although most thread-starters sought and/or offered assistance, the "match" of sought-to-offered assistance was present for informational support but not present for emotional support. Commenters tended to offer informational rather than emotional support. Furthermore, some posts offered topics of discussion, although no thread-starter requested such topics or a change of topic.

Figure 1. Objectives of using family forum (family-related posts)

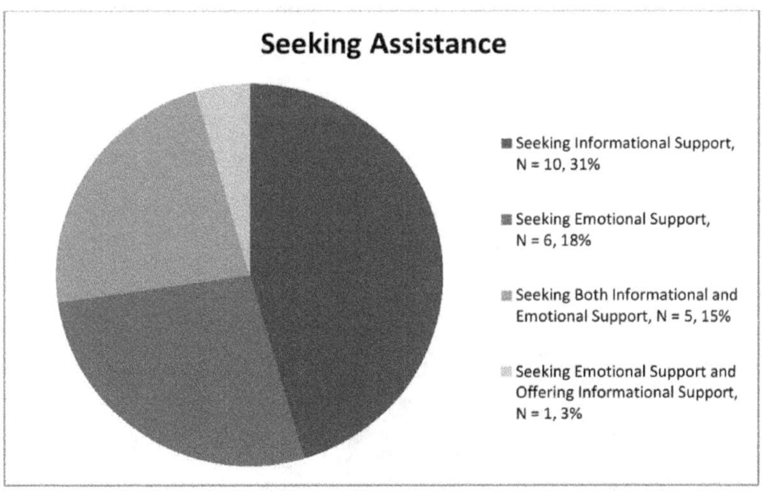

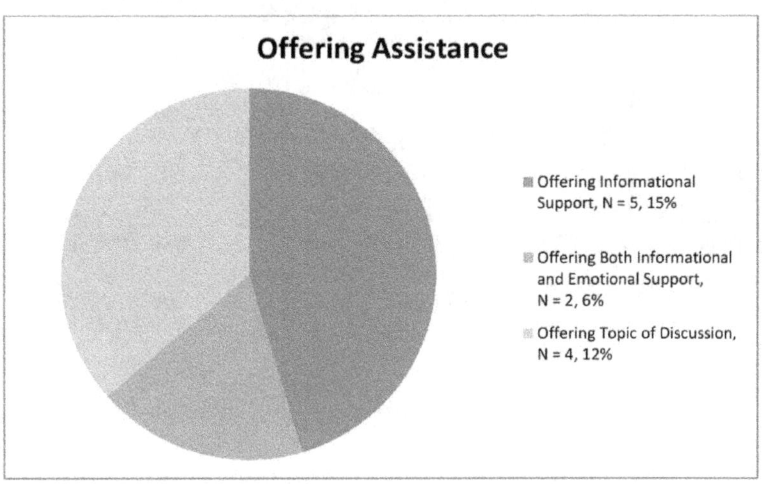

Results Relevant to RQ2: Family Issues Discussed on the Forum

The 33 family-related posts discussed a variety of family members. Husband/boyfriend/father were the most popular family members mentioned in the posts, as 20 posts were related to husband/boyfriend/father. Wife was mentioned in 10 posts and parents/parents in-law were mentioned in 9 posts. Only 7 posters mentioned children. One post involved an additional family member, a sister, and another post involved a non-family member.

Within the 33 family-related posts, twelve were related to family members in the United States, two concerned family back home; eight talked about both family members here in the United States and back home. The remaining eleven posts discussed abstract family concepts. It is interesting to note that only 7 of the 33 family-related posts were related to acculturation issues and the other 26 were about non-acculturation issues.

Six family issues were discussed (see Figure 2), including conflict, primarily conflicts with spouses and issues related to children. Some family-related posts included multiple issues (i.e., conflicts with parents and child rearing/education).

Males and females used the Family Forum about equally but they posted about different issues. Female thread-starters mainly sought help solving conflicts and problems, typically involving relationships with husband/boyfriends/father and sometimes discussing the contemporary home. Male thread-starters mainly posted about family problems; they also offered suggestions and information to others rather than seeking help. Other male posts addressed real estate, computers, cars, and business.

Figure 2. Types of family related issues discussed

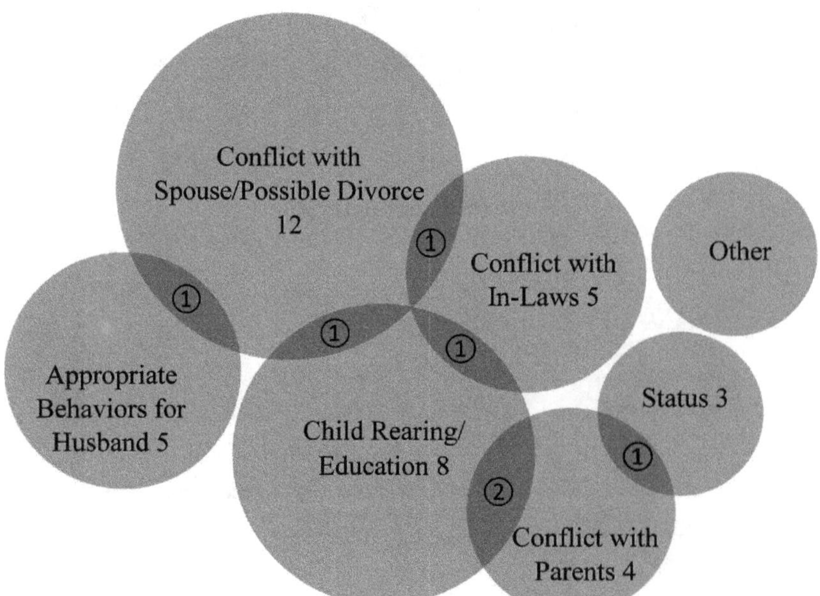

Results Relevant to RQ3: Types of Assistance Provided on the Family Forum

The most common follow-up post was a supportive comment, providing either informational or emotional support. Questions based on the original topic ranked as the next most frequently response; thus, users on the Family Forum actively raised questions further promoting the flow of the conversation and discussion. Less frequently occurring responses included negative feedback (e.g., statements assigning blame) and statements adding additional topics to the conversation.

In our sample, the Family Forum posters received replies and most of the replies provided assistance; 98% of the 50 selected posters received at least one response and 100% of the sampled posts were clicked and read by users. Most (58%) of the 50 thread-starters replied to their own posts, joining the conversations with other users. The majority (92%) of the 50 posts received informational and/or emotional support from other Family Forum users.

Within the 33 family related posts, 11 of the thread-starters appeared simply to want to complain and garner emotional support, as 14 did not post a thank-you comment or join the discussion. Nonetheless, fellow forum users provided emotional or informational support, if original posters returned to read the responses to their posts. In contrast, another 22 thread-starters seeking comments or information came back, led the discussion, and received help or support. Within the seven kinds of responses to posts (question based on the original topic, emotional support, informational support, self-disclosure, positive feedback, negative feedback, and off topic), informational support was the most commonly received form of feedback. The distribution of the received responses is displayed in Figure 3.

Figure 3. Frequency of responses

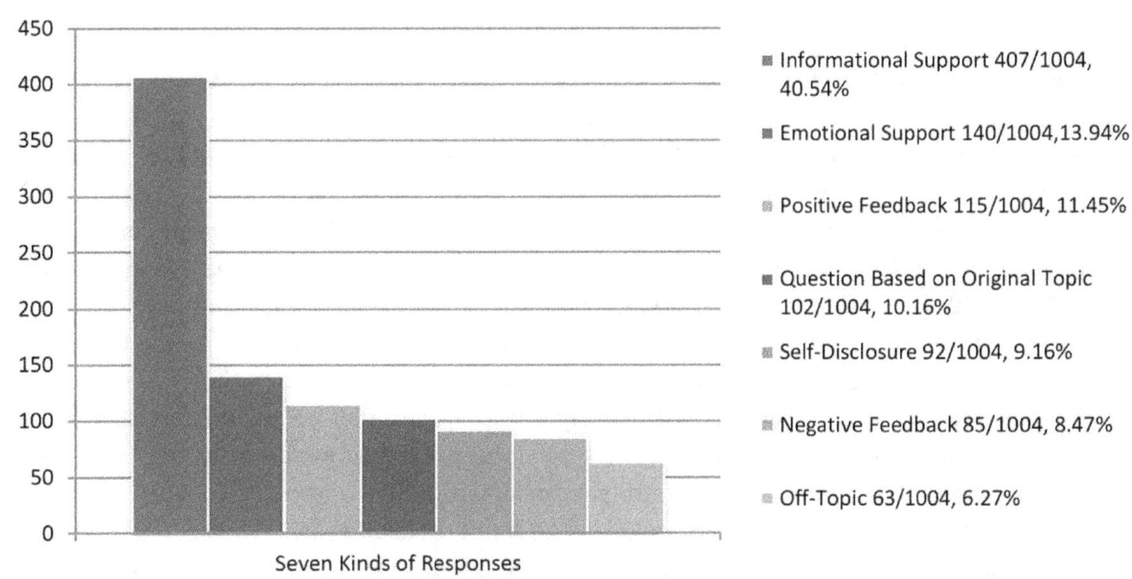

DISCUSSION

Summary

More than two-third of the sampled Family Forum users (66%) sought or offered family-related assistance (e.g., informational or emotional support, topic of discussion). Among 33 sampled family-related posts:

1. Husband/boyfriend/father was most commonly mentioned family member (20/33);
2. Six family issues were discussed, primarily conflicts with spouses and issues related to children;
3. Family member in the United States were more likely to be involved in the family issues than family members back home; and
4. Acculturation issues were rarely discussed on Family Forum (7/33).

Users on Family Forum received various types of assistance, most commonly informational support (40.54%) and emotional support (13.94%).

Interpretation

- **Assistance from Family Forum:** Due to the "face" and "harmony" principles, it is unlikely that emerging adults who are Chinese nationals in the United States talk face-to-face about family issues with their friends or contact other family members in distant locations to seek help. Family Forum provides a free-of-charge context to release stress and share information with other users in similar circumstances. Many forum users employed symbolic names (e.g., WinderDancer) that preserved their anonymity. Thus, users of Family Forum could express their concerns without fear of losing face or sacrificing harmony in their face-to-face relationships. The results of our study document that posts on Family Forum were widely viewed and garnered high response rates with multiple users involved in each thread—thus documenting the interactional nature and conversational dynamics of Family Forum.
- **Family Form as a Place for Family-Related Assistance and Discussion:** When studying abroad in the United States, Chinese nationals experience multiple stressors during their acculturation process (Brown, 2009; Wang & Sun, 2008; Zhang, 2009) in addition to "normal stress" associated with addressing the issues of emerging adulthood (e.g., identity exploration). Thus, these students can benefit from assistance provided by their ethnic group (Kim, 2001) in online formats (Cao & Bathhurst, 2012; Kim, Izumi, & McKay-Semmler, 2009; Wang & Sun, 2008; Yang, Wu, Zhu, & Southwell, 2004; Ye, 2006; Zhang, 2009; Zhou & Cai, 2002). In addition to blogs and Internet services, our results document that the Family Forum provides a venue for Chinese nationals who are living in the United States to share information and help one another as they experience similar situations living abroad and coping with family related issues. Our results document that users of Family Forum mainly sought assistance (e.g., help and informational/emotional support) when dealing with problems/conflicts with family members, offered assistance to others (informational or emotional support), and started discussions on family related topics. Consistent with previous studies examining both IM and message boards for Chinese users (Qian & Mao, 2010; Xie, 2008), the most commonly provided form of support was informational support followed by emotional support (Quan & Ren, 2010).

- **Various Family Issues Discussed:** Working or studying while caring for family in the United States can present challenges to Chinese couples. Indeed, 20 of the 33 family-related posts in our sample mentioned conflicts or problems with family members in the United States. Perhaps because of the nuclear family model (spouse and child live together without parents), conflicts with spouses and conflicts related to child rearing/education ranked as the most frequently mentioned conflicts. Given that instability is a major feature of emerging adulthood, including instability in relationships (Munsey, 2006), this finding is not surprising.

Sometimes parents and parents-in-law were involved in the conflicts between spouses and/or in the conflicts on child rearing/education, as family members who reside "back home" nonetheless can maintain a daily, virtual presence within their family residing in the United States via email, text, cell calls, and video-conferencing such as Skype. Such conflicts with in-laws could result from prioritizing the care of seniors versus the child in 4-2-1 families and/or multiple adults attempting to decide together on children's education. Additionally, emerging adults must redefine family relationships to work functionally as adult-adult relationships including relationships with parents (Hays & Metts, 2015; Milevsky, 2005; Padilla-Walker, Nelson, & Knapp, 2014; Willoughby, Olson, Carroll, Nelson, & Miller, 2012) and parents-in-law. Advice from the Family Forum may assist in that developmental task.

- **Acculturation Not a Major Issue:** Acculturation stress was not a frequently discussed concern on the family forum compared to family-oriented problems. The lack of acculturation-related conversations may be the result of multiple factors including the following:
    - Users may consider Family Forum a place to discuss family-related issues and they may employ other forums for discussions on acculturation stress.
    - Perhaps Americans and Chinese cultures valuing of family is so similar that Chinese nationals experience very little acculturation stress related to family issues. Nonetheless, our results indicate that scholars and practitioners interested in assisting Chinese international students who are studying in the United States might reasonably look beyond acculturation to include additional pressing issues including the challenges of emerging adulthood, especially those related to family concerns, in their examination of challenges faced by these students.
- **Sex Differences:** Lastly, our study documents that husbands mainly discussed financial issues (e.g., real estate, cars, and business); wives talked more about household issues. This finding may reflect traditional gender roles of males and females in Chinese families--that the husband oversees financial matters, while the wife cares for the children and the household. Our discovery of gender- and sex-based differences in online discourse is consistent with previous research (Webb & Temple, 2015). For example, Lee (2013) observed differences in gendered discourses within online communities of Korean immigrants (Lee, 2013). Furthermore, compared to males, female Chinese immigrants are more likely to seek help from others, perhaps because they experience more family stress (Franks & Faux, 1990).

LIMITATIONS AND SUGGESTIONS FOR FUTURE STUDIES

This study was not without its limitations. The translation process may have introduced inaccuracies; most information on the Family Forum was in Mandarin than English but this paper is written in English. Because English is the coders' second language, they may have failed to represent some original meanings adequately in English. A future study could employ a translation and back–translation method (Brislin, 1970) to verify the equivalent meanings of the Chinese and English versions of the posts.

The website provided limited information on thread-starters' ages and educational background, as personal information is not required on forum user registration. Furthermore, information on the thread-starters (e.g., biological sex of their avatars) can be faked. Finally, one person can register as multiple users.

The sample was not necessarily representative of all Chinese students studying in the United States, given that the majority of users in the Family Forum reported living in the eastern part of the United States and many of the users in the study self-reported as partners in young married couples. Furthermore, our sample was drawn from only one forum on one website and that website contains many sub-forums; thus, our results may not reflect MITBBS as a whole, all forums, or all forum-type websites. Finally, our sample was relatively small, but given our random sampling technique, should be representative of the contemporary posts on Family Forum. Future studies could include samples from additional forums to represent emerging adults living in other parts of the United States and users from multiple age groups.

CONCLUSION

Despite its limitations, this study contributes to our understanding of Chinese international students as emerging adults, specifically their use of the internet to address family issues in multiple ways:

1. The results demonstrate that an online forum can provide a venue for Chinese internationals to discuss family issues and receive emotional and informational assistance.
2. Our analysis revealed that various types of assistance for family problems can be obtained from Family Forum, including emotional support, informational support, and discussion.
3. In our data set, most family-related issues mentioned on the Family Forum were not related to acculturative stress (26/33).
4. In this sample, posters were far more likely to write about family members in the United States than family members "back home."
5. The analysis revealed that the users discussed primarily conflicts with parents and parent in-laws, conflicts with spouses, and conflicts on child rearing/education.

Taken as a whole, our findings provide a warrant for further exploration of websites that provide assistance to emerging young adults, especially Chinese international students studying in the United States.

REFERENCES

Arnett, J. J. (2000). Emerging adulthood: A theory of development from the late teens through the twenties. *The American Psychologist*, *55*(5), 469–480. doi:10.1037/0003-066X.55.5.469

Arnett, J. J. (2015). *Emerging adulthood: The winding road from the late teens through the twenties* (2nd ed.). New York: Oxford University Press. doi:10.1093/oxfordhb/9780199795574.013.9

Arseth, A. K., Kroger, J., Martinussen, M., & Bakken, G. (2009). Intimacy status, attachment, separation-individuation patterns, and identity status in female university students. *Journal of Social and Personal Relationships*, *26*(5), 697–712. doi:10.1177/0265407509347927

Badger, S., Nelson, L. J., & Barry, C. M. (2006). Perceptions of the transition to adulthood among Chinese and American emerging adults. *International Journal of Behavioral Development*, *30*(1), 84–93. doi:10.1177/0165025406062128

Bakardjieva, M. (2003). Virtual togetherness: An everyday-life perspective. *Media Culture & Society*, *25*, 291–313. doi:10.1177/0163443703025003001

Baym, N. K. (2001). Interpersonal life online. In S. Livingston & L. Lievrouw (Eds.), *The handbook of new media* (pp. 62–76). London: Sage.

Bigham, D. S. (2012). Emerging adulthood in sociolinguists. *Language and linguistics. Compass*, *6*, 533–544. doi:10.1002/lnc3.350

Brislin, R. W. (1970). Back-translation for cross-cultural research. *Journal of Cross-Cultural Psychology*, *1*(3), 185–216. doi:10.1177/135910457000100301

Brockhage, K., & Phillips, K. E. (2016). (Re)negotiating our relationship: How contradictions emerge in sibling privacy boundaries. *The Southern Communication Journal*, *81*(2), 79–91. doi:10.1080/1041794X.2015.1095231

Brown, L. (2009). A failure of communication on the cross-cultural campus. *Journal of Studies in International Education*, *13*(4), 439–454. doi:10.1177/1028315309331913

Cao, L., David, P., & Bathhurst, R. (2012). Social support network and use of SNSs among Chinese international students: An exploratory study in New Zealand. *Information Engineering Letters*, *2*, 2160–4114. doi:10.5729/iel.vol2.issue4.29

Chang, Y. Y. (2010). Are you my guest or my child? Mothers uncertainties in interacting with their returnee children in China. *Chinese Journal of Communication*, *3*(2), 167–184. doi:10.1080/17544751003740367

Chen, L. K. (2009). Negotiating identity between career and family roles: A study of international graduate students wives in the US. *International Journal of Lifelong Education*, *28*(2), 211–226. doi:10.1080/02601370902757075

Corbin, J., & Strauss, A. (2008). *Basics of qualitative research: Grounded theory procedure and techniques* (3rd ed.). Newbury Park, CA: Sage. doi:10.4135/9781452230153

Davis, K. (2012). Tensions of identity in a networked era: Young peoples perspectives on the risks and rewards of online self-expression. *New Media & Society*, *14*(4), 634–651. doi:10.1177/1461444811422430

Franks, F., & Faux, S. A. (1990). Depression, stress, mastery, and social resources in four ethnocultural womens groups. *Research in Nursing & Health*, *13*(5), 283–292. doi:10.1002/nur.4770130504

Gallagher, H. C. (2013). Willingness to communicate and cross-cultural adaptation: L2 communication and acculturative stress as transaction. *Applied Linguistics*, *34*(1), 53–73. doi:10.1093/applin/ams023

Halliwell, D. (2016). I know you, but I dont know who you are: Siblings discursive struggles surrounding experiences of transition. *Western Journal of Communication*, *80*(3), 327–347. doi:10.1080/10570314.2015.1091493

Hayes, A., & Metts, S. (2015). Support, closeness, and influence tactics as predictors of acceptance of unsolicited parental advice regarding a romantic relationship during emerging adulthood. *Ohio Communication Journal, 53,* 62-69. Available at http://connection.ebscohost.com/c/articles/110152582/support-closeness-influence-tactics-as-predictors-acceptance-unsolicited-parental-advice-regarding-romantic-relationship-during-emerging-adulthood

Hazen, H. D., & Alberts, H. C. (2006). Visitors or immigrants? International students in the United States. *Population Space and Place*, *12*(3), 201–216. doi:10.1002/psp.409

Hendry, L. B., & Kloep, M. (2007). Conceptualizing emerging adulthood: Inspecting the emperors new clothes? *Child Development Perspectives*, *1*(2), 74–79. doi:10.1111/j.1750-8606.2007.00017.x

IIE (Institute of International Education). (2010). *International student enrollments rose modestly in 2009/10, led by strong increase in students from China.* Retrieved from http://www.iie.org/en/Who-We-Are/News-and-Events/Press-Center/Press Releases/2010/2010-11-15-Open-Doors-International-Students-In-The-US

Jiang, Q., & Sanchez-Barricarte, J. J. (2011). The 4 – 2 – 1 family structure in China: A survival analysis based on life tables. *European Journal of Ageing*, *8*(2), 119–127. doi:10.1007/s10433-011-0189-1

Kim, Y. Y. (2001). *Becoming intercultural: An integrative theory of communication and cross cultural adaptation*. Thousand Oaks, CA: Sage.

Kim, Y. Y., Izumi, S., & McKay-Semmler, K. (2009, November). *The role of direct and mediated interpersonal communication in cross-cultural adaptation: A study of educated and long-term non-native residents in the United States.* Paper presented at the annual meeting of the National Communication Association, Chicago, IL.

Lee, E. K. (2013). Formation of a talking space and gender discourses in digital diaspora space: Case of a female Korean im/migrants online community in the USA. *Asian Journal of Communication*, *23*(5), 472–488. doi:10.1080/01292986.2013.772216

Lei, Y., Liu, Y., Zhou, X., & Zhang, B. (2008). *MITBBS project final report.* School of information, University of Michigan. Retrieved from http://www-personal.umich.edu/~ladamic/courses/networks/si508si708cs608/projects/MITBBS.pdf

Lewthwaite, M. (1996). A study of international students perspectives on cross-cultural adaptation. *International Journal for the Advancement of Counseling*, *19*(2), 167–185. doi:10.1007/BF00114787

Li, J. Q., Liu, X., Wei, T., & Lan, W. (2013). Acculturation, Internet use, and psychological well-being among Chinese international students. *Journal of International Students*, *3*, 155–166. Retrieved from http://cdigital.uv.mx/bitstream/123456789/38135/1/journalstudents.pdf#page=78

Liao, K. Y., & Wei, M. (2014). Academic stress and positive affect: Asian value and self-worth contingency as moderators among Chinese international students. *Cultural Diversity & Ethnic Minority Psychology*, *20*(1), 107–115. doi:10.1037/a0034071

Lim, S. L., & Lim, B. K. (2012). Po Xi Wen Ti: The mother-in-law problem. *Journal of Family Psychotherapy*, *23*(3), 202–216. doi:10.1080/08975353.2012.705649

Lim, S. L., Lim, B. K. H., Michael, R., Cai, R., & Schock, C. K. (2010). The trajectory of counseling in China: Past, present, and future trends. *Journal of Counseling and Development*, *88*(1), 4–8. doi:10.1002/j.1556-6678.2010.tb00141.x

Lin, A., & Tong, A. (2009). Constructing cultural *Self* and *Other* in the Internet discussion of a Korean historical TV drama. *Journal of Asian Pacific Communication*, *19*(2), 289–312. doi:10.1075/japc.19.2.03lin

Lin, C. (2006). Culture shock and social support: An investigation of a Chinese student organization on a U.S. campus. *Journal of Intercultural Communication Research, 35,* 117-137. dio:10.1080/17475750600909279

Logan, J. R., Bian, F., & Bian, Y. (1998). Tradition and change in the urban Chinese family: The case of living arrangements. *Social Forces*, *76*(3), 851–882. doi:10.1093/sf/76.3.851

Milevsky, A. (2005). Compensatory patterns of sibling support in emerging adulthood: Variations in loneliness, self-esteem, depression and life satisfaction. *Journal of Social and Personal Relationships*, *22*(6), 743–755. doi:10.1177/0265407505056447

Montgomery, C., & Borg, M. (2010). *Understanding the international student experience*. London: Palgrave MacMillan.

Munsey, C. (2006). Emerging adults: The in-between age. *Monitor, 37*, 68. Retrieved from http://www.apa.org/monitor/jun06/emerging.aspx

NAFSA Association of International Educators. (2010). *The economic benefits of international education to the United States: A statistical analysis, 2009-2010.* Retrieved from http://www.nafsa.org/publicpolicy/default.aspx?id=23158

Nelson, L. J., Badger, S., & Wu, B. (2004). The influence of culture in emerging adulthood: Perspectives of Chinese college students. *International Journal of Behavioral Development*, *28*(1), 26–36. doi:10.1080/01650250344000244

Padilla-Walker, L. M., Nelson, L. J., & Knapp, D. J. (2014). Because Im still the parent, thats why! Parental legitimate authority during emerging adulthood. *Journal of Social and Personal Relationships*, *31*(3), 293–313. doi:10.1177/0265407513494949

Qian, Y., & Mao, Y. (2010). A content analysis of online social support behaviors of overseas Chinese prenatal and postnatal women. *China Media Research, 6*(4), 43-54. Retrieved from http://hdl.handle.net/1765/39898

Quan, C., & Ren, F. (2010). A blog emotion corpus for emotional expression analysis in Chinese. *Computer Speech & Language, 24*(4), 726–749. doi:10.1016/j.csl.2010.02.002

Stephenson-Abetz, J., & Holman, A. (2012). Home iş where the heart is: Facebook and the negotiation of old and new during the transition to college. *Western Journal of Communication, 76*(2), 176–193. doi:10.1080/10570314.2011.654309

Sullivan, C. (2010). *Predictors of acculturative stress for international students in the United States* (Unpublished doctoral dissertation). University of Missouri, St. Louis, MO.

Sumter, S. R., Vanderbosch, L., & Ligtenberg, L. (2017). Love me Tinder: Untangling emerging adults motivations for using the dating application Tinder. *Telematics and Informatics, 34*(1), 67–78. doi:10.1016/j.tele.2016.04.009

Turner, J. W., Grube, J. A., & Meyers, J. (2001). Developing an optimal match within online communities: An exploration of CMC support communities and traditional support. *Journal of Communication, 51*(2), 231–251. doi:10.1111/j.1460-2466.2001.tb02879.x

United States Department of Homeland Security. (2010). *Yearbook of immigration statistics: 2009.* Washington, DC: U. S. Department of Homeland Security, Office of Immigration Statistics. Retrieved from https://www.dhs.gov/xlibrary/assets/statistics/yearbook/2009/ois_yb_2009.pdf

United States Department of State. (2009). *International students come to United States in record numbers, 16% increase in new foreign student enrollment is largest since 1980.* Retrieved from http://www.state.gov/r/pa/prs/ps/2009/nov/131995.htm

Unknown Space. (2003). *About US.* Retrieved from: http://www.mitbbs.com/about_us.htm

Wang, K. T., Wei, M., & Chen, H. H. (2015). Social factors in cross-national adjustment subjective well-being trajectories among Chinese international students. *The Counseling Psychologist, 43*(2), 272–298. doi:10.1177/0011000014566470

Wang, Y., & Sun, S. (2009). Examining Chinese students Internet use and cross-cultural adaptation: Does loneliness speak much? *Asian Journal of Communication, 19*(1), 80–96. doi:10.1080/01292980802618494

Webb, L. M., & Temple, N. (2015). Gender issues and digital technology: Challenges and opportunities for empowerment and enactment. In B. Guzzetti & M. Lesley (Eds.), *Handbook of research on the social impact of digital media* (pp. 638–669). Hershey, PA: IGI Global.

Webb, L. M., & Wang, Y. X. (2013). Techniques for analyzing blogs and micro-blogs. In N. Sappleton (Ed.), *Advancing research methods with new technologies* (pp. 183–204). Hershey, PA: IGI Global Publishers; doi:10.4018/978-1-4666-3918-8.ch012

Wei, M., Liao, Y. H., Heppner, P. P., Chao, R. C. L., & Ku, T. Y. (2012). Forbearance coping, identification with heritage culture, acculturative stress, and psychological distress among Chinese international students. *Journal of Counseling Psychology, 59*(1), 97–106. doi:10.1037/a0025473

Willoughby, B. J., Olson, C. D., Carroll, J. S., Nelson, L. J., & Miller, R. B. (2012). Sooner or later? The marital horizons of parents and their emerging adult children. *Journal of Social and Personal Relationships*, *29*(7), 967–981. doi:10.1177/0265407512443637

Xie, B. (2008). Multimodal computer-mediated communication and social support among older Chinese internet users. *Journal of Computer-Mediated Communication*, *13*(3), 728–750. doi:10.1111/j.1083-6101.2008.00417.x

Xie, X., DeFrain, J., Meredith, W., & Combs, R. (1996). Family strengths in the People's Republic of China: As perceived by the university students and government employees. *International Journal of Sociology of the Family*, *26*, 7–27. Retrieved from http://www.jstor.org/stable/23029686

Xie, X., Xia, Y., & Zhou, Z. (2004). Strengths and challenges in Chinese immigrant families. *Great Plains Research*, *14*, 203–218. Retrieved from http://www.jstor.org/stable/23779478

Xu, A., Xie, X., Liu, W., Xia, Y., & Liu, D. (2007). Chinese family strengths and resiliency. *Marriage & Family Review*, *41*(1-2), 143–164. doi:10.1300/J002v41n01_08

Xu, J. (2010). Health orientation and media exposure among Chinese college students: Family, Internet and life satisfaction. *China Media Research, 6,* 8-14. Retrieved from http://www.chinamediaresearch.net/index.php/back-issues

Xu, X., & Martin, K. W. (1990). Love matches and arranged marriages: A Chinese replication. *Journal of Marriage and the Family*, *52*(3), 709–222. Retrieved from http://www.jstor.org/stable/352936 doi:10.2307/352936

Yan, K., & Berliner, D. C. (2013). Chinese international students personal and sociocultural stressors in the United States. *Journal of College Student Development*, *54*(1), 62–84. doi:10.1353/csd.2013.0010

Yang, A. (2010). From "silent minority" to collective protests in real life: Tension, resistance, and online identity discourse of overseas Chinese. *Journal of intercultural Communication, 22,* 2. Retrieved from http://www.immi.se/intercultural/nr22/aimei.htm

Yang, C., Wu, H., Zhu, M., & Southwell, G. B. (2004). Tuning in to fit in? Acculturation and media use among Chinese students in the United States. *Asian Journal of Communication*, *14*(1), 81–94. doi:10.1080/01292980420001951512

Ye, J. (2006a). An examination of acculturative stress, interpersonal social support, and use of online ethnic social groups among Chinese international students. *The Howard Journal of Communications*, *17*(1), 1–20. doi:10.1080/10646170500487764

Ye, J. (2006b). Traditional and online support networks in the cross-cultural adaptation of Chinese international students in the United States. *Journal of Computer-Mediated Communication*, *11*(3), 863–876. doi:10.1111/j.1083-6101.2006.00039.x

Zhang, J., Smith, S., Swisher, M., Fu, D., & Fogarty, K. (2010). Gender role disruption and marital satisfaction among wives of Chinese international students in the United States. *Journal of Comparative Family Studies*, *42*, 523–542. Retrieved from jstor.org/stable/41604466

Zhang, L. (2009, May). *Virtual story, real life: An Examination of Chinese students' acculturation in the United States through blogs.* Paper presented at the annual meeting of the International Communication Association, Chicago, IL. Retrieved from http://www.allacademic.com/meta/p298830_index.html

Zhang, Y. J. (2001). Support networks for urban and rural senior citizens. *Social Sciences Study*, *4*, 11–21.

Zhou, M., & Cai, G. (2002). Chinese language media in the United States: Immigration and assimilation in American life. *Qualitative Sociology, 25*, 419-441. doi::101609013146310.1023/A

KEY TERMS AND DEFINITIONS

4-2-1 Family Mode: A three generation family consisting of four grandparents, a marital dyad, and their one child.

Chinese International Students: Chinese nationals who are living legally in another country for a set period of time to pursue training or an advanced college degree.

Cultural Adaptation: Individual experiencing the process or orienting to living in a culture that is unfamiliar to them.

MITBBS: A large, multi-faceted online forum for Chinese national studying in the United States.

Online Forum: A website designed to promote text-based interaction among its members who join the network to discuss a common interest and who often share common demographic characteristics.

Self-Disclosure: An individual reveals information about the self that others are unlikely to know or discover from other sources.

Social Support: Discourse designed to offer the target recipient(s) positive feedback or information that might lead to a positive outcome.

APPENDIX

Table 1. Selected list of unknown space online forums

Arts and Sciences					
Arts	Belief	Biology	Business	Chemistry	Chinese Classics
Computation	Economics	Engineering	Ghost	Law	Literature
Macromolecules	Mathematics	ME	On Stage	Paladin	Physics
Poetry	Prose	Psycho Analysis	Qigong	Reader	Science
SciFiction	Thoughts	Wisdom			
Cities and States					
Boston	Carolinas	Chicago	Connecticut	Florida	Georgia
Great Lakes	Indiana	Los Angeles	Louisiana	Michigan	Missouri
Montreal	New Jersey	New York	Ohio	Philadelphia	Pittsburgh
Rocky Mountain	San Francisco	Seattle	Tennessee	Texas	Toronto
Vancouver	Virginia	Washington D.C.			
Information Technology					
Apple	Building Web	Database	EE	Hardware	Internet
IT News	Java	Linux	PDA	Programming	Security
Software	Unix	Windows	XML		
Jobs and Financials					
Investment	Job Hunting	Money	Start-up	Stock	Working
Tax					
Leisure and Entertainment					
Astrology	Comic	Classical Music	Dance	Fashion	Game
Hi-Fi	Joke	Movie	MUD	MTV	Photographer
Photo Forum	Rock n' Roll	Travel	TV	TV Game	
Life					
Automobile	Banquet	Family	Fitness	Food	Gardening
Go West	Immigration	Living	Medicine	Next Generation	Overseas
Pets	Reunion	Travel	Shopping		
Love and Heart					
Girl	Heart	Love	Memory	Single	Whisper
Sports					
Badminton	Baseball	Basketball	Bridge	Chess	Fishing
Football	Go	Golf	Hockey	MJ	Pingpong

Chapter 10
Diverse Disabilities and Dating Online

Elizabeth Mazur
Penn State – Greater Allegheny, USA

ABSTRACT

Although research indicates that almost all emerging adults in the U.S. use the internet, little is known about the online dating experiences of persons with disabilities. Particularly in developed countries, online dating currently accounts for a substantial proportion of the initiation of romantic relationships and promises numerous advantages for persons with disabilities. Online dating includes a way to escape disability stigma, at least initially, access to a wide network of potential partners, and a convenient, private, and efficient method of meeting them. Online daters can be strategic in how they present both themselves and their disabilities, the manner in which they communicate with potential partners, and whether they join a large, popular dating site or a specialized disability-oriented one. The chapter discusses how the nine-step process of online dating might differ for or challenge emerging adults with various types of disabilities, sharing relevant research and media examples when available.

INTRODUCTION

Online dating is hard enough. Try doing it with a disability. (Sykes, 2014, p. 1)

According to the Census Bureau in 2010, approximately 10.2 percent of Americans ages 15 to 24 had some type of disability, and about 5.3% reported a severe disability (Brault, 2012). Much research suggests that in Western nations emerging adults with disabilities have more difficulty dating and finding romantic and sexual partners than do their peers without disabilities (Miller, Chen, Glover-Graf, & Kranz, 2009; Wiegerink, Roebroeck, Donkervoort, Stam, & Cohen-Kettenis, 2006). This is distressing and unfortunately ironic because the quality of close relationships strongly contributes to happiness, health, and longevity (Holt-Lunstad, Smith, & Layton, 2010; Myers, 1999). College students in committed romantic relationships experience fewer mental health problems (Braithwaite, Delevi, & Fincham, 2010);

DOI: 10.4018/978-1-5225-1856-3.ch010

furthermore, emerging adults report spending more time with romantic partners than with friends, and they are significantly more likely than adolescents to consider their partner a source of influence and reference (Giordano, Longmore, Schroeder, & Seffrin, 2008).

The challenges for people with disabilities (PWDs) in forming long-term romantic relationship are demonstrated by their low marriage rates. According to the National Longitudinal Transition Study-2, the marriage rate for emerging adults with disabilities (13%) during the first eight years after high school is significantly lower than that of their peers (19%) without disabilities (Newman et al., 2011). For people between ages 18 and 34, the percent never married among those with disabilities is 74%, compared to 65% for those without disabilities (Schur, Kruse, & Blanck, 2013). The marriage rate for PWDs never reaches a similar percent as that for individuals without disabilities; according to the 2010 U.S. Census, just 41% of U.S. adults ages 18 and older with disabilities are married as compared to 52% of U.S. adults without disabilities (Schur et al., 2013).

Not all types of disabilities have a similar influence on people's chances of getting married. Using data from the National Longitudinal Study of Adolescent Health, MacInnes (2011) found that among individuals between the ages of 24 and 32 in the U.S., 43% of individuals with learning disabilities, 37% of those with mental disabilities, and 21% of those with multiple disabilities reported having experienced a first marriage as compared to 53% of their peers with physical disabilities and 50% of those without disabilities. In the National Longitudinal Transition Study-2, marriage rates eight years after high school graduation ranged from 1% for U.S. emerging adults with Autism Spectrum Disorder (ASD) or multiple disabilities to 11% for those with mental retardation, emotional disturbances, hearing impairment, or traumatic brain injury, 13% for those with speech/language impairment, and 15% for those with other health impairments and with learning disabilities (Newman et al., 2011).

PWDs in Western nations are also less likely than those without disabilities to socialize with friends, relatives, or neighbors (McDonald, 2010, Pfeiffer & Pinquart, 2011; Wiegerink et al., 2006). Children and adolescents with disabilities are less likely than their peers without disabilities to engage in developmentally appropriate social endeavors outside of school, such as organized and informal peer group activities and dating (Nosek, Howland, Rintala, Young, & Chanpong, 2001; Pinquart & Pfeiffer, 2012). These activities create opportunities for adolescents and emerging adults to develop romantic relationships and learn helpful social skills, such as flirting (Shuttleworth, 2000; Wiegerink, Roebroeck, Van Der Slot, Stam, & Cohen-Kettenis, 2010). In addition, people without disabilities are often reluctant or unwilling to engage in a meaningful or intimate manner with PWDs and appear to hold negative attitudes and stereotypes, especially when the disability is severe or includes cognitive or psychiatric impairments (Miller et al., 2009).

Women with disabilities are much more likely to have problems finding and keeping partners than men with disabilities and women without disabilities (Gill, 1996; Howland & Rintala, 2001; Nosek et al., 2001). Gender and disability stereotypes interact in unique ways, especially when forming social judgments of women. According to traditional societal stereotypes, women with physical disabilities do not, and should not, engage in dating behavior, and they are typically considered asexual and ineligible for the attentions of those who desire a romantic relationship (Gill,1996; Howland & Rintala, 2001; Olkin, 1999). However, the type of disability matters in terms of this desire. For example, research with American undergraduates found that they viewed women with intellectual disabilities as more physically attractive than those with physical disabilities, although students felt more comfortable with the idea of interacting with the latter (Coleman, Brunell, & Haugen, 2015). However, students' attitudes did not differ when judging men with the same two types of disabilities. In addition, culture matters in terms of the perceiver; there is evidence that emerging adult American women have fewer stereotypes of PWDs than do American men and Asian men and women. In a study of male and female undergraduates in the U.S., Taiwan, and Singapore, American women showed the most favorable attitudes toward people with disabilities in the context of dating and marriage (Chen, Brodwin, Cardoso, & Chan, 2002).

One way that both men and women with disabilities may escape such stigma is to use the internet. Online dating, particularly in developed countries, currently accounts for a substantial proportion of the initiation of romantic relationships. Recent data by Pew Internet indicates that 27% of 18-24-year-olds in the U.S. have used online dating (Smith, 2016). Over half (57%) of Pew's respondents ages 18-24 knew someone who had used online dating sites or mobile dating apps, and 34% of them knew someone who had entered into a long-term relationship or marriage in which they had met their partner online. Furthermore, a majority of adult online daters considered the online dating experience to be positive; specifically, they agreed that online dating is a good way to meet people, helps people find a better match for themselves, and is easier and more efficient than other ways of dating.

There are many examples of how individuals with disabilities use the internet for social interaction and support. For example, online support groups offer social interaction for groups of PWDs, typically consisting of discussion forums specifically for the individual with the disability and/or their families and friends (Gozza-Cohen & May, 2012). For PWDs who are unable to leave home, have limited access to others with the same or similar disability, are challenged by learning disabilities, or who live in more rural areas, these online sites can provide emotional support and assist with building relationships with people with similar concerns and interests (Gozza-Cohen & May, 2012, Homes & O'Loughlin, 2012).

Little is known about emerging adults with disabilities' internet use for romance. Because research indicates that almost all (97%) of 18 to 29-year-olds in the U.S. report using the internet (Anderson & Perrin, 2015), PWDs in this age group are likely to use social media sites that are popular with their peers, such as Facebook, Instagram, and Snapchat (Lenhart, 2015). For example, a study of adolescents in the Netherlands found that access to and use of the internet is similar between physically disabled and nondisabled adolescents (Lathouwers, de Moor, & Didden, 2009). A qualitative study in Sweden also indicated that young adults with intellectual disabilities use the internet in similar ways as their peers, mainly for social and romantic reasons (Lofgren-Martenson, 2008).

The objective of this chapter is to draw on the accumulated scientific literature on emerging adults' personal relationships, internet interactions, and online dating to consider how online dating might be similar or different for PWDs during emerging adulthood as compared to their peers without disabilities. Because there are only a handful of studies that directly address the topic of online dating for PWDs, and even fewer that include emerging adults, the author will often extrapolate from related topics to examine how internet dating is likely to affect the process and outcomes relevant to the romantic relationships of PWDs. This literature spans multiple research domains such as clinical psychology, developmental psychology, social psychology, personality psychology, rehabilitation, sociology, communications, medicine, and computer and information studies. The chapter will culminate with an analysis of daters' progression through the nine steps of online dating.

BACKGROUND

A unique component of internet interactions for emerging adults is that it allows them to play with their public persona, an important aspect of identity exploration while engaging with others (Mazur & Kozarian, 2010). More specifically, research suggests that such social interactions can be considered to a large extent as conscientious public performance (Bargh, McKenna, & Fitzsimons, 2002, Mazur & Kozarian, 2010). Given this conscientious public performance, emerging adults with physical disabilities have the opportunity to not reveal their disability (Gozza-Cohen & May, 2012). The few empirical studies suggest that on the internet young people with disabilities find themselves caught in a bind between concealment and disclosure, even though their disability is a natural part of their everyday lives (Soderstrom, 2013).

These issues of identity and representation of self come to the fore with online dating. A number of PWDs have explained how they can be strategic in the way they present themselves and interact on Internet dating sites (Goodman, 2012; Heideman, 2014; Sykes, 2014). Results from research on this topic are similar; for example, most of the Swedish adults ages 18 to 31 years that Lofgren-Martenson (2008) interviewed reported that they presented themselves in cyberspace, typically on a popular virtual meeting-place called LunarStorm, without mentioning their intellectual disability. Many participants explained that they wanted to meet friends and partners without intellectual disabilities. Thus, they informed others only about their age, interests, and purpose for using the Internet.

Online dating offers other benefits in terms of finding romantic relationships for PWDs. One advantage is that online dating provides access to a wider network of potential partners who would have been previously unknown or inaccessible to PWDs; individuals do not need to leave home to find a potential date (Finkel, Eastwick, Karney, Reis, & Sprecher, 2012; Roth & Gillis, 2015). Furthermore, dating sites provide convenient computer-mediated communication as a way to learn about potential partners. However, these considerable advantages are mitigated somewhat by the strategy of introducing users to potential partners through profiles, which according to Levitin (2014) and Finkel and his colleagues (2012), typically fail to capture the essence of a person.

THE NINE STEPS OF ONLINE DATING: CHALLENGES AND DIFFERNCES FOR PWDS

For people with disabilities, dating is Mount Everest. (Olkin, 1999, p. 223)

In their seminal analysis of online dating, Finkel and his colleagues (2012) delineated a nine-step process of online dating. The remainder of the chapter will discuss in turn how these nine steps might differ for or challenge PWDs during emerging adulthood, including relevant research and media examples as available.

Seeking Information about One or More Dating Sites

The two strongest predictors of American adults engaging in online dating, being an Internet user and being single (Finkel et al., 2012), are likely to be as true of PWDs as people without disabilities; online daters typically have difficulty locating potential romantic partners (Finkel et al., 2012). According to personality research, people who are more sensitive to rejection are more likely to use online dating sites than those who are less sensitive (Blackhart, Fitzpatrick, & Williamson, 2014). As the research about disability suggests, this vulnerability is likely to be grounded in reality for PWDs, especially for women (Coleman et al., 2014; Gill, 1996; Rintala et al., 1997)

In terms of garnering information, a British survey of internet daters ages 16 and older found that the most frequently mentioned sources of information about online dating were advertising seen on the internet and visiting an online dating website (Gunter, 2007). Users of online dating websites, especially women, were most likely to have considered using such services following a personal recommendation. For example, one 26-year-old British man explained in a news article, "I had felt a bit snobby about internet dating but some friends had tried it, so it felt less intimidating" (Urquhart & Fraser-Thoms, 2012, p. 11). Because research is lacking, one can only surmise that disability-only dating sites are promoted primarily by word of mouth rather than by mass advertising.

Registering for Dating Sites

There is little research available that has studied the decisions of emerging adults to choose one specific dating site over another. The general site Plenty of Fish (POF), which claims "more dates, more relationships, more visits than any other dating site," suggests that adults will choose dating sites that their friends have used successfully when it asserts that the site visitor will "know of at least 1 person that has found someone on POF" (Plentyoffishmedia, 2015, para. 1). In Gunter's (2007) study of British dating site users of all ages, choice of dating service was influenced by cost, quality of contacts, and the potential number and variety of contacts a site may be able to supply. For women, the site's reputation and the preservation of anonymity were also particularly important.

The consideration for PWDs is whether to register for large, popular dating sites, such as OkCupid, Match.com, eHarmony, and Plenty Of Fish (POF), that include mostly people without disabilities, or to register with smaller free or low-cost websites that are aimed specifically at heterosexual and homosexual PWDs with a variety of disabilities. For example, the sites Whispers4u and Dating 4 Disabled target people with physical and mobility-related disabilities. In addition to targeting people with physical and mobility-related disabilities, Disabled Passions includes daters with chronic health conditions and depression. Other specialty sites include NoLongerLonely for adults with mental illness, POZ Personals for people who are H.I.V. positive, Deaf Singles Connection, and Prescription4Love, which is dedicated to individuals with a variety of physical and mental health conditions, including sexually transmitted diseases and those "that don't conjure images of romance and intimacy, like diabetes and Parkinson's disease" (Barrow, 2010, para. 14).

The major advantage of such specialized sites is the commonality of disability. As one man with H.I.V. explained, "Getting to know someone in an online community of people with H.I.V. allows relationships to form without the burden of the big reveal hovering overhead. Here everyone knows you have H.I.V., so it gets the barrier out of the way" (Barrow, 2010, paras. 12-13). However, other online users with disabilities believe that dating sites targeting different disabilities are limiting. Writing for *The Daily Beast*, Heideman (2014) noted that the women she interviewed believed that their disability should not restrict them to a smaller dating pool of only people with disabilities.

Finkel and his colleagues (2012) proposed that users choose a particular dating site after conducting a cost/benefit analysis. For example, a user might ask himself or herself, "Do the benefits, such as efficiency, access to attractive potential partners, and the possibility of forming strong relationships outweigh the costs, money, time, and the potential awkwardness of having one's dating profile available to strangers"

(p. 15)? It is unclear whether this type of cost/benefit analysis occurs among emerging adults with disabilities. Furthermore, this cost/benefit analysis might be impacted by other variables, such as gender, type of disability, and time since acquiring the disability. Gill (1996) suggests that heterosexual women with disabilities are often open to the idea of partnering with a PWD but that men with disabilities are often more interested in finding a partner without a disability. In one study, Olkin (1999) suggested that daters with early-acquired disabilities may have a fear of rejection based on real experiences with rejection in childhood, particularly during adolescence. Thus, while most emerging adults with disabilities will seek out dating opportunities, the choice of dating site appears much more fraught than it is for their peers without disabilities (Schover & Jensen, 1988).

Strategically Creating a Profile and, Possibly, Completing a Matching Questionnaire

Strategic presentation is a challenging issue for many online daters, of whom 22% have asked someone else to help them create or review their profile (Smith & Anderson, 2016). Women are especially likely to enlist a friend in helping them craft the perfect profile. In particular, 30% of female online daters have asked a friend for help when creating a profile as compared to 16% of men (Smith & Anderson, 2016). Whitty (2008) found that crafting an attractive profile is considered important by nearly all online daters and that the physical image was more important than any other characteristic.

Research with people without obvious disabilities suggests that the information that online users present tends not to be entirely truthful, partly because people of all ages, consciously or not, typically engage in strategic self-presentation when constructing their profiles (Finkel et al., 2012). On an online Australian dating site, adults without obvious physical disabilities most commonly misrepresented themselves in terms of their physical appearance; this is the characteristic that daters most highly value in their potential partners (Whitty, 2008). Online dating sites that offer matching, such as EHarmony and Match.com, require users to complete extensive questionnaires that potential partners cannot view. One's answers can be crucial because such sites only allow users to view profiles of potential partners whom the algorithm declares, based on the responses, to be a match (Finkel et al., 2012). Online users' motivation for strategic presentation while completing these questionnaires is likely to be as strong as their desire to represent themselves well in their profiles.

The stakes for creating a "perfect" profile or questionnaire are likely to be high for PWDs, who are aware that people without disabilities tend to be socially uncomfortable around them. Americans often associate disability with charity campaigns, poster children, and telethons that depict people with disabilities as objects of pity. As Jaeger (2012) explains, "It is a rare person with an obvious disability whose personal interactions with new acquaintances aren't dictated by the expectations of being viewed as a pathetic wretch burdened by the disability, or an amazing overachiever who can serve as an inspiring story" (p. 150). Saltes (2013), who queried 108 former and current disabled users of online dating sites ages 18 to 75, found that users' anticipation of rejection carried over from the offline environment into the online dating environment. However, participants explained that profile information about impairment could be balanced with other information, such as interests, activities, educational background, and desired personal traits in a partner.

An online dater's profile construction need not be a static process. Whitty (2007) found that online daters experiment with self-descriptions and photos to increase their success at attracting others to their profile as did Sykes (2014), who described his own online dating experience. He noted that after adding disability status to his Match.com profile, he received as much online attention as before the update, yet felt more secure in the knowledge that people were interested in him despite his disability. It appears that constructing an online dating profile is, at least in part, an exercise in self-identity through the perception of potential partners' opinions.

Browsing Others' User Profiles

Research on mate preferences in online dating has found that dating site users prefer partners who are similar to them on numerous attributes (Hitsch, Hortacsu, & Ariely, 2010). These variables include education level, ethnicity, race, religion, marital status, political views, smoking habits, the presence or absence of children, and the desire for a long term relationship. Women show a stronger preference than men for income relative to physical attributes, such as facial attractiveness, height, and body mass index, and they are less willing to date someone of a different race (Hitsch et al., 2010; Hwang, 2013; Whitty, 2008). There is little research about whether such preferences would differ for emerging adults with disabilities. In one study that addressed this topic, Pinquart and Pfeiffer (2012) found that German adolescents with visual impairments were less likely than their sighted peers to consider physical attractiveness and material resources when seeking a partner on an online dating site. Rather, they were more likely to consider emotional maturity as important for partner selection.

The concern for PWDs who use dating sites is likely to relate to being accepting of those with different disabilities than their own as well as evaluating others' profiles for likely acceptance of their disabilities. The anonymity of the internet allows online users to be honest about what traits they are truly seeking in a partner. According to Barrow (2010), many of the almost 12,000 members of Dating 4 Disabled specify the types of disabilities they would accept when seeking a long-term relationship. Barrow (2010) quotes the head of member services, "Like anyone else, people with disabilities have different preferences. Someone with good mobility may prefer someone also mobile, others don't limit at all" (para. 19.).

People tend to be comfortable with the disability that they know (Wright, 1983); thus, emerging adults with mobility limitations might fear reactions from potential partners with cognitive or sensory disabilities, or might stereotype people with those disabilities in a way similar to daters without disabilities. Dunn (2015) summarized the research on this topic, revealing that attitudes of individuals without disabilities become increasingly negative as one moves on the continuum from physical to cognitive and mental health-related disabilities as well as the presence of other factors, such as the disability's perceived severity, visibility, contagiousness, and unpredictability. U.S. college students who were uncertain whether they would date a person who stutters reported that they would base their decision partly on the prospective partner's level of stuttering severity, in addition to personality, appearance, and intelligence (Mayo & Mayo, 2013). Unfortunately, there is no research that specifically studies the variables that attracts PWDs to view certain online profiles and not others.

Initiating Contact through the Dating Site

As in traditional dating, online users' decisions regarding whether to contact potential partners are not random; users are especially likely to initiate contact with people who appear physically attractive or even more physically attractive than they, have similar interests and values as them, and are similar in age and educational attainment (Finkel et al., 2012; Kreager, Cavanaugh, Yen, & Yu, 2014; Whitty,

2008). However, this last variable of educational attainment may be complicated for PWDs. High school graduation and four-year college attendance and graduation rates are lower for emerging adults with disabilities when compared to emerging adults without disabilities (Newman et al., 2011; Yettick & Lloyd, 2015). These rates also vary among those emerging adults with different disabilities. Eight years after high school, emerging adults with visual and hearing impairments were more likely to have attended college or university than those with emotional disturbances, ASD, other health impairments, multiple disabilities, or mental retardation (Newman et al., 2011).

Some online daters with disabilities may decline to initiate any contact with people with disabilities, viewing their decision as refusing to "settle" (Nemeth, 2000). Olkin (1999) argues that a PWD's decision to date a person with or without a disability can represent either self-acceptance or self-loathing. Similar to the decision to register for a large, popular dating site or a smaller disability-focused one, "neither choice is inherently right or wrong or better or worse" (p. 225), although Olkin believes that the decision is likely to be grounded in the dater's self-esteem.

Receiving Contact through the Dating Site

According to the large online dating site OkCupid, female users are more likely to get responses to their first contacts (40% chance) than are males (25% chance), and half of those responses are sent to women within 7 hours after the initial message (May, 2013). Neither women or men appear to have difficultly ignoring requests from less desirable suitors (Yeager et al., 2014). Unlike people without disabilities, PWDs experience a challenge to their self-concept if "disability trolls" reply to their profiles. Daters with obvious disabilities often sift through "the literally hundreds of messages … from people who… simply want to know how exactly you're 'broken' and whether or not you can still have sex" (Heideman, 2014, para 7). After continually fielding such questions, users with visible disabilities "begin to feel like the people online are dating your wheelchair, rather than dating you" (paras. 7-8)." In Saltes' (2013) study, female PWDs discussed the challenge of "devotees," people who are specifically interested in and sexually aroused by PWDs. Men with disabilities did not report such experiences. According to Solvang (2007), some women with amputations dismiss devotees, whereas others welcome the sexual way in which their bodies are desired. The internet provides a relatively easy opportunity for devotees to connect with PWDs, especially those who use disability dating web sites. For emerging adults who may just be learning how to get people to see them as people rather than as their disabilities, comments from disability trolls might have a profound effect on their online and offline dating experiences (Heideman, 2014). It may be enlightening, however, for some PWDs to see the myth that able-bodied daters will never find PWDs desirable as romantic and sexual partners demolished. Yet, some emerging adults with disabilities may feel suspicious of people without disabilities who desire to initiate a romantic relationship with them (Nemeth, 2000). Some of that prejudice may be based on experience or may occur because of the internalized stigma that something must be wrong with a person without disability who voluntarily desires to be with a person with a disability (Dunn, 2015; Nemeth, 2000).

Engaging in Mutual Mediated Communication

There is only about a 30% chance that a reply to a first message will turn into an actual conversation (May, 2013). An actual conversation is defined as a correspondence that lasts for at least three exchanges. Once a conversation begins, the internet facilitates disclosure and may be especially helpful for those people who are socially anxious, shy, or lack social skills (McKenna, Green, & Gleason, 2002). Users are more likely to feel that they can better express their real selves. Research has found that people are likely to disclose more information about themselves online than when face-to-face (Bargh et al., 2002; Joinson, 2001). Because of the reciprocity norm surrounding self-disclosure, online daters who consciously disclose more about themselves may enable "deal breakers" for themselves and for their potential dating partners to surface before the first face-to-face meeting (Gibbs, Ellison, & Heino, 2006). Saltes (2013) argues that online dating may enable a level of interaction with others that is more difficult offline for some PWDs. In particular, the privacy and asynchronous online interactions enable PWDs to communicate more effectively and feel more at ease and comfortable disclosing their impairment. However, online interactions are not always as efficient and effective as offline interactions. In particular, online conversations can be a fertile source of misunderstandings and insults, intentional or not (Seymour & Lupton, 2004).

The process of mutual mediated communication may differ depending on the type of disability. For example, people with intellectual disabilities, those who display speech difficulties, and those with visual impairment may have an easier time writing texts and emails with voice-recognition software, spelling with software spelling and grammar assistance, and communicating orally with text-to-speech software (Lofgren-Martenson, 2008), although the latter might disconcert people without similar disabilities. Screen readers may assist people with reading disabilities, intellectual disabilities, or visual impairments to listen aurally to content on the dating website and in their received emails and messages.

Yet these new technologies, however advantageous, may limit the online dating opportunities of PWDs if they are too expensive or are inaccessible (Schur et al., 2013). For multiple practical reasons, such as unreliable technology and lack of technical support and training, individuals with disabilities often do not use or discontinue using assistive technology (Alper & Raharinirina, 2006; Bowker, 2010; Reiss & Wacher, 2000). They also may resist use for psychological reasons, viewing assistive devices, such as hearing aids and speech synthesizers, as markers of dependency and stigmatization (Blood, 1997; Ravneberg, 2012). The mere presence of a hearing aid triggers negative social reactions in oneself and in others (Blood, 1997; Blood, Blood, & Danhauer, 1978). Thus, while utilizing assistive technology may allow a person with speech and language disabilities to communicate online with other daters, accessing and acknowledging the use of an assistive device can be large psychological steps for many PWDs. Also, due to likely experience with stigma, PWDS are typically aware that assistive technology may produce prejudicial reactions from potential daters as well as curiosity and embarrassment.

Meeting Face-to-Face

One-third of adult online daters in the U.S. have never progressed to the date stage (Smith & Anderson, 2016). Most of the Australian online daters that Whitty (2008) interviewed claimed that the first face-to-face meeting was the true beginning of the screening out process. However, the first offline meeting may be especially complicated for those with mobility challenges, disfigurement issues, and stigmatized illnesses, such as bowel disease, who do not disclose their disability in their profiles or online communications. For example, Mathias and Harcourt (2014) described how women ages 18 to 29 with below-knee amputation preferred potential partners to be aware of their prosthesis from the outset, helping to reduce anxiety about how and when to "reveal" it. On the other hand, other online daters may conceal disability as long as possible; as one media informant explained about his nondisclosing brother who suffered from Crohn's disease: "He was a good-looking boy. But when do you tell a girl that you have a colostomy bag? The first date? The third? There's no good time" (Barrow, 2010, para. 15). Adolescents between the ages of 13 and 20 with a variety of visible differences, such as cleft lip and skin conditions, worried about what partners might think of their difference, but only if they were concerned about their appearance; adolescents who valued other aspects of their selves besides physical attractiveness displayed more confidence in their ability to attract a partner (Griffiths, Willamson, & Rumsey, 2011).

Emerging adults with disabilities who have communication problems, such as hearing or oral speech limitations, are likely to find it more difficult to meet a potential dating partner in person than those without communication problems, and they are less satisfied with dating overall (Nosek et al., 2001). Rintala and her colleagues (1997) found that communication problems often interact with low self-esteem. A person with low self-esteem may be unable to effectively communicate interest in a potential dating partner or to maintain a relationship through clearly understood communication (Nosek et al., 2001).

The first date is likely to be awkward for most emerging adults, but having to figure out clear pathways for communication and physical accessibility can be additional stressors. There is little research on deaf-hearing adult relationships. In one study, McIntosh (1999) found that hearing people welcome a hearing-impaired person who speaks, but experience discomfort in most deaf-hearing interactions. Allard and Williams (2008) revealed college students' negative stereotypes about the self-esteem, intelligence, and employability of individuals with speech and language disorders, such as stuttering and poor articulation. Furthermore, people who stutter view their stuttering as an obstacle to forming relationships that often makes it difficult for them to talk to potential romantic partners (Mayo & Mayo, 2013). Similarly, Shuttleworth (2000) found that men with cerebral palsy and speech impairments often perceive communication as a barrier to developing intimacy, but may employ nonverbal strategies such as making "puppy dog eyes" and giving back rubs, even with ones' feet. People who are visually impaired yet skilled oral communicators report frequently interacting with fully sighted people who display unease or confusion. Smith and Kandath (1999) provide multiple examples of sighted people's inappropriate responses, such as speaking too loudly or not treating the visually impaired person as an adult peer. For daters with mobility challenges, meeting in public can be complicated by accessibility issues, such as steps into a building or bathroom, or whether or how easily a wheelchair, power chair, or scooter will fit into a car or public transportation. Olkin (1999) explains that people with disabilities need a unique skill for social interactions, that of getting others to view them as people, not as disabilities and, thus, how to comfortably present their disability to others. Emerging adults' feelings of ease with their disability will set the tone for the potential dating relationship much more than the extent of their disability (Olkin, 1999).

Developing an Offline Relationship by Proceeding to a Second Date and/or Removing Their Online Dating Profile

Having a physical disability may present challenges at the start of a relationship. As Elizabeth, a 23-year-old female amputee explained, "I need someone who won't be weird about my scars, who will carry my purse if I'm on crutches, who doesn't mind when I ask him to get me stuff because I already took my leg off" (Mathias & Harcourt, 2014, p. 398). In addition, for some emerging adults with physical and intellectual disabilities there may be issues that they might need to discuss sooner than is typical for their peers without disabilities, such as independent living, pregnancy, childbirth, and raising children. For example, Elizabeth clarifies that the qualities she is looking for in her ideal partner include "considering the long-term, like the fact that I might be physically dependent earlier in life, childbirth, raising a child, things like that" (p. 398). According to Nemeth (2000), couples with at least one partner with a disability must understand that they have disability-related "baggage" before they can negotiate relationships that work. Part of this negotiation can include a redefinition of or a complete rejection of traditional gender roles and attitudinal shifts in definitions of acceptable and fulfilling sex.

Gill (1996) describes how stigma contagion and the fear of gender and disability stereotypes are powerful variables when women with disabilities try to establish romantic relationships. Partners without disabilities commonly report that strangers treat them differently because of their relationship with a PWD. Olkin (1999) notes that a commonly held belief is that no able-bodied person will find a PWD desirable as a sex partner, and if they do, it is because there is either something wrong with the nondisabled partner or they are "settling"; thus, the partner without disability is often seen as either a loser or a saint (Smart, 2011). It may be difficult for individuals without a disability to cope with such prejudice, especially if there are other online dating profiles waiting to be considered. As with traditional offline dating, a romantic relationship can proceed for a long time, only to founder when the issue of long-term commitments, such as marriage or starting a family, forces the partner of a PWD to reassess his or her desires for a particular life partner (Gil, 1996). At the same time, most PWDs state that people without disabilities typically ascribe far more importance and limitations to their disability than they do (Smart, 2000).

Research with online daters has found that success in finding a partner may be partially a "numbers game" of multiple first dates, as reported by many of the interview participants in Gibbs' and her colleagues' (2006) survey of heterosexual Match.com members in the U.S. Romantic success, the researchers suggest, also requires the cognitive ability to reflect and learn from one's encounters, which people with intellectual disabilities might find difficult. Because they are less likely than their peers to be experienced daters, emerging adults with other disabilities whose relationships founder also may find it challenging to process the termination (Howland & Rintala, 2001). PWDs commonly feel angry and helpless in reaction to the real and perceived pervasive rejection and discrimination of dating situations (Olkin, 1999). They may not know whether their lack of success was due to their specific impairment, a more general disability stigma, or for the same reasons that relationships end for emerging adults without disabilities. It is likely that some PWDS, similar to daters without disabilities, will develop a committed relationship with someone they have met online. Other emerging adults with disabilities may become discouraged if they perceive fewer dating opportunities than their nondisabled peers, especially in an online environment with "plenty of fish."

FUTURE RESEARCH DIRECTIONS

Online dating is much more culturally acceptable than it was a decade ago (Smith & Anderson, 2016). Yet, despite the preponderance of online dating sites and, more recently, mobile dating apps, which are particularly popular among American emerging adults, most marriages and committed relationships still begin offline. Only 12% of Americans who have been with their spouse or partners for 5 years or less, the ones most likely to have used online services, report that they met their partner with the help of an internet dating site (Smith & Anderson, 2016). There is no frequency of use information for PWDs to guide them or comparisons of success for emerging adults between the large internet sites, like Match.com, and the smaller specialty disability dating sites, between men and women with disabilities, or between heterosexual and homosexual users of online sites. There is no research to support recommendations about the best time or manner to disclose one's disability during the process of online dating and the ramifications for long-term success. In fact, as is likely evident throughout the chapter, there has been little research published about online dating for PWDs and even less that includes more than a few emerging adults.

Emerging adults appear to be migrating to mobile phone apps for online dating, such as Tinder, and those begun by traditional dating sites such as Match.com, eHarmony, and OkCupid (Smith & Anderson, 2016). As the president of Match.com in North America reveals, Tinder "opened up this young demographic – 18- to -25-year-olds – that no product could open up before" (Wood, 2015, p. B8). Because Tinder profiles are significantly shorter and photos are more emphasized (Wood, 2015), the implications for PWDs are likely to be complicated. Apps like Tinder facilitate more frequent meetings with nearby daters as compared to traditional dating websites because they discourage communication via a laptop screen and encourage face-to-face interaction. For a PWD, there is likely much worrying over construction of the brief dating profiles, less time spent profile browsing, and quicker disclosure of disability, either through the profile photos or during the in-person meeting. Thus, dating apps like Tinder might challenge the dating prospects of emerging adults with disabilities by elevating the importance of their physical appearance and presence of visible disabilities as early as the first meeting over their personality attributes and common interests. This is a fertile area for new research.

CONCLUSION

Online dating has the potential to improve what is an often frustrating activity for PWDs: the pursuit of a committed, emotionally satisfying romantic relationship during one's emerging adulthood. Online dating provides the opportunity to communicate with multiple potential partners conveniently and efficiently, an appealing alternative to relying on more traditional ways of seeking romantic relationships. Online communication also allows users to "meet" without an initial focus on disability. However, there are many online dating challenges for PWDs. Some of these challenges are similar to those for people without disabilities, such as the creation of attractive profiles. Some are unique, such as the question of when and how to disclose one's disability. Some challenges may differ depending on the type of disabilities one experiences. Despite these complexities, online dating, with its opportunity to interact with multiple interested daters, appears to offer emerging adults with disabilities a positive venue for relationship development.

REFERENCES

Allard, E. R., & Willimas, D. F. (2008). Listeners perceptions of speech and language disorders. *Journal of Communication Disorders*, *41*(2), 108–123. doi:10.1016/j.jcomdis.2007.05.002 PMID:17586521

Alper, S., & Raharinirina, S. (2006). Assistive technology for individuals with disabilities: A review and synthesis of the literature. *Journal of Special Education Technology*, *21*, 47–64.

Anderson, M., & Perrin, A. (2015, July 28). *15% of Americans don't use the internet. Who are they?* Pew Research Center's Internet & American Life Project. Retrieved from http://www.pewresearch.org/fact- tank/2015/07/28/15-of-americans-dont-use-the-internet-who-are-they/

Bargh, J. A., McKenna, K. Y. A., & Fitzsimons, G. M. (2002). Can you see the real me? Activation and expression of the true self on the Internet. *The Journal of Social Issues*, *58*(1), 33–48. doi:10.1111/1540-4560.00247

Barrow, K. (2010, December 27). Difference is the norm on these dating sites. *The New York Times*. Retrieved from http://www.nytimes.com

Blackhart, G. C., Fitzpatrick, J., & Williamson, J. (2014). Dispositional factors predicting use of online dating sites and behaviors related to online dating. *Computers in Human Behavior*, *33*, 113–118. doi:10.1016/j.chb.2014.01.022

Blood, G. W., Blood, I. M., & Danhauer, J. L. (1978). Listeners impressions of normal-hearing and hearing-impaired children. *Journal of Communication Disorders*, *11*(6), 513–518. doi:10.1016/0021-9924(78)90025-4 PMID:739066

Blood, I. M. (1997). The hearing aid effect: Challenges for counseling. *Journal of Rehabilitation*, *63*, 59–62.

Bowker, N. I. (2010). Understanding barriers to online experience for people with physical and sensory disabilities using discursive social psychology. *Universal Access in the Information Society*, *9*(2), 121–136. doi:10.1007/s10209-009-0162-3

Braithwaite, S. R., Delevi, R., & Fincham, F. D. (2010). Romantic relationships and the physical and mental health of college students. *Personal Relationships*, *17*(1), 1–12. doi:10.1111/j.1475-6811.2010.01248.x

Brault, M. W. (2012, July). *Americans with disabilities: 2010. Current Population Reports*. Retrieved from http://www.census.gov/prod/2012pubs/p70- 131.pdf

Chen, R. K., Brodwin, M. G., Cardoso, E., & Chan, F. (2002). Attitudes toward people with disabilities in the social context of dating and marriage: A comparison of American, Taiwanese, and Singaporean college students. *Journal of Rehabilitation*, *68*, 5–11.

Coleman, J. M., Brunell, A. B., & Haugen, I. M. (2015). Multiple forms of prejudice: How gender and disability stereotypes influence judgments of disabled men and women. *Current Psychology (New Brunswick, N.J.)*, *34*(1), 177–189. doi:10.1007/s12144-014-9250-5

Dunn, D. (2015). *The social psychology of disability*. New York: Oxford University Press.

Finkel, E. J., Eastwick, P. W., Karney, B. R., Reis, H. T., & Sprecher, S. (2012). Online dating: A critical analysis from the perspective of psychological science. *Psychological Science in the Public Interest*, *13*(1), 3–66. doi:10.1177/1529100612436522 PMID:26173279

Fox, S. (2011, January 21). *Americans living with disability and their technology profile*. Pew Research Center's Internet & American Life Project. Retrieved from http://pewinternet.org/Reports/2011/Disability.aspx

Gibbs, J. L., Ellison, N. B., & Heino, R. D. (2006). Self-presentation in online personals: The role of anticipated future interaction, self-disclosure, and perceived success in internet dating. *Communication Research*, *33*(2), 152–177. doi:10.1177/0093650205285368

Gill, C. J. (1996). Dating and relationship issues. *Sexuality and Disability*, *14*(3), 183–190. doi:10.1007/BF02590076

Giordano, P. C., Longmore, M. A., Schroeder, R. D., & Seffrin, P. M. (2008). A life-course perspective on spirituality and desistance from crime. *Criminology*, *46*(1), 99–132. doi:10.1111/j.1745-9125.2008.00104.x

Goodman, S. (2012, March 22). Online dating with a disability. *The Guardian*. Retrieved from http://www.theguardian.com/lifeandstyle/2012/mar/22/online-dating-with-disability

Gozza-Cohen, M., & May, D. (2012). Individuals with disabilities and internet use. In Z. Yan (Ed.), *Encyclopedia of Cyber Behavior* (pp. 242–258). Hershey, PA: IGI Global. doi:10.4018/978-1-4666-0315-8.ch021

Gunter, B. (2007). Internet dating: a British survey. *Aslib Proceedings: New Information perspectives, 60*, 88-98.

Heideman, E. (2014, August 1). Disabled woman tackles the dating site trolls. *The Daily Beast*. Retrieved from http://www.thedailybeast.com/articles/2014/08/01/dropping-the-d-bomb- online-dating-with-a-disability.html

Hitsch, G. J., Hortacsu, A., & Ariely, D. (2010). What makes you click? – Mate preferences in online dating. *Quantitative Marketing and Economics*, *8*(4), 393–427. doi:10.1007/s11129-010-9088-6

Holmes, K. M., & O'Loughlin, N. (2012). The experience of people with learning disabilities on social networking sites. *British Journal of Learning Disabilities*, *42*, 3–7.

Holt-Lunstad, J., Smith, T. B., & Layton, J. B. (2010). Social relationships and mortality risk: A meta-analytic review. *PLoS Medicine*, *7*(7), 1–20. doi:10.1371/journal.pmed.1000316 PMID:20668659

Howland, C. A., & Rintala, D. H. (2001). Dating behaviors of women with physical disabilities. *Sexuality and Disability*, *19*(1), 41–70. doi:10.1023/A:1010768804747

Hwang, W. (2013). Who are people willing to date? Ethnic and gender patterns in online dating. *Race and Social Problems*, *5*(1), 28–40. doi:10.1007/s12552-012-9082-6

Jaeger, P. T. (2012). *Disability and the internet: Confronting a digital divide*. Boulder, CO: Lynne Rienner Publishers.

Joinson, A. N. (2001). Self-disclosure in computer-mediated communication: The role of self-awareness and visual anonymity. *European Journal of Social Psychology*, *31*(2), 170–192. doi:10.1002/ejsp.36

Kreager, D. A., Cavanagh, S. E., Yen, J., & Yu, M. (2014). Where have all the good men gone? Gendered interactions in online dating. *Journal of Marriage and the Family*, *76*(2), 387–410. doi:10.1111/jomf.12072 PMID:24910472

Lathouwers, K., de Moor, J., & Didden, R. (2009). Access to and use of Internet by adolescents who have a physical disability: A comparative study. *Research in Developmental Disabilities*, *30*(4), 702–711. doi:10.1016/j.ridd.2008.09.003 PMID:19022618

Lenhart, A. (2015, April 9). *Teen, social media and technology overview 2015*. Pew Research Center. Retrieved from http://www.pewinternet.org/files/2015/04/PI_TeensandTech_Update2015_0409151.pdf

Levitin, D. J. (2014). *The Organized Mind.* New York: Penguin Random House.

Limoncin, E., Carta, R., Gravina, G. L., Carosa, E., Ciocca, G., Di Sante, S., & Jannini, E. A. et al. (2014). The sex.ual attraction toward disabilities: A preliminary internet- based study. *International Journal of Impotence Research, 26*(2), 51–54. doi:10.1038/ijir.2013.34 PMID:24048013

Lofgren-Martenson, L. (2008). Love in cyberspace: Swedish young people with intellectual disabilities and the internet. *Scandinavian Journal of Disability Research, 10*(2), 125–138. doi:10.1080/15017410701758005

MacInnes, M. (2011). Altar-bound? The effect of disability on the hazard of entry into a first marriage. *International Journal of Sociology, 41*(1), 87–103. doi:10.2753/IJS0020-7659410105 PMID:23946548

Mathias, Z., & Harcourt, D. (2014). Dating and intimate relationships of women with below-knee amputation: An exploratory study. *Disability and Rehabilitation, 36*(5), 395–402. doi:10.3109/09638288.2013.797509 PMID:23721496

May, K. T. (2013, February 14). *7 things we learned about online dating from the co-founder of OKCupid* [blog post]. Retrieved from http://blog.ted.com/7- things-we-learned-about-online-dating-from-the-co-founder-of-okcupid/

Mayo, R., & Mayo, C. M. (2013). College students' perspectives on dating a person who stutters. *College Student Journal, 47*, 169–177.

Mazur, E., & Kozarian, L. (2010). Self-presentation and interaction in blogs of adolescents and young emerging adults. *Journal of Adolescent Research, 25*(1), 124–144. doi:10.1177/0743558409350498

McDonald, S. M. (2010, July 26). *As ADA turns 20, Harris interactive survey finds lifestyle and economic gaps still remain between Americans with and without disabilities.* The Kessler Foundation. Retrieved from http://www.2010disabilitysurveys.org/

McIntosh, A. (1999). When the deaf and the hearing interact: Communication features, relationship, and disability issues. In D. O. Braithwaite & T. L. Thompson (Eds.), *Handbook of Communication and People with Disabilities: Research and Application* (pp. 353–368). Mahwah, NJ: Routledge.

McKenna, K. Y., Green, A. S., & Gleason, M. E. J. (2002). Relationship formation on the Internet: What's the big attraction? *The Journal of Social Issues, 58*(1), 9–31. doi:10.1111/1540-4560.00246

Miller, E., Chen, R., Glover-Graf, N. M., & Kranz, P. (2009). Willingness to engage in personal relationships with persons with disabilities. *Rehabilitation Counseling Bulletin, 52*(4), 211–224. doi:10.1177/0034355209332719

Myers, D. G. (1999). Close relationships and quality of life. In D. Kahneman, E. Diener, & N. Schwarz (Eds.), *Well-being: The foundations of hedonic psychology* (pp. 376–393). New York: Russell Sage Foundation.

Nemeth, S. A. (2000). Society, sexuality, and disabled/ablebodied romantic relationships. In D. O. Braithwaite & T. L. Thompson (Eds.), *Handbook of communication and people with disabilities* (pp. 37–48). Mahwah, NJ: Lawrence Erlbaum.

Newman, L., Wagner, M., Knokey, A. M., Marder, C., Nagle, K., Shaver, D., … Schwarting, M. (2011). *The Post-High School Outcomes of Young Adults With Disabilities up to 8 Years After High School. A Report From the National Longitudinal Transition Study-2 (NLTS2)* (NCSER 2011-3005). Menlo Park, CA: SRI International.

Nosek, M. A., Howland, B. A., Rintala, D. H., Young, M. E., & Chanpong, G. (2001). National study of women with physical disabilities: Final report. *Sexuality and Disability, 19*, 5-39.

Pfeiffer, J. P., & Pinquart, M. (2011). Attainment of developmental tasks by adolescent with visual impairments and sighted adolescents. *Journal of Visual Impairment & Blindness, 105*, 33–44.

Pinquart, M., & Pfeiffer, J. P. (2012). What is essential is invisible to the eye: Intimate relationships of adolescents with visual impairment. *Sexuality and Disability, 30*(2), 139–147. doi:10.1007/s11195-011-9248-y

Plentyoffishmedia. (2015, October 23). Retrieved from http://www.pof.com/

Ravneberg, B. (2012). Usability and abandonment of assistive technology. *Journal of Assistive Technologies, 6*(4), 259–269. doi:10.1108/17549451211285753

Riemer-Reiss, M. L., & Wacher, R. R. (2000). Factors associated with assistive technology discontinuance among individuals with disabilities. *Journal of Rehabilitation, 66*, 44–50.

Rintala, D. H., Howland, C. A., Nosek, M. A., Bennett, J. L., Young, M. E., Foley, C. C., & Chanpong, G. et al. (1997). Dating issues for women with physical disabilities. *Sexuality and Disability, 15*(4), 219–242. doi:10.1023/A:1024717313923

Roth, M. E., & Gillis, J. M. (2015). Convenience with the click of a mouse: A survey of adults with autism spectrum disorder on online dating. *Sexuality and Disability, 33*(1), 133–150. doi:10.1007/s11195-014-9392-2

Saltes, N. (2013). Disability, identity, and disclosure in the online dating environment. *Disability & Society, 28*(1), 96–109. doi:10.1080/09687599.2012.695577

Schover, L. R., & Jensen, S. B. (1988). *Sexuality and chronic illness: A comprehensive approach.* New York: Guilford.

Schur, L., Kruse, D., & Blanck, P. (2013). *People with disabilities: Sidelined or mainstreamed?* New York: Cambridge University Press. doi:10.1017/CBO9780511843693

Seymour, W., & Lupton, D. (2004). Holding the line online: Exploring wired relationships for people with disabilities. *Disability & Society, 19*(4), 291–305. doi:10.1080/09687590410001689421

Shuttleworth, R. P. (2000). The search for sexual intimacy for men with cerebral palsy. *Sexuality and Disability, 18*(4), 263–282. doi:10.1023/A:1005646327321

Smart, J. (2011). *Disability across the developmental lifespan*. New York: Springer.

Smith, A. (2016, February 11). *15% of American adults have used online dating sites or mobile dating apps.* Pew Research Center. Retrieved from http://www.pewinternet.org/2016/02/11/15-percent-of-american-adults- have-used-online-dating-sites-or-mobile-dating-apps/

Smith, A., & Anderson, M. (2016, February 29). *5 facts about online dating*. Pew Research Center. Retrieved from http://www.pewresearch.org/fact-tank/2016/02/29/5-facts-about-online- dating/

Smith, J. W., & Kandath, K. (1999). Communication and the blind or visually impaired. In D. O. Braithwaite & T. L. Thompson (Eds.), *Handbook of communication and people with disabilities: Research and application* (pp. 389–404). Mahwah, NJ: Routledge.

Soderstrom, S. (2013). Digital differentiation in young peoples internet use – eliminating or reproducing disability stereotypes. *Future Internet*, *5*(2), 190–204. doi:10.3390/fi5020190

Solvang, P. (2007). The amputee body desired: Beauty destabilized? Disability re-valued? *Sexuality and Disability*, *25*(2), 51–64. doi:10.1007/s11195-007-9036-x

Sykes, T. (2014, January 18). Online dating is hard enough. Try doing it with a disability. *The Guardian*. Retrieved from http://www.theguardian.com/commentisfree/2014/jan/18/online-dating-with-disability-match

Urquhart, C., & Frawer, E. (2012, December 30). Online dating surges as lonely hearts look to kickstart some post-Christmas romance. *The Observer*. Retrieved from http://www.theguardian.com/lifeandstyle/2012/dec/29/online-dating-christmas-romance

Whitty, M. T. (2008). Revealing the real me, searching for the actual you: Presentations of self on an internet dating site. *Computers in Human Behavior*, *24*(4), 1707–1723. doi:10.1016/j.chb.2007.07.002

Wiegerink, D., Roebroeck, M. E., Donkervoort, M., Stam, H. J., & Cohen-Kettenis, P. T. (2006). Social and sexual relationships of adolescents and young adults with cerebral palsy: A review. *Clinical Rehabilitation*, *20*(12), 1023–1031. doi:10.1177/0269215506071275 PMID:17148513

Wiegerink, D., Roebroeck, M. E., Van Der Slot, W. M., Stam, H. J., & Cohen-Kettenis, P. T. (2010). Importance of peers and dating in the development of romantic relationships and sexual activity of young adults with cerebral palsy. *Developmental Medicine and Child Neurology*, *52*(6), 576–582. doi:10.1111/j.1469-8749.2010.03620.x PMID:20187888

Wood, M. (2015, February 4). Led by Tinder, the mobile dating game surges. *The New York Times,* p. B8.

Wright, B. (1983). *Physical disability: A psychosocial approach*. New York: Harper & Row. doi:10.1037/10589-000

Yettick, H., & Lloyd, S. C. (2015, May29). Graduation rate hits high, but some groups lag. *Education Week*, *34*, 18.

KEY TERMS AND DEFINITIONS

Disabilities: An umbrella term, covering impairments, activity limitations, and participation restrictions.

Mutual Mediated Communication: Ways of communicating through and around dating sites, such as by email-like messages and instant messaging on the dating site, personal email, text messaging, webcam conversations, or speaking on the phone.

Online Dating: The use of commercial or nonprofit internet sites that provide dating services to users seeking romantic relationships.

Profile: An online user's description and summary of themselves typically including basic demographic information, behaviors and interests, description of the traits sought in a potential partner, and one or more photos of oneself.

Self-Disclosure: Confiding intimate aspects of oneself to others.

Self-Esteem: Individuals' feelings of high or low self-worth.

Self-Presentation: Behaviors that are designed to convey an image about one's self to other people.

Stigma: An attribute or identity that is perceived by others to have a broadly negative quality within a culture or situation.

Chapter 11
Influence of Social Media on Dating Relationships of Emerging Adults in Nigerian Universities:
Social Media and Dating in Nigeria

Olufemi Adeniyi Fawole
University of Ilorin, Nigeria

Olasunkanmi Adebiyi Osho
University of Ilorin, Nigeria

ABSTRACT

Social media play important roles in creating a person's sense of reality, recreating face-to-face interactions on the web by allowing people to interact either publicly of privately. Social networking sites helps in maintaining relationship with individuals who may not be closer to one; used to express romantic relationships through profile pictures or posts on social networking sites like Facebook, Twitter, Uber Social etc. This chapter focused on the influence of Facebook on communication between emerging adults in dating relationships. A total of seventy-seven participants comprising students from the University of Lagos, Nigeria aged between 19 and 29 years, took part in different focus group discussions. Data was analyzed using thematic analysis. The results revealed that majority of the dating couples spent long hours on Facebook daily and they did not feel comfortable with the hours spent on Facebook by their partner chatting with friends on a regular basis.

INTRODUCTION

Social media, such as Twitter, WhatsApp, Facebook, and the like, have grown rapidly over the years in terms of popularity. Furthermore, social media impact our lives and sometimes determine how we might react to issues and situations. Social media also shape our attitudes and values, and perceptions of others,

DOI: 10.4018/978-1-5225-1856-3.ch011

situations, places, and events. Social media have a significant influence on people and their cultural lives (Wood, 2009). Social media provide surveillance for individuals who scan local and global environments for information that helps them make decisions to live better. In addition, social media serves a socialization function, contributing to togetherness by creating commonality and helping individuals to maintain social relationships by giving them something in common. Consequently, social media are important in creating community and global communication. However, people can fully immerse themselves in social media, thereby having stimulation, relaxation, or emotional release. These feelings can be seen as a diversion function of social media. Using the mass media as a stimulant, relaxant, or release is quick, healthy escapism but when individuals perceive themselves as characters in a story and live their lives as those characters, it becomes a serious psychological disorder (Vivian, 2001).

Emerging adulthood offers more independence and freedom, unlike adolescence, and unlike adulthood, it offers less responsibility. Arnett (2000) posited a new perspective on the period widely known as late adolescence or young adulthood. He describes this stage as the period of change, in which the emerging adult is able to explore issues that emerged during adolescence, such as relationships, love, work, and general world views.

This study sought to examine the influence of social media on communication between emerging adults in dating relationship. It also attempts to determine whether emerging adults in dating relationship feel safe or comfortable sharing relationship problems with others through social media chats/post. The social networking site, Facebook, is a rapidly expanding occurrence that is changing the nature of social relationships. Personal opinion, instead of facts, as well as information described in the popular media, suggests that Facebook may be responsible for creating jealousy and suspicion in romantic relationships (Liebert, 2012). The belief has always been that communication nurtures a healthy relationship. This is commonly referred to as traditional offline communication, whereby couples in relationships maintain intimacy mainly through face-to-face interaction. However, the spread of the Internet, mobile phones, and social media has reformed the way the world communicates within social networks. Social media, in particular, make it possible for people to extend beyond two-way communication by allowing networks of people to instantly connect across the globe by exchanging personal information online (Williams, 2012). Social networking allows users to connect and interact with likeminded people. While these tools were originally developed for individual use, the aspects of information sharing and instant responsiveness of social media lend themselves well to corporate communications (CCG, Investors Relations, 2012).

Scholars, such as Elphinston and Noller (2011), Manner, Bakley, Lawrence, O'Neill and Raines (2011), and Farrugia (2013), have criticized the negative impact of social media on society, relationships, and even marriages, saying that the quality of relationships is deteriorating and the strength of social connections is weakening. Previous studies conducted with emerging adults and adolescents had focused on parenting and delinquent behaviors. Ekpo (1996) and Uwe and Obot (2000) argued that when parents fail to teach their children the necessary social skills for successful interaction in the world, they tend to develop the skills through unfavorable means.

In 2015, an online statistic site on internet users, "Statmonkey", simply put it that 93.72% of Nigerians are active users of the internet; while Facebook recently revealed that it has 16 million active users in Nigeria, a 6.3% increase from June 30, 2015. The network giant, Facebook, further revealed that 7.2 million people in Nigeria visit Facebook each day and that 97% of those access the social networking site on their mobile devices (Financial Nigeria, 2016). A poll released from Social Media Week in Lagos,

Nigeria in 2016 identified Facebook as the leading online dating platform in Nigeria with 72% of all internet users in Nigeria, followed by WhatsApp (15%), 2go (8%), and Badoo (5%). Facebook was the most used social platform used by Nigerians.

Social media or networking site users are connected in the way they develop relationships through the Internet, even though they may not have a face-to-face relationship with those connections offline (Rau, et al., 2008). Utz and Beukeboom (2011) argue that social networking sites have become part of many daily routines. Rau et al. (2008) further stated that users find value in social networking sites because these sites allow users to post about their personal life and opinions. These posts can provide validation to individuals when they receive feedback from their online friends. These authors further stated that social networking sites gratify social-emotional needs rather than informational needs, and that these sites are connected in a person-to-person manner which is more direct and interpersonal.

Farrugia (2013) stated that as relationships have branched into online environments, the components of love have new influences. Papp, Danielewicz, and Cayemberg (2012) concluded that the use of Facebook has altered the way people interact and develop relationships. They stated that people no longer disregard the potential connections between Facebook and intimate relationships, which serve as one of the most important contexts of individual growth and development. Seeing a profile picture online is comparable to seeing a person from across the room where the viewers can then decide if they are attracted to the person. Facebook allows users to add the individual as a friend, inbox message them, or 'poke' them with just a few clicks (Farrugia, 2013). Identifying factors, such as groups and interests, initiate a relationship. Depending on how much a person or their partner reveals, Marshall et al. (2012) argue that the insecurity of individuals can play a direct factor in relationship stability.

Farrugia (2013) further states that public displays of commitment mean displaying such things as liking pictures or status updates, posting pictures, or sharing inside jokes on a future partner's social meda wall. This feature allows the users to like the public display of commitment that their friends have uploaded. Liking a picture on Facebook is an interactive way to virtually indicate approval. Liking uploaded content is as simple as clicking the thumbs up button at the bottom of the picture. Furthermore, uploading photos of a significant other is a demonstration of commitment to others online. Bowe (2010) as cited in Farrugia (2013) further suggests in his study that couples found it important to reciprocate actions of posting about their relationship online, though women were more likely to express their affections online than men (Mansson & Myers, 2011; Marshall et al., 2009).

Researchers have shown several results of Facebook on interpersonal relationships, among married couples and adolescents. Valenzuela, Park and Kee (2008) concluded in their research that there were positive relationships between intensity of Facebook use, Facebook Groups use, and students' life satisfaction, social trust, and civic and political participation. Facebook gives users the platform to rediscover old friends and relationship on Facebook could lead to physical contact (Edegoh, Asemah & Ekanem, 2013).

Muise, Christofides, and Desmarais (2009) concluded that Facebook users are more prone to jealousy. They further stated that exposure to information about a romantic partner's friends and social interactions may result in an environment that enhances jealousy. Facebook creates opportunities to expose users to information about their partners that they may not have had without Facebook, which then increases their surveillance of their partner on Facebook (Muise et al., 2009). In the same vein, Elphinston and Noller (2011) found that individuals who are more highly involved with Facebook may have relationship difficulties such as jealousy and dissatisfaction; furthermore, these individuals believed that the amount of time spent on Facebook would predict jealousy. Manner, Bakley, Lawrence, O'Neill, and Raines (2011) concluded that frequency of Facebook use is positively associated with negative relationship experiences.

According to Valverde and Davis (2010), one of the major reasons why relationships fail is poor communication. This observation reinforces the central role which communication plays in any healthy relationship. Others are loss of feeling, financial problems, lack of time, sexual issues, marrying too young, loss of respect and admiration, poor boundaries with extended family, and substance and alcohol abuse. Some of these reasons account for the high mortality rate of Facebook relationships.

The ease and freedom associated with sharing information with a huge audience, with very little effort, has made social media a tool through which couples make private issues public, rekindle old flames, snoop, stalk, and retaliate against their spouses (Edmunds, 2014). Not much research is available to provide evidence regarding how social media influence normative socialization of emerging adults' relationships. Therefore, it is important to identify if the use of social media, particularly Facebook, has any influence on relationships among emerging adults in Nigeria. The use of social networking sites (Facebook, Myspace, Twitter etc) involves interacting with others and also meeting new friends at home and abroad. However, such sites also have a negative effect on courtships and intimate relationships. This research is important in identifying the use of Facebook among emerging adults in dating relationships in Nigeria, and it will allow couples to know whether the use of Facebook by emerging adults in such relationships will really foster the relationship they have with their respective partners.

METHODOLOGY

The sample for the study was comprised of emerging adults aged between 19 and 29 years, who were final year students of Faculty of Social Sciences, University of Lagos, Lagos State, Nigeria. There were 77 undergraduate students (41 males and 36 females) included in this study. Data analysis strategy used in this study included a thematic analysis using inductive techniques to identify themes across seven focus groups. Each focus group had 11 members drawn from different faculties from the University, and all in the final year of their different degree programs. The analysis concentrated on themes related to Facebook and communication between emerging adults in dating relationship.

RESULTS

Table 1 presents characteristics of respondents on the basis of questions asked about the use of Facebook and how it affects their relationship with their dating partner. For time spent daily on Facebook, a total of 6.49% ($n = 5$) of the respondents spend 0 to 2hrs on Facebook daily, 46.75% ($n = 36$) of the respondents spend 3 – 5hrs on Facebook daily, 44.16% (n = 34) spend about 6 – 9hrs, and 2.60% ($n = 2$) of the respondents spend 10hrs or more on Facebook daily. This shows that the majority of the respondents spend about 3 – 5hrs on Facebook daily. Ellison, Steinfield, and Lampe (2007) conducted a study among U.S. college students where they found that students reported using Facebook on an average of 10 – 30 minutes daily. Also from the study, 31.17% ($n = 24$) of the respondents maintained that they made new friend regularly on Facebook, 40.26% ($n = 31$) stated they made new friends occasionally, 18.18% ($n = 14$) reported never to have made friends on Facebook, and 10.39% ($n = 8$) of the respondents were undecided This shows that the majority of the respondents made new friends occasionally on Facebook. Lenhart and Madden (2007) found that half of teenagers who use social networking sites make new friends. A total of 36.36% ($n = 28$) of the respondents reported that they listed their relationship status on Facebook for everyone to see, 53.25% (*n* = 41) of the respondents said they did not list their relationship status on Facebook, and 10.39% (*n* = 8) of the respondents were undecided. The study equally revealed that 27.27% (*n* = 21) of the respondents stated they felt safe with their partner chatting with friends on Facebook, 53.25% (*n* = 41) of the respondents disagreed with the statement, and 19.48% (*n* = 15) of the respondents were undecided. A total of 32.47% (*n* = 25) of the respondents reported not feeling comfortable when their partner posted or uploaded any information about them or their relationship on his/her wall, 53.25% (*n* = 41) of the respondents stated they felt comfortable, and 14.29% (*n* = 11) of the respondents were indifferent. About half of the participants, 50.65% (*n* = 39) reported that they regularly checked their partner's Facebook profile, 38.96% (*n* = 30) of the respondents reported that they did not check their partner's Facebook profile on a regular basis, and 10.39% (*n* = 8) of the respondents were undecided.

ANALYSIS, INTERPRETATION, AND DISCUSSION

The following analysis and interpretation is guided by two core themes: time spent by dating couples on social media and their tendency to discuss private issues with friends on Facebook.

Time Spent on Facebook

Participants in dating relationship indicated that their partners spent long hours using Facebook. They did not feel comfortable with the hours their partner spent on social media. Typical activities involved chatting with friends on a regular basis and meeting new friends. This even made respondents feel jealous of their partners. These concerns were voiced among the following participants:

Female 1: *I get scared at times, with the way he spends so much time on Facebook. Sometimes, I even try to see if he is chatting with some girls…*

Male 5: *When she is on Facebook, she goes on and on and on to the extent that we even have quarrels. She would not give me attention at all. It is like an addiction…and we don't even have the chance to communicate together…*

Male 14: *Whenever she is on Facebook, I feel lonely most times because she is always engrossed in it such that if she's cooking, the food at times get burnt...*

Female 52: *He hardly sleeps at night because of his addiction to Facebook… chatting with his friends without giving me any attention… so I often pray for his phone to run-out of battery...*

Female 43: *…because of his love for Facebook even when not chatting with friends, we have broken up twice, only just reunited few weeks ago because I couldn't bear the loneliness.*

These findings are supported by the Muise, Christofides, and Desmarais (2009) who found out that Facebook users were more prone than others to jealousy due to the exposure to information about a romantic partner's friends and social interactions. Elphinston and Noller (2011) concluded that individuals who were highly involved with Facebook may have relationship difficulties, such as jealousy and dissatisfaction, and these individuals also believed that the amount of time spent on Facebook contributed to jealousy.

Table 1. Characteristics of respondents on use of Facebook

Variable	Frequency	Percentage
Gender		
Male	41	53.25
Female	36	46.75
Total	77	100
Time Spent		
0-2hrs	5	6.49
3-5hrs	36	46.75
6-9hrs	34	44.16
10hrs and above	2	2.60
Total	77	100.0
Made New Friends		
Regularly	24	31.17
Occasionally	31	40.26
Never	14	18.18
Undecided	8	10.39
Total	77	100.0
Made Relationship Status Public		
Yes	28	36.36
No	41	53.25
Undecided	8	10.39
Total	77	100.0
Felt Safe		
Yes	21	27.27
No	41	53.25
Undecided	15	19.48
Total	77	100.0
Felt Comfortable		
Yes	25	32.47
No	41	53.25
Undecided	11	14.29
Total	77	100.0
Regularly Checked Partner's Profile		
Yes	39	50.65
No	30	38.96
Undecided	8	10.39
Total	77	100.0

Discussion of Private Issues on Facebook

Individuals in dating relationship also indicated that their partners engaged in discussions of private issues with friends on Facebook. The majority of the participants reported that their partners discussed private matters with friends on Facebook because they do not feel safe and this may lead to the breakdown of the dating relationship. For instance, most of the participants did not feel comfortable when their partner posted or uploaded anything about their relationship information on social media, such as Facebook wall. Another participant indicated that her partner knows the ramifications of discussing personal matters on Facebook:

Female 23: *I can't allow him to put our personal issues on Facebook! In fact, he knows he dares not. Or else I will just break up with him! Personal issues are just that: personal!*

Other participants indicated that their partner did not post personal information online because their partner valued their relationship or due to societal norms to keep relationships difficulties private:

Female 51: *He doesn't post our personal or private issues on Facebook. He, like me, cherishes our relationship. Besides, he is someone that likes keeping his personal life personal.*

Male 20: *Our private issues are addressed between ourselves because we don't know what others are also further passing on about our relationship, and so she always keeps them safe.*

Female 38: *While growing up, my parents always say to my elderly ones that are married – never allow any third-party interferes in your relationship, so, I've always adapted that ideology with my partner.*

These findings are supported by the works of Manner et al. (2011) who concluded that the frequency of Facebook use is grossly associated with undesirable relationship experiences on Facebook. The study also found that spending a considerable amount of time on social media contributed to the jealousy, suspicion, and surveillance between dating couples due to the long hours they spend chatting with friends on such media. This has limited the medium of communication between dating couples because they feel neglected because of the hours spent on the site. The intimacy in the relationship with each other starts deteriorating because of new friends they meet daily and the long hours of conversation they have with these friends.

IMPLICATIONS AND FUTURE OUTLOOK

This study has several limitations. First, only one social medium was examined, which was Facebook. It is quite possible that emerging adults in Nigeria prefer using other forms of social media. Second, the study concentrated on a specific group of undergraduate university students from only one department. It is possible that not all the students in the university primarily use Facebook. The accessibility to fast and easy internet services among emerging adults who participated in this study may differ from that of students from other universities. Additional studies should be conducted to address the limitations of this study. For instance, Facebook is only one social networking site. Researchers should consider other forms of social media, such as Twitter, Instagram, WhatsApp, and so on. Little research exists on the factors that guide the stability and maintenance of relationships among Nigerian emerging adults. Follow-up research should be conducted to better understand relationship development among these individuals.

CONCLUSION

The purpose of this study was to examine the influence of Facebook on communication among emerging adults in dating relationships. Overall, the findings revealed that emerging adults engaged in jealousy, suspicion, and surveillance when their partners spent long hours chatting with friends on Facebook. These emerging adults felt neglected by their partners' behaviors. Their intimacy deteriorated because of new friends their partners' met daily and the long hours of conversation partner had with friends. These emerging adults do not feel secure or comfortable when their significant other uploaded or posted any of their relationship issues on Facebook.

REFERENCES

Arnett, J. J. (2000). Emerging Adulthood: A theory of development from the late teens through the twenties. *The American Psychologist*, *55*(5), 469–480. doi:10.1037/0003-066X.55.5.469 PMID:10842426

Bowe, G. (2010). Reading Romance: The impact Facebook Rituals can have on a Romantic Relationship. *Journal of Comparative Research in Anthropology & Sociology*, *1*(2), 61–77.

Brenner, J. (2012). *Social networking*. Pew Internet and American Life Project. http://pewinternet.org/Commentary/2012/March/Pew-Internet-Social-Networking-fulldetail.aspx

Edegoh, L. O. N., Asemah, E. S., & Ekanem, I. B. (2013). Facebook and Relationship Management among Students of Anambra State University, Uli, Nigeria. *International Review of Social Sciences and Humanities*, *6*(1), 205–216.

Edmunds, A. (2014). *Weekly Publication: San Diego Divorce Center, The Edmunds Law Firm*. Retrieved September 13, 2015, from Available at www.sandiegodivorcecenter.com/category/press-releases

Ekpo, S. (1996). *Juvenile Delinquency in Nigeria*. ABBNNY Educational Publishers.

Ellison, N. B., Steinfield, C., & Lampe, C. (2007). The benefits of Facebook friends: Social capital and college students use of online social network sites. *Journal of Computer-Mediated Communication*, *12*(4), 1143–1168. doi:10.1111/j.1083-6101.2007.00367.x

Elphinston, R. A., & Noller, P. (2011). Time to Face It! Facebook Intrusion and the Implications for Romantic Jealousy and Relationship Satisfaction. *Cyberpsychology, Behavior, and Social Networking*, *14*(11), 631–635. doi:10.1089/cyber.2010.0318 PMID:21548798

Farrugia, R. C. (2013). *Facebook and Relationships: A Study of How Social Media Use is Affecting Long – Term Relationships*. Rochester Institute of Technology.

Financial Nigeria. (2016). *Facebook records 16 million active users*. Retrieved from www.financialnigeria.com

Investor Relations, C. C. G. (2011). *Social Media Strategy for Investor Relations*. Investor Relations Strategic Communications.

Lenhart, A., & Madden, M. (2007). *Teens, privacy & online social networks: How teens manage their online identities and personal information in the age of MySpace*. Washington, DC: Pew Internet & American Life Project.

M A Liebert, Inc., Publishers. (2012, September 19). Can Post-Breakup Facebook Surveillance Delay Emotional Recovery? *ScienceDaily*. Retrieved August 16, 2015 from www.sciencedaily.com/releases/2012/09/120919124941.htm

Manner, C. (2011). Understanding the Predictors of Negative Personal Relationship Experiences on Facebook. *International Journal of Humanities and Social Science*.

Mansson, D. H., & Myers, S. A. (2011). An Initial Examination of College Students Expressions of Affection through Facebook. *The Southern Communication Journal*, *76*(2), 155–168. doi:10.1080/10417940903317710

Marshall, T. C., Bejanyan, K., Di Castro, G., & Lee, R. A. (2012). Attachment Styles as Predictors of Facebook-Related Jealousy and Surveillance in Romantic Relationships. *Social Psychology*, *20*(1).

Muise, A., Christofides, E., & Desmarais, S. (2009). More Information than you ever Wanted: Does Facebook Bring out the Green-Eyed Monster of Jealousy? *Cyberpsychology & Behavior*, *12*(4), 441–445. doi:10.1089/cpb.2008.0263 PMID:19366318

Papp, L. M., Danielewicz, J., & Cayemberg, C. (2012). Are we Facebook Official? Implications of Dating Partners Facebook Use and Profiles for Intimate Relationship Satisfaction. *Cyberpsychology, Behavior, and Social Networking*, *15*(2), 85–90. doi:10.1089/cyber.2011.0291 PMID:21988733

Rau, P. P., Gao, Q., & Ding, Y. (2008). Relationship between the Level of Intimacy and Lurking in Online Social Network Services. *Computers in Human Behavior*, *24*(6), 2757–2770. doi:10.1016/j.chb.2008.04.001

Rideout, V. J., Foehr, U. G., & Roberts, D. F. (2010). *Generation M: Media in the lives of 8-to 18-year-olds*. Henry J. Kaiser Family Foundation. Retrieved from http://www.eric.ed.gov/PDFS/ED527859.pdf

Utz, S., & Beukeboom, C. J. (2011). The Role of Social Network Sites in Romantic Relationships: Effects on Jealousy and Relationship Happiness. *Journal of Computer-Mediated Communication*, *16*(4), 511–527. doi:10.1111/j.1083-6101.2011.01552.x

Uwe, E. A., & Obot, A. E. (2000). *Marriage Counselling: Issues and Solutions. Calabar*. Pyramid Publishers.

Valenzuela, S., Park, N., & Kee, K. F. (2008). Lessons from Facebook: The Effect of Social Network Sites on College Students' Social Capital. *9th International Symposium on Online Journalism*, Austin, TX.

Valverde, L., & Davis, L. (2010). 10 Reasons Relationships Fail. *Loss Angeles Therapy Group: Articles Base*. Retrieved from http://m.articlebase.com/relationships-articles/10-reasonsrelationship-fail-and-how-to-succeed-2625111.html

Vivian, J. (2001). *The media of mass communication (updated online edition)*. Boston: Allyn & Bacon.

Williams, L. M. (2012). *Facebook Ruined My Marriage: Digital Intimacy Interference on Social Networking Sites*. Media Studies – Theses. Paper 7.

Wood, J. T. (2009). *Communication in our lives* (5th ed.). Boston: Wardsworth Cengage Learning.

Chapter 12
The Influence of Pornography on Romantic Relationships of Emerging Adults

Bonnie Young-Petersen
Brigham Young University, USA

Brian J. Willoughby
Brigham Young University, USA

ABSTRACT

Scholars have studied emerging adults and pornography extensively, but to date there is no research on how pornography influences how emerging adults approach and act in relationships. The purpose of this chapter is to explore the nature of pornography use among emerging adults, as well as to look at the relationship between pornography use and porn-related relational anxiety among emerging adults. The authors describe existing research on pornography and emerging adults, introduce their own study, and explain the results and implications.

INTRODUCTION

Researchers have been drawn to the study of emerging adulthood since Dr. Jeffrey Arnett introduced the term over 15 years ago (Arnett, 2000). Defined as the stage from the late teens through the twenties, emerging adulthood has attracted scholars because today's emerging adults act differently compared to previous generations. Scholars have noted how this cohort differs in attachment patterns (Umemura, Lacinova, & Macek, 2014), sexual behavior (Bersamin, et al., 2014), ideas about marriage (Willoughby & Hall, 2015), technology use (Swanson & Walker, 2015), and religiosity (Salas-Wright, Vaughn, & Maynard, 2014). While extensive research has been conducted on multiple aspects of emerging adult life, scholars have paid special attention to the changing romantic relationship and sexuality patterns of this group (Stanley, Rhoades, & Fincham, 2011; Carroll et al., 2007; Willoughby, Hall, & Luczak, 2013; Lefkowitz & Gillen, 2006). Our particular study will examine pornography use patterns of emerging adults, as well as how pornography influences attitudes and feelings experienced in emerging adult romantic relationships.

DOI: 10.4018/978-1-5225-1856-3.ch012

Similar to the outburst of research on emerging adults, sexuality scholars have increasingly studied the effects of pornography on its consumers. Around the same time Arnett articulated his ideas about a new pre-adulthood phase, the Internet boom took over the western world, increasing pornography's accessibility and use (Young, 2008). Today's emerging adults are some of the most frequent consumers of pornography (Traen, Nilsen, & Stigum, 2006; Stack, Wasserman, & Kern, 2004; Coyne, Padilla-Walker, & Howard, 2013; Carroll et al., 2008). Yet scholarship explicitly linking emerging adults and pornography use is still limited and scholars have not addressed how changing trends in romantics among emerging adults are influenced by pornography use. In this chapter, we will look at what connections exist between pornography use and how emerging adults think about and act in romantic relationships. More specifically, our chapter will address the following questions:

1. What is the nature of pornography use (including type, frequency, compulsive behaviors, and gender differences) among emerging adults?
2. What is the relationship between pornography use and pornography-related anxiety in emerging adult romantic relationships?

Emerging Adults and Romantic Relationships

The romantic s of today's emerging adults (mostly Millennials or Gen Z-ers) look significantly different from their predecessors' relationships. Previously, the ages between 18 and 30 were viewed as the period where young people would make major decisions of marriage, occupation, and assume their position as an adult in society (Levinson, 1978). Scholars have also noted that in contrast to generations past, today's young people are delaying those major decisions, and spend their twenties preparing for their futures *individually.* According to Schulman and Connolly (2013), the romantic relationships of today's emerging adults are characterized by postponement of marriage and heavily influenced by individualistic ambitions. Many emerging adults believe it is important to travel extensively or to have an experience of self-discovery before settling down. Others postpone marriage until they have become financially secure. Most emerging adults today also believe that it is important to "test run" their relationships before marriage, and cohabit with their potential partner, adding another step into the path to marriage (Fincham & Cui, 2010).

But emerging adults aren't unique simply because of waiting to tie the knot or postponing the transition to adulthood. Popular culture portrays that while many of our young people in the United States are waiting to marry, they are replacing stable, committed relationships with "friends with benefits" and "harmless hook-ups" (defined as brief, uncommitted sexual encounters involving kissing to intercourse without an understood promise of a continued relationship) (Garcia, Reiber, Massey, Merriweather, 2012). Books like "The Happy Hook Up: A Single Girl's Guide to Casual Sex" (Sherman & Tocantins, 2004) or "The Hookup Handbook: A Single Girl's Guide to Living it Up" (Rozler & Lavinthal, 2010) perpetuate this idea, and reflect Millenials' ideas about how to approach and behave in relationships during this relatively new stage of life. While recent research has suggested that "hook-up culture" might be not as prevalent as supposed (Monto & Carey, 2014), other studies suggest that up to 80% of college students have engaged in a hook-up (Garcia, Reiber, Massey, Merriweather, 2012; Owen, Fincham, Moore, 2011). One study of undergraduate college students showed that both men and women had nearly double the number of hook-ups compared to first dates (Bradshaw, Kahn, & Saville, 2010).

These sexual practices are often void of emotional ties or expectations of permanence. In fact, research suggests that emerging adults engaging in hook-ups do not disclose their feelings about sex with their partners, and communicate their sexual likes more than their dislikes (Byers & Demmons, 1999). This falls in line well with sexual communication research that has found that sexual communication becomes more common as the relationship progresses and becomes exclusive (Fincham & Cui, 2010). Combined, these results suggest that emerging adults are seeking the sexual experiences traditionally shared in committed relationships in non-committal hook-ups. But how does pornography relate to these behaviors?

Like the general increases seen in both premarital sex and general sexual behaviors among emerging adults, the availability and use of pornography have also increased and such growth has implications for sexuality more generally. One recent study revealed that nearly 90% of emerging adult males reported using pornography (Carroll et al., 2008). One scholar argued that the widespread availability and popularity of porn serves to drive down the "price of sex" with real women as high-speed digital porn gives men attractive sexual options and experiences without relationship commitments (Regnerus & Uecker, 2010). The same scholars proposed that pornography has perpetuated abnormal ideas about sexual practices among emerging adults. They report that the rate of heterosexual emerging adult couples who had anal sex with their partners has increased over the last few decades. According to their research, by the age of 23, around 30% of emerging adults experienced anal sex. This increase in popularity of anal sex is viewed as evidence of porn-inspired scripts available on pornographic websites (Fincham & Cui, 2010). Because of the influence of pornography on relationships and sexuality reported here, it can be expected that pornography will also influence how emerging adults will approach and experience anxiety in romantic relationships.

Approaches to Pornography Research

While pornography outcome research in the last decade has been prolific, (Tolman et al., 2014) not all results point to the same outcomes. Because of the diversity of moral perspectives regarding pornography, scholars have taken multiple positions in pornography outcome research. Often the values and background of researchers will inform the questions they will ask about pornography's effects. As Hald, Seaman, and Linz (2014) suggest, the three most common approaches have been the "liberal," "conservative-moralistic," and "radical feminist" perspectives. All three perspectives have different views on how pornography may interact with emerging adult development. The liberal perspective, which commonly supports positive outcomes of pornography use, is often supported by research focused on the neutrality or positive sexual outcomes of pornography use. For example, some research has showed that while male pornography use is negatively associated with both male and female sexual quality, female pornography use may be positively associated with female sexual quality (Poulsen, Busby, & Galovan, 2013). Another study supported that pornography is a source of knowledge and a resource for intimate practices (Attwood, 2005). This finding would be especially relevant among today's emerging adults, as they are the generation that has had the most exposure to the wide array of available Internet pornography. From this perspective, increased pornography use may help emerging adults become more sexually knowledgeable and help improve their sexual communication.

Pornography outcome research from the conservative-moralistic perspective focuses heavily on negative sexual and relational outcomes. For example, a 2011 study conducted by E.M. Morgan showed that higher use of pornography among emerging adults was associated with more risky sexual behavior, such as more casual sex encounters, and lower age at first intercourse. Another study found that less progressive gender role attitudes, more permissive sexual norms, and sexual harassment perpetration were predicted by early exposure to pornography (Brown & L'Engle, 2009). Similarly, Stewart and Szymanski's 2012 study found that women's reports of their male partner's frequency of pornography use were negatively associated with their relationship quality, and that perceptions of problematic use of pornography were negatively correlated with self-esteem, relationship quality, and sexual satisfaction. From this perspective, pornography use during emerging adulthood may elevate harmful or risk-taking behaviors and be associated with negative individual and relational developmental outcomes.

Research from what Hald, Seaman, and Linz (2014) refer to as the "radical feminist perspective" is most concerned with pornography's effects on attitudes and treatment of women. One 2007 study showed that for both males and females, exposure to online pornography was significantly related to beliefs that women are sex objects (Peter & Valkenburg, 2007). Similarly, Malamuth, Hald, and Koss (2011) examined porn use and attitudes supporting violence against women, and found that among emerging adult males, an overall positive association between these factors existed. These attitudes, however, were moderated by individual differences such as a propensity for sexual aggression against women and high pornography consumption. Yet other studies have found that exposure to pornography was a non-significant predictor of misogynist attitudes (McKee, 2007; Padgett, Brislin-Slutz, Neal, 1989; Barak, Fisher, Belfry, & Lashambe, 1999). This perspective would suggest the emerging adults (mostly men) who use pornography frequently may be more likely to harbor negative or inaccurate beliefs about women, and that these beliefs that may influence their ability to have healthy relationships with those of the opposite sex.

The liberal, conservative, and feminist approaches to pornography research provide unique understandings of pornography during emerging adulthood, but alone, these perspectives are limited in their ability to produce or support a comprehensive framework for organizing the effects of pornography. To this end, more inclusive approaches for pornography outcomes have been found when scholars have grounded their outcome research in social science theory.

Theoretical Foundations

Approaching research theoretically provides scaffolding for understanding the scholarly validity of outcome research. Further, using theory enables scholars to extend and connect their results to other research findings. Pornography outcome scholars have begun to use an array of theories to put their findings into context, as well as to connect their findings with other research. Generally, scholars have used theory to organize the outcomes of pornography use. Below we summarize two of the major theories used to date when examining pornography use during emerging adulthood.

Social Learning Theory

One theory that researchers have used to explain the effects of pornography is social learning theory. Social learning theory (Bandura, 1977; Check & Malamuth, 1986) states that individuals learn not only by their own experiences, but also through the observation of others' behaviors. When applied in a sexual context, social learning theory suggests that sexual behaviors, attitudes, role models, and sex roles can be influenced and even created by pornography, and that this happens in a context where no punishment or social norms can prevent or negatively reinforce such ideas, attitudes, and behaviors

(Malamuth & Check, 1985; Seto, Maric, & Barbaree, 2001). Some scholars feel that sexual behaviors and attitudes are likely to be influenced by pornography because of the non-normative material found in today's popular pornography.

One content analysis of best-selling pornography videos found that of the 304 scenes analyzed, 88.2% contained physical aggression (spanking, gagging, slapping), and 48.7% contained verbal aggression. The targets of this behavior responded neutrally or showed pleasure to this aggression (Bridges, Wosnitzer, Scharrer, Sun, & Liberman, 2010). Because the majority of today's most popular pornography includes verbal and physical aggression, and the targets of this behavior show pleasure or neutrality, some scholars say that this behavior is bound to be learned and acted out – even if at a small level—in sexual imaginations and relationships. A recent meta-analysis of pornography consumption and acts of sexual aggression found that pornography consumption was associated with sexual aggression, in the United States and internationally, among males and females, and in longitudinal and cross-sectional studies (Wright, Tokunaga, & Kraus, 2015). Another recent meta-analysis found pornography use to be positively correlated with attitudes supporting violence against women, even when individuals consumed nonviolent pornography (Hald, Malamuth, & Yuen, 2010).

Hald, Kuyper, Adam, and Wit (2013) found that even when controlling for important other factors, pornography consumption influenced sexual behaviors of young people. These sexual behaviors included experience with threesomes, sex with a same sex partner, real-life sex with a partner met online, ever being paid for sex, and ever paying money for sex. These associations were small to moderate, however, and results showed that pornography is just one factor among many that may influence the sexual behaviors of youth. But media exposure does not just lead to changed sexual behaviors. Another study, for example, showed that sexual television content that portrayed negative consequences of sex lead to more negative attitudes towards premarital intercourse, and even more negative judgments of characters involved in premarital intercourse (Eyal & Kunkel, 2008).

Sexual Script Theory

Social learning theory shares multiple ideas with sexual script theory, and like social learning theory, sexual script theory is used by researchers to explain outcomes of pornography use (Štulhofer, Buško, & Landripet, 2010). Sexual script theory is rooted in the widely used script theory, which teaches that human behavior is dictated by patterns called "scripts" that individuals "act out" due to exposure and conditioning. According to sexual script theory, sexual scripts, or culturally available messages that define what 'counts' as sex, or how to act during a sexual encounter, may be altered by messages and images portrayed in pornography (Frith & Kitzinger, 2001). While it is acknowledged that pornography is not the only element influencing sexual scripts, this theory proposes that it may be used as a guide or educational tool for many users, young and old.

According to this theory, pornography leads users to "act out" new sexual behaviors or adopt differing attitudes about sexuality due to the "scripts" they have observed. One study conducted by Braithwaite, Couslon, Keddington, and Fincham (2015) examined how pornography influenced emerging adults' hooking up behavior via sexual scripts. These researchers found that more frequent viewing of pornography was associated with more frequent hook ups and higher numbers of hook up partners, and plans to have higher numbers of sexual partners, and that more permissive sexual scripts mediated the association between more frequent pornography viewing and hooking up. A 2010 study that utilized scripting theory found that viewing pornography normalized new sexual behaviors and influenced willingness to explore sexual relationships. This study, however, found that viewing pornography extended sexual scripts rather than replacing them completely (Weinberg, Williams, Kleiner, & Irizarry).

In conclusion, scholars who include theory in their scope of pornography outcome research find more universal and applicable findings. In addition to the importance of theory, scholars also acknowledge the importance of individual and contextual factors in pornography outcomes related to emerging adults. These factors give a more comprehensive scope and understanding of pornography use, explaining and providing nuance for different outcomes.

Major Individual and Contextual Factors in Pornography Research

Perhaps even more important than the outcomes associated with pornography use itself are the context of the use and the traits of the user. Several scholars have now suggested that individual and contextual factors are vital to understanding the correlates and outcomes of pornography. Important factors that have been addressed include gender, age, religiosity, beliefs about pornography, and relationship status (individual factors), as well as if pornography is used alone vs. with partner and discrepancy in partner use (contextual factors) (Hald, 2006; Willoughby, Carroll, Nelson, & Padilla-Walker, 2014; Willoughby, Carroll, Busby, & Brown, 2015; Patterson & Price, 2012). Such results have demonstrated that pornography outcome research is multifaceted and complicated.

Among the most important individual factors is gender. Social scientists have repeatedly highlighted the differences between males and females in pornography outcomes (Malamuth, 1996; Romito, Beltramini, 2001) and very few studies exclude gender from analyses. One study examining perceived effects of Internet pornography found that females perceived greater negative effects of viewing pornography than males, and were also ready to support stricter guidelines for internet pornography (Lo & Wei, 2002). In 2006, Hald looked at consumption differences among young heterosexual Danish adults. He found significant differences between genders in pornography consumption patterns, including age of exposure (men were younger), frequency of viewing pornography (men viewed more), and patterns of viewing pornography with partners (women more likely to view with partners). Men and women were also found to vary in their pornographic preferences: men showed more interest in hardcore pornography than women, and also were found to masturbate to pornography more than women. Another study assessing sexual arousal, affecting response, absorption, and sexual behavior as an outcome of watching X-rated videos found that emerging adult males reported more positive psychosexual responses than women (Mosher & Maclan, 1994). Clearly, the context of gender is one of the most – if not the most – important characteristic in approaching pornography outcomes (Carroll et al., 2008).

Another important individual factor that influences pornography outcomes is that of religion. This is for multiple reasons. For one, religious individuals often receive negative messages about pornography that non-religious individuals seldom hear. Religious organizations often have strict rules about sexuality both outside and within marriage, and using pornography is rarely a part of what is deemed an appropriate script of either context. It seems logical, then, that religious individuals would use less pornography – and the research supports that (Nelson, Padilla-Walker, & Carroll, 2010). Recent studies have shown that while nearly two thirds of young men and one half of young women in the United States agree that viewing pornography is acceptable, and nearly ninety percent of young men and one third of women report using it (Carroll et. al., 2008), studies on religious young adults have found a negative relationship between pornography use and religiosity, and that this group unanimously believes that pornography use is unacceptable (Nelson, Padilla-Walker, & Carroll, 2010).

But what about religious individuals who *do* use pornography? Because of religious teachings and moral restrictions, religiously devout individuals who compulsively – or even willfully – use pornography often experience unique feelings of guilt or shame. This idea is supported by a 2012 study by Patterson and Price which showed that the mental health costs of using pornography was greater for religious individuals than non-religious individuals. Another study found that religious emerging adults experienced extreme distress as a result of their pornography use, and commonly perceived their use to be addictive, even without clinical evidence of addiction (Sessoms, 2011). Conversely, religious emerging adults who "stick to their morals" regarding pornography report higher levels of self-worth as well as lower levels of depression (Nelson, Padilla-Walker, & Carroll, 2010). Further, religious emerging adults define pornography and interpret pornographic material differently than non-religious emerging adults, and often have a lower threshold for what types of sexual media constitute "pornography" (Willoughby & Busby, 2015).

Relationship contexts, including if one is in a relationship or if pornography use is utilized individually versus relationally, have also been seen to influence pornography acceptability and use. One study exploring pornography use of college students in committed romantic relationships found that three main groups emerged from the sample. First, a group (70.8% of men, 45.5% of women) that reported that solo and partner use was acceptable. Second, a group (22.3% of men, 26.2% of women) the viewed pornography unacceptable because of being in a committed relationship. Third, a group (5.4% men, 12.9% women) that reported that pornography use was unacceptable in any context or circumstance (Olmstead, Negash, Pasley, & Fincham, 2013). Other studies have shown that in a relationship context, discrepancies in pornography use at the couple level are related to negative outcomes (Willoughby, Carroll, Busby, & Brown, 2016).

As can be seen, previous research on pornography use and emerging adults offers a wide array of findings and perspectives. Despite growing research this area, continued work is needed to address a multitude of scholarly gaps. For example, most research has focused exclusively on individual outcomes or relational outcomes. No research to date has explored how pornography use may alter an emerging adult's attitudes about forming romantic relationships or communicating about pornography in those relationships. In addition, since Carroll et al.'s landmark study on emerging adults and pornography in 2008, no scholarship has given a detailed account of the current pornography use patterns of emerging adults. Having reviewed previous literature on pornography use outcomes and emerging adults, we will now turn to a new analysis to provide us more information regarding pornography use patterns of emerging adults and the unique influence that pornography has on emerging adults' attitudes about and behaviors in forming romantic relationships.

METHODS

Participants

This study is based on data collected in 2015 from an international sample of 929 emerging adults (437 male, 488 female) who took an online survey via Amazon's Mechanical Turk (MTurk) website. MTurk is a website dedicated to online labor and is used to employ ''workers'' from around the world to complete specific tasks. Scholars have noted that samples from MTurk are very similar to other diverse behavioral research samples, and several scholars have replicated previous research results on MTurk to provide evidence for the validity of the sample (Paolacci, Chandler, & Ipeirotis, 2010; Suri & Watts, 2011). The participants were predominately from Southeast Asia and the United States. For the purpose of this study (to compare pornography use among female and male emerging adults), we excluded transgender individuals from our analyses. The participants ranged in age from 18-30 with the mean age of the sample being 25.25 years (*SD*=3.22). Fifty percent of the sample was White, 34.1% were Asian, 6.3% were Black, and 5.4% were Latino. Participants reported a variety of religious affiliations: 25.7% reported Hindu, 15.8% reported Catholic, 15.1% reported Protestant, 3.5% reported Muslim, 3.4% reported Latter-day Saint, 1.2% reported Jewish, and 31.1% reported no religious affiliation. Four percent reported an "other" religious affiliation. Twenty-eight percent of the sample were dating and never married, 29.3% were married, and 33.6% were single.

Procedures

Participants were recruited to take an online survey via Amazon's Mturk website in the spring of 2015. Informed consent was obtained online, and only after participants indicated consent were they able to take the 20-30 minute survey and receive the compensation (.25$) through Mturk. Sections of the survey addressed areas such as religiosity, life satisfaction, depression, impulsivity, risky behavior, history of pornography use, compulsive pornography use, attitudes about pornography, and relationship history.

Measures

Pornography

In the survey participants took, pornography was defined as "any material intended for the sexual arousal of its viewer." Pornography use was measured by frequency of viewing as well as by type of pornography viewed. Participants indicated if they had (1) or had not (0) ever viewed pornography. Of those who indicated that they had ever viewed pornography, participants indicated if they had viewed pornography daily (7), 2-6 times a week (6), about every other week (5), about every month (4), about once every few months (3), about twice a year (2), or about once a year or less (1). Specific types of pornography were explained in different items on the survey, with items asking participants to indicate whether they had (1) or had not (0) viewed photos of women in lingerie or swimsuits, photos of women exposing breasts, photos of women exposing breasts and genitals, photos of men exposing genitals, photos of sexual intercourse, videos depicting sexual intercourse, or videos depicting other sexual acts.

Control Variables

Previous research has suggested that there are several individual characteristics that are associated with pornography use and outcomes including gender, impulsivity, relationship status, culture, and religiosity (Carroll et al., 2008). Thus, the control variables used when running our regressions included gender, race, relationship status, impulsivity, age, and religiosity. Categorical variables were recoded into bivariate controls. Gender was measured by male (0) and female (1). Because approximately 50 percent of our sample was white, race was simplified into two categories: white (0) and non-white (1). Relationship status also divided into two categories. Those who were engaged, in a committed relationship, married, or cohabiting were "in a relationship" (1) and individuals who were divorced, separated, widowed, or single were "not in a relationship" (0).

Individuals were asked, "How important is your religious faith to you?" and were able to chose from "very important," "important," "somewhat important," and "not important." They also were asked to indicate their religious affiliation, and were able to choose from "Catholic," "Protestant," "Hindu," "Muslim," "LDS," "Jewish," "None," or "Other." Using these items, we divided our sample into "religious" (1) and "non-religious" (0) categories. Those who reported high religious importance (religious faith was "very important" or "important") *and* a religious affiliation were labeled as "religious." Non-religious individuals where those who either did not report a religious affiliation *or* scored low on religious importance ("somewhat important" or "not important") were labeled as "non-religious." Thus, "religious" individuals were those who scored high on religious importance and also identified with an organized religion, while those who were "not religious" either did not identify with a religious affiliation or did belong to a religion but did not consider their religion personally important.

We measured impulsive behavior with the impulsivity scale validated by Novak and Clayton (2001). The scale was reliable (Chronbach's $\alpha = .879$) and items on this scale included "I have difficulty controlling my temper," "I get so frustrated I am ready to explode," "I get upset easily," "Often I am afraid I will lose control over my feelings," and "I slam doors when I am mad." Participants responded on a five-point Likert scale from "Never true" (1) to "Always true" (5).

Anxiety Related to Pornography

For the purposes of this study and to explore how pornography may associate with relational fears and anxieties, the research team created items measuring pornography-related relational anxiety. Through a collaborative effort of the research team, and drawing from previous research, the items were created. After collecting our data, a principal axis factor analysis using a varimax rotation procedure was computed on the proposed items of the dataset analyzed. Two factors were extracted with eigenvalues greater than 1 that accounted for 70.66% of the total factor variance. All items loaded on their specified scales with no cross-loadings between factors. Additional analyses indicated that the two measures were reliable (see below).

The first measure, which we called "Relationship Anxiety," measured an individual's belief that his/her pornography use negatively impacts their ability to form and maintain romantic relationships. "Relationship Anxiety," was reliable (Chronbach's $\alpha = .954$) and was composed of 9 items. Items on this scale included questions statements such as "My pornography use affects the way I see my dates," "I stop dating when I am using pornography," "I feel uncomfortable around the opposite gender after I use pornography," and "I feel that my relationship will end if I disclose my pornography use to my partner." Responses were on a 6-point agreement scale from "very strongly disagree" (1) to "very strongly agree" (6). Individuals who scored higher on this scale had more beliefs that his/her pornography use impaired their relationship formation and maintenance.

The second factor that emerged we named "Communication Anxiety." "Communication Anxiety" refers to an individual's stress about or fear of talking about pornography with their partner. This measure was also reliable (Chronbach's $\alpha = .848$) and was composed of 4 items (see Table 2). Items included statements such as "I feel anxious talking about pornography with my romantic partners," "I have withheld details about my pornography use because I am afraid my partner will react negatively," "I have withheld details about my pornography use because I do not know how to communicate about it," and "My partner would react negatively if I disclosed pornography use to him/her." Responses were on a

6-point agreement scale from "very strongly agree" (1) to "very strongly disagree" (6). Individuals who scored higher on this scale experienced or believed they would experience more anxiety when talking about pornography with their romantic partner.

Other Variables

Other measures we used included items reflecting individuals' past experiences and beliefs of pornography use. These items were not used in a scale but were used to gather preliminary data and to observe trends in our sample. These items included: "Have you ever had a relationship end solely because of pornography use?" "Have you ever had a relationship end partially because of pornography use?" "Have you discussed your pornography use with your spouse, fiancée, significant other, friend of the same gender, and friend of the opposite gender?" Participants responded "yes" (1) or "no" (0) to each of these items. We used these items in our T-tests analysis to compare male and female emerging adults' experience with pornography.

NATURE OF PORNOGRAPHY USE AMONG EMERGING ADULTS

Of our emerging adult sample including men and women from ages 18-30, 86% percent reported "ever viewing pornography." This statistic aligns well with other reports of emerging adult pornography-viewing behaviors: other studies have found that 60% to 87% of young people have consumed pornography (Carroll et al., 2008; Braun-Courville & Rojas, 2009). Of the 86% in our study that had ever viewed pornography, 88.4% had viewed pornography in the last 12 months: 8.9% reported daily use, 25.4% 2-5 times per week, 19% every other week, 16.3% once a month, 12.2% every few months, 5% twice a year, and 13.1% about

Figure 1. Emerging adults' agreement to the item "I am addicted to pornography"

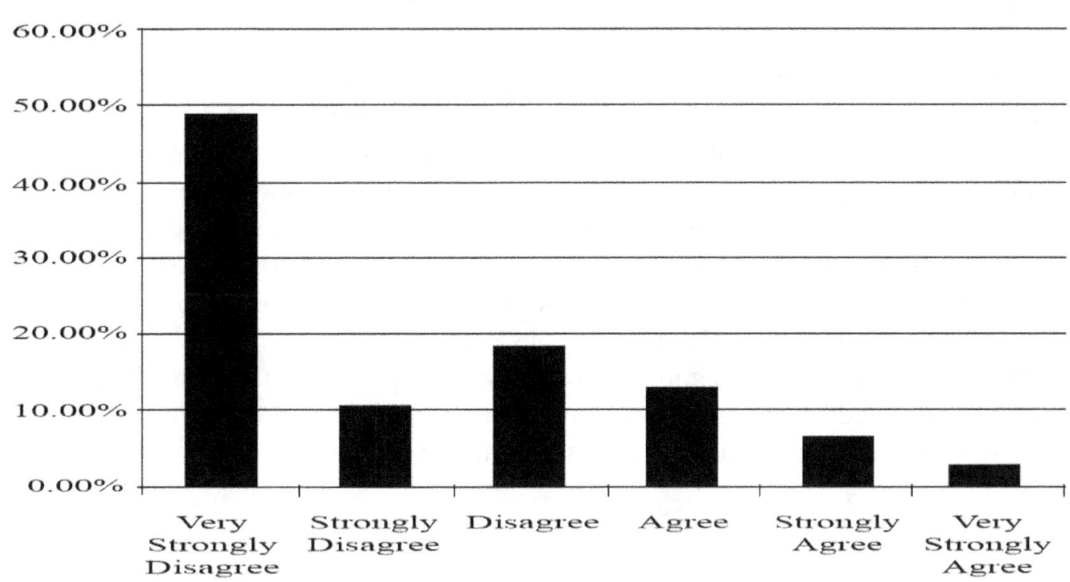

Figure 2. Emerging adults who have/have not ever viewed pornography, by gender

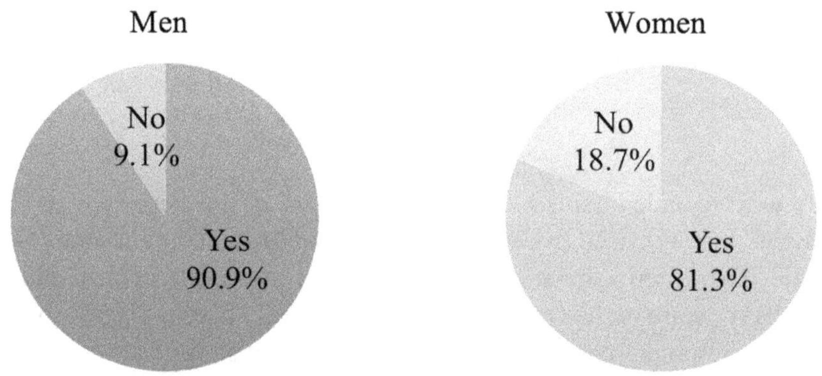

Figure 3. Emerging adults who have/have not viewed pornography in the last 12 months, by gender

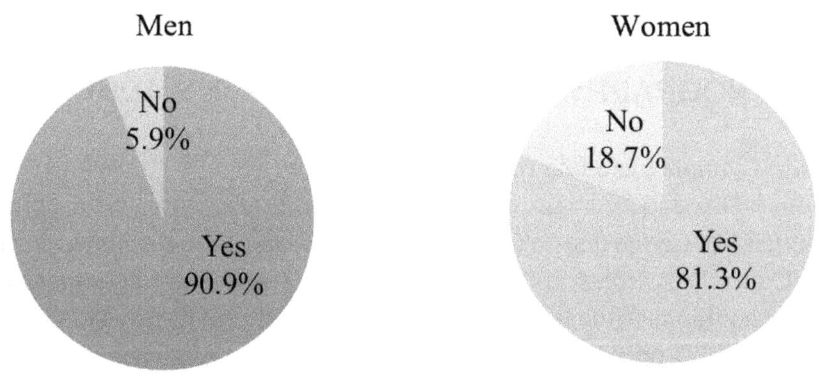

once a year or less. Despite the frequency of pornography consumption, most emerging adults disagree that this behavior is compulsive. Almost half of our sample (48.5%) "very strongly disagreed" that they were "addicted" to pornography. Only thirteen percent agreed, 6.5% "strongly agreed," and 2.8% "very strongly" agreed that they were addicted to pornography (see Figure 1).

Of the 86% of emerging adults that reported ever viewing pornography, 34.3% used pornography daily or weekly. Despite a lack of self-reported addictive behavior, twenty-two percent of emerging adults responded positively to having compulsive behaviors related to viewing pornography. To systematically measure compulsive pornography use (as opposed to trusting self-report of compulsive behaviors), we combined scores from the pornography compulsion scale (translated from the sexual compulsion scale) with weekly or daily use. Those who scored above the median for compulsive pornography use and also reported using pornography daily or weekly were considered to be "compulsive" pornography users. According to this criteria, almost 9% of our sample reported behaviors necessary to be considered "compulsive" pornography users. These numbers give us an idea of the pornography viewing behavior of today's emerging adults, but the data is better understood when put in the context of gender.

Figure 4. Emerging adults and frequency of viewing pornography, by gender

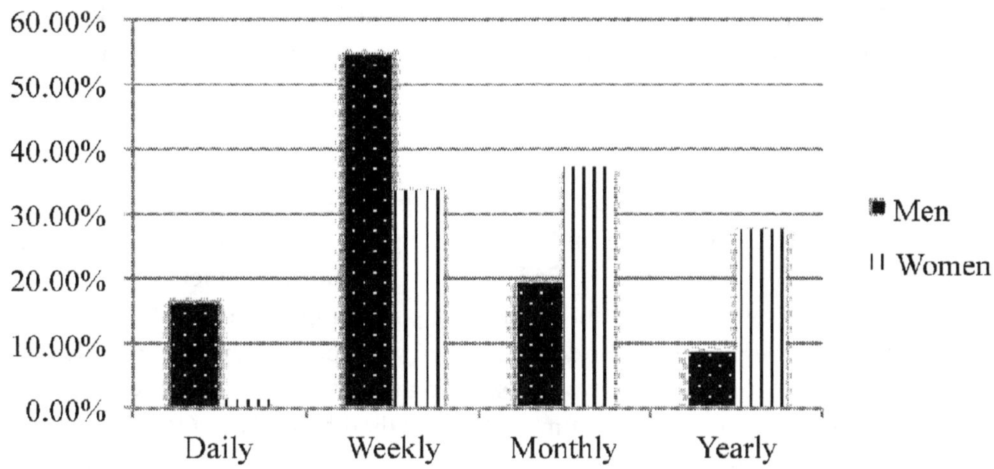

Differences in Gender

Perhaps the most influential factor explaining differences between groups of individuals is gender. To explore the differences between male and female emerging adults' pornography patterns, we performed an MANOVA analysis. Significant multivariate differences were found between men and women on our dependent variables (Wilks $\lambda = .670$, $F(1, 748) = 36.321$, $p < .001$). We therefore proceed to univariate results. Univariate F-tests were significant for viewing pornography in the last 12 months ($F(1, 748) = 24.66$, $p < .001$; partial $\eta^2 = .032$), overall frequency of viewing pornography ($F(1, 748) = 151.55$, $p < .001$; partial $\eta^2 = .17$), viewing photos of women in lingerie ($F(1, 748) = 53.33$, $p < .001$; partial $\eta^2 = .067$), viewing photos of women showing breasts and/or genitals ($F(1, 748) = 53.92$, $p < .001$; partial $\eta^2 = .067$), viewing photos of men showing their genitals ($F(1, 748) = 25.05$, $p < .001$; partial $\eta^2 = .033$), viewing photos of sexual intercourse ($F(1, 748) = 43.07$, $p < .001$; partial $\eta^2 = .054$), viewing videos of sexual intercourse ($F(1, 748) = 10.90$, $p < .001$; partial $\eta^2 = .014$), viewing videos of other explicit sexual acts ($F(1, 748) = 7.76$, $p < .01$; partial $\eta^2 = .010$), and viewing violent sex, child sex, and rape ($F(1, 748) = 22.73$, $p < .001$; partial $\eta^2 = .029$).

Post-hoc tests were run using the Bonferonni method to control for multiple comparisons.

These analyses showed that generally, emerging adult males viewed pornography more frequently. Men were more likely than women to have viewed pornography in the last 12 months (men: $M = 1.058$; women: $M = 1.172$) and to view pornography more frequently in that time (men: $M = 5.106$; women: $M = 3.597$). There were also significant differences between men and women in the type of pornography viewed (see Table 1 depicting percentages of men and women viewing different types of pornography. The MANOVA analyses confirm the significant differences depicted all tables below). As is expected with traditional heterosexual sexual attraction (i.e. women physically attracted to men, men physically attracted to women), men were more likely than women to view pictures of women in lingerie (men: $M = .775$; women: $M = .530$) and photos of women exposing breasts and/ or genitals (men: $M = .783$; women: $M = .538$). Similarly, women were more likely than men to view photos of men exposing genitals (men: $M = .354$; women: $M = .535$). However, more men (75.2%) than women (48.5%) reported viewing pictures of the opposite sex exposing genitals. Men also reported higher levels of consuming media portraying sexual acts than women. Men were more likely than women to view photos of sexual intercourse (men: $M = .767$; women: $M = .546$), videos of sexual intercourse (men: $M = .844$; women: $M = .747$), and videos of other explicit sexual acts than women (men: $M = .778$; women: $M = .688$).

Differences in Religiosity

To explore differences in religious vs. non-religious emerging adults, we performed a MANOVA analysis. Significant multivariate differences were found between religious and non-religious emerging adults on our dependent variables (Wilks $\lambda = .890$, $F(1, 747) = 9.135$, $p < .001$). We therefore proceed to univariate results. Univariate F-tests were significant for viewing pornography in the last 12 months ($F(1, 747) = 7.53$, $p < .01$; partial $\eta^2 = .010$), overall frequency of viewing pornography ($F(1, 747) = 17.12$, $p < .001$; partial $\eta^2 = .022$), viewing photos of women showing breasts and/or genitals ($F(1, 747) = 6.774$, $p < .01$; partial $\eta^2 = .009$), viewing photos of men showing their genitals ($F(1, 747) = 6.056$, $p < .05$; partial $\eta^2 = .008$), viewing photos of sexual intercourse ($F(1, 747) = 9.554$, $p < .01$; partial $\eta^2 = .013$), viewing videos of sexual intercourse ($F(1, 747) = 12.852$, $p < .001$; partial $\eta^2 = .017$), and viewing videos of other explicit sexual acts ($F(1, 747) = 10.567$, $p < .01$; partial $\eta^2 = .014$).

Post-hoc tests were run using the Bonferonni method to control for multiple comparisons.

These analyses showed that generally, non-religious emerging adults viewed pornography more frequently than religious emerging adults. Religious emerging adults (R) were more likely than non-religious (NR) emerging adults to have viewed pornography in the last 12 months (NR: $M = 1.086$; R: $M = 1.149$), but non-religious emerging adults viewed pornography more frequently than religious emerging adults (NR: $M = 4.596$; R: $M = 4.043$). There were also significant differences between religious and non-religious emerging adults in the type of pornography consumed. Non-religious emerging adults were more likely than religious emerging adults to view pictures of women in lingerie (NR: $M = 6.82$; R: $M = 6.25$), photos of women exposing breasts and/ or genitals (NR: $M = .703$; R: $M = .613$), photos of men exposing genitals (NR: $M = .489$; R: $M = .399$), photos of intercourse (NR: $M = .708$; R: $M =.601$), videos of intercourse (NR: $M = .843$; R: $M = .738$), and videos of other sexually explicit acts (NR: $M = .779$; R: $M = .674$).

PORNOGRAPHY USE AND RELATIONAL ANXIETY AMONG EMERGING ADULTS

We also explored feelings of pornography-related anxiety among emerging adults. From our findings, it is apparent that pornography is generally a significant factor in the levels of anxiety that emerging adults experience when forming or maintaining romantic relationships.

Relational Anxiety and Gender

First, we ran MANOVA analyses to explore the differences between men and women who ended romantic relationships because of pornography use. Significant multivariate differences were found between men and women on our dependent variables (Wilks $\lambda = .992$, $F(1, 860) = 3.471$, $p < .05$). We therefore proceed to univariate results. Univariate F-tests were significant for "ending a relationship solely because of pornography use" ($F(1, 860) = 6.339$, $p < .05$; partial $\eta^2 = .007$), but not for "ending a relationship partially because of pornography use" (F (1, 860) = .994, p =.319; partial η^2 = .001). Post-hoc tests were run using the Bonferonni method to control for multiple comparisons. These analyses showed that while the differences were small, women were more likely than men to report that a relationship ended solely because of pornography use (men: M= 1.898, women: M= 1.841). From these results, it may be suggested that emerging adult females are more reactive to pornography use than emerging adult males, and are reporting that more relationships have ended because of pornography use than men.

We also ran a MANOVA analysis to explore the differences between genders in disclosing/ discussing pornography use with others. Participants indicated whether or not they had talked about their pornography use with spouses, fiancées, significant others, friends of the same gender, and friends of the opposite gender. Significant multivariate differences were found between men and women on our dependent variables (Wilks λ = .900, F (1, 717) = 11.227, p < .001). We therefore proceed to univariate results. Univariate F-tests were significant for discussing one's pornography use with a significant other (F (1, 717) = 30.510, p < .001; partial η^2 = .041) and with a spouse (F (1, 717) = 7.765, p < .01; partial η^2 = .011). Post-hoc tests using the Bonferonni method controlling for multiple comparisons indicated that men who had used pornography were more likely than women who had used pornography discuss their pornography use with a significant other (men: M= 1.539 women: M= 1.339) and with a spouse (men: M= 1.728, women: M= 1.631). From these results, it appears that men are more likely than women to disclose their pornography use to individuals they are in a committed relationship with. Such findings may suggest that men are being compelled to speak about pornography in relationships more than females, or that men simply use pornography more, and thus will report more conversation than women.

Predictors of Relational Anxiety

Next, we conducted a multiple analysis with gender, race, impulsivity, relationship status, age, and religiosity as predictors of "relationship anxiety." All measures were entered simultaneously into the model. As outlined above, "relationship anxiety" refers to an individual's belief that he or she is capable of forming and maintaining a healthy relationship. The higher the relationship anxiety of an individual, the less likely he or she believes themselves capable of having a successful relationship. The linear combination of the six predictors was significantly related to relationship anxiety, R^2 = .343, adjusted R^2 = .337, F (6,713) = 61.421, *p*< .001. Of all of the measures, religiosity was the strongest predictor of relationship anxiety (β= .594, SE=.082, *p*< .001), followed by gender (β= -.523, SE=.079, *p*< .001). More religious emerging adults were more likely to believe that their pornography use would negatively influence their ability to initiate or carry on a committed relationship. Emerging adult males were also more likely than emerging adult women to believe that their consumption of pornography would have a negative impact on their relationships.

Impulsivity was the third strongest predictor of relationship anxiety (β= .406, SE=.041, *p*< .001). The more impulsive an emerging adult was, the more he believed that his pornography use could negatively influence his relationships. Race (β= .345, SE=.083, *p*< .001) and relationship status (β= -.312, SE=.085, *p*< .001) were also significant predictors of relationship anxiety. Non-white and single individuals were more likely to experience "relationship anxiety" than white individuals or emerging adults in a committed relationship. Age was not a significant predictor of relationship anxiety among emerging adults (see Table 3).

We also conducted a multiple regression analysis with gender, race, impulsivity, relationship status, age, and religiosity as predictors of anxiety of pornography-related communication anxiety. As outlined above, "communication anxiety" refers to an individual's stress about or fear of talking about pornography with their partner. The linear combination of the six predictors was significantly related to communication anxiety, $R^2 = .207$, adjusted $R^2 = .201$, $F(6,821) = 35.310$, $p < .001$. Of all of the measures, gender was the strongest predictor of communication anxiety ($\beta = -.577$, $SE = .084$, $p < .001$), followed by religiosity ($\beta = .435$, $SE = .087$, $p < .001$). This indicates that, of all the predictors, gender is the factor that most explains differences of anxiety among emerging adults. Emerging adults males are significantly more anxious about discussing pornography in romantic relationships than women. More religious emerging adults are more anxious about talking about pornography than less religious emerging adults.

Impulsivity was the third strongest predictor of communication anxiety ($\beta = .360$, $SE = .043$, $p < .001$), indicating that more impulsive individuals feel higher amounts of anxiety around talking about pornography in relationships. Relationship status ($\beta = -.255$, $SE = .090$, $p < .05$) was also a significant (yet weak) predictor of communication anxiety. Emerging adults in romantic relationships were slightly less anxious talking about pornography with a significant other than those not in relationships. Neither age nor race were significant predictors of communication anxiety among emerging adults (see Table 4).

CONCLUSION

It is inaccurate and unwise to assume that *all* emerging adults are experiencing anxiety because of pornography use in their relationships. However, we see from our results that certain individual and contextual variables influence levels of anxiety for emerging adults. Specifically and similar to previous studies focused on pornography use, being male and religious appeared to be key individual factors and predicted more pornography-related anxiety for emerging adults.

Gender

Generally, gender was the strongest predictor of pornography related anxiety differences in emerging adults. Notwithstanding the widely accepted cultural script that men are more sexual than women (Crawford & Popp, 2003), men may feel that they have to hide their pornography use more than women. Men were also more likely than women to believe that their pornography use will negatively influence their ability to form and maintain a relationship. For male emerging adults, it seems that pornography use is something that feels vulnerable, uncomfortable, or intimidating to share in a committed relationship.

Perhaps this is because of male's perception that women find their partners' pornography use hurtful, inappropriate, or dishonest. From cultural or societal norms, emerging adult males may feel that pornography is an acceptable pastime for single, not committed, males. Thus, to fit into existing norms, males may decline from disclosing such information to their partner. Here, secrecy may explain the anxiety that many men may be experiencing. In addition, a male's perceptions of his female partner's eagerness to discuss pornography may add to the levels of anxiety that he feels, especially if that readiness is not matched or felt by the male. However, avoiding anxiety-producing topics (such as pornography) in romantic relationships often leads to lower relationship satisfaction (Velotti et al., 2015), so it is imperative that today's young adults engage in such conversations. Despite its widespread use, pornography seems to be something that today's emerging adult males are not wanting to bring to (or bring up in) relationships. To explore these ideas further, future research should look at pornography acceptance by relationship status.

Religiosity

In our analysis, we found that religiosity was a more significant predictor than gender for emerging adults' beliefs that their pornography use made them inadequate partners in committed relationships. Religiosity was also a strong predictor for anxiety related to communicating about pornography. These findings can be explained by the social (and sexual) scripts that are often learned in religious settings. Religious emerging adults may hold strong beliefs about the importance of "worthiness" when forming a committed relationship. Pornography use that would make a religious individual "unworthy," is also bound to lead him or her to feeling more anxiety in forming, and communicating their "unworthiness" in relationships. Communicating in healthy ways about pornography in romantic relationships will also be vital for religious emerging adults, especially because of the negative labels and reactions attached to pornography use in religious circles.

LIMITATIONS AND FUTURE DIRECTIONS

Using Amazon's mechanical Turk online crowdsourcing system may have introduced sample bias into our study. There may be certain characteristics of individuals who utilized Amazon's mechanical Turk site that made them more or less likely to report their attitudes and behaviors relating to pornography use and relationships. Further, because we utilized individual data (vs. dyadic data), the study should not be interpreted to measure couple outcomes, but rather individual outcomes/ individuals' perceptions of couple outcomes. Future research should employ dyadic data from romantic partners to further examine relationship outcomes.

Also, although our sample demographics reflect an impressive level of diversity on relationship and religious factors, our sample was predominantly white. Thus, our sample may not be as internationally representative as possible. For future studies, it may be important to analyze differences in behavior between emerging adults in different parts of the world, or to compare emerging adults in America with emerging adults from other countries.

In terms of religious representation, because our sample was comprised predominantly of Christian (Catholic & Protestant together added up to about 30%) and Hindu individuals (about 30%), we are unable to generalize these findings to all religious circles. There may be specific scripts and rules within in Hinduism and Christianity that teach about pornography in a way that the effects of its use are magnified compared to other religious groups. In order to produce more generalizable results, we would employ random stratified sampling and include equal proportions of major religious groups. In the future, it would be valuable to study the differences between religious groups regarding pornography use. Further, no variables representing cultural attitudes toward pornography were included in this study. Taking cultural and societal norms surrounding pornography into consideration will be an important factor for researchers to consider when looking at pornography outcomes, as different cultural attitudes and beliefs about pornography and sexuality have been seen to alter its effects (Löfgren-Mårtenson & Månsson, 2010).

Despite these limitations, the data presented here, combined with previous scholarship on emerging adults suggests that pornography has a significant influence on emerging adult's behaviors and relationships. While only a small proportion display compulsive pornography-viewing behaviors, the majority of today's emerging adults use pornography, and most emerging adult males use pornography frequently. Emerging adult males also consume a wider spectrum of pornographic material with higher frequency than women. Pornography use seems to be associated with anxiety in relationship formation and a certain discomfort for emerging adults in established relationships. This anxiety is most apparent among male and religious emerging adults, but also exists among non-religious and female emerging adults. As pornography use becomes more widespread, emerging adults may experience more pornography-related anxieties and relational dynamics in romantic relationships.

In order to address the issues at hand, emerging adults will need to learn to talk about pornography in healthy ways as to lessen the anxiety they experience in the relationship, and thereby improve overall quality of their relationships. Further, relationship and sexual educators should consider including curriculum that can prepare young people and emerging adults to address the topic of pornography with romantic partners. Individual and couple therapists can also help their young clients to explore these topics in a safe and structured atmosphere, allowing them to practice and prepare to discuss them with future partners. Doing so will help lessen the anxiety or discomfort that these individuals experience, and prepare them for healthier relationships.

REFERENCES

Arnett, J. J. (2000). Emerging adulthood: A theory of development from the late teens through the twenties. *The American Psychologist*, *55*(5), 469–480. doi:10.1037/0003-066X.55.5.469

Attwood, F. (2005). What do people do with porn? Qualitative research into the consumption, use, and experience of pornography and other sexually explicit media. *Sexuality & Culture*, *9*(2), 65–86. doi:10.1007/s12119-005-1008-7

Bandura, A. (1977). *Social Learning Theory*. Englewood Cliffs, NJ: Prentice-Hall.

Barak, A., Fisher, W. A., Belfry, S., & Lashambe, D. R. (1999). Sex, guys, and cyberspace: Effects of internet pornography and individual differences on mens attitudes toward women. *Journal of Psychology & Human Sexuality*, *11*(1), 63–91. doi:10.1300/J056v11n01_04

Bartholomew, K., & Horowitz, L. M. (1991). Attachment styles among young adults: A test of a four-category model. *Journal of Personality and Social Psychology*, *61*(2), 226–244. doi:10.1037/0022-3514.61.2.226

Bersamin, M. M., Zamboanga, B. L., Schwartz, S. J., Donnellan, M. B., Hudson, M., Weisskirch, R. S., & Caraway, S. J. (2014). Risky business: Is there an association between casual sex and mental health among emerging adults? *Journal of Sex Research*, *51*(1), 43–51. doi:10.1080/00224499.2013.772088

Bradshaw, C., Kahn, A. S., & Saville, B. K. (2010). To hook up or date: Which gender benefits? *Sex Roles*, *62*(9-10), 661–669. doi:10.1007/s11199-010-9765-7

Braithwaite, S. R., Coulson, G., Keddington, K., & Fincham, F. D. (2015). The influence of pornography on sexual scripts and hooking up among emerging adults in college. *Archives of Sexual Behavior*, *44*(1), 111–123. doi:10.1007/s10508-014-0351-x

Braun-Courville, D. K., & Rojas, M. (2009). Exposure to sexually explicit websites and adolescent sexual attitudes and behaviors. *The Journal of Adolescent Health*, *45*(2), 156–162. doi:10.1016/j.jadohealth.2008.12.004

Bridges, A. J., Wosnitzer, R., Scharrer, E., Sun, C., & Liberman, R. (2010). Aggression and sexual behavior in best-selling pornography videos: A content analysis update. *Violence Against Women*, *16*(10), 1065–1085. doi:10.1177/1077801210382866

Brown, J. D., & LEngle, K. L. (2009). X-rated sexual attitudes and behaviors associated with US early adolescents exposure to sexually explicit media. *Communication Research*, *36*(1), 129–151. doi:10.1177/0093650208326465

Byers, E. S., & Demmons, S. (1999). Sexual satisfaction and sexual self-disclosure within dating relationships. *Journal of Sex Research*, *36*(2), 180–189. doi:10.1080/00224499909551983

Carroll, J. S., Padilla-Walker, L. M., Nelson, L. J., Olson, C. D., Barry, C. M., & Madsen, S. D. (2008). Generation XXX: Pornography acceptance and use among emerging adults. *Journal of Adolescent Research*, *23*(1), 6–30. doi:10.1177/0743558407306348

Carroll, J. S., Willoughby, B., Badger, S., Nelson, L. J., Barry, C. M., & Madsen, S. D. (2007). So close, yet so far away: The impact of varying marital horizons on emerging adulthood. *Journal of Adolescent Research*, *22*(3), 219–247. doi:10.1177/0743558407299697

Check, J. V., & Malamuth, N. M. (1986). Pornography and sexual aggression: A social learning theory analysis. *Annals of the International Communication Association*, *9*(1), 181–213. doi:10.1080/23808985.1986.11678607

Coleman, E. (2011). Impulsive/compulsive sexual behavior: Assessment and treatment. The Oxford Handbook of Impulse Control Disorders, 375.

Coyne, S. M., Padilla-Walker, L. M., & Howard, E. (2013). Emerging in a digital world: A decade review of media use, effects, and gratifications in emerging adulthood. *Emerging Adulthood*, *1*(2), 125–137. doi:10.1177/2167696813479782

Crawford, M., & Popp, D. (2003). Sexual double standards: A review and methodological critique of two decades of research. *Journal of Sex Research*, *40*(1), 13–26. doi:10.1080/00224490309552163

Eyal, K., & Kunkel, D. (2008). The effects of sex in television drama shows on emerging adults sexual attitudes and moral judgments. *Journal of Broadcasting & Electronic Media*, *52*(2), 161–181. doi:10.1080/08838150801991757

Feeney, J. A., & Noller, P. (1990). Attachment style as a predictor of adult romantic relationships. *Journal of Personality and Social Psychology*, *58*(2), 281–291. doi:10.1037/0022-3514.58.2.281

Fincham, F. D., & Cui, M. (Eds.). (2010). *Romantic relationships in emerging adulthood.* Cambridge University Press. doi:10.1017/CBO9780511761935

Frith, H., & Kitzinger, C. (2001). Reformulating sexual script theory: Developing a discursive psychology of sexual negotiation. *Theory & Psychology*, *11*(2), 210. doi:10.1177/0959354301112004

Garcia, F. D., & Thibaut, F. (2010). Sexual addictions. *The American Journal of Drug and Alcohol Abuse*, *36*(5), 254–260. doi:10.3109/00952990.2010.503823

Giugliano, J. R. (2013). Sex addiction as a mental health diagnosis: Coming together or coming apart? *Sexologies*, *22*(3), e77–e80. doi:10.1016/j.sexol.2012.08.018

Hald, G. M. (2006). Gender differences in pornography consumption among young heterosexual Danish adults. *Archives of Sexual Behavior*, *35*(5), 577–585. doi:10.1007/s10508-006-9064-0

Hald, G. M., Kuyper, L., Adam, P. C., & Wit, J. B. (2013). Does viewing explain doing? Assessing the association between sexually explicit materials use and sexual behaviors in a large sample of Dutch adolescents and young adults. *Journal of Sexual Medicine*, *10*(12), 2986–2995. doi:10.1111/jsm.12157

Hald, G. M., & Malamuth, N. M. (2008). Self-perceived effects of pornography consumption. *Archives of Sexual Behavior*, *37*(4), 614–625. doi:10.1007/s10508-007-9212-1

Hald, G. M., Malamuth, N. M., & Yuen, C. (2010). Pornography and attitudes supporting violence against women: Revisiting the relationship in non-experimental studies. *Aggressive Behavior*, *36*(1), 14–20. doi:10.1002/ab.20328

Hald, G. M., Seaman, C., & Linz, D. (2014). Sexuality and pornography. In D. Tolman, L. Diamond, J. Bauermeister, W. George, J. Pfaus, & L. Ward, (Eds.), APA handbook of sexuality and psychology, Vol. 1: Person-based approaches. American Psychological Association. doi:10.1037/14194-001

Hall, P. (2014). Sex addiction–An extraordinarily contentious problem. *Sexual and Relationship Therapy*, *29*(1), 68–75. doi:10.1080/14681994.2013.861898

Kalichman, S. C., & Rompa, D. (1995). Sexual sensation seeking and sexual compulsivity scales: Validity, and predicting HIV risk behavior. *Journal of Personality Assessment*, *65*(3), 586–601. doi:10.1207/s15327752jpa6503_16

Kelley, H. H., & Thibaut, J. W. (1978). *Interpersonal relations: A theory of interdependence*. New York: Wiley-Interscience.

Kingston, D. A., & Malamuth, N. M. (2011). Problems with aggregate data and the importance of individual differences in the study of pornography and sexual aggression: Comment on Diamond, Jozifkova, and Weiss (2010). *Archives of Sexual Behavior*, *40*(5), 1045–1048. doi:10.1007/s10508-011-9743-3

Kuzma, J. M., & Black, D. W. (2008). Epidemiology, prevalence, and natural history of compulsive sexual behavior. *The Psychiatric Clinics of North America*, *31*(4), 603–611. doi:10.1016/j.psc.2008.06.005

Lefkowitz, E. S., & Gillen, M. M. (2006). *"Sex is just a normal part of life": Sexuality in emerging adulthood*. Academic Press.

Levinson, D. J. (1978). *The seasons of a man's life*. Random House LLC.

Lo, V. H., & Wei, R. (2002). Third-person effect, gender, and pornography on the internet. *Journal of Broadcasting & Electronic Media*, *46*(1), 13–33. doi:10.1207/s15506878jobem4601_2

Löfgren-Mårtenson, L., & Månsson, S. A. (2010). Lust, love, and life: A qualitative study of Swedish adolescents perceptions and experiences with pornography. *Journal of Sex Research*, *47*(6), 568–579. doi:10.1080/00224490903151374

Malamuth, N. M. (1996). Sexually explicit media, gender differences, and evolutionary theory. *Journal of Communication*, *46*(3), 8–31. doi:10.1111/j.1460-2466.1996.tb01486.x

Malamuth, N. M., & Check, J. V. (1985). The effects of aggressive pornography on beliefs in rape myths: Individual differences. *Journal of Research in Personality*, *19*(3), 299–320. doi:10.1016/0092-6566(85)90021-2

Malamuth, N. M., Hald, G. M., & Koss, M. (2012). Pornography, individual differences in risk and mens acceptance of violence against women in a representative sample. *Sex Roles*, *66*(7-8), 427–439. doi:10.1007/s11199-011-0082-6

McKee, A. (2007). The relationship between attitudes towards women, consumption of pornography, and other demographic variables in a survey of 1,023 consumers of pornography. *International Journal of Sexual Health*, *19*(1), 31–45. doi:10.1300/J514v19n01_05

Mikulincer, M. (2006). Attachment, caregiving, and sex within romantic relationships. *Dynamics of Romantic Love: Attachment, Caregiving, and Sex*, 23-42.

Monto, M. A., & Carey, A. G. (2014). A new standard of sexual behavior? Are claims associated with the hookup culture supported by general social survey data? *Journal of Sex Research*, *51*(6), 605–615. doi:10.1080/00224499.2014.906031

Morgan, E. M. (2011). Associations between young adults use of sexually explicit materials and their sexual preferences, behaviors, and satisfaction. *Journal of Sex Research*, *48*(6), 520–530. doi:10.1080/00224499.2010.543960

Mosher, D. L., & MacIan, P. (1994). College men and women respond to X-rated videos intended for male or female audiences: Gender and sexual scripts. *Journal of Sex Research*, *31*(2), 99–113. doi:10.1080/00224499409551736

Nelson, L. J., Padilla-Walker, L. M., & Carroll, J. S. (2010). I believe it is wrong but I still do it: A comparison of religious young men who do versus do not use pornography. *Psychology of Religion and Spirituality*, *2*(3), 136–147. doi:10.1037/a0019127

Novak, S. P., & Clayton, R. R. (2001). The influence of school environment and self-regulation on transitions between stages of cigarette smoking: A multilevel analysis. *Health Psychology*, *20*(3), 196–207. doi:10.1037/0278-6133.20.3.196

Olmstead, S. B., Negash, S., Pasley, K., & Fincham, F. D. (2013). Emerging adults expectations for pornography use in the context of future committed romantic relationships: A qualitative study. *Archives of Sexual Behavior*, *42*(4), 625–635. doi:10.1007/s10508-012-9986-7

Owen, J., Fincham, F. D., & Moore, J. (2011). Short-term prospective study of hooking up among college students. *Archives of Sexual Behavior*, *40*(2), 331–341. doi:10.1007/s10508-010-9697-x

Padgett, V. R., Brislin-Slütz, J. A., & Neal, J. A. (1989). Pornography, erotica, and attitudes toward women: The effects of repeated exposure. *Journal of Sex Research*, *26*(4), 479–491. doi:10.1080/00224498909551529

Paolacci, G., Chandler, J., & Ipeirotis, P. G. (2010). Running experiments on amazon mechanical turk. *Judgment and Decision Making*, *5*(5), 411–419.

Patterson, R., & Price, J. (2012). Pornography, religion, and the happiness gap: Does pornography impact the actively religious differently? *Journal for the Scientific Study of Religion*, *51*(1), 79–89. doi:10.1111/j.1468-5906.2011.01630.x

Paul, E. L., McManus, B., & Hayes, A. (2000). Hookups: Characteristics and correlates of college students spontaneous and anonymous sexual experiences. *Journal of Sex Research*, *37*(1), 76–88. doi:10.1080/00224490009552023

Peter, J., & Valkenburg, P. M. (2007). Adolescents exposure to a sexualized media environment and their notions of women as sex objects. *Sex Roles*, *56*(5-6), 381–395. doi:10.1007/s11199-006-9176-y

Phillips, B., Hajela, R., & Hilton, D. L. Jr. (2015). Sex addiction as a disease: Evidence for assessment, diagnosis, and response to critics. *Sexual Addiction & Compulsivity*, *22*(2), 167–192. doi:10.1080/10720162.2015.1036184

Poulsen, F. O., Busby, D. M., & Galovan, A. M. (2013). Pornography use: Who uses it and how it is associated with couple outcomes. *Journal of Sex Research*, *50*(1), 72–83. doi:10.1080/00224499.2011.648027

Regnerus, M., & Uecker, J. (2010). *Premarital sex in America: How young americans meet, mate, and think about marrying*. Oxford University Press. doi:10.1093/acprof:oso/9780199743285.001.0001

Reich, R. R., Cummings, J. R., Greenbaum, P. E., Moltisanti, A. J., & Goldman, M. S. (2015). *The temporal "pulse" of drinking: Tracking 5 years of binge drinking in emerging adults*. Academic Press.

Resch, M. N., & Alderson, K. G. (2014). Female partners of men who use pornography: Are honesty and mutual use associated with relationship satisfaction? *Journal of Sex & Marital Therapy*, *40*(5), 410–424. doi:10.1080/0092623X.2012.751077

Romito, P., & Beltramini, L. (2011). Watching pornography: Gender differences, violence and victimization. An exploratory study in Italy. *Violence Against Women*.

Rozler, J., & Lavinthal, A. (2010). *The hookup handbook: A single girl's guide to living it up*. Simon and Schuster.

Salas-Wright, C. P., Vaughn, M. G., & Maynard, B. R. (2014). Profiles of religiosity and their association with risk behavior among emerging adults in the United States. *Emerging Adulthood.*

Sessoms, J. (2011). *The cyber pornography use inventory: Comparing a religious and secular sample.* Academic Press.

Seto, M. C., Maric, A., & Barbaree, H. E. (2001). The role of pornography in the etiology of sexual aggression. *Aggression and Violent Behavior*, *6*(1), 35–53. doi:10.1016/S1359-1789(99)00007-5

Shaver, P., & Hazan, C. (1987). Being lonely, falling in love: Perspectives from attachment theory. *Journal of Social Behavior and Personality*.

Sherman, A. J., & Tocantins, N. (2004). *The happy hook up: A single girl's guide to casual sex*. Springer Science & Business.

Shulman, S., & Connolly, J. (2013). The challenge of romantic relationships in emerging adulthood: Reconceptualization of the field. *Emerging Adulthood*, *1*(1), 27–39. doi:10.1177/2167696812467330

Stack, S., Wasserman, I., & Kern, R. (2004). Adult social bonds and use of Internet pornography. *Social Science Quarterly*, *85*(1), 75–88. doi:10.1111/j.0038-4941.2004.08501006.x

Stanley, S. M., Rhoades, G. K., & Fincham, F. D. (2011). *Understanding romantic relationships among emerging adults: The significant roles of cohabitation and ambiguity*. Cambridge University Press.

Stewart, D. N., & Szymanski, D. M. (2012). Young adult womens reports of their male romantic partners pornography use as a correlate of their self-esteem, relationship quality, and sexual satisfaction. *Sex Roles*, *67*(5-6), 257–271. doi:10.1007/s11199-012-0164-0

Štulhofer, A., Buško, V., & Landripet, I. (2010). Pornography, sexual socialization, and satisfaction among young men. *Archives of Sexual Behavior*, *39*(1), 168–178. doi:10.1007/s10508-008-9387-0

Suri, S., & Watts, D. J. (2011). Cooperation and contagion in web-based, networked public goods experiments. *PLoS ONE*, *6*(3), e16836. doi:10.1371/journal.pone.0016836

Swanson, J. A., & Walker, E. (2015) Academic versus non-academic emerging adult college student technology use. *Technology, Knowledge and Learning*, 1-12.

Tolman, D. L., Diamond, L. M., Bauermeister, J. A., George, W. H., Pfaus, J. G., & Ward, L. (2014). APA Handbook of Sexuality and Psychology, Vol. 2: Contextual approaches. APA.

Traen, B., Nilsen, T. S., & Stigum, H. (2006). Use of pornography in traditional media and on the internet in Norway. *Journal of Sex Research*, *43*(3), 245–254. doi:10.1080/00224490609552323

Umemura, T., Lacinová, L., & Macek, P. (2014). Is emerging adults' attachment preference for the romantic partner transferred from their attachment preferences for their mother, father, and friends?. *Emerging Adulthood*.

Velotti, P., Balzarotti, S., Tagliabue, S., English, T., Zavattini, G. C., & Gross, J. J. (2015). Emotional suppression in early marriage: Actor, partner, and similarity effects on marital quality. *Journal of Social and Personal Relationships*.

Weinberg, M. S., Williams, C. J., Kleiner, S., & Irizarry, Y. (2010). Pornography, normalization, and empowerment. *Archives of Sexual Behavior*, *39*(6), 1389–1401. doi:10.1007/s10508-009-9592-5

Willoughby, B. J., & Busby, D. M. (2015). In the eye of the beholder: Exploring variations in the perceptions of pornography. *Journal of Sex Research*, 1–11.

Willoughby, B. J., Carroll, J. S., Busby, D. M., & Brown, C. C. (2015). Differences in pornography use among couples: Associations with satisfaction, stability, and relationship processes. *Archives of Sexual Behavior*, 1–14.

Willoughby, B. J., Carroll, J. S., Busby, D. M., & Brown, C. C. (2016). Differences in pornography use among couples: Associations with satisfaction, stability, and relationship processes. *Archives of Sexual Behavior*, *45*(1), 145–158. doi:10.1007/s10508-015-0562-9

Willoughby, B. J., Carroll, J. S., Nelson, L. J., & Padilla-Walker, L. M. (2014). Associations between relational sexual behaviour, pornography use, and pornography acceptance among US college students. *Culture, Health & Sexuality*, *16*(9), 1052–1069. doi:10.1080/13691058.2014.927075

Willoughby, B. J., & Hall, S. S. (2015). Enthusiasts, delayers, and the ambiguous middle: Marital paradigms among emerging adults. *Emerging Adulthood*, *3*(2), 123–135. doi:10.1177/2167696814548478

Willoughby, B. J., Hall, S. S., & Luczak, H. P. (2013). Marital paradigms: A conceptual framework for marital attitudes, values, and beliefs. *Journal of Family Issues*.

Wright, P. J., Tokunaga, R. S., & Kraus, A. (2015). A meta-analysis of pornography consumption and actual acts of sexual aggression in general population studies. *Journal of Communication*.

Young, K. S. (2008). Internet sex addiction risk factors, stages of development, and treatment. *The American Behavioral Scientist*, *52*(1), 21–37. doi:10.1177/0002764208321339

KEY TERMS AND DEFINITIONS

Compulsive Pornography Use: In this study, compulsive pornography use was measured by combining the pornography compulsion scale (translated from the sexual compulsion scale) with weekly or daily use. Those who scored above the median for compulsive pornography use and also reported using pornography daily or weekly were considered to be "compulsive" pornography users.

Emerging Adulthood: The stage from the late teens through the twenties, encompassing 18 to 30 year-olds.

Hook-Up: A brief, uncommitted sexual encounter involving kissing to intercourse without an understood promise of a continued relationship.

Pornography: Sexually explicit words, images, or videos that have the intent to arouse the user.

Religiosity: In this study, religiosity was measured by self-reports of religious importance and religious affiliations. "Religious" individuals were those who scored high on religious importance and also identified with an organized religion, while those who were "not religious" either did not identify with a religious affiliation or did belong to a religion but did not consider their religion personally important.

Sexual Script Theory: Rooted in the widely used script theory, which teaches that human behavior is dictated by patterns called "scripts" that individuals "act out" due to exposure and conditioning. Sexual scripts are culturally available messages that define what 'counts' as sex, or how to act during a sexual encounter.

Social Learning Theory: States that individuals learn not only by their own experiences, but also through the observation of others' behaviors.

APPENDIX: TABLES

Table 1. Type of pornography viewed in the last twelve months

	Female	Male
Women in Lingerie	47.4%**	74.4%
Photos of women exposing breasts and/or genitals	46.3%**	75.2%
Photos of men exposing genitals	45.8%**	35.5%
Photos of sexual intercourse	47.3%**	72.4%
Videos of sexual intercourse	63.5%**	79.8%
Videos of other explicit sexual acts	58.1%*	73.9%

**$p<.001$, *p<.01

Table 2. Percentages of emerging adults that have ended relationships solely and partially because of pornography use

	Male	Female
Solely b/c porn	15.9%**	10.2%
Partially b/c porn	15.1%*	12.7%

Table 3. Regression model predicting relationship anxiety

Variable	Model 1		
	b	SE	β
Gender	-.523**	.079	-.209
Race	.345**	.083	.138
Impulsivity	.406**	.041	.310
Relationship Status	-.312**	.085	-.117
Age	.014	.012	.037
Religiosity	.594**	.082	.236

$R^2 = .343$
**$p<.001$

Table 4. Regression model predicting communication anxiety

Variable	Model 1		
	b	SE	β
Gender	-.577**	.084	-.221
Race	.104	.089	.040
Impulsivity	.360**	.043	.268
Relationship Status	-.255*	.090	-.092
Age	.017	.013	.043
Religiosity	.435**	.087	.166

$R^2 = .024$
*$p<.01$, **$p<.001$

Chapter 13

Victimization or Entertainment?

How Attachment and Rejection Sensitivity Relate to Sexting Experiences, Evaluations, and Victimization

Alaina Brenick
University of Connecticut, USA

Kaitlin M. Flannery
University of Connecticut, USA

Emily Rankin
Central Connecticut State University, USA

ABSTRACT

As texting continues to serve as an increasingly common method of communication among emerging adults, increases in rates of sexting, or sending sexually explicit messages, pictures, or videos, have also been observed. While consensual sexting can facilitate intimacy in relationships, when used as a tool to victimize others, it has been shown to yield a range of negative outcomes- from embarrassment to severe depression and suicide. This chapter aims to review the existing literature on emerging adults' engagement in and evaluations of sexting, while also considering the risks associated with sexting victimization. The role that individual characteristics, such as attachment style and rejection sensitivity, play in the relationship between experiences with and evaluations of using sexting as a tool for victimization will also be explored.

INTRODUCTION

As technology use increasingly dominates the social lives of emerging adults (EAs), intimate communication—and potentially victimization—between romantic partners is transforming. This shift is especially apparent in rates of sexting, or the sending or receiving of sexually suggestive written messages, pictures, or videos. Sexting has become an increasingly common relationship ritual in young adults' romantic

DOI: 10.4018/978-1-5225-1856-3.ch013

lives, with a conservative estimate of nearly 43% of youth between the ages of 18-24 years having sexted (Gordon-Messer, Bauermeister, Grodzinski, & Zimmerman, 2013). In another sample, 80.9% of 697 undergraduate participants reported having sent a sext at least once in their lifetime, and nearly half of the entire sample (48.5%) had sent a sext within the last 30 days (Hudson & Fetro, 2015). Given its ubiquity in emerging adulthood, it is essential to consider that although consensual sexting can facilitate intimacy in relationships (e.g., Burkett, 2015), when individuals are coerced into sexting or when sexting is used as a tool to victimize others, it can yield a range of negative outcomes from embarrassment to severe depression and suicide (Celizic, 2009; Judge, 2012). Nonetheless, little research has examined EAs' actual engagement in and evaluations of sexting as they relate to individual characteristics that might be associated with heightened vulnerability to the potential negative outcomes of sexting. In an attempt to understand those individuals who might be most at risk, this chapter presents an original study that addresses this gap in the literature by assessing EAs' engagement in and evaluations of sexting and sexting victimization, together with individual characteristics—insecure attachment and rejection sensitivity—that have been demonstrated to be associated with other types of relational victimization (e.g., Downey & Feldman, 1996; Drouin & Tobin, 2014), and which therefore might be linked to heightened vulnerability to the negative aspects of sexting, such as sexting victimization.

BACKGROUND

General Trends in Sexting

Though sexting prevalence rates vary from study to study (see Klettke, Hallford, & Mellor, 2014), even conservative estimates (e.g., Gordon-Messer et al., 2013) indicate that sexting has become common practice among EAs. The variability in estimates of sexting behaviors is likely due to the complexity in operationalizing sexting altogether (Klettke et al., 2014). In a review of young adults' sexting, Klettke and colleagues (2014) found on average 53% of young adults send sexual texts and photos (49% reported sending sexts specifically with photo images), while 56% of young adults report having received sexts. Klettke and colleagues (2014) emphasized the importance of breaking down sexting prevalence rates by type of sext (e.g., text or image) and the role of the individual (e.g., sender or recipient). In line with this recommendation, this chapter's authors assessed EAs' sexting in terms of sending and receiving text, image, and video messages. Similar to Klettke and colleagues' (2014) results, this chapter's authors found that 57% of EAs sent or received text based sexts, 43% sent and 49% received photo sexts, and 17% sent and 20% received video sexts.

As sexting in all forms has become a more normative manner of communication within relationships, a body of literature has emerged suggesting that sexting can be not only a normative, but also a positive experience in emerging adulthood, fostering intimacy and pleasure within a close relationship (Burkett, 2015; Parker, Blackburn, Perry & Hawks, 2013), as evidenced in studies assessing EAs' motivations for sexting. For instance, Hudson and Fetro (2015) found that in a sample of college students, attitudes toward sexting, perceptions of sexting norms, and behavioral intentions of sexting all significantly predicted activity with sexting; Kopecký (2011) found that individuals reported sexting to be viewed as arousing or to initiate sexual activity. Additionally, for those who were considered current sexters (i.e., had sent a sext within the last 30 days), the strongest predictor of their sexting activity was their attitude toward sexting, which the authors suggest indicated that current sexters were intentional in their sexting, and were motivated to sext because they wanted to and not because they felt social pressure to do so (Hudson

& Fetro, 2015). These motivations to sext were mirrored in work by Lee and Crofts (2015), who argued that the gendered discourse surrounding females' motivations to engage in sexting does not accurately reflect the motivations most females actually express. Lee and Crofts (2015) acknowledge the existence of the widely discussed scenarios involving females experiencing pressure to send sexts to males; however, they suggest that most females decide to engage in sexting to pursue pleasure or because they desire to do so. Work by Dir and Cyders (2015) similarly implies that, although many people discuss sexting in terms of negative outcomes, these were rarely reported in that sample (the most common negative experience was having sexts shared with others, which happened to 12% of the sample). Renfrow and Rollo (2014) suggested that undergraduates were aware of the risk of having their sexts shared, but engaged in sexting anyway and attempted to minimize these risks by keeping sexts fun and less explicit, maintaining deniability in their sexts, and citing the normalcy of their actions. These participants also suggested that they saw benefits to sexting, such that it helped maintain their relationships, especially long distance relationships (Burkett, 2015; Drouin et al., 2013). From these studies, it is clear that sexting can serve a unique purpose in romantic relationships, and despite an overwhelmingly negative narrative surrounding sexting, EAs do not all perceive it to be victimizing or risky.

Sexting Victimization

Despite the perceived benefits of sexting, research has established that there can be significant risks associated with sexting victimization. Contrary to Lee and Crofts (2015), work by Drouin, Ross, and Tobin (2015), for instance, demonstrated that approximately one fifth of a sample of EAs felt coerced into engaging in sexting. In fact, across a number of studies (e.g., Englander, 2012; Kopecký, 2011; Walker, Sanci, Temple-Smith, 2013), pressure or coercion from peers or partners was listed as a frequent motivation for sexting. Drouin and colleagues (2015) found that although the reported coercion was typically subtle, as opposed to containing threats, participants still reported trauma associated with this coercion, especially when looking back at the events. This study also revealed that sexting coercion was associated with intimate partner violence, as well as coercion into engaging in physical sex, indicating that sexting is another outlet through which intimate partner violence can be perpetrated (Drouin et al, 2015). Thus, even rare occurrences of sexting victimization should be addressed diligently.

Moreover, victimization can occur through the unauthorized sharing of sexts—an occurrence that is often viewed as a peer-encouraged means to obtain popularity amongst young men (Burkett, 2015; Ringrose, Harvey, Gill, & Livingstone, 2013). Media coverage offers additional evidence for such sexting victimization, although typically with extreme cases, for example, the widely broadcast story of an 18-year-old female who sent a sexual photo to her boyfriend. When the couple ended their relationship, the boyfriend distributed the sexual photo to their peers at school. Peers then began to humiliate the female, calling her degrading names, which left her feeling depressed, and afraid to attend school; soon after, she committed suicide (Celizic, 2009). Although suicide is an extreme and rare outcome associated with sexting, the evidence for this possibility of victimization clearly necessitates an understanding of what individual characteristics might place a person at greater risk for the negative rather than positive outcomes of sexting. Two such risk factors might be the attachment security of an individual as well as their sensitivity to rejection. Both of these characteristics have been shown to increase vulnerability to and expectations of interpersonal victimization through personal experiences of loneliness, exclusion, abandonment, or worry about partner availability (Weisskirch & Delevi, 2011; Zimmer-Gembeck, Trevaskis, Nesdale, & Downey, 2013; Drouin & Tobin, 2014), and therefore necessitate further study into their relationship to sexting and sexting victimization.

ATTACHMENT, REJECTION SENSITIVITY, AND SEXTING

Individuals with insecure attachment or rejection sensitivity experience higher levels of victimization and vulnerability in their romantic relationships (Drouin & Tobin, 2014). However, to date, only two studies have assessed attachment in relation to sexting (see Klettke et al., 2014), and no research has examined the potentially moderating relation of attachment and rejection sensitivity with participants' engagement in and attitudes about sexting and sexting victimization. In this chapter, the authors will review the extant literature on engagement in and evaluations of sexting and sexting victimization as well as present findings from a recent study that assessed EAs' engagement in sexting, their perceptions of sexting and sexting victimization, and their self-reports of attachment security and rejection sensitivity. Gaining a deeper understanding of the relationship between these individual characteristics and individuals' engagement in and evaluations of sexting will be important in order to identify those most at risk for sexting victimization and inform potential intervention or awareness strategies for those individuals, in particular.

Insecure Attachment

Attachment refers to how individuals process and reflect on their thoughts and feelings regarding their own intimate relationship experiences. A wealth of previous research has demonstrated the relation between attachment and experiences of victimization and vulnerability in romantic relationships (see Drouin & Tobin, 2014). Attachment can be defined as a deep and enduring emotional bond between two people developed through the interactions a child has with his/her caregivers; such interactions can result in that child developing either a secure or insecure (e.g., anxious or avoidant) attachment. Whereas attachment is often used to describe the relationship a child has with his/her caregivers, many theorists have examined adult and couple attachment as well, noting many similarities in the unique context of adult romantic attachment, including the need for close physical contact, deep interest in one another, and experiencing a sense of safety when the other is nearby (see George, 2009). Adults often integrate their childhood attachment experiences into their adult relationships by seeking out similar characteristics in their partners that they experienced with their caregivers (Cassidy, 2001). Attachment classification, or the pattern of relating to others, develops into an internal working model that is thought to be the foundation for an individual's intimate relationships in the present and in the future (see Weisskirch & Delevi, 2011).

Previous research has shown that individuals with insecure attachment experience higher levels of victimization and vulnerability in their romantic relationships (Drouin & Tobin, 2014). However, to date, only a few studies have assessed attachment in relation to sexting (see Klettke et al., 2014). From those studies, there is evidence to suggest that EAs who demonstrate insecure attachment (i.e., anxious; Weisskirch & Delevi, 2011, or avoidant; Drouin & Landgraff, 2012), are more likely to engage in sexting, and to view their sexting experiences as more victimizing (Delevi & Weisskirch, 2013). As such, it is a logical extension of attachment theory to further investigate how an individual's anxious or avoidant attachment style relates to his or her experiences of sexting within intimate relationships.

Sexting can be used for a variety of reasons in romantic relationships, and those with differing attachment styles may vary in their motivations for sexting, which may in turn relate to sexting victimization. For some, sexting may serve as a new way to explore romantic relationships by providing a means of connection and reassurance, whereas for others sexting may provide distance within a relationship while also sustaining intimacy. Regardless of these potential uses and benefits, sexting can also leave a sexter vulnerable to victimization. By utilizing sexting as a tool for intimacy, or lack thereof, a sexter may be exposing him or herself to the potential for victimization through the distribution of their sexual images and messages. Below, the authors discuss the relation between anxious and avoidant attachment with motivations for and experiences of sexting and sexting victimization.

Anxious attachment, on one hand, is characterized as having a strong desire for intimacy with others but also an intense fear of being abandoned. Individuals with anxious attachment are likely to seek approval from others and will attempt to build closeness with their partner out of fear that their partner will lose interest in the relationship. These individuals may be worried or preoccupied about the availability and responsiveness of their romantic partner (see Delevi & Weisskirch, 2013; Weisskirch & Delevi, 2011). Those with anxious attachment often experience more pressure to send sexual messages to keep a romantic partner's interest or to satisfy relational expectations (Drouin & Tobin, 2014). Anxious individuals may use sexting to gain reassurance from their romantic partner and to ensure that their partner is emotionally invested (Drouin & Landgraff, 2012).

Those with anxious attachment also are more likely to experience sexting victimization in the form of unwanted but consensual sexting. In this context, individuals sext, but do so only because they feel obliged to participate. Heterosexual women who participate in unwanted but consensual sexting may display characteristics such as passivity, feeling responsible for maintaining relationship bonds, perceiving men's sexual urges as being uncontrollable and therefore unable to be resisted, and, for men, experiencing social pressure to have sex (Delevi & Weisskirch, 2012; Drouin & Tobin, 2014).

Avoidant attachment, on the other hand, is characterized as having a fear of being intimate or dependent on others. Individuals with avoidant attachment attempt to distance themselves from their partners to avoid being dependent or relied upon for emotional closeness and support (Drouin & Landgraff, 2012). Those with avoidant attachment styles may be less likely to talk on the phone with their partner and often try to distance themselves, perhaps utilizing sexting as preferred means of communication (Weisskirch & Delevi, 2011; Drouin & Landgraff, 2012). Thus, sexting could be appealing to avoidant individuals because it serves as a reasonable substitute for physical intimacy (Drouin & Landgraff, 2012).

Attachment theory also states that individuals develop expectations about whether loved ones will fulfill their needs or reject them (Erozkan, 2009). Insecure attachment has been linked to rejection sensitivity, which is characterized by fear of being deserted, abused, betrayed or victimized with a high degree of sensitivity towards rejection (Natarajan, Somasundaram, & Sundaram, 2011). A person with an insecure attachment also may be influenced by feelings of rejection and be more likely to experience victimization when they encounter rejection. Therefore, it is important to consider the interaction between insecure attachment styles and levels of rejection sensitivity when considering one's positive and negative experiences of sexting and sexting victimization and one's evaluations of such experiences.

Rejection Sensitivity

Rejection sensitivity is defined as a disposition to cognitively and affectively process information in such a way that rejection is both expected and perceived in the actions of others (Downey & Feldman, 1996). People who are highly sensitive to rejection fear being deserted, abused, or betrayed by others, and tend to react very strongly to instances of actual and perceived rejection (Downey & Feldman, 1996). Rejection sensitivity is associated with a range of problematic behaviors in intimate relationships. For instance, these individuals are likely to believe that their partner is dissatisfied with their relationship, and have been found to rate partners' behaviors as being more conflictual than do third-party observers (Norona, Salvatore, Welsh, & Darling, 2014). Consequently, those high in rejection sensitivity react accordingly and display behaviors such as jealousy, suspicion, and seeking control over a partner (Downey & Feldman, 1996). Alternatively, individuals high in rejection sensitivity may act submissively toward their partner and defer to their wishes in hopes of avoiding rejection (Hafen, Spilker, Chango, Marston, & Allen, 2014; Young & Furman, 2007). High levels of rejection sensitivity also have been linked to higher levels of depression, loneliness, exclusion, and, of particular importance for the present chapter, victimization from others (Zimmer-Gembeck et al., 2013). Given these characteristics associated with rejection sensitivity, it is unsurprising that rejection sensitivity is linked to both an increased risk for victimization and a greater negative response to the experience of victimization in the form of self-rated negative moods, and experimenter rated reactions of confusion, anger, or sadness (Downey & Feldman, 1996; Zimmer-Gembeck et al., 2014).

Because young people who are sensitive to rejection are highly motivated to avoid experiencing rejection, they may engage in behaviors that put them at risk for victimization (Young & Furman, 2007). In fact, rejection sensitivity has been linked to increased risk of victimization in multiple contexts including peer networks, friendships, and romantic relationships (Hafen et al., 2014; Zimmer-Gembeck & Duffy, 2014; Zimmer-Gembeck et al., 2014). Rejection sensitivity also has implications for the quality of these relationships, such that young adults who were high in rejection sensitivity in adolescence were less likely to be engaged in romantic relationships in emerging adulthood, and those who were in romantic relationships tended to report more negativity and anxiety within that relationship (Hafen et al., 2014); this study also revealed that females who increased in rejection sensitivity from adolescence to emerging adulthood were more likely to take on a role of submissiveness within their relationship, and defer power within the relationship to their partner.

Although these risks for victimization are clear, perhaps most related to patterns of sexting in emerging adulthood is the relation between rejection sensitivity and risk for sexual victimization as reported by Young and Furman (2007). Just as adolescent girls were more likely to act in ways that they believed were 'wrong' as a means to avoid losing their partner (Purdie & Downey, 2000), this study found that adolescents high in rejection sensitivity were more likely to experience sexual aggression into emerging adulthood (Young & Furman, 2007). However, as stressed by Edwards and Barber (2010), it is critically important to consider the context of sexual victimization; they astutely highlight that not just physically forced sexual interactions, but also compliant or consensual engagement in an activity in which someone does not really wish to partake, constitute sexual victimization, though contextually variant. While it is readily apparent that forced sexual interaction is victimization, coercion into consensual acts is also a form of victimization. Evaluations of victimization and responses to victimization differ based on the context in which victimization occurs (see Brenick & Romano, 2016; Rutland, Killen, & Abrams, 2010). Edwards and Barber (2010), examined sexual victimization in the context of condom use during intercourse, and the study found that those rejection sensitive individuals who wanted to use condoms during intercourse were less likely to use condoms if they believed that their partner did not want to use them. Similarly, sexual victimization also can take place through sexting, a context that also does not include forced sexual interaction. Given Edwards and Barber's (2010) findings on condom use, it is likely that those EAs who are highly rejection sensitive would be much more likely to yield to their partner's wishes to engage in sexting if that is what they believed their partner would want. Furthermore, this allows for potential continued victimization through unauthorized sharing of those sexts with unintended recipients. Although sexting is becoming an important part of relationships that inherently requires negotiations of roles within a relationship, no research thus far has considered sexting as a context for victimization that might be influenced by an individual's rejection sensitivity.

Beyond the direct influence of rejection sensitivity on the potential for victimization, rejection sensitivity is also highly related to insecure attachment styles (Natarajan et al., 2011). Given the literature linking attachment style to victimization both theoretically and empirically (Natarajan et al., 2011), and the clear association between rejection sensitivity and attachment (Erozkan, 2009; Natarajan et al., 2011), it is important to consider both individual characteristics in tandem. This was demonstrated in a study by Ozen, Sumer, and Demir (2010) in which relationship satisfaction (in this case, friendship) was predicted by both attachment and rejection sensitivity. Attachment had a direct effect on relationship satisfaction; however, rejection sensitivity moderated this effect such that rejection sensitivity influenced friendship satisfaction only for adolescents highly avoidant in their attachment style (Ozen et al., 2010). As suggested above, it is possible that rejection sensitivity might act as a moderator with insecure attachment to predict negative sexting experiences. If so, this situation sets the stage for individuals to be vulnerable to victimization, such as coercion into sexting, and then experience its negative outcomes as highly rejection sensitive individuals experience in their relationships. Altogether, it is clear that both attachment and rejection sensitivity are important individual characteristics to consider in relation to sexting patterns and victimization in emerging adulthood, but further research is needed to more clearly understand the relationship.

Current Research on Insecure Attachment, Rejection Sensitivity, and Sexting

The authors' present work set out to address these gaps in the literature by administering an online survey comprised of Collins' (1996) attachment scale, Downey and Feldman's (1996) rejection sensitivity questionnaire, and Alderson and Samimi's (2014) sexting experiences questionnaire. A sample of 169 EAs between 18-25 years of age (M_{age}=20.70, *SD*=.96; 4.7% African-American, 9.5% Asian-American, 77.5% European-American, 7.7% Hispanic-Latino) was obtained through online recruitment using email listservs sent out to the entire student body of a large public university in New England. The majority of participants self-identified as female (79.8%), as heterosexual (93.2%), and as being in a relationship (55.3%).

Measures

The online survey assessed participant demographics, attachment style, level of rejection sensitivity, and beliefs about and experiences with sexting. First participants were asked to report their gender, ethnicity, sexuality, age, and relationship status. Participants then completed the attachment, rejection sensitivity, and sexting experiences scales detailed below. Although the three measures have been widely used and are well established and validated, we pilot tested the combined instrument. Test fatigue was minimal, and comprehension was high, so no changes were made to the protocol.

Attachment

The *Revised Adult Attachment Scale* (Collins, 1996; alternative scoring) was used to assess participants' levels of insecure attachment. In the 18-item questionnaire, participants were asked to think about all of their relationships (past and present), and then respond to items in terms of how they experience their relationships. A scale of 1 (not at all characteristic of me) to 5 (very characteristic of me) was used to respond to items such as, "I find that people are never there when you need them" and "I often wonder whether romantic partners really care about me." The measure addressed two components of attachment: attachment anxiety (M=2.91, SD=1.02) and attachment avoidance (M=2.78, SD=0.74). Previous studies have demonstrated that this is a reliable and valid measure (Mikulincer & Shaver, 2016), and the Cronbach's alpha for the current sample was .87.

Rejection Sensitivity

Participants were administered the 18-item *Adult Rejection Sensitivity Questionnaire* (Downey & Feldman, 1996) to assess rejection sensitivity. The questionnaire asks participants to imagine themselves in hypothetical social situations and rate how concerned or anxious they would be about potential rejection in the scenarios. A scale of 1 (very unconcerned) to 6 (very concerned) was used to evaluate situations such as "Your boyfriend/ girlfriend has plans to go out with friends tonight, but you really want to spend the evening with him/her, and you tell him/her so." Participants were then asked to rate how concerned or anxious they would be over whether or not their boyfriend or girlfriend would decide to stay in. Scoring for this measure ranges from 2.00 to 26.00; the current participants' average score was 8.84 (SD=3.32). Previous studies have demonstrated that this is a reliable and valid measure (Downey & Feldman, 1996), and the Cronbach's alpha for the current sample was .85.

Sexting Experiences

A subsample of questions from Alderson and Samimi's (2014) questionnaire of potential sexting outcomes was used to assess participants' sexting experiences. This instrument provides a previously validated multifaceted conceptualization of sexting, assessing both the behaviors and beliefs of the participant in regards to the positive, negative, and neutral aspects of sexting. Specifically, the measure includes questions on five distinct sexting themes: *sexting entertainment*- participants' ratings of sexting as enjoyable and fun, Cronbach's alpha = .86; *sexting expectation*- participants' ratings of how typical and expected it is to engage in sexting, Cronbach's alpha = .78; *sexting sharing*- participants' reports of sharing sexts that they have received, Cronbach's alpha = .78; *sexting risk*- participants' beliefs that sexting is risky and could yield negative outcomes, Cronbach's alpha = .86; and *sexting regret*- participants' reports of having sent a sext that they later regretted sending (1 item). Responses were scaled from 1 (strongly disagree) to 7 (strongly agree). Sample questions include: "Sexting is a regular part of romantic relationships nowadays" (expectation; M=3.15, SD=1.08); "Sexting is fun" (entertainment; M=3.93, SD=1.34); "Sending sexually suggestive photos or videos is risky" (risk; M=6.25, SD=0.77); "I share the sexts I receive with my friends" (sharing; M=1.79; SD=1.28); "I have sent a sext and then regretted sending it later on" (regret; M=3.44, SD=1.97).

Results

For each of the dependent measures of sexting experiences, hierarchical multiple regressions were conducted with four steps: the first model included the control variables—gender and relationship status—as predictors. The second model added rejection sensitivity, anxious attachment, and avoidant attachment as predictors. The third and fourth models added all two- and three-way interaction terms, respectively, between the three predictor variables of interest. The data met all relevant statistical assumptions for this analysis. Given that interaction terms were examined in these regressions, all variables were mean centered (the variable mean was subtracted from each variable value) prior to analyses to increase interpretability of the results and reduce multicollinearity. This analysis revealed significant findings for three dependent variables: sexting entertainment, expectation, and sharing. Surprisingly, no significant results emerged for sexting risk or regret. Below we detail the significant results.

Sexting Entertainment

First, it is possible that insecure attachment and rejection sensitivity might not only leave an individual more likely to experience the negative and victimizing experiences of sexting, but also less likely to experience the positive experiences of sexting (e.g. seeing it as enjoyable and fun). To assess this possible influence, the authors analyzed the relation between insecure attachment, rejection sensitivity, and sexting entertainment. The results of the multiple regression analysis were significant in the highest model ($F(1,151)=5.62, p<.05$) with the following significant predictors: relationship status, rejection sensitivity, anxious attachment, and avoidant attachment. The last three effects were qualified by a significant 2-way interaction (anxious attachment by rejection sensitivity) and a significant 3-way interaction (anxious attachment by rejection sensitivity by avoidant attachment; see Table 1 for all coefficients). These results reveal that individuals in a romantic relationship, as compared to those who are single, were more likely to find sexting entertaining. In general, individuals who were higher in rejection sensitivity or avoidant attachment, or lower in anxious attachment found sexting to be less entertaining and enjoyable. However, the significant 3-way interaction (anxious attachment by rejection sensitivity by avoidant attachment) qualifies these findings such that higher levels of rejection sensitivity only relate to decreased entertainment value of sexting among participants who are either high in anxious or avoidant attachment; in cases where participants were only highly rejection sensitive in the absence of both anxious or avoidant attachment, they rated sexting as significantly more entertaining (see Figure 1).

Sexting Expectations

Next, sexting expectations were assessed as participants' beliefs about the typicality in which sexting is engaged among EAs. The multiple regression analysis was significant in the highest model ($F(1,151)=5.11$, $p<.05$) with anxious attachment as the only significant independent predictor, a significant 2-way interaction (anxious attachment by rejection sensitivity), and a significant 3-way interaction (anxious attachment by rejection sensitivity by avoidant attachment; see Table 1 for coefficients). Individuals who were higher in anxious attachment rated sexting as a highly typical experience in which they are expected to engage in intimate relationships. The significant 3-way interaction (anxious attachment by rejection sensitivity by avoidant attachment) provides a more nuanced picture; overall, participants who were lower in rejection sensitivity were moderately accepting of sexting as a normative expectation in relationships regardless of their levels of anxious or avoidant attachment. However, participants with higher rejection sensitivity and either higher anxious or avoidant attachment were less likely to rate sexting as typical and expected, whereas participants with higher levels of rejection sensitivity in the absence of both anxious and avoidant attachment, instead rated sexting as increasingly expected and typical (see Figure 2).

Figure 1. Sexting entertainment: 3-way interaction between avoidant attachment, anxious attachment, and rejection sensitivity

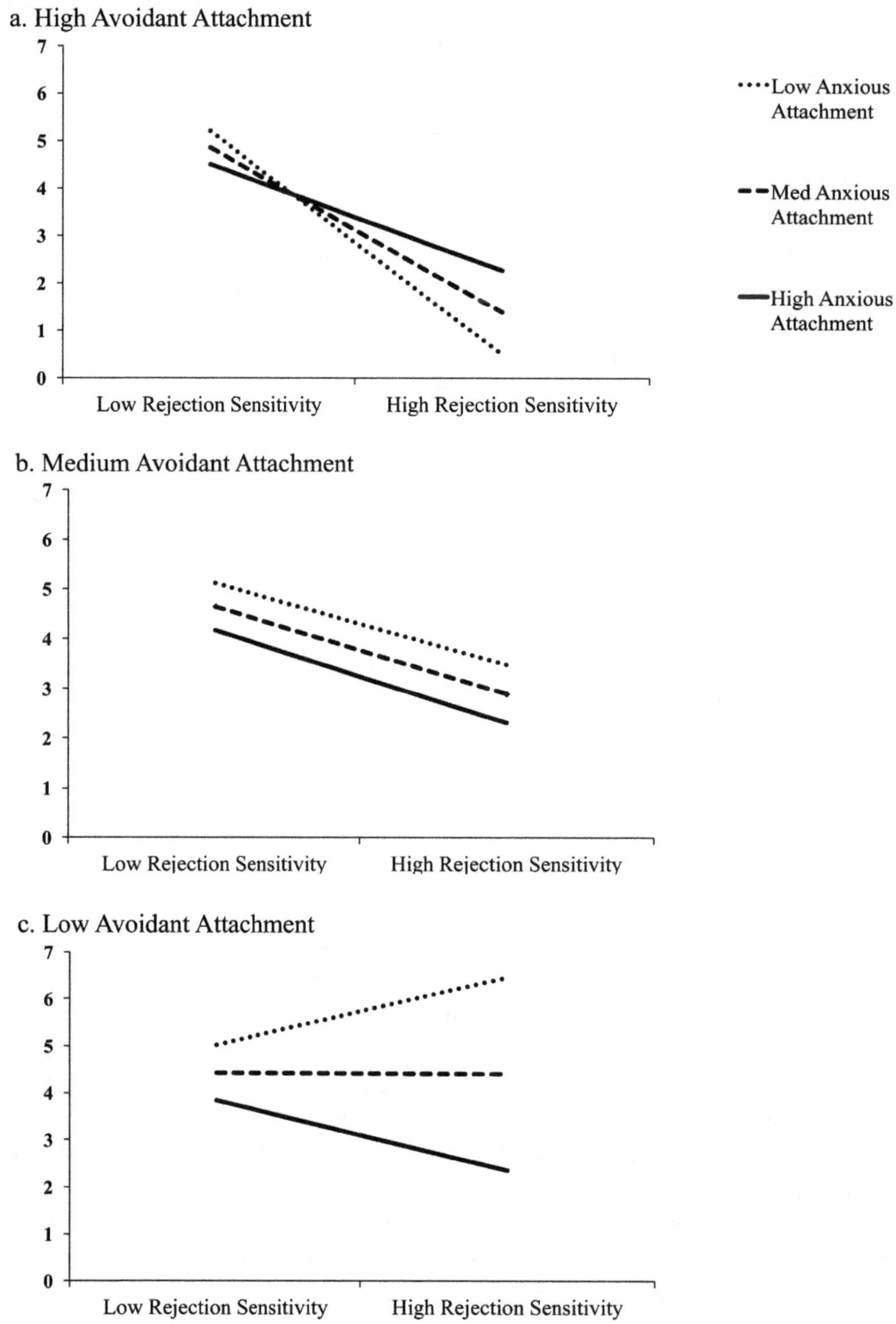

Figure 2. Sexting expectations: 3-way interaction between avoidant attachment, anxious attachment, and rejection sensitivity

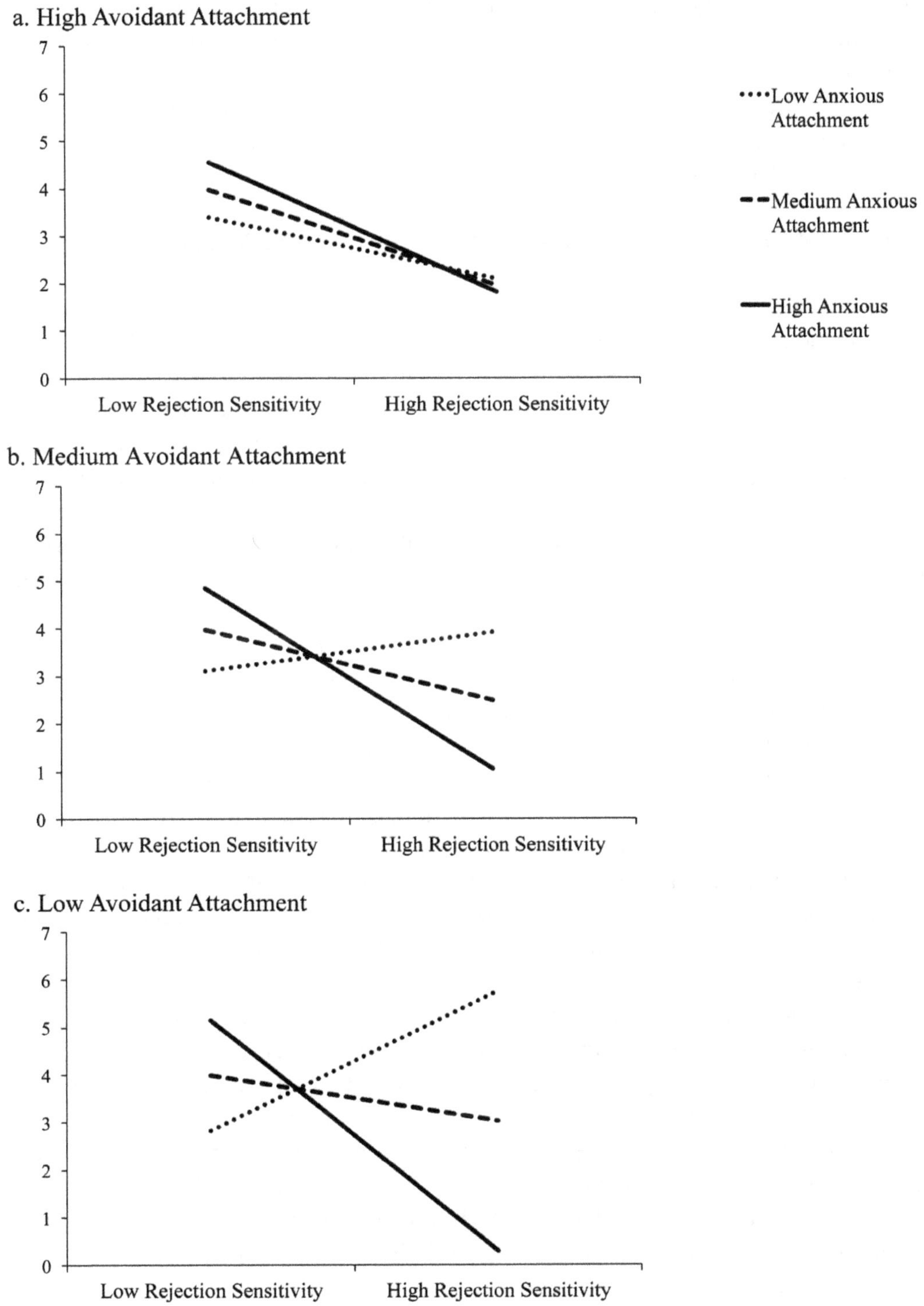

Sexting Sharing

The last set of significant findings resulted from multiple regression analysis on participants' experiences of sharing a sext that they received from someone else. Only the first model was significant ($F(2,158)=8.70$, $p<.001$), with both gender and relationship status as significant predictors (see Table 1 for coefficients). Males are more likely than females to share the sexts they receive with others. Individuals who are single, as compared to those who are in a relationship, are more likely to share the sexts they receive with others.

The Social Domain Theory and Evaluations of Sexting Victimization

These findings clearly demonstrate the benefit of examining both insecure attachment and rejection sensitivity in relation to EAs' engagement in and attitudes about sexting. It is equally important, though, to consider EAs' social and moral evaluations of sexting victimization. The Social Domain Theory (see Smetana, Jambon, & Ball, 2014; Turiel, 1983) provides a theoretical and methodological framework through which this can be accomplished. The theory asserts that "morality is primarily about ways of approaching social relationships and how people ought to treat each other" (Turiel, 2014, p.19). This framework has been utilized extensively to assess children's, adolescents', and adults' social and moral evaluations of a myriad of social interactions—and potential transgressions—ranging from interpersonal rejection (Park & Killen, 2010) and exclusion (Brenick & Killen, 2014), to harassment (Horn & Nucci, 2006), retribution (Ardila-Rey, Killen, & Brenick, 2009), and deception (Perkins, & Turiel, 2007). However, to date, no research has focused on evaluations of victimization through sexting.

The Social Domain Theory conceptualizes social interactions as the quintessential context in which individuals coordinate three distinct domains of social thought: *the moral, the societal,* and *the psychological.* Research guided by the Social Domain Theory often employs the use of real or hypothetical scenarios of social interactions involving transgressions. Participants are asked to comprehensively evaluate the rightness or wrongness of the transgression; these evaluations are directly related to the coordination of the three domains of social knowledge.

Moral constructs manifest as universal, generalizable concerns regarding potential harm, welfare, and justice. Such moral concerns are used to determine and justify the level of acceptability or objection warranted by a social transgression (Smetana et al., 2014; Turiel, 1983); for instance, the unauthorized sharing of a sext beyond the intended recipient.

The *societal* domain involves conventions that define acceptable social interaction based on group norms, expectations, and authority within a given context. Transgressions within the societal domain are considered wrong only so long as the social norms and rules dictate, but would be evaluated as acceptable if those rules and norms were removed or changed (Smetana et al., 2014; Turiel, 1983). As an example, consider a high school with the following rule: cellphone use is banned in the classroom and any student caught using their cellphone in class must show school administrators their phone content. In this situation, a sext might be shared beyond the intended recipient, but it would be viewed as a more acceptable transgression due to the context defined rules governing cellphone usage.

Finally, *psychological* constructs deal with personal preferences. Issues within the psychological domain are considered "rights…grounded in notions of self and personal agency" (Smetana et al., 2014, p.25) rather than transgressions. An EA might believe that a sext that was sent to him is now his property to do with as he pleases- that it is his personal choice.

When a social interaction falls squarely within the moral domain, a transgression will be viewed as highly unacceptable, regardless of societal rules or personal preferences (see Brenick & Killen, 2014; Crystal, Killen, & Ruck, 2008; Heinze & Horn, 2014; Horn & Nucci, 2006). Transgressions in the societal domain are seen as less wrong than moral transgressions, as the context specificity of the acceptability of the transgression is taken into account in the former. Psychological transgressions are often not even considered to be wrong, but rather personal prerogatives (Smetana et al., 2014). However, social interactions are complex and typically appeal to multiple domains of social thought; multifaceted transgressions are often viewed as more acceptable given that moral concerns are coordinated with competing societal or psychological concerns (Brenick & Romano, 2016; Killen, Lee-Kim, McGlothlin, & Stangor, 2002;). The coordination of these competing concerns relates directly to whether an act is even viewed as victimizing, and, if so, what action, if any, should be taken in response (see Rutland et al., 2010). At its core, EAs may believe it is wrong to victimize the original sext creator by sharing a sext without permission (a transgression squarely in the moral domain), but what if peer conventions dictate that everyone shares sexts they receive (societal domain)?

Does it matter if a sext is simply shown to a friend in close physical proximity rather than forwarded to the cellphone of another individual in any location? In the former, the sext, though shared, does not transfer possession again and cannot be shared further, yet the opposite is true for the latter. Moreover, do EAs differentiate between the sharing of sexts in which the person depicted in the sext is known from those in which the person depicted is a stranger? Finally, how might these evaluations relate to an individual's attachment and rejection sensitivity? The current study provides empirical assessment of participants' evaluations of hypothetical sexting victimization scenarios.

Current Research on Evaluations of Sexting Victimization

In addition to assessing EAs' attachment styles, rejection sensitivity, and sexting experiences, the study presented here also assessed participants' evaluations of sexting victimization. In collaboration with an EA research assistant, two scenarios and the accompanying follow-up questions were developed specifically for use in this study. The measure was pilot tested with a sample of EAs to assess testing fatigue, comprehension, and ecological validity of the scenarios as presented. Only minor changes were made to the scenario wording.

Participants were presented with two hypothetical scenarios depicting scenes in which one male individual, while out with male friends, received a picture sext of a woman. The scenarios differed in only one way; in the unknown condition the sext recipient and his friends did not know the woman depicted in the sext, but in the known condition, the sext recipient and his friends knew the female depicted in the sext. In line with Social Domain Theory established methodological protocol (see Brenick & Killen, 2014; Killen et al, 2002), the unknown condition was always presented first so that the scenario order reflected increasing levels of intimacy (from an unknown woman to a known woman). The text of the unknown scenario read as follows: "Bob is hanging out with his best friends Sean and Mike. Bob's phone rings, he has just received a message from his friend AJ. AJ just forwarded Bob a sexual picture of a female that none of them know." For both scenarios, participants rated the acceptability (i.e., how good or bad) of two potential responses by the scenario protagonist: 1. showing the sext to his friends nearby, or 2. electronically forwarding the sext to others. Participants also justified their answers in open-ended responses.

A mixed within- and between- subjects design was used to investigate participants' evaluations of sexting scenarios. A 2 (gender: female, male) x 2 (relationship status: single, in a relationship) x 2 (familiarity of target: known, unknown) x 2 (sharing type: show sext, forward sext) repeated measures analysis of variance (ANOVA), with anxious attachment, avoidant attachment, and rejection sensitivity as covariates, was conducted for the following dependent measures: showing acceptability and forwarding acceptability.

The vast majority of participants considered sharing sexts through methods of both showing the sext to friends close-by (74% when the sext depicts someone unknown to the group, 89% when known) and forwarding the sext to others electronically (96% unknown; 98% known) to be wrong and unacceptable. However, the actual ratings of acceptability differed significantly by scenario type ($F(1,153)=22.75$, $p<.001$; $\eta_p^2=.13$); and by gender ($F(1,153)=18.47$; $p<.001$; $\eta_p^2=.10$). These findings indicate that participants rate it as more wrong for the scenario protagonist to share a sext when the scenario target is known to the group than when the target is unknown. In addition, females think it is significantly worse to share a sext than do males.

Two significant interaction effects, however, yield a more complex understanding of EAs' evaluations of sexting victimization. First, a significant 2-way interaction between scenario type and scenario action revealed that while participants think it is less acceptable to show a sext of a known, rather than an unknown, scenario target, participants think it is equally bad to forward a sext regardless of whether the scenario target is known or unknown, ($F(1,153)=11.56$, $p<.001$; $\eta_p^2=.07$). Second, a significant 2-way interaction between scenario action and gender revealed that the effect of gender is much more striking in the show condition than in the forward condition; though males are only slightly more accepting than females of forwarding a sext, when the scenario target is simply showing a sext to friends nearby, females rate this as significantly less acceptable than males ($F(1,153)=20.02$, $p<.001$; $\eta_p^2=.12$).

Participants offered a number of justifications for their evaluations of sexting victimization. When the scenario target was known to the protagonist and his friends, participants often appealed to moral concerns for the victimization and rights violations experienced directly by the scenario target. When the scenario target was unknown to the protagonist and his friends, participants appealed more to moral concerns as well, but at a general level not specific to harm or rights violations of the target. For example, participants in the known condition reasoned: "The photo could have devastating effects on the woman's future"; "Because now there's an even larger chance they will come in contact with this girl that they personally know and ruin her life." Conversely, in the unknown condition, moral appeals were made on a broader societal scale, rather than concerns for the scenario target: "It's not acceptable [to] promote this type of sexual objectification" and "It's an invasion of privacy."

Additionally, in the unknown condition participants often appealed to the psychological and societal domain as well. In reference to the psychological domain, participants responded, "They then have the photo on their phone and can do whatever they want with it" and "Because it's his property," indicating that the sext was now the personal property of the recipient to do with as he pleased. In relation to the societal domain, participants responded, "It's just a social convention to share something to those around you on your phone if you weren't expecting such a message. It probably would be done without even thinking twice about who saw it," indicating that sharing sexts is the viewed as the status quo.

Perhaps what is most striking though, is the discrepancy between individuals' perceptions of sexting victimization, their actual sexting activity, and their perceptions of others' sexting activity. Clearly, participants found unauthorized sharing of sexts as wrong—a harmful moral violation of privacy and decency. At the same time, 98% of our participants reported to having shared or forwarded a sext they received. In relation to the scenarios, 42% of participants believed it was likely or very likely that the scenario protagonist would forward the sext of an unknown woman—37% for a known woman. Incredibly, 98% of participants believed it was likely or very likely the scenario protagonist would show his friends the sext of an unknown person—69% for a known person. Participants see not just sexting, but this type of sexting *victimization* as a typical and expected occurrence.

SOLUTIONS AND RECOMMENDATIONS

The findings reviewed and newly presented in this chapter further establish the scientific knowledge that sexting, particularly with text and images, is an increasingly common behavior among young adults. In line with Klettke and colleagues' (2014) charge to the field, the newly presented findings in this chapter extend our knowledge by assessing EAs' engagement in multiple, clearly defined acts of sexting-breaking sexting down by content (i.e. text, image, video) and by the act of sending or receiving a sext. Additionally, sexting experiences were broken down into multiple dimensions reflecting both positive (entertainment) and negative (risk and regret) qualities of sexting experiences, as well as expectations surrounding sexting behaviors. Although the literature reports varying rates of the negative experiences of victimization through sexting, the present review emphasizes that even rare instances of sexting victimization have been shown to yield highly detrimental consequences (Drouin et al., 2015). As a result, it is imperative to explore all aspects of the multifaceted nature of sexting as well as potential indicators of vulnerability toward sexting victimization.

Accordingly, this chapter presented anxious and avoidant attachment and rejection sensitivity as three such significant predictors of sexting experiences and evaluations of sexting and sexting victimization. Previously, only a handful of studies had explored attachment and sexting, yet those findings indicate a significant relation between the two; specifically, individuals with insecure attachment may engage in sexting more frequently because of overestimated beliefs that sexting is expected of them. This result was replicated in the findings of the current study, but also expanded upon by examining both insecure attachment and rejection sensitivity as they relate independently and interactively to young adults' experiences and evaluations of sexting. The novel results demonstrate that individuals with higher levels of avoidant attachment or rejection sensitivity found sexting to be less entertaining and were less accepting of the idea that sexting was typical and expected. Individuals with higher levels of anxious attachment, however, found sexting to be more entertaining and were more accepting of the expectation to sext in relationships. This is in line with the few previous studies in the field that have described persons with anxious attachment as using sexual intimacy as a way to reduce tension, maintain a romantic partner's interest, and to build closeness with a romantic partner (Delevi & Weisskirch, 2011; Delevi & Weisskirch, 2013). Sexting may be a novel technological advancement that allows an individual with anxious attachment to maintain intimacy with a partner. However, interactions between insecure attachment and rejection sensitivity revealed a more complex relation; rejection sensitivity related to ratings of sexting as less entertaining and more expected only when an individual was also neither avoidantly nor anxiously attached. As a result, the interplay between rejection sensitivity and insecure attachment offers more comprehensive and precise insights about the proclivities toward and experiences of sexting and sexting victimization.

Beyond this, the authors have presented new insight into how EAs *evaluate* sexting and sexting victimization to complement our understanding of EAs' own *experiences* with sexting. To best address sexting victimization, it is essential to understand the ways in which EAs find sexting to be victimizing. For instance, when societal convention dictates the expectation to sext with an intimate partner, is it viewed as victimizing to be coerced into sexting? Similarly, when it is the real and perceived norm to share sexts with others without permission, is this form of victimization still viewed as a moral transgression? EAs view sexting as something that is risky, but they also feel obliged to engage in it within their relationships—thus, demonstrating a tendency to knowingly engage in risky behaviors. They rate it as wrong, as a violation of privacy and decency, to share sexts without permission, yet the vast majority also admitted to having shared a sext and believing others would as well. This demonstrates a clear disconnect between their behaviors and beliefs. Providing a comprehensive account of how EAs make sense of their own and others' sexting experiences is critical to addressing any discrepancies in frequency of sexting victimization as well as preventing and effectively responding to sexting victimization.

These conceptual and methodological approaches had not previously been reported in the published literature, but can help identify individuals who are more likely to experience the negative consequences (and less likely to experience the positive outcomes) of sexting. Additionally, these approaches clarify the ways in which sexting is enacted and viewed as victimizing. This knowledge not only has the power to inform the ways in which EAs approach sexting, but also can reveal the most effective methods of preventing and responding to sexting victimization.

FUTURE RESEARCH DIRECTIONS

This chapter has clearly delineated the need for additional research examining EAs' engagement in and evaluations of sexting and sexting victimization—including how both of these factors relate to attachment dimensions and sensitivity to rejection. The presented study contributed valuable information about the influence of individual characteristics on evaluations of sexting; however, though comparable to other late-adolescent/EA samples (e.g., Norona, Roberson, & Welsh, 2016), rates of rejections sensitivity were relatively low in the current sample. Future research could target samples with a larger range of rejection sensitivity, including those who are extremely rejection sensitive, and, to a lesser extent, a sample with a wider array of attachment styles; results from such studies could expand the field's understanding of the effects of these individual characteristics across a larger spectrum. Furthermore, our sample, like many before it, was predominantly female and heterosexual; future research would benefit from including a larger sample of males, as well as transgender, gender non-conforming, and non-heterosexual individuals. Despite the sample demographic, the current study did uncover striking gender differences in participants' evaluations of situations in which sexts were shared. Detailed analyses and further interpretation of these findings are imprudent due to the disproportionate sizes of the gender sub-samples. Due to space limitations, they are also beyond the scope of the current study and chapter. The results, however, do suggest that future research should consider the effects of gender on sexting behavior and evaluation. Future research also should identify additional individual characteristics that influence sexting and sexting victimization; such identification may provide a deeper understanding of which individuals are at greatest risk following engagement in sexting. Such individual characteristics might include factors such as a history of victimization, social competence, and other instances of risk-taking behavior.

In addition to continuing to examine individual characteristics that predispose EAs for risk of victimization through sexting, the dyadic context within which sexting occurs also may be important to examine. Another limitation of the current study is the reliance on a single reporter design. This presents the potential of inflated correlations between measures when relying on self-report, but also misses valuable information that can be obtained from other sources, especially given that sexting often takes place in dyads. A dyadic design would reveal much needed information about the relationship contexts in which sexting takes place. For instance, victimization might occur more readily when partners have discrepant desires for sexting, and, despite their reservations, one partner agrees to sext the other because they believe it is what the other wants. In these instances, it would be important to examine how accurately partners guessed the desires of their partners. The pressure experienced by one partner may be imposed by other sources, such as general social convention, and, in fact, may not be coming from their partner. Moreover, certain types of dyads may engage in more or more varied sexting behaviors, and, in turn, those behaviors may be evaluated differently (e.g., whether people judge sexting within committed relationships less negatively or as less risky than sexting between casual sexual partners). Future research might aim to answer questions including whether the quality of the relationship, experienced intimacy, status, or trust between partners influences engagement in, evaluations of, and risk for experiencing victimization via sexting.

Additional avenues of research that could expand our understanding of sexting include a fuller examination of social and moral reasoning about sexting victimization. For instance, how do young adults coordinate societal, moral, and psychological concerns (Smetana et al., 2014; Turiel, 1983) when pertaining to contexts of sexting victimization? Does an EA's own engagement in sexting relate to reasoning about the likelihood and acceptability of sexting victimization? Studies addressing research questions of this type may provide a more detailed assessment of the perceived risks of sexting and a more explicit conceptualization of what sexting victimization entails.

Finally, though the study presented in this chapter provides valuable insight into how current university students evaluate sexting and sexting victimization, a much broader understanding of the changing societal landscape in terms of engagement in and acceptance of sexting and sexting victimization is warranted. This suggested research would require a more complex operationalization of sexting and sexting victimization, including risk and regret, than is typically used, and could not just lump the sending, receiving, sharing, or forwarding of texts together under the broad umbrella of sexting. Additionally, future research should examine sexting among people in many different stages of life beyond emerging adulthood.

CONCLUSION

As the prevalence of sexting and presumed typicality of sexting victimization continue to increase, continued research and the treatment of sexting as a multifaceted phenomenon are warranted. The current chapter explored how often EAs reported engaging in different modes of sexting (e.g., text, image, or video) and their judgments of various sexting scenarios. Our findings revealed that many EAs reported engaging in sexting. Furthermore, they viewed sexting as risky, but nonetheless obligatory in their intimate relationships—demonstrating a tendency to knowingly engage in risky behaviors. Importantly, these results were influenced by participants' attachment and rejection sensitivity. Individuals with insecure attachment and rejection sensitivity possess characteristics that might leave them more vulnerable to sexting victimization, pointing to the need for future research to examine these potential areas of risk.

This research could inform future education and intervention efforts aimed at providing training to EAs on how to address and avoid coercion into sexting and combat norms of victimization through unauthorized sharing of sexts. These training efforts could be tailored to individuals who experience attachment insecurity and sensitivity to rejection, avoiding a one-size-fits-all approach. For instance, on the one hand, individuals who are insecurely attached and sensitive to rejection might benefit the most from communication (e.g., about expectations) and boundary-setting skills training. On the other hand, efforts targeting all EAs more broadly might be most successful by working to change societal norms about sexting and sexting victimization (e.g., challenging the notion that women are expected by men to sext; taking action as a bystander to stop unauthorized sharing of sexts). Intervention efforts also might be effective with younger adolescent populations, and encompass more detailed preventative education about the multiple ways in which sexting can pose a risk to their social, emotional, and professional lives, while highlighting ways in which they may be more vulnerable to those negative consequences. Overall, sexting has become a common means of communication and expression within the intimate relationships of EAs, and given the significant developmental implications this has for EAs' cognition and behavior, as well as social and emotional well-being, the topic warrants further examination.

REFERENCES

Alderson, K., & Samimi, P. (2014). Sexting among undergraduate students. *Computers in Human Behavior, 31*, 230–241. doi:10.1016/j.chb.2013.10.027

Ardila-Rey, A., Killen, M., & Brenick, A. (2009). Moral reasoning in violent contexts: Displaced and non-displaced Colombian childrens evaluations of moral transgressions, retaliation, and reconciliation. *Social Development, 18*(1), 181–209. doi:10.1111/j.1467-9507.2008.00483.x PMID:25722543

Brenick, A., & Killen, M. (2014). Moral judgments about Jewish–Arab intergroup exclusion: The role of cultural identity and contact. *Developmental Psychology, 50*(1), 86–99. doi:10.1037/a0034702 PMID:24188040

Brenick, A., & Romano, K. (2016). Perceived peer and parent outgroup norms, cultural identity, and adolescents reasoning about peer intergroup exclusion. *Child Development, 87*(5), 1392–1408. doi:10.1111/cdev.12594 PMID:27684394

Burkett, M. (2015). Sex(t) talk: A qualitative analysis of young adults negotiations of the pleasures and perils of sexting. *Sexuality & Culture: An Interdisciplinary Quarterly, 19*(4), 835–863. doi:10.1007/s12119-015-9295-0

Cassidy, J. (2001). Truth, lies, and intimacy: An attachment perspective. *Attachment & Human Development, 3*(2), 121–155. doi:10.1080/14616730110058999 PMID:11708734

Celizic, M. (2009). *Her Teen Committed Suicide Over Sexting*. Retrieved from http://www.today.com/parents/her-teen-committed-suicide-over-sexting-2D80555048#.VRwMLvnF-So

Collins, N. (1996). *Revised Adult Attachment Scale* [Measurement Instrument]. Retrieved from https://labs.psych.ucsb.edu/collins/nancy/UCSB_Close_Relationships_Lab/Resources_files/Adult%20Attachment%20Scale.doc

Crystal, D. S., Killen, M., & Ruck, M. (2008). It is who you know that counts: Intergroup contact and judgments about race-based exclusion. *The British Journal of Developmental Psychology*, *26*(1), 51–70. doi:10.1348/026151007X198910 PMID:25505355

Dake, J., Price, J., Maziarz, L., & Ward, B. (2012). Prevalence and correlates of sexting behavior in adolescents. *American Journal of Sexuality Education*, *7*(1), 1–15. doi:10.1080/15546128.2012.650959

Delevi, R., & Weisskirch, R. (2012). Its ovr b/n u n me: Technology use, attachment styles, and gender roles in relationship dissolution. *Cyberpsychology, Behavior, and Social Networking*, *15*(9), 486–490. doi:10.1089/cyber.2012.0169 PMID:22823329

Delevi, R., & Weisskirch, R. (2013). Attachment style and conflict resolution skills predicting technology use in relationship dissolution. *Computers in Human Behavior*, *29*(6), 2530–2534. doi:10.1016/j.chb.2013.06.027

Dir, A. L., & Cyders, M. A. (2015). Risks, risk factors, and outcomes associated with phone and Internet sexting among university students in the United States. *Archives of Sexual Behavior*, *44*(6), 1675–1684. doi:10.1007/s10508-014-0370-7 PMID:25358950

Downey, G., & Feldman, S. (1996). Implications of rejection sensitivity for intimate relationships. *Journal of Personality and Social Psychology*, *70*(6), 1327–1343. doi:10.1037/0022-3514.70.6.1327 PMID:8667172

Downey, G., Freitas, A., Michaelis, B., & Khouri, H. (1998). The self-fulfilling prophecy in close relationships: Rejection sensitivity and rejection by romantic partners. *Journal of Personality and Social Psychology*, *75*(2), 545–560. doi:10.1037/0022-3514.75.2.545 PMID:9731324

Downey, G., Nesdale, D., Trevaskis, S., & Zimmer-Gembeck, M. (2014). Relational victimization, loneliness and depressive symptoms: Indirect associations via self and peer reports of rejection sensitivity. *Journal of Youth and Adolescence*, *43*(4), 568–582. doi:10.1007/s10964-013-9993-6 PMID:23955324

Drouin, M., & Landgraff, C. (2012). Texting, sexting, and attachment in college students romantic relationships. *Computers in Human Behavior*, *28*(2), 444–449. doi:10.1016/j.chb.2011.10.015

Drouin, M., Ross, J., & Tobin, E. (2015). Sexting: A new, digital vehicle for intimate partner aggression? *Computers in Human Behavior*, *50*, 197–204. doi:10.1016/j.chb.2015.04.001

Drouin, M., & Tobin, E. (2014). Unwanted but consensual sexting among young adults: Relations with attachment and sexual motivations. *Computers in Human Behavior*, *31*, 412–418. doi:10.1016/j.chb.2013.11.001

Drouin, M., Vogel, K. N., Surbey, A., & Stills, J. R. (2013). Lets talk about sexting, baby: Computer-mediated sexual behaviors among young adults. *Computers in Human Behavior*, *29*(5), A25–A30. doi:10.1016/j.chb.2012.12.030

Edwards, G., & Barber, B. (2010). The relationship between rejection sensitivity and compliant condom use. *Archives of Sexual Behavior*, *39*(6), 1381–1388. doi:10.1007/s10508-009-9520-8 PMID:19760145

Erozkan, A. (2009). Rejection sensitivity levels with respect to attachment styles, gender, and parenting styles: A study with Turkish students. *Social Behavior and Personality*, *37*(1), 1–14. doi:10.2224/sbp.2009.37.1.1

Gordon-Messer, D., Bauermeister, J. A., Grodzinski, A., & Zimmerman, M. (2013). Sexting among young adults. *The Journal of Adolescent Health*, *52*(3), 301–306. doi:10.1016/j.jadohealth.2012.05.013 PMID:23299018

Hafen, C., Spilker, A., Chango, J., Marston, E., & Allen, J. (2014). To accept or reject? The impact of adolescent rejection sensitivity on early adult romantic relationships. *Journal of Research on Adolescence*, *24*(1), 55–64. doi:10.1111/jora.12081 PMID:24729668

Heinze, J., & Horn, S. (2014). Do adolescents evaluations of exclusion differ based on gender expression and sexual orientation? *The Journal of Social Issues*, *70*(1), 63–80. doi:10.1111/josi.12047

Horn, S. S., & Nucci, L. (2006). Harassment of gay and lesbian youth and school violence in America: An analysis and directions for intervention. In C. Daiute, Z. F. Beykont, C. Higson-Smith, & L. Nucci (Eds.), *International perspectives on youth conflict and development* (pp. 139–155). New York, NY: Oxford University Press. doi:10.1093/acprof:oso/9780195178425.003.0009

Hudson, H. K., & Fetro, J. V. (2015). Sextual activity: Predictors of sexting behaviors and intentions to sext among selected undergraduate students. *Computers in Human Behavior*, *49*, 615–622. doi:10.1016/j.chb.2015.03.048

Judge, A. (2012). Sexting among U.S. adolescents: Psychological and legal perspectives. *Harvard Review of Psychology*, *20*(2), 86–96. doi:10.3109/10673229.2012.677360 PMID:22512742

Killen, M., Lee-Kim, J., McGlothlin, H., Stangor, C., & Helwig, C. C. (2002). How children and adolescents evaluate gender and racial exclusion. *Monographs of the Society for Research in Child Development*, *67*(4), i-129. PMID:12557595

Killen, M., & Rutland, A. (2011). *Children and Social Exclusion: Morality, Prejudice, and Group Identity*. Hoboken, NJ: Wiley. doi:10.1002/9781444396317

Klettke, B., Hallford, D., & Mellor, D. (2014). Sexting prevalence and correlates: A systematic literature review. *Clinical Psychology Review*, *34*(1), 44–53. doi:10.1016/j.cpr.2013.10.007 PMID:24370714

Kopecký, K. (2014). Cyberbullying and sexting between children and adolescents –Comparative study. *Procedia: Social and Behavioral Sciences*, *149*, 467–471. doi:10.1016/j.sbspro.2014.08.292

Lee, M., & Crofts, T. (2015). Gender, pressure, coercion and pleasure: Untangling motivations for sexting between young people. *The British Journal of Criminology*, *55*(3), 454–473. doi:10.1093/bjc/azu075

Mikulincer, M., & Shaver, P. R. (2016). *Attachment in adulthood: Structure, dynamics, and change* (2nd ed.). New York: Guilford Press.

Natarajan, G., Somasundaram, C. P., & Sundaram, K. R. (2011). Relationship between attachment security and rejection sensitivity in early adolescence. *Psychological Studies*, *56*(4), 378–386. doi:10.1007/s12646-011-0108-8

Norona, J. C., Roberson, P. N. E., & Welsh, D. P. (2016). Rejection sensitivity and depressive symptoms: Longitudinal actor-partner effects in adolescent romantic relationships. *Journal of Adolescence*, *51*, 6–18. doi:10.1016/j.adolescence.2016.05.007 PMID:27254083

Norona, J. C., Salvatore, J. F., Welsh, D. P., & Darling, N. (2014). Rejection sensitivity and adolescents perceptions of romantic interactions. *Journal of Adolescence*, *37*(8), 1257–1267. doi:10.1016/j.adolescence.2014.09.003 PMID:25282535

Ozen, A., Sumer, N., & Demir, M. (2010). Predicting friendship quality with rejection sensitivity and attachment security. *Journal of Social and Personal Relationships*, 163–181. doi:10.1177/0265407510380607

Park, Y., & Killen, M. (2010). When is peer rejection justifiable? Childrens understanding across two cultures. *Cognitive Development*, *25*(3), 290–301. doi:10.1016/j.cogdev.2009.10.004 PMID:21076660

Parker, T. S., Blackburn, K. M., Perry, M. S., & Hawks, J. M. (2013). Sexting as an intervention: Relationship satisfaction and motivation considerations. *The American Journal of Family Therapy*, *41*(1), 1–12. doi:10.1080/01926187.2011.635134

Perkins, S. A., & Turiel, E. (2007). To lie or not to lie: To whom and under what circumstances. *Child Development*, *78*(2), 609–621. doi:10.1111/j.1467-8624.2007.01017.x PMID:17381793

Purdie, V., & Downey, G. (2000). Rejection sensitivity and adolescent girls vulnerability to relationship-centred difficulties. *Child Maltreatment*, *5*(4), 338–349. doi:10.1177/1077559500005004005 PMID:11232261

Renfrow, D. G., & Rollo, E. A. (2014). Sexting on campus: Minimizing perceived risks and neutralizing behaviors. *Deviant Behavior*, *35*(11), 903–920. doi:10.1080/01639625.2014.897122

Ringrose, J., Harvey, L., Gill, R., & Livingstone, S. (2013). Teen girls, sexual double standards and sexting: Gendered value in digital image exchange. *Feminist Theory*, *14*(3), 305–323. doi:10.1177/1464700113499853

Rutland, A., Killen, M., & Abrams, D. (2010). A new social-cognitive developmental perspective on prejudice: The interplay between morality and group identity. *Perspectives on Psychological Science*, *5*(3), 279–291. doi:10.1177/1745691610369468 PMID:26162160

Smetana, J. G., Jambon, M., & Ball, C. (2014). The social domain approach to children's moral and social judgments. In M. Killen & J. G. Smetana (Eds.), *Handbook of moral development* (2nd ed.; pp. 23–45). New York, NY: Psychology Press. doi:10.4324/9780203581957.ch2

Turiel, E. (1983). *The Development of Social Knowledge: Morality and Convention*. Cambridge University Press.

Turiel, E. (2014). Morality: Epistemology, development, and social opposition. In M. Killen & J. G. Smetana (Eds.), *Handbook of moral development* (2nd ed.; pp. 3–22). New York, NY: Psychology Press. doi:10.4324/9780203581957.ch1

Vanden Abeele, V., Campbell, M., Eggermont, S., & Roe, K. (2014). Sexting, mobile porn use, and peer group dynamics: Boys and girls self-perceived popularity, need for popularity, and perceived peer pressure. *Media Psychology*, *17*(1), 6–33. doi:10.1080/15213269.2013.801725

Walker, S., Sanci, L., & Temple-Smith, M. (2013). Sexting: Young womens and mens views on its nature and origins. *The Journal of Adolescent Health*, *52*(6), 697–701. doi:10.1016/j.jadohealth.2013.01.026 PMID:23587784

Weisskirch, R., & Delevi, R. (2011). Sexting and adult romantic attachment. *Computers in Human Behavior*, *27*(5), 1697–1701. doi:10.1016/j.chb.2011.02.008

Young, B. J., & Furman, W. (2007). Interpersonal factors in the risk for sexual victimization and its recurrence during adolescence. *Journal of Youth and Adolescence*, *37*(3), 297–309. doi:10.1007/s10964-007-9240-0

Zimmer-Gembeck, M., & Duffy, A. (2014). Heightened emotional sensitivity intensifies associations between relational aggression and victimization among girls but not boys: A longitudinal study. *Development and Psychopathology*, *26*(3), 661–673. doi:10.1017/S0954579414000303 PMID:25047290

Zimmer-Gembeck, M., Trevaskis, S., Nesdale, D., & Downey, G. (2014). Relational victimization, loneliness and depressive symptoms: Indirect associations via self and peer reports of rejection sensitivity. *Journal of Youth and Adolescence*, *43*(4), 568–582. doi:10.1007/s10964-013-9993-6 PMID:23955324

KEY TERMS AND DEFINITIONS

Anxious Attachment: An insecure attachment style that is characterized by having a deep desire for intimacy, while simultaneously fearing abandonment.

Attachment: The lasting emotional and affectionate bond (either secure or insecure in nature) that we develop in childhood with our caregiver and that manifests through the lifespan with the most important people in our lives (e.g. romantic partners).

Avoidant Attachment: An insecure attachment style that is characterized by having an aversion to being dependent on another individual, or having another individual dependent on you.

Evaluations of Sexting: The ways in which people judge and reason about the positive, negative, and neutral aspects of sexting behaviors.

Rejection Sensitivity: The tendency to expect or perceive others to act in ways that reject the individual.

Sexting Victimization: Being harmed by sexting. Sexting victimization can occur in various ways, ranging from feelings of coercion and pressure to sext, to the threat or act of having a sext shared with others without the prior consent of the individual depicted.

Sexting: Sending or receiving sexually suggestive text, picture, or video messages.

APPENDIX

Table 1. Multiple regression analysis for sexting experiences by attachment and rejection sensitivity

Step	Predictors	Sexting Expectations		Sexting Entertainment		Sexting Sharing		Sexting Risk	
		ΔR^2	β	ΔR^2	β	ΔR^2	β	ΔR^2	β
1	Gender	0.01	-0.09	0.09**	-0.13	0.10***	-0.20**	0.02	-
	Relationship Status		-0.09		-0.23**		-0.25**		-
2	RS	0.03	-0.19	0.08**	-0.26*	0.02	-	0.03	-
	ANX		0.21*	0.04	0.21*	0.00	-	0.02	-
	AVOID		-0.14		-0.35***		-		-
3	RS x ANX	0.06*	-0.34**		-0.29**		-		-
	RS x AVOID		-0.08		-0.02		-		-
	ANX x AVOID		0.13	0.03*	0.05	0.00	-	0.00	-
4	RS x ANX x AVOID	0.03*	0.32*		0.31*		-		-
	Total R^2	0.13		0.24		0.13		0.07	

Note. $n = 161$. RS: Rejection Sensitivity; ANX = Anxious Attachment; AVOID = Avoidant Attachment.

Gender entered as a "dummy" variable: 0= male; 1= female. Relationship status entered as a "dummy" variable: 0= in a relationship, 1= single.

$*p < .05$; $**p < .01$; $***p < .001$. Tables show βs for all predictors in highest significant step.

Variables excluded from tables were not significant in any model.

Chapter 14
Being Online in Emerging Adulthood:
Between Problematic or Functional Use of the Internet

Martina Benvenuti
University of Bologna, Italy

Elvis Mazzoni
University of Bologna, Italy

Gioele Piobbico
University of Bologna, Italy

ABSTRACT

Internet revolutionized our lifestyle. New generation devices like smartphones and tablets allow us to be always connected: the web represents a significant part of our days. These epochal changes bring with them questions about the potentialities and the risks of web 2.0. This chapter introduces a research whose purpose is to investigate the relationships between Online and Offline lives in Emerging Adulthood. Starting by the concept of functional organ (Leont'ev, 1972) and inverse instrumentality (Ekbia & Nardi, 2012), the goal of the study is to go beyond the research on web addiction, and start to explore a model able to predict why some emerging adults have their life empowered by the web and while others get trapped in the problematic use.

INTRODUCTION

The Internet is an important part of our daily lives and it represents a basic tool for information searching, social interactions, and the consequent knowledge construction (Frozzi & Mazzoni, 2011; Mazzoni & Zanazzi, 2014). The benefits that derive from the Internet to perform daily activities are enormous; information and communication have never been so easy to access and fast. However, there is one downside. Web 2.0 requires a lot of our attention during use (due to the network of relations and information

DOI: 10.4018/978-1-5225-1856-3.ch014

processing on which we are absorbed) and it often distracts us from tasks in which we are involved in during daily activities, such as studying, working, or cultivating offline relationships. The integration between being online and offline is an important part of the psychology of human beings (Turkle, 2012). In some cases, it is possible to find a balance between these two aspects of human life. The web is functional to work, to study, and to carry out daily activities. In other cases, people run the risk of pursuing behaviors that lead to problematic use (Davis, 2001).

Considering the previous positive and negative aspects of the Internet use, the theoretical perspective of this chapter is based on the assumption that the Internet is not good or bad: it could become problematic or empowering based on how it is used and depending on the reasons behind such a use (Mazzoni, Baiocco, Cannata & Dimas, 2016; Mazzoni, Cannata & Baiocco, 2016). This chapter relies on the theoretical framework that allows the researchers to take into account both the positive and negative outcomes of Web 2.0. Leontev's (1972) proposed the construct of functional organ to describe an artificial tool that is integrated into the behavior and the cognition of a human being to become an extended part of his/her biology. On the other hand, Ekbia and Nardi (2012) explained that web technologies might enable situations of inverse instrumentality, a process of objectification of users that regulates their behavior in a non-expectant manner, drawing them in or pushing them away from certain kinds of activities. By means of a cross-sectional study, the objective of this chapter is to analyze which processes are related to a massive and pervasive use of the web to be a source of empowerment (functional organ) or a source of problematic use (inverse instrumentality) during emerging adulthood.

BACKGROUND

In the last decades, the increased availability and the increasingly rapid and constant technological developments have led to significant changes in peoples' lifestyle in many countries (Ngai, Tao, & Moon, 2015). Web 2.0 has revolutionized the traditional ways of communication, interactions, and the flow of information between people and organizations, allowing easy access to an unprecedented amount of data and allowing the spread of news in real time, offering interactive virtual spaces where millions of people are quickly reachable (Kaplan & Haenlein, 2010). The immediacy and the convenience of communication on the Web have forever changed the history of human communication. Millions of people have chosen to interact by means of virtual platforms, such as blogs, social networking sites, chat programs, and e-mail (Lee, 2014). Thanks to the rapid diffusion of Information and Communication Technologies (ICT), the Internet has rapidly evolved into a tool for ordinary use which allows the development of new applications that facilitate and enable not only communication but also many and different activities (Khang, Kim, & Kim, 2013; Odaci & Çıkrıkçı, 2014). The use of the web and Social Networking Sites (SNSs) greatly facilitates the spread of multimedia audio and video (pictures, movies, music). The availability of communications technologies also increases the possibility of having access to information and knowledge between different cultures. However, some studies have found controversial aspects between the use of digital media and wellbeing. In particular, one's psychological wellbeing has been indicated as a better predictor of poor outcomes when compared to how intensely digital media are used (see Weigle, 2014; Lee & Leeson, 2015; Caplan, Williams, & Yee, 2009). Consequently, the debate that arose in recent years between many scholars on the use of the social web has become increasingly heated, and two different perspectives can broadly characterize it. Some scholars have highlighted the possible negative effects of the social web whereas other scholars have stressed its potential for human development. One of the major exponent of the negative aspect of the use of the Internet is Kimberly Young (1998), who conceptualized the concept of Internet Addiction Disorder (IAD). In her studies, she showed that people addicted to the Internet have personal problems similar to other people with addictions to gambling, alcoholism, and food disorders. However, it is still unclear when and why Internet addiction can be considered a real independent syndrome and when, instead, it occurs as a comorbidity symptom of other diseases (Mazzoni, Baiocco, Cannata& Dimas, 2016).

Other scholars (Ellison, Steinfield and Lampe, 2007; Mazzoni & Iannone, 2014; Mazzoni, Baiocco, Cannata, Dimas, 2016; Mazzoni, Cannata, Baiocco, 2016) focus their attention on the functional use of the Internet, showing how its use, particularly the use of Social Networking Sites (SNSs), supports the construction and maintenance of social capital as well as eases the transition between school, college/ university, and work. In one study, Steinfield and colleagues (2008) analyzed the relationship between social capital (i.e., the possible benefits that flow from the creation and maintenance of interpersonal relationships), self-esteem and the use of SNSs in U.S. college students. They found that college students with low self-esteem had the most benefit from the use of Facebook in terms of maintaining social capital than those college students who had higher self-esteem.

The need to go beyond the dualism between negative and positive use of the Internet requires a different approach to understand the effects of the Internet in everyday life or an integration between the online life and the offline one. Leont'ev (1974) who emphasized the dual nature of the fundamental aspects of human activities proposes a cultural-historical perspective that could help us in this integration. He starts with the Vygotskian idea that every human activity is mediated by tools that shape the way in which humans act, but also the way in which they think. Leont'ev defines these tools that act as mediators in human activity as functional organs, i.e. artifacts that represent extensions of physical and mental human abilities (Mazzoni & Iannone, 2014). Therefore, we can imagine the Internet (and its applications) as functional organs that enhance human capabilities, including the ability to search information, interact, connect with others, construct knowledge, and learn. However, sometimes the use of the Internet could have a negative counterpart represented by the inverse instrumentality (Ekbia & Nardi, 2012). This problematic aspect is characterized by a double mediation: people act intentionally to pursue their goals through technology; at the same time, individuals would be partially objectified by the interaction. From this point of view, it is necessary to consider two types of technologies: fragmentation technologies (the person performs mechanically the same actions) and totalizing technologies (the instrument takes control on human activities). The first type of technology acts as a process that dematerializes the human being, reducing him or her to a set of functions related to the technical system. The second type of technologies includes tools that can establish a strong connection with the subject in terms of frequency, time of use, and emotional commitment, as well as the impact on offline life (Ekbia & Nardi, 2011). For instance, it is difficult to determine whether the motivation to attend some events (such as parties, concerts, conferences) is a real interest on the events or on the positive feedback (e.g., "Likes" on Facebook) received after posting pictures of the events on the web.

THE USE OF THE INTERNET DURING THE EMERGING ADULTHOOD: PROCESSES OF EXPERIMENTATION, EXPLORATION, AND CHANGE

Some studies (Ellison, Steinfield and Lampe, 2007; Frozzi & Mazzoni, 2011; Mazzoni & Iannone, 2014) demonstrated the positive aspects of the use of Internet during Emerging Adulthood. As defined in the literature, emerging adulthood is a specific phase of development that takes place from the end of high school until around the age of 30 in industrialized western countries (Arnett & Tanner, 2006; Arnett, 2000; Douglass, 2007). This period is developed in cultural, social, and economic contexts that allow people to extend the exploration period that is characterized mainly by years of frequent changes and transitions, such as moving to another town to attend university. Thus, emerging adulthood is marked by instability and the consequent search for stability (Mazzoni & Zanazzi, 2014). In this regard, Emerging Adulthood is characterized by experimentation, exploration, change, and diversity. Moreover, following Arnett's proposals (Arnett, 2012; Arnett & Fishel, 2013; Clark University Poll, 2015), it is possible to separate this period in two phases: Younger Emerging Adulthood from 21 to 24 years old and Older Emerging Adulthood, from 25 to 29 years old. The youngers are characterized by the end of adolescence, entrance into the adult legal age (such as in many European countries like Italy), the first experiences in university and in jobs, and independence from family. "Gradually, over the course of the launching period, they learn to stand more on their own and they feel comfortable about living independently" (Arnett & Fischel, 2013, p. 12). The older emerging adults are characterized by the search of more stability, since they have finished their studies or they found a job they like; thus "during the last years of their twenties, most emerging adults make the important choices that will form the structure of their adult lives in love and work" (Arnett & Fishel, 2013, p. 13).

Despite the differences between various countries concerning education, culture, and economy, emerging adults in different countries with advanced economies seem to share these characteristics. In addition, this period of life is typical of countries with emerging economy in which education and training play an important role in personal and career development. In most of the industrialized countries, at the end of their studies, adolescents face a delicate and unstable period characterized by one or more transitions, such as the transition from school to university or from school/university to work (Tuomi-Gröhn & Engeström, 2003; Arnett, 2015). During these transitions, emerging adults face a gap between their background of knowledge and skills and those required by the new activity system (e.g. the new organization in which a person will work). Often emerging adults do not have effective and appropriate information and knowledge to overcome the boundaries between these different activity systems (Wenger, 2000). Furthermore, as these transitions also include residential changes (in many cases also to another town), maintaining existing social networks and constructing new connections represent two important challenges for emerging adults (Steinfield, Ellison & Lampe, 2008; Mazzoni & Iannone, 2014). The new connections are very important for receiving and sharing relevant information (e.g., about the life in a new university or about the new work environment). From this point of view, the Internet, particularly SNSs, might play a very important role as mediation tools to construct a bridge between schools and university or schools and work environments, so that knowledge acquired and constructed meets the request of the new activity system. The SNSs are also very important as a sort of pre-socialization virtual environments to the new activity system, by creating contacts with those people who already work in the new activity system to ask them for information. SNSs might be considered an extension of the human ability to create and maintain relationships, particularly with regards to people who are facing major transitions in different activity systems during the life period from adolescence to adulthood (Frozzi &

Mazzoni, 2011). SNSs can also be seen as virtual cultural artifacts that allow emerging adults to expand their zone of proximal development beyond the limits of space and time that characterize the physical presence, allowing them to expand their potential to build and maintain social capital, and to access and share information and knowledge (Vygotsky, 1978; Griffin & Cole, 1984; Frozzi & Mazzoni, 2011).

Factors Connected to the Use of the Internet

The main factors connected to the use of the Internet that will be considered in this study are: self-esteem, social support, self-control, cognitive absorption, and mindfulness.

Regarding self-esteem, many scholars have examined the relationship between the use of the Internet and self-esteem. For example, Forest and Wood (2012) have found that people with low self-esteem considered Facebook an appealing venue for self-disclosure, the low positivity and high negativity of their disclosures elicited undesirable responses from other people. Although various studies have suggested an inverse relationship between self-esteem and problematic use of the Internet (e.g., Johnson, 2011; Widyanto & Griffiths, 2011), other studies have shown that this relationship is not so straightforward (Kuss & Griffiths, 2011; Zywica & Danowski, 2008). Kuss and Griffiths (2011) found that low and high self-esteem do not influence the frequency of web use. They proposed that these findings could be explained by social enhancement and compensation. Such proposal is not new in the literature. Other researchers (e.g., Żywica & Danowski, 2008) have found that people characterized by greater extroversion and higher self-esteem perceive themselves as more popular both in online life and in offline life (hypothesis of social enhancement). On the other hand, people with less self-esteem perceive themselves as less popular both on the Web and in real life (hypothesis of social compensation). One possible hypothesis to explain these results is that if individuals do not receive adequate social support in daily life, in order to compensate for this shortage, they tend to create a parallel life to activate contacts and build relationships online.

Thus, social support could be a factor that plays an important role in regulating the use of the Internet. Although social support may seem like a phenomenon inseparable from face-to-face relationships, some studies have shown that online social support plays an important role in people's life. Using the constructs of online social support and offline social support, Wang and Wang (2013) investigated whether the way people relate to their contacts affects Internet Addiction. The results revealed that having a higher amount of relationship and greater support online increases the risk of IAD, while more support in offline life is negatively correlated with this addiction. The explanation given by the authors is that the construction of bonds predominantly online means that you can rely mainly on people in the online world, implying a growing need to stay connected.

Many studies have been conducted using (low) self-control as a predictor of problematic Internet use (PIU) or Internet addiction. Khang, Kim, and Kim (2013) found that when tested together with other self-traits, self-control was predictive of PIU. A low level of self-directedness is also a predictor of Internet addiction in several studies (Ha et al., 2007; Montag, Montag, Jurkiewicz & Reuter, 2010; Montag et al. 2011; Sariyska et al., 2015). This personality trait represents an individual's ability to regulate his or her behavior according to the situation (Cloninger, Svrakic & Przybeck, 1993). Although Cloninger and colleagues consider self-directedness in broader terms, the latest theories regarding self-regulation (Heatherton, 2011) proposes that self-directedness is the sum of different factors with self-control being just one of them.

In order to succeed in regulating one's behavior it is not only necessary to have control over it, but also to be aware of the difference between the action one performs and the action he or she wishes to perform. Therefore, mindfulness may also be an important aspect of behavioral regulation as it "can broadly be described as objective experiential awareness and is believed to be a psychological property that can be cultivated or depleted" (MacKillop & Anderson, 2007, pg. 289). Indeed, another theory considers Mindfulness to be the core characteristic of self-regulation (Vago & Silbersweig, 2012; Ghorbani, Watson, Farhadi, & Chen, 2014). Self-control and self-regulation allow people to manage a situation while the mindfulness of what you are doing allows for constant monitoring on the progress of the situation. The term mindfulness defines precisely the presence or absence of attention relatively to what happens in the present (Walach et al., 2006).

Since mindfulness plays an important role in maintaining a certain amount of attention and avoid negative behaviors, we can certainly speculate an effect of this factor, combined with self-regulation, on the problematic use of the Internet as well as on cognitive absorption. Indeed, one of the most common experiences during the time spent online is the unawareness of time passing. The term cognitive absorption (Agarwal & Karahanna, 2000) means a strong involvement with five dimensions (temporal dissociation, focused immersion, enjoy, control, curiosity).

AN EXPLORATORY STUDY ON EMERGING ADULTS: FROM PROBLEMATIC INTERNET USE TO FUNCTIONAL INTERNET USE

Methods

Based on the previously reviewed theoretical background, the second part of this chapter is devoted to the analysis of data from a large sample of Italian emerging adults. The purpose of this study was to investigate the impact of web tools and Internet connections in their life. The study investigates whether the previously described factors (self-esteem, social support, self-control, cognitive absorption, and mindfulness) play a role, and to what extent, to move the balance from Problematic Internet Use (PIU) to Functional Internet Use (FIU).

To achieve this objective, we distributed an online questionnaire (constructed by means the Qualtrics platform[1]) through several social networking websites (Facebook, Twitter, Google +, Linkedin). This method yielded a sample of 588 Younger Emerging Adults and 118 Older Emerging Adults. This exploratory study had two goals:

1. Describe the use of web artifacts in this sample of Italian emerging adults;
2. Investigate the connection between Problematic Internet Use, self-esteem, online and offline social support, self-control, cognitive absorption and mindfulness;
3. Verify if the offline social support is a protective factor of the Problematic Internet Use and online social support is predictor of the PIU in younger and older emerging adults;
4. Verify if self-control and Mindfulness are protective factors towards PIU.

The study uses a cross-sectional research design that was approved by the ethical committee of the Alma Mater Studiorum - University of Bologna. A convenience sample of emerging adults who utilized social networking websites was used. The online questionnaire was hosted on a website[2]. The main criteria for the choice of the scales were: their validity, their brevity, and the theoretical background.

A part of the questionnaire included questions asking participants about daily time spent online, amount of time that they were reachable via the web, what kind of devices they used and the amount of time they spent using these devices, and the most used web tools, the time per day dedicated to using these web tools, and the number of times participants checked these web tools per day. Junco (2013) studied the reliability of self-reported objective measures of Internet use. His results showed that although it is highly correlated, the self-reported time of use was higher than the time measured by monitoring software. Junco proposed a different explanation of this phenomenon. He explained that there is difficulty when measuring a non-linear parceled time. To account for these effects, the questionnaire differentiated between the time in which the web is used actively and the time in which a person is simply connected without using the web (considering also the time spent "being reachable"). Furthermore, the questionnaire included specific questions about the types of tool used, and the time spent online with each tool, and with each application.

Sample Description

The total number of respondents was 706 (age mean = 21.6; SD = 2.9). There were 588 (48.4%; age mean = 20.6, SD = 2.0) Younger Emerging Adults, which included 353 females (60%; age mean = 20.7; SD = 1,9) and 235 are males (40%; age mean = 20.5; SD = 2,1). There were 118 Older Emerging Adults (16.7%; age mean = 26.4; SD = 1.4), with 73 females (61.9%; age mean = 26.3; SD = 1.4) and 45 are males (38.1%; age mean = 26.7; SD = 1.3).

Measures

The questionnaire includes items related to dimensions which could be ideally divided in three sections. Some questions concerned demographic measures; others evaluate several dimensions of the offline life and some analyze dimensions related to the online life. Only the scales which are relevant for the objectives of this chapter on emerging adults will be described in detail. These are described next:

Demographic Measures

The respondents are asked to answer questions regarding their gender, age, nationality, country of residence, occupation, educational qualification, and relationship status.

Offline Life Measures

Studies on self-esteem rely on the pioneering work of Rosenberg (1995) who created a validated scale for measuring general self-esteem. The scale has been translated and validated in different languages, including Italian which is composed by ten likert-scale items with 4 points each (1=strongly agree to 4=strongly disagree) and has been used in this study.

Social Support online and offline was assessed using the Social Support Scale created by Wang and Wang (2013) and adapted by Leung and Lee (2005). Items were answered using 7-points likert scale (1=strongly disagree to 7=agree).

The Brief Self-Control Scale was used to assess self-control, which was edited by Tangey, Baumeister, and Boone (2004), re-validated by Maloney, Grawitch, and Barber (2012), and based on a 5-points likert scale (1= not at all like me to 5= very much like me). The two authors, through exploratory and confirmatory factor analysis, identified two different dimensions of self-control: restraint and impulsivity. According to these scholars, these two dimensions have different impact on the outcomes of self-control (11 items).

Measures of mindfulness are complex as various measuring instruments toll do not assess the same concept (Walach, Buchheld, Buttenmüller, Kleinknecht, & Schmidt, 2006). Among the different possibilities, the Mindfulness Attention Awarness Scale (MAAS) was chosen. This questionnaire was created by Brown and Ryan (2003) and validated by MacKillop and Anderson (2007). The authors define mindfulness as a state of *objective experiential awareness*. The MAAS does not include other dimensions of mindfulness often explored by other scales, "like the non-judgmental, accepting attitude, dis-identification, insightful understanding, or an attitude of having no specific goals" (Walach et al., 2006, p. 1545). It consists of a mono-dimensional score, with 15 items measured with a 6-points Likert system (1=almost always to 6=almost never).

Online Life Measures

The Problematic Use of the Internet was measured by the Generalized Problematic Internet Use Scale 2 (Caplan, 2010), which consists of 15 items that are measured on a 7-points likert scale (1 = Strongly disagree, 4 = Neutral, 7 = Strongly agree.). The definition of problematic use was preferred compared to concepts related to pathological addiction since it embraces a wide range of experiences and it is closer to the experience of the users. The theoretical background on which the PIU scale relies on is the cognitive-behavioral theory of Davis (2001). The scale was recently validated with an Italian sample (Fioravanti, Primi & Casale, 2013). The tool differentiates four sub-dimensions: Preference for online Social Interactions, Mood Regulation, Loss of Control, and Negative Outcomes.

Results

Descriptive Analysis

Following the first purpose of this chapter, below the use of web tools and Internet connections are described in our sample of Italian emerging adults. Given that no gender differences have been found as regards the use of different devices to connect to the web and the use of web applications in the Italian sample of emerging adults, we did not consider gender differences in the analysis to concentrate mainly on differences between younger and older emerging adults. Following these considerations, Figure 1 shows the type of devices used to be online. There are no essential differences in the type of devices used: the computer is the most used tool for both Younger Emerging Adults (95.60%) and the Older Emerging Adults (99.20%), followed by 91.50% for Young Emerging Adults and 83.90% for Older Emerging Adults. The tablet and console/videogames (i.e. play station, x-box, etc.) were not common devices used to connect on the Internet.

Regarding the most commonly used applications during the day (directly from the web or in App versions), emerging adults prefer Facebook, both for Younger (92.90%) and Older Emerging Adults (93.20). Data (see Figure 2) show a relevant difference in the use of e-mail between Older (82.20%) and

Figure 1. Type of devices used to be online

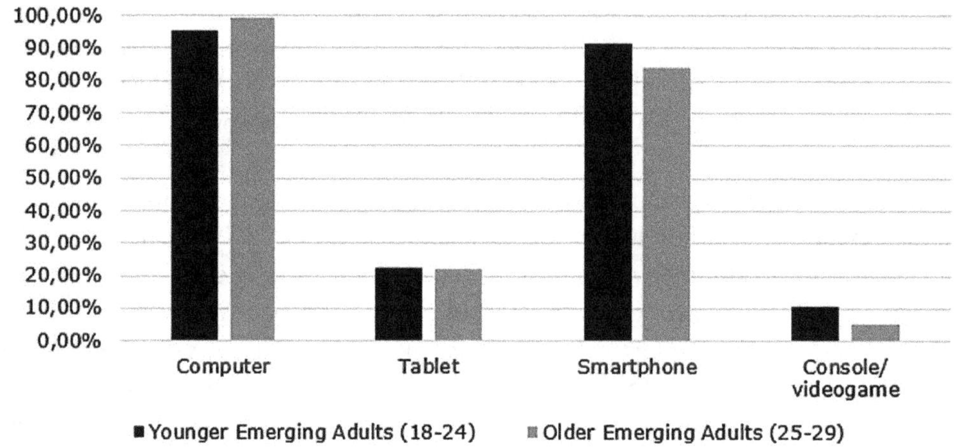

Figure 2. Web tools used during the day

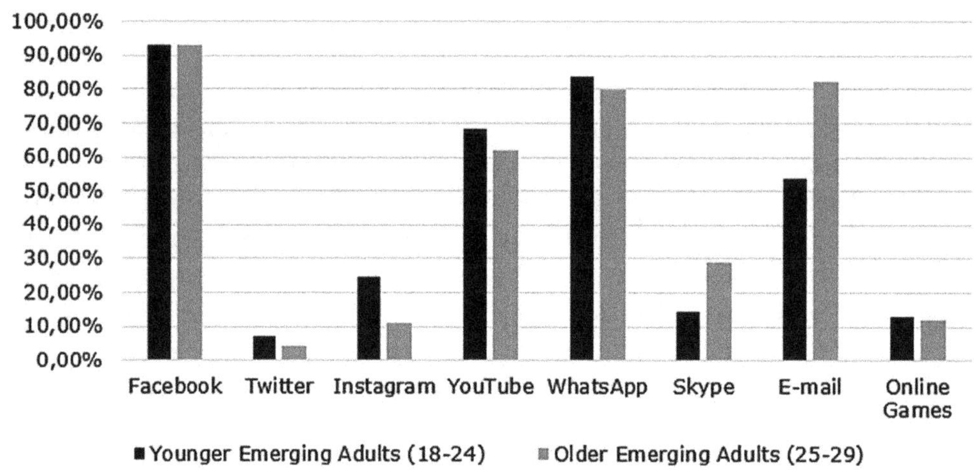

Younger (53.90%) emerging adults. Skype was also used more by Older Emerging Adults (28.80%) than Younger Emerging Adults (14.50%). There were no differences between the two groups in regards to their use of Twitter, Instagram, Youtube, WhatsApp, and online games.

There were no relevant differences in the hours spent online, the hours ready to interact during free time, and during study/work time between Younger and Older Emerging Adults (see Figure 3).

Regarding the use of Web tools during free time (see Figure 4), the use of Facebook was high in both groups like the use of e-mail. Despite these similarities, there were some relevant differences: the Younger Emerging Adults used Skype more than the Older Emerging Adults, (Younger 5.40 hours; Older 3.58 hours), while the Older Emerging Adults used Twitter (Younger 1.20; Older 4.0), WhatsApp (Younger 2.82; Older 4.25), and online games (Younger 3.79 hours; Older 1.82 hours) more than the Young Emerging Adults.

Figure 3. Total hours spent online during free time and study

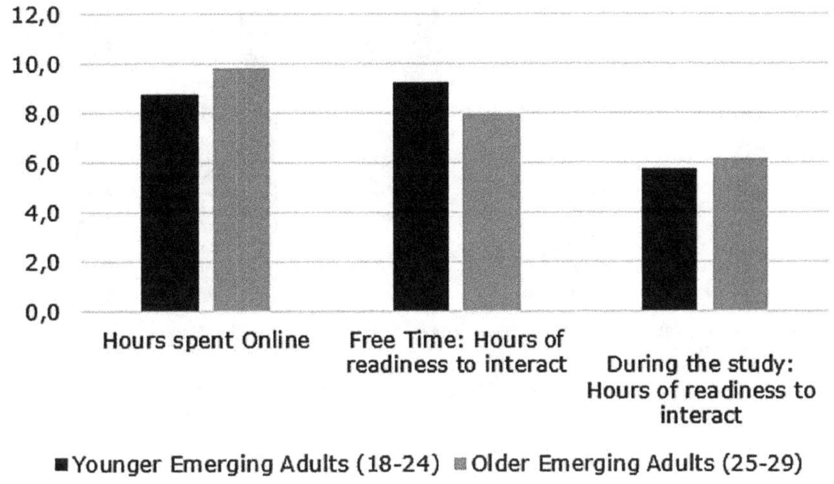

Figure 4. Web tools used during free time

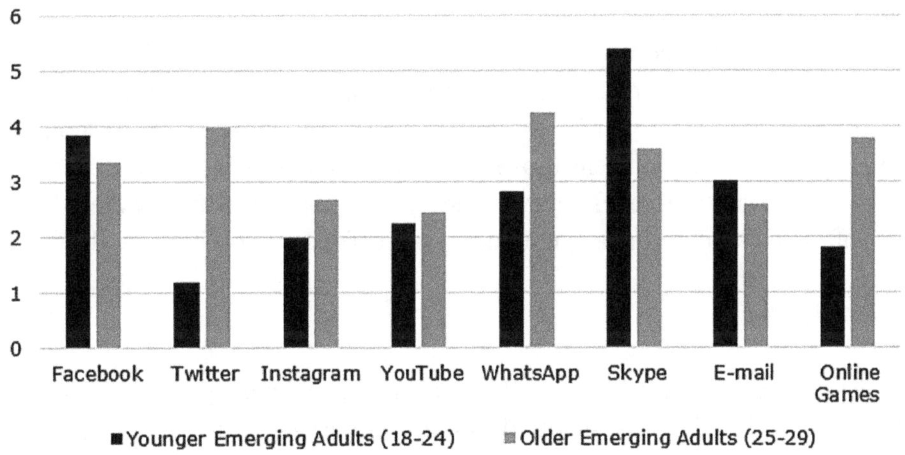

Figure 5. Web Tools use during work/study time

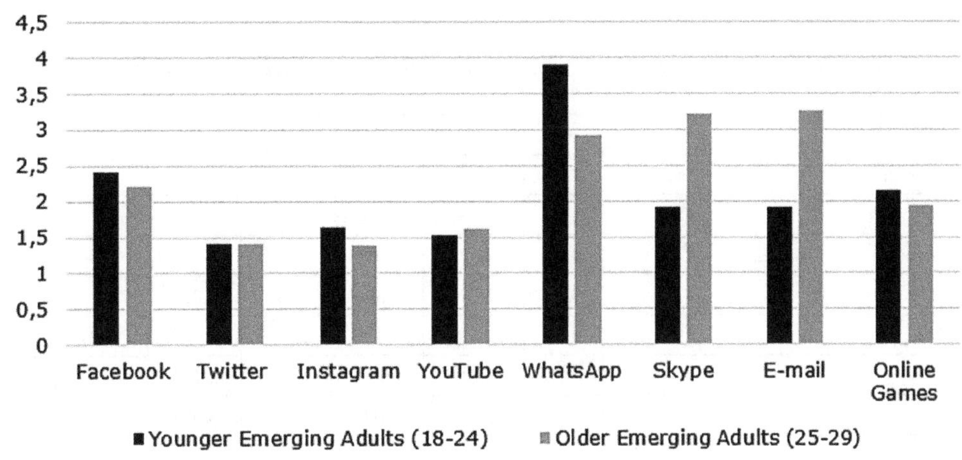

Figure 6. Sum of contact in the Online Life and Offline Life

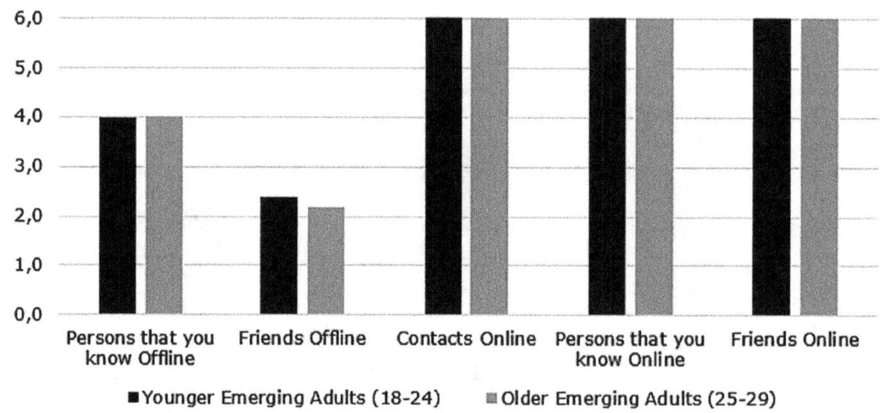

When comparing the hours spent to use the web tools of Figure 2 during free time with the use during study or work (see Figure 5), it is possible to note that the more relevant differences concern WhatsApp (younger 3.90 hours; older 2.91 hours), Skype (younger 1.90 hours; older 3.22 hours) and e-mail (younger 1.90 hours; older 3.26 hours).

Figure 6 concerns the sum of contacts that Younger and Older Emerging Adults have both in online and offline life. The scale goes from 1 (0-20) to 6 (more than 300) for acquaintances (both online and offline), and 1 (less than five) to 6 (81-150) for friends. Obviously the measure of "contacts" is possible only for online life since these represent those latent ties typical of web contexts (Haythornthwaite, 2005), There are no relevant differences between the two groups, while there were differences between both the number of offline and online acquaintances and offline and online friends.

Correlations Analysis

Turning now to the second objective of this exploratory study, i.e. investigating the connections between the Problematic Internet Use, the self-esteem, the online and offline social support, the self-control and the mindfulness, Tables 1 and 2 show the correlations of Younger Emerging Adults (Table 1) and Older Emerging Adults (Table 2).

Table 1. Correlations of younger emerging adults and scales' reliability (Cronbach's Alpha)

	M	SD	1	2	3	4	5	6	7
1. Problematic Internet Use	2.87	1.32	(.90)						
2. Online Social Support	3.17	1.04	.16**	(.95)					
3. Cognitive Absorption	4.48	0.87	.43**	.24**	(.80)				
4. Mindfulness	4.065	0.69	-.30**	-.02	-.04	(.82)			
5. Offline Social Support	3.93	0.79	-.27**	.37**	.00	.06	(.93)		
6. Self-Esteem	3.06	0.50	-.35**	.09*	-.03	.21**	.32**	(.84)	
7. Self-Control	41.8	7.2	-.44**	.07	-.09*	.40**	.20**	.40**	(.77)

Table 2. Correlation and scales' reliability (Cronbach's Alpha) of older emerging adults

	M	SD	1	2	3	4	5	6	7
1. Problematic Internet Use	2.61	1.14	(.92)						
2. Online Social Support	2.98	0.93	.17	(.97)					
3. Cognitive Absorption	4.38	0.81	.50**	.12	(.82)				
4. Mindfulness	4.01	0.74	-.39**	.09	-.23*	(.76)			
5. Offline Social Support	3.89	0.75	-.28**	.14	.13	.16	(.93)		
6. Self-Esteem	3.19	0.47	-.23*	-.07	.01	.23*	.26**	(.83)	
7. Self-Control	43.7	6,.41	-.32**	-.08	-.22*	.41**	.16	.25**	(.80)

The results show positive correlations between PIU and online social support, and PIU and cognitive absorption. Furthermore, PIU correlates negatively with Mindfulness, Offline Social Support, Self-Esteem, and Self-Control. Online Social Support correlates positively with Cognitive Absorption, Offline Social Support, and Self-Esteem (although this last correlation is low). Cognitive Absorption also shows a negative correlation (although low) with Self-Control. Mindfulness, as well as Offline Social Support, has positive correlations with Self-Esteem and Self-Control, and these last two dimensions are correlated with each other.

In general, the results of the Older Emerging Adults are almost the same correlations previously described for Younger Emerging Adults. However, some differences are evident, such as the fact that online social support was not associated with any of the variables. At the same time, Cognitive Absorption was correlated negative with Mindfulness, which was not found for Younger Emerging Adults, while the correlation between Offline Social Support and Self-Control was not found for Older Emerging Adults.

Regressions Analysis

Following the third goal of this study, a hierarchical multiple linear regression has been applied to data. Gender and age were introduced as predictors in the first model, while Offline Social Support and Online Social Support were introduced in the second model. Afterwards, we verified if the Offline Social Support is a protective factor in the PIU in the Younger Emerging Adults (Table 3) and in the Older Emerging Adults (Table 4).

The results show that the Offline Social Support negatively predicts the PIU and the Online Social Support predicts it positively both in Younger and Older Emerging Adults.

Finally, considering the last purpose of this chapter we verified if Self-Control and Mindfulness are protective factors towards the PIU in the Younger Emerging Adults (Table 5) and in the Older Emerging Adults (Table 6), by using hierarchical multiple linear regression. Like in the previously analysis, gender and age were predictors in the first model, while Mindfulness and Self-Control were tested as predictors in second model.

The results show that Mindfulness and Self-Control negatively predicts the PIU in Early Emerging Adults even if, in the group of Older Emerging Adults, despite the Self-Control appears inversely related to the PIU, only Mindfulness proves to be a factor that significantly predicts a lower level of PIU.

Table 3. Hierarchical multiple regression using as dependent variable Problematic Internet Use in Younger Emerging Adults

Model		Unstandardized Coefficients		Standardized Coefficients	t	Sig.
		B	Std. Error	Beta		
1	Predictors	2.71	.61		4.47	.000
	Gender	.38	.11	.14	3.44	.001
	Age	-.02	.03	-.03	-.66	.512
2	Predictors	4.07	.65		6.24	.000
	Gender	.19	.11	.07	1.78	.076
	Age	-.02	.03	-.02	-.63	.529
	Offline Social Support	-.60	.08	-.36	-8.39	.000
	Online Social Support	.38	.05	.30	7.27	.000

** p>.001

Table 4. Hierarchical multiple regression using as dependent variable Problematic Internet Use in Older Emerging Adults

Model		Unstandardized Coefficients		Standardized Coefficients	t	Sig.
		B	Std. Error	Beta		
1	Predictiors	.20	2.07		.08	.923
	Gender	.38	,22	.17	1.75	.083
	Age	.07	.08	.08	.90	.369
2	Predictors	2.05	2.28		.90	.372
	Gender	.21	.23	.09	.92	.362
	Age	.04	.08	.05	.54	.594
	Offline Social Support	-.41	.16	-.27	-2.65	.009
	Online Social Support	.27	.11	.22	2.48	.014

** p>.001

Table 5. Hierarchical multiple regression using as dependent variable Problematic Internet Use in Younger Emerging Adults

Model		Unstandardized Coefficients		Standardized Coefficients	t	Sig.
		B	Std. Error	Beta		
1	Predictors	2.68	.60		4.45	.000
	Gender	.39	.11	.14	3.47	.001
	Age	-.02	.03	-.03	-.62	.538
2	Predictors	6.00	.62		9.72	.000
	Gender	.31	.10	.11	3.08	.002
	Age	.02	.03	.04	.93	.352
	Mindfulness	-.30	.08	-.15	-3.83	.000
	Self-Control	-,.07	.01	-.37	-9.06	.000

** p>.001

Table 6. Hierarchical multiple regression using as dependent variable Problematic Internet Use in Older Emerging Adults

Model		Unstandardized Coefficients		Standardized Coefficients	t	Sig.
		B	Std. Error	Beta		
1	Predictors	.20	2.07		.10	.923
	Gender	.38	.22	.16	1.75	.083
	Age	.07	.08	.08	.90	.369
2	Predictors	4.47	2.12		2.10	.038
	Gender	.32	.20	.14	1.60	.113
	Age	.04	.07	.04	.49	.627
	Mindfulness	-.46	.15	-.29	-3.09	.003
	Self-Control	-.03	.02	-.18	-1.94	.055

** p>.001

DISCUSSION

The aim of the study was to investigate which dimensions play a role in Functional Internet Use (i.e. its positive integration in everyday life) or in the Problematic Internet Use (that has been conceptualized as inverse instrumentality) in emerging adulthood. From this point of view, one of the most important aspect to take into account is the reason behind the use of certain web technologies. Online behavior could be a way to compensate deficiencies in offline life and, consequently, the use of the Internet could lead to negative outcomes. On the other hand, if the Internet becomes a tool to enhance and improve one's abilities in the offline life, its use would have positive effects.

Results of the study, those concerning correlations and regressions, seem to support this views. For Younger Emerging Adults, Online Social Support play an important role in maintaining and constructing social capital during transitions from school to university or work or from university to work, and this suggests some types of problematic Internet use. However, this is true only in the case of a deficient Offline Social Support, since this dimension correlates negatively with Problematic Internet Use. In case of high online social support, but with a high offline social support, the risk of problematic internet use is diminished (Mazzoni, Baiocco, Cannata, & Dimas, 2016). This critical aspect of online social support is not present for Older Emerging Adults, characterized by a more stable time.

Moreover, for all emerging adults considered in this study, Mindfulness, Self-Esteem and Self-Control seem to play an important role in reducing Problematic Internet Use. From this point of view, emerging adults with high self-esteem, high self-control, and high mindfulness do not seem to manifest online behaviors that lead to a dysfunctional use of the Internet with negative outcomes in their offline life. Thus, a Younger Emerging Adult, with high self-esteem, probably perceives himself/herself as having high social support principally offline, but also online. This dynamic preserves him/her from trying to construct an online network of relationships simply because he/she has a lack of relations in the offline life.

The Social Enhancement hypothesis (Zwynca & Danowksi, 2008) explains that "those with more developed offline social networks enhance them with more extensive online social networks", whereas the Social Compensation hypothesis suggests that "those who perceive their offline social networks to be inadequate compensate for them with more extensive online social networks" (p.3). The online environment might allow people with strong offline social network to improve them, by allowing them to integrate their two networks (offline and online) and enhancing their capacity to further connect with people. This is exactly what Leont'ev (1974) calls functional organ.

SOLUTIONS AND RECOMMENDATIONS

Although much research has highlighted the negative impact of online life on human development (see Caplan, 2005; Davis, 2001; Young, 2004), studies have also found that online life has a positive effect on the offline one (Barker, 2009; Ellison, Steinfield & Lampe, 2007; Mazzoni & Iannone, 2014; Mazzoni, Baiocco, Cannata & Dimas, 2016; Stern & Taylor, 2007; Valkenburg & Peter, 2009). The results described in this chapter show which factors have to be developed to prevent emerging adults from experiencing the negative effects of Problematic Internet Use. Working on the development of Mindfulness, Self-Control and Self-Esteem of emerging adults will increase these individuals' ability to integrate Internet applications in their daily life in positive ways.

FUTURE RESEARCH DIRECTIONS

Future research should clarify some concepts which have only been touched on in this exploratory study and can further explore some issues suggested by the theoretical work and by the empirical results. For a better understanding of Internet use, studies should be conducted on different cultural, social, and economic contexts to investigate the connections between Problematic Internet Use, Self-Esteem, online and offline Social Support, Self-Control, Cognitive Absorption, and Mindfulness. Also, future research should investigate these connections during the adolescence and adulthood, because the factors explored in this study (self-esteem, social support, self-control, cognitive absorption, and mindfulness) change significantly during the lifespan.

Moreover, the findings from our study revealed differences between older and younger emerging adults. Considering that most of the research literature about Internet addiction are based on samples of students, it would be important to better analyze the situation in different segments of the population as the results could differ significantly.

CONCLUSION

This research is relevant because it aims to address a gap in the literature by providing an understanding of relationships between online and offline life and trying to balance the excessive imbalance of research focused on the pathological side of human-technology interactions. In this regard, the main goal was to focus attention not only on understanding factors that determine a problematic use of the Internet, but also on those factors that allow emerging adults to integrate it into a functional organ to achieve the developmental and career goals that characterize their daily activities. This perspective, that was born into the wider field of positive psychology (Riva et al., 2012), could have important implications to improve the effectiveness of certain human functions in everyday contexts, thanks to the attention placed on the awareness of the negative and positive aspects of the Internet.

Nonetheless, this study presents three kinds of limitations: sample limitations, structural limitations and theoretical limitations. The sample limitations are a direct consequence of the data collection method. Although the number of participants is high for statistical purposes it is not representative of the large and diverse population to which it refers. The channels used (principally social networking sites) to reach participants limits the sample to people belonging to middle/high social class, highly educated, and with good ability in the use of technology.

Structural limitations are due to the very nature of the phenomenon studied. The Internet is a huge thing; it has entered into the life of most people pervasively, and in many different aspects. Moreover, the Internet changes at an extremely high rate, and there is already talk about a web 3.0 online. The psychological research of the last 15 years converge son the importance of variables like self-control and self-esteem to predict the dysfunctional use of the web. We can ask, in the future, for a better collaboration between software engineers, web sociologists, and cyber-psychologists to study the new changes that will occur in the web before they become obsolete. It is important to acknowledge that in this study activity theory is used as a metaphor and not as a research tool. Activity theory is in fact a post-cognitive theory that uses a peculiar construct and focuses its attention not on the individual but on his or her activity. In order to obtain these goals, emerging adults interact with media technology, with gains and losses in terms of empowerment, health, freedom, security, and happiness.

REFERENCES

Agarwal, R., & Karahanna, E. (2000). Time flies when youre having fun: Cognitive absorption and beliefs about information technology usage. *Management Information Systems Quarterly*, *24*(4), 665–694. doi:10.2307/3250951

Arnett, J. J. (2000). Emerging adulthood: A theory of development from the late teens through the twenties. *The American Psychologist*, *55*(5), 469–480. doi:10.1037/0003-066X.55.5.469 PMID:10842426

Arnett, J. J. (2012). New Horizons in Research on Emerging and Young Adulthood. In A. Booth, S. L. Brown, N. S. Landale, W. D. Manning, & S. M. McHale (Eds.), *Younger Adulthood in a Family Context* (pp. 231–244). New York, NY: Springer. doi:10.1007/978-1-4614-1436-0_15

Arnett, J. J. (2015). *Emerging Adulthood: The Winding Road from the Late Teens Through the Twenties*. New York, NY: Oxford University Press. doi:10.1093/oxfordhb/9780199795574.013.9

Arnett, J. J., & Fishel, E. (2013). *When Will My Grown-up Kid Grow Up? Loving and Understanding Your Emerging Adult*. Workman Publishing.

Arnett, J. J., & Tanner, J. L. (2006). *Emerging adults in America: Coming of age in the 21st century*. Washington, DC: American Psychological Association.

Barker, V. (2009). Older adolescents motivations for social network site use: The influence of gender, group identity, and collective self-esteem. *Cyberpsychology & Behavior*, *12*(2), 209–213. doi:10.1089/cpb.2008.0228 PMID:19250021

Brown, K. W., & Ryan, R. M. (2003). The benefits of being present: Mindfulness and its role in psychological well-being. *Journal of Personality and Social Psychology, 84*(4), 822–848. doi:10.1037/0022-3514.84.4.822 PMID:12703651

Caplan, S., Williams, D., & Yee, N. (2009). Problematic Internet use and psychosocial well-being among MMO players. *Computers in Human Behavior, 25*(6), 1312–1319. doi:10.1016/j.chb.2009.06.006

Caplan, S. E. (2005). A social skill account of problematic Internet use. *Journal of Communication, 55*(4), 721–736. doi:10.1111/j.1460-2466.2005.tb03019.x

Caplan, S. E. (2010). Theory and measurement of generalized problematic Internet use: A two-step approach. *Computers in Human Behavior, 25*(5), 1089–1097. doi:10.1016/j.chb.2010.03.012

Clark University Poll of Emerging Adults. (2015). *Work, Education and Identity*. Worcester, MA: Clark University.

Cloninger, C. R., Svrakic, D. M., & Przybeck, T. R. (1993). A psychobiological model of temperament and character. *Archives of General Psychiatry, 50*(12), 975–990. doi:10.1001/archpsyc.1993.01820240059008 PMID:8250684

Davis, R. A. (2001). A cognitive-behavioral model of pathological Internet use. *Computers in Human Behavior, 17*(2), 187–195. doi:10.1016/S0747-5632(00)00041-8

Douglass, C. B. (2007). From Duty to Desire: Emerging Adulthood in Europe and Its Consequences. *Child Development Perspectives, 1*(2), 101–108. doi:10.1111/j.1750-8606.2007.00023.x

Ekbia, H., & Nardi, B. A. (2012). Inverse instrumentality: How technologies objectify patients and players. In P. Leonardi, B. Nardi, & J. Kallinikos (Eds.), Materiality and organizing: social interactions in a technological world. Oxford, UK: Oxford University Press.

Ellison, N., Steinfield, C., & Lampe, C. (2007). The benefits of Facebook friends: Social capital and college students use of online social network sites. *Journal of Computer-Mediated Communication, 12*(4), 1143–1168. doi:10.1111/j.1083-6101.2007.00367.x

Fioravanti, G., Primi, C., & Casale, S. (2013). Psychometric evaluation of the generalized Problematic Internet Use Scale 2 in an Italian sample. *Cyberpsychology, Behavior, and Social Networking, 16*(10), 761–766. doi:10.1089/cyber.2012.0429 PMID:23742149

Forest, A. L., & Wood, J. V. (2012). When social networking is not working individuals with low self-esteem recognize but do not reap the benefits of self-disclosure on Facebook. *Psychological Science, 23*(3), 295–302. doi:10.1177/0956797611429709 PMID:22318997

Frozzi, G., & Mazzoni, E. (2011). On the importance of social network sites in the transitions which characterize "emerging adulthood.". *ICST Transactions on E-Education and E-Learning, 11*(7-9), 1–11.

Ghorbani, N., Watson, P. J., Farhadi, M., & Chen, Z. (2014). A multi-process model of self-regulation: Influences of mindfulness, integrative self-knowledge and self-control in Iran. *International Journal of Psychology, 49*(2), 115–122. doi:10.1002/ijop.12033 PMID:24811882

Griffin, P., & Cole, M. (1984). Current activity for the future: The zo-ped. In B. Rogoff & J. V. Wertsch (Eds.), *Children's learning in the zone of proximal development* (pp. 276–295). San Francisco: Jossey-Bass. doi:10.1002/cd.23219842306

Ha, J. H., Kim, S. Y., Bae, S. C., Bae, S., Kim, H., Sim, M., & Cho, S. C. (2007). Depression and Internet addiction in adolescents. *Psychopathology*, *40*(6), 424–430. doi:10.1159/000107426 PMID:17709972

Haythornthwaite, C. (2005). Social networks and Internet connectivity effects. *Information Communication and Society*, *8*(2), 125–147. doi:10.1080/13691180500146185

Heatherton, T. F. (2011). Neuroscience of self and self-regulation. *Annual Review of Psychology*, *62*(1), 363–390. doi:10.1146/annurev.psych.121208.131616 PMID:21126181

Johnson, G. M. (2011). Self-esteem and use of the Internet among young school-age children. *International Journal of Psychological Studies*, *3*(2), 48–53. doi:10.5539/ijps.v3n2p48

Junco, R. (2013). Comparing actual and self-reported measures of Facebook use. *Computers in Human Behavior*, *29*(3), 626–631. doi:10.1016/j.chb.2012.11.007

Kaplan, A., & Haenlein, M. (2010). Users of the world, unite! The challenges and opportunities of Social Media. *Business Horizons*, *53*(1), 59–68. doi:10.1016/j.bushor.2009.09.003

Kaptelinin, V., & Nardi, B. A. (2006). *Acting with technology: Activity theory and interaction design*. MIT Press.

Khang, H., Kim, J., & Kim, Y. (2013). Self-traits and motivations as antecedents of digital media flow and addiction: The Internet, mobile phones, and video games. *Computers in Human Behavior*, *29*(6), 2416–2424. doi:10.1016/j.chb.2013.05.027

Kuss, D., & Griffiths, M. (2011). Addiction to social networks on the Internet: A literature review of empirical research. *International Journal of Environment and Public Health*, *8*, 3528–3552. doi:10.3390/ijerph8093528

Lee, B. W., & Leeson, P. R. (2015). Online gaming in the context of social anxiety. *Psychology of Addictive Behaviors*, *29*(2), 473–482. doi:10.1037/adb0000070 PMID:25938630

Lee, S. (2014). How do people compare themselves with others on social network sites? The case of Facebook. *Computers in Human Behavior*, *32*, 253–260. doi:10.1016/j.chb.2013.12.009

Leont'ev, A. N. (1972). Activity and Consciousness. *Voprosy Filosofii*, *12*, 129–140.

Leontev, A. N. (1974). The problem of activity in psychology. *Journal of Russian & East European Psychology*, *13*(2), 4–33. doi:10.2753/RPO1061-040513024

Leung, L., & Lee, P. S. (2005). Multiple determinants of life quality: The roles of Internet activities, use of new media, social support, and leisure activities. *Telematics and Informatics*, *22*(3), 161–180. doi:10.1016/j.tele.2004.04.003

MacKillop, J., & Anderson, E. J. (2007). Further psychometric validation of the mindful attention awareness scale (MAAS). *Journal of Psychological Behavior Assessment*, *29*(4), 289–293. doi:10.1007/s10862-007-9045-1

Maloney, P. W., Grawitch, M. J., & Barber, L. K. (2012). The multi-factor structure of the Brief Self-Control Scale: Discriminant validity of restraint and impulsivity. *Journal of Research in Personality*, *46*(1), 11–115. doi:10.1016/j.jrp.2011.10.001

Mazzoni, E., Baiocco, L., Benvenuti, M., Cannata, D., Fossi, E., & Zanazzi, L. (2014). Beyond Internet addiction. A new framework to understand risks and benefits of being online. In *Proceedings of the International Conferences on ICT, Society and Human Beings 2014*. IADIS.

Mazzoni, E., Baiocco, L., Cannata, D., & Dimas, I. (2016). Is Internet the cherry on top or a crutch? Offline social support as moderator of the outcomes of online social support on Problematic Internet Use. *Computers in Human Behavior*, *56*, 369–374. doi:10.1016/j.chb.2015.11.032

Mazzoni, E., Cannata, D., & Baiocco, L. (2016). Focused, not lost: The mediating role of Temporal Dissociation and Focused Immersion on Problematic Internet Use. *Behaviour & Information Technology*, 1–10. doi:10.1080/0144929X.2016.1159249

Mazzoni, E., & Iannone, M. (2014). From high school to university: Impact of social networking sites on social capital in the transitions of emerging adults. *British Journal of Educational Technology*, *45*(2), 303–315. doi:10.1111/bjet.12026

Mazzoni, E., & Zanazzi, L. (2014). Comparing the Use of SNSs Among Adults and Emerging Asults. *Journal of e-Learning and Knowledge Society*, *10*, 25-36.

Montag, C., Flierl, M., Markett, S., Walter, N., Jurkiewicz, M., & Reuter, M. (2011). Internet addiction and personality in first-person-shooter video gamers. *Journal of Media Psychology*, *23*(4), 163–173. doi:10.1027/1864-1105/a000049

Montag, C., Jurkiewicz, M., & Reuter, M. (2010). Low self-directedness is a better predictor for problematic Internet use than high neuroticism. *Computers in Human Behavior*, *26*(6), 1531–1535. doi:10.1016/j.chb.2010.05.021

Ngai, E., Tao, S., & Moon, K. (2015). Social media research: Theories, constructs, and conceptual frameworks. *International Journal of Information Management*, *35*(1), 33–44. doi:10.1016/j.ijinfomgt.2014.09.004

Odaci, H., & Çıkrıkçı, Ö. (2014). Problematic Internet use in terms of gender, attachment styles and subjective well-being in university students. *Computers in Human Behavior*, *32*, 61–66. doi:10.1016/j.chb.2013.11.019

Riva, G., Banos, R. M., Botella, C., Wiederhold, B. K., & Gaggioli, A. (2012). Positive technology: Using interactive technologies to promote positive functioning. *Cyberpsychology, Behavior, and Social Networking*, *15*(2), 69–77. doi:10.1089/cyber.2011.0139 PMID:22149077

Rosenberg, M., Schooler, C., Schoenbach, C., & Rosenberg, F. (1995). Global self-esteem and specific self-esteem: Different concepts, different outcomes. *American Sociological Review*, *60*(1), 141–156. doi:10.2307/2096350

Sariyska, R., Reuter, M., Lachmann, B., & Montag, C. (2015). Attention deficit/hyperactivity disorder is a better predictor for problematic Internet use than depression: Evidence from Germany. *Journal of Addiction Research & Therapy*, *6*(209), 2.

Steinfield, C., Ellison, N. B., & Lampe, C. (2008). Social capital, self-esteem, and use of online social network sites: A longitudinal analysis. *Journal of Applied Developmental Psychology*, *29*(6), 435–445. doi:10.1016/j.appdev.2008.07.002

Stern, L. A., & Taylor, K. (2007). Social networking on Facebook. *Journal of the Communication. Speech & Theatre Association of North Dakota*, *20*, 9–20.

Tangney, J. P., Baumeister, R. F., & Boone, A. L. (2004). High self-control predicts good adjustment, less pathology, better grades, and interpersonal success. *Journal of Personality*, *72*(2), 271–322. doi:10.1111/j.0022-3506.2004.00263.x PMID:15016066

Tuomi-Gröhn, T., & Engeström, Y. (2003). *Between school and work: New perspectives on transfer and boundary crossing*. Amsterdam: Pergamon.

Turkle, S. (2012). *Alone together: Why we expect more from technology and less from each other*. New York, NY: Basic books.

Vago, D. R., & Silbersweig, D. A. (2012). Self-awareness, self-regulation, and self-transcendence (S-ART): A framework for understanding the neurobiological mechanisms of mindfulness. *Frontiers in Human Neuroscience*, *6*, 1–30. doi:10.3389/fnhum.2012.00296 PMID:23112770

Valkenburg, P. M., & Peter, J. (2009). Social consequences of the Internet for adolescents a decade of research. *Current Directions in Psychological Science*, *18*(1), 1–5. doi:10.1111/j.1467-8721.2009.01595.x

Vygotsky, L. (1978). *Mind and society: The development of higher psychological processes*. Cambridge, MA: Harvard University Press.

Walach, H., Buchheld, N., Buttenmüller, V., Kleinknecht, N., & Schmidt, S. (2006). Measuring mindfulness - the Freiburg mindfulness inventory (FMI). *Personality and Individual Differences*, *40*(8), 1543–1555. doi:10.1016/j.paid.2005.11.025

Wang, E. S.-T., & Wang, M. C.-H. (2013). Social Support and Social Interaction Ties on Internet Addiction: Integrating Online and Offline Contexts. *Cyberpsychology, Behavior, and Social Networking*, *16*(11), 843–849. doi:10.1089/cyber.2012.0557 PMID:23848959

Weigle, P. (2014). Internet and Video Game Addiction: Evidence & Controversy. *Adolescent Psychiatry*, *4*(2), 81-91.

Wenger, E. (2000). Communities of Practice and Social Learning Systems. *Organization*, *7*(2), 225–246. doi:10.1177/135050840072002

Widyanto, L., & Griffiths, M. (2011). An empirical study of problematic Internet use and self-esteem. *International Journal of Cyber Behavior, Psychology and Learning*, *1*(1), 13–24. doi:10.4018/ijcbpl.2011010102

Young, K. (1998). Internet addiction: The emergence of a new clinical disorder. *Cyberpsychology & Behavior*, *1*(3), 237–244. doi:10.1089/cpb.1998.1.237

Young, K. S. (2004). Internet addiction a new clinical phenomenon and its consequences. *The American Behavioral Scientist*, *48*(4), 402–415. doi:10.1177/0002764204270278

Zywica, J., & Danowski, J. (2008). The faces of Facebookers: Investigating social enhancement and social compensation hypotheses; predicting Facebook™ and offline popularity from sociability and self-esteem, and mapping the meanings of popularity with semantic networks. *Journal of Computer-Mediated Communication*, *14*(1), 1–34. doi:10.1111/j.1083-6101.2008.01429.x

KEY TERMS AND DEFINITIONS

Activity System: The structure of a human activity representing the interaction of the main aspects: subject, object, artefacts, community, division of labor and rules.

Cognitive Absorption: A strong involvement within a specific activity that takes all the attention of a person (temporal dissociation, diving focused, fun, control, curiosity).

Functional Organ: The integration of a specific tool and a certain human skill which allows it to achieve better performance than the use of only the personal skills.

Inverse Instrumentality: A process of objectification of users that regulates their behavior in an expectant manner, drawing them in or pushing them away from certain kinds of activities.

Mindfulness: The presence or absence of attention relatively to what happens in the present.

Offline Life: The set of actions and relationships that a person performs and has when he's disconnected to the Internet.

Online Life: The set of actions and relationships that a person performs and has when he's connected to the Internet.

Self-Control: A measure of how much people control themselves and their actions.

Self-Esteem: A measure of how much people perceive to be popular and successful in their social interactions.

Social Support: The set of information that come to a person thanks to social interactions and that transmit to the individual the feeling of being loved, valued and able, as well as being part of a network from which derive mutual obligations.

ENDNOTES

1 www.qualtrics.com

2 https://sites.google.com/site/onlineliferesearch/

Chapter 15
Cyberstalking Victimization and Perpetration among Greek College Students

Argyroula Kalaitzaki
Technological Educational Institute of Crete, Greece & Laboratory of Interdisciplinary Approaches for the Enhancement of Quality of Life, Greece

ABSTRACT

Cyberstalking is a rapidly growing phenomenon, which is becoming more common among youth nowadays. The study aimed at investigating: 1) the prevalence, behaviors, and tactics of both victims and perpetrators among a sample of Greek undergraduate students, 2) the correlates of victimization and perpetration with personality, attachment style, and relating to others, and 3) the impact of cyberstalking on victims' mental health. Results showed that 23.9% of the students were victims and 9% were perpetrators, with females, disproportionately both experiencing and inflicting cyberstalking. Negatively close relating (i.e., intrusive, restrictive and possessive relating) increased the risk of cyberstalking perpetration, whereas negatively distant relating (suspicious, avoidant, and self-reliant relating) decreased the risk of cyberstalking victimization. Agreeableness decreased the risk of perpetration. Mother's affectionless control increased the risk of both perpetration and victimization and mother's neglectful parenting increased the risk of perpetration only.

INTRODUCTION

Although stalking is not a new behavior, as it has been reported since the 19th century, its emergence into the cyber-world is (Lewis, Fremouw, Ben, & Farr, 2001). Stalking is defined as engaging in a pattern of harassing or threatening behavior, such as following a person, appearing at a person's home or place of business, making harassing phone calls, leaving written messages or objects, or vandalizing a person's property (Ashcroft, 2001; Tjaden & Thoennes, 1998). The advancement of information and communication technologies, such as the Internet, has offered stalkers an additional and perhaps more effective, though dubious and insidious, way to target their victims and commit their malevolent acts. Thus, some stalkers have become cyberstalkers.

DOI: 10.4018/978-1-5225-1856-3.ch015

Despite experts' and legislators' attempts to define cyberstalking, still there is no commonly accepted definition of *cyberstalking* or *technology-aided stalking*. However, the term is generally used to refer to the "behaviors that involve repeated threats and harassment by the use of electronic mail or other computer-based communication that would make a reasonable person afraid or concerned for their safety" (Finn, 2004, p. 469). Similar definitions involve the repeated pursuit or monitoring of an individual utilizing electronic means (e.g., e-mails, blogs, instant messaging, video, chat rooms, on-line social networks, or other websites) or tracking technologies that induces the victim to feel distress, fear, alarm, or concerned for his/her safety (Bocij, 2006; D'Ovidio & Doyle, 2003; Reyns, 2010). This may involve threatening, coercive, harassing, or intimidating messages or sexual overtones or other unwanted, persistent, and intrusive contact.

To the author's knowledge there is no study up until this date which describes cyberstalking in Greece. The prevalence of both cyberstalking perpetration and victimization worldwide is also unknown because of the different definitions employed and study samples, which results in variant prevalence rates. Few estimates concerning the perpetration of cyberstalking are readily available (Roberts 2008), particularly due to the difficulty in obtaining offending data. It has been reported that approximately 1 in 4 stalking victims reported some form of cyberstalking (Baum, Catalano, Kristina, Michael, 2009). Cyberstalkers are primarily male (Working to Halt Online Abuse; WHOA, 2011), with a mean age of 24 years (D'Ovidio & Doyle, 2003) and they usually know the victim (e.g., a friend, coworker, fellow student, or an ex-partner) (WHOA, 2011).

Several studies among university students have reported relatively high, though diverse prevalence rates of cyberstalking victimization too, ranging from 18.9% (Holt & Bossler, 2009) to 45.2% (Alexy et al., 2005), Estimates of cyberstalking victimization range between 2% to 13% of males and 8% to 32% of females (Spitzberg & Cupach, 2007). Risk factors for cyberstalking vicitmization include being females (e.g., Reyns, Henson, & Fisher, 2012) and in young adtuldhood (between 18 and 30 years of age; e.g., Brownstein, 2000).

Cyberstalking behaviours are likely to be more prevalent in the population of emerging adults (aged between 18–25 years old; Arnett, 2000), than in any other age group as they are the highest users of social media. They are also more likely to connect with partners in their intimate relationships through digital technologies (Boyle & O'Sullivan, 2014; Dewing, 2010), Moreover, the relationships in this age group are characterized by greater emotional intensity and importance or commitment compared to earlier ages (Collins, 2003), which might be the cause of the potential distress of letting go during the process of adjusting to a breakup (Lee & O'Sullivan, 2014).

Scarce research exists on the personality of cyberstalkers and cyberstalking victims. Cyberstalkers are low on agreeableness, conscientiousness, and emotional stability, and high on extraversion (O'Riordan & O'Connell, 2014), while other studies have described cyberstalkers as introverted (Wall, 2007). The personality correlations associated with cyberstalking victims is currently unknown. However, victims of cyberbullying have been described as low on agreeableness and high on extraversion and openness (Festl & Quandt, 2013; Peluchette, Karl, Wood, & Williams, 2015).

Studies have revealed that cyberstalkers have an insecure-anxious adult attachment style (MacKenzie, Mullen, Ogloff, McEwan, & James, 2008; Patton, Nobles, & Fox, 2010; Tonin, 2004). Fox and Warber (2014) found that people with "preoccupied" and "fearful" attachment styles reported higher levels of "relationship uncertainty" within a romantic relationship and higher levels of interpersonal electronic surveillance (IES) of romantic partners (i.e., checking up more often on their romantic partners). Interpersonal electronic surveillance of a partner after breaking up could lead to cyberstalking provided that it is not just checking up or seeking information about the partner but also instilling fear to the victim. Furthermore, research has shown that attachment styles influence reactions to breakups, with anxious attachment styles having a longer recovery period and continuing to seek information about their partner after the breakup (e.g., Fagundes, 2012).

There is inconsistent evidence regarding the responses victims use to deal with cyberstalking. WHOA (2011) and Alexy, Burgess, Baker, & Smoyak (2005) found that the majority of victims do not report cyberstalking, whereas other studies have found that victims do report cyberstalking (e.g., Finn, 2004). Cyberstalking can have major psychosocial impacts on individuals. Victims have reported increased suicidal ideation, fear, anger, depression, and post traumatic stress disorder (PTSD) symptomology (Short, Linford, Wheatcroft, & Maple, 2014). In addition, poorer well-being has also been resported (Dreßing, Bailer, Anders, Wagner, & Gallas, 2014). To the author's knowledge, the psychological effects of cyberstalking perpetration is unknown. However, cyberbullies have poorer quality of life and psychological difficulties, such as more hyperactivity and conduct problems (Fletcher et al., 2014). Due to its serious negative implications, cyberstalking should be an issue of great concern by both legal authorities and victim assistance professionals.

The current study will add to this limited, yet growing body of research on cyberstalking, by investigating:

1. The prevalence, behaviors, and tactics/responses of cyberstalking perpetration and victimization,
2. Personality, attachment style, and type of relating to others as risk factors associated with cyberstalking perpetration and victimization, and
3. The impact of cyberstalking on victims' mental health.

The findings will address the gaps in the empirical literature, provide new insights into the field, and make recommendations for further research on cyberstalking and the prevention of these behaviors.

METHOD

Participants

Data were collected via a Web-based survey administered to a random sample of undergraduate college students at the Technological Education Institute of Crete in the southern Greece. The sample consists of 442 undergraduate students (78.7% woman) aged 17-21 (42.2%), 22-27 (44.12%) or 28 and over (13.7%).

Procedure

The questionnaire was prepared using Google Forms and the link to the online questionnaire was posted on personal and group webpages and social networks available to the students (e.g., Facebook). Once volunteers read the informed consent, which assured them that all information was confidential and anonymous, they were invited to complete the questionnaire which asked about their experience with cyberstalking, both as victims or offenders.

Measures

The questionnaire asked participants their demographic characteristics (e.g., gender, age, and department) as well as questions regarding traditional (offline) stalking. Next, the definition of cyberstalking was introduced along with examples of cyberstalking acts (e.g., compiling online information, stealing a person's online identity, threatening, faulse accusations, defamation). The following questionnaires were administered to participants:

The Big Five Inventory (BFI; John & Srivastava, 1999) was administered to measure the Big Five factors (i.e., dimensions) of personality (i.e., extraversion, agreeableness, conscientiousness, neuroticism, openess). It is a self-report inventory of 44 items initiated with the phrase "I see myself as someone who..." Particpants responded to each item using a five-point Likert type scale ranging from 1 (*Strongly Disagree*) to 5 (*Strongly Agree*). Certain items were reverse scored and scores were summed to produce five subscale scores, which corresponded to the five dimensions of personality. Extraversion encompasses traits like talkative, energetic, and assertive. Agreeableness includes traits like sympathetic, kind, and affectionate. Conscientiousness includes traits like organized, thorough, and planful. Neuroticism encompasses traits like tense, moody, and anxious. Openness to Experience includes traits like having wide interests, being imaginative, and insightful. This questionnaire has been shown to have good convergent and discriminant validity, acceptable reliability, and factorial structure across 56 nations, Greece included (John, Donahue, & Kentle, 1999; Schmitt, Allik, McCrae, & Benet-Martinez, 2007). The Greek reliabilities were satisfactory (extraversion: 0.92, agreeableness: 0.91, conscientiousness: 0.89, neuroticism: 0.90, openness: 0.89).

The Person's Relating to Others Questionnaire – Shortened version (PROQ3; Birtchnell, Hammond, Horn, De Jong, & Kalaitzaki, 2013; Kalaitzaki & Birtchnell, 2016) measures a persons' negative (i.e. maladaptive) tendencies to relate to others. It is a 48-item, self-administered questionnaire, with six items contributing to each of the eight scales: upper neutral (e.g., domination), upper close (e.g., intrusiveness), neutral close (e.g., clingy), lower close (e.g., fear of rejection), lower neutral (e.g., helplessness), lower distant (e.g., subservience), neutral distant (e.g., withdral), and upper distant (e.g., tyranny). These scales correspond to the negative relating styles within the eight octants of a theoretical structure called the interpersonal octagon, proposed by Relating Theory (Birtchnell, 1993/1996). The six items for each subscale comprise five negative items that contribute to the score and one unscored positive item. The response options include "Nearly always true," "Quite often true," "Sometimes true" and "Rarely true," which carry a score of 3, 2, 1 or 0, respectively. The PROQ3 is scored by computer and the scores are represented both numerically and graphically as shaded areas across the eight octants of an octagon. Higher scores represent more relating deficits. Example items for each scale are:

- **Upper Neutral (UN):** *I try to arrange things so that people do what I want,*
- **Upper Close (UC):** *I keep a firm hold on someone who is close to me,*
- **Neutral Close (NC):** *I have a tendency to cling to people,*
- **Lower Close (LC):** *I have a dread of being rejected,*
- **Lower Neutral (LN):** *I prefer it when someone else is in control,*
- **Lower Distant (LD):** *I easily give in to people,*
- **Neutral Distant (ND):** *I do not let people get too close to me*, and
- **Upper Distant (UD):** *I tend to get back at people who offend me.*

The PROQ3 has been found to possess good psychometric properties (Birtchnell et al., 2013; Newberry & Birtchnell, 2011). In this study the reliabilities were satisfactory (UN: 0.88, UC: 0.89, NC: 0.90, LC: 0.87, LN: 0.86, LD: 0.84, ND: 0.93, UD: 0.84).

The Parental Bonding Instrument (mother-father version) (PBI; Parker, Tupling, & Brown, 1979) was used to assess participants' retrospective assessment of care and protection during their first 16 years of life. It consists of two identical forms (one for each parent) of 25 items each rated on a 4-point Likert scale. A care score, measured by 12 items, and a control score, measured by 13 items, is obtained for each parent. Low scores on the care scale reflect parental indifference, neglect, and rejection whereas high scores reflect parental warmth and affection, and high scores on the protection scale reflect excessive control and intrusive parenting whereas low scores reflect encouragement of autonomy and independence. Four types of bonding were extracted: Optimal bonding / parenting (high care and low protection), weak or absent bonding / neglectful parenting (low care and low protection), affectionate constraint (high care and high protection), affectionless control (low care and high protection). In the present study, the Greek-validated PBI was used, which possesses satisfactory test–retest reliability and internal consistency (Avagianou & Zafiropoulou, 2008). In this study the reliabilities were satisfactory for both mother's and father's version, respectively (optimal parenting: 0.87 and 0.85, neglectful parenting: 0.86 and 0.84, affectionate constraint: 0.89 and 0.90, affectionless control: 0.86 and 0.87).

The Brief Symptom Inventory (BSI-18; Derogatis, 2001) is a short 18-item self-report questionnaire adapted from the 53-item Brief Symptom Inventory (BSI; Derogatis, 1993) to measure psychological distress and psychiatric disorders using three symptom scales of six items each, including Somatization (i.e., distress caused by the perception of bodily dysfunction, focusing on symptoms arising from cardiovascular, gastrointestinal, and other physiological systems that have powerful autonomic mediation), Depression (i.e., symptoms of disaffection and dysphoric mood, such as those reflecting self deprecation, anhedonia, loss of hope, and suicidal ideation), and Anxiety (i.e., symptoms of nervousness, tension, motor restlessness, apprehension, and panic states). It also includes an overall summary score, the Global Severity Index (GSI). The scale possesses satisfactory reliability indexes (Derogatis, 2001) and psychometric structure (Meijer, de Vries, & van Bruggen, 2011). In this study, the reliabilities were very good (somatization: 0.95, depression: 0.97, anxiety: 0.97, overall scale: 0.95).

The victims of cyberstalking also completed the *Impact of Event Scale-Revised* (IES-R; Weiss & Marmar, 1996). This is a 22-item self-report questionnaire to measure subjective distress caused by traumatic events (i.e., post traumatic stress). Respondents rated their degree of distress during the past seven days and items were rated on a 5-point scale ranging from 0 (*not at all*) to 4 (*extremely*). A sample item is "Any reminders brought back feelings about it". The IES-R yields a total score (ranging from 0 to 88) and subscale scores can also be calculated for the Intrusion (intrusive thoughts, nightmares, intrusive feelings and imagery, dissociative-like re-experiencing), Avoidance (numbing of responsiveness, avoidance of feelings, situations, and ideas), and Hyperarousal (anger, irritability, hypervigilance, difficulty concentrating, heightened startle) scales. Scores over 24 are indicative of at least some Post Traumatic Stress Disorder (PTSD) symptoms, whereas scores over 33 are indicative of a probable diagnosis of PTSD. In this study, the reliabilities were very good (intrusion: 0.94, avoidance: 0.92, hyperarousal: 0.91, overall scale: 0.93).

RESULTS

Victimization

Results show that 43.3% were victims of stalking (N = 190) and 21.8% were victims of cyberstalking (N = 95), with 2.1% being victims currently (N = 9). Females (80.7%) and younger participants (17-21; 58.1%) were disproportionately cyberstalked. Cyberstalking was most likely to be experienced less than 4 times in one's lifetime (84.3%), mainly by one person (60.0%), who had a close proximity to the victim (38.6%; e.g., friend, (ex)-partner, classmate) as opposed to an unknown person (31.6%). Cyberstalking lasted 1 to 2 weeks (64.7%), one month (13.7%), or up to one year (19.6%). The incidence was not reported in 82.5% of the cases. Those who did report the incidence typically told a friend (45.6%). The victims were likely to have experienced the following behaviors (once to three times a year): harassment (42.7%), web exclusion (34.7%), theft of personal code (29.2%), defamation/denigration (22.7%), publishing personal data (18.1%), and fraudulence and video recording through cell-phone (14.3% each). Cyberstalking occurred predominantly (42.1%) through social networking websites (i.e., Facebook, MySpace, Twitter) or text messages (28.1%).

Victims were predominantly intrusive, restrictive, and possessive to others, which are features of relating from an upper close position (M = 13.9, SD = 3.4). They were open (M = 34.3, SD = 5.3), conscientious (M = 29.6, SD = 4.8) and agreeable (M = 28.8, SD = 5) in terms of their personality characteristics. Victims recalled both their mothers and fathers as being low in care and high in protection (i.e., affectionless control) (M = 0.3, SD = 0.5 and M = 0.4, SD = 0.5, respectively).

Cyberstalking reportedly instilled fear among victims in 58.6% of the cases, and symptoms of anxiety (M = 6.8, SD = 5.7) and depression (M = 6.6, SD = 6.5). Hyperarousal was the predominant response by those who had experienced cyberstalking (M = 1.2, SD = 0.8), as opposed to avoidance (M = 1.1, SD = 0.8) and intrusion (M = 1.0, SD = 0.8). In paritcular, the most likely responses by victims were 'behaved more carefully than before' (66.6%), 'limited the disclosure of personal data / information online' (62.8%), and 'reduced the importance of the problem or refused it' (49%). Not at all likely to be reported were the following responses: 'retaliated using electronic methods' (82.0%), 'met with the police to estimate the cyberstalking' (76.0%), 'substantiated a legal case' (72.0%), and 'negotiated the relationship with the cyberstalker' (64.7%).

Perpetration

A percentage of 19.1% admitted to being stalkers in the offline environment (N = 84) and 8.2% were cyberstalkers (N = 34), with 1.0% being presently involved as cyberstalkers (N = 4). An unexpected finding was that female students were statistically more likely (60.7%) than male students to perpetrate cyberstalking. They were typically between the ages of 22 and 27 years old (46.7%) or younger (17 – 21: 40%). Offending occurred less than 4 times (69.2%) or more than 10 times (19.2%) in one's lifetime, predominantly at the age of 17-21 (69.2%), against one victim (53.8%) and cyberstalking lasted for 1 to 2 weeks (53.8%) or approximately one month (34.6%). Cyberstalkers were engaged in the following behaviors a few times a year (up to 7 times), including: interception of personal code (36.9%), web exclusion (34.6%), harassment (30.8%), defamation/denigration (30.7%), publishing personal data and fraudulence (26.9% each), and video recording through cell-phone (19.2%). Cyberstalking occurred predominantly through social networking websites (i.e., Facebook, MySpace, Twitter) and text messages (32.1% each) or emails (21.4%).

Like victims, offenders' predominant type of relating to others ($M = 13.9$, $SD = 3.4$) was negative relating from a position of upper closeness (i.e., being intrusive, restrictive, and possessive). In addition, they were open ($M = 36.4$, $SD = 4.8$), conscientious ($M = 29.9$, $SD = 4.5$) and agreeable ($M = 29.6$, $SD = 3.4$). They recalled affectionless control by their mother that was low in care and high in protection ($M = 0.4$, $SD = 0.5$) and affectionate constraint by father that was high in care and high in protection ($M = 0.3$, $SD = 0.5$).

Differences between Victims and Perpetrators

One-way ANOVA was conducted to compare types of relating, personality and parenting types between victims and perpetrators. Perpetrators demonstrated significant higher negative lower distant (LD) relating scores than victims; they were also less agreeable, but the difference failed to reach statistical significance (see Table 1). No differences were found regarding the parenting types among perpetrators and victims (optimal, neglectful, affectionate constraint, and affectionless control).

Risk Factors

A binary logistic regression was performed to examine the effects of the eight types of negative relating to others (i.e., upper neutral, upper close, neutral close, lower close, lower neutral, lower distant, neutral distant, and upper distant) and the five personality factors (i.e., extraversion, agreeableness, conscientiousness, neuroticism, and openness) on the likelihood that students were perpetrators of cyberstalking. Personality and relating variables were entered in the same model as they are both intrapersonal features. The logistic regression model (Table 2) was statistical significant ($\chi^2_{(2)} = 16.685$, $p < .001$). The model explained 21.5% (Nagelkerke R^2) of the variance in cyberstalking perpetration and corrected classified 91.0% of cases. Higher scores in negative neutral close (NC) relating were associated with a higher likelihood of cyberstalking perpetration, but higher scores on agreeableness were associated with reduced likelihood of perpetration. A separate binary logistic regression examined the effects of the four attachments styles (i.e., affectionate constraint, affectionless control, optimal parenting, and neglectful parenting) on perpetration. The model was statistical significant ($\chi^2_{(2)} = 9.25$, $p < .01$). It explained 8.3% (Nagelkerke R^2) of the variance and corrected classified 91.1% of cases. Higher scores in mother's affectionless control and neglectful parenting were associated with a higher likelihood of cyberstalking perpetration.

Two binary logistic regressions were also performed to examine the effects of the same independent variables on cyberstalking victimization (Table 3). The first logistic regression model was statistical significant ($\chi^2_{(2)} = 4.125$, $p = .042$), and it explained 3.8% of the variance and corrected classified 76.1% of cases. Higher scores on negative distant relating (ND) were associated with reduced likelihood of cyberstalking victimization. Personality factors failed to be associated with cyberstalking victimization. The second logistic regression model was also statistical significant ($\chi^2_{(2)} = 4.177$, $p = .041$), and it explained 2.5% of the variance and corrected classified 78.0% of cases. Affectionless control by mothers increased cyberstalking victimization.

Table 1. Differences between victims (N=95) and perpetrators (N=34)

	Victims	Perpatrators	*F* (p)
	Relating to Others (PROQ3)		
Upper Neutral (UN)	12.3 (3.5)	12.4 (2.1)	.001 (.977)
Upper Close (UC)	13.9 (3.4)	15.0 (1.9)	1.105 (.297)
Neutral Close (NC)	12.4 (3.1)	14.1 (2.0)	2.802 (.099)
Lower Close (LC)	12.8 (3.2)	13.5 (1.6)	.485 (.489)
Lower Neutral (LN)	13.4 (3.1)	13.9 (2.5)	.321 (.573)
Lower Distant (LD)	13.0 (2.4)	14.5(1.4)	4.437 (.039)
Neutral Distant (ND)	12.3 (3.8)	12.5(3.6)	.051 (.821)
Upper Distant (UD)	12.7 (2.9)	12.7(3.0)	.004 (.951)
Total score (TOT)	102.6 (17.7)	108.6 (7.6)	1.201 (.277)
	Personality Facrors (BFI)		
Extraversion	24.7 (4.4)	24.5 (5.2)	.065 (.799)
Agreeableness	28.8 (5.0)	27.0 (3.9)	3.318 (.071)
Conscientiousness	29.6 (4.8)	28.4 (5.9)	1.189(.278)
Neuroticism	25.0 (5.4)	24.7 (5.2)	.064 (.801)
Openness	34.4 (5.2)	33.6 (7.6)	.324(.571)
	Parenting Styles (PBI)		
Affectionate constraint (Mother)	0.3 (0.4)	0.1 (0.3)	2.550(.113)
Affectionate constraint (Father)	0.2 (0.4)	0.3 (0.4)	.104(.748)
Affectionless control (Mother)	0.4 (0.5)	0.5 (0.5)	2.040 (.156)
Affectionless control (Father)	0.4 (0.5)	0.4 (0.5)	.081 (.777)
Optimal parenting (Mother)	0.3 (0.4)	0.2 (0.4)	.369(.545)
Optimal parenting (Father)	0.2 (0.4)	0.1 (0.4)	.036(.849)
Neglectful parenting (Mother)	0.1 (0.3)	0.2 (0.4)	1.214(.273)
Neglectful parenting (Father)	0.2 (0.4)	0.2 (0.4)	.032(.859)

Table 2. Negative relating styles, personality factors (first regression model) and parenting styles (second regression model) as independent variables (sorted by effect size) in the logistic regressions where the dependent variable is cyberstalking perpetration

Variables	B	S.E.	Wald	p	Exp(B)	95% C.I. for EXP(B)	
						Lower	Upper
			Model A				
Agreeableness	-.184	.058	10.159	.001	.832	.742	.931
PROQ3 (NC)	.192	.077	6.164	.013	1.211	1.041	1.409
			Model B				
Mother's affectionless control	1.138	.405	7.886	.005	3.121	1.410	6.906
Mother's neglectful parenting	1.068	.537	3.959	.047	2.909	1.016	8.329

Table 3. Negative relating styles, personality factors (first regression model) and parenting styles (second regression model) as independent variables (sorted by effect size) in the logistic regressions where the dependent variable is cyberstalking victimization

Variables	B	S.E.	Wald	p	Exp(B)	95% C.I.for EXP(B)	
						Lower	Upper
Model A							
PROQ3 (ND)	- 0.85	.042	4.040	.044	.919	.846	.998
Model B							
Mother's affectionless control	5.19	.252	4.264	.039	1.681	1.027	2.752

DISCUSSION

Consistent with the results of other studies (e.g., Finn, 2004), cyberstalking occurred commonly among participants (23.9%) and females were more likely to be cyberstalked than males (e.g., Reyns et al., 2012). Although literature review has revealed high rates of cyberstalking (e.g., Alexy et al., 2005; Holt & Bossler, 2009), in this study a lower than expected rate was revealed (9%). It is believed that the true prevalence of offending might have been under-estimated. Respondents might have been unwilling to conceal unpleasant information such as cyberstalking. Unexpectedly, higher rates of women engaged in cyberstalking perpetration. There is sufficient research evidence indicating that the majority of cyber-stalkers are males (e.g., WHOA, 2011), although a few other studies have suggested that females admit higher rates of cyberstalking (e.g., Strawhun, Adams, & Huss, 2013). Another finding that was consistent with other studies was that cyberstalking most frequently occurred via social networking websites and that perpetrators were usually known to the victim (WHOA, 2011)). In this study, the majority of the victims did not report the incidence (e.g., Finn, 2004).

Negatively neutral close (NC) relating was the predominant type of relating to others by both victims and offenders, which reflects an instrusive, restrictive, and possessive type of relating and a need of attention and admiration. This may suggest the need by victims and offenders to cling to others and fear of separation and of being alone. This makes absolute sense only in cases where offenders and victims were known, such as ex partners. NC relating was also found to increase the odds of cyberstalking perpetration. Newberry (2016) found that NC was significantly correlated with psychopathy (i.e., which reflects one's callousness of caring about the pain that inflicts to others). The findings of the present study suggest that cyberstalkers need to maintain a close, though negative, relationship with the victim in order to inflict their malicious acts. It can also be assumed that students might resort to cyberstalking as a reaction to being fearful of separation and/or rejection. These findings coincide with Ganck and Vanheule's (2015) assertion that people react with violence in their interpersonal relationships as a result of the threat they experience coming from untrustworthy other persons.

On the other hand, negative distant (ND) relating was associated with reduced likelihood of cyberstalking victimization. ND relating reflects suspiciousness, avoidance, fear of invasion and intrusion, need of personal space, and privacy. It seems that this type of relating is a protective factor against victimization. It might be that people with this type of predominant relating style might limit the extent of inappropriate disclosure of personal information. Avoiding being a target of cyberstalking requires revealing nothing personal about oneself and maintaining a certain distance from the offender.

Of the personality factors, agreeableness (i.e., sympathy, kindness, and affection) was associated with a lower likelihood of one being a cyberstalker, which is consistent with other findings (e.g., O'Riordan & O'Connell, 2014). No statistically significant results were found for victims. It might be that another instrument for measuring personality might be more appropriate and could provide statistical significant results for victims. There might also be some other variables not included in this study that might affect victimization. For instance, Fox, Gover, and Kaukinen (2009) found that the lack of self-control was associated with stalking victimization for college women.

In this study, cyberstalking perpetration was associated with mother's affectionless control and neglectful parenting, and cyberstalking victimization was associated only with mother's affectionless control. Affectionless control predicted both perpetration and victimization. Parental monitoring has protective effects against offending, whereas negative parental control reflectss rejection and hostility and increases delinquency (Hoeve et al., 2009). Morevoer, authoritative parenting (i.e., high control and responsiveness) has been found to predict lower levels of cyberbullying, while permissive parenting (i.e., low control and high responsiveness) has been found to predict higher levels of risk taking behaviour, such as disclosing personal information and meeting people only known by text (Carson, 2014). Similar patterns might be found for cyberstalking.

Parenting styles are associated with attachment (Karavasilis, Doyle, & Markiewicz, 2003) and attachment is associated with cyberstalking-related behaviors (Fox & Warber, 2014; Strawhun, et al., 2013). For instance, studies have linked anxious attachment to cyberstalking (e.g., Ménard & Pincus, 2012; Strawhun, et al., 2013). Fox and Tokunaga (2015) found that avoidantly attached people employ distance in their relationships, evade relational commitment, and are more likely to look for alternatives to the relationship, in comparison to anxiously attached people who demand intimacy and approval from partners, and who become overly dependent or exessively attached to partners and are more likely to try to establish a reconnection and resort to Facebook stalking following a break-up. Moreover, Zeinali, Sharifi, Enayati, Asgari, and Pasha (2011) found that authoritative and permissive parenting styles were associated with secure partner attachment, which in turn was associated with high levels of self-regulation and decreased addiction susceptibility, whereas authoritarian and neglectful parenting styles were associated with insecure attachment, which in turn was associated with a low level of self-regulation and increased addiction susceptibility. Self-regulation might be an important factor in cyberstalking as well.

The primary limitations of this study are the use of a convenience sample rather than a representative one and its limited size, which may have affected sampling error. Perpetrators were particularly underrepresented. It is possible that with a larger sample of offenders and victims might produce different results. Prevalence rates may have been underestimated due to a tendency for social desirable responding. However, because the findings are in accordance with those of other studies, they may be considered to provide an accurate account of the situation in Greece. This sample was also heavily skewed toward females and heterosexual participants. Future research should address homosexual participants and samples equally spread across genders. Because of the cross-sectional type of this study, causal inferences are not warranted without longitudinal verification. It would have been interesting to have compared scores between perpetrators, victims and those that were both perpetrators and victims or those that neither perpetrators nor victims, but the smallness of the size of the sampling groups did not permit the comparison. The potential moderating relationship of resilient coping on the association between cyberstalking victimization and the outcome variables needs to be explored, since there is a vast literature indicating the signifance of this variable (e.g., Spitzberg & Cupach, 2001; Spitzberg & Hoobler, 2002). Future studies need to address other mediating variables too.

Despite these limitations, the implications drawn from the results of this study extend the knowledge of this phenomenon in Greece. Given the increased prevalence of cyberstalking worldwide, future studies should be conducted to determine its psychological, interpersonal, and social consequences. Continued research will maximize the likelihood of an accurate and comprehensive understanding of cyberstalking, the implications of which would be to establish effective prevention and appropriate intervention programs to prevent cyberstalking or mitigate its effects. Recommendations for law enforcement and criminal justice officials include training service providers to recognize the tactics used by cyberstalkers and to respond to the needs of victims). Service providers should develop websites for victims to exchange information and design or expand formal and informal support networks to meet the needs of victims and enhance their safety.

Efforts should also target the perpetrators of cyberstalking. Enhancing their interpersonal skills and modifying cyberstalkers'negative relating styles to positive styles would be useful. Counselors can also assist people from disandvantaged backgrounds to acquire positive perceptions of their stressful developmental trajectories and help them develop a strong identity, fulfilling intimate relationships and skills to adapt to the constantly changing environments. Moreover, buffering or strengthening resiliency against negative parenting rearing could have positive impacts in overcoming adversity. Counseling centers can adopt therapeutic interventions and approaches to address parenting issues and provide advices on positive parenting practices. Raising public awareness about the tactics used by cyberstalkers, the detrimental impact of cyberstalking on victims, and the steps that can be taken to prevent this phenomenn are important for preventing and/or combating cyberstalking.

REFERENCES

Alexy, E. M., Burgess, A. W., Baker, T., & Smoyak, S. A. (2005). Perceptions of cyberstalking among college students. *Brief Treatment and Crisis Intervention*, *5*(3), 279–289. doi:10.1093/brief-treatment/mhi020

Arnett, J. J. (2000). Emerging adulthood. A theory of development from the late teens through the twenties. *The American Psychologist*, *55*(5), 469–480. doi:10.1037/0003-066X.55.5.469 PMID:10842426

Ashcroft, J. (2001). *Stalking and domestic violence: A report to Congress (No. NCJ 186157)*. Washington, DC: U.S. Department of Justice.

Avagianou, P. A., & Zafiropoulou, M. (2008). Parental bonding and depression: Personality as a mediating factor. *International Journal of Adolescent Medicine and Health*, *20*(3), 261–270. doi:10.1515/IJAMH.2008.20.3.261 PMID:19097563

Baum, K., Catalano, S. M., Kristina, R., & Michael, R. (2009). *Stalking victimization in the United States*. Washington, DC: Bereau of Justice Statistics. U.S. Department of Justice. Available from: https://www.justice.gov/sites/default/files/ovw/legacy/2012/08/15/bjs-stalking-rpt.pdf

Birtchnell, J., Hammond, S., Horn, E., De Jong, C., & Kalaitzaki, A. (2013). A cross-national comparison of a shorter version of the Persons Relating to Others Questionnaire. *Clinical Psychology & Psychotherapy*, *20*(1), 36–48. doi:10.1002/cpp.789 PMID:21960317

Bocij, P. (2006). *The Dark Side Of The Internet*. Greenwood Publishing Group.

Boyle, A. M., & O'Sullivan, L. F. (2016). Staying connected: Computer-mediated and face-to-face communication in college students' dating relationships. *Cyberpsychology, Behavior, and Social Networking, 19*(5), 299–307. doi:10.1089/cyber.2015.0293

Brownstein, A. (2000). In the campus shadows, women are stalkers as well as the stalked. *The Chronicle of Higher Education, 47*(15), 40–42.

Carson, R. (2014). *Adolescent cyberbullying in New Zealnd and the implications of parenting styles* (Unpublished doctoral thesis). University of Canterbury.

Collins, W. A. (2003). More than myth: The developmental significance of romantic relationships during adolescence. *Journal of Research on Adolescence, 13*(1), 1–24. doi:10.1111/1532-7795.1301001

D'Ovidio, R., & Doyle, J. (2003). A study on cyberstalking: Understanding investigative hurdles. *FBI Law Enforcement Bulletin, 72*(3), 10–17.

De Ganck, J., & Vanheule, S. (2015). Bad boys dont cry: A thematic analysis of interpersonal dynamics in interview narratives of young offenders with psychopathic traits. *Frontiers in Psychology, 6*, 1–11. doi:10.3389/fpsyg.2015.00960 PMID:26217279

Derogatis, L. R. (1993). *BSI, Brief Symptom Inventory: Administration, scoring & procedures manual.* Minneapolis, MN: National Computer Systems.

Derogatis, L. R. (2001). *Brief Symptom Inventory (BSI)-18. Administration, scoring and procedures manual.* Minneapolis, MN: NCS Pearson, Inc.

Dewing, M. (2010). *Social media: Who uses them?* Library of Parliament Background Paper. Retrieved from publications.gc.ca/site/eng/370191/publication.html

Dreßing, H., Bailer, J., Anders, A., Wagner, H., & Gallas, C. (2014). Cyberstalking in a large sample of social network users: Prevalence, characteristics, and impact upon victims. *Cyberpsychology, Behavior, and Social Networking, 17*(2), 61–67. doi:10.1089/cyber.2012.0231

Fagundes, C. P. (2012). Getting over you: Contributions of attachment theory for postbreakup emotional adjustment. *Personal Relationships, 19*, 37–50.

Festl, R., & Quandt, T. (2013). Social relations and cyberbullying: The influence of individual and structural attributes on victimization and perpetration via the internet. *Human Communication Research, 39*, 101–126. doi:10.111/j.1468-2958.2012.01442.x

Finn, J. (2004). A survey of online harassment at a university campus. *Journal of Interpersonal Violence, 19*(4), 468–483. doi:10.1177/0886260503262083 PMID:15038885

Fletcher, A., Fitzgerald-Yau, N., Jones, R., Allen, E., Viner, R. M., & Bonell, C. (2014). Brief report: Cyberbullying perpetration and its associations with socio-demographics, aggressive behaviour at school, and mental health outcomes. *Journal of Adolescence, 37*(8), 1393–1398. doi:10.1016/j.adolescence.2014.10.005 PMID:25448835

Fox, J., & Tokunaga, R. S. (2015). Romantic Partner Monitoring After Breakups: Attachment, Dependence, Distress, and Post-Dissolution Online Surveillance via Social Networking Sites. *Cyberpsychology, Behavior, and Social Networking*, *18*(9), 491–498. doi:10.1089/cyber.2015.0123 PMID:26348808

Fox, J., & Warber, K. M. (2014). Social networking sites in romantic relationships: Attachment, uncertainty, and partner surveillance on facebook. *Cyberpsychology, Behavior, and Social Networking*, *17*(1), 3–7. doi:10.1089/cyber.2012.0667

Fox, K. A., Gover, A. R., & Kaukinen, C. (2009). The rffects of low self control and childhood maltreatment on stalking victimization among men and women. *American Journal of Criminal Justice*, *34*(3-4), 181–197. doi:10.1007/s12103-009-9064-4

Hoeve, M., Dubas, J. S., Eichelsheim, V. I., van der Laan, P. H., Smeenk, W., & Gerris, J. R. M. (2009). The relationship between parenting and delinquency: A meta-analysis. *Journal of Abnormal Child Psychology*, *37*, 749–775.

Holt, T. J., & Bossler, A. M. (2009). Examining the applicability of lifestyle-routine activities theory for cybercrime victimization. *Deviant Behavior*, *30*(1), 1–25. doi:10.1080/01639620701876577

John, O. P., Donahue, E. M., & Kentle, R. L. (1991). *TheBig Five Inventory--Versions 4a and 54*. Berkeley, CA: Institute of Personality and Social Research.

John, O. P., & Srivastava, S. (1999). The Big Five trait taxonomy: History, measurement, and theoretical perspectives. In L. A. Pervin & O. P. John (Eds.), *Handbook of personality: Theory and research* (pp. 102–138). New York: Guilford Press.

Kalaitzaki, A. E., & Birtchnell, J. (2016). The Person's Relating to Others Questionnaire (PROQ). In J. Birtchnell, M. Newberry, & A. E. Kalaitzaki (Eds.), *Relating Theory: Clinical, Forensic and other Applications*. London: Palgrave Macmillan.

Karavasilis, L., Doyle, A. B., & Markiewicz, D. (2003). Associations between parenting style and attachment to mother in middle childhood and adolescence. *International Journal of Behavioral Development*, *27*(2), 153–164. doi:10.1080/0165025024400015

Lee, B. H., & OSullivan, L. F. (2014). The ex-factor: Characteristics of online and offline post-relationship contact and tracking among canadian emerging adults. *The Canadian Journal of Human Sexuality*, *23*(2), 96–105. doi:10.3138/cjhs.2415

Leontopoulou, S. (2006). Resilience of Greek youth at an educational transition point: The role of locus of control and coping strategies as resources. *Social Indicators Research*, *76*(1), 95–126. doi:10.1007/s11205-005-4858-3

Lewis, S. F., Fremouw, W. J., Del Ben, K., & Farr, C. (2001). An investigation of the psychological characteristics of stalkers: Empathy, problem-solving, attachment and borderline personality features. *Journal of Forensic Sciences*, *46*(1), 80–84. doi:10.1520/JFS14915J PMID:11210929

MacKenzie, R. D., Mullen, P. E., Ogloff, J. R. P., McEwan, T. E., & James, D. V. (2008). Parental bonding and adult attachment styles in different types of stalker. *Journal of Forensic Sciences*, *53*(6), 1443–1449. doi:10.1111/j.1556-4029.2008.00869.x PMID:18798773

Mechanic, M. B., Uhlmansiek, M. H., Weaver, T. L., & Resick, P. A. (2000). The impact of severe stalking experienced by acutely battered women: An examination of violence, psychological symptoms, and strategic responding. *Violence and Victims*, *15*, 443–458. PMID:11288940

Meijer, R. R., de Vries, R. M., & van Bruggen, V. (2011). An evaluation of the Brief Symptom Inventory-18 using item response theory: Which items are most strongly related to psychological distress? *Psychological Assessment*, *23*(1), 193–202. doi:10.1037/a0021292

Menard, K. S., & Pincus, A. L. (2012). Predicting overt and cyber stalking perpetration by male and female college students. *Journal of Interpersonal Violence*, *27*(11), 2183–2207. doi:10.1177/0886260511432144

Neill, J. T., & Dias, K. L. (2001). Adventure Education and Resilience: The Double-Edged Sword. *Journal of Adventure Education and Outdoor Learning*, *12*(2), 35–42. doi:10.1080/14729670185200061

Newberry, M. (2016). Negative Relating and Psychopathy. In J. Birtchnell, M. Newberry, & A. E. Kalaitzaki (Eds.), *Relating Theory: Clinical, Forensic and other Applications*. London: Palgrave Macmillan. doi:10.1057/978-1-137-50459-3_20

ORiordan, C., & OConnell, M. (2014). Predicting adult involvement in crime: Personality measures are significant, socio-economic measures are not. *Personality and Individual Differences*, *68*, 98–101. doi:10.1016/j.paid.2014.04.010

Parker, G., Tupling, H., & Brown, L. B. (1979). A Parental Bonding Instrument. *The British Journal of Medical Psychology*, *52*(1), 1–10. doi:10.1111/j.2044-8341.1979.tb02487.x

Patton, C. L., Nobles, M. R., & Fox, K. A. (2010). Look who's stalking: Obsessive pursuit and attachment theory. *Journal of Criminal Justice*, *38*(3), 282–290. doi:10.1016/j.jcrimjus.2010.02.013

Peluchette, J. V., Karl, K., Wood, C., & Williams, J. (2015). Cyberbullying victimization: Do victims' personality and risky social network behaviors contribute to the problem? *Computers in Human Behavior*, *52*, 424–435. doi:10.1016/j.chb.2015.06.028

Reyns, B. W. (2010). A situational crime prevention approach to cyberstalking victimization: Preventive tactics for Internet users and online place managers. *Crime Prevention and Community Safety*, *12*(2), 99–118. doi:10.1057/cpcs.2009.22

Reyns, B. W., Henson, B., & Fisher, B. S. (2012). Stalking in the twilight zone: Extent of cyberstalking victimization and offending among college students. *Deviant Behavior*, *33*(1), 1–25. doi:10.1080/01639625.2010.538364

Roberts, L. (2008). Jurisdictional and definitional concerns with computer related interpersonal crimes: An analysis on cyber stalking. *International Journal of Cyber Criminology*, *2*, 271–285.

Schmitt, D. P., Allik, J., McCrae, R. R., & Benet-Martinez, V. (2007). The geographic distribution of Big Five personality traits: Patterns and profiles of human self-description across 56 nations. *Journal of Cross-Cultural Psychology*, *38*(2), 173–212. doi:10.1177/0022022106297299

Short, E., Linford, S., Wheatcroft, J. M., & Maple, C. (2014). The impact of cyberstalking: The lived experience-a thematic analysis. *Studies in Health Technology and Informatics*, *199*, 133–137. doi:10.3233/978-1-61499-401-5-133 PMID:24875706

Spitzberg, B. H. (2002). The tactical topography of stalking victimization and management. *Trauma, Violence & Abuse*, *3*(4), 261–288. doi:10.1177/1524838002237330

Spitzberg, B. H., & Cupach, W. R. (2001). Paradoxes of pursuit: Toward a relational model of stalking-related phenomena. In J. A. Davis (Ed.), *Stalking crimes and victim protection: Prevention, intervention, threat assessment, and case management* (pp. 97–136). Boca Raton, FL: CRC Press. doi:10.1201/9781420041743.ch6

Spitzberg, B. H., & Cupach, W. R. (2007). The state of the art of stalking: Taking stock of the emerging literature. *Aggression and Violent Behavior*, *12*(1), 64–86. doi:10.1016/j.avb.2006.05.001

Spitzberg, B. H., & Hoobler, G. (2002). Cyberstalking and the technologies of interpersonal terrorism. *New Media & Society*, *4*(1), 71–92. doi:10.1177/14614440222226271

Straus, M. A., & Fauchier, A. (2007). *Manual for the Dimensions of Discipline Inventory (DDI)*. Durham, NH: Family Research Laboratory, University of New Hampshire.

Strawhun, J., Adams, N., & Huss, M. T. (2013). The assessment of cyberstalking: An expanded examination including social networking, attachment, jealousy, and anger in relation to violence and abuse. *Violence and Victims*, *28*(4), 715–730. doi:10.1891/0886-6708.11-00145 PMID:24047049

Tjaden, P., & Thoennes, N. (1998). *Stalking in America: Findings from the National Violence Against Women Survey (Research in Brief NCJ 169592)*. Washington, DC: National Institute of Justice and Centers for Disease Control and Prevention.

Tonin, E. (2004). The attachment styles of stalkers. *Journal of Forensic Psychiatry & Psychology*, *15*(4), 584–590. doi:10.1080/14789940410001729644

Wagnild, G. M., & Young, H. M. (1993). Development and psychometric evaluation ofthe resilience scale. *Journal of Nursing Measurement*, *1*(2), 165–178. PMID:7850498

Wall, D. (2007). *Cybercrime: The Transformation of Crime in the Information Age*. Polity.

Weiss, D. S., & Marmar, C. R. (1996). The Impact of Event Scale - Revised. In J. Wilson & T. M. Keane (Eds.), *Assessing psychological trauma and PTSD* (pp. 399–411). New York: Guilford.

Westrup, D., Fremouw, W. J., Thompson, R. N., & Lewis, S. F. (1999). The Psychological impact of stalking in female undergraduates. *Journal of Forensic Sciences*, *44*(3), 554–557. doi:10.1520/JFS14507J PMID:10408109

Working to Halt Online Abuse. (2011). *Cyberstalking statistics*. Retrieved on 8th January, 2015, from http://www.haltabuse.org/resources/stats/2011Statistics.pdfZeinali

Zeinali, A., Sharifi, H., Enayati, M., Asgari, P., & Pasha, G. (2011). The mediational pathway among parenting styles, attachment styles and self-regulation with addiction susceptibility of adolescents. *Journal of Research in Medical Sciences*, *16*(9), 1105–1121.

Chapter 16
Cyber Aggression and Victimization among Emerging Adults:
The Associated Adjustment Difficulties

Michelle F. Wright
Masaryk University, Czech Republic

ABSTRACT

This chapter describes a study with the objective to examine cyber aggression involvement among emerging adults across technologies and relationships. Another purpose was to investigate the bidirectional associations between emerging adults' cyber aggression involvement and adjustment difficulties over four years. Participants were 1,483 emerging adults (Mage = 24.67; 60% female) from Southeastern universities in the United States. Emerging adults completed questionnaires on their cyber aggression involvement and adjustment difficulties. The most frequently utilized digital technologies and tool to harm others were text messages. Ex-friends were frequently involved in cyber aggression. Cyber aggression involvement predicted all adjustment difficulties across four years and all adjustment difficulties predicted cyber aggression involvement, suggesting bidirectional relationships among these variables. There were magnitude differences such that the bidirectional relationships were stronger when predicting all adjustment difficulties from cyber aggression and cyber victimization.

INTRODUCTION

Emerging adults are enmeshed in a digitally connected world. Being digitally connected to just about anyone in a matter of seconds and having access to an assortment of information at the "click of a button" are just a few of the benefits associated with emerging adults' internet and digital technology use. Many emerging adults go online or utilize digital technologies at least once a day (Smith, Rainie, & Zickuhr, 2011). Although the internet and digital technologies provide various opportunities and conveniences in emerging adults' lives, they might be at risk for internet addiction, identity theft, sexual predation

DOI: 10.4018/978-1-5225-1856-3.ch016

and exploitation, and cyber aggression (Copes, Kerby, Huff, & Kane, 2010; Finn, 2004; Weigman & van Schie, 1998; Wright & Li, 2012). Utilizing digital technologies increases the likelihood of experiencing or perpetrating cyber aggression (Alvarez-Garcia, Nunez Perez, Gonzalez, & Perez, 2015; Holt, Fitzgerald, Bossler, Chee, & Nq, 2016; Mishna, Khoury-Kassabri, Gadalla, & Daciuk, 2012; Perrin & Duggan, 2015). Emerging adults' high levels of internet and digital technology consumption increase their online risks, particularly their risk of cyber aggression.

Despite emerging adults using the internet and digital technologies at similar or higher levels than children and adolescents, little attention has been devoted to their exposure and perpetration of cyber aggression. High profile cases of cyber aggression sometimes involve emerging adults, although the general public typically believes that these behaviors are a concern for children and adolescents. Failure to acknowledge emerging adults' vulnerability to cyber aggression might neglect the development of intervention programs aimed at reducing risks among this population. Furthermore, not recognizing that cyber aggression is a concerned for emerging adults might exacerbate their psychological, social, academic, and behavioral difficulties. Research on cyber aggression and emerging adults is increasing, although much of this research involves studies utilizing cross-sectional research designs, which limits our understanding of the long-term predictors and consequences of these behaviors. The first objective of the present study was to describe the nature of cyber aggression and victimization among emerging adults by focusing on what digital technologies are used and the relationship between the perpetrator and the victim. The second objective of the present study was to investigate the longitudinal, reciprocal relationships between cyber victimization, cyber aggression, suicidal ideation, non-suicidal self-harm, depression, loneliness, anxiety, and grade point average among emerging adults over four years, using cross-lagged modeling.

BACKGROUND

Definition of Emerging Adulthood

More and more high school students plan to attend college nowadays, delaying their plans for marriage and families (Badger, Nelson, & Barry, 2006). Consequently, many people in college do not consider themselves to be adults. Coalescing together, these factors have created a unique developmental period, often referred to as "emerging adulthood" (Arnett, 2000). Emerging adulthood is characterized by an increased level of exploration and instability until one reaches their mid to late twenties, before taking on adult roles and responsibilities. Other characteristics of emerging adulthood include pursuing personal goals (e.g., traveling, school), creating an identity that is influenced by work, school, or interpersonal relationships, becoming involved in intimate relationships, and engaging in risky behaviors, such as using illegal drugs or driving while drunk (Arnett & Jensen, 2002; Nelson & Barry, 2005). Given these characteristics, many researchers consider emerging adulthood a unique developmental period, separate from adolescence and adulthood.

Definition of Cyber Aggression and Victimization

Typically conceptualized as an extension of face-to-face traditional aggression, cyber aggression involves purposefully and hostilely embarrassing or intimidating others (Ferdon & Hertz, 2007; Kowalski & Limber, 2007; Topcu, Erdur-Baker, & Aydin, 2008; Wolak, Mitchell, & Finkelhor, 2007; Ybarra, Diener-West, & Leaf, 2007). Unlike the traditional definition of face-to-face aggression and victimization, cyber aggressive behaviors do not necessarily have to include repetition or an imbalance of power between the perpetrator and the victim (Grigg, 2010). Cyber aggressive behaviors are usually malicious, and might include sending abusive emails, impersonating others, and sending harassing messages via text messages, instant messenger, and social networking sites (Walker, Sockman, & Koehn, 2011; Wolak et al., 2007; Wright & Li, 2012; Ybarra & Mitchell, 2004). Other cyber aggressive behaviors include harassment, insults, physical threats, verbal taunts, malicious teasing, social exclusion, and humiliation. There are also more severe forms of cyber aggressive behaviors, such as distributing explicit videos or images of others, happy slapping, hacking, and flaming (Rideout, Roberts, & Foehr, 2005; Smith et al., 2008). Happy slapping is defined as a group of people insulting another person, while filming the incidence on a mobile phone, and then later posting the images or videos online. Hacking is defined as gaining access to someone's computer system or other online accounts in an effort to get information. Flaming is defined as posting provocative and/or offensive messages in a public forum with the intention to provoke angry responses or agreement from members of the public forum. Cyber aggression can be perpetuated or experienced through a variety of digital technologies and tools, including cell phones, social networking sites, emails, gaming consoles, chatrooms, blogs, Youtube, and chat programs.

Cyber Aggression and Victimization among Emerging Adults

Research on cyber aggression is advancing, with many of the earliest studies focused on the prevalence rates of these behaviors among children and adolescents. One of the first studies conducted on cyber aggression among emerging adults was published by Finn in 2004. In her study, she found that 10-15% of her sample experienced email and/or instant messenger victimization, equating to 1 in 10 emerging adults being targeted by cyber victimization. Changes in emerging adults' access to an assortment of digital technologies have transformed the avenues to perpetrate cyber aggression. Therefore, more current research has focused on cyber aggression through various digital technologies. In particular, Walker, Sockman, and Koehn (2011) focused on cyber victimization among emerging adults via Facebook and text messages. They found that 56% of their sample reported that they were harassed through Facebook. Furthermore, 45% of their participants experienced victimization through text messages. In another study, Wright and Li (2012) investigated how often emerging adults experience cyber aggression, with the majority of their participants reporting cyber victimization every 2 to 4 months. Less attention has been given to the frequency of cyber aggression perpetration among emerging adults. Dilmac (2009) examined Turkish emerging adults' engagement in cyber aggression. His findings revealed that 22.5% of emerging adults in his study perpetrated cyber aggression at least once in their lifetime. Ultimately, emerging adults' involvement in cyber aggression ranges from 8.6% to 43.3% (Crosslin & Crosslin, 2014; Finn, 2014; Hinduja & Patchin, 2010; Schenk & Fremouw, 2012). It is worth noting that the differences between the frequency rates of these studies is not important as variations in these rates reflect differences in the samples used, the measurement of cyber aggression involvement, and the definitions of cyber aggression and cyber victimization. Other research has focused on the consequences associated with cyber aggression and victimization among emerging adults.

Consequences of Cyber Aggression Involvement

Few studies have focused on the consequences associated with cyber aggression involvement among emerging adults. In this literature, emerging adults' cyber victimization was related to eating disorders, suicidal ideation, and depression (Cowie, 2013). Furthermore, emerging adults who were victims of cyber aggression experienced depression, anxiety, phobias, and paranoia (Cowie, 2013; Schenk & Fremouw, 2012). Their feelings of isolation and loneliness increased, resulting in diminished opportunities for forming new friendships (Crosslin & Crosslin, 2014). Problematic alcohol use is also increased among female emerging adults who were involved in cyber aggression (Selkie, Kota, Chan, & Moreno, 2015). Like cybervictims, emerging adults who were cyberaggressors also experienced depression. Less attention has been given to how cyber aggression involvement might impact the academic performance of emerging adults. The literature on this topic among adolescents indicates that cyberaggressors and cybervictims experienced more academic difficulties and engaged in more non-suicidal self-harm than uninvolved adolescents (Tang et al., 2013; Wright, 2015).

Present Study

The first goal of the study was to understand the nature of cyber aggression involvement among emerging adults through examining the digital technologies used to harm others and the relationship between the perpetrator and the victim. Another goal of the study was to investigate the longitudinal, reciprocal relationships between cyber victimization, cyber aggression, suicidal ideation, non-suicidal self-harm, depression, loneliness, anxiety, and grade point average over four years, while accounting for prior levels of these variables and face-to-face aggression and victimization. Bidirectional or reciprocal relationships were hypothesized because research indicates that cyber victimization and cyber aggression are predictors of suicidal ideation, non-suicidal self-harm, depression, loneliness, anxiety and grade point average, and that these variables also predict cyber victimization and cyber aggression (Cappadocia, Craig, & Pepler, 2013; Cowie, 2013; Crosslin & Crosslin, 2014; Schenk & Fremouw, 2012; Wright, 2015; Ybarra & Mitchell, 2004; Ybarra et al., 2007). Magnitudes or ordering of the variables were not hypothesized due to a lack of research on this topic. An important consideration of the present study was to include time parameters for emerging adults' self-reported cyber aggression involvement. Many studies focusing on emerging adults do not specify time parameters, with many of these studies examining lifetime prevalence versus estimates of cyber aggression involvement within the past 60 days or the past year. By specifying time parameters, it is possible to determine whether cyber aggression and victimization are important developmental concerns for emerging adults. The present study had the following aims:

1. Describe the frequency of cyber aggression involvement among emerging adults through various technologies over four years.
2. Describe the frequency of who perpetrates cyber aggression among emerging adults over four years.
3. Examine the reciprocal and longitudinal associations between cyber victimization, cyber aggression, suicidal ideation, non-suicidal self-harm, depression, loneliness, anxiety, and grade point average among emerging adults over four years, while controlling for face-to-face aggression and victimization.

METHOD

Participants

There were 1,483 emerging adults (ages 21-29; M_{age} = 24.67 years; 60% female) who participated in this study. The sample was from one of three 4-year universities located in the Southeastern United States. These universities enrolled between 29,636 to 59,770 students in 2014. The participants self-identified as White (65%), Black/African American (15%), Latino/a (10%), Asian (6%), and biracial (4%). The majority of participants were classified as college seniors, with 10% classified as juniors. Family incomes ranged from $23,000 to $461,000. Most of the participants were from middle-class families and 85% received financial assistance, typically student loans, scholarships, or work-study programs. The demographic background of the participants reflects the overall general student population at each of the universities.

Procedures

Recruitment began during participants' first year of college. The information about the study was posted on the universities' psychology subject pool websites, which included a short description of the study, how long students would be expected to participate, and what they would do (i.e., answer questionnaires). The recruitment ad explained that the study would take place over four years and that students would be expected to complete a set of questionnaires per year.

The first wave of data was collected during the fall of participants' first year in college. Participants came to a research laboratory for the first wave of data collection. During this data collection session, participants had to be first-year college students to be eligible for the study. Thirty-five students were not eligible for the study. These students still received credit for attending the session. After determining eligibility, participants read and completed an informed consent document, which included information about the nature of the study, length of the study, what they would do over the four years, and how much they would be compensated ($10 per wave for a total of $40 over the course of the study). Research assistants explained to participants that they could still participate in the study even if they were unsure whether they wanted to commit to the four-year duration of the study. Participants were informed that their participation was voluntary and that they could stop participating in the study at any time, while still receiving credit through the psychology subject pool. There were thirty-five students who declined to participate for various reasons, and they were thanked for their time and given subject pool credit. Two thousand and twenty-seven first-year college students provided their consent to participate in the study. Before completing questionnaires, participants were interviewed regarding demographic information. They were asked again to confirm that they were first-year college students as well as provide their gender, ethnicity, family income (348 participants were unsure), and information about their financial assistance. Research assistants also asked participants for their permanent home address, a school-affiliated email address, a personal email address, and their phone number. This information was used to contact participants over the four years of the study and research assistants routinely contacted participants via a school-affiliated email address to confirm contact information. All participants were assigned an ID that was used throughout the duration of the study. The study was approved by the universities' institutional review boards, and APA standards were followed throughout the completion of this study. At all waves of data collection, participants completed measures on self-reported cyber aggression and victimization, self-reported face-to-face aggression and victimization, suicidal ideation, non-suicidal self-harm, depression, loneliness, anxiety, and grade point average (GPA).

The psychology subject pool was used at Wave 1 only. Other waves of data collection occurred after 2 years (Wave 2), 3 years (Wave 3), and 4 years (Wave 4). Before sending participants an email with a website address directing them to the online questionnaires for waves two through four, research assistants contacted them via the phone. During the phone conversation, research assistants verified their home address, school-affiliated email address, and personal email address. The information was updated as needed over the next three years. In the second year, 52 participants did not have a working phone number. Research assistants were able to reconnect with 10 of these participants, and a phone meeting was scheduled to verify their personal information. Once contact information was verified, emails were sent to participants. When participants clicked on the website address in the email, they were then taken to the informed consent document. If they agree to participate, they were taken to the questionnaires. If participants did not agree to participate, they were not taken to the questionnaires and thanked for their time. On the last page of the website, participants were asked to provide an email address that they checked frequently, if they wanted to receive the gift card. A $10 Amazon gift card was emailed to participants who wished to receive one after each wave of data collection. The same procedure was used for data collection in the third and fourth years. Depending on the year of data collection, around 60-73% of participants requested the gift card. Attrition during the second year was 154, with 112 declining to participate and 42 who were unreachable. The third year attrition rate was 138, with 78 declining to participate and 60 who were unreachable. For the fourth year, the attrition rate was 230, with 167 declining to participate and 63 who were unreachable. Thus, the attrition rate for the full study was between 9% and 15%, such that 522 of the 2,227 participants from the first wave did not participate by the end of the fourth wave. Attrition for the first school was 521, 514 for the second school, and 501 for the third school. Typical attrition for longitudinal studies is between 30-70%, indicating that attrition from the present study was much less than previous longitudinal studies (Fischer, Dornelas, & Goethe, 200).

Measures

Self-Reported Cyber Aggression and Victimization

Participants were asked to report how often they experienced or perpetrated aggression online or through text messages. Ten items were included for cyber victimization and ten items were included for cyber aggression. Some of the cyber aggression behaviors included having rumors spread about oneself / spreading rumors about someone, being teased / teasing someone, having mean or hurtful comments posted about oneself / posting mean or hurtful comments about someone, and having someone threaten to hurt them / threatening to hurt someone (Wright & Li, 2012). All items were rated on a scale of 1 (*never*) to 9 (*daily*). Before answering the items, participants were asked to respond to the questionnaires according to what has happened to them in the last 60 days. Behaviors for cyber victimization and cyber aggression were combined separately, with acceptable Cronbach's alphas at Wave 1 (.88 for cyber victimization and .86 for cyber aggression), Wave 2 (.87 for cyber victimization and .86 for cyber aggression), Wave 3 (.91 for cyber victimization and .87 for cyber aggression), and Wave 4 (.90 for cyber victimization and .88 for cyber aggression).

Cyber Aggression and Victimization across Various Technologies

Participants were asked how often they experienced cyber aggression for ten items across seven technologies and tools (i.e., social networking sites, chat programs, email, chatrooms, blogs, online gaming, and text messages), which resulted in seventy items for cyber victimization. The same items were included for cyber aggression perpetration, across the seven technologies. A sample item included: Having rumors spread about oneself through social networking sites / spreading rumors about someone through social networking sites (e.g., Twitter, Facebook, Myspace). The behavior stem was replaced with a different behavior for each of the items and the technology stem was replaced with each of the digital technologies or tools. Items were answered using yes or no. All items were combined separately for each of the technologies for cyber aggression (seven total scores for each of the four waves) and cyber victimization (seven total scores for each of the four waves).

Cyber Aggression and Victimization within the Relationship between the Aggressor and the Perpetrator

Like the previous questionnaire, participants answered ten items according to how often six different individuals (i.e., ex-significant other, ex-friend, current significant other, current friend, acquaintance, and someone whom they did not know) victimized the participants online or through text messages, resulting in 60 items. The same items were used for cyber aggression, except these items were reworded to indicate who the participants targeted. The behavior stem was replaced with a different behavior for each of the items and the relationship stem was replaced with each of the individuals. Items were answered using yes or no. All items were combined separately for each of the relationships for cyber aggression (seven total scores for each of the four waves) and cyber victimization (seven total scores for each of the waves).

Self-Reported Face-to-Face Aggression and Victimization

Like the self-reported cyber aggression and victimization questionnaire, participants also reported how often they were victimized or perpetrated aggression in the offline world (Wright, Li, & Shi, 2014). These items were the same as those used for the previous questionnaire, except the "online or through text messages" portion of the item was removed. Twenty items were included for this questionnaire (10 items for face-to-face aggression and 10 items for face-to-face victimization), which were rated on a scale of 1 (*never*) to 9 (*daily*). Before answering the items, participants were asked to respond to the questions according to what they have experienced or perpetrated within the last 60 days. The items for face-to-face aggression and face-to-face victimization were averaged separately to form separate scores. Cronbach's alphas were acceptable for Wave 1 (.90 for face-to-face victimization and .89 for face-to-face aggression), Wave 2 (.86 for face-to-face victimization and .86 for face-to-face aggression), Wave 3 (.86 for face-to-face victimization and .85 for face-to-face aggression), and Wave 4 (.88 for face-to-face victimization and .87 for face-to-face aggression).

Suicidal Ideation

To assess suicidal ideation, participants were asked to respond to two questions (i.e., during the past 12 months, how often have you seriously considered attempting suicide, and during the past 12 months, did you make a plan about how you would attempt suicide; Center for Disease Control, 2011). The original items included yes or no responses, and these responses were updated to a 5-point Likert-type scale for this study, with ratings on a scale of 1 (*never*) to 5 (*very often*). The two items were combined to form scores on suicidal ideation. Cronbach's alphas were acceptable for Wave 1 (.73), Wave 2 (.73), Wave 3 (.71), and Wave 4 (.70).

Non-Suicidal Injury

Participants completed the Self-Harm Inventory. This questionnaire consists of 22 items asking participants if they have ever intentionally engaged in a described behavior (Sansome, Wiederman, & Sansone, 1998). All 22 items were answered with yes or no responses. These responses were updated to a 5-point Likert-type scale for this study, with ratings on a scale of 1 (*never*) to 5 (*very often*). Sample items included: Hit yourself, Cut yourself on purpose, and Prevented wounds from healing. All items were combined to form a final score on non-suicidal self-harm. Cronbach's alpha was acceptable for Wave 1 (.81), Wave 2 (.78), Wave 3 (.78), and Wave 4 (.80).

Depression

The Beck Depression Inventory was used to assess depression among emerging adults (Beck, Steer, & Brown, 1996). The questionnaire included 21 items with four statements per item. Participants rated each statement on a scale of 0 (*I do not feel sad*) to 3 (*I am sad and unhappy that I can't stand it*) on how they felt in the past 2 weeks. Items were combined to form a final score on depression, with Cronbach's alphas of .86 for Wave 1, .88 for Wave 2, .88 for Wave 3, and .86 for Wave 4.

Loneliness

The Revised UCLA Loneliness Scale was used to measure participants' feelings and experience of loneliness (Russell, 1996). There were 20 items included for this questionnaire, which were rated on a scale of 1 (*never*) to 4 (*often*). A sample item included: I feel isolated from others. The items were combined to form a final score on loneliness, with acceptable Cronbach's alphas of .83 for Wave 1, .84 for Wave 2, .80 for Wave 3, and .81 for Wave 4.

Anxiety

The Beck Anxiety Inventory was used to measure participants' symptoms of anxiety over the past month, including the day they completed the questionnaire (Beck & Steer, 1993). Participants responded to 21 items representing symptoms of anxiety (e.g., numbness or tingling and feeling hot). The items were rated on a scale of 0 (*not at all*) to 3 (*severely - it bothered me a lot*). All 21 items were combined to form a final score for anxiety, with acceptable Cronbach's alphas of .83 for Wave 1, .81 for Wave 2, .81 for Wave 3, and .84 for Wave 4.

Grade Point Average

Participants responded to an open-ended question that asked them their cumulative GPA using a 4.0 grading system. During the first wave, participants were asked for their final high school cumulative GPA. For the second through the fourth waves, they were asked for their current cumulative GPA in the previous semester. They wrote in their cumulative GPA.

Analytic Plan

To investigate cyber aggression and cyber victimization for various technologies and the relationship between the aggressor and the victim, frequencies were calculated (Aims 1 through 2). To examine the longitudinal, reciprocal relationships among cyber aggression, cyber victimization, suicidal ideation, non-suicidal self-harm, depression, loneliness, anxiety, and GPA over four years, various autoregressive cross-lagged path models were constructed using *Mplus* 7.31 (Aim 3; Bollen & Curran, 2006). All variables were regressed on proceeding variables, which allows for the ability to examine bivariate effects between variables, while accounting for previous levels of these variables over time. Face-to-face aggression and victimization were controlled for in the analyses by allowing these two variables to predict all variables in the models. Accounting for face-to-face aggression and victimization is important because these variables are highly correlated with cyber aggression and victimization (Wright & Li, 2012). Paths were added from cyber aggression and cyber victimization to suicidal ideation, non-suicidal self-harm, depression, loneliness, anxiety, and GPA for each of the waves. A missing at random test was performed to determine whether the data were missing completely at random (Little & Rubin, 1989; Rubin & Coplan, 2010). The findings revealed that all data were missing completely at random, $\chi^2 = 91.03$, $df = 116$, $p = .96$. Therefore, only complete cases were included in the analyses. There was missing data for 53 participants and therefore these cases were dropped from the analyses, resulting in a final sample size of 1,483.

RESULTS

Descriptive Statistics

Before conducting the autoregressive cross-lagged models, descriptive statistics were computed for each of the study's variables. Next, correlational analyses were conducted among all variables examined in the study (see Table 1). The findings revealed that cyber aggression and cyber victimization at all waves were associated positively with suicidal ideation, non-suicidal self-harm, depression, loneliness, anxiety, and GPA. On the other hand, cyber aggression and cyber victimization were related negatively to GPA for all waves. Furthermore, all adjustment variables were related positively to each other, except for GPA. GPA was associated negatively with suicidal ideation, depression, loneliness, and anxiety, but it was unrelated to non-suicidal self-harm.

The frequencies of cyber aggression and victimization occurring through various technologies and tools, such as social networking sites, chat programs, email, chatrooms, blogs, online gaming, and text messages, were conducted (see Table 2). The most used technology for cyber aggression was text messages, followed by social networking sites, chat programs and email, chatrooms, blogs, and online gaming across all four waves. Similar patterns were found for cyber victimization across all four waves as well. Frequencies were conducted for the relationship between the perpetrator and the victim (see Table 3). For cyber aggression, the most frequently targeted individual was an ex-friend, followed by ex-significant other, someone they did not know offline, current friend, and current significant other. The same patterns were found for cyber victimization. Overall, the frequency of cyber aggression and cyber victimization diminished from wave one through wave four for all technologies and across each of the relationships between the perpetrator and the victim.

Cyber Aggression

The model fit for suicidal ideation (χ^2 = 98.54, df = 12, CFI = .98, $RMSEA$ = .06, $SRMR$ = .04), non-suicidal self-harm (χ^2 = 106.13, df = 12, CFI = .97, $RMSEA$ = .05, $SRMR$ = .05), depression (χ^2 = 114.01, df = 12, CFI = .97, $RMSEA$ = .06, $SRMR$ = .05), loneliness (χ^2 = 118.69, df = 12, CFI = .97, $RMSEA$ = .06, $SRMR$ = .05), anxiety (χ^2 = 125.71, df = 12, CFI = .99, $RMSEA$ = .05, $SRMR$ = .05), and GPA (χ^2 = 89.89, df = 12, CFI = .99, $RMSEA$ = .05, $SRMR$ = .05) demonstrated excellent fit indices (see Figure 2 for all path models). The coefficients for the paths revealed stability for cyber aggression, suicidal ideation, non-suicidal self-harm, depression, loneliness, anxiety, and GPA over time. Wave 1, Wave 2, Wave 3, and Wave 4 of cyber aggression predicted all adjustment outcomes, after accounting for previous levels of these variables and face-to-face aggression, while all adjustment outcomes predicted cyber aggression for each wave as well. The strengths of the magnitudes were weaker when all adjustment outcomes predicted cyber aggression than when cyber aggression predicted all adjustment outcomes.

Figure 1. Autoregressive cross-lagged model of cyber aggression with suicidal ideation, non-suicidal self-harm, depression, lonliness, anxiety, and GPA across all waves
Note: W1 = Wave 1; W2 = Wave 2; W3 = Wave 3; W4 = Wave 4. Standard coefficients are displayed.
**p<.05.*

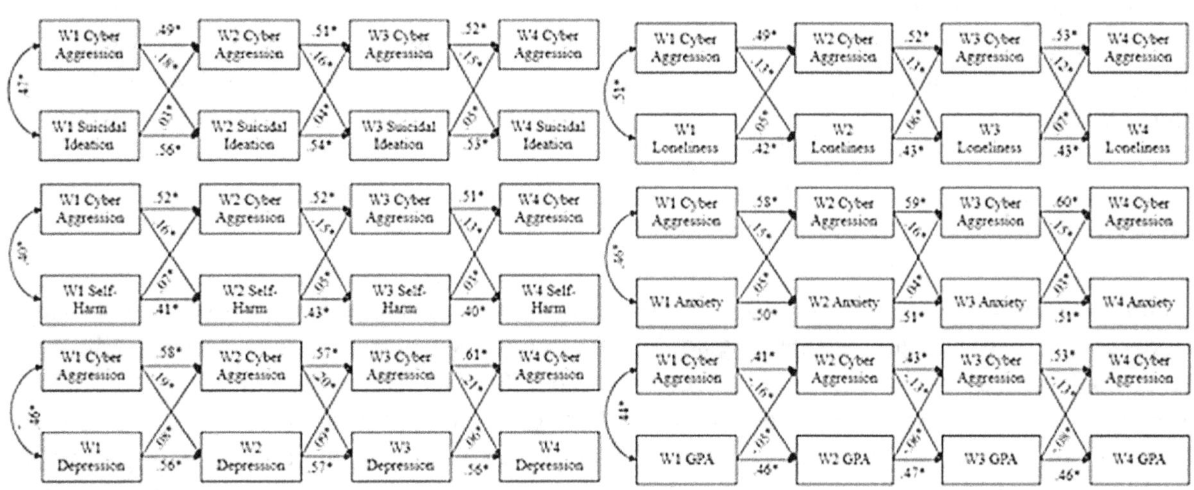

Figure 2. Autoregressive cross-lagged model of cyber victimization with suicidal ideation, non-suicidal self-harm, depression, lonliness, anxiety, and GPA across all waves
Note: W1 = Wave 1; W2 = Wave 2; W3 = Wave 3; W4 = Wave 4. Standard coefficients are displayed.
**p<.05.*

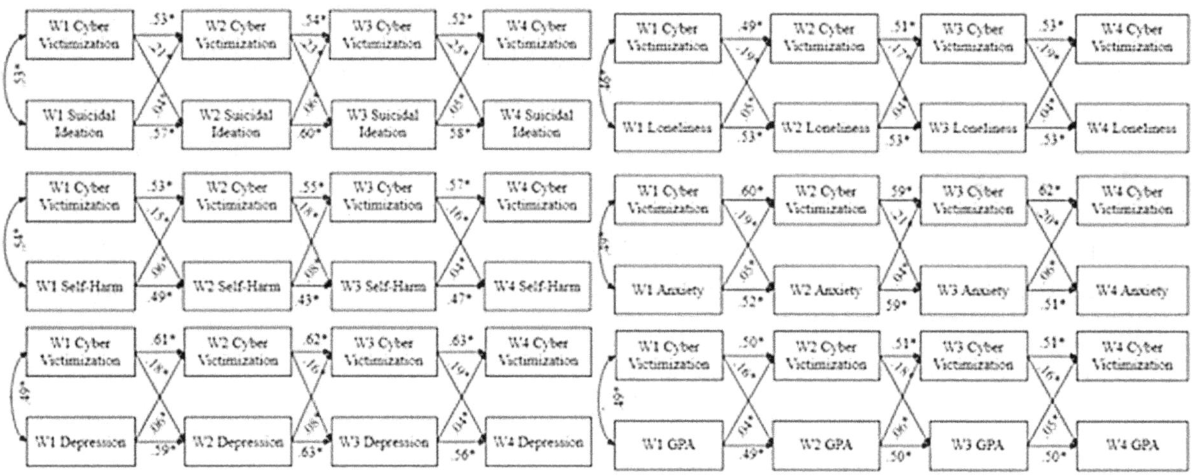

Cyber Victimization

The model fit for suicidal ideation (χ^2 = 96.13, *df* = 12, *CFI* = .99, *RMSEA* = .05, *SRMR* = .04), non-suicidal self-harm (χ^2 = 106.78, *df* = 12, *CFI* = .95, *RMSEA* = .05, *SRMR* = .05), depression (χ^2 = 119.23, *df* = 12, *CFI* = .97, *RMSEA* = .06, *SRMR* = .05), loneliness (χ^2 = 113.69, *df* = 12, *CFI* = .98, *RMSEA* = .05, *SRMR* = .05), anxiety (χ^2 = 123.03, *df* = 12, *CFI* = .96, *RMSEA* = .06, *SRMR* = .05), and GPA (χ^2 = 88.67, *df* = 12, *CFI* = .98, *RMSEA* = .05, *SRMR* = .05) demonstrated excellent fit indices (see Figure 2 for all path models). The coefficients for the paths revealed stability for cyber victimization, suicidal ideation, non-suicidal self-harm, depression, loneliness, anxiety, and GPA over time. Wave 1, Wave 2, Wave 3, and Wave 4 of cyber victimization predicted all adjustment outcomes, after accounting for previous levels of these variables and face-to-face victimization, while all adjustment outcomes predicted cyber victimization for all waves as well. The strengths of the magnitudes were weaker when all adjustment outcomes predicted cyber victimization than when cyber victimization predicted all adjustment outcomes.

DISCUSSION

Findings from a handful of studies have linked cyber aggression and cyber victimization to suicidal ideation, depression, and anxiety among emerging adults, utilizing cross-sectional research designs (Kokkinos, Antoniadou, & Markos, 2014; Schenk & Fremouw, 2012; Tennant, Demaray, Coyle, & Malecki, 2015; Wright & Li, 2012, 2013). Most of the available research on the longitudinal relationships between cyber aggression involvement and adjustment difficulties (i.e., suicidal ideation, depression, anxiety) have been conducted among children and adolescents (Bannink, Broeren, van de Looij-Jasen, de Waart, & Raat, 2014; Hay & Meldrum, 2010; Shpiegel, Klomek, & Apter, 2015). These studies revealed that suicidal ideation, depression, and anxiety increased after children and adolescents experienced or perpetrated cyber aggression. Finding that suicidal ideation, non-suicidal self-harm, depression, loneliness, anxiety, and GPA are antecedents and consequences of cyber aggression and victimization among emerging adults demonstrates the importance of understanding more about this topic. Cyber aggression and victimization are typically considered problems for primary and secondary school students. Acknowledging that these behaviors occur among emerging adults is an important step in the prevention of cyber aggression involvement and helping to alleviate the negative consequences associated with such behaviors. The first purpose of the present study was to describe the digital technologies and tools that emerging adults utilize more often to harm others and to understand the nature of the relationship between the perpetrator and the victim. The second purpose of the study was to investigate the longitudinal and reciprocal relationship of cyber aggression and cyber victimization to suicidal ideation, non-suicidal self-harm, depression, loneliness, anxiety, and GPA across fours year among emerging adults, while accounting for previous levels of these variables and face-to-face aggression and victimization.

The findings from the present study were similar to those found in cross-sectional studies on the associations of cyber victimization to various psychological, social, academic, and behavioral difficulties among emerging adults (Feinstein, Bhatia, & Davila, 2014; Kokkinos et al., 2014; Landoll, La Greca, & Lai, 2013; Schenk & Fremouw, 2012; Tennant et al., 2015). Furthermore, the results of the present study expand on the existing literature by demonstrating longitudinal and bidirectional associations between cyber victimization, suicidal ideation, non-suicidal self-harm, depression, loneliness, anxiety, and GPA. Such relationships were highly stable over the four years of the study, revealing that prior levels of cyber aggression and cyber victimization predicted later cyber aggression involvement and psychosocial and academic difficulties. Prolonged exposure to cyber aggression might potentially weaken emerging adults' ability to effectively cope with victimization. Utilizing maladaptive coping strategies might lead emerging adults to suicidal ideation, non-suicidal self-harm, depression, loneliness, anxiety, and GPA. Stable patterns of cyber victimization were experienced by some emerging adults in this study, combined with poor coping strategies, which might increase their risk for additional victimization and further adjustment difficulties (Ybarra, Alexander, & Mitchell, 2005).

Less attention has been given in the literature to cyber aggression perpetration among children, adolescents, and emerging adults, with even fewer studies conducted on the association between cyber aggression perpetration and adjustment difficulties among emerging adults. Cyber aggression perpetration is linked to depression, anxiety, and loneliness, findings that are consistent with the current study's results (Brighi et al., 2012; Gradinger, Strohmeier, & Spiel, 2009; Sontag, Clemans, Graber, & Lyndon, 2011). Research also indicates that adolescent cyberaggressors experience academic difficulties, such as failing grades, classroom disruptions, and poor achievement scores (Wright, 2015). This finding can also be applied to the current study's results, revealing connections between cyber aggression perpetration and lower GPA. Thus far, no research has focused on the association between cyber aggression perpetration, suicidal ideation, and non-suicidal self-harm. In the face-to-face aggression literature, the perpetration of aggression is correlated with suicidal ideation and self-harm among adolescents (Barker, Arsenault, Brendgen, Fontaine, Maughan, 2008; Kim, Leventhal, Koh, & Boyce, 2009). It is proposed that individuals with externalizing problems, like aggression, are more impulsive and indulge in anger-related behaviors, which increases their suicide and self-harm risk (Apter et al., 1991). Therefore, cyber aggression perpetrators might be more impulsive and anger-prone, leading them more vulnerable to suicidal ideation and self-harm.

The magnitudes of the associations of cyber aggression and cyber victimization to suicidal ideation, non-suicidal self-harm, depression, loneliness, anxiety, and GPA were stronger than the reciprocal associations. Tennant and colleagues (2015) consider cyber aggression to be "a more persistent and pervasive form of aggression." Due to the pervasiveness of cyber aggression, emerging adults' psychological and academic difficulties might increase over time. Cyber victimization might lead some emerging adults to continuously experience a cycle of victimization, leading to repeated exposure to negative messages. The repeated exposure to negative messages and interactions might make it difficult for victims to perceive positive social interactions. The inability to perceive positive social interactions might reduce cybervictims' self-concept, leading to greater levels of suicidal ideation, non-suicidal self-harm, depression, loneliness, anxiety, and lower GPAs (Lipton, 2011). Victims of cyber aggression might find it more difficult to escape from victimization as they are not able to receive sanctuary in their homes (Kowalski & Limber, 2012). Furthermore, emerging adults are typically away from home and experience changes in their social relationships and identity. These changes in emerging adults' lives might make them more vulnerable to the adjustment difficulties associated with cyber victimization.

SOLUTIONS AND RECOMMENDATIONS

Raising awareness of cyber aggression and cyber victimization on college and university campuses is needed. Colleges and universities need to develop clear policies concerning cyber aggression involvement and provide details about the sanctions against perpetrators at the school level. It might be helpful to distribute materials on cyber aggression involvement and the associated adjustment difficulties during freshmen orientations. The resource can explain the dangers related to cyber victimization, what constitutes cyber aggression, and include contact information for the counseling center that students. The counseling center should also employ trained and knowledge staff regarding recognizing the signs of cyber aggression and the psychological, academic, and behavioral consequences.

FUTURE RESEARCH DIRECTIONS

The four-wave longitudinal design of the present study is a strength of this research. More attention should be given to investigating cyber aggression and cyber victimization among emerging adults, as findings from the present study indicate that these experiences and behaviors are harmful to emerging adults' psychological health. This study employed self-reports of both face-to-face and cyber aggression and victimization. Follow-up research should be conducted using multi-informants, such as friends and parents. This research might also consider investigating clinical forms of suicidality, non-suicidal self-harm, depression, anxiety, and loneliness to better understand their linkages to cyber aggression and cyber victimization over time. This study relied on a convenience sample of emerging adults. More attention should be given to conducting follow-up studies on cyber aggression and cyber victimization among other adults as well.

CONCLUSION

This study adds to the growing body of literature on cyber aggression and cyber victimization among emerging adults, and how such experiences relate to psychological and academic difficulties. The findings of the study were consistent with cross-sectional studies, with the present study revealing longitudinal and reciprocal relationships between cyber aggression, cyber victimizations, suicidal ideation, non-suicidal self-harm, depression, anxiety, and GPA over four years. Additional research attention should be given to understanding more about these associations. More awareness should be given to cyber aggression and cyber victimization among emerging adults as oftentimes these behaviors are considered concerns associated with children and adolescence. This mentality prevents additional research conducted on cyber aggression and cyber victimization among emerging adults, which diminishes our ability to deal with these behaviors and the associated psychological and academic difficulties. Awareness of cyber aggression and cyber victimization among emerging adults is necessary to prevent these behaviors and to alleviate the negative outcomes of such behaviors.

REFERENCES

Alvarez-Garcia, D., Nunez Perez, J. C., Gonzalez, A. D., & Perez, C. R. (2015). Risk factors associated with cyber victimization in adolescence. *International Journal of Clinical and Health Psychology*, *15*(3), 226–235. doi:10.1016/j.ijchp.2015.03.002

Apter, A., Kotler, M., Sevy, S., Plutchik, R., Brown, S. L., Foster, H., & van Praag, H. M. et al. (1991). Correlates of risk of suicide in violent and nonviolent psychiatric patients. *The American Journal of Psychiatry*, *148*(7), 883–837. doi:10.1176/ajp.148.7.883 PMID:2053628

Arnett, J. (2000). Emerging adulthood: A theory of development from late teens through the twenties. *The American Psychologist*, *55*(5), 469–480. doi:10.1037/0003-066X.55.5.469 PMID:10842426

Arnett, J., & Jensen, L. (2002). A congregation of one: Individualized religious beliefs among emerging adults. *Journal of Adolescent Research*, *17*(5), 451–467. doi:10.1177/0743558402175002

Badger, S., Nelson, L., & Barry, C. M. (2006). Perceptions of the transition to adulthood among Chinese and American emerging adults. *International Journal of Behavioral Development*, *30*(1), 84–93. doi:10.1177/0165025406062128

Bannink, R., Broeren, S., van de Looij-Jansen, P. M., de Waart, F. G., & Raat, H. (2014). Cyber and traditional bullying victimization as a risk factor for mental health problems in adolescents. *PLoS ONE*, *9*, e94026. doi:10.1371/journal.pone.0094026 PMID:24718563

Barker, E. D., Arseneault, L., Brendgen, M., Fontaine, N., & Maughan, B. (2008). Joint development of bullying and victimization in adolescence: Relations to delinquency and self-harm. *Journal of the American Academy of Child and Adolescent Psychiatry*, *47*(9), 1030–1038. PMID:18665001

Beck, A. T., & Steer, R. A. (1993). *Beck anxiety inventory manual*. San Antonio, TX: Harcourt Brace.

Beck, A. T., Steer, R. A., & Brown, G. K. (1996). *Manual for the beck inventory-II*. San Antonio, TX: Psychological Corporation.

Bollen, K. A., & Curran, P. J. (2006). *Latent curve models: A structural equation perspective.* New York, NY: Wiley.

Brighi, A., Melotti, G., Guarini, A., Genta, M. L., Ortega, R., Mora-Merchan, J., … Thompson, F. (2012). Self-esteem and loneliness in relation to cyberbullying in three European countries. In Q. Ling, D. Cross, & P. K. Smith (Eds.), Cyberbullying in the global playground (pp. 52-56). West Sussex, UK: Blackwell Publishing.

Cappadocia, M. C., Craig, W. M., & Pepler, D. (2013). Cyberbullying: Prevalence, stability and risk factors during adolescence. *Canadian Journal of School Psychology*, *28*, 171–192.

Center for Disease Control and Prevention (CDC). (2011). *Self-directed violence surveillance: Uniform definitions and recommended data elements.* Retrieved from: http://www.cdc.gov/violenceprevention/pdf/SelfDirected-Violence-a.pdf

Copes, H., Kerley, K., Huff, R., & Kane, J. (2010). Differentiating identity theft: An exploratory study of victims using a national victimization survey. *Journal of Criminal Justice*, *38*(5), 1045–1052. doi:10.1016/j.jcrimjus.2010.07.007

Cowie, H. (2013). Cyberbullying and its impact on young peoples emotional health and well-being. *Psychiatrist*, *37*(5), 167–170. doi:10.1192/pb.bp.112.040840

Crosslin, K. L., & Crosslin, M. B. (2014). Cyberbullying at a Texas university—A mixed-methods approach to examining online aggression. *Texas Public Health Journal*, *66*, 26–31.

Dilmac, N. (2009). Psychological needs as a predict of cyber bullying: A preliminary report on college students. *Educational Sciences: Theory and Practice*, *9*(3), 1307–1325.

Feinstein, B. A., Bhatia, V., & Davila, J. (2014). Rumination mediates the association between cybervictimization and depressive symptoms. *Journal of Interpersonal Violence*, *29*(9), 1732–1746. doi:10.1177/0886260513511534 PMID:24346650

Ferdon, C. D., & Hertz, M. F. (2007). Electronic media, violence, and adolescents. An emerging public health problem. *The Journal of Adolescent Health*, *41*(6), 1–5. doi:10.1016/j.jadohealth.2007.08.020 PMID:17577527

Finn, J. (2004). A survey of online harassment at a university campus. *Journal of Interpersonal Violence*, *19*(4), 468–483. doi:10.1177/0886260503262083 PMID:15038885

Fischer, E. H., Dornelas, E. A., & Goethe, J. W. (2001). Characteristics of people lost to attrition in psychiatric follow-up studies. *The Journal of Nervous and Mental Disease*, *189*(1), 49–55. doi:10.1097/00005053-200101000-00009 PMID:11206665

Gradinger, P., Strohmeier, D., & Spiel, C. (2015). Traditional bullying and cyberbullying: Identification of risk groups for adjustment problems. *The Journal of Psychology*, *217*, 205–213.

Grigg, D. W. (2010). Cyber-aggression: Definition and concept of cyberbullying. *Australian Journal of Guidance & Counselling*, *20*(02), 143–156. doi:10.1375/ajgc.20.2.143

Hay, C., & Meldrum, R. (2010). Bullying victimization and adolescent self-harm: Testing hypotheses from General Strain Theory. *Journal of Youth and Adolescence*, *39*(5), 446–459. doi:10.1007/s10964-009-9502-0 PMID:20072852

Hinduja, S., & Patchin, J. W. (2010). Bullying, cyberbullying, and suicide. *Archives of Suicide Research*, *14*(3), 206–221. doi:10.1080/13811118.2010.494133 PMID:20658375

Holt, T. J., Fitzgerald, S., Bossler, A. M., Chee, G., & Nq, E. (2016). Assessing the risk factors of cyber and mobile phone bullying victimization in a nationally representative sample of Singapore youth. *International Journal of Offender Therapy and Comparative Criminology*, *60*(5), 598–615. doi:10.1177/0306624X14554852 PMID:25326463

Kim, Y. S., Leventhal, B. L., Koh, Y. J., & Boyce, W. T. (2009). Bullying increased suicide risk: Prospective study of Korean adolescents. *Archives of Suicide Research*, *13*(1), 15–30. doi:10.1080/13811110802572098 PMID:19123106

Kokkinos, C. M., Antoniadou, N., & Markos, A. (2014). Cyber-bullying: An investigation of the psychological profile of university student participants. *Journal of Applied Developmental Psychology*, *35*(3), 204–214. doi:10.1016/j.appdev.2014.04.001

Kowalski, R. M., & Limber, S. P. (2007). Electronic bullying among middle school students. *The Journal of Adolescent Health*, *41*(6), 22–30. doi:10.1016/j.jadohealth.2007.08.017 PMID:18047942

Kowalski, R. M., & Limber, S. P. (2012). Psychological, physical, and academic correlates of cyberbullying and traditional bullying. *The Journal of Adolescent Health*, *53*, 513–520. PMID:23790195

Landoll, R. R., La Greca, A. M., & Lai, B. S. (2013). Aversive peer experiences on social networking sites: Development of the Social Networking-Peer Experiences Questionnaires (SN-PEQ). *Journal of Research on Adolescence*, *23*(4), 695–705. doi:10.1111/jora.12022 PMID:24288449

Lipton, J. D. (2011). Combating cyber-victimization. *Berkeley Technology Law Journal*, *26*, 1104–1126.

Little, R. J. A., & Rubin, D. B. (1989). The analysis of social science data with missing values. *Sociological Methods & Research*, *18*(2-3), 292–326. doi:10.1177/0049124189018002004

Mishna, F., Khoury-Kassabri, M., Gadalla, T., & Daciuk, J. (2012). Risk factors for involvement in cyber bullying: Victims, bullies and bully-victims. *Children and Youth Services Review*, *34*(1), 63–70. doi:10.1016/j.childyouth.2011.08.032

Nelson, L., & Barry, C. (2005). Distinguishing features of emerging adulthood: The role of self-classification as an adult. *Journal of Adolescent Research*, *20*(2), 242–262. doi:10.1177/0743558404273074

Perrin, A., & Duggan, M. (2015). *Americans' internet access: 2000-2015*. Retrieved from: http://www.pewinternet.org/2015/06/26/americans-internet-access-2000-2015/

Rideout, V. J., Roberts, D. F., & Foehr, U. G. (2005). *Generation M: Media in the lives of 8-18-year-olds: Executive summary*. Menlo Park, CA: Henry J. Kaiser Family Foundation.

Rubin, K. H., & Coplan, R. (2010). *The development of shyness and social withdrawal*. New York, NY: Guilford Press.

Russell, D. (1996). UCLA Loneliness Scale (Version 3): Reliability, validity, and factor structure. *Journal of Personality Assessment*, *66*(1), 20–40. doi:10.1207/s15327752jpa6601_2 PMID:8576833

Sansone, R. A., Wiederman, M. W., & Sansone, L. A. (1998). The Self-Harm Inventory (SHI): Development of a scale of identifying self-destructive behaviors and borderline personality disorder. *Journal of Clinical Psychology*, *54*(7), 973–983. doi:10.1002/(SICI)1097-4679(199811)54:7<973::AID-JCLP11>3.0.CO;2-H PMID:9811134

Schenk, A. M., & Fremouw, W. J. (2012). Prevalence, psychological impact, and coping of cyberbully victims among college students. *Journal of School Violence*, *11*(1), 21–37. doi:10.1080/15388220.2011.630310

Selkie, E. M., Kota, R., Chan, Y., & Moreno, M. (2015). Cyberbullying, depression, and problem alcohol use in female college students: A multisite study. *Cyberpsychology, Behavior, and Social Networking*, *18*(2), 79–86. doi:10.1089/cyber.2014.0371 PMID:25684608

Shpiegel, Y., Klomek, A. B., & Apter, A. (2015). Bullying, cyberbullying, depression and suicide ideation among youth. Comparing online to paper-and-pencil questionnaires. *International Journal of Child and Adolescent Health*, *8*, 161–167.

Smith, A., Rainie, L., & Zickuhr, K. (2011). *College students and technology*. Retrieved from http://www.pewinternet.org/2011/07/19/college-students-and-technology/

Smith, P. K., Mahdavi, J., Carvalho, M., Fisher, S., Russell, S., & Tippett, N. (2008). Cyberbullying: Its nature and impact in secondary school pupils. *Journal of Child Psychology and Psychiatry, and Allied Disciplines*, *49*(4), 376–385. doi:10.1111/j.1469-7610.2007.01846.x PMID:18363945

Sontag, L. M., Clemans, K. H., Graber, J. A., & Lyndon, S. T. (2011). Traditional and cyber aggressors and victims: A comparison of psychosocial characteristics. *Journal of Youth and Adolescence*, *40*(4), 392–404. doi:10.1007/s10964-010-9575-9 PMID:20680425

Tang, J., Ma, Y., Guo, T., Ahmed, N. I., Yu, Y., & Wang, J. (2013). Association of aggression and non-suicidal self-injury: A school-based sample of adolescents. *PLoS ONE*, *8*(1), e78149. doi:10.1371/journal.pone.0078149 PMID:24205132

Tennant, J. E., Demaray, M. K., Coyle, S., & Malecki, C. K. (2015). The dangers of the webs: Cybervictimization, depression, and social support in college students. *Computers in Human Behavior*, *50*, 348–357. doi:10.1016/j.chb.2015.04.014

Topcu, C., Erdur-Baker, O., & Capa, A. Y. (2008). Examination of cyber-bullying experiences among Turkish students from different school types. *Cyberpsychology & Behavior*, *11*(6), 644–648. doi:10.1089/cpb.2007.0161 PMID:18783345

Walker, C., Sockman, B., & Koehn, S. (2011). An exploratory study of cyberbullying with undergraduate university students. *TechTrends*, *55*(2), 31–38. doi:10.1007/s11528-011-0481-0

Weigman, O., & Schie, E. (1998). Video game playing and its relations with aggressive and prosocial behaviors. *The British Journal of Social Psychology*, *37*(3), 367–378. doi:10.1111/j.2044-8309.1998.tb01177.x PMID:9738313

Wolak, J., Mitchell, K., & Finkelhor, D. (2007). Does online harassment constitute bullying? An exploration of online harassment by known peers and online-only contacts. *The Journal of Adolescent Health*, *41*(6), 51–58. doi:10.1016/j.jadohealth.2007.08.019 PMID:18047945

Wright, M. F. (2015). Cyber victimization and perceived stress: Linkages to late adolescents cyber aggression and psychological functioning. *Youth & Society*, *47*(6), 789–810. doi:10.1177/0044118X14537088

Wright, M. F., & Li, Y. (2012). Kicking the digital dog: A longitudinal investigation of young adults victimization and cyber-displaced aggression. *Cyberpsychology, Behavior, and Social Networking*, *15*(9), 44–454. doi:10.1089/cyber.2012.0061 PMID:22974350

Wright, M. F., & Li, Y. (2013). Normative beliefs about aggression and cyber aggression among young adults: A longitudinal investigation. *Aggressive Behavior*, *39*(3), 161–170. doi:10.1002/ab.21470 PMID:23440595

Wright, M. F., Li, Y., & Shi, J. (2014). Chinese adolescents social status goals: Associations with behaviors and attributions for relational aggression. *Youth & Society*, *46*(4), 566–588. doi:10.1177/0044118X12448800

Ybarra, M. L., Alexander, C., & Mitchell, K. J. (2005). Depressive symptomology, youth internet use, and online interactions: A national survey. *The Journal of Adolescent Health*, *36*(1), 9–18. doi:10.1016/j.jadohealth.2003.10.012 PMID:15661591

Ybarra, M. L., Diener-West, M., & Leaf, P. J. (2007). Examining the overlap in internet harassment and school bullying: Implications for school intervention. *The Journal of Adolescent Health*, *41*(6), S42–S50. doi:10.1016/j.jadohealth.2007.09.004 PMID:18047944

Ybarra, M. L., & Mitchell, K. J. (2004). Online aggressor/targets, aggressors, and targets: A comparison of associated youth characteristics. *Journal of Child Psychology and Psychiatry, and Allied Disciplines*, *45*(7), 1308–1316. doi:10.1111/j.1469-7610.2004.00328.x PMID:15335350

ADDITIONAL READING

Bauman, S. (2011). *Cyberbullying: What counselors need to know*. Alexandria, VA: American Counseling Association.

Bauman, S., Cross, D., & Walker, J. (2013). *Principles of cyberbullying research: Definitions, measures, and methodology*. New York, NY: Routledge.

Feinberg, T., & Robey, N. (2010). Cyberbullying: Intervention and prevention strategies. Retrieved from: http://www.nasponline.org/resources/bullying/cyberbullying.pdf

Hinduja, S., & Patchin, J. W. (2015). *Bullying beyond the schoolyard: Preventing and responding to cyberbullying*. Thousand Oaks, CA: Sage Publications.

Li, Q., Cross, D., & Smith, P. K. (2012). *Cyberbullying in the global playground*. Malden, MA: Blackwell Publishing. doi:10.1002/9781119954484

Menesini, E., & Spiel, C. (2012). *Cyberbullying: Development, consequences, risk and protective factors*. New York, NY: Psychology Press.

Shariff, S., & Churchill, A. H. (2010). *Truths and myths of cyber-bullying: International perspectives on stakeholder responsibility and children's safety*. New York, NY: Peter Lang Publishing, Inc.

Tokunaga, R. S. (2010). Following you home from school: A critical review and synthesis of research on cyberbullying victimization. *Computers in Human Behavior*, *26*(3), 277–287. doi:10.1016/j.chb.2009.11.014

APPENDIX: TABLES

Table 1. Correlations among all waves of the variables in the study

	Cyber Aggression				Cyber Victimization			
	Wave 1	Wave 2	Wave 3	Wave 4	Wave 1	Wave 2	Wave 3	Wave 4
W1 CA	---	---	---	---	---	---	---	---
W2 CA	.51***	---	---	---	---	---	---	---
W3 CA	.43***	.43***	---	---	---	---	---	---
W4 CA	.37***	.37***	.41***	---	---	---	---	---
W1 CV	.35***	.35***	.36***	.35***	---	---	---	---
W2 CV	.34***	.34***	.33***	.30***	.54***	---	---	---
W3 CV	.34***	.33***	.34***	.30***	.46***	.50***	---	---
W4 CV	.30***	.33***	30***	.31***	.42***	.47***	.44***	---
W1 SI	.29***	.29**	.28**	.24*	.39***	.37***	.42***	.48***
W2 SI	.27**	.26**	.26**	.22*	.36***	.36***	.43***	.48***
W3 SI	.25*	.25*	.24*	.19*	.34***	.33***	.45***	.46***
W4 SI	.20*	.22*	.23*	.18*	.35***	.41***	.42***	.41***
W1 SH	.31***	.33***	.30***	.29**	.32***	.30***	.29***	.31***
W2 SH	.29**	.28**	.29**	.26**	.29**	.31***	.31***	.30***
W3 SH	.26*	.26*	.25*	.23*	.30***	.31***	.28**	.27**
W4 SH	.23*	.21*	.19*	.20*	.27**	.26**	.27**	.23*
W1 DEP	.41***	.37***	.33***	.29**	.51***	.53***	.49***	.50***
W2 DEP	.33***	.42***	.33***	.30***	.48***	.49***	.46***	.50***
W3 DEP	.36***	.37***	.39***	.36***	.46***	.51***	.50***	.51***
W4 DEP	.35***	.33***	.31***	.36***	.46***	.56***	.46***	.46***
W1 LONE	.33***	.31***	.27**	.27**	.30***	.27**	.25*	.22*
W2 LONE	.30***	.30***	.27**	.25*	.29**	.28**	.25*	.22*
WE LONE	.28**	.27**	.25*	.19*	.27**	.29**	.26**	.21*
W4 LONE	.25*	.20*	.19*	.19*	.23*	.23*	.26**	.19*
W1 ANX	.27**	.30***	.28**	.25*	.26***	.29***	.30***	.29***
W2 ANX	.25*	.29**	.27**	.21*	.21**	.31***	.32***	.29***
W3 ANX	.19*	.21*	.20*	.23*	.25***	.22**	.28***	.27***
W4 ANX	.19*	.19*	.20*	.19*	.18*	.17*	.24**	.25**
W1 GPA	-.36***	-.31***	-.27**	-.25*	-.31***	-.26**	-.23*	-.19*
W2 GPA	-.31***	-.30***	-.28**	-.26*	-.30***	-.29**	-.27**	-.25*
W3 GPA	-.31***	-.29**	-.23*	-.23*	-.30***	-.27**	-.29**	-.27**
W4 GPA	-.27**	-.27**	-.26*	-.21*	-.26**	-.26**	-.21*	-.25*

Note. W1 = Wave 1; W2 = Wave 2; W3 = Wave 3; W4 = Wave 4; CA = cyber aggression; CV = cyber victimization; SI = suicidal ideation; SH = non-suicidal self-harm; DEP = depression; LONE = loneliness; ANX = anxiety; GPA = grade point average.
*p < .05. **p < .01. ***p < .001.

Table 2. Frequency of cyber aggression and cyber victimization across digital technologies and tools

	Cyber Aggression				Cyber Victimization			
	Wave 1	**Wave 2**	**Wave 3**	**Wave 4**	**Wave 1**	**Wave 2**	**Wave 3**	**Wave 4**
SNS	24.6%	22.3%	21.6%	20.2%	30.7%	30.1%	28.9%	28.1%
Chat	12.7%	10.9%	10.0%	8.9%	9.1%	8.7%	7.3%	6.9%
Email	12.7%	11.1%	9.6%	8.8%	4.5%	4.0%	4.0%	3.8%
Chatrooms	3.1%	2.9%	2.2%	1.9%	1.6%	1.3%	1.1%	0.8%
Blogs	1.3%	1.1%	0.9%	0.9%	1.6%	0.9%	0.6%	0.6%
Online Gaming	3.0%	3.0%	2.7%	2.0%	10.3%	10.1%	9.5%	9.0%
Text Messages	39.1%	37.8%	35.8%	33.4%	28.2%	28.2%	27.8%	26.3%

Table 3. Frequency of cyber aggression and cyber victimization across different relationships between the perpetrator and the victim

	Cyber Aggression				Cyber Victimization			
	Wave 1	**Wave 2**	**Wave 3**	**Wave 4**	**Wave 1**	**Wave 2**	**Wave 3**	**Wave 4**
Ex-significant other	15.2%	15.0%	14.5%	13.3%	21.4%	19.8%	19.0%	18.4%
Ex-friend	16.8%	16.1%	15.6%	15.0%	35.3%	33.8%	32.8%	30.9%
Current significant other	1.0%	0.8%	0.8%	0.7%	1.3%	1.0%	0.8%	0.6%
Current friend	7.7%	7.1%	6.4%	6.1%	8.4%	8.1%	7.6%	7.1%
Acquaintance	11.3%	10.8%	10.1%	8.8%	11.3%	10.8%	9.2%	8.3%
Someone do not know offline	10.3%	9.8%	8.6%	8.0%	15.9%	15.0%	14.1%	13.5%

Compilation of References

Abreu, C. (2013). Dependência de internet. In *Vivendo esse mundo digital* (pp. 95–103). Porto Alegre: Artmed.

Adams, G. R., & Marshall, S. K. (1996). A developmental social psychology of identity: Understanding the person-in-context. *Journal of Adolescence*, *19*(5), 429–442. doi:10.1006/jado.1996.0041 PMID:9245296

Afif, J. C. B. A. (1997). *Futebol 100% profissional*. São Paulo: Editora Gente.

Agarwal, R., & Karahanna, E. (2000). Time flies when youre having fun: Cognitive absorption and beliefs about information technology usage. *Management Information Systems Quarterly*, *24*(4), 665–694. doi:10.2307/3250951

Agergaard, S., & Ryba, T. V. (2014). Migration and Carrer Transition in professional sport: Transitional athletic careers in a psychological and sociological perspective. *Sociology of Sport Journal*, *31*(2), 228–247. doi:10.1123/ssj.2013-0031

Ajrou, K. J., Blandon, A. Y., & Antonucci, T. C. (2005). Social networks among men and women: The effects of age and socioeconomic status. *The Journals of Gerontology. Series B, Psychological Sciences and Social Sciences*, *60*(6), S311–S317. doi:10.1093/geronb/60.6.S311 PMID:16260713

Ajzen, I. (1991). The theory of planned behavior. *Organizational Behavior and Human Decision Processes*, *50*(2), 179–211. doi:10.1016/0749-5978(91)90020-T

Alderson, K., & Samimi, P. (2014). Sexting among undergraduate students. *Computers in Human Behavior*, *31*, 230–241. doi:10.1016/j.chb.2013.10.027

Alexy, E. M., Burgess, A. W., Baker, T., & Smoyak, S. A. (2005). Perceptions of cyberstalking among college students. *Brief Treatment and Crisis Intervention*, *5*(3), 279–289. doi:10.1093/brief-treatment/mhi020

Allard, E. R., & Willimas, D. F. (2008). Listeners perceptions of speech and language disorders. *Journal of Communication Disorders*, *41*(2), 108–123. doi:10.1016/j.jcomdis.2007.05.002 PMID:17586521

Alper, S., & Raharinirina, S. (2006). Assistive technology for individuals with disabilities: A review and synthesis of the literature. *Journal of Special Education Technology*, *21*, 47–64.

Alpizar, K., Islas-Alvarado, R., Warren, C., & Fiebert, M. (2012). 'Gender, Sexuality and Impression Management on Facebook'. *International Review of Social Sciences and Humanities*, *4*(1), 121–125.

Alvarez-Garcia, D., Nunez Perez, J. C., Gonzalez, A. D., & Perez, C. R. (2015). Risk factors associated with cyber victimization in adolescence. *International Journal of Clinical and Health Psychology*, *15*(3), 226–235. doi:10.1016/j.ijchp.2015.03.002

American Association of Intellectual and Developmental Disabilities. (2013). *Definition of intellectual disability*. Retrieved from http://aaidd.org/intellectual-disability/definition#.Vd0xTKaZ5EI

American Diabetes Association. (2015). *Diabetes symptoms*. Retrieved from http://www.diabetes.org/diabetes-basics/symptoms/

American Psychiatric Association. (2013). *Diagnostic and statistical manual of mental disorders* (5th ed.). Arlington, VA: American Psychiatric Publishing.

Anderson, M., & Perrin, A. (2015, July 28). *15% of Americans don't use the internet. Who are they?* Pew Research Center's Internet & American Life Project. Retrieved from http://www.pewresearch.org/fact- tank/2015/07/28/15-of-americans-dont-use-the-internet-who-are-they/

Andreason, A. W. (2003). Expatriate adjustment to foreign assignments. *International Journal of Commerce & Management, 1*(1), 42–60. doi:10.1108/eb047459

Andriani, I. (2016). *Model of cyberbullying behavior influenced by external and internal factors* (Unpublished Doctoral Dissertation). University of Gunadarma, Jakarta.

Angermeyer, M. C., & Matschinger, H. (1997). Social distance towards the mentally ill: Results of representative surveys in the Federal Republic of Germany. *Psychological Medicine, 27*(1), 131–141. doi:10.1017/S0033291796004205

Angermeyer, M. C., & Matschinger, H. (2003). Public beliefs about schizophrenia and depression: Similarities and differences. *Social Psychiatry and Psychiatric Epidemiology, 38*(9), 526–534. doi:10.1007/s00127-003-0676-6

Anthenunis, M. L., Valkenburg, P. M., & Peter, J. (2012). The quality of online, offline, and mixed-mode friendships among users of a social net- working site. *Cyberpsychology: Journal of Psychosocial Research on Cyberspace, 6,* Article 6. Retrieved from http://www.cyberpsychology.eu/view.php? cisloclanku=2012120304&article=6

Apter, A., Kotler, M., Sevy, S., Plutchik, R., Brown, S. L., Foster, H., & van Praag, H. M. et al. (1991). Correlates of risk of suicide in violent and nonviolent psychiatric patients. *The American Journal of Psychiatry, 148*(7), 883–837. doi:10.1176/ajp.148.7.883 PMID:2053628

Aquilino, W. S. (2006). Family relationships and support systems in emerging adulthood. In J. J. Arnett, J. L. Tanner, J. J. Arnett, & J. L. Tanner (Eds.), *Emerging adults in America: Coming of age in the 21st century* (pp. 193–217). Washington, DC: American Psychological Association. doi:10.1037/11381-008

Arakali, H. (2015). *Emerging Markets Like Indonesia, India Top US In Facebook Mobile Access*. Retrieved January 30, 2016 from http://www.ibtimes.com/emerging-markets-indonesia-india-top-us-facebook-mobile-access-1792686Bolt

Ardila-Rey, A., Killen, M., & Brenick, A. (2009). Moral reasoning in violent contexts: Displaced and non-displaced Colombian childrens evaluations of moral transgressions, retaliation, and reconciliation. *Social Development, 18*(1), 181–209. doi:10.1111/j.1467-9507.2008.00483.x PMID:25722543

Arnett, J. (2004). *Emerging adulthood: The winding road from the late teens through the twenties*. New York, NY: Oxford University Press.

Arnett, J. J. (1992). Reckless Behaviour in Adolescence: A developmental Perspective. *Developmental Review, 12*(4), 339–373. doi:10.1016/0273-2297(92)90013-R

Arnett, J. J. (2000). Emerging adulthood: A theory of development from the late teens through the twenties. *The American Psychologist, 55*(5), 469–480. doi:10.1037/0003-066X.55.5.469 PMID:10842426

Arnett, J. J. (2004). *Emerging adulthood: The winding road from the late tens through the twenties*. New York, NY: Oxford University Press.

Arnett, J. J. (2005). The Developmental Context of Substance Use in Emerging Adulthood. *Journal of Drug Issues*, *35*(2), 235–254. doi:10.1177/002204260503500202

Arnett, J. J. (2006). Emerging adulthood: Understanding the new way of coming of age. In J. J. Arnett & J. L. Tanner (Eds.), *Emerging adults in America: Coming of age in the 21st century* (pp. 1–19). Washington, DC: American Psychological Association. doi:10.1037/11381-001

Arnett, J. J. (2007). Emerging adulthood: What is it, and what is it good for? Child Devlopment. *Perspectives*, *1*, 68–73. doi:10.1111/j.1750-8606.2007.00016.x

Arnett, J. J. (2012). New Horizons in Research on Emerging and Young Adulthood. In A. Booth, S. L. Brown, N. S. Landale, W. D. Manning, & S. M. McHale (Eds.), *Younger Adulthood in a Family Context* (pp. 231–244). New York, NY: Springer. doi:10.1007/978-1-4614-1436-0_15

Arnett, J. J. (2015). *Emerging Adulthood: The Winding Road from the Late Teens Through the Twenties*. Oxford, UK: Oxford University Press. doi:10.1093/oxfordhb/9780199795574.013.9

Arnett, J. J., & Fishel, E. (2013). *When Will My Grown-up Kid Grow Up? Loving and Understanding Your Emerging Adult*. Workman Publishing.

Arnett, J. J., & Tanner, J. L. (2006). *Emerging adults in America: Coming of age in the 21st century*. Washington, DC: American Psychological Association.

Arnett, J., & Jensen, L. (2002). A congregation of one: Individualized religious beliefs among emerging adults. *Journal of Adolescent Research*, *17*(5), 451–467. doi:10.1177/0743558402175002

Arseth, A. K., Kroger, J., Martinussen, M., & Bakken, G. (2009). Intimacy status, attachment, separation-individuation patterns, and identity status in female university students. *Journal of Social and Personal Relationships*, *26*(5), 697–712. doi:10.1177/0265407509347927

Asberg, K. K., Bowers, C., Renk, K., & McKinney, C. (2008). A structural equation modeling approach to the study of stress and psychological adjustment in emerging adults. *Child Psychiatry and Human Development*, *39*(4), 481–501. doi:10.1007/s10578-008-0102-0

Ashcroft, J. (2001). *Stalking and domestic violence: A report to Congress (No. NCJ 186157)*. Washington, DC: U.S. Department of Justice.

Atkinson, R., & Flint, J. (2001). Accessing hidden and hard-to-reach populations: Snowball research strategies. *Social Research Update*, *33*(1), 1–4.

Attwood, F. (2005). What do people do with porn? Qualitative research into the consumption, use, and experience of pornography and other sexually explicit media. *Sexuality & Culture*, *9*(2), 65–86. doi:10.1007/s12119-005-1008-7

Avagianou, P. A., & Zafiropoulou, M. (2008). Parental bonding and depression: Personality as a mediating factor. *International Journal of Adolescent Medicine and Health*, *20*(3), 261–270. doi:10.1515/IJAMH.2008.20.3.261 PMID:19097563

Baams, L., Jonas, K. J., Utz, S., Bos, H. M. W., & van der Vuurst, L. (2013). Internet use and online social support among same sex attracted individuals of different ages. *Computers in Human Behavior*, *27*(5), 1820–1827. doi:10.1016/j.chb.2011.04.002

Badger, S., Nelson, L. J., & Barry, C. M. (2006). Perceptions of the transition to adulthood among Chinese and American emerging adults. *International Journal of Behavioral Development*, *30*(1), 84–93. doi:10.1177/0165025406062128

Baines, R. (2013). Translation, Globalization and the Elite Migrant Athlete. *The Translator*, *19*, 207-228.

Bakardjieva, M. (2003). Virtual togetherness: An everyday-life perspective. *Media Culture & Society*, *25*, 291–313. doi:10.1177/0163443703025003001

Balfe, M., Doyle, F., Smith, D., Sreenan, S., Brugha, R., Hevey, D., & Conroy, R. (2013). Whats distressing about having type 1 diabetes? A qualitative study of young adults perspectives. *BMC Endocrine Disorders*, *13*(1), 1–14. doi:10.1186/1472-6823-13-25

Bandura, A. (1977). *Social Learning Theory*. Englewood Cliffs, NJ: Prentice-Hall.

Bannink, R., Broeren, S., van de Looij-Jansen, P. M., de Waart, F. G., & Raat, H. (2014). Cyber and traditional bullying victimization as a risk factor for mental health problems in adolescents. *PLoS ONE*, *9*, e94026. doi:10.1371/journal.pone.0094026 PMID:24718563

Barak, A., Fisher, W. A., Belfry, S., & Lashambe, D. R. (1999). Sex, guys, and cyberspace: Effects of internet pornography and individual differences on mens attitudes toward women. *Journal of Psychology & Human Sexuality*, *11*(1), 63–91. doi:10.1300/J056v11n01_04

Barclay, D. C., Higgins, C., & Thompson, R. (1995). The partial least squares approach to causal modelling: Personal computer adoption and use as an illustration. *Technology Studies*, *2*, 285–308.

Bargh, J. A., McKenna, K. Y. A., & Fitzsimons, G. M. (2002). Can you see the real me? Activation and expression of the true self on the Internet. *The Journal of Social Issues*, *58*(1), 33–48. doi:10.1111/1540-4560.00247

Barker, E. D., Arseneault, L., Brendgen, M., Fontaine, N., & Maughan, B. (2008). Joint development of bullying and victimization in adolescence: Relations to delinquency and self-harm. *Journal of the American Academy of Child and Adolescent Psychiatry*, *47*(9), 1030–1038. PMID:18665001

Barker, V. (2009). Older adolescents motivations for social network site use: The influence of gender, group identity, and collective self-esteem. *Cyberpsychology & Behavior*, *12*(2), 209–213. doi:10.1089/cpb.2008.0228 PMID:19250021

Barrow, K. (2010, December 27). Difference is the norm on these dating sites. *The New York Times*. Retrieved from http://www.nytimes.com

Bartholomew, K., & Horowitz, L. M. (1991). Attachment styles among young adults: A test of a four-category model. *Journal of Personality and Social Psychology*, *61*(2), 226–244. doi:10.1037/0022-3514.61.2.226

Baum, K., Catalano, S. M., Kristina, R., & Michael, R. (2009). *Stalking victimization in the United States*. Washington, DC: Bereau of Justice Statistics. U.S. Department of Justice. Available from: https://www.justice.gov/sites/default/files/ovw/legacy/2012/08/15/bjs-stalking-rpt.pdf

Baumeister, R. F. (1993). Conceptions of self and identity: A modern retrospective on Allport's view. In K. H. Craik, R. Hogan, R. N. Wolfe, K. H. Craik, R. Hogan, & R. N. Wolfe (Eds.), *Fifty years of personality psychology* (pp. 177–186). New York, NY: Plenum Press. doi:10.1007/978-1-4899-2311-0_12

Baym, N. K. (1995). The emergence of community in computer-mediated interaction. In S. G. Jones (Ed.), *Cybersociety: Computer-mediated communication and community* (pp. 138–163). Thousand Oaks, CA: Sage.

Baym, N. K. (2001). Interpersonal life online. In S. Livingston & L. Lievrouw (Eds.), *The handbook of new media* (pp. 62–76). London: Sage.

Beaudoin, C. E., & Tao, C. C. (2007). Benefiting from social capital in online support groups: An empirical study of cancer patients. *Cyberpsychology & Behavior*, *10*(4), 587–590. doi:10.1089/cpb.2007.9986

Beck, A. T., & Steer, R. A. (1993). *Beck anxiety inventory manual*. San Antonio, TX: Harcourt Brace.

Beck, A. T., Steer, R. A., & Brown, G. K. (1996). *Manual for the beck inventory-II*. San Antonio, TX: Psychological Corporation.

Bender, J. L., Jimenez-Marroquin, M. C., & Jadad, A. R. (2011). Seeking support on facebook: A content analysis of breast cancer groups. *Journal of Medical Internet Research*, *13*(1), e16. doi:10.2196/jmir.1560

Bersamin, M. M., Zamboanga, B. L., Schwartz, S. J., Donnellan, M. B., Hudson, M., Weisskirch, R. S., & Caraway, S. J. (2014). Risky business: Is there an association between casual sex and mental health among emerging adults? *Journal of Sex Research*, *51*(1), 43–51. doi:10.1080/00224499.2013.772088

Berzonsky, M. D. (2003a). Identity style and well-being: Does commitment matter? *Identity*, *3*(2), 131–142. doi:10.1207/S1532706XID030203

Berzonsky, M. D. (2003b). The structure of identity: Commentary on Jane Krogers view of identity status transition. *Identity*, *3*(3), 231–245. doi:10.1207/S1532706XID0303_04

Bickley, S. R. (1990). Dental hygienists' attitudes towards dental care for people with a mental handicap and the perceptions of adequacy of their training. *Dental Education*, *168*, 361–364.

Bigham, D. S. (2012). Emerging adulthood in sociolinguists. *Language and linguistics. Compass*, *6*, 533–544. doi:10.1002/lnc3.350

Birkett, M., Espelage, D., & Koenig, B. (2009). LGB and questioning students in schools: The moderating effects of homophobic bullying and school climate on negative outcomes. *Journal of Youth and Adolescence*, *38*(7), 989–1000. doi:10.1007/s10964-008-9389-1 PMID:19636741

Birtchnell, J., Hammond, S., Horn, E., De Jong, C., & Kalaitzaki, A. (2013). A cross-national comparison of a shorter version of the Persons Relating to Others Questionnaire. *Clinical Psychology & Psychotherapy*, *20*(1), 36–48. doi:10.1002/cpp.789 PMID:21960317

Blackhart, G. C., Fitzpatrick, J., & Williamson, J. (2014). Dispositional factors predicting use of online dating sites and behaviors related to online dating. *Computers in Human Behavior*, *33*, 113–118. doi:10.1016/j.chb.2014.01.022

Blanchard, A. L. (2007). Developing a sense of virtual community measure. *CyberPsychology & Behaviour*, *10*(6), 827–830. doi:10.1089/cpb.2007.9946 PMID:18085972

Blodgett, A. T., Schinke, R. J., McGannon, K. R., Caholic, D. A., Enosse, L., Peltier, D., & Pheasant, C. (2014). Navigating the inseder-outsider hyphen: A qualitative exploration of the acculturation challenges on aboriginal athletes pursuing sport in Euro-Canadian context. *Psychology of Sport and Exercise*, *15*(4), 345–355. doi:10.1016/j.psychsport.2014.02.009

Blood, G. W., Blood, I. M., & Danhauer, J. L. (1978). Listeners impressions of normal-hearing and hearing-impaired children. *Journal of Communication Disorders*, *11*(6), 513–518. doi:10.1016/0021-9924(78)90025-4 PMID:739066

Blood, I. M. (1997). The hearing aid effect: Challenges for counseling. *Journal of Rehabilitation*, *63*, 59–62.

Bloom, J. R., & Kessler, L. (1994). Emotional support following cancer: A test of the stigma and social activity hypotheses. *Journal of Health and Social Behavior*, *35*(2), 118–133. doi:10.2307/2137360

Blumler, J. G., & Katz, E. (Eds.). (1974). *The Uses of Mass Communications: Current Perspectives on Gratifications Research* (Vol. 3). Beverly Hills, CA: Sage Annual Reviews of Communication Research.

Bocij, P. (2006). *The Dark Side Of The Internet*. Greenwood Publishing Group.

Bolding, G., Davis, M., Hart, G., Sherr, L., & Elford, J. (2007). Where young MSM meet their first sexual partner: The role of the Internet. *AIDS and Behavior*, *11*(4), 522–526. doi:10.1007/s10461-007-9224-9 PMID:17347876

Bollen, K. A., & Curran, P. J. (2006). *Latent curve models: A structural equation perspective*. New York, NY: Wiley.

Bolt, J. (2010, August 9). How to Wreck Your Self Esteem: Compare Yourself with Others. *Psychology Today*. Retrieved from http://www.psychologytoday.com/blog/your-zesty- self/201008/how-wreck-your-self-esteem-compare-youself-others

Bond, B. J., Hefner, V., & Drogos, K. L. (2009). Information-seeking practices during the sexual development of lesbian, gay, and bisexual individuals: The influence and effects of coming out in a mediated environment. *Sexuality & Culture*, *13*(1), 32–50. doi:10.1007/s12119-008-9041-y

Bos, H. M., Sandfort, T. G., de Bruyn, E. H., & Hakvoort, E. M. (2008). Same-sex attraction, social relationships, psychosocial functioning, and school performance in early adolescence. *Developmental Psychology*, *44*(1), 59–68. doi:10.1037/0012-1649.44.1.59 PMID:18194005

Bowe, G. (2010). Reading Romance: The impact Facebook Rituals can have on a Romantic Relationship. *Journal of Comparative Research in Anthropology & Sociology*, *1*(2), 61–77.

Bowker, N. I. (2010). Understanding barriers to online experience for people with physical and sensory disabilities using discursive social psychology. *Universal Access in the Information Society*, *9*(2), 121–136. doi:10.1007/s10209-009-0162-3

Bowlby, J. (1969). Attachment and loss:Vol. I.*Attachment*. New York, NY: Basic Books.

boyd, d. & Ellison, N. (2007): Social network sites: Definition, history, and scholarship. *Journal of Computer-Mediated Communication, 13*(1).

boyd, d. (2014). *It's complicated: The social lives of networked teens*. New Haven, CT: Yale University Press.

boyd, d., & Heer, J. (2006, January). Profiles as conversation: Networked identity performance on Friendster. In *System Sciences, 2006. HICSS'06. Proceedings of the 39th Annual Hawaii International Conference on* (Vol. 3, pp. 59c-59c). IEEE.

Boyle, A. M., & O'Sullivan, L. F. (2016). Staying connected: Computer-mediated and face-to-face communication in college students' dating relationships. *Cyberpsychology, Behavior, and Social Networking*, *19*(5), 299–307. doi:10.1089/cyber.2015.0293

Bradshaw, C., Kahn, A. S., & Saville, B. K. (2010). To hook up or date: Which gender benefits? *Sex Roles*, *62*(9-10), 661–669. doi:10.1007/s11199-010-9765-7

Braithwaite, S. R., Coulson, G., Keddington, K., & Fincham, F. D. (2015). The influence of pornography on sexual scripts and hooking up among emerging adults in college. *Archives of Sexual Behavior*, *44*(1), 111–123. doi:10.1007/s10508-014-0351-x

Braithwaite, S. R., Delevi, R., & Fincham, F. D. (2010). Romantic relationships and the physical and mental health of college students. *Personal Relationships*, *17*(1), 1–12. doi:10.1111/j.1475-6811.2010.01248.x

Brandão, M. R. F., Magnani, A., Tega, E., & Medina, J. P. (2013). Além da cultura nacional: O expatriado no futebol. *Revista Brasileira Ciência e Movimento*, *21*(2), 177–182. doi:10.18511/0103-1716/rbcm.v21n2p177-182

Brault, M. W. (2012, July). *Americans with disabilities: 2010. Current Population Reports*. Retrieved from http://www.census.gov/prod/2012pubs/p70- 131.pdf

Braun-Courville, D. K., & Rojas, M. (2009). Exposure to sexually explicit websites and adolescent sexual attitudes and behaviors. *The Journal of Adolescent Health*, *45*(2), 156–162. doi:10.1016/j.jadohealth.2008.12.004

Brenick, A., & Killen, M. (2014). Moral judgments about Jewish–Arab intergroup exclusion: The role of cultural identity and contact. *Developmental Psychology*, *50*(1), 86–99. doi:10.1037/a0034702 PMID:24188040

Brenick, A., & Romano, K. (2016). Perceived peer and parent outgroup norms, cultural identity, and adolescents reasoning about peer intergroup exclusion. *Child Development*, *87*(5), 1392–1408. doi:10.1111/cdev.12594 PMID:27684394

Brenner, J. (2012). *Social networking*. Pew Internet and American Life Project. http://pewinternet.org/Commentary/2012/March/Pew-Internet-Social-Networking-fulldetail.aspx

Bridges, A. J., Wosnitzer, R., Scharrer, E., Sun, C., & Liberman, R. (2010). Aggression and sexual behavior in best-selling pornography videos: A content analysis update. *Violence Against Women*, *16*(10), 1065–1085. doi:10.1177/1077801210382866

Brighi, A., Melotti, G., Guarini, A., Genta, M. L., Ortega, R., Mora-Merchan, J., … Thompson, F. (2012). Self-esteem and loneliness in relation to cyberbullying in three European countries. In Q. Ling, D. Cross, & P. K. Smith (Eds.), Cyberbullying in the global playground (pp. 52-56). West Sussex, UK: Blackwell Publishing.

Brislin, R. W. (1970). Back-translation for cross-cultural research. *Journal of Cross-Cultural Psychology*, *1*(3), 185–216. doi:10.1177/135910457000100301

Brockhage, K., & Phillips, K. E. (2016). (Re)negotiating our relationship: How contradictions emerge in sibling privacy boundaries. *The Southern Communication Journal*, *81*(2), 79–91. doi:10.1080/1041794X.2015.1095231

Brod, M., Kongso, J. H., Lessard, S., & Christensen, T. L. (2009). Psychological insulin resistance: Patient beliefs and implications for diabetes management. *Quality of Life Research: An International Journal of Quality of Life Aspects of Treatment, Care and Rehabilitation*, *18*(1), 23–32. doi:10.1007/s11136-008-9419-1

Bronk, K. C. (2011). The role of purpose in life in healthy identity formation: A grounded model. *New Directions for Youth Development*, *132*(132), 31–44. doi:10.1002/yd.426 PMID:22275277

Brooks-Gunn, J., & Paikoff, R. (1993). *Sex is a gamble, kissing is a game: Adolescent sexuality and health promotion. In Promoting the health of adolescents: New directions for the twenty-first century* (pp. 180–208). New York, NY: Oxford University Press.

Brown, J. D., & LEngle, K. L. (2009). X-rated sexual attitudes and behaviors associated with US early adolescents exposure to sexually explicit media. *Communication Research*, *36*(1), 129–151. doi:10.1177/0093650208326465

Brown, K. W., & Ryan, R. M. (2003). The benefits of being present: Mindfulness and its role in psychological well-being. *Journal of Personality and Social Psychology*, *84*(4), 822–848. doi:10.1037/0022-3514.84.4.822 PMID:12703651

Brown, L. (2009). A failure of communication on the cross-cultural campus. *Journal of Studies in International Education*, *13*(4), 439–454. doi:10.1177/1028315309331913

Brownstein, A. (2000). In the campus shadows, women are stalkers as well as the stalked. *The Chronicle of Higher Education*, *47*(15), 40–42.

Buhi, E. R., Daley, E., Oberne, A., Smith, S., Schneider, T., & Fuhrmann, H. (2010). Quality and accuracy of sexual health information web sites visited by young people. *The Journal of Adolescent Health*, *47*(2), 206–208. doi:10.1016/j.jadohealth.2010.01.002 PMID:20638014

Burke, M., Marlow, C., & Thomas, L. (2010). Social Networking Activity and Social Wellbeing. *CHI 2010 April 10-15*. Atlanta, GA: CHI.

Burkett, M. (2015). Sex(t) talk: A qualitative analysis of young adults negotiations of the pleasures and perils of sexting. *Sexuality & Culture: An Interdisciplinary Quarterly*, *19*(4), 835–863. doi:10.1007/s12119-015-9295-0

Butler, J. (1993). *Bodies that matter: On the discursive limits of sex*. London: Routledge.

Butler, J. (1999). *Gender trouble. Feminism and the subversion of identity*. New York: Routledge.

Byers, E. S., & Demmons, S. (1999). Sexual satisfaction and sexual self-disclosure within dating relationships. *Journal of Sex Research*, *36*(2), 180–189. doi:10.1080/00224499909551983

Cane, D. B., & Gotlib, I. H. (1985). Implicit conceptualizations of depression: Implications for an interpersonal perspective. *Social Cognition*, *3*(4), 341–368. doi:10.1521/soco.1985.3.4.341

Cao, L., David, P., & Bathhurst, R. (2012). Social support network and use of SNSs among Chinese international students: An exploratory study in New Zealand. *Information Engineering Letters*, *2*, 2160–4114. doi:10.5729/iel.vol2.issue4.29

Caplan, S. E. (2005). A social skill account of problematic Internet use. *Journal of Communication*, *55*(4), 721–736. doi:10.1111/j.1460-2466.2005.tb03019.x

Caplan, S. E. (2010). Theory and measurement of generalized problematic Internet use: A two-step approach. *Computers in Human Behavior*, *25*(5), 1089–1097. doi:10.1016/j.chb.2010.03.012

Caplan, S., Williams, D., & Yee, N. (2009). Problematic Internet use and psychosocial well-being among MMO players. *Computers in Human Behavior*, *25*(6), 1312–1319. doi:10.1016/j.chb.2009.06.006

Cappadocia, M. C., Craig, W. M., & Pepler, D. (2013). Cyberbullying: Prevalence, stability and risk factors during adolescence. *Canadian Journal of School Psychology*, *28*, 171–192.

Carroll, J. S., Padilla-Walker, L. M., Nelson, L. J., Olson, C. D., Barry, C. M., & Madsen, S. D. (2008). Generation XXX: Pornography acceptance and use among emerging adults. *Journal of Adolescent Research*, *23*(1), 6–30. doi:10.1177/0743558407306348

Carroll, J. S., Willoughby, B., Badger, S., Nelson, L. J., Barry, C. M., & Madsen, S. D. (2007). So close, yet so far away: The impact of varying marital horizons on emerging adulthood. *Journal of Adolescent Research*, *22*(3), 219–247. doi:10.1177/0743558407299697

Carson, R. (2014). *Adolescent cyberbullying in New Zealnd and the implications of parenting styles* (Unpublished doctoral thesis). University of Canterbury.

Case, A. (2010, December). *Amber Case: We are all cyborgs now* [video file]. Retrieved from https://www.ted.com/talks/amber_case_we_are_all_cyborgs_now/transcript?language=en

Cassidy, J. (2001). Truth, lies, and intimacy: An attachment perspective. *Attachment & Human Development*, *3*(2), 121–155. doi:10.1080/14616730110058999 PMID:11708734

Celizic, M. (2009). *Her Teen Committed Suicide Over Sexting*. Retrieved from http://www.today.com/parents/her-teen-committed-suicide-over-sexting-2D80555048#.VRwMLvnF-So

Center for Disease Control and Prevention (CDC). (2011). *Self-directed violence surveillance: Uniform definitions and recommended data elements*. Retrieved from: http://www.cdc.gov/violenceprevention/pdf/SelfDirected-Violence-a.pdf

Centers for Disease Control & Prevention. (2016). *HIV Among Youth.* Retrieved from http://www.cdc.gov/hiv/group/age/youth/

Chang, Y. Y. (2010). Are you my guest or my child? Mothers uncertainties in interacting with their returnee children in China. *Chinese Journal of Communication*, *3*(2), 167–184. doi:10.1080/17544751003740367

Chapman, J., Turner, W., & Prochnow, J. (2000). Early reading related to performance, reading self-concept and the development of academic self-concept. *Journal of Educational Psychology*, *92*(4), 703–708. doi:10.1037/0022-0663.92.4.703

Chapple, A., Ziebland, S., & McPherson, A. (2004). Stigma, shame, and blame experienced by patients with lung cancer: Qualitative study. *British Medical Journal*, *328*(7454), 1470–1473. doi:10.1136/bmj.38111.639734.7C

Check, J. V., & Malamuth, N. M. (1986). Pornography and sexual aggression: A social learning theory analysis. *Annals of the International Communication Association*, *9*(1), 181–213. doi:10.1080/23808985.1986.11678607

Chen, L. K. (2009). Negotiating identity between career and family roles: A study of international graduate students wives in the US. *International Journal of Lifelong Education*, *28*(2), 211–226. doi:10.1080/02601370902757075

Chen, R. K., Brodwin, M. G., Cardoso, E., & Chan, F. (2002). Attitudes toward people with disabilities in the social context of dating and marriage: A comparison of American, Taiwanese, and Singaporean college students. *Journal of Rehabilitation*, *68*, 5–11.

Chen, Y., & Katz, J. E. (2009). Extending family to school life: College students use of the mobile phone. *International Journal of Human-Computer Studies*, *67*(2), 179–191. doi:10.1016/j.ijhcs.2008.09.002

Chesney, M. A., & Smith, A. W. (1999). Critical delays in HIV testing and care: The potential role of stigma. *The American Behavioral Scientist*, *42*(7), 1162–1174. doi:10.1177/00027649921954822

Cheung, B. Y., Chudek, M., & Heine, S. J. (2011). Evidence for a sensitive period for acculturation: Younger immigrants report acculturating at faster rate. *Psychological Science*, *22*(2), 146–152. doi:10.1177/0956797610394661 PMID:21189354

Child, J. T., & Westermann, D. A. (2013). Lets be Facebook friends: Exploring parental Facebook friend requests from a Communication Privacy Management (CPM) perspective. *Journal of Family Communication*, *13*(1), 46–59. doi:10.1080/15267431.2012.742089

Chin, W. W. (1998). The partial least squares approach for structural equation modelling. In G. A. Marcoulides (Ed.), Modern Methods for Business Research (pp. 295-336). London: Lawrence Erlbaum Associates.

Ciampa, A. C., Leme, C. G., & Souza, R. F. (2010). Considerações sobre a formação e transformação da identidade profissional de atleta de futebol no Brasil. *Diversidade. Perspectiva em Psicologia*, *6*, 27–36.

Clark University Poll of Emerging Adults. (2015). *Work, Education and Identity*. Worcester, MA: Clark University.

Clark, L. S. (2011). Parental mediation theory for the digital age. *Communication Theory*, *21*(4), 323–343. doi:10.1111/j.1468-2885.2011.01391.x

Clemens, C., Atkin, D., & Krishnan, A. (2015). The influence of biological and personality traits on gratification obtained through online dating websites. *Computers in Human Behavior*, *49*, 120–129. doi:10.1016/j.chb.2014.12.058

Cloninger, C. R., Svrakic, D. M., & Przybeck, T. R. (1993). A psychobiological model of temperament and character. *Archives of General Psychiatry*, *50*(12), 975–990. doi:10.1001/archpsyc.1993.01820240059008 PMID:8250684

Coleman, E. (2011). Impulsive/compulsive sexual behavior: Assessment and treatment. The Oxford Handbook of Impulse Control Disorders, 375.

Coleman, J. M., Brunell, A. B., & Haugen, I. M. (2015). Multiple forms of prejudice: How gender and disability stereotypes influence judgments of disabled men and women. *Current Psychology (New Brunswick, N.J.)*, *34*(1), 177–189. doi:10.1007/s12144-014-9250-5

Coleman, J. S. (1988). Social Capital in the Creation of Human Capital. *American Journal of Sociology*, *94*, S95–S120. doi:10.1086/228943

Collins, N. (1996). *Revised Adult Attachment Scale* [Measurement Instrument]. Retrieved from https://labs.psych.ucsb.edu/collins/nancy/UCSB_Close_Relationships_Lab/Resources_files/Adult%20Attachment%20Scale.doc

Collins, W. A. (2003). More than myth: The developmental significance of romantic relationships during adolescence. *Journal of Research on Adolescence*, *13*(1), 1–24. doi:10.1111/1532-7795.1301001

Collins, W., & Laursen, B. (2004). Changing relationships, changing youth. *The Journal of Early Adolescence*, *24*(1), 55–62. doi:10.1177/0272431603260882

Confederação Brasileira de Futebol. (2015, Março 15). Retrieved from http://www.cbf.com.br/stjd/publicacoes-pautas#.VYA3V-eXHeQ

Cooney, G., Jahoda, A., Gumley, A., & Knott, F. (2006). Young people with learning disabilities attending mainstream and segregated schooling: Perceived stigma, social comparisons and future aspirations. *Journal of Intellectual Disability Research*, *50*(6), 432–445. doi:10.1111/j.1365-2788.2006.00789.x

Cooper, R. M., & Blumenfeld, W. J. (2012). Responses to cyberbullying: A descriptive analysis of the frequency of and impact on LGBT and allied youth. *Journal of LGBT Youth*, *9*(2), 153–177. doi:10.1080/19361653.2011.649616

Copes, H., Kerley, K., Huff, R., & Kane, J. (2010). Differentiating identity theft: An exploratory study of victims using a national victimization survey. *Journal of Criminal Justice*, *38*(5), 1045–1052. doi:10.1016/j.jcrimjus.2010.07.007

Corbin, J., & Strauss, A. (2008). *Basics of qualitative research: Grounded theory procedure and techniques* (3rd ed.). Newbury Park, CA: Sage. doi:10.4135/9781452230153

Correa, T., Hinsley, A. W., & Gil de Zuniga, H. (2010). Who Interacts on the Web? The Intersection of Users Personality and Social Media Use. *Computers in Human Behavior*, *26*(2), 247–253. doi:10.1016/j.chb.2009.09.003

Cote, J. E. (2009). *Identity formation and self-development in adolescence*. In R. M. Lerner & L. D. Steinberg (Eds.), Handbook of adolescent psychology (3rd ed.; pp. 266–304). Hoboken, NJ: John Wiley & Sons, Inc.

Cottingham, R. (2007, June 23). *"On Facebook, nobody knows…"* [web log post; cartoon]. Retrieved from http://www.socialsignal.com/blog/rob-cottingham/on-facebook-nobody-knows

Couch, D., & Liamputtong, P. (2008). Online dating and mating: The use of the Internet to meet sexual partners. *Qualitative Health Research*, *18*(2), 268–279. doi:10.1177/1049732307312832 PMID:18216345

Cowie, H. (2013). Cyberbullying and its impact on young peoples emotional health and well-being. *Psychiatrist*, *37*(5), 167–170. doi:10.1192/pb.bp.112.040840

Coyne, S. M., Padilla-Walker, L. M., & Howard, E. (2013). Emerging in a digital world: A decade review of media use, effects, and gratifications in emerging adulthood. *Emerging Adulthood*, *1*(2), 125–137. doi:10.1177/2167696813479782

Crawford, M., & Popp, D. (2003). Sexual double standards: A review and methodological critique of two decades of research. *Journal of Sex Research*, *40*(1), 13–26. doi:10.1080/00224490309552163

Crosslin, K. L., & Crosslin, M. B. (2014). Cyberbullying at a Texas university—A mixed-methods approach to examining online aggression. *Texas Public Health Journal*, *66*, 26–31.

Crystal, D. S., Killen, M., & Ruck, M. (2008). It is who you know that counts: Intergroup contact and judgments about race-based exclusion. *The British Journal of Developmental Psychology*, *26*(1), 51–70. doi:10.1348/026151007X198910 PMID:25505355

Cuadrado, E., Tabernero, C., & Briones, E. (2014). Dispositional and psychosocial variables as longitudinal predictors of acculturative stress. *Applied Psychology*, *63*(3), 441–479. doi:10.1111/j.1464-0597.2012.00531.x

D'Ovidio, R., & Doyle, J. (2003). A study on cyberstalking: Understanding investigative hurdles. *FBI Law Enforcement Bulletin*, *72*(3), 10–17.

Dake, J., Price, J., Maziarz, L., & Ward, B. (2012). Prevalence and correlates of sexting behavior in adolescents. *American Journal of Sexuality Education*, *7*(1), 1–15. doi:10.1080/15546128.2012.650959

Damo, A. S. (2007). *Do dom à profissão: a formação de futebolistas no Brasil e na França*. São Paulo: Anpocs.

Damo, A. S. (2014). Training soccer players in Brazil. *Soccer and Society*, *15*(1), 93–107. doi:10.1080/14660970.2013.854570

Damon, W., Menon, J., & Cotton, B. K. (2003). The development of purpose during adolescence. *Applied Developmental Science*, *7*(3), 119–128. doi:10.1207/S1532480XADS0703_2

DAugelli, A. R. (2012). Restoring Lives: Developmental Research on Sexual Orientation. *Human Development*, *55*(1), 1–3. doi:10.1159/000336251

Davis, K. (2010). Coming of age online: The developmental underpinnings of girls blogs. *Journal of Adolescent Research*, *25*(1), 145–171. doi:10.1177/0743558409350503

Davis, K. (2012a). Friendship 2.0: Adolescents experiences of belonging and self-disclosure online. *Journal of Adolescence*, *35*(6), 1527–1536. doi:10.1016/j.adolescence.2012.02.013 PMID:22475444

Davis, K. (2012b). Tensions of identity in a networked era: Young peoples perspectives on the risks and rewards of online self-expression. *New Media & Society*, *14*(4), 634–651. doi:10.1177/1461444811422430

Davis, K. (2013). Young peoples digital lives: The impact of interpersonal relationships and digital media use on adolescents sense of identity. *Computers in Human Behavior*, *29*(6), 2281–2293. doi:10.1016/j.chb.2013.05.022

Davis, K. (2014). Youth identities in a digital age: The anchoring role of friends in youth's approaches to online identity expression. In A. Bennett & B. Robards (Eds.), *Mediated youth cultures: The internet, belonging, and new cultural configurations* (pp. 11–25). New York, NY: Palgrave Macmillan. doi:10.1057/9781137287021_2

Davis, R. A. (2001). A cognitive-behavioral model of pathological Internet use. *Computers in Human Behavior*, *17*(2), 187–195. doi:10.1016/S0747-5632(00)00041-8

De Beauvoir, S. (1989). *The second sex*. New York: Vintage Books.

De Ganck, J., & Vanheule, S. (2015). Bad boys dont cry: A thematic analysis of interpersonal dynamics in interview narratives of young offenders with psychopathic traits. *Frontiers in Psychology*, *6*, 1–11. doi:10.3389/fpsyg.2015.00960 PMID:26217279

De Lauretis, T. (1991). Queer theory. Lesbian and gay sexualities. *Differences: A Journal of Feminist Cultural Studies*, *3*(2), 3–18.

De Valck, K., Van Bruggen, G. H., & Wierenga, B. (2009). Virtual communities: A marketing perspective. *Decision Support Systems*, *47*(3), 185–203. doi:10.1016/j.dss.2009.02.008

Deci, E. L., & Ryan, R. M. (2002). *Handbook of self-determination research*. Rochester, NY: University of Rochester Press.

DeHann, S., Kuper, L. E., Magee, J. C., Bigelow, L., & Mustanski, B. S. (2013). The interplay between online and offline explorations of identity, relationships, and sex: A mixed-method study with LGBT youth. *Journal of Sex Research*, *50*(5), 421–434. doi:10.1080/00224499.2012.661489 PMID:22489658

Delevi, R., & Weisskirch, R. (2012). Its ovr b/n u n me: Technology use, attachment styles, and gender roles in relationship dissolution. *Cyberpsychology, Behavior, and Social Networking*, *15*(9), 486–490. doi:10.1089/cyber.2012.0169 PMID:22823329

Delevi, R., & Weisskirch, R. (2013). Attachment style and conflict resolution skills predicting technology use in relationship dissolution. *Computers in Human Behavior*, *29*(6), 2530–2534. doi:10.1016/j.chb.2013.06.027

Derogatis, L. R. (1993). *BSI, Brief Symptom Inventory: Administration, scoring & procedures manual*. Minneapolis, MN: National Computer Systems.

Derogatis, L. R. (2001). *Brief Symptom Inventory (BSI)-18. Administration, scoring and procedures manual*. Minneapolis, MN: NCS Pearson, Inc.

DeSousa, D. A., Salum, G. A., Isolan, R. L., & Manfro, G. G. (2013). Sensitivity and Specificity of the Screen for Child Anxiety Related Emotional Disorders (SCARED): A Community-Based Study. *Child Psychiatry and Human Development*, *44*(3), 391–399. doi:10.1007/s10578-012-0333-y PMID:22961135

Dewing, M. (2010). *Social media: Who uses them?* Library of Parliament Background Paper. Retrieved from publications.gc.ca/site/eng/370191/publication.html

Dholakia, U. M., Bagozzi, R., & Pearo, L. (2004). A social influence model of consumer participation in network and small group based virtual communities. *International Journal of Research in Marketing*, *21*(3), 241–263. doi:10.1016/j.ijresmar.2003.12.004

Dilmac, N. (2009). Psychological needs as a predict of cyber bullying: A preliminary report on college students. *Educational Sciences: Theory and Practice*, *9*(3), 1307–1325.

Dir, A. L., & Cyders, M. A. (2015). Risks, risk factors, and outcomes associated with phone and Internet sexting among university students in the United States. *Archives of Sexual Behavior*, *44*(6), 1675–1684. doi:10.1007/s10508-014-0370-7 PMID:25358950

Douglass, C. B. (2007). From Duty to Desire: Emerging Adulthood in Europe and Its Consequences. *Child Development Perspectives*, *1*(2), 101–108. doi:10.1111/j.1750-8606.2007.00023.x

Downes, M., Varner, I. I., & Masoud, H. (2010). Indvidual profile as predictors of expatriate effectiveness. *International Business Journal*, *20*, 235–247.

Downey, G., & Feldman, S. (1996). Implications of rejection sensitivity for intimate relationships. *Journal of Personality and Social Psychology*, *70*(6), 1327–1343. doi:10.1037/0022-3514.70.6.1327 PMID:8667172

Downey, G., Freitas, A., Michaelis, B., & Khouri, H. (1998). The self-fulfilling prophecy in close relationships: Rejection sensitivity and rejection by romantic partners. *Journal of Personality and Social Psychology*, *75*(2), 545–560. doi:10.1037/0022-3514.75.2.545 PMID:9731324

Downey, G., Nesdale, D., Trevaskis, S., & Zimmer-Gembeck, M. (2014). Relational victimization, loneliness and depressive symptoms: Indirect associations via self and peer reports of rejection sensitivity. *Journal of Youth and Adolescence*, *43*(4), 568–582. doi:10.1007/s10964-013-9993-6 PMID:23955324

Dreßing, H., Bailer, J., Anders, A., Wagner, H., & Gallas, C. (2014). Cyberstalking in a large sample of social network users: Prevalence, characteristics, and impact upon victims. *Cyberpsychology, Behavior, and Social Networking*, *17*(2), 61–67. doi:10.1089/cyber.2012.0231

Drouin, M., & Landgraff, C. (2012). Texting, sexting, and attachment in college students romantic relationships. *Computers in Human Behavior*, *28*(2), 444–449. doi:10.1016/j.chb.2011.10.015

Drouin, M., Ross, J., & Tobin, E. (2015). Sexting: A new, digital vehicle for intimate partner aggression? *Computers in Human Behavior*, *50*, 197–204. doi:10.1016/j.chb.2015.04.001

Drouin, M., & Tobin, E. (2014). Unwanted but consensual sexting among young adults: Relations with attachment and sexual motivations. *Computers in Human Behavior*, *31*, 412–418. doi:10.1016/j.chb.2013.11.001

Drouin, M., Vogel, K. N., Surbey, A., & Stills, J. R. (2013). Lets talk about sexting, baby: Computer-mediated sexual behaviors among young adults. *Computers in Human Behavior*, *29*(5), A25–A30. doi:10.1016/j.chb.2012.12.030

Drushel, B. E. (2010). Virtually supportive: Self-disclosure of minority sexualities through online social networking sites. In C. Pullen & M. Cooper (Eds.), *LGBT Identity and Online New Media* (pp. 62–72). New York: Routledge.

Duggan, M., Ellison, N. B., Lampe, C., Lenhart, A., & Madden, M. (2015). Social media update 2014. Washington, DC: Pew Research Center. Retrieved from http://www.pewinternet.org/2015/01/09/social-media-update-2014/

Dunbar, R. (1998). *Grooming, Gossiping and the Evolution of Language*. Cambridge, MA: Harvard University Press.

Dunn, D. (2015). *The social psychology of disability*. New York: Oxford University Press.

Dutra-Thomé, L. (2013). *Emerging adulthoodin Southern Brazilians from differing socioeconomic status: social e subjective markers* (Unpublished doctoral dissertation). Universidade Federal do Rio Grande do Sul, Porto Alegre, Brazil.

Dutra-Thomé, L., & Koller, S. H. (2014). Emerging adulthood in brazilians of differing socioeconomic status: Transition to adulthood. *Paidéia*, *24*, 313–322.

Dutra-Thomé, L., Koller, S. H., McWhirter, E., & McWhirter, B. (2015). Application of the Future Expectation Scale for Adolescents (FESA) in Brazil. *Psicologia: Reflexão e Crítica*, *28*(2), 331–339. doi:10.1590/1678-7153.201528213

Edegoh, L. O. N., Asemah, E. S., & Ekanem, I. B. (2013). Facebook and Relationship Management among Students of Anambra State University, Uli, Nigeria. *International Review of Social Sciences and Humanities*, *6*(1), 205–216.

Edmunds, A. (2014). *Weekly Publication: San Diego Divorce Center, The Edmunds Law Firm*. Retrieved September 13, 2015, from Available at www.sandiegodivorcecenter.com/category/press-releases

Edwards, G., & Barber, B. (2010). The relationship between rejection sensitivity and compliant condom use. *Archives of Sexual Behavior*, *39*(6), 1381–1388. doi:10.1007/s10508-009-9520-8 PMID:19760145

Ekbia, H., & Nardi, B. A. (2012). Inverse instrumentality: How technologies objectify patients and players. In P. Leonardi, B. Nardi, & J. Kallinikos (Eds.), Materiality and organizing: social interactions in a technological world. Oxford, UK: Oxford University Press.

Ekpo, S. (1996). *Juvenile Delinquency in Nigeria*. ABBNNY Educational Publishers.

Eliason, M. J., & Schope, R. (2007). Shifting sands or solid foundation? Lesbian, gay, bisexual, and transgender identity formation. In The health of sexual minorities (pp. 3-26). Springer US.

Ellison, N. B., Heino, R., & Gibbs, J. (2006). Managing Impression Online: Self-Presentation Process in the Online Dating Environment. *Journal of Computer-Mediated Communication*, *11*(2), 415–441. doi:10.1111/j.1083-6101.2006.00020.x

Ellison, N. B., Steinfield, C., & Lampe, C. (2007). The benefits of Facebook friends: Social capital and college students use of online social network sites. *Journal of Computer-Mediated Communication*, *12*(4), 1143–1168. doi:10.1111/j.1083-6101.2007.00367.x

Elphinston, R. A., & Noller, P. (2011). Time to Face It! Facebook Intrusion and the Implications for Romantic Jealousy and Relationship Satisfaction. *Cyberpsychology, Behavior, and Social Networking*, *14*(11), 631–635. doi:10.1089/cyber.2010.0318 PMID:21548798

Erikson, E. H. (1950). *Childhood and society* (1st ed.). New York, NY: Norton.

Erikson, E. H. (1968). *Identity, youth, and crisis* (1st ed.). New York, NY: Norton.

Erikson, E. H. (1968).*Identity: Youth and crisis*. New York, NY: Norton; doi:10.1007/978-0-387-31334-4_1

Erikson, E. H. (1980). *Identity and the life cycle*. New York, NY: Norton.

Erikson, E. H. (1997). *The life cycle completed*. New York: W. W. Norton.

Erosheva, E. A., Kim, H.-J., Emlet, C., & Fredriksen-Goldsen, K. I. (2016). Social networks of lesbian, gay, bisexual, and transgender older adults. *Research on Aging*, *38*(1), 98–123. doi:10.1177/0164027515581859 PMID:25882129

Erozkan, A. (2009). Rejection sensitivity levels with respect to attachment styles, gender, and parenting styles: A study with Turkish students. *Social Behavior and Personality*, *37*(1), 1–14. doi:10.2224/sbp.2009.37.1.1

Espelage, D. L., & Swearer, S. M. (2008). Addressing research gaps in the intersection between homophobia and bullying. *School Psychology Review*, *37*(2), 155–159.

Evans, A. B., & Stead, D. E. (2014). Its long way to the super leaguw: The experiences of Australisian professional rugby league migrants in the United Kingdon. *International Review for the Sociology of Sport*, *49*(6), 707–727. doi:10.1177/1012690212464700

Eyal, K., & Kunkel, D. (2008). The effects of sex in television drama shows on emerging adults sexual attitudes and moral judgments. *Journal of Broadcasting & Electronic Media*, *52*(2), 161–181. doi:10.1080/08838150801991757

Facebook. (2015). *Terms of service*. Retrieved from https://www.facebook.com/legal/terms

Fagundes, C. P. (2012). Getting over you: Contributions of attachment theory for postbreakup emotional adjustment. *Personal Relationships*, *19*, 37–50.

Fairbairn, J., Bivens, R., & Dawson, M. (2013). *Sexual Violence and Social Media: Building a Framework for Prevention*. Ottawa: Crime Prevention Ottawa.

Falk, R. F., & Miller, N. B. (1992). *A primer for soft modeling*. Akron, OH: University of Akron Press.

Fardouly, J., Diedrichs, P. C., Vartanian, L. R., & Halliwell, E. (2015). Social comparison on social media: The impact of Facebook on young womans body image concern and mood. *Body Image*, *13*, 38–45. doi:10.1016/j.bodyim.2014.12.002

Farrugia, R. C. (2013). *Facebook and Relationships: A Study of How Social Media Use is Affecting Long – Term Relationships*. Rochester Institute of Technology.

Fearnow, B. (2014, May 25). *Study: Facebook Users Who Share Too Much Information More Lonely, Depressed*. Retrieved August 9, 2016, from CBS Atlanta: http://atlanta.cbslocal.com/2014/05/25/study-facebook-users-who-share-too-much-information-more-lonely-depressed/

Feeney, J. A., & Noller, P. (1990). Attachment style as a predictor of adult romantic relationships. *Journal of Personality and Social Psychology*, *58*(2), 281–291. doi:10.1037/0022-3514.58.2.281

Feinstein, B. A., Bhatia, V., & Davila, J. (2014). Rumination mediates the association between cybervictimization and depressive symptoms. *Journal of Interpersonal Violence*, *29*(9), 1732–1746. doi:10.1177/0886260513511534 PMID:24346650

Ferdon, C. D., & Hertz, M. F. (2007). Electronic media, violence, and adolescents. An emerging public health problem. *The Journal of Adolescent Health*, *41*(6), 1–5. doi:10.1016/j.jadohealth.2007.08.020 PMID:17577527

Fergus, S., & Zimmerman, M. A. (2005). Adolescent resilience: A framework for understanding healthy development in the face of risk. *Annual Review of Public Health*, *26*(1), 399–419. doi:10.1146/annurev.publhealth.26.021304.144357 PMID:15760295

Ferreira, A. B. H. (1997). *Minidicionário Aurélio de língua portuguesa*. Rio de janeiro: Nova Fronteira.

Festl, R., & Quandt, T. (2013). Social relations and cyberbullying: The influence of individual and structural attributes on victimization and perpetration via the internet. *Human Communication Research*, *39*, 101–126. doi:10.111/j.1468-2958.2012.01442.x

File, B. L., & Wright, E. R. (2000). The dimensionality of stigma: A comparison of its impact on the self of persons with HIV/AIDS and cancer. *Journal of Health and Social Behavior*, *41*(1), 50–67. doi:10.2307/2676360

Financial Nigeria. (2016). *Facebook records 16 million active users.* Retrieved from www.financialnigeria.com

Fincham, F. D., & Cui, M. (Eds.). (2010). *Romantic relationships in emerging adulthood.* Cambridge University Press. doi:10.1017/CBO9780511761935

Finkel, E. J., Eastwick, P. W., Karney, B. R., Reis, H. T., & Sprecher, S. (2012). Online dating: A critical analysis from the perspective of psychological science. *Psychological Science in the Public Interest*, *13*(1), 3–66. doi:10.1177/1529100612436522 PMID:26173279

Finn, J. (2004). A survey of online harassment at a university campus. *Journal of Interpersonal Violence*, *19*(4), 468–483. doi:10.1177/0886260503262083 PMID:15038885

Fioravanti, G., Primi, C., & Casale, S. (2013). Psychometric evaluation of the generalized Problematic Internet Use Scale 2 in an Italian sample. *Cyberpsychology, Behavior, and Social Networking*, *16*(10), 761–766. doi:10.1089/cyber.2012.0429 PMID:23742149

Fischer, E. H., Dornelas, E. A., & Goethe, J. W. (2001). Characteristics of people lost to attrition in psychiatric follow-up studies. *The Journal of Nervous and Mental Disease*, *189*(1), 49–55. doi:10.1097/00005053-200101000-00009 PMID:11206665

Fletcher, A., Fitzgerald-Yau, N., Jones, R., Allen, E., Viner, R. M., & Bonell, C. (2014). Brief report: Cyberbullying perpetration and its associations with socio-demographics, aggressive behaviour at school, and mental health outcomes. *Journal of Adolescence*, *37*(8), 1393–1398. doi:10.1016/j.adolescence.2014.10.005 PMID:25448835

Foo, C. T. (2003). Child of the internet. *Cyberpsychology & Behavior*, *6*(2), 195–199. doi:10.1089/109493103321640392

Forest, A. L., & Wood, J. V. (2012). When social networking is not working individuals with low self-esteem recognize but do not reap the benefits of self-disclosure on Facebook. *Psychological Science*, *23*(3), 295–302. doi:10.1177/0956797611429709 PMID:22318997

Fornell, C., & Larcker, D. F. (1981). Evaluating structural equation models with unobservable variables and measurement error. *JMR, Journal of Marketing Research*, *18*(1), 39–50. doi:10.2307/3151312

Foucault, M. (1978). The history of sexuality:Vol. 1. *An introduction.* New York: Pantheon Books.

Fox, S. (2011, January 21). *Americans living with disability and their technology profile.* Pew Research Center's Internet & American Life Project. Retrieved from http://pewinternet.org/Reports/2011/Disability.aspx

Fox, S., & Jones, S. (2009). The social life of health information. Washington, DC: Pew Internet and American Life Project. Retrieved from http://www.pewinternet.org/2009/06/11/the-social-life-of-health-information/

Fox, J., & Tokunaga, R. S. (2015). Romantic Partner Monitoring After Breakups: Attachment, Dependence, Distress, and Post-Dissolution Online Surveillance via Social Networking Sites. *Cyberpsychology, Behavior, and Social Networking*, *18*(9), 491–498. doi:10.1089/cyber.2015.0123 PMID:26348808

Fox, J., & Warber, K. M. (2014). Social networking sites in romantic relationships: Attachment, uncertainty, and partner surveillance on facebook. *Cyberpsychology, Behavior, and Social Networking*, *17*(1), 3–7. doi:10.1089/cyber.2012.0667

Fox, J., & Warber, K. M. (2015). Queer identity management and political self-expression on social networking sites: A co-cultural approach to the spiral of silence. *Journal of Communication*, *65*(1), 79–100. doi:10.1111/jcom.12137

Fox, J., Warber, K. M., & Makstaller, D. (2013). The role of Facebook in romantic relationship development: An exploration of Knapps relational stage model. *Journal of Social and Personal Relationships*, *30*(6), 771–794. doi:10.1177/0265407512468370

Fox, K. A., Gover, A. R., & Kaukinen, C. (2009). The rffects of low self control and childhood maltreatment on stalking victimization among men and women. *American Journal of Criminal Justice*, *34*(3-4), 181–197. doi:10.1007/s12103-009-9064-4

Franks, F., & Faux, S. A. (1990). Depression, stress, mastery, and social resources in four ethnocultural womens groups. *Research in Nursing & Health*, *13*(5), 283–292. doi:10.1002/nur.4770130504

Frith, H., & Kitzinger, C. (2001). Reformulating sexual script theory: Developing a discursive psychology of sexual negotiation. *Theory & Psychology*, *11*(2), 210. doi:10.1177/0959354301112004

Frozzi, G., & Mazzoni, E. (2011). On the importance of social network sites in the transitions which characterize "emerging adulthood.". *ICST Transactions on E-Education and E-Learning*, *11*(7-9), 1–11.

Gallagher, H. C. (2013). Willingness to communicate and cross-cultural adaptation: L2 communication and acculturative stress as transaction. *Applied Linguistics*, *34*(1), 53–73. doi:10.1093/applin/ams023

Garcia, F. D., & Thibaut, F. (2010). Sexual addictions. *The American Journal of Drug and Alcohol Abuse*, *36*(5), 254–260. doi:10.3109/00952990.2010.503823

Gardner, H., & Davis, K. (2013). *The App Generation: How today's youth navigate identity, intimacy, and imagination in a digital world.* New Haven, CT: Yale University Press.

Gardner, M., & Steinberg, L. (2005). Peer influence on risk taking, risk preference, and risky decision making in adolescence and adulthood: An experimental study. *Developmental Psychology*, *41*(4), 625–635. doi:10.1037/0012-1649.41.4.625 PMID:16060809

Gentzler, A. L., Oberhauser, A. M., Westerman, D., & Nadorff, D. K. (2011). College students use of electronic communication with parents: Links to loneliness, attachment, and relationship quality. *Cyberpsychology, Behavior, and Social Networking*, *14*(1-2), 71–74. doi:10.1089/cyber.2009.0409

Gergen, K. J. (2000). *The saturated self: Dilemmas of identity in contemporary life*. New York, NY: Basic Books.

Ghorbani, N., Watson, P. J., Farhadi, M., & Chen, Z. (2014). A multi-process model of self-regulation: Influences of mindfulness, integrative self-knowledge and self-control in Iran. *International Journal of Psychology*, *49*(2), 115–122. doi:10.1002/ijop.12033 PMID:24811882

Gibbs, J. L., Ellison, N. B., & Heino, R. D. (2006). Self-presentation in online personals: The role of anticipated future interaction, self-disclosure, and perceived success in internet dating. *Communication Research*, *33*(2), 152–177. doi:10.1177/0093650205285368

Giddens, A. (1991). *Modernity and self-identity: Self and society in the late modern age*. Stanford, CA: Stanford University Press.

Gill, C. J. (1996). Dating and relationship issues. *Sexuality and Disability*, *14*(3), 183–190. doi:10.1007/BF02590076

Giordano, C., Wood, J. V., & Michela, J. L. (2000). Depressive personality style, dysphoria, and social comparison in everyday life. *Journal of Personality and Social Psychology*, *79*(3), 438–451. doi:10.1037/0022-3514.79.3.438

Giordano, P. C., Longmore, M. A., Schroeder, R. D., & Seffrin, P. M. (2008). A life-course perspective on spirituality and desistance from crime. *Criminology*, *46*(1), 99–132. doi:10.1111/j.1745-9125.2008.00104.x

Giugliano, J. R. (2013). Sex addiction as a mental health diagnosis: Coming together or coming apart? *Sexologies*, *22*(3), e77–e80. doi:10.1016/j.sexol.2012.08.018

Giulianotti, R. (2010). *Sociologia do Futebol: Dimensões históricas e socioculurais do esporte das multidões*. São Paulo: Nova Alexandria.

GLSEN, CiPHR, & CCRC. (2013). *Out online: The experiences of lesbian, gay, bisexual and transgender youth on the Internet*. New York: GLSEN. Retrieved from http://www.glsen.org/sites/default/files/Out%20Online%20FINAL.pdf

Goffman, E. (1963). *Stigma: Notes on the management of spoiled identity*. Englewood Cliffs, NJ: Prentice Hall.

Goldenberg, I., & Goldenberg, H. (1996). *Family therapy: An overview* (4th ed.). Pacific Grove, CA: Brooks/Cole Publishing.

González, J. M. R., & Oliveira, J. A. (2011). Os efeitos da expatriação sobre a identidade: Estudo de caso. *Caderno EBAPE*, *9*(4), 1122–1135. doi:10.1590/S1679-39512011000400011

Goodman, S. (2012, March 22). Online dating with a disability. *The Guardian*. Retrieved from http://www.theguardian.com/lifeandstyle/2012/mar/22/online-dating-with-disability

Google. (2012). *Hyper-connected teens and twenty-somethings*. Retrieved from https://www.thinkwithgoogle.com/infographics/the-media-habits-of-teens-and-young-adults.html

Gordon-Messer, D., Bauermeister, J. A., Grodzinski, A., & Zimmerman, M. (2013). Sexting among young adults. *The Journal of Adolescent Health*, *52*(3), 301–306. doi:10.1016/j.jadohealth.2012.05.013 PMID:23299018

Gosling, S. (2009, March 20). *The Ancient Psychological Roots of Facebook Behaviour*. Retrieved August 9, 2016, from Harvard Business Review: https://hbr.org/2009/03/the-ancient-psychological-root.html

Gotlib, I. H., & Beatty, M. E. (1985). Negative responses to depression: The role of attribution style. *Cognitive Therapy and Research*, *9*(1), 91–103. doi:10.1007/BF01178753

Gowen, L. K., Deschaine, M., Gruttadaro, D., & Markey, D. C. (2012). Young adults with mental health conditions and social networking websites: Decreasing social isolation. *Psychiatric Rehabilitation Journal*, *35*, 245–250. doi:10.2975/35.3.2012.245.250

Gozza-Cohen, M., & May, D. (2012). Individuals with disabilities and internet use. In Z. Yan (Ed.), *Encyclopedia of Cyber Behavior* (pp. 242–258). Hershey, PA: IGI Global. doi:10.4018/978-1-4666-0315-8.ch021

Gradinger, P., Strohmeier, D., & Spiel, C. (2015). Traditional bullying and cyberbullying: Identification of risk groups for adjustment problems. *The Journal of Psychology*, *217*, 205–213.

Greene, J. A., Choudhry, N. K., Kilabuk, E., & Shrank, W. H. (2010). Online social networking by patients with diabetes: A qualitative evaluation of communication with facebook. *Journal of General Internal Medicine*, *26*(3), 287–292. doi:10.1007/s11606-010-1526-3

Greene, K. (2009). An integrated model of health disclosure decision-making. In T. D. Afifi & W. A. Afifi (Eds.), *Uncertainty, information management, and disclosure decisions: Theories and applications* (pp. 226–253). New York: Routledge.

Greene, K., & Faulkner, S. L. (2002). Self-disclosure in relationships of HIV-positive African American adolescent females. *Communication Studies*, *53*, 297–317. doi:10.1080/10510970209388595

Grieve, R., Indian, M., Witteveen, K., Tolan, G. A., & Marrington, J. (2013). Face-to-face or Facebook: Can social connectedness be derived online? *Computers in Human Behavior*, *29*(3), 604–609. doi:10.1016/j.chb.2012.11.017

Griffin, P., & Cole, M. (1984). Current activity for the future: The zo-ped. In B. Rogoff & J. V. Wertsch (Eds.), *Children's learning in the zone of proximal development* (pp. 276–295). San Francisco: Jossey-Bass. doi:10.1002/cd.23219842306

Grigg, D. W. (2010). Cyber-aggression: Definition and concept of cyberbullying. *Australian Journal of Guidance & Counselling*, *20*(02), 143–156. doi:10.1375/ajgc.20.2.143

Gross, E. F. (2004). Adolescent Internet use: What we expect, what teens report. *Journal of Applied Developmental Psychology*, *25*(6), 633–649. doi:10.1016/j.appdev.2004.09.005

Gudelunas, D. (2012). Theres an app for that: The uses and gratifications of online social networks for gay men. *Sexuality & Culture*, *16*(4), 347–365. doi:10.1007/s12119-012-9127-4

Gunter, B. (2007). Internet dating: a British survey. *Aslib Proceedings: New Information perspectives, 60*, 88-98.

Guterman, M. (2009). *O futebol explica o Brasil – Uma história da maior expressão popular do país*. São Paulo: Contexto.

Hafeez, K. (2015, February 23). Remember when, on the Internet, nobody knew who you were. [Cartoon]. *The New Yorker.* Retrieved from http://www.condenaststore.com/-sp/Remember-when-on-the-Internet-nobody-knew-who-you-were-New-Yorker-Cartoon-Prints_i13126074_.htm

Hafen, C., Spilker, A., Chango, J., Marston, E., & Allen, J. (2014). To accept or reject? The impact of adolescent rejection sensitivity on early adult romantic relationships. *Journal of Research on Adolescence*, *24*(1), 55–64. doi:10.1111/jora.12081 PMID:24729668

Hair, J. F., Hult, G. T. M., Ringle, C. M., & Sarstedt, M. (2014). *A primer on partial least squares structural equation modeling (PLS-SEM)*. Thousand Oaks, CA: Sage.

Ha, J. H., Kim, S. Y., Bae, S. C., Bae, S., Kim, H., Sim, M., & Cho, S. C. (2007). Depression and Internet addiction in adolescents. *Psychopathology*, *40*(6), 424–430. doi:10.1159/000107426 PMID:17709972

Halberstam, J. (2005). *In a queer time and place. Transgender bodies, subcultural lives*. New York: New York University Press.

Hald, G. M., Seaman, C., & Linz, D. (2014). Sexuality and pornography. In D. Tolman, L. Diamond, J. Bauermeister, W. George, J. Pfaus, & L. Ward, (Eds.), APA handbook of sexuality and psychology, Vol. 1: Person-based approaches. American Psychological Association. doi:10.1037/14194-001

Hald, G. M. (2006). Gender differences in pornography consumption among young heterosexual Danish adults. *Archives of Sexual Behavior*, *35*(5), 577–585. doi:10.1007/s10508-006-9064-0

Hald, G. M., Kuyper, L., Adam, P. C., & Wit, J. B. (2013). Does viewing explain doing? Assessing the association between sexually explicit materials use and sexual behaviors in a large sample of Dutch adolescents and young adults. *Journal of Sexual Medicine*, *10*(12), 2986–2995. doi:10.1111/jsm.12157

Hald, G. M., & Malamuth, N. M. (2008). Self-perceived effects of pornography consumption. *Archives of Sexual Behavior*, *37*(4), 614–625. doi:10.1007/s10508-007-9212-1

Hald, G. M., Malamuth, N. M., & Yuen, C. (2010). Pornography and attitudes supporting violence against women: Revisiting the relationship in non-experimental studies. *Aggressive Behavior*, *36*(1), 14–20. doi:10.1002/ab.20328

Halliwell, D. (2016). I know you, but I dont know who you are: Siblings discursive struggles surrounding experiences of transition. *Western Journal of Communication*, *80*(3), 327–347. doi:10.1080/10570314.2015.1091493

Hall, P. (2014). Sex addiction–An extraordinarily contentious problem. *Sexual and Relationship Therapy*, *29*(1), 68–75. doi:10.1080/14681994.2013.861898

Hamer, J. S. (2003). Coming-out: Gay males' information seeking. *School Libraries Worldwide*, *9*(2), 73–89.

Harper, G. W., Serrano, P. A., Bruce, D., & Bauermeister, J. A. (2015). The Internet's multiple roles in facilitating the sexual orientation identity development of gay and bisexual male adolescents. *American Journal of Men's Health*. PMID:25585861

Harter, S. (2003). The development of self-representations during childhood and adolescence. In M. R. Leary & J. P. Tangney (Eds.), *Hand-book of self and Identity* (pp. 610–642). New York: Guilford.

Hawk, S. T., Keijsers, L., Hale, W. I., & Meeus, W. (2009). Mind your own business! Longitudinal relations between perceived privacy invasion and adolescent-parent conflict. *Journal of Family Psychology*, *23*(4), 511–520. doi:10.1037/a0015426

Hay, C., & Meldrum, R. (2010). Bullying victimization and adolescent self-harm: Testing hypotheses from General Strain Theory. *Journal of Youth and Adolescence*, *39*(5), 446–459. doi:10.1007/s10964-009-9502-0 PMID:20072852

Hayes, A., & Metts, S. (2015). Support, closeness, and influence tactics as predictors of acceptance of unsolicited parental advice regarding a romantic relationship during emerging adulthood. *Ohio Communication Journal, 53,* 62-69. Available at http://connection.ebscohost.com/c/articles/110152582/support-closeness-influence-tactics-as-predictors-acceptance-unsolicited-parental-advice-regarding-romantic-relationship-during-emerging-adulthood

Haythornthwaite, C. (2005). Social networks and internet connectivity effects. *Information Communication and Society*, *8*(2), 125–147. doi:10.1080/13691180500146185

Hazen, H. D., & Alberts, H. C. (2006). Visitors or immigrants? International students in the United States. *Population Space and Place*, *12*(3), 201–216. doi:10.1002/psp.409

Heatherton, T. F. (2011). Neuroscience of self and self-regulation. *Annual Review of Psychology*, *62*(1), 363–390. doi:10.1146/annurev.psych.121208.131616 PMID:21126181

Heideman, E. (2014, August 1). Disabled woman tackles the dating site trolls. *The Daily Beast*. Retrieved from http://www.thedailybeast.com/articles/2014/08/01/dropping-the-d-bomb- online-dating-with-a-disability.html

Heinze, J., & Horn, S. (2014). Do adolescents evaluations of exclusion differ based on gender expression and sexual orientation? *The Journal of Social Issues*, *70*(1), 63–80. doi:10.1111/josi.12047

Hendry, L. B., & Kloep, M. (2007). Conceptualizing emerging adulthood: Inspecting the emperors new clothes? *Child Development Perspectives*, *1*(2), 74–79. doi:10.1111/j.1750-8606.2007.00017.x

Henseler, J., Ringle, C. M., & Sinkovics, R. R. (2009). The use of partial least squares modeling in international marketing. *Advances in International Marketing*, *20*, 277–319.

Herek, G. M. (2014). HIV-related stigma. In P. W. Corrigan (Ed.), *The stigma of disease and disability: Empirical models and implications for change* (pp. 121–138). Washington, DC: American Psychological Association.

Hillier, L., & Harrison, L. (2007). Building realities less limited than their own: Young people practicing same-sex attraction on the Internet. *Sexualities*, *10*(1), 82–100. doi:10.1177/1363460707072956

Hillier, L., Mitchell, K. J., & Ybarra, M. L. (2012). The Internet as a safety net: Findings from a series of online focus groups with LGB and non-LGB young people in the U.S. *Journal of LGBT Youth*, *9*(3), 225–246. doi:10.1080/19361653.2012.684642

Hill, J. P. (1983). Early Adolescence: Research agenda. *The Journal of Early Adolescence*, *3*(1-2), 1–21. doi:10.1177/027243168331002

Hinduja, S., & Patchin, J. W. (2010). Bullying, cyberbullying, and suicide. *Archives of Suicide Research*, *14*(3), 206–221. doi:10.1080/13811118.2010.494133 PMID:20658375

Hitsch, G. J., Hortacsu, A., & Ariely, D. (2010). What makes you click? – Mate preferences in online dating. *Quantitative Marketing and Economics*, *8*(4), 393–427. doi:10.1007/s11129-010-9088-6

Hodges, E. V. E., Boivin, M., Vitaro, F., & Bukowski, W. M. (1999). The power of friendship: Protection against an escalating cycle of peer victimization. *Developmental Psychology*, *35*(1), 94–101. doi:10.1037/0012-1649.35.1.94 PMID:9923467

Hoeve, M., Dubas, J. S., Eichelsheim, V. I., van der Laan, P. H., Smeenk, W., & Gerris, J. R. M. (2009). The relationship between parenting and delinquency: A meta-analysis. *Journal of Abnormal Child Psychology*, *37*, 749–775.

Hofer, B. K. (2008). The electronic tether: Parental regulation, self-regulation, and the role of technology in college transitions. *Journal of the First-Year Experience & Students in Transition*, *20*(2), 9–24.

Hofer, B. K., & Moore, A. S. (2010). *The iConnected parent: Staying close to your kids in college (and beyond) while letting them grow up*. New York: The Free Press.

Holmes, K. M., & O'Loughlin, N. (2012). The experience of people with learning disabilities on social networking sites. *British Journal of Learning Disabilities*, *42*, 3–7.

Holt-Lunstad, J., Smith, T. B., & Layton, J. B. (2010). Social relationships and mortality risk: A meta-analytic review. *PLoS Medicine*, *7*(7), 1–20. doi:10.1371/journal.pmed.1000316 PMID:20668659

Holt, T. J., & Bossler, A. M. (2009). Examining the applicability of lifestyle-routine activities theory for cybercrime victimization. *Deviant Behavior*, *30*(1), 1–25. doi:10.1080/01639620701876577

Holt, T. J., Fitzgerald, S., Bossler, A. M., Chee, G., & Nq, E. (2016). Assessing the risk factors of cyber and mobile phone bullying victimization in a nationally representative sample of Singapore youth. *International Journal of Offender Therapy and Comparative Criminology*, *60*(5), 598–615. doi:10.1177/0306624X14554852 PMID:25326463

Horn, S. S., & Nucci, L. (2006). Harassment of gay and lesbian youth and school violence in America: An analysis and directions for intervention. In C. Daiute, Z. F. Beykont, C. Higson-Smith, & L. Nucci (Eds.), *International perspectives on youth conflict and development* (pp. 139–155). New York, NY: Oxford University Press. doi:10.1093/acprof:oso/9780195178425.003.0009

Horowitz, L. M., French, R. de S., Lapid, J. S., & Weckler, D. A. (1982). Symptoms and interpersonal problems: The prototypes as an integrating concept. In J. C. Anchin & D. J. Kiesler (Eds.), Handbook of interpersonal psychotherapy (pp. 168-189). New York: Pergamon.

Horvath, K. J., Danilenko, G. P., Williams, M. L., Simoni, J., Amico, K. R., Oakes, J. M., & Rosser, B. R. S. (2012). Technology use and reasons to participate in social networking health websites among people living with HIV in the US. *AIDS and Behavior*, *16*(4), 900–910. doi:10.1007/s10461-012-0164-7

Hosek, S. G., Harper, G. W., & Domanico, R. (2000). Psychological and social difficulties of adolescents living with HIV: A qualitative analysis. *Journal of Sex Education and Therapy*, *25*, 269–276.

Howland, C. A., & Rintala, D. H. (2001). Dating behaviors of women with physical disabilities. *Sexuality and Disability*, *19*(1), 41–70. doi:10.1023/A:1010768804747

Hudson, H. K., & Fetro, J. V. (2015). Sextual activity: Predictors of sexting behaviors and intentions to sext among selected undergraduate students. *Computers in Human Behavior*, *49*, 615–622. doi:10.1016/j.chb.2015.03.048

Hunt, E. (2015, November 3). Essena O'Neill quits Instagram claiming social media 'is not real life'. *The Guardian*. Retrieved from http://www.theguardian.com/media/2015/nov/03/instagram-star-essena-oneill-quits-2d-life-to-reveal-true-story-behind-images

Hwang, W. (2013). Who are people willing to date? Ethnic and gender patterns in online dating. *Race and Social Problems*, *5*(1), 28–40. doi:10.1007/s12552-012-9082-6

IIE (Institute of International Education). (2010). *International student enrollments rose modestly in 2009/10, led by strong increase in students from China.* Retrieved from http://www.iie.org/en/Who-We-Are/News-and-Events/Press-Center/Press Releases/2010/2010-11-15-Open-Doors-International-Students-In-The-US

Imai, T. (in press). Influences of mental illness stigma in a computer-mediated communication context: Investigating mediating roles of predicted outcome value and negative affect. *Japanese Journal of Communication Studies, 45.*

Imai, T., & Dailey, R. M. (2015). Influences of mental illness stigma on perceptions of and responses to requests for favors. *Health Communication.*

Indian, M., & Grieve, R. (2014). When Facebook is easier than face-to-face: Social support derived from Facebook in socially anxious individuals. *Personality and Individual Differences*, *59*, 102–106. doi:10.1016/j.paid.2013.11.016

Ingis, S., Signorelli, M., & Wolf, A. (2014). California eraser button law. *The Download.* Retrieved from http://www.lexology.com/library/detail.aspx?g=5112686b-104a-46fc-8091-09aca02b2b1b

International Agency for Research on Cancer. (2008). *World Cancer Report 2008* (P. Boyle & B. Levin, Eds.). Lyon, France: Author.

Internet Live Stats. (2016, August 9). *Internet Live Stats.* Retrieved August 9, 2016, from Uganda Internet Users: http://www.internetlivestats.com/internet-users/uganda/

Investor Relations, C. C. G. (2011). *Social Media Strategy for Investor Relations.* Investor Relations Strategic Communications.

Jackson, D. D. (1965). The study of the family. *Family Process*, *4*(1), 1–20. doi:10.1111/j.1545-5300.1965.00001.x

Jackson, L. A., Zhao, Y., Witt, E. A., Fitzgerald, H. E., Von Eye, A., & Harold, R. (2009). Self-concept, self-esteem, gender, race, and information technology use. *Cyberpsychology & Behavior*, *12*(4), 437–440. doi:10.1089/cpb.2008.0286

Jacobsen, W. C., & Forste, R. (2011). The wired generation: Academic and social outcomes of electronic media use among university students. *Cyberpsychology, Behavior, and Social Networking*, *14*(5), 275–280. doi:10.1089/cyber.2010.0135

Jaeger, P. T. (2012). *Disability and the internet: Confronting a digital divide.* Boulder, CO: Lynne Rienner Publishers.

Jahoda, A., Wilson, A., Stalker, K., & Cairney, A. (2010). Living with stigma and the self perceptions of people with mild learning disabilities. *The Journal of Social Issues*, *66*(3), 521–534. doi:10.1111/j.1540-4560.2010.01660.x

James, W. (1890). *The principles of psychology.* New York, NY: H. Holt. doi:10.1037/11059-000

Jarvis, C. B., MacKenzie, S. B., & Podsakoff, P. M. (2003). A critical review of construct indicators and measurement model misspecification in marketing and consumer research. *The Journal of Consumer Research*, *30*(2), 199–218. doi:10.1086/376806

Jenkins, J. H., & Carpenter-Song, E. A. (2009). Awareness of stigma among persons with schizophrenia: Marking the contexts of lived experience. *The Journal of Nervous and Mental Disease*, *197*(7), 520–529. doi:10.1097/NMD.0b013e3181aad5e9

Jiang, Q., & Sanchez-Barricarte, J. J. (2011). The 4 – 2 – 1 family structure in China: A survival analysis based on life tables. *European Journal of Ageing*, *8*(2), 119–127. doi:10.1007/s10433-011-0189-1

John, O. P., Donahue, E. M., & Kentle, R. L. (1991). *TheBig Five Inventory--Versions 4a and 54*. Berkeley, CA: Institute of Personality and Social Research.

John, O. P., & Srivastava, S. (1999). The Big Five trait taxonomy: History, measurement, and theoretical perspectives. In L. A. Pervin & O. P. John (Eds.), *Handbook of personality: Theory and research* (pp. 102–138). New York: Guilford Press.

Johnson, G. M. (2011). Self-esteem and use of the Internet among young school-age children. *International Journal of Psychological Studies*, *3*(2), 48–53. doi:10.5539/ijps.v3n2p48

Joinson, A. N. (2008). 'Looking at', 'Looking up', or 'Keeping Up' with People? Motives and Uses of Facebook. CHI 2008 Proceedings: Online Social Newtworks (pp. 1027-1036). Florence, Italy: ACM.

Joinson, A. N. (2001). Self-disclosure in computer-mediated communication: The role of self-awareness and visual anonymity. *European Journal of Social Psychology*, *31*(2), 170–192. doi:10.1002/ejsp.36

Jones, S. (2002). The Internet goes to college: How students are living in the future with today's technology. Washington, DC: Pew Internet & American Life Project. Retrieved from http://files.eric.ed.gov/fulltext/ED472669.pdf

Jones, E. E., Farina, A., Hastorf, A. H., Markus, H., Miller, D. T., & Scott, R. A. (1984). *Social stigma: The psychology of marked relationships*. New York: Freeman.

Judge, A. M. (2012). Sexting among U.S. adolescents: Psychological and legal implications. *Harvard Review of Psychiatry*, *20*(2), 86–96. doi:10.3109/10673229.2012.677360 PMID:22512742

Junco, R. (2013). Comparing actual and self-reported measures of Facebook use. *Computers in Human Behavior*, *29*(3), 626–631. doi:10.1016/j.chb.2012.11.007

Kabaabetswe, P., & Norr, K. F. (2002). Behavioural Change, Goals and Means. In *Aids in Africa* (2nd ed.). New York: Kluwer Academic Publishers. doi:10.1007/0-306-47817-X_33

Kalaitzaki, A. E., & Birtchnell, J. (2016). The Person's Relating to Others Questionnaire (PROQ). In J. Birtchnell, M. Newberry, & A. E. Kalaitzaki (Eds.), *Relating Theory: Clinical, Forensic and other Applications*. London: Palgrave Macmillan.

Kalichman, S. C., & Rompa, D. (1995). Sexual sensation seeking and sexual compulsivity scales: Validity, and predicting HIV risk behavior. *Journal of Personality Assessment*, *65*(3), 586–601. doi:10.1207/s15327752jpa6503_16

Kaplan, A., & Haenlein, M. (2010). Users of the world, unite! The challenges and opportunities of Social Media. *Business Horizons*, *53*(1), 59–68. doi:10.1016/j.bushor.2009.09.003

Kaptelinin, V., & Nardi, B. A. (2006). *Acting with technology: Activity theory and interaction design*. MIT Press.

Karavasilis, L., Doyle, A. B., & Markiewicz, D. (2003). Associations between parenting style and attachment to mother in middle childhood and adolescence. *International Journal of Behavioral Development*, *27*(2), 153–164. doi:10.1080/0165025024400015

Katz, E., Blumler, J. G., & Gurevitch, M. (2003). Utilization of mass communication by the individual. In V. Nigthingale & K. Ross (Eds.), *Critical Readings: Media and Audiences* (pp. 35–51). Maidenhead, UK: Open University Press.

Kelley, H. H., & Thibaut, J. W. (1978). *Interpersonal relations: A theory of interdependence*. New York: Wiley-Interscience.

Kemp, S. (2011). *Social, digital, and mobile in Indonesia*. Retrieved January 5, 2016 from http://wearesocial.sg/blog/2011/12/social-digital-mobile-indonesia/

Kendall, L. (1999). Recontextualizing "cyberspace": Methodological considerations for on-line research. In S. G. Jones (Ed.), *Doing Internet research: Critical issues and methods for examining the Net* (pp. 57–74). Thousand Oaks, CA: Sage. doi:10.4135/9781452231471.n3

Kennedy, H. (2006). Beyond anonymity, or future directions for internet identity research. *New Media & Society*, *8*(6), 859–876. doi:10.1177/1461444806069641

Kenya National Bureau of Statistics (KNBS). (2015). *Kenya National Bureau of Statistics*. Retrieved August 9, 2016, from 2014 Kenya Demographic and Health Survey (2014 KDHS): http://www.knbs.or.ke/index.php?option=com_content&view=article&id=308:2014-kenya-demographic-and-health-survey-2014-kdhs&catid=82:news&Itemid=593

Khang, H., Kim, J., & Kim, Y. (2013). Self-traits and motivations as antecedents of digital media flow and addiction: The Internet, mobile phones, and video games. *Computers in Human Behavior*, *29*(6), 2416–2424. doi:10.1016/j.chb.2013.05.027

Killen, M., Lee-Kim, J., McGlothlin, H., Stangor, C., & Helwig, C. C. (2002). How children and adolescents evaluate gender and racial exclusion. *Monographs of the Society for Research in Child Development*, *67*(4), i-129. PMID:12557595

Killen, M., & Rutland, A. (2011). *Children and Social Exclusion: Morality, Prejudice, and Group Identity*. Hoboken, NJ: Wiley. doi:10.1002/9781444396317

Kim, Y. Y., Izumi, S., & McKay-Semmler, K. (2009, November). *The role of direct and mediated interpersonal communication in cross-cultural adaptation: A study of educated and long-term non-native residents in the United States.* Paper presented at the annual meeting of the National Communication Association, Chicago, IL.

Kimbrough, A. M., Guadagno, R. E., Muscanell, N. L., & Dill, J. (2013). Gender differences in mediated communication:Women connect more than do men. *Computers in Human Behavior*, *29*(3), 896–900. doi:10.1016/j.chb.2012.12.005

Kim, H. W., Zheng, J. R., & Gupta, S. (2011). Examining knowledge contribution from the perspective of an online identity in blogging communities. *Computers in Human Behavior*, *27*(5), 1760–1770. doi:10.1016/j.chb.2011.03.003

Kim, J., & Lee, J. R. (2011). The Facebook paths to happiness: Effects of the number Facebook friends and self-presentation on subjective well-being. *Cyberpsychology, Behavior, and Social Networking*, *14*(6), 359–364. doi:10.1089/cyber.2010.0374

Kim, Y. S., Leventhal, B. L., Koh, Y. J., & Boyce, W. T. (2009). Bullying increased suicide risk: Prospective study of Korean adolescents. *Archives of Suicide Research*, *13*(1), 15–30. doi:10.1080/13811110802572098 PMID:19123106

Kim, Y. Y. (2001). *Becoming intercultural: An integrative theory of communication and cross cultural adaptation.* Thousand Oaks, CA: Sage.

Kingston, D. A., & Malamuth, N. M. (2011). Problems with aggregate data and the importance of individual differences in the study of pornography and sexual aggression: Comment on Diamond, Jozifkova, and Weiss (2010). *Archives of Sexual Behavior*, *40*(5), 1045–1048. doi:10.1007/s10508-011-9743-3

Kirkpatrick, D. (2012). *The Facebook effect: The real inside story of Mark Zuckerberg and the world's fastest growing company*. New York, NY: Simon Schuster.

KISSmetrics. (2013). *Infographics: How to Get More Likes on Facebook*. Retrieved August 9, 2016, from KISSmetrics: https://blog.kissmetrics.com/more-likes-on-facebook/

Klettke, B., Hallford, D. J., & Mellor, D. J. (2014). Sexting prevalence and correlates: A systematic literature review. *Clinical Psychology Review*, *34*(1), 44–53. doi:10.1016/j.cpr.2013.10.007 PMID:24370714

Kokkinos, C. M., Antoniadou, N., & Markos, A. (2014). Cyber-bullying: An investigation of the psychological profile of university student participants. *Journal of Applied Developmental Psychology*, *35*(3), 204–214. doi:10.1016/j.appdev.2014.04.001

Kopecký, K. (2014). Cyberbullying and sexting between children and adolescents –Comparative study. *Procedia: Social and Behavioral Sciences*, *149*, 467–471. doi:10.1016/j.sbspro.2014.08.292

Korzenny, F. (1978). A theory of electronic propinquity: Mediated communications in organizations. *Communication Research*, *5*(1), 3–24. doi:10.1177/009365027800500101

Kosciw, J. G., Palmer, N. A., & Kull, R. M. (2014). Reflecting resiliency: Openness about sexual orientation and/or gender identity and its relationship to well-being and educational outcomes for LGBT students. *American Journal of Community Psychology*, *55*(1-2). doi:10.1007/s10464-014-9642-6 PMID:24691967

Kowalski, R. M., Giumetti, G. W., Schroeder, A. N., & Lattanner, M. R. (2012). Bullying in the digital age: A critical review and meta-analysis of cyberbullying research among youth. *Psychological Bulletin*, *140*(4), 1073–1137. doi:10.1037/a0035618 PMID:24512111

Kowalski, R. M., & Limber, S. P. (2007). Electronic bullying among middle school students. *The Journal of Adolescent Health*, *41*(6), 22–30. doi:10.1016/j.jadohealth.2007.08.017 PMID:18047942

Kowalski, R. M., & Limber, S. P. (2012). Psychological, physical, and academic correlates of cyberbullying and traditional bullying. *The Journal of Adolescent Health*, *53*, 513–520. PMID:23790195

Krasnova, H., Wenninger, H., Widjaja, T., & Buxmann, P. (2013). "Envy on Facebook: A Hidden Threat to Users' Life Satisfaction?" (2013). *Wirtschaftsinformatik Proceedings 2013*. Retrieved from http://www.ara.cat/tecnologia/facebook_ARAFIL20130128_0001.pdf

Krayer, A., Ingledew, D. K., & Iphofen, R. (2008). Social comparison and body image in adolescence: A grounded theory approach. *Health Education Research*, *23*(5), 892–903. doi:10.1093/her/cym076

Kreager, D. A., Cavanagh, S. E., Yen, J., & Yu, M. (2014). Where have all the good men gone? Gendered interactions in online dating. *Journal of Marriage and the Family*, *76*(2), 387–410. doi:10.1111/jomf.12072 PMID:24910472

Kreutz, C. (2009, June). *The Next Billion-The Rise of Social Networking sites in Developing Countries*. Retrieved November 17, 2015, from Web2forDev.com: http://www.web2fordev.net/en/component/content/article/1-latest-news/69-social-networks

Kuss, D., & Griffiths, M. (2011). Addiction to social networks on the Internet: A literature review of empirical research. *International Journal of Environment and Public Health*, *8*, 3528–3552. doi:10.3390/ijerph8093528

Kuzma, J. M., & Black, D. W. (2008). Epidemiology, prevalence, and natural history of compulsive sexual behavior. *The Psychiatric Clinics of North America*, *31*(4), 603–611. doi:10.1016/j.psc.2008.06.005

Landoll, R. R., La Greca, A. M., & Lai, B. S. (2013). Aversive peer experiences on social networking sites: Development of the Social Networking-Peer Experiences Questionnaires (SN-PEQ). *Journal of Research on Adolescence*, *23*(4), 695–705. doi:10.1111/jora.12022 PMID:24288449

Lanigan, J. D. (2009). A sociotechnological model for family research and intervention: How information and communication technologies affect family life. *Marriage & Family Review*, *45*(6-8), 587–609. doi:10.1080/01494920903224194

Lanigan, J. D., Bold, M., & Chenoweth, L. (2009). Computers in the family context: Perceived impact on family time and relationships. *Family Science Review*, *14*, 16–32.

Lapidot-Lefler, N., & Barak, A. (2012). Effects of anonymity, invisibility, and lack of eye-contact on toxic online disinhibition. *Computers in Human Behavior*, *28*(2), 434–443. doi:10.1016/j.chb.2011.10.014

Lariscy, R. W., Tinkham, S. F., & Sweetser, K. D. (2011). Kids these days: Examining differences in political uses and gratifications, internet political participation, political information efficacy, and cynicism on the basis of age. *The American Behavioral Scientist*, *55*(6), 749–764. doi:10.1177/0002764211398091

Lasswell, H. D. (1948). The structure and function of communication in society. *The Communication of Ideas*, *37*, 215–228.

Lathouwers, K., de Moor, J., & Didden, R. (2009). Access to and use of Internet by adolescents who have a physical disability: A comparative study. *Research in Developmental Disabilities*, *30*(4), 702–711. doi:10.1016/j.ridd.2008.09.003 PMID:19022618

Lawlor, D. A., & Rowley, M. (2010). Young Peoples Use of Online Social Networking Sites - a Uses and Gratifications Perspective. *Journal of Research in Interactive Marketing*, *4*(1), 46–58. doi:10.1108/17505931011033551

Lawson, H., & Leck, K. (2006). Dynamics of internet dating. *Social Science Computer Review*, *24*(2), 189–208. doi:10.1177/0894439305283402

Lee, B. H., & OSullivan, L. F. (2014). The ex-factor: Characteristics of online and offline post-relationship contact and tracking among canadian emerging adults. *The Canadian Journal of Human Sexuality*, *23*(2), 96–105. doi:10.3138/cjhs.2415

Lee, B. W., & Leeson, P. R. (2015). Online gaming in the context of social anxiety. *Psychology of Addictive Behaviors*, *29*(2), 473–482. doi:10.1037/adb0000070 PMID:25938630

Lee, E. K. (2013). Formation of a talking space and gender discourses in digital diaspora space: Case of a female Korean im/migrants online community in the USA. *Asian Journal of Communication*, *23*(5), 472–488. doi:10.1080/01292986.2013.772216

Lee, H. J., Lee, D. H., Taylor, C. R., & Lee, J. H. (2011). Do online brand communities help build and maintain relationships with consumers? A network theory approach. *Journal of Brand Management*, *19*(3), 213–227. doi:10.1057/bm.2011.33

Lee, L., & Kartika, N. (2014). The influence of individual, family, and social capital factors on expatriate adjustment and performance: The moderating effect of psychology contract and organizational support. *Expert Systems with Applications*, *41*(11), 5483–5494. doi:10.1016/j.eswa.2014.02.030

Lee, M., & Crofts, T. (2015). Gender, pressure, coercion and pleasure: Untangling motivations for sexting between young people. *The British Journal of Criminology*, *55*(3), 454–473. doi:10.1093/bjc/azu075

Lee, S. (2014). How do people compare themselves with others on social network sites? The case of Facebook. *Computers in Human Behavior*, *32*, 253–260. doi:10.1016/j.chb.2013.12.009

Lee, S., Meszaros, P. S., & Colvin, J. (2009). Cutting the wireless cord: College student cell phone use and attachment to parents. *Marriage & Family Review*, *45*(6-8), 717–739. doi:10.1080/01494920903224277

Lefkowitz, E. S., & Gillen, M. M. (2006). *"Sex is just a normal part of life": Sexuality in emerging adulthood.* Academic Press.

Lei, Y., Liu, Y., Zhou, X., & Zhang, B. (2008). *MITBBS project final report*. School of information, University of Michigan. Retrieved from http://www-personal.umich.edu/~ladamic/courses/networks/si508si708cs608/projects/MITBBS.pdf

Lenhart, A. (2015). Teens, social media & technology. Washington, DC: Pew Research Center. Retrieved from http://www.pewinternet.org/2015/04/09/teens-social-media-technology- 2015/

Lenhart, A. (2015, April 9). *Teen, social media and technology overview 2015*. Pew Research Center. Retrieved from http://www.pewinternet.org/files/2015/04/PI_TeensandTech_Update2015 _0409151.pdf

Lenhart, A., & Madden, M. (2007). *Teens, privacy & online social networks: How teens manage their online identities and personal information in the age of MySpace*. Washington, DC: Pew Internet & American Life Project.

Leont'ev, A. N. (1972). Activity and Consciousness. *Voprosy Filosofii*, *12*, 129–140.

Leontev, A. N. (1974). The problem of activity in psychology. *Journal of Russian & East European Psychology*, *13*(2), 4–33. doi:10.2753/RPO1061-040513024

Leontopoulou, S. (2006). Resilience of Greek youth at an educational transition point: The role of locus of control and coping strategies as resources. *Social Indicators Research*, *76*(1), 95–126. doi:10.1007/s11205-005-4858-3

Leung, L., & Lee, P. S. (2005). Multiple determinants of life quality: The roles of Internet activities, use of new media, social support, and leisure activities. *Telematics and Informatics*, *22*(3), 161–180. doi:10.1016/j.tele.2004.04.003

Levinson, D. J. (1978). *The seasons of a man's life*. Random House LLC.

Levitin, D. J. (2014). *The Organized Mind*. New York: Penguin Random House.

Lewis, S. F., Fremouw, W. J., Del Ben, K., & Farr, C. (2001). An investigation of the psychological characteristics of stalkers: Empathy, problem-solving, attachment and borderline personality features. *Journal of Forensic Sciences*, *46*(1), 80–84. doi:10.1520/JFS14915J PMID:11210929

Lewthwaite, M. (1996). A study of international students perspectives on cross-cultural adaptation. *International Journal for the Advancement of Counseling*, *19*(2), 167–185. doi:10.1007/BF00114787

Liao, K. Y., & Wei, M. (2014). Academic stress and positive affect: Asian value and self-worth contingency as moderators among Chinese international students. *Cultural Diversity & Ethnic Minority Psychology*, *20*(1), 107–115. doi:10.1037/a0034071

Liau, A., Millett, G., & Marks, G. (2006). Meta-analytic examination of online sex-seeking and sexual risk behavior among men who have sex with men. *Sexually Transmitted Diseases*, *33*(9), 576–584. doi:10.1097/01.olq.0000204710.35332.c5 PMID:16540884

Lifton, R. J. (1993). *The protean self: Human resilience in an age of fragmentation*. New York, NY: BasicBooks.

Li, H. (Ed.). (2012). *Virtual community motivation and participation: Cross-disciplinary theories*. Hershey, PA: Information Science Reference. doi:10.4018/978-1-4666-0312-7

Li, J. Q., Liu, X., Wei, T., & Lan, W. (2013). Acculturation, Internet use, and psychological well-being among Chinese international students. *Journal of International Students*, *3*, 155–166. Retrieved from http://cdigital.uv.mx/bitstream/123456789/38135/1/journalstudents.pdf#page=78

Limoncin, E., Carta, R., Gravina, G. L., Carosa, E., Ciocca, G., Di Sante, S., & Jannini, E. A. et al. (2014). The sex.ual attraction toward disabilities: A preliminary internet- based study. *International Journal of Impotence Research*, *26*(2), 51–54. doi:10.1038/ijir.2013.34 PMID:24048013

Lim, S. L., & Lim, B. K. (2012). Po Xi Wen Ti: The mother-in-law problem. *Journal of Family Psychotherapy*, *23*(3), 202–216. doi:10.1080/08975353.2012.705649

Lim, S. L., Lim, B. K. H., Michael, R., Cai, R., & Schock, C. K. (2010). The trajectory of counseling in China: Past, present, and future trends. *Journal of Counseling and Development*, *88*(1), 4–8. doi:10.1002/j.1556-6678.2010.tb00141.x

Lin, C. (2006). Culture shock and social support: An investigation of a Chinese student organization on a U.S. campus. *Journal of Intercultural Communication Research, 35,* 117-137. dio:10.1080/17475750600909279

Lin, A., & Tong, A. (2009). Constructing cultural *Self* and *Other* in the Internet discussion of a Korean historical TV drama. *Journal of Asian Pacific Communication*, *19*(2), 289–312. doi:10.1075/japc.19.2.03lin

Link, B. G. (1982). Mental patient status, work, and income: An examination of the effects of a psychiatric label. *American Sociological Review*, *47*(2), 202–215. doi:10.2307/2094963

Link, B. G. (1987). Understanding labeling effects in the area of mental disorders: An assessment of the effects of expectations of rejection. *American Sociological Review*, *52*(1), 96–112. doi:10.2307/2095395

Link, B. G., Cullen, F. T., Struening, E., Shrout, P. E., & Dohrenwend, B. P. (1989). A modified labeling theory approach to mental disorders: An empirical assessment. *American Sociological Review*, *54*(3), 400–423. doi:10.2307/2095613

Link, B. G., & Phelan, J. C. (2001). Conceptualizing stigma. *Annual Review of Sociology*, *27*(1), 363–385. doi:10.1146/annurev.soc.27.1.363

Link, B. G., Phelan, J. C., Bresnahan, M., Stueve, A., & Pescosolido, B. A. (1999). Public conceptions of mental illness: Labels, causes, dangerousness and social distance. *American Journal of Public Health*, *89*(9), 1328–1333. doi:10.2105/AJPH.89.9.1328

Lipton, J. D. (2011). Combating cyber-victimization. *Berkeley Technology Law Journal*, *26*, 1104–1126.

Little, R. J. A., & Rubin, D. B. (1989). The analysis of social science data with missing values. *Sociological Methods & Research*, *18*(2-3), 292–326. doi:10.1177/0049124189018002004

Lofgren-Martenson, L. (2008). Love in cyberspace: Swedish young people with intellectual disabilities and the internet. *Scandinavian Journal of Disability Research*, *10*(2), 125–138. doi:10.1080/15017410701758005

Löfgren-Mårtenson, L., & Månsson, S. A. (2010). Lust, love, and life: A qualitative study of Swedish adolescents perceptions and experiences with pornography. *Journal of Sex Research*, *47*(6), 568–579. doi:10.1080/00224490903151374

Logan, J. R., Bian, F., & Bian, Y. (1998). Tradition and change in the urban Chinese family: The case of living arrangements. *Social Forces*, *76*(3), 851–882. doi:10.1093/sf/76.3.851

Lo, V. H., & Wei, R. (2002). Third-person effect, gender, and pornography on the internet. *Journal of Broadcasting & Electronic Media*, *46*(1), 13–33. doi:10.1207/s15506878jobem4601_2

Luna, C. (2013). Uma *web* perturbada pela violência. In *Vivendo esse mundo digital* (pp. 60–71). Porto Alegre: Artmed.

Lysaker, P. H., Roe, D., & Yanos, P. T. (2007). Toward understanding the insight paradox: Internalized stigma moderates the association between insight and social functioning, hope, and self-esteem among people with schizophrenia spectrum disorders. *Schizophrenia Bulletin*, *33*(1), 192–199. doi:10.1093/schbul/sbl016

Lyubormirsky, S., & Ross, L. (1997). Hedonic consequnces of social comparison: A contrast of happy and unhappy people. *Journal of Personality and Social Psychology*, *73*(6), 1141–1157. doi:10.1037/0022-3514.73.6.1141

M A Liebert, Inc., Publishers. (2012, September 19). Can Post-Breakup Facebook Surveillance Delay Emotional Recovery? *ScienceDaily*. Retrieved August 16, 2015 from www.sciencedaily.com/releases/2012/09/120919124941.htm

MacInnes, M. (2011). Altar-bound? The effect of disability on the hazard of entry into a first marriage. *International Journal of Sociology*, *41*(1), 87–103. doi:10.2753/IJS0020-7659410105 PMID:23946548

MacKenzie, R. D., Mullen, P. E., Ogloff, J. R. P., McEwan, T. E., & James, D. V. (2008). Parental bonding and adult attachment styles in different types of stalker. *Journal of Forensic Sciences*, *53*(6), 1443–1449. doi:10.1111/j.1556-4029.2008.00869.x PMID:18798773

MacKenzie, S. B., Podsakoff, P. M., & Jarvis, C. B. (2005). The problem of measurement model misspecification in behavioural and organizational research and some recommended solutions. *The Journal of Applied Psychology*, *90*(4), 710–730. doi:10.1037/0021-9010.90.4.710 PMID:16060788

MacKillop, J., & Anderson, E. J. (2007). Further psychometric validation of the mindful attention awareness scale (MAAS). *Journal of Psychological Behavior Assessment*, *29*(4), 289–293. doi:10.1007/s10862-007-9045-1

Madden, M., Lenhart, A., Duggan, M., Cortesi, S., & Gasser, U. (2013). Teens and technology. Washington, DC: Pew Research Center. Retrieved from http://www.pewinternet.org/files/old-media/Files/Reports/2013/PIP_TeensandTechnology2013.pdf

Magee, J. C., Bigelow, L., DeHann, S., & Mustanski, B. S. (2012). Sexual health information seeking online: A mixed-method study among lesbian, gay, bisexual, and transgender young people. *Health Education & Behavior*, *39*(3), 276–289. doi:10.1177/1090198111401384 PMID:21490310

Magoon, K. (2010). *Sex Education in Schools*. Abdo Consulting Inc.

Malamuth, N. M. (1996). Sexually explicit media, gender differences, and evolutionary theory. *Journal of Communication*, *46*(3), 8–31. doi:10.1111/j.1460-2466.1996.tb01486.x

Malamuth, N. M., & Check, J. V. (1985). The effects of aggressive pornography on beliefs in rape myths: Individual differences. *Journal of Research in Personality*, *19*(3), 299–320. doi:10.1016/0092-6566(85)90021-2

Malamuth, N. M., Hald, G. M., & Koss, M. (2012). Pornography, individual differences in risk and mens acceptance of violence against women in a representative sample. *Sex Roles*, *66*(7-8), 427–439. doi:10.1007/s11199-011-0082-6

Maloney, P. W., Grawitch, M. J., & Barber, L. K. (2012). The multi-factor structure of the Brief Self-Control Scale: Discriminant validity of restraint and impulsivity. *Journal of Research in Personality*, *46*(1), 11–115. doi:10.1016/j.jrp.2011.10.001

Manner, C. (2011). Understanding the Predictors of Negative Personal Relationship Experiences on Facebook. *International Journal of Humanities and Social Science*.

Mansson, D. H., & Myers, S. A. (2011). An Initial Examination of College Students Expressions of Affection through Facebook. *The Southern Communication Journal*, *76*(2), 155–168. doi:10.1080/10417940903317710

Marcelli, D., & Branconnier, A. (2007). *Adolescência e Psicopatologia*. Porto Alegre: Artmed.

Markus, H., & Nurius, P. (1986). Possible selves. *The American Psychologist*, *41*(9), 954–969. doi:10.1037/0003-066X.41.9.954

Marshall, T. C., Bejanyan, K., Di Castro, G., & Lee, R. A. (2012). Attachment Styles as Predictors of Facebook-Related Jealousy and Surveillance in Romantic Relationships. *Social Psychology*, *20*(1).

Masten, A. S., Obradović, J., & Burt, K. B. (2006). Resilience in emerging adulthood: Developmental perspectives on continuity and transformation. In J. J. Arnett, J. L. Tanner, J. J. Arnett, & J. L. Tanner (Eds.), *Emerging adults in America: Coming of age in the 21st century* (pp. 173–190). Washington, DC: American Psychological Association; doi:10.1037/11381-007

Mathias, Z., & Harcourt, D. (2014). Dating and intimate relationships of women with below-knee amputation: An exploratory study. *Disability and Rehabilitation*, *36*(5), 395–402. doi:10.3109/09638288.2013.797509 PMID:23721496

Matos, M. (2015). *Adolescentes em navegação segura, por águas desconhecidas.* Lisboa: Coisas de ler.

May, K. T. (2013, February 14). *7 things we learned about online dating from the co-founder of OKCupid* [blog post]. Retrieved from http://blog.ted.com/7- things-we-learned-about-online-dating-from-the-co-founder-of-okcupid/

Mayo, R., & Mayo, C. M. (2013). College students' perspectives on dating a person who stutters. *College Student Journal*, *47*, 169–177.

Mazur, E., & Kozarian, L. (2010). Self-presentation and interaction in blogs of adolescents and young emerging adults. *Journal of Adolescent Research*, *25*(1), 124–144. doi:10.1177/0743558409350498

Mazzoni, E., & Zanazzi, L. (2014). Comparing the Use of SNSs Among Adults and Emerging Asults. *Journal of e-Learning and Knowledge Society, 10*, 25-36.

Mazzoni, E., Baiocco, L., Benvenuti, M., Cannata, D., Fossi, E., & Zanazzi, L. (2014). Beyond Internet addiction. A new framework to understand risks and benefits of being online. In *Proceedings of the International Conferences on ICT, Society and Human Beings 2014*. IADIS.

Mazzoni, E., Baiocco, L., Cannata, D., & Dimas, I. (2016). Is Internet the cherry on top or a crutch? Offline social support as moderator of the outcomes of online social support on Problematic Internet Use. *Computers in Human Behavior*, *56*, 369–374. doi:10.1016/j.chb.2015.11.032

Mazzoni, E., Cannata, D., & Baiocco, L. (2016). Focused, not lost: The mediating role of Temporal Dissociation and Focused Immersion on Problematic Internet Use. *Behaviour & Information Technology*, 1–10. doi:10.1080/0144929X.2016.1159249

Mazzoni, E., & Iannone, M. (2014). From high school to university: Impact of social networking sites on social capital in the transitions of emerging adults. *British Journal of Educational Technology*, *45*(2), 303–315. doi:10.1111/bjet.12026

Mazzoni, E., & Zanazzi, L. (2014). Comparing the use of SNSs among adults and emerging adults. *Journal of e-Learning and knowledge. Society*, *10*(3), 25–36.

McAdams, D. P. (1996). Personality, modernity, and the storied self: A contemporary framework for studying persons. *Psychological Inquiry*, *7*(4), 295–321. doi:10.1207/s15327965pli0704_1

McAdams, D. P. (1997). The case for unity in the (post)modern self: A modest proposal. In R. D. Ashmore, L. J. Jussim, R. D. Ashmore, & L. J. Jussim (Eds.), *Self and identity: Fundamental issues* (pp. 46–78). New York, NY: Oxford University Press.

McDonald, S. M. (2010, July 26). *As ADA turns 20, Harris interactive survey finds lifestyle and economic gaps still remain between Americans with and without disabilities.* The Kessler Foundation. Retrieved from http://www.2010disabilitysurveys.org/

McIntosh, A. (1999). When the deaf and the hearing interact: Communication features, relationship, and disability issues. In D. O. Braithwaite & T. L. Thompson (Eds.), *Handbook of Communication and People with Disabilities: Research and Application* (pp. 353–368). Mahwah, NJ: Routledge.

McIntyre, L. L., Blacher, J., & Baker, B. L. (2006). Transition to school: Adaptation in young children with and without developmental delays. *Journal of Intellectual Disability Research*, *50*, 349–361. doi:10.1111/j.1365-2788.2006.00783.x

McKee, A. (2007). The relationship between attitudes towards women, consumption of pornography, and other demographic variables in a survey of 1,023 consumers of pornography. *International Journal of Sexual Health*, *19*(1), 31–45. doi:10.1300/J514v19n01_05

McKenna, K. Y., Green, A. S., & Gleason, M. E. J. (2002). Relationship formation on the Internet: What's the big attraction? *The Journal of Social Issues*, *58*(1), 9–31. doi:10.1111/1540-4560.00246

McKenna, K.-Y. A., & Bargh, J. A. (1998). Coming out in the age of the Internet: Identity demarginalization through virtual group participation. *Journal of Personality and Social Psychology*, *7*(3), 681–694. doi:10.1037/0022-3514.75.3.681

McMahon, F. (2010). Use Social Media. *Sound and Video Contractor*, *28*(3), 50–53.

McMillan, D. W. (1996). Sense of community. *Journal of Community Psychology*, *24*(4), 315–325. doi:10.1002/(SICI)1520-6629(199610)24:4<315::AID-JCOP2>3.0.CO;2-T

McWhirter, E. H., & McWhirter, B. T. (2008). Adolescente future expectations of work, education, Family and community: Development of a nem measure. *Youth & Society*, *40*(2), 182–202. doi:10.1177/0044118X08314257

Mechanic, M. B., Uhlmansiek, M. H., Weaver, T. L., & Resick, P. A. (2000). The impact of severe stalking experienced by acutely battered women: An examination of violence, psychological symptoms, and strategic responding. *Violence and Victims*, *15*, 443–458. PMID:11288940

Meijer, R. R., de Vries, R. M., & van Bruggen, V. (2011). An evaluation of the Brief Symptom Inventory-18 using item response theory: Which items are most strongly related to psychological distress? *Psychological Assessment*, *23*(1), 193–202. doi:10.1037/a0021292

Menard, K. S., & Pincus, A. L. (2012). Predicting overt and cyber stalking perpetration by male and female college students. *Journal of Interpersonal Violence*, *27*(11), 2183–2207. doi:10.1177/0886260511432144

Mendenhall, M., & Oddou, G. (2014). The dimensions of expatriate acculturation: A review. *Academy of Management Review*, *10*, 39–47.

Meyer, I. H. (2003). Prejudice, social stress, and mental health in lesbian, gay, and bisexual populations: Conceptual issues and research evidence. *Psychological Bulletin*, *129*(5), 674–697. doi:10.1037/0033-2909.129.5.674 PMID:12956539

Meyrowitz, J. (1985). *No sense of place. The impact of social electronic in social behavior*. Oxford, UK: Oxford University Press.

Michikyan, M., Dennis, J., & Subrahmanyam, K. (2015). Can you guess who I am? Real, ideal, and false self-presentation on Facebook among emerging adults. *Emerging Adulthood*, *3*(1), 55–64. doi:10.1177/2167696814532442

Miedema, J. (2009). *Slow Reading*. Duluth, MN: Litwin.

Mikulincer, M. (2006). Attachment, caregiving, and sex within romantic relationships. *Dynamics of Romantic Love: Attachment, Caregiving, and Sex*, 23-42.

Mikulincer, M., & Shaver, P. R. (2016). *Attachment in adulthood: Structure, dynamics, and change* (2nd ed.). New York: Guilford Press.

Milevsky, A. (2005). Compensatory patterns of sibling support in emerging adulthood: Variations in loneliness, self-esteem, depression and life satisfaction. *Journal of Social and Personal Relationships*, *22*(6), 743–755. doi:10.1177/0265407505056447

Miller, H. (1995, June). The presentation of self in electronic life: Goffman on the Internet. In Embodied knowledge and virtual space conference (Vol. 9). Academic Press.

Miller, A. N., & Rubin, D. L. (2007). Factors leading to self-disclosure of a positive HIV diagnosis in Nairobi, Kenya. *Qualitative Health Research, 17*(5), 586–598. doi:10.1177/1049732307301498

Miller, E., Chen, R., Glover-Graf, N. M., & Kranz, P. (2009). Willingness to engage in personal relationships with persons with disabilities. *Rehabilitation Counseling Bulletin, 52*(4), 211–224. doi:10.1177/0034355209332719

Miller-Ott, A. E., Kelly, L., & Duran, R. L. (2014). Cell phone usage expectations, closeness, and relationship satisfaction between parents and their emerging adults in college. *Emerging Adulthood, 2*(4), 313–323. doi:10.1177/2167696814550195

Mishna, F., Khoury-Kassabri, M., Gadalla, T., & Daciuk, J. (2012). Risk factors for involvement in cyber bullying: Victims, bullies and bully-victims. *Children and Youth Services Review, 34*(1), 63–70. doi:10.1016/j.childyouth.2011.08.032

Modzelewski, R. (2013). Virtual togetherness: Sense of identity and community in cyberspace. *Crossroads: A Journal of English Studies, 1,* 37–53.

Moningka, C. (2015). *The use of social media in Jakarta. Unpublished research.* Jakarta: Gunadarma University.

Montag, C., Flierl, M., Markett, S., Walter, N., Jurkiewicz, M., & Reuter, M. (2011). Internet addiction and personality in first-person-shooter video gamers. *Journal of Media Psychology, 23*(4), 163–173. doi:10.1027/1864-1105/a000049

Montag, C., Jurkiewicz, M., & Reuter, M. (2010). Low self-directedness is a better predictor for problematic Internet use than high neuroticism. *Computers in Human Behavior, 26*(6), 1531–1535. doi:10.1016/j.chb.2010.05.021

Montgomery, C., & Borg, M. (2010). *Understanding the international student experience.* London: Palgrave MacMillan.

Monto, M. A., & Carey, A. G. (2014). A new standard of sexual behavior? Are claims associated with the hookup culture supported by general social survey data? *Journal of Sex Research, 51*(6), 605–615. doi:10.1080/00224499.2014.906031

Mo, P. K. H., & Coulson, N. S. (2008). Exploring the communication of social support within virtual communities: A content analysis of messages posted to an online HIV/AIDS support group. *Cyberpsychology & Behavior, 11*(3), 371–374. doi:10.1089/cpb.2007.0118

Moreno, M. A., Jelenchick, L. A., Egan, K. G., Cox, E., Young, H., Gannon, K. E., & Becker, T. (2011). Feeling bad on Facebook: Depression disclosures by college students on a social networking site. *Depression and Anxiety, 28*(6), 447–455. doi:10.1002/da.20805

Morgan, E. M. (2011). Associations between young adults use of sexually explicit materials and their sexual preferences, behaviors, and satisfaction. *Journal of Sex Research, 48*(6), 520–530. doi:10.1080/00224499.2010.543960

Mor, S., Morris, M., & Joh, J. (2013). Identifying and training adaptive cross-cultural management skills: The crucial role of cultural metacognition. *Academy of Management Learning & Education, 12*(3), 453–475. doi:10.5465/amle.2012.0202

Mosher, D. L., & MacIan, P. (1994). College men and women respond to X-rated videos intended for male or female audiences: Gender and sexual scripts. *Journal of Sex Research, 31*(2), 99–113. doi:10.1080/00224499409551736

Muise, A., Christofides, E., & Desmarais, S. (2009). More Information than you ever Wanted: Does Facebook Bring out the Green-Eyed Monster of Jealousy? *Cyberpsychology & Behavior, 12*(4), 441–445. doi:10.1089/cpb.2008.0263 PMID:19366318

Munsey, C. (2006). Emerging adults: The in-between age. *Monitor, 37,* 68. Retrieved from http://www.apa.org/monitor/jun06/emerging.aspx

Mustanski, B., Newcomb, M., & Garofalo, R. (2011). Mental health of lesbian, gay, and bisexual youth: A developmental resiliency perspective. *Journal of Gay and Lesbian Social Services, 23*, 204– 225. doi: 10.1080=10538720.2011.561474

Mustanski, B., Birkett, M., Greene, G. J., Hatzenbuehler, M. L., & Newcomb, M. E. (2014). Envisioning an American without sexual orientation inequities in adolescent health. *American Journal of Public Health, 104*(2), 218–225. doi:10.2105/AJPH.2013.301625 PMID:24328618

Mustanski, B., Garofalo, R., Herrick, A., & Donenberg, G. (2007). Psychosocial health problems increase risk for HIV among urban young men who have sex with men: Preliminary evidence of a syndemic in need of attention. *Annals of Behavioral Medicine, 34*(1), 37–45. doi:10.1007/BF02879919 PMID:17688395

Mustanski, B., Greene, G. J., Ryan, D., & Whitton, S. W. (2015). Feasibility, acceptability, and initial efficacy of an online sexual health promotion program for LGBT youth: The Queer Sex Ed intervention. *Journal of Sex Research, 52*(2), 220–230. doi:10.1080/00224499.2013.867924 PMID:24588408

Mustanski, B., Lyons, T., & Garcia, S. C. (2011a). Internet use and sexual health of young men who have sex with men: A mixed- methods study. *Archives of Sexual Behavior, 40*(2), 289–300. doi:10.1007/s10508-009-9596-1 PMID:20182787

Muuss, R. E. (1969). *Teorias da Adolescência*. Belo Horizonte: Editora do Professor.

Myers, D. G. (1999). Close relationships and quality of life. In D. Kahneman, E. Diener, & N. Schwarz (Eds.), *Well-being: The foundations of hedonic psychology* (pp. 376–393). New York: Russell Sage Foundation.

Nabi, R. L., Prestin, A., & So, J. (2013). Facebook Friends with (Health) Benefits?: Exploring the Palliative Effects of Social Network Sites Compared to Interpersonal Networks. *Cyberpsychology, Behavior, and Social Networking, 16*, 721–727. doi:10.1089/cyber.2012.0521

NAFSA Association of International Educators. (2010). *The economic benefits of international education to the United States: A statistical analysis, 2009-2010*. Retrieved from http://www.nafsa.org/publicpolicy/default.aspx?id=23158

Natarajan, G., Somasundaram, C. P., & Sundaram, K. R. (2011). Relationship between attachment security and rejection sensitivity in early adolescence. *Psychological Studies, 56*(4), 378–386. doi:10.1007/s12646-011-0108-8

Neal, C., Beckjord, E., Rechis, R., Schaeffer, J., Berno, D., & Duchover, Y. (2010). *Cancer stigma and silence around the world: A LIVESTRONG report*. Retrieved from http://images.livestrong.org/downloads/flatfiles/what-we-do/our-approach/reports/cancer-stigma/LSGlobalResearchReport.pdf

Neill, J. T., & Dias, K. L. (2001). Adventure Education and Resilience: The Double-Edged Sword. *Journal of Adventure Education and Outdoor Learning, 12*(2), 35–42. doi:10.1080/14729670185200061

Nelson, L. J., Badger, S., & Wu, B. (2004). The influence of culture in emerging adulthood: Perspectives of Chinese college students. *International Journal of Behavioral Development, 28*(1), 26–36. doi:10.1080/01650250344000244

Nelson, L. J., & Chen, X. (2007). Emerging Adulthood in China: The Role of Social and Cultural Factors. *Society for Research in Child Development, 1*(2), 86–91.

Nelson, L. J., Padilla-Walker, L. M., & Carroll, J. S. (2010). I believe it is wrong but I still do it: A comparison of religious young men who do versus do not use pornography. *Psychology of Religion and Spirituality, 2*(3), 136–147. doi:10.1037/a0019127

Nelson, L., & Barry, C. (2005). Distinguishing features of emerging adulthood: The role of self-classification as an adult. *Journal of Adolescent Research, 20*(2), 242–262. doi:10.1177/0743558404273074

Nemeth, S. A. (2000). Society, sexuality, and disabled/ablebodied romantic relationships. In D. O. Braithwaite & T. L. Thompson (Eds.), *Handbook of communication and people with disabilities* (pp. 37–48). Mahwah, NJ: Lawrence Erlbaum.

Newberry, M. (2016). Negative Relating and Psychopathy. In J. Birtchnell, M. Newberry, & A. E. Kalaitzaki (Eds.), *Relating Theory: Clinical, Forensic and other Applications*. London: Palgrave Macmillan. doi:10.1057/978-1-137-50459-3_20

Newman, L., Wagner, M., Knokey, A. M., Marder, C., Nagle, K., Shaver, D., … Schwarting, M. (2011). *The Post-High School Outcomes of Young Adults With Disabilities up to 8 Years After High School. A Report From the National Longitudinal Transition Study-2 (NLTS2)* (NCSER 2011-3005). Menlo Park, CA: SRI International.

Newman, M. W., Lauterbach, D., Munson, S. A., Resnick, P., & Morris, M. E. (2011). It's not that I don't have problems, I'm just not putting them on Facebook: Challenges and opportunities in using online social networks for health. In *Proceedings of the ACM 2011 Conference on Computer Supported Cooperative Work* (pp. 341- 350). Hangzhou, China: ACM. doi:10.1145/1958824.1958876

Ngai, E., Tao, S., & Moon, K. (2015). Social media research: Theories, constructs, and conceptual frameworks. *International Journal of Information Management*, *35*(1), 33–44. doi:10.1016/j.ijinfomgt.2014.09.004

Nicholson, K. J., & Sacco, W. P. (1999, August). *Interpersonal responses to depression: Negative social-cognition, affect, and non-genuine support.* Poster session presented at the annual meeting of the American Psychological Association, Boston, MA.

Nitzburg, G., & Farber, B. A. (2013). Putting Up Emotional (Facebook) Walls? Attachment Status and Emerging Adults Experiences of Social Networking Sites. *Journal of Clinical Psychology*, *69*(11), 1183–1190. doi:10.1002/jclp.22045 PMID:23996299

Norman, R. M. G., Gawronski, G., Hampson, E., Sorrentno, R. M., Szeto, A., & Ye, Y. (2010). Physical proximity in anticipation of meeting someone with schizophrenia: The role of explicit evaluations, implicit evaluations and cortisol levels. *Schizophrenia Research*, *124*(1-3), 74–80. doi:10.1016/j.schres.2010.07.021

Norona, J. C., Roberson, P. N. E., & Welsh, D. P. (2016). Rejection sensitivity and depressive symptoms: Longitudinal actor-partner effects in adolescent romantic relationships. *Journal of Adolescence*, *51*, 6–18. doi:10.1016/j.adolescence.2016.05.007 PMID:27254083

Norona, J. C., Salvatore, J. F., Welsh, D. P., & Darling, N. (2014). Rejection sensitivity and adolescents perceptions of romantic interactions. *Journal of Adolescence*, *37*(8), 1257–1267. doi:10.1016/j.adolescence.2014.09.003 PMID:25282535

Nosek, M. A., Howland, B. A., Rintala, D. H., Young, M. E., & Chanpong, G. (2001). National study of women with physical disabilities: Final report. *Sexuality and Disability, 19*, 5-39.

Novak, S. P., & Clayton, R. R. (2001). The influence of school environment and self-regulation on transitions between stages of cigarette smoking: A multilevel analysis. *Health Psychology*, *20*(3), 196–207. doi:10.1037/0278-6133.20.3.196

Nsibirano, R., & Consolata, K. (2014). Internet Use and Reconstruction of Gender Identity Among University Students in Uganda. In G. B. Kyomuhendo, F. K. Muhanguzi, S. Gerrard, & J. Ahikire (Eds.), *Gender, Poverty and Social Transformation: Reflections on Fractures and Continuities in Contemporary Uganda* (pp. 139–168). Kampala: Fountain Publishers.

Odaci, H., & Çıkrıkçı, Ö. (2014). Problematic Internet use in terms of gender, attachment styles and subjective well-being in university students. *Computers in Human Behavior*, *32*, 61–66. doi:10.1016/j.chb.2013.11.019

Odek, T. (2007). *Cultural Challenges and Sex Education in Mageta Island, Kenya: Post Sexuality Leadership Development Report Series 3*. Nairobi: Africa Sexuality Centre.

Oestreicher-Singer, G., & Zalmanson, L. (2013). Content or community? A digital business strategy for content providers in the social age. *Management Information Systems Quarterly*, *37*(2), 591–616.

Olmstead, S. B., Negash, S., Pasley, K., & Fincham, F. D. (2013). Emerging adults expectations for pornography use in the context of future committed romantic relationships: A qualitative study. *Archives of Sexual Behavior*, *42*(4), 625–635. doi:10.1007/s10508-012-9986-7

ORiordan, C., & OConnell, M. (2014). Predicting adult involvement in crime: Personality measures are significant, socio-economic measures are not. *Personality and Individual Differences*, *68*, 98–101. doi:10.1016/j.paid.2014.04.010

Owen, J., Fincham, F. D., & Moore, J. (2011). Short-term prospective study of hooking up among college students. *Archives of Sexual Behavior*, *40*(2), 331–341. doi:10.1007/s10508-010-9697-x

Ozen, A., Sumer, N., & Demir, M. (2010). Predicting friendship quality with rejection sensitivity and attachment security. *Journal of Social and Personal Relationships*, 163–181. doi:10.1177/0265407510380607

Padgett, V. R., Brislin-Slütz, J. A., & Neal, J. A. (1989). Pornography, erotica, and attitudes toward women: The effects of repeated exposure. *Journal of Sex Research*, *26*(4), 479–491. doi:10.1080/00224498909551529

Padilla-Walker, L. M., Nelson, L. J., Carroll, J. S., & Jensen, A. C. (2010). More than a just a game: Video game and Internet use during emerging adulthood. *Journal of Youth and Adolescence*, *39*(2), 103–113. doi:10.1007/s10964-008-9390-8 PMID:20084557

Padilla-Walker, L. M., Nelson, L. J., & Knapp, D. J. (2014). Because Im still the parent, thats why! Parental legitimate authority during emerging adulthood. *Journal of Social and Personal Relationships*, *31*(3), 293–313. doi:10.1177/0265407513494949

Pai, P., & Arnott, D. C. (2012). User adoption of social networking sites: Eliciting uses and gratifications through a means–end approach. *Computers in Human Behavior*, *29*(3), 1039–1053. doi:10.1016/j.chb.2012.06.025

Paolacci, G., Chandler, J., & Ipeirotis, P. G. (2010). Running experiments on amazon mechanical turk. *Judgment and Decision Making*, *5*(5), 411–419.

Papp, L. M., Danielewicz, J., & Cayemberg, C. (2012). Are we Facebook Official? Implications of Dating Partners Facebook Use and Profiles for Intimate Relationship Satisfaction. *Cyberpsychology, Behavior, and Social Networking*, *15*(2), 85–90. doi:10.1089/cyber.2011.0291 PMID:21988733

Parker, G., Tupling, H., & Brown, L. B. (1979). A Parental Bonding Instrument. *The British Journal of Medical Psychology*, *52*(1), 1–10. doi:10.1111/j.2044-8341.1979.tb02487.x

Parker, T. S., Blackburn, K. M., Perry, M. S., & Hawks, J. M. (2013). Sexting as an intervention: Relationship satisfaction and motivation considerations. *The American Journal of Family Therapy*, *41*(1), 1–12. doi:10.1080/01926187.2011.635134

Park, N., Kee, K. F., & Valenzuela, S. (2009). Being immersed in social networking environment: Facebook groups, uses and gratifications, and social outcomes. *Cyberpsychology & Behavior*, *12*(6), 729–733. doi:10.1089/cpb.2009.0003 PMID:19619037

Park, Y., & Killen, M. (2010). When is peer rejection justifiable? Childrens understanding across two cultures. *Cognitive Development*, *25*(3), 290–301. doi:10.1016/j.cogdev.2009.10.004 PMID:21076660

Patchin, J. W., & Hinduja, S. (2010). Changes in Adolescent Online Social Networking Behaviours from 2006 to 2009. *Computers in Human Behavior*, *26*(6), 1818–11821. doi:10.1016/j.chb.2010.07.009

Patterson, P., Millar, B., Desille, N., & McDonald, F. (2012). The unmet needs of emerging adults with a cancer diagnosis: A qualitative study. *Cancer Nursing*, *35*(3), 32–40. doi:10.1097/NCC.0b013e31822d9105

Patterson, R., & Price, J. (2012). Pornography, religion, and the happiness gap: Does pornography impact the actively religious differently? *Journal for the Scientific Study of Religion*, *51*(1), 79–89. doi:10.1111/j.1468-5906.2011.01630.x

Patton, C. L., Nobles, M. R., & Fox, K. A. (2010). Look who's stalking: Obsessive pursuit and attachment theory. *Journal of Criminal Justice*, *38*(3), 282–290. doi:10.1016/j.jcrimjus.2010.02.013

Paul, E. L., McManus, B., & Hayes, A. (2000). Hookups: Characteristics and correlates of college students spontaneous and anonymous sexual experiences. *Journal of Sex Research*, *37*(1), 76–88. doi:10.1080/00224490009552023

Pavlou, P. A., & El Sawy, O. A. (2006). From IT competence to competitive advantage in turbulent environments: The case of new product development. *Information Systems Research*, *17*(3), 198–227. doi:10.1287/isre.1060.0094

Peer, J. W., Hillman, S. B., & Van Hoet, E. (2015). The effects of stress on the lives of emerging adult college students: An exploratory analysis. *Adultspan Journal*, *14*(2), 90–99. doi:10.1002/adsp.12007

Peer, J. W., & McAuslan, P. (2016). Self-doubt during emerging adulthood: The conditional mediating influence of mindfulness. *Emerging Adulthood*, *4*(3), 176–185. doi:10.1177/2167696815579828

Peluchette, J. V., Karl, K., Wood, C., & Williams, J. (2015). Cyberbullying victimization: Do victims' personality and risky social network behaviors contribute to the problem? *Computers in Human Behavior*, *52*, 424–435. doi:10.1016/j.chb.2015.06.028

Pereira, N. A. F., Pimentel, R., & Kato, H. T. (2005). Expatriação e estratégia internacional: O papel da família como fator de equilíbrio na adaptação do expatriado. *Revista de administração. Contemporanea (Bologna, Italy)*, *9*, 53–71.

Perkins, S. A., & Turiel, E. (2007). To lie or not to lie: To whom and under what circumstances. *Child Development*, *78*(2), 609–621. doi:10.1111/j.1467-8624.2007.01017.x PMID:17381793

Perrin, A. (2015). *Social media usage 2005-2015.* Retrieved from http://www.pewinternet.org/2015/10/08/social-networking-usage-2005-2015/

Perrin, A., & Duggan, M. (2015). *Americans' internet access: 2000-2015.* Retrieved from: http://www.pewinternet.org/2015/06/26/americans-internet-access-2000-2015/

Peter, J., & Valkenburg, P. M. (2007). Adolescents exposure to a sexualized media environment and their notions of women as sex objects. *Sex Roles*, *56*(5-6), 381–395. doi:10.1007/s11199-006-9176-y

Petter, S., Straub, D. W., & Rai, A. (2007). Specifying formative constructs in information systems research. *Management Information Systems Quarterly*, *31*, 623–656.

Pew Research Center. (2014). *Social networking fact sheet.* Retrieved from http://www.pewinternet.org/fact-sheets/social-networking-fact-sheet/

Pew Research Center. (2015). *The demographics of social media users.* Retrieved from http://www.pewinternet.org/2015/08/19/the-demographics-of-social-media-users/

Pfeiffer, J. P., & Pinquart, M. (2011). Attainment of developmental tasks by adolescent with visual impairments and sighted adolescents. *Journal of Visual Impairment & Blindness*, *105*, 33–44.

Phillips, B., Hajela, R., & Hilton, D. L. Jr. (2015). Sex addiction as a disease: Evidence for assessment, diagnosis, and response to critics. *Sexual Addiction & Compulsivity*, *22*(2), 167–192. doi:10.1080/10720162.2015.1036184

Piaget, J. (1960). *The psychology of intelligence.* Patterson: Littlefield-Adams.

Pinquart, M., & Pfeiffer, J. P. (2012). What is essential is invisible to the eye: Intimate relationships of adolescents with visual impairment. *Sexuality and Disability*, *30*(2), 139–147. doi:10.1007/s11195-011-9248-y

Plentyoffishmedia. (2015, October 23). Retrieved from http://www.pof.com/

Postmes, T., Spears, R., & Lea, M. (2000). The formation of group norms in computermediated communication. *Human Communication Research*, *26*(3), 341–371. doi:10.1111/j.1468-2958.2000.tb00761.x

Poulsen, F. O., Busby, D. M., & Galovan, A. M. (2013). Pornography use: Who uses it and how it is associated with couple outcomes. *Journal of Sex Research*, *50*(1), 72–83. doi:10.1080/00224499.2011.648027

Prensky, M. (2001). Digital Natives, Digital Immigrants. *On the Horizon*, *9*(5), 1–6. doi:10.1108/10748120110424816

Purdie, V., & Downey, G. (2000). Rejection sensitivity and adolescent girls vulnerability to relationship-centred difficulties. *Child Maltreatment*, *5*(4), 338–349. doi:10.1177/1077559500005004005 PMID:11232261

Qian, Y., & Mao, Y. (2010). A content analysis of online social support behaviors of overseas Chinese prenatal and postnatal women. *China Media Research, 6*(4), 43-54. Retrieved from http://hdl.handle.net/1765/39898

Quan, C., & Ren, F. (2010). A blog emotion corpus for emotional expression analysis in Chinese. *Computer Speech & Language*, *24*(4), 726–749. doi:10.1016/j.csl.2010.02.002

Quan-Haase, A., & Young, A. L. (2010). Uses and Gratifications of Social Media: A Comparison of Facebook and Instant Messaging. *Bulletin of Science and Technology*, *30*(5), 350–361. doi:10.1177/0270467610380009

Rafferty, J., Boettcher, C., & Griffin, K. W. (2001). Benefits and risks of reverse inclusion for preschoolers with and without disabilities: Parents perspectives. *Journal of Early Intervention*, *24*(4), 266–286. doi:10.1177/105381510102400403

Ramsey, M. A., Gentzler, A. L., Morey, J. N., Oberhauser, A. M., & Westerman, D. (2013). College students use of communication technology with parents: Comparisons between two cohorts in 2009 and 2011. *Cyberpsychology, Behavior, and Social Networking*, *16*(10), 747–752. doi:10.1089/cyber.2012.0534

Rau, P., Gao, Q., & Ding, Y. (2008). Relationship Between the Level of Intimacy and Lurking in Online Social Network Services. *Computers in Human Behavior*, *24*(6), 2757–2770. doi:10.1016/j.chb.2008.04.001

Ravizza, K. (2002). A philosophical costruct: A framework for performance enhancement. *International Journal of Sport Psychology*, *33*, 4–18.

Ravneberg, B. (2012). Usability and abandonment of assistive technology. *Journal of Assistive Technologies*, *6*(4), 259–269. doi:10.1108/17549451211285753

Regnerus, M., & Uecker, J. (2010). *Premarital sex in America: How young americans meet, mate, and think about marrying*. Oxford University Press. doi:10.1093/acprof:oso/9780199743285.001.0001

Reich, R. R., Cummings, J. R., Greenbaum, P. E., Moltisanti, A. J., & Goldman, M. S. (2015). *The temporal "pulse" of drinking: Tracking 5 years of binge drinking in emerging adults*. Academic Press.

Reifman, A., Arnett, J. J., & Colwell, M. J. (2007). *Emerging Adulthood*: Theory, assessment and application. *Journal of Youth Development*, *2*(1).

Renfrow, D. G., & Rollo, E. A. (2014). Sexting on campus: Minimizing perceived risks and neutralizing behaviors. *Deviant Behavior*, *35*(11), 903–920. doi:10.1080/01639625.2014.897122

Resch, M. N., & Alderson, K. G. (2014). Female partners of men who use pornography: Are honesty and mutual use associated with relationship satisfaction? *Journal of Sex & Marital Therapy*, *40*(5), 410–424. doi:10.1080/0092623X.2012.751077

Reyns, B. W. (2010). A situational crime prevention approach to cyberstalking victimization: Preventive tactics for Internet users and online place managers. *Crime Prevention and Community Safety*, *12*(2), 99–118. doi:10.1057/cpcs.2009.22

Reyns, B. W., Henson, B., & Fisher, B. S. (2012). Stalking in the twilight zone: Extent of cyberstalking victimization and offending among college students. *Deviant Behavior*, *33*(1), 1–25. doi:10.1080/01639625.2010.538364

Rial, C. (2008). *Rodar*: A circulação dos jogadores de futebol brasileiros no exterior. *Horizontes Antropológicos*, *14*(30), 21–75. doi:10.1590/S0104-71832008000200002

Rice, E., Rhoades, H., Winetrobe, H., Sanchez, M., Montoya, J., Plant, A., & Kordic, T. (2012). Sexually explicit cell phone messaging associated with sexual risk among adolescents. *Pediatrics*, *130*(4), 667–673. doi:10.1542/peds.2012-0021 PMID:22987882

Richardson, D., Litterwood, M., Nesti, M., & Benstead, L. (2012). An examination of the migratory transition of elite young European soccer players to the english premier league. *Journal of Sports Sciences*, *30*(15), 1605–1618. doi:10.1080/02640414.2012.733017 PMID:23098129

Rick, W. (2015, September 10). *Reuters*. Retrieved August 9, 2016, from Facebook Rakes in Users in Nigeria and Kenya, Eyes Rest of Africa: http://www.reuters.com/article/us-facebook-africa-idUSKCN0RA17L20150910

Rideout, V. J., Foehr, U. G., & Roberts, D. F. (2010). *Generation M: Media in the lives of 8-to 18-year-olds*. Henry J. Kaiser Family Foundation. Retrieved from http://www.eric.ed.gov/PDFS/ED527859.pdf

Rideout, V. J., Roberts, D. F., & Foehr, U. G. (2005). *Generation M: Media in the lives of 8-18-year-olds: Executive summary*. Menlo Park, CA: Henry J. Kaiser Family Foundation.

Ridini, S. P. (1998). *Health and Sexuality Education in Schools*. West Port: Green Wood Publishing Group, Inc.

Riemer-Reiss, M. L., & Wacher, R. R. (2000). Factors associated with assistive technology discontinuance among individuals with disabilities. *Journal of Rehabilitation*, *66*, 44–50.

Ringrose, J., Harvey, L., Gill, R., & Livingstone, S. (2013). Teen girls, sexual double standards and sexting: Gendered value in digital image exchange. *Feminist Theory*, *14*(3), 305–323. doi:10.1177/1464700113499853

Rintala, D. H., Howland, C. A., Nosek, M. A., Bennett, J. L., Young, M. E., Foley, C. C., & Chanpong, G. et al. (1997). Dating issues for women with physical disabilities. *Sexuality and Disability*, *15*(4), 219–242. doi:10.1023/A:1024717313923

Rippere, V. (1977). Commonsense beliefs about depression and antidepressive behaviour: A study of social consensus. *Behaviour Research and Therapy*, *15*(6), 465–473. doi:10.1016/0005-7967(77)90002-X

Riva, G., Banos, R. M., Botella, C., Wiederhold, B. K., & Gaggioli, A. (2012). Positive technology: Using interactive technologies to promote positive functioning. *Cyberpsychology, Behavior, and Social Networking*, *15*(2), 69–77. doi:10.1089/cyber.2011.0139 PMID:22149077

Roberts, D., Foehr, U., & Rideout, V. (2005). *Generation M: Media in the lives of 8-18 year olds*. Menlo Park, CA: Kaiser Family Foundation. Retrieved from http://kff.org/other/event/generation-m-media-in-the-lives-of/

Roberts, L. (2008). Jurisdictional and definitional concerns with computer related interpersonal crimes: An analysis on cyber stalking. *International Journal of Cyber Criminology*, *2*, 271–285.

Rodrigues, N. (2013). *A pátria das chuteiras*. Rio de Janeiro: Nova Fronteira.

Rodríguez, S. N., & Damásio, B. F. (2014). Desenvolvimento da identidade e sentindo de vida na adolescência. In L. F. Habigzang, E. Diniz, & S. H. Koller (Eds.), *Trabalhando com adolescentes: teoria e intervenção psicológica* (pp. 30–41). Porto Alegre: Artmed.

Romito, P., & Beltramini, L. (2011). Watching pornography: Gender differences, violence and victimization. An exploratory study in Italy. *Violence Against Women.*

Romm, C., Pliskin, N., & Clarke, R. (1997). Virtual communities and society: Toward an integrative three phase model. *International Journal of Information Management*, *11*(4), 261–270. doi:10.1016/S0268-4012(97)00004-2

Roose, K. (2014, June 13). The complete guide to anonymous apps. *New York Magazine.* Retrieved from http://nymag.com/daily/intelligencer/2014/06/complete-guide-to-anonymous-apps.html

Rosenberg, M., Schooler, C., Schoenbach, C., & Rosenberg, F. (1995). Global self-esteem and specific self-esteem: Different concepts, different outcomes. *American Sociological Review*, *60*(1), 141–156. doi:10.2307/2096350

Roth, M. E., & Gillis, J. M. (2015). Convenience with the click of a mouse: A survey of adults with autism spectrum disorder on online dating. *Sexuality and Disability*, *33*(1), 133–150. doi:10.1007/s11195-014-9392-2

Rozler, J., & Lavinthal, A. (2010). *The hookup handbook: A single girl's guide to living it up*. Simon and Schuster.

Rubin, K. H., & Coplan, R. (2010). *The development of shyness and social withdrawal.* New York, NY: Guilford Press.

Rubin, R. B., & Martin, M. M. (1994). Development of a measure of interpersonal communication competence. *Communication Research Reports*, *11*(1), 33–44. doi:10.1080/08824099409359938

Ruggiero, T. E. (2000). Uses and gratifications theory in the 21st century. *Mass Communication & Society*, *3*(1), 3–37. doi:10.1207/S15327825MCS0301_02

Russell, D. (1996). UCLA Loneliness Scale (Version 3): Reliability, validity, and factor structure. *Journal of Personality Assessment*, *66*(1), 20–40. doi:10.1207/s15327752jpa6601_2 PMID:8576833

Rutland, A., Killen, M., & Abrams, D. (2010). A new social-cognitive developmental perspective on prejudice: The interplay between morality and group identity. *Perspectives on Psychological Science*, *5*(3), 279–291. doi:10.1177/1745691610369468 PMID:26162160

Sacco, W. P., & Vaughan, C. A. (2006). Depression and the response of others: A social-cognitive interpersonal process model. In T. E. Joiner, J. S. Brown, & J. Kistner (Eds.), *The interpersonal, social and cognitive nature of depression.* Mahwah, NJ: Lawrence Erlbaum Associates.

Safranova, V. (2015, November 18). On fake Instagram, a chance to be real. *The New York Times.* Retrieved from http://www.nytimes.com/2015/11/19/fashion/instagram-finstagram-fake-account.html?_r=0

Sagioglou, C., & Greitemeyer, T. (2014). Facebooks emotional consequences: Why Facebook causes a decrease in mood and why people still use it. *Computers in Human Behavior*, *35*, 359–363. doi:10.1016/j.chb.2014.03.003

Salas-Wright, C. P., Vaughn, M. G., & Maynard, B. R. (2014). Profiles of religiosity and their association with risk behavior among emerging adults in the United States. *Emerging Adulthood.*

Salgado, P. G., Boubeta, A. R., Tobío, T. B., Mallou, J. V., & Couto, C. B. (2014). Evaluation and early detection of problematic Internet use in adolescents. *Psicothema*, *26*(1), 21–26. PMID:24444725

Saltes, N. (2013). Disability, identity, and disclosure in the online dating environment. *Disability & Society*, *28*(1), 96–109. doi:10.1080/09687599.2012.695577

Samakow, J. (2013). *Japan Internet 'Fasting Camps' Aim To Treat Screen-Addicted Kids*. Retrieved January, 8, 2016 from http://www.huffingtonpost.com/2013/08/28/japan-internet-fasting-camp_n_3824697.html

Sanderson, C. A. (2010). *Social psychology*. New York: John Wiley & Sons, Inc.

Sandra, L. (2012). *The dynamics interaction of psychological self-concept and on-line identity* (Unpublished Doctoral Dissertation). University of Gajah Mada, Yogyakarta.

Sansone, R. A., Wiederman, M. W., & Sansone, L. A. (1998). The Self-Harm Inventory (SHI): Development of a scale of identifying self-destructive behaviors and borderline personality disorder. *Journal of Clinical Psychology*, *54*(7), 973–983. doi:10.1002/(SICI)1097-4679(199811)54:7<973::AID-JCLP11>3.0.CO;2-H PMID:9811134

Santos, E. C., Neto, O. C. M., & Koller, S. H. (2014). Adolescentes e Adolescências. In Trabalhando com adolescentes: teoria e intervenção psicológica. Porto Alegre: Artmed.

Sarigiani, P. A., Trumbell, J. M., & Camarena, P. M. (2013). Electronic communications technologies and transition to college: Links to parent-child attachment and adjustment. *Journal of the First-Year Experience & Students in Transition*, *25*(1), 35–60.

Sariyska, R., Reuter, M., Lachmann, B., & Montag, C. (2015). Attention deficit/hyperactivity disorder is a better predictor for problematic Internet use than depression: Evidence from Germany. *Journal of Addiction Research & Therapy*, *6*(209), 2.

Sarup, M. A. (1993). *Introductory guide to Poststructuralism and Postmodernism*. Athens, GA: University of Georgia Press.

Sato, E., Ohsawa, I., Kataoka, J., Miwa, M., Tsukagoshi, F., Sato, J., & Sato, Y. et al. (2003). Socio-psychological problems of patients with late adolescent onset type 1 diabetes – analysis by qualitative research. *Nagoya Journal of Medical Science*, *66*, 21–29.

Savin-Williams, R. C. (1994). Verbal and physical abuse as stressors in the lives of lesbian, gay male, and bisexual youths: Associations with school problems, running away, substance abuse, prostitution, and suicide. *Journal of Consulting & Clinical Psychology*, *62*, 261–269. doi: .26110.1037/0022-006X.62.2

Savin-Williams, R. C. (2005). *The new gay teenager*. Cambridge, MA: Harvard University Press. doi:10.4159/9780674043138

Schabert, J., Browne, J. L., Mosely, K., & Speight, J. (2005). Social stigma in diabetes: A framework to understand a growing problem for an increasing epidemic. *Patient*, *6*(1), 1–10. doi:10.1007/s40271-012-0001-0

Schenk, A. M., & Fremouw, W. J. (2012). Prevalence, psychological impact, and coping of cyberbully victims among college students. *Journal of School Violence*, *11*(1), 21–37. doi:10.1080/15388220.2011.630310

Schinke, R. J., McGannon, K. R., Battochio, R. C., & Wells, G. D. (2013). Acculturation in elite sport: A thematic analysis of immigrant athletes and coaches. *Journal of Sports Sciences*, *31*(15), 1676–1686. doi:10.1080/02640414.2013.794949 PMID:23688005

Schmitt, D. P., Allik, J., McCrae, R. R., & Benet-Martinez, V. (2007). The geographic distribution of Big Five personality traits: Patterns and profiles of human self-description across 56 nations. *Journal of Cross-Cultural Psychology*, *38*(2), 173–212. doi:10.1177/0022022106297299

Schneider, D. J. (2005). *The psychology of stereotyping*. New York: Guilford Press.

Schon, J. (2014). Dad doesnt text: Examining how parents use of information communication technologies influences satisfaction among emerging adult children. *Emerging Adulthood*, *2*(4), 304–312. doi:10.1177/2167696814551786

Schoon, E. W., & Cain, C. (2011). Facebooks Boundaries. *Contexts*, *10*(2), 70–71. doi:10.1177/1536504211408925

Schover, L. R., & Jensen, S. B. (1988). *Sexuality and chronic illness: A comprehensive approach.* New York: Guilford.

Schur, L., Kruse, D., & Blanck, P. (2013). *People with disabilities: Sidelined or mainstreamed?* New York: Cambridge University Press. doi:10.1017/CBO9780511843693

Schwartz, S. J., Donnellan, M. B., Ravert, R. D., Luyckx, K., & Zamboanga, B. L. (2013). Identity development, personality, and well-being in adolescence and emerging adulthood: Theory, research, and recent advances. In Handbook of psychology: Developmental psychology (vol. 6, pp. 339-364). New York: John Wiley and Sons.

Schwartz, S. J. (2007). The structure of identity consolidation: Multiple correlated constructs or one superordinate construct? *Identity*, *7*(1), 27–49. doi:10.1080/15283480701319583

Schwartz, S. J., Unger, J. B., Zamboanga, B. L., & Szapocznik, J. (2010). Rethinking the concept of acculturation: Implications for theory and research. *The American Psychologist*, *65*(4), 237–251. doi:10.1037/a0019330 PMID:20455618

Seeman, N. (2008). Web 2.0 and chronic illness: New horizons, new opportunities. *ElectronicHealthcare*, *6*, 104–110.

Selkie, E. M., Kota, R., Chan, Y., & Moreno, M. (2015). Cyberbullying, depression, and problem alcohol use in female college students: A multisite study. *Cyberpsychology, Behavior, and Social Networking*, *18*(2), 79–86. doi:10.1089/cyber.2014.0371 PMID:25684608

Sessoms, J. (2011). *The cyber pornography use inventory: Comparing a religious and secular sample.* Academic Press.

Seto, M. C., Maric, A., & Barbaree, H. E. (2001). The role of pornography in the etiology of sexual aggression. *Aggression and Violent Behavior*, *6*(1), 35–53. doi:10.1016/S1359-1789(99)00007-5

Setyawan, D. (2014). *KPAI ingatkan orang tua: waspadai kejahatan seksual pada anak melalui media sosial.* Retrieved, January, 8, 2016 from http://www.kpai.go.id/berita/kpai-ingatkan-orang-tua-waspadai-kejahatan-seksual-pada-anak-melalui-media-sosial/

Seymour, W., & Lupton, D. (2004). Holding the line online: Exploring wired relationships for people with disabilities. *Disability & Society*, *19*(4), 291–305. doi:10.1080/09687590410001689421

Sharp, E. H., Coatsworth, J. D., Darling, N., Cumsille, P., & Ranieri, S. (2007). Gender Differences in the Self-Defining Activities and Identity Experiences of Adolescents and Emerging Adults. *Journal of Adolescence*, *30*(2), 251–269. doi:10.1016/j.adolescence.2006.02.006 PMID:16600358

Shaver, P., & Hazan, C. (1987). Being lonely, falling in love: Perspectives from attachment theory. *Journal of Social Behavior and Personality.*

Sherman, A. J., & Tocantins, N. (2004). *The happy hook up: A single girl's guide to casual sex.* Springer Science & Business.

Shiu, A. T., Kwan, J. J. Y., & Wong, R. Y. (2003). Social stigma as a battier to diabetes self-management: Implications for multi-level interventions. *Journal of Clinical Nursing*, *12*(1), 149–150. doi:10.1046/j.1365-2702.2003.00735.x

Short, E., Linford, S., Wheatcroft, J. M., & Maple, C. (2014). The impact of cyberstalking: The lived experience-a thematic analysis. *Studies in Health Technology and Informatics*, *199*, 133–137. doi:10.3233/978-1-61499-401-5-133 PMID:24875706

Shpiegel, Y., Klomek, A. B., & Apter, A. (2015). Bullying, cyberbullying, depression and suicide ideation among youth. Comparing online to paper-and-pencil questionnaires. *International Journal of Child and Adolescent Health*, *8*, 161–167.

Shpigelman, C.-N., & Gill, C. J. (2014a). Facebook use by persons with disabilities. *Journal of Computer-Mediated Communication*, *19*(3), 610–624. doi:10.1111/jcc4.12059

Shpigelman, C.-N., & Gill, C. J. (2014b). How do adults with intellectual disabilities use Facebook? *Disability & Society, 29*(10), 1601–1616. doi:10.1080/09687599.2014.966186

Shulman, S., & Connolly, J. (2013). The challenge of romantic relationships in emerging adulthood: Reconceptualization of the field. *Emerging Adulthood, 1*(1), 27–39. doi:10.1177/2167696812467330

Shuttleworth, R. P. (2000). The search for sexual intimacy for men with cerebral palsy. *Sexuality and Disability, 18*(4), 263–282. doi:10.1023/A:1005646327321

Sibicky, M., & Dividio, J. F. (1986). Stigma of psychological therapy: Stereotypes, interpersonal reactions, and the self-fulfilling prophecy. *Journal of Counseling Psychology, 33*(2), 148–154. doi:10.1037/0022-0167.33.2.148

Singer, N. (2013, November 9). They loved your GPA then they saw your tweets. *The New York Times*. Retrieved from http://www.nytimes.com/2013/11/10/business/they-loved-your-gpa-then-they-saw-your-tweets.html

Slevin, E., & Sines, D. (1996). Attitudes of nurses in general hospital towards people with learning disabilities: Influences of contact, and graduate – non-graduate status, a comparative study. *Journal of Advanced Nursing, 24*(6), 1116–1126. doi:10.1111/j.1365-2648.1996.tb01016.x

Šmahel, D. (2003). *Psychology and Internet: Children being adults, adults being children*. Prague: Triton.

Smart, J. (2011). *Disability across the developmental lifespan*. New York: Springer.

Smetana, J. G., Jambon, M., & Ball, C. (2014). The social domain approach to children's moral and social judgments. In M. Killen & J. G. Smetana (Eds.), *Handbook of moral development* (2nd ed.; pp. 23–45). New York, NY: Psychology Press. doi:10.4324/9780203581957.ch2

Smith, A. (2015). U.S. smartphone use in 2015. Washington, DC: Pew Research Center. Retrieved from http://www.pewinternet.org/2015/04/01/us-smartphone-use-in-2015/

Smith, A. (2016, February 11). *15% of American adults have used online dating sites or mobile dating apps*. Pew Research Center. Retrieved from http://www.pewinternet.org/2016/02/11/15-percent-of-american-adults- have-used-online-dating-sites-or-mobile-dating-apps/

Smith, A., & Anderson, M. (2016, February 29). *5 facts about online dating*. Pew Research Center. Retrieved from http://www.pewresearch.org/fact-tank/2016/02/29/5-facts-about-online- dating/

Smith, A., Rainie, L., & Zickuhr, K. (2011). *College students and technology*. Retrieved from http://www.pewinternet.org/2011/07/19/college-students-and-technology/

Smith, C. (2013, September 18). *Facebook Users Are Uploading 350 Million New Photos Each Day*. Retrieved August 9, 2016, from Business Insider: Tech: http://mybilliondollarapp.com/how-many-photos-on-facebook-how-about-240-billion/

Smith, J. (2013, April 16). How your social media can help (or hurt) you in your job search. *Forbes*. Retrieved from http://www.forbes.com/sites/jacquelynsmith/2013/04/16/how-social-media-can-help-or-hurt-your-job-search/

Smith, J. W., & Kandath, K. (1999). Communication and the blind or visually impaired. In D. O. Braithwaite & T. L. Thompson (Eds.), *Handbook of communication and people with disabilities: Research and application* (pp. 389–404). Mahwah, NJ: Routledge.

Smith, P. K. (2011). *Understanding children's development* (5th ed.). Chichester, UK: John Wiley & Sons Ltd.

Smith, P. K., Mahdavi, J., Carvalho, M., Fisher, S., Russell, S., & Tippett, N. (2008). Cyberbullying: Its nature and impact in secondary school pupils. *Journal of Child Psychology and Psychiatry, and Allied Disciplines, 49*(4), 376–385. doi:10.1111/j.1469-7610.2007.01846.x PMID:18363945

Smith, R. H., & Kim, S. H. (2007). Comprehending envy. *Psychological Bulletin, 133*(1), 46–64. doi:10.1037/0033-2909.133.1.46

Soderstrom, S. (2013). Digital differentiation in young peoples internet use – eliminating or reproducing disability stereotypes. *Future Internet, 5*(2), 190–204. doi:10.3390/fi5020190

Soliha, S. F. (2015). Tingkat ketergantungan pengguna media sosial dan kecemasan sosial. *Jurnal Interaksi, 4*(1), 1–10.

Solvang, P. (2007). The amputee body desired: Beauty destabilized? Disability re-valued? *Sexuality and Disability, 25*(2), 51–64. doi:10.1007/s11195-007-9036-x

Sontag, L. M., Clemans, K. H., Graber, J. A., & Lyndon, S. T. (2011). Traditional and cyber aggressors and victims: A comparison of psychosocial characteristics. *Journal of Youth and Adolescence, 40*(4), 392–404. doi:10.1007/s10964-010-9575-9 PMID:20680425

Special Olympics. (2015). *What is intellectual disability?* Retrieved from http://www.specialolympics.org/Sections/Who_We_Are/What_Is_Intellectual_Disability.aspx

Spitz, C. (2012). PIB do esporte cresce mais do que o do país. *O Globo*. Retrieved from http://oglobo.globo.com/economia/pib-do-esporte-cresce-mais-do-que-do-pais-5028799#ixzz3AHwi5EIJ

Spitzberg, B. H. (2002). The tactical topography of stalking victimization and management. *Trauma, Violence & Abuse, 3*(4), 261–288. doi:10.1177/1524838002237330

Spitzberg, B. H., & Cupach, W. R. (2001). Paradoxes of pursuit: Toward a relational model of stalking-related phenomena. In J. A. Davis (Ed.), *Stalking crimes and victim protection: Prevention, intervention, threat assessment, and case management* (pp. 97–136). Boca Raton, FL: CRC Press. doi:10.1201/9781420041743.ch6

Spitzberg, B. H., & Cupach, W. R. (2007). The state of the art of stalking: Taking stock of the emerging literature. *Aggression and Violent Behavior, 12*(1), 64–86. doi:10.1016/j.avb.2006.05.001

Spitzberg, B. H., & Hoobler, G. (2002). Cyberstalking and the technologies of interpersonal terrorism. *New Media & Society, 4*(1), 71–92. doi:10.1177/14614440222226271

Srivastava, R., & Joshi, S. (2014). Relationship between self-concept and self-esteem in adolescent. *Journal of Advanced Research, 2*(2), 36–43.

Stack, S., Wasserman, I., & Kern, R. (2004). Adult social bonds and use of Internet pornography. *Social Science Quarterly, 85*(1), 75–88. doi:10.1111/j.0038-4941.2004.08501006.x

Stanley, S. M., Rhoades, G. K., & Fincham, F. D. (2011). *Understanding romantic relationships among emerging adults: The significant roles of cohabitation and ambiguity*. Cambridge University Press.

Stapel, D. A., & Blanton, H. (2004). From seeing to being: Subliminal social comparison affect implicit and explicit self-evaluation. *Journal of Personality and Social Psychology, 87*(4), 468–481. doi:10.1037/0022-3514.87.4.468

Starke, M. (2013). Everyday life of young adults with intellectual disabilities: Inclusionary and exclusionary processes among young adults of parents with intellectual disability. *Intellectual and Developmental Disabilities, 51*(3), 164–175. doi:10.1352/1934-9556-51.3.164

Stastica. (2016, August 9). *Stastica*. Retrieved August 9, 2016, from Statistical Online Portal: http://www.statista.com/statistics/264810/number-of-monthly-active-facebook-users-worldwide/

Stats, I. W. (2015, November 15). *Internet World Stats*. Retrieved August 9, 2016, from Usage and Population Statistics: http://www.internetworldstats.com/stats1.htm

Steel, Z., Marnane, C., Iranpour, C., Chey, T., Jackson, J. W., Patel, V., & Silove, D. (2014). The global prevalence of common mental disorders: A systematic review and meta-analysis 19802013. *International Journal of Epidemiology*, *43*(2), 476–493. doi:10.1093/ije/dyu038

Steers, M. N., Wickham, R. E., & Acitelli, L. K. (2014). Seeing everyone elses highlight reels: How Facebook usage is linked to depressive symptoms. *Journal of Social and Clinical Psychology*, *33*(8), 701–731. doi:10.1521/jscp.2014.33.8.701

Steinberg, L. (2008). *Adolescence*. New York, NY: McGraw-Hill.

Stein, D. J., Phillips, K. A., Bolton, D., Fulford, K. W. M., Sadler, J. Z., & Kendler, K. S. (2010). What is a mental/psychiatric disorder? From DSM-IV to DSM-V. *Psychological Medicine*, *40*(11), 1759–1765. doi:10.1017/S0033291709992261

Steiner, P. (1993). On the Internet, nobody knows you're a dog. *The New Yorker, 69*(20), 61.

Steinfield, C., Ellison, N. B., & Lampe, C. (2008). Social capital, self-esteem, and use of online social network sites: A longitudinal analysis. *Journal of Applied Developmental Psychology*, *29*(6), 435–445. doi:10.1016/j.appdev.2008.07.002

Stephenson-Abetz, J., & Holman, A. (2012). Home is where the heart is: Facebook and the negotiation of old and new during the transition to college. *Western Journal of Communication*, *76*(2), 176–193. doi:10.1080/10570314.2011.654309

Stern, L. A., & Taylor, K. (2007). Social networking on Facebook. *Journal of the Communication. Speech & Theatre Association of North Dakota*, *20*, 9–20.

Stewart, D. N., & Szymanski, D. M. (2012). Young adult womens reports of their male romantic partners pornography use as a correlate of their self-esteem, relationship quality, and sexual satisfaction. *Sex Roles*, *67*(5-6), 257–271. doi:10.1007/s11199-012-0164-0

Stone, A. R. (1991). Will the real body please stand up?. *Cyberspace: First Steps*, 81-118.

Straus, M. A., & Fauchier, A. (2007). *Manual for the Dimensions of Discipline Inventory (DDI)*. Durham, NH: Family Research Laboratory, University of New Hampshire.

Strawhun, J., Adams, N., & Huss, M. T. (2013). The assessment of cyberstalking: An expanded examination including social networking, attachment, jealousy, and anger in relation to violence and abuse. *Violence and Victims*, *28*(4), 715–730. doi:10.1891/0886-6708.11-00145 PMID:24047049

Štulhofer, A., Buško, V., & Landripet, I. (2010). Pornography, sexual socialization, and satisfaction among young men. *Archives of Sexual Behavior*, *39*(1), 168–178. doi:10.1007/s10508-008-9387-0

Subrahmanyam, K., & Greenfield, P. M., & Tynes, B. M. (2004). Constructing sexuality and identity in an online teen chat room. *Journal of Applied Developmental Psychology, an International Lifespan Journal, 25*, 651-666. doi:10.1016/j.appdev.2004.09.007

Subrahmanyam, K. S., & Šmahel, D. (2012). *Digital youth: The role of media in development*. New York, NY: Springer.

Subrahmanyam, K., Reich, S. M., Waechter, N., & Espinoza, G. (2008). Online and offline social networks: Use of social networking sites by emerging adults. *Journal of Applied Developmental Psychology*, *29*(6), 420–433. doi:10.1016/j.appdev.2008.07.003

Subrahmanyam, K., Šmahel, D., & Greenfield, P. M. (2006). Connecting developmental constructions to the internet: Identity presentation and sexual exploration in online teen chat rooms. *Developmental Psychology*, *42*(3), 395–406. doi:10.1037/0012-1649.42.3.395 PMID:16756432

Suler, J. (2004). The online disinhibition effect. *Cyberpsychology & Behavior*, *7*(3), 2004. doi:10.1089/1094931041291295 PMID:15257832

Sullivan, C. (2010). *Predictors of acculturative stress for international students in the United States* (Unpublished doctoral dissertation). University of Missouri, St. Louis, MO.

Sumter, S. R., Vanderbosch, L., & Ligtenberg, L. (2017). Love me Tinder: Untangling emerging adults motivations for using the dating application Tinder. *Telematics and Informatics*, *34*(1), 67–78. doi:10.1016/j.tele.2016.04.009

Suri, S., & Watts, D. J. (2011). Cooperation and contagion in web-based, networked public goods experiments. *PLoS ONE*, *6*(3), e16836. doi:10.1371/journal.pone.0016836

Swallow, S. R., & Kuiper, N. A. (1992). Mild depression and frequency of social comparison behavior. *Journal of Social and Clinical Psychology*, *11*(2), 167–180. doi:10.1521/jscp.1992.11.2.167

Swanson, J. A., & Walker, E. (2015) Academic versus non-academic emerging adult college student technology use. *Technology, Knowledge and Learning*, 1-12.

Sykes, T. (2014, January 18). Online dating is hard enough. Try doing it with a disability. *The Guardian.* Retrieved from http://www.theguardian.com/commentisfree/2014/jan/18/online-dating-with-disability-match

Tajfel, H., & Turner, J. C. (1986). The social identity theory of intergroup behaviour. In S. Worchel & W. G. Austin (Eds.), *Psychology of Intergroup Relations* (2nd ed.; pp. 7–24). Chicago, IL: Nelson-Hall.

Tang, J., Ma, Y., Guo, T., Ahmed, N. I., Yu, Y., & Wang, J. (2013). Association of aggression and non-suicidal self-injury: A school-based sample of adolescents. *PLoS ONE*, *8*(1), e78149. doi:10.1371/journal.pone.0078149 PMID:24205132

Tangney, J. P., Baumeister, R. F., & Boone, A. L. (2004). High self-control predicts good adjustment, less pathology, better grades, and interpersonal success. *Journal of Personality*, *72*(2), 271–322. doi:10.1111/j.0022-3506.2004.00263.x PMID:15016066

Tennant, J. E., Demaray, M. K., Coyle, S., & Malecki, C. K. (2015). The dangers of the webs: Cybervictimization, depression, and social support in college students. *Computers in Human Behavior*, *50*, 348–357. doi:10.1016/j.chb.2015.04.014

Tetzlaff, D. (2000). Yo-ho-ho and a server of warez. In *The World Wide Web and contemporary cultural theory*, (pp. 99-126). Academic Press.

Tibbert, S. J., Andersen, M. B., & Morris, T. (2015). What a difference a Mentally Toughening year makes: The acculturation of a rookie. *Psychology of Sport and Exercise*, *17*, 68–78. doi:10.1016/j.psychsport.2014.10.007

Tickle, M., Adebanjo, D., & Michaelides, Z. (2011). Developmental approaches to B2B virtual communities. *Technovation*, *31*(7), 296–308. doi:10.1016/j.technovation.2011.04.002

Tjaden, P., & Thoennes, N. (1998). *Stalking in America: Findings from the National Violence Against Women Survey (Research in Brief NCJ 169592).* Washington, DC: National Institute of Justice and Centers for Disease Control and Prevention.

Tolman, D. L., Diamond, L. M., Bauermeister, J. A., George, W. H., Pfaus, J. G., & Ward, L. (2014). APA Handbook of Sexuality and Psychology, Vol. 2: Contextual approaches. APA.

Tonin, E. (2004). The attachment styles of stalkers. *Journal of Forensic Psychiatry & Psychology*, *15*(4), 584–590. doi:10.1080/14789940410001729644

Topcu, C., Erdur-Baker, O., & Capa, A. Y. (2008). Examination of cyber-bullying experiences among Turkish students from different school types. *Cyberpsychology & Behavior*, *11*(6), 644–648. doi:10.1089/cpb.2007.0161 PMID:18783345

Traen, B., Nilsen, T. S., & Stigum, H. (2006). Use of pornography in traditional media and on the internet in Norway. *Journal of Sex Research*, *43*(3), 245–254. doi:10.1080/00224490609552323

Tuomi-Gröhn, T., & Engeström, Y. (2003). *Between school and work: New perspectives on transfer and boundary crossing*. Amsterdam: Pergamon.

Turiel, E. (1983). *The Development of Social Knowledge: Morality and Convention.* Cambridge University Press.

Turiel, E. (2014). Morality: Epistemology, development, and social opposition. In M. Killen & J. G. Smetana (Eds.), *Handbook of moral development* (2nd ed.; pp. 3–22). New York, NY: Psychology Press. doi:10.4324/9780203581957.ch1

Turkle, S. (1995). *Life on the screen: Identity in the age of the Internet*. New York, NY: Simon & Schuster.

Turkle, S. (2012). *Alone together: Why we expect more from technology and less from each other*. New York, NY: Basic books.

Turner, J. W., Grube, J. A., & Meyers, J. (2001). Developing an optimal match within online communities: An exploration of CMC support communities and traditional support. *Journal of Communication*, *51*(2), 231–251. doi:10.1111/j.1460-2466.2001.tb02879.x

U.S. Bureau of Labor Statistics. (2010). *Employment status of the civilian population by sex, age, and disability status, not seasonally adjusted* [Data file]. Retrieved from http://www.bls.gov

Uganda Bureau of Statistics (UBOS), & ICF International Inc. (2012). *Uganda Demographic and Health Survey 2011.* UBOS and Calverton.

Uganda Communications Commission. (2014). *Uganda Communications Commission*. Retrieved August 9, 2016, from Uganda Communications Commission: http://www.ucc.co.ug/data/qmenu/3/Facts-and-Figures.html

Uhlir, J. L. (2016). *Social comparison and self-presentation on social media of depressive symptoms*. Scripps Senior Theses Paper 756. Retrieved, August 18, 2016 from http://scolarship.claremont.edu/scripps_theses/756

Umemura, T., Lacinová, L., & Macek, P. (2014). Is emerging adults' attachment preference for the romantic partner transferred from their attachment preferences for their mother, father, and friends?. *Emerging Adulthood.*

Underwood, M., & Faris, R. (2015). *#Being thirteen: Social media and the hidden world of young adolescents' peer culture*. Retrieved from https://assets.documentcloud.org/documents/.../being-13-report.pdf

United States Department of Homeland Security. (2010). *Yearbook of immigration statistics: 2009.* Washington, DC: U. S. Department of Homeland Security, Office of Immigration Statistics. Retrieved from https://www.dhs.gov/xlibrary/assets/statistics/yearbook/2009/ois_yb_2009.pdf

United States Department of State. (2009). *International students come to United States in record numbers, 16% increase in new foreign student enrollment is largest since 1980.* Retrieved from http://www.state.gov/r/pa/prs/ps/2009/nov/131995.htm

Unknown Space. (2003). *About US.* Retrieved from: http://www.mitbbs.com/about_us.htm

Urquhart, C., & Frawer, E. (2012, December 30). Online dating surges as lonely hearts look to kickstart some post-Christmas romance. *The Observer.* Retrieved from http://www.theguardian.com/lifeandstyle/2012/dec/29/online-dating-christmas-romance

Utz, S., & Beukeboom, C. J. (2011). The Role of Social Network Sites in Romantic Relationships: Effects on Jealousy and Relationship Happiness. *Journal of Computer-Mediated Communication*, *16*(4), 511–527. doi:10.1111/j.1083-6101.2011.01552.x

Uwe, E. A., & Obot, A. E. (2000). *Marriage Counselling: Issues and Solutions. Calabar*. Pyramid Publishers.

Vago, D. R., & Silbersweig, D. A. (2012). Self-awareness, self-regulation, and self-transcendence (S-ART): A framework for understanding the neurobiological mechanisms of mindfulness. *Frontiers in Human Neuroscience*, *6*, 1–30. doi:10.3389/fnhum.2012.00296 PMID:23112770

Valenzuela, S., Park, N., & Kee, K. F. (2008). Lessons from Facebook: The Effect of Social Network Sites on College Students' Social Capital.*9th International Symposium on Online Journalism*, Austin, TX.

Valkenburg, P. M., & Peter, J. (2009). Social consequences of the Internet for adolescents a decade of research. *Current Directions in Psychological Science*, *18*(1), 1–5. doi:10.1111/j.1467-8721.2009.01595.x

Valkenburg, P. M., & Peter, J. (2011). Online communication among adolescents: An integrated model of its attraction, opportunities, and risks. *The Journal of Adolescent Health*, *48*(2), 121–127. doi:10.1016/j.jadohealth.2010.08.020 PMID:21257109

Valverde, L., & Davis, L. (2010). 10 Reasons Relationships Fail. *Loss Angeles Therapy Group: Articles Base*. Retrieved from http://m.articlebase.com/relationships-articles/10-reasonsrelationship-fail-and-how-to-succeed-2625111.html

Van Alphen, L. M., Dijker, A. J. M., Bos, A. E. R., Van den Borne, B., & Curfs, L. M. G. (2012). The influence of group size and stigma severity on social acceptance: The case of people with intellectual disability moving into neighborhoods. *Journal of Community & Applied Social Psychology*, *22*(1), 38–50. doi:10.1002/casp.1094

Vanden Abeele, V., Campbell, M., Eggermont, S., & Roe, K. (2014). Sexting, mobile porn use, and peer group dynamics: Boys and girls self-perceived popularity, need for popularity, and perceived peer pressure. *Media Psychology*, *17*(1), 6–33. doi:10.1080/15213269.2013.801725

Vaswani, K. (2012). *Indonesia's love affair with social media*. Retrieved, January 8, 2016 from http://www.bbc.com/news/world-asia-17054056

Vaterlaus, J. M., Beckert, T. E., & Bird, C. V. (2015). At a certain age its not appropriate to monitor ones child: Perceptions of parental mediation of emerging adult interactive technology use. *Emerging Adulthood*, *3*(5), 353–358. doi:10.1177/2167696815581277

Velotti, P., Balzarotti, S., Tagliabue, S., English, T., Zavattini, G. C., & Gross, J. J. (2015). Emotional suppression in early marriage: Actor, partner, and similarity effects on marital quality. *Journal of Social and Personal Relationships*.

Vivian, J. (2001). *The media of mass communication (updated online edition)*. Boston: Allyn & Bacon.

Vogel, E. A., Rose, J. P., Roberts, L. R., & Eckles, K. (2014). Social comparison, social media, and self-esteem. *Psychology of Popular Media Culture*, *3*(4), 206–222. doi:10.1037/ppm0000047

von Bertalanffy, L. (1968). *General systems theory: Foundation, development, applications*. New York: Braziller.

Vygotsky, L. (1978). *Mind and society: The development of higher psychological processes*. Cambridge, MA: Harvard University Press.

Wachira, K. (2010). Kenya Digital Life 2010. *MSRA Conference*. Nairobi: TNS Research International.

Wagnild, G. M., & Young, H. M. (1993). Development and psychometric evaluation ofthe resilience scale. *Journal of Nursing Measurement*, *1*(2), 165–178. PMID:7850498

Wakeford, N. (2002). New technologies and 'cyber-queer' research. In D. Richardson & S. Seidman (Eds.), *The Handbook of Lesbian and Gay Studies* (pp. 115–144). Thousand Oaks, CA: Sage Publications. doi:10.4135/9781848608269.n9

Walach, H., Buchheld, N., Buttenmüller, V., Kleinknecht, N., & Schmidt, S. (2006). Measuring mindfulness - the Freiburg mindfulness inventory (FMI). *Personality and Individual Differences*, *40*(8), 1543–1555. doi:10.1016/j.paid.2005.11.025

Walker, C., Sockman, B., & Koehn, S. (2011). An exploratory study of cyberbullying with undergraduate university students. *TechTrends*, *55*(2), 31–38. doi:10.1007/s11528-011-0481-0

Walker, S., Sanci, L., & Temple-Smith, M. (2013). Sexting: Young womens and mens views on its nature and origins. *The Journal of Adolescent Health*, *52*(6), 697–701. doi:10.1016/j.jadohealth.2013.01.026 PMID:23587784

Wall, D. (2007). *Cybercrime: The Transformation of Crime in the Information Age*. Polity.

Walther, J. B. (1996). Computer-mediated communication: Impersonal, interpersonal, and hyperpersonal interaction. *Communication Research*, *23*(1), 3–43. doi:10.1177/009365096023001001

Walther, J. B., & Parks, M. R. (2002). Cues filtered out, cues filtered in: Computer-mediated communication and relationships. In M. L. Knapp & J. A. Daly (Eds.), *Handbook of interpersonal communication* (3rd ed.; pp. 529–563). Thousand Oaks, CA: Sage.

Wang, C., & Chang, Y. (2010). Cyber relationship motives: Scale development and validation. *Social Behavior and Personality: An International Journal*, *38*(3), 289–300. doi:10.2224/sbp.2010.38.3.289

Wang, E. S.-T., & Wang, M. C.-H. (2013). Social Support and Social Interaction Ties on Internet Addiction: Integrating Online and Offline Contexts. *Cyberpsychology, Behavior, and Social Networking*, *16*(11), 843–849. doi:10.1089/cyber.2012.0557 PMID:23848959

Wang, K. T., Wei, M., & Chen, H. H. (2015). Social factors in cross-national adjustment subjective well-being trajectories among Chinese international students. *The Counseling Psychologist*, *43*(2), 272–298. doi:10.1177/0011000014566470

Wang, Y., & Sun, S. (2009). Examining Chinese students Internet use and cross-cultural adaptation: Does loneliness speak much? *Asian Journal of Communication*, *19*(1), 80–96. doi:10.1080/01292980802618494

Ward, P., Clark, T., Zabriskie, R., & Morris, T. (2014). Paper/pencil versus online data collection: An exploratory study. *Journal of Leisure Research*, *46*(1), 84–105.

Washington Post-Kaiser Family Foundation. (2012). *2012 survey of Americans of HIV/AIDS*. Retrieved from https://kaiserfamilyfoundation.files.wordpress.com/2013/01/8334-f.pdf

Waskul, D., & Douglass, M. (1997). Cyberself: The emergence of self in on-line chat. *The Information Society*, *13*(4), 375–397. doi:10.1080/019722497129070

Webb, L. M., & Temple, N. (2015). Gender issues and digital technology: Challenges and opportunities for empowerment and enactment. In B. Guzzetti & M. Lesley (Eds.), *Handbook of research on the social impact of digital media* (pp. 638–669). Hershey, PA: IGI Global.

Webb, L. M., & Wang, Y. X. (2013). Techniques for analyzing blogs and micro-blogs. In N. Sappleton (Ed.), *Advancing research methods with new technologies* (pp. 183–204). Hershey, PA: IGI Global Publishers; doi:10.4018/978-1-4666-3918-8.ch012

Weigle, P. (2014). Internet and Video Game Addiction: Evidence & Controversy. *Adolescent Psychiatry*, *4*(2), 81-91.

Weigman, O., & Schie, E. (1998). Video game playing and its relations with aggressive and prosocial behaviors. *The British Journal of Social Psychology*, *37*(3), 367–378. doi:10.1111/j.2044-8309.1998.tb01177.x PMID:9738313

Wei, M., Liao, Y. H., Heppner, P. P., Chao, R. C. L., & Ku, T. Y. (2012). Forbearance coping, identification with heritage culture, acculturative stress, and psychological distress among Chinese international students. *Journal of Counseling Psychology*, *59*(1), 97–106. doi:10.1037/a0025473

Weinberg, M. S., Williams, C. J., Kleiner, S., & Irizarry, Y. (2010). Pornography, normalization, and empowerment. *Archives of Sexual Behavior*, *39*(6), 1389–1401. doi:10.1007/s10508-009-9592-5

Weinstein, E. (2014). The personal is political on social media: Online civic expression patterns and pathways among civically engaged youth. *International Journal of Communication*, *8*(24), 210–233.

Weinstein, E., Rundle, M., & James, C. (2015). A hush Falls over the crowd: Diminished online civic expression among young civic actors. *International Journal of Communication*, *9*(23), 84–105.

Weiss, D. S., & Marmar, C. R. (1996). The Impact of Event Scale - Revised. In J. Wilson & T. M. Keane (Eds.), *Assessing psychological trauma and PTSD* (pp. 399–411). New York: Guilford.

Weisskirch, R., & Delevi, R. (2011). Sexting and adult romantic attachment. *Computers in Human Behavior*, *27*(5), 1697–1701. doi:10.1016/j.chb.2011.02.008

Wellard, S. J., Rennie, S., & King, R. (2008). Perceptions of people with type 2 diabetes about self-management and the efficiency of community based services. *Contemporary Nurse*, *29*(2), 218–226. doi:10.5172/conu.673.29.2.218

Wellman, B., & Guilia, M. (1999). Net surfers don't ride alone: Virtual communities as communities. In P. Kollock & M. Smith (Eds.), *Communities and cyberspace* (pp. 167–194). New York: Routledge.

Wendt, G., & Lisboa, C. (2014). Adolescência no contexto das novas tecnologias de informação e comunicação. In *Trabalhando com adolescentes: teoria e intervenção psicológica* (pp. 180–190). Porto Alegre: Artmed.

Wenger, E. (2000). Communities of Practice and Social Learning Systems. *Organization*, *7*(2), 225–246. doi:10.1177/135050840072002

Westrup, D., Fremouw, W. J., Thompson, R. N., & Lewis, S. F. (1999). The Psychological impact of stalking in female undergraduates. *Journal of Forensic Sciences*, *44*(3), 554–557. doi:10.1520/JFS14507J PMID:10408109

White, J. B., Langer, E. J., Yariv, L., & Welch, J. C. IV. (2006). Frequent social comparison and destructive emotions and behaviors: The dark side of social comparison. *Journal of Adult Development*, *13*(1), 36–44. doi:10.1007/s10804-006-9005-0

Whiting, A., & Williams, D. (2013). Why people use social media: A uses and gratifications approach. *Qualitative Market Research: An International Journal*, *16*(4), 362–369. doi:10.1108/QMR-06-2013-0041

Whitty, M. T. (2008). Revealing the real me, searching for the actual you: Presentations of self on an internet dating site. *Computers in Human Behavior*, *24*(4), 1707–1723. doi:10.1016/j.chb.2007.07.002

Widyanto, L., & Griffiths, M. (2011). An empirical study of problematic Internet use and self-esteem. *International Journal of Cyber Behavior, Psychology and Learning*, *1*(1), 13–24. doi:10.4018/ijcbpl.2011010102

Wiedeman, R. (2015, September 23). The prom queen of Instagram. *New York Magazine*. Retrieved from http://nymag.com/thecut/2015/09/lilli-hymowitz-prom-queen-of-instagram.html#

Wiegerink, D., Roebroeck, M. E., Donkervoort, M., Stam, H. J., & Cohen-Kettenis, P. T. (2006). Social and sexual relationships of adolescents and young adults with cerebral palsy: A review. *Clinical Rehabilitation*, *20*(12), 1023–1031. doi:10.1177/0269215506071275 PMID:17148513

Wiegerink, D., Roebroeck, M. E., Van Der Slot, W. M., Stam, H. J., & Cohen-Kettenis, P. T. (2010). Importance of peers and dating in the development of romantic relationships and sexual activity of young adults with cerebral palsy. *Developmental Medicine and Child Neurology*, *52*(6), 576–582. doi:10.1111/j.1469-8749.2010.03620.x PMID:20187888

Wiener, L. S., & Battles, H. B. (2006). Untangling the web: A close look at diagnosis disclosure among HIV-infected adolescents. *The Journal of Adolescent Health*, *38*(3), 307–309. doi:10.1016/j.jadohealth.2005.03.024

Williams, L. M. (2012). *Facebook Ruined My Marriage: Digital Intimacy Interference on Social Networking Sites*. Media Studies – Theses. Paper 7.

Williams, T., Connolly, J., Pepler, D., & Craig, W. (2005). Peer victimization, social support, and psychosocial adjustment of sexual minority adolescents. *Journal of Youth and Adolescence*, *34*(5), 471–482. doi:10.1007/s10964-005-7264-x

Willoughby, B. J., Hall, S. S., & Luczak, H. P. (2013). Marital paradigms: A conceptual framework for marital attitudes, values, and beliefs. *Journal of Family Issues*.

Willoughby, B. J., & Busby, D. M. (2015). In the eye of the beholder: Exploring variations in the perceptions of pornography. *Journal of Sex Research*, 1–11.

Willoughby, B. J., Carroll, J. S., Busby, D. M., & Brown, C. C. (2015). Differences in pornography use among couples: Associations with satisfaction, stability, and relationship processes. *Archives of Sexual Behavior*, 1–14.

Willoughby, B. J., Carroll, J. S., Nelson, L. J., & Padilla-Walker, L. M. (2014). Associations between relational sexual behaviour, pornography use, and pornography acceptance among US college students. *Culture, Health & Sexuality*, *16*(9), 1052–1069. doi:10.1080/13691058.2014.927075

Willoughby, B. J., & Hall, S. S. (2015). Enthusiasts, delayers, and the ambiguous middle: Marital paradigms among emerging adults. *Emerging Adulthood*, *3*(2), 123–135. doi:10.1177/2167696814548478

Willoughby, B. J., Olson, C. D., Carroll, J. S., Nelson, L. J., & Miller, R. B. (2012). Sooner or later? The marital horizons of parents and their emerging adult children. *Journal of Social and Personal Relationships*, *29*(7), 967–981. doi:10.1177/0265407512443637

Wilson, R. E., Graham, S. D., & Graham, L. T. (2012). A Review of Facebook Research in Social Sciences. *Perspectives of Pyschology Science*, *7*(3), 203–220. doi:10.1177/1745691612442904 PMID:26168459

Wolak, J., Mitchell, K., & Finkelhor, D. (2007). Does online harassment constitute bullying? An exploration of online harassment by known peers and online-only contacts. *The Journal of Adolescent Health*, *41*(6), 51–58. doi:10.1016/j.jadohealth.2007.08.019 PMID:18047945

Wold, H. (1985). Introduction to the second generation of multivariate analysis. In H. Wold (Ed.), *Theoretical Empiricism: A general rationale for scientific model-building* (pp. 9–11). New York: Paragon House.

Wood, M. (2015, February 4). Led by Tinder, the mobile dating game surges. *The New York Times,* p. B8.

Wood, J. T. (2009). *Communication in our lives* (5th ed.). Boston: Wardsworth Cengage Learning.

Working to Halt Online Abuse. (2011). *Cyberstalking statistics*. Retrieved on 8th January, 2015, from http://www.haltabuse.org/resources/stats/2011Statistics.pdfZeinali

World Health Organization. (2012). *Cancer fact sheet.* Retrieved from http://globocan.iarc.fr/Pages/fact_sheets_cancer.aspx

World Health Organization. (2014a). *The top 10 causes of death.* Retrieved from http://www.who.int/mediacentre/factsheets/fs310/en/

World Health Organization. (2014b). *Diabetes.* Retrieved from http://www.who.int/mediacentre/factsheets/fs312/en/

World Health Organization. (2015). *HIV/AIDS.* Retrieved from http://www.who.int/mediacentre/factsheets/fs360/en/

Wright, B. (1983). *Physical disability: A psychosocial approach.* New York: Harper & Row. doi:10.1037/10589-000

Wright, M. F. (2015). Cyber victimization and perceived stress: Linkages to late adolescents cyber aggression and psychological functioning. *Youth & Society*, *47*(6), 789–810. doi:10.1177/0044118X14537088

Wright, M. F., & Li, Y. (2012). Kicking the digital dog: A longitudinal investigation of young adults victimization and cyber-displaced aggression. *Cyberpsychology, Behavior, and Social Networking*, *15*(9), 44–454. doi:10.1089/cyber.2012.0061 PMID:22974350

Wright, M. F., & Li, Y. (2013). Normative beliefs about aggression and cyber aggression among young adults: A longitudinal investigation. *Aggressive Behavior*, *39*(3), 161–170. doi:10.1002/ab.21470 PMID:23440595

Wright, M. F., Li, Y., & Shi, J. (2014). Chinese adolescents social status goals: Associations with behaviors and attributions for relational aggression. *Youth & Society*, *46*(4), 566–588. doi:10.1177/0044118X12448800

Wright, P. J., Tokunaga, R. S., & Kraus, A. (2015). A meta-analysis of pornography consumption and actual acts of sexual aggression in general population studies. *Journal of Communication.*

Xie, B. (2008). Multimodal computer-mediated communication and social support among older Chinese internet users. *Journal of Computer-Mediated Communication*, *13*(3), 728–750. doi:10.1111/j.1083-6101.2008.00417.x

Xie, X., DeFrain, J., Meredith, W., & Combs, R. (1996). Family strengths in the People's Republic of China: As perceived by the university students and government employees. *International Journal of Sociology of the Family*, *26*, 7–27. Retrieved from http://www.jstor.org/stable/23029686

Xie, X., Xia, Y., & Zhou, Z. (2004). Strengths and challenges in Chinese immigrant families. *Great Plains Research*, *14*, 203–218. Retrieved from http://www.jstor.org/stable/23779478

Xu, J. (2010). Health orientation and media exposure among Chinese college students: Family, Internet and life satisfaction. *China Media Research, 6,* 8-14. Retrieved from http://www.chinamediaresearch.net/index.php/back-issues

Xu, A., Xie, X., Liu, W., Xia, Y., & Liu, D. (2007). Chinese family strengths and resiliency. *Marriage & Family Review*, *41*(1-2), 143–164. doi:10.1300/J002v41n01_08

Xu, C., Ryan, S., Prybutok, V., & Wen, C. (2012). It is not for fun: An examination of social network site usage. *Information & Management*, *49*(5), 210–217. doi:10.1016/j.im.2012.05.001

Xu, X., & Martin, K. W. (1990). Love matches and arranged marriages: A Chinese replication. *Journal of Marriage and the Family*, *52*(3), 709–222. Retrieved from http://www.jstor.org/stable/352936 doi:10.2307/352936

Yang, A. (2010). From "silent minority" to collective protests in real life: Tension, resistance, and online identity discourse of overseas Chinese. *Journal of intercultural Communication, 22,* 2. Retrieved from http://www.immi.se/intercultural/nr22/aimei.htm

Yang, C., Wu, H., Zhu, M., & Southwell, G. B. (2004). Tuning in to fit in? Acculturation and media use among Chinese students in the United States. *Asian Journal of Communication*, *14*(1), 81–94. doi:10.1080/01292980420001951512

Yan, K., & Berliner, D. C. (2013). Chinese international students personal and sociocultural stressors in the United States. *Journal of College Student Development*, *54*(1), 62–84. doi:10.1353/csd.2013.0010

Yarkin, K. L., Harvey, J. H., & Bloxom, B. M. (1981). Cognitive sets, attribution, and social interaction. *Journal of Personality and Social Psychology*, *41*(2), 243–252. doi:10.1037/0022-3514.41.2.243

Ybarra, M. L., Alexander, C., & Mitchell, K. J. (2005). Depressive symptomology, youth internet use, and online interactions: A national survey. *The Journal of Adolescent Health*, *36*(1), 9–18. doi:10.1016/j.jadohealth.2003.10.012 PMID:15661591

Ybarra, M. L., Diener-West, M., & Leaf, P. J. (2007). Examining the overlap in internet harassment and school bullying: Implications for school intervention. *The Journal of Adolescent Health, 41*(6), S42–S50. doi:10.1016/j.jadohealth.2007.09.004 PMID:18047944

Ybarra, M. L., & Mitchell, K. J. (2004). Online aggressor/targets, aggressors, and targets: A comparison of associated youth characteristics. *Journal of Child Psychology and Psychiatry, and Allied Disciplines, 45*(7), 1308–1316. doi:10.1111/j.1469-7610.2004.00328.x PMID:15335350

Ybarra, M. L., Mitchell, K. J., Kosciw, J. G., & Korchmaros, J. D. (2015). Understanding linkages between bullying and suicidal ideation in a national sample of LGB and heterosexual youth in the United States. *Prevention Science, 16*(3), 451–462. doi:10.1007/s11121-014-0510-2 PMID:25322949

Ybarra, M. L., Mitchell, K. J., Palmer, N. A., & Reisner, S. L. (2015). Online social support as a buffer against online and offline peer and sexual victimization among US LGBT and non-LGBT youth. *Child Abuse & Neglect, 39*, 123–136. doi:10.1016/j.chiabu.2014.08.006 PMID:25192961

Ye, J. (2006a). An examination of acculturative stress, interpersonal social support, and use of online ethnic social groups among Chinese international students. *The Howard Journal of Communications, 17*(1), 1–20. doi:10.1080/10646170500487764

Ye, J. (2006b). Traditional and online support networks in the cross-cultural adaptation of Chinese international students in the United States. *Journal of Computer-Mediated Communication, 11*(3), 863–876. doi:10.1111/j.1083-6101.2006.00039.x

Yettick, H., & Lloyd, S. C. (2015, May29). Graduation rate hits high, but some groups lag. *Education Week, 34*, 18.

Young, K. S. (1999). Internet addiction: symptoms, evaluation and treatment. *Innovations in clinical practice: A source book, 17*, 19-31.

Young, B. J., & Furman, W. (2007). Interpersonal factors in the risk for sexual victimization and its recurrence during adolescence. *Journal of Youth and Adolescence, 37*(3), 297–309. doi:10.1007/s10964-007-9240-0

Young, K. (1998). Internet addiction: The emergence of a new clinical disorder. *Cyberpsychology & Behavior, 1*(3), 237–244. doi:10.1089/cpb.1998.1.237

Young, K. S. (2004). Internet addiction a new clinical phenomenon and its consequences. *The American Behavioral Scientist, 48*(4), 402–415. doi:10.1177/0002764204270278

Young, K. S. (2008). Internet sex addiction risk factors, stages of development, and treatment. *The American Behavioral Scientist, 52*(1), 21–37. doi:10.1177/0002764208321339

Zeinali, A., Sharifi, H., Enayati, M., Asgari, P., & Pasha, G. (2011). The mediational pathway among parenting styles, attachment styles and self-regulation with addiction susceptibility of adolescents. *Journal of Research in Medical Sciences, 16*(9), 1105–1121.

Zhang, L. (2009, May). *Virtual story, real life: An Examination of Chinese students' acculturation in the United States through blogs.* Paper presented at the annual meeting of the International Communication Association, Chicago, IL. Retrieved from http://www.allacademic.com/meta/p298830_index.html

Zhang, J., Smith, S., Swisher, M., Fu, D., & Fogarty, K. (2010). Gender role disruption and marital satisfaction among wives of Chinese international students in the United States. *Journal of Comparative Family Studies, 42*, 523–542. Retrieved from jstor.org/stable/41604466

Zhang, Y. J. (2001). Support networks for urban and rural senior citizens. *Social Sciences Study, 4*, 11–21.

Zhao, S., Grasmuck, S., & Martin, J. (2008). Identity construction on Facebook: Digital empowerment in anchored relationships. *Computers in Human Behavior*, *24*(5), 1816–1836. doi:10.1016/j.chb.2008.02.012

Zhou, M., & Cai, G. (2002). Chinese language media in the United States: Immigration and assimilation in American life. *Qualitative Sociology, 25*, 419-441. doi::101609013146310.1023/A

Zimmer-Gembeck, M., & Duffy, A. (2014). Heightened emotional sensitivity intensifies associations between relational aggression and victimization among girls but not boys: A longitudinal study. *Development and Psychopathology*, *26*(3), 661–673. doi:10.1017/S0954579414000303 PMID:25047290

Zywica, J., & Danowski, J. (2008). The faces of Facebookers: İnvestigating social enhancement and social compensation hypotheses; predicting Facebook™ and offline popularity from sociability and self-esteem, and mapping the meanings of popularity with semantic networks. *Journal of Computer-Mediated Communication*, *14*(1), 1–34. doi:10.1111/j.1083-6101.2008.01429.x

About the Contributors

Michelle Wright is a postdoctoral research fellow at Masaryk University. Her research interests include the contextual factors, such as familial and cultural, which influence children's and adolescents' aggression and victimization as well as their pursuit, maintenance, and achievement of peer status. She also has an interest in peer rejection and unpopularity and how such status relate to insecurity with one's peer standing, aggression, and victimization.

* * *

Leonor Acosta (PhD) is Associate Professor in Cultural Studies and Gender Studies at the University of Cadiz. Her research interests are mass media, social media and popular culture from a trans-feminist point of view. She has published several contributions in collective books as well in journals devoted to English Studies with a focus on Gender Studies. She is a member of an international network of researchers for developing Gender Studies within Social Sciences.

Martina Benvenuti is a second year Phd Student in Psychological science at S.E.Fo.R.A. Lab at the Departement of Psychology of the ALMA MATER STUDIORUM - University of Bologna. Her research interests concern: Emerging Adulthood and Education and Information and Communication Technologies (ICT); The co-evolution characterizing human activity systems (in the Activity Theory perspective) and the Information and Communication Technologies (ICT): analysis of the changes produced by ICT (specifically by Web Artifacts) on human acitivity systems involving educational training and knowledge construction; Human-robot interaction in educational context: psychological aspects connected to development, learning and knowledge construction; Social Network Analysis applied to educational, vocational training contexts and public administration system.

Michelle Birkett, Ph.D., is faculty in the Department of Medical Social Sciences at Northwestern University, and a Research Scientist within the Institute of Sexual and Gender Minority Health. Dr. Birkett's research uses network and quantitative methodologies to understand the social contextual influence of prejudice on adolescent health and well-being, and in particular, the health of LGBT adolescents.

Alaina Brenick, PhD, is currently an Assistant Professor of Human Development and Family Studies at the University of Connecticut. She was awarded a traineeship from the National Institute of Child Health and Human Development/National Institutes of Health to obtain her PhD at the University of Maryland prior to becoming a postdoctoral fellow at the Friedrich Schiller University in Jena, Germany. Broadly, Dr. Brenick's research interests include how youth experience, make sense of, and respond to peer victimization and group conflict. Her research examines children, adolescent, and young adults' social and moral reasoning regarding victimization, bullying, discrimination, and exclusion, and the roles of individual characteristics, perceptions of group norms, contact, identity, and culture in these evaluations.

Katie Davis is an Assistant Professor at The University of Washington Information School, where she studies the role of networked technologies in teens' lives. She holds two master's degrees and a doctorate in Human Development and Education from Harvard Graduate School of Education. In addition to publishing and presenting her research in scholarly venues, Katie regularly shares her work with parents, teachers, industry leaders, and policymakers in an effort to build connections between research and practice.

Fernanda Faggiani received her MS in Sport Psychology from the Liverpool John Moores University in 2009. She is currently a PhD student and a Lecture at Pontifícia Universidade Católica do Rio Grande do Sul (PUCRS). Also works as a Sport Psychology in the Academy of a Brazilian Soccer Team. She writes and presents on issues of sport psychology, developmental psychology, acculturation and cognitive interventions.

Olufemi Adeniyi Fawole is a lecturer in the Department of Sociology, University of Ilorin. He holds a Ph.D. in Sociology with areas of interest in Adolescence, Delinquency, Emerging adulthood as well as Family issues.

Kaitlin Flannery earned her master's degree and is currently a doctoral candidate in Developmental Psychology in the Department of Psychological Sciences at the University of Connecticut. Her research is focused on social and emotional development among adolescents and emerging adults. Specifically, she is interested in the development of social cognition and its role in friendships and friendship dissolution. Her research also examines how individual characteristics influence dyadic relationships, and their effects on the social and emotional well-being of adolescents and young adults.

Beatriz Gomez-Ortiz is a PhD candidate of the Doctoral Programme in Economics and Business at the University of Malaga (Spain). She has a degree in Business Management. She main research interests focus on the broad framework of digital marketing.

Tyler Hatchel is a second year doctoral student in the Department of Psychology at the University of Florida. He completed this work at California State University, Los Angeles. Tyler is primarily interested in the health and well-being of LGBTQ youth. In particular, he has completed a number of studies examining risk and protective factors that shape the relation between various forms of victimization and poor outcomes. He is also interested in suicidality, tele-health, and digital media.

Tatsuya Imai is an assistant professor in the Department of British and American Studies of Nanzan University. His recent work "Influences of mental illness stigma in a computer-mediated communication context: Investigating mediating roles of predicted outcome value and negative affect" will be published soon in Japanese Journal of Communication. He has researched interpersonal communication in various contexts such as stereotype, romantic relationships, and international education. He earned his Master's degree in Communication from Michigan State University (2008) and Ph.D. in Communication Studies in University of Texas at Austin (2013).

Argyroula Kalaitzaki, BA, MSc, PhD, CPsychol, is an Assistant Professor of Clinical Psychology at the Technological Educational Institute of Crete, Greece and a Chartered Psychologist. She is the head of the Laboratory of Interdisciplinary Approaches for the Enhancement of Quality of Life. Her studies (BA, MSc, and PhD) were undertaken at the University of Crete. She has also a second PhD in Psychology from the University of Sunderland, UK. She is the author of many papers in peer-reviewed journals and she has presented her research at numerous national and international scientific conferences. She is the co-editor of the book 'Relating Theory: Clinical and Forensic Applications' (2016). Her primary research interests include interpersonal (inter)relating within couples and families, the effectiveness of psychotherapy, dating violence and abuse, parenting, social networks and problems of misuse (e.g., internet addiction, cyberstalking) and recently, positive psychology.

Ruth Kendagor is a PhD student in Communication and holds a Masters Degree in Communication Studies from Moi University- Kenya. Presently, she is a Lecturer at Karatina University in Kenya.

Carolina Saraiva de Macedo Lisboa received her PhD in Psychology from the Universidade Federal do Rio Grande do Sul with an Internship in the Universidade do Minho in Portugal in 2005. She has a level 2/CNPq Productivity scholarship and and is currently a Professor in the Postgraduate program in psychology of the Pontifícia Universidade Católica do Rio Grande do Sul. She is a Therapist certified by Brazilian Federation of Cognitive Therapies, having experience in the field of clinical psychology, cognitive-behavioral approach, developmental psychology and School and Educational Psychology. She writes and presentes widely on issues of bullying and cyberbullying, as well as social development and managing partner cognitions in virtual contexts.

Elizabeth Mazur is an Associate Professor of Psychology at Penn State University, Greater Allegheny campus. She received her M.A. and Ph.D. in Developmental Psychology from University of Michigan, completed a postdoc at Arizona State University's Center for Prevention Research, and previously taught at Eastern Kentucky University and University of Michigan, Flint. She is currently on the Committee for Disability Issues in Psychology of the American Psychological Association.

Elvis Mazzoni is PhD researcher of developmental and educational psychology and social networks analyst at the ALMA MATER STUDIORUM - University of Bologna. He is managing editor of the European Journal of Psychology of Education and editorial board member of Cyperpsychology, Behaviour and Social Networking. Thanks to his studies on the role played by ICT in lifelong learning and lifespan development, he collaborates with many scientific committees of International congresses and conferences.

Sebastian Molinillo (PhD) is Associate Professor in Marketing at University of Malaga. His research interests are social media and technology adoption. He has published papers at peer reviewed journals such as Journal of Business Research, Tourism and Management Studies, Dos Algarves. He has presented several papers at the annual conferences of the Academy of Marketing, Global Innovation and Knowledge Academy, European Academy of Management and Business Economics, AEMARK, among others.

Clara Moningka is a Ph.D. Candidate of Doctoral Programme in Psychology at Gunadarma University, Indonesia. Her research is focus on social change in Indonesia, including the impact of the use of technology.

Esperanza Moreno is a PhD Candidate of the Doctoral Programme in Art and Humanities at the University of Cadiz. She has a degree in Fine Arts and a Masters Degree in Visual Arts and Multimedia. Her research interests are LGBT artistic expression on digital environments.

David Mugambe Mpiima holds a Masters in Gender Studies and a BA (Social Sciences) both degrees attained from Makerere University. He is an Assistant Lecturer in the School of Women and Gender Studies, College of Humanities and Social Sciences, Makerere University where he mainly teaches both Social and Feminist Research at Undergraduate and Post Graduate levels; Gender, Politics and the State as well as Gender and the Information Society at PGD Local Economic Development. His research interests include gender analysis of; governance, politics as well as Information Communication Technologies (ICT).

Sarah Njau has an Msc. Development Studies from Moi University in Kenya and a BA (Social Sciences-majoring in Gender and Development) from Makerere University in Uganda.

Olasunkanmi Adebiyi Osho is a Masters student in the Department of Sociology, University of Ilorin, Kwara State, Nigeria.

Justin W. Peer is a Lecturer within the Department of Psychology at the University of Michigan-Dearborn. His research focuses on the influence of stress on the attainment of developmental goals and mental/physical health during emerging adulthood.

Emily Rankin is currently seeking certification in Special Education at Central Connecticut State University. She graduated magna cum laude from The University of Connecticut as an honors scholar with a Bachelor of Arts degree in Human Development and Family Studies. Ms. Rankin's interest in attachment theory and its role in child development led to her interest in the field of special education. Her research interests include attachment theory specifically as it impacts learning, fostering positive relationships among students with special needs and their typically developing peers, assistive technology as a tool for learning, bullying, and victimization in the school setting.

Kaveri Subrahmanyam, Ph.D., is a Professor of Psychology at California State University, Los Angeles and Associate Director of the Children's Digital Media Center @ Los Angeles. She is a recipient of the Cal State LA Outstanding Professor award in 2013. Dr. Subrahmanyam studies the cognitive and social implications of interactive media use and is currently studying the relation between digital communication and well-being, the cognitive implications of digital media and multitasking, and the link between children's home media use and their oral language development. Dr. Subrahmanyam has published numerous research articles and book chapters on youth and digital media and has co-edited a special issue on social networking for the Journal of Applied Developmental Psychology (2008) and a special section on interactive media and human development for Developmental Psychology (2012). She is a co-author (with Dr. David Smahel) of Digital Youth: The Role of Media in Development (Springer, 2010).

Lynne M. Webb (PhD, University of Oregon, 1980) serves as Professor in Communication, Florida International University, Miami, Florida. Her research examines three objects of study: social media, family communication, and romantic communication. She has published three scholarly readers and over 80 essays, including multiple theories, research reports, pedagogical essays, and methods pieces. Her work has appeared in numerous national and international journals including the Journal of Family Communication, Journal of Applied Communication, Health Communication, Computers in Human Behavior, and the International Journal of Social Research and Methodology as well as in prestigious edited volumes including the Handbook of Family Communication (Sage, 2014) and numerous IGI Global collections. She has presented over 100 papers at conferences in the U.S. and abroad. Dr. Webb has received numerous research, teaching, and service awards during her 35 years as a university professor; she is the 2015 recipient of the Southern States Communication Association's highest award, the Osborn Teacher/Scholar Award for excellence in teaching, research, and service.

Emily Weinstein is an advanced doctoral student in Human Development and Education at Harvard Graduate School of Education, where she studies the social, emotional, and civic lives of adolescents and emerging adults. She holds a master's degree in Prevention Science and Practice, also from Harvard Graduate School of Education. Outside of her academic work, Emily develops program resources and works directly with teens, schools, and families related to youth digital and social media use.

Brian Willoughby is an associate professor in the School of Family Life at Brigham Young University. Dr. Willoughby is also the Director of the RELATE Institute, a non-profit organization dedicated to studying and improving romantic relationships. Dr. Willoughby's research focuses on young adult dating and relationship patterns. Dr. Willoughby's specific expertise areas include dating, sexuality, cohabitation, marriage formation, and marital attitudes/beliefs.

Chenwei Wu (MA, University of Arkansas, 2012) is a PhD candidate in Comparative Literature and Cultural Studies at the University of Arkansas. Her MA thesis in Communication examined how interpersonal communication and computer mediated communication influence cross-cultural adaptation among Chinese nationals studying in the United States. Her research primarily focuses on the areas of cross cultural, interpersonal, family, gender, and computer mediated communication. Her research has been presented at the 82nd annual conference of the Southern States Communication Association.

Bonnie Young-Petersen is a master's student in Brigham Young University's Marriage and Family Therapy program. Bonnie's research focuses on pornography use, emerging adults, and relationships.

Index

F

G

H

I

J

L

M

N

O

P

Q

R

S

T

V

W

www.ingramcontent.com/pod-product-compliance
Lightning Source LLC
LaVergne TN
LVHW060415300926
849162LV00006B/1433